Sales Force Management

Sales Force Management

Second Edition

Joe F. Hair, Jr.
University of South Alabama

Rolph E. Anderson
Drexel University

Rajiv Mehta
New Jersey Institute of Technology

Barry J. Babin
University of Mississippi

WILEY

VP AND EDITORIAL DIRECTOR	Mike McDonald
PUBLISHER	Lise Johnson
SENIOR MANAGING EDITOR	Judy Howarth
DIRECTOR OF CONTENT OPERATIONS	Martin Tribe
SENIOR MANAGER OF CONTENT OPERATIONS	Mary Corder
PRODUCTION EDITOR	Padmapriya Soundararajan
COVER PHOTO CREDIT	© MR.Cole_Photographer/Getty Images

This book was set in 10/12pts STIX Two Text by SPi Global

Founded in 1807, John Wiley & Sons, Inc. has been a valued source of knowledge and understanding for more than 200 years, helping people around the world meet their needs and fulfill their aspirations. Our company is built on a foundation of principles that include responsibility to the communities we serve and where we live and work. In 2008, we launched a Corporate Citizenship Initiative, a global effort to address the environmental, social, economic, and ethical challenges we face in our business. Among the issues we are addressing are carbon impact, paper specifications and procurement, ethical conduct within our business and among our vendors, and community and charitable support. For more information, please visit our website: www.wiley.com/go/citizenship.

Evaluation copies are provided to qualified academics and professionals for review purposes only, for use in their courses during the next academic year. These copies are licensed and may not be sold or transferred to a third party. Upon completion of the review period, please return the evaluation copy to Wiley. Return instructions and a free of charge return shipping label are available at: www.wiley.com/go/returnlabel. If you have chosen to adopt this textbook for use in your course, please accept this book as your complimentary desk copy. Outside of the United States, please contact your local sales representative.

ISBN: 978-1-119-70283-2 (PBK)
ISBN: 978-1-119-70876-6 (EVALC)

Library of Congress Cataloging in Publication Data:

Names: Hair, Joseph F., Jr., 1944- author. | Anderson, Rolph E., author. | Mehta, Rajiv, author. | Babin, Barry J., author.
Title: Sales force management / Joseph F. Hair, Rolph E. Anderson, Rajiv Mehta, Barry J. Babin.
Description: 2nd edition. | Hoboken, NJ : Wiley, [2020] | Includes
   bibliographical references and index.
Identifiers: LCCN 2020022654 (print) | LCCN 2020022655 (ebook) | ISBN 9781119702832 (paperback) | ISBN 9781119708728 (adobe pdf) | ISBN 9781119702825 (epub)
Subjects: LCSH: Sales force management—Textbooks. | Sales management—Textbooks.
Classification: LCC HF5439.5 .H35 2020 (print) | LCC HF5439.5 (ebook) | DDC 658.8/1—dc23
LC record available at https://lccn.loc.gov/2020022654
LC ebook record available at https://lccn.loc.gov/2020022655

The inside back cover will contain printing identification and country of origin if omitted from this page. In addition, if the ISBN on the back cover differs from the ISBN on this page, the one on the back cover is correct.

*To my family, colleagues, and students – thanks for
your support over the years.*
—Joe Hair

*To Martha, Rachel, and Stuart for their unfaltering love
and support.*
—Rolph Anderson

*To the memory of a wonderful father, R.K., for his
unconditional love; and to my mother, Kamlesh.*
—Rajiv Mehta

*To my family and to all my students who've gone on to
a scholarly career.*
—Barry Babin

BRIEF CONTENTS

CONTENTS

2   Managing Ethics in a Sales Environment   30

8   Recruiting and Selecting the Sales Force   215

10 Sales Force Leadership   285

13 Sales Organization Audit and Sales Analytics   403

14 Sales Force Performance Evaluation   438

PREFACE

It's an exciting time to learn about and prepare for a career in sales management – those crucial managers who lead the sales force responsible for generating revenue, i.e., money, which is the lifeblood of any organization. Today, there are more opportunities and challenges for sales managers and their salespeople than at any previous time. Not only are sales managers and salespeople among the most highly paid members of an organization but surveys consistently find that sales jobs are among the most rewarding and satisfying, with the fastest potential routes to senior level management – all the way up to CEO. What's more, few jobs will be as important as those in sales as companies strive to survive and thrive in intensely competitive domestic and global markets. With rapidly advancing technology and ever-evolving tastes and preferences of customers, the sales force will provide an essential connection between selling organizations and their buying organization customers. Today's sales managers must play pivotal, multifaceted roles in planning, organizing, managing, directing, leading, and controlling the sales departments of their organizations. As the critical managers directly responsible for generating revenues and profits, sales managers are responsible for one of the most important of all functions in determining company success.

Probably the most obvious developments impacting sales force management today and in the foreseeable future are technological innovations, "big data," marketing analytics, and artificial intelligence (AI). The roles of sales managers and their salespeople will need to continually evolve and adapt to dynamic developments in communicating with customers and various stakeholders who influence the sales process, the growing empowerment of prospects and customers with computer access to much of the same information as salespeople, continually rising customer expectations for product quality and service, increased global competition especially from China and Pacific Rim countries, cultural and generational diversity of the sales force as well as that of customers, impact of climate and environmental concerns, and the diverse attitudes among customers, salespeople, and stakeholders about various ethical and political issues. Old school sales managers will not be able to rely on their past knowledge, experience, or success in the future. Instead, they will have to endeavor to keep pace with rapid, often unexpected and dynamic changes that will require them to establish and monitor a continuous learning environment for the entire sales department. There will be much closer interaction between marketing and sales activities in organizations. Sales managers will need greater knowledge about marketing strategy, and the marketing team must make sure to include selling and sales force management perspectives in their strategic planning efforts. The most successful sales managers will develop and apply marketing concepts, strategic planning processes, financial analysis techniques, motivation and leadership skills, effective compensation methods for changing goals and economic conditions, advance technology applications, marketing analytics, and improved communication methods including effective use of social media, plus greater "soft skills" for interacting with customers, stakeholders, and salespeople from diverse cultures and backgrounds. Our primary goal for *Sales Force Management is to help college students prepare for an exciting, prosperous career via sales and sales management, whether in a profit-oriented or nonprofit-oriented organization.*

Sales Force Management goes beyond learning about basic buyer–seller transactions to developing long-run relationships and partnerships with customers based on professionalism, mutual respect, trust, quality products and service, candid information sharing, and negotiations leading to "win–win" outcomes. We give more attention to Business-to-Business (B2B) selling than to Business-to-Consumer (B2C) selling because most college graduates who go into sales will be working for a business selling products and services to other businesses who are represented by highly educated professional buyers, so hardball selling or manipulation of prospects and customers will never be appropriate or successful. Professional B2B salespeople must operate more like solutions oriented consultants than mere sellers of products and services because the sales goal is to help prospects and customers find solutions for their problems and satisfy their ongoing business needs. In this way, long-term relationships can be cultivated and developed between sellers and buyer organizations. Of course, professional salespeople would like to sell their own company's products and services but the higher goal is to find solutions for the customer and maintain the long-term relationship. By keeping in mind the life-time value of a customer, not just the profit from each transaction, salespeople can better further the relationship and encourage repeat purchases which will be the most profitable approach over the long-run. Knowledge of sales principles, concepts, issues, and activities are critical to successful selling and sales management and we strive to provide an appropriate balance among theoretical, analytical, and pragmatic approaches by blending the latest knowledge and most progressive applications from the sales practitioner's environment with the latest research findings from academia.

Though *Sales Force Management* is designed primarily for use at upper level colleges and universities, some progressive junior colleges may wish to adopt it for students planning to enter sales careers. All chapters of the text have been pre-tested by undergraduate and masters level students at several universities, and their suggested improvements have been included where appropriate.

To provide both instructors and students an exciting, up-to-date text and a comprehensive set of supplements, we conducted interviews with professors, students, salespeople, and sales managers. Their feedback was used to develop the comprehensive instructor resource material for this edition of *Sales Force Management*. We summarize below what you will find when you examine this book which we hope you will want to adopt as we believe it offers the best total package of any text currently available on sales force management.

Organization of the Book

The overall goal of the book is to help sales managers and salespeople prepare for the challenging and exciting years ahead, so that the transition from personal selling to sales force management and/or marketing management is a natural progression, not a traumatic step. To this end, *Sales Force Management* is divided into four major parts, with a total of 14 chapters.

Part One, **Twenty-First-Century Sales Force Management**, provides an overview and integration of personal selling and sales force management. Chapter 1, **Introduction to Sales Force Management and Its Evolving Roles,** covers the eclectic, expanding role of professional sales force managers who are becoming respected members of the marketing management team and increasingly assuming a long run, strategic perspective for their organizations. Chapter 2, **Managing Ethics in a Sales Environment**, focuses on the diverse, evolving ethical and legal issues faced by salespeople and sales managers. It provides an overview of the concepts of business ethics and the conflicts confronted in responding to the ever-changing marketing environment, including dealing with the company, co-workers, customers, and various external stakeholders. Finally, legislation affecting selling and sales force management in local, state, federal, and global selling environments and situations is examined. Chapter 3, **Customer Relationship Management (CRM)**

and Building Partnerships, begins with a discussion of the different ways companies deal with customers in an effort to build customer relationships that lead to repeat business and loyalty. Next we relate customer loyalty to customer lifetime value, with particular emphasis on applying marketing analytics and other technology to improve the selling process, and more effectively prepare and guide salespeople. Chapter 4, **The Selling Process**, provides a comprehensive, in-depth analysis of the personal selling process and presents a variety of techniques and real-world examples of ways to improve selling performance with diverse prospects and customers to find "win–win" outcomes .

Part Two, **Organizing and Developing the Sales Force**, covers planning, organizing, and developing the sales force. Chapter 5, **Sales Forecasting and Budgeting**, focuses on using different convergent methods for sales forecasting then developing and monitoring the budgeting process for allocating resources and efforts to achieve the forecast. Sales forecasting is viewed as the starting point or required "cornerstone" for all sales and marketing planning, production scheduling, cash-flow projections, financial planning, capital investment, procurement, channel and supply chain management, human resource planning, and budgeting. After analyzing the major concepts and methods for accurately estimating demand, we illustrate the application of the most widely used forecasting techniques. Finally, the purpose, benefits, and process for preparing an annual sales budget are discussed. Chapter 6, **Sales Force Planning and Organizing**, explains strategic sales planning and organizing while considering the underlying assumptions. Planning is represented as a basic function of sales managers because it creates the essential framework for all other sales decision-making. The value and use of a sales force management information system for strategic and tactical planning is illustrated, and the proactive planning process is explained step-by-step. Various approaches for organizing the sales force are summarized and illustrated, as well as techniques for determining the optimal sales force size. Chapter 7, **Time and Territory Management**, presents alternative approaches for assigning and managing sales territories to achieve sales objectives effectively and efficiently. It also outlines the procedures for equitably setting up and revising sales territories, and for routing and maximizing productive sales time. Chapter 8, **Recruiting and Selecting the Sales Force**, explains the various sources of sales force recruitment and tools for improving the selection process. The sources of good sales candidates, the legal rights of sales applicants, the differences between job analysis and a job description, and the basic qualifications necessary for the emerging types and requirements for sales positions are all covered. These are followed by a description of the procedures and tools used to select the best applicants and an explanation of what sales managers look for in application forms and interviews. Legal considerations in interviewing and testing are summarized, as is the important step of socialization of new recruits.

Part Three, **Managing and Directing Sales Force Efforts**, covers managing and directing sales force efforts to achieve organizational goals under changing market conditions. Chapter 9, **Training the Sales Force**, presents the many aspects of training and retraining sales reps. The major topics include who is responsible for training, training program content, approaches for training, evaluation of training, and the benefits of continuous training and retraining. Chapter 10, **Sales Force Leadership**, is concerned with the critically important topic of how to successful lead the diverse members of modern sales forces. First, the essential differences between leadership and management are considered, and the sources of leader power are identified. Major classical and contemporary leadership theories are discussed in-depth first. Then, we analyze the emergent and increasingly popular concepts of empowerment, shared leadership, and servant leadership used by some proactive sales managers to lead the ever more diverse and multi-talented members of the modern sales force towards the attainment of challenging sales and organizational goals. The chapter concludes with a discussion of how both verbal and nonverbal communication can be effectively used by salespeople and sales managers. Chapter 11, **Sales Force Motivation**, focuses on how to motivate a continually evolving sales force to meet varying organization goals. It describes the various theories of motivation and considers nonfinancial as well as financial rewards that can be used to increase the effort of salespeople for achieving sales goals. Perhaps most important, it demonstrates why blanket approaches to motivation are ineffective and recommends unique ways to individualize motivation using incentives based on the career stages of salespeople. Chapter 12, **Sales Force Compensation**, examines the major types of compensation plans and how they need to be regularly modified with changing market conditions. We also consider what can be done to slow the rise in sales costs, and analyze alternative ways to determine the optimum balance of sales calls and other means of managing customer relationships, particularly digital communications. The chapter ends with a discussion of different approaches, including their advantages and disadvantages, to reimbursing sales expenses incurred by sales reps.

Part Four, **Controlling and Evaluating Sales Force Performance**, discusses methods for controlling and evaluating sales force performance to achieve organization goals while accommodating the influence of various internal and external stakeholders. Chapter 13, **Sales Organization Audit and Sales Analytics**, begins by assessing the benefits, process, and procedures for conducting a sales organization audit that includes the sales planning process, overall selling environment, sales functions, and performance of sales management. Next, the relationship between sales volume, costs, and profitability are discussed and analyzed. Sources of sales information and the collection of sales data are described. Then, the value of cooperation between marketing and the information technology group is shown, as well as procedures for obtaining, analyzing, and applying data on sales, cost, and profitability. Methods of allocating costs and measuring return on assets by market segments, including territories, customers, products, and salespeople, are examined in terms of their influence on productivity and profits. Chapter 14, **Sales Force Performance Evaluation**, summarizes techniques for setting performance standards for salespeople and objectively measuring performance, including the topics of potential evaluator biases and methods to better ensure salesperson evaluation fairness across ratings by different sales managers.

Objectives and Features

We developed Sales Force Management because of our belief the market needed a comprehensive, up-to-date text on the emerging and evolving roles of sales managers and salespeople as they face the opportunities and challenges of rapidly advancing technology, evolving customer preferences, and the growing diversity of customers and salespeople. As a result, we believe we have achieved the following objectives:

- Emphasize the role of selling and sales force management in the tough, highly competitive selling environment companies face today and in the future.
- Analyze key behavioral, technological, and managerial forces affecting selling and sales management along with long-run trends in domestic and global markets.
- Underscore the increasing importance of ethical considerations for sales managers and salespeople in dealing with customers and diverse stakeholders.
- Stress the important analytical, communication, relationship, motivation, leadership, and evaluation skills needed by today's and tomorrow's salespeople and sales managers.
- Illustrate the latest data and information technology developments and innovations impacting the sales manager's job, particularly in the areas of recruitment, selection, training, sales force planning, forecasting, leading, compensating, and evaluating performance.
- Emphasize the importance of developing long-run, "win–win" customer relationships and even partnerships.

- Summarize the latest statistics, analytics, and trends in sales force management.
- Communicate the necessity for sales managers to learn and integrate marketing, finance, and analytical techniques in order to contribute to marketing strategy development.

To accomplish these objectives, we have incorporated a number of innovative features to assist instructors in achieving *Assurance of Learning Objectives*, including:

- Real-world examples summarized in *Sales Management in Action* boxes.
- *Ethics in Sales Management* scenarios.
- Exercises to illustrate and develop sales management skills.
- Role-play exercises to facilitate understanding sales management challenges.
- Chapter cases by leading sales management scholars to reinforce the chapter material.
- Pedagogical supplements to help students learn and professors to teach; specifically developed for the text are a set of Digital Multimedia PowerPoint Video Lectures with Voice-Over Recordings for each chapter, which we believe is a pioneering supplement. The full array of the ancillaries package also includes a detailed Instructor's Resource Manual, Test Bank, and PowerPoint Slide Decks that are unmatched in comprehensiveness and quality by any other text on sales force management.

Innovative, Cutting-Edge Ancillaries Package for *Sales Force Management, 2nd ed.* Adopters

To dynamically increase student learning and effective instruction, this textbook provides a comprehensive set of supplements that enable delivery of text-specific online content available from the instructor website at www.wiley.com/go/hair/salesforcemanagement2e. The innovative, cutting edge ancillaries package includes:

- *Digital Multimedia PowerPoint Video Lectures with Voice-Over Recordings.* We are excited and proud to announce that *Sales Force Management, 2nd ed.* introduces an innovative feature that we believe is a pioneering supplement for sales management textbooks: *Digital Multimedia PowerPoint Video Lectures with Voice-Over Recordings.* One of our coauthors has developed PowerPoint video lectures with voice-over recordings for each chapter so that adopters of this text do not need to develop their own multimedia lectures, thereby eliminating the time consuming efforts usually required in adopting a new sales management textbook, i.e., developing new PowerPoint slides, writing narratives for each slide, and learning to record and edit files using complicated video recording software. With student demand increasing rapidly for digital online courses and more universities offering distance learning courses, our text's Digital Multimedia PowerPoint Video Lectures with Voice-Over Recordings will free-up instructor time to focus on other required activities, including research and institutional service. The Digital Multimedia PowerPoint Video Lectures offered with our text will make it seamlessly easy for potential adopters to migrate to teaching courses online by integrating the links to the innovative lectures on course management platforms, such as Moodle and Canvas. What's more, the recorded lectures will be especially beneficial for instructors that would like to employ the proven "flipped classroom" in which students come prepared in advance and come to class to cooperatively solve business problems – an innovative approach that has shown considerable promise of increasing student learning.
- *PowerPoint Slide Decks.* PowerPoint slide decks for each chapter provide an effective presentation tool for lectures that will be highly beneficial to instructors and students alike. The PowerPoint slide decks provide an outline of each chapter with key figures and tables from the main text, and students can add their own notes to each slide.

- *Instructor's Resource Manual.* For each chapter, the *Instructor's Resource Manual* includes the list of learning objectives, detailed lecture outlines, and suggested answers to all Assurance of Learning exercises, such as end-of-chapter discussion questions, and knowledge application activities that include cases, ethical exercises, and role-playing exercises.
- *Test Bank.* A printable Test Bank includes a wealth of pre-tested both recall and application-oriented multiple-choice, true-false, and essay questions. Suggested answers and explanations – both practical and theoretical – for the questions are offered to facilitate grading as well as advance student learning and concept retention. Questions selected for tests can be uploaded, administered, graded, and recorded online by your institution's course management system.
- *Wiley Computerized Test Bank.* The electronic version of the printed Test Bank allows instructors to easily generate and edit tests.
- *Wiley Student Website.* The Wiley Student Website includes complete chapter-by-chapter glossaries, flashcards, and crossword puzzles for reviewing key terms, and ACE self-tests.
- *Wiley Instructor Website.* At the Wiley Instructor Website, downloadable versions of the complete array of ancillaries are included, as follows:
  - Digital Multimedia PowerPoint Video Lectures with Voice-Over Recordings for each chapter
  - Instructor's Resource Manual by chapter (in MS Word) that can be edited by instructors
  - PowerPoint slide decks for each chapter
  - Comprehensive Test Bank with various questions types and formats
  - Sample syllabi for 10- and 15-week semesters

Acknowledgments

Extensive efforts are required from many talented people to write a college level textbook. The authors gratefully acknowledge the contributions made by those who helped in finalizing *Sales Force Management, 2nd ed.* First, many scholars and practitioners advanced the study and practice of selling and sales force management over the years and thereby enabled us to make our own contribution. Second, we are especially appreciative to our marketing colleagues who contributed case material or reviewed early versions of the book and offered candid and constructive suggestions. Among these people our special thanks go to:

Jennifer Barr, Stockton University
Nicole Dilg Beachum, University of Alabama, Birmingham
Charles Besio, Southern Methodist University
Jim Boles, University of North Carolina, Greenville
Aberdeen Leila Borders, University of New Orleans
José Casal, New Jersey Institute of Technology
Paul Christ, West Chester University
Alex H. Cohen, West Chester University
Mary Collins, Strayer University
Peter Dahlin, Mälardalen University, Sweden
Bobby Davis, Florida A&M University
Barry Dickinson, Holy Family University
Khalid Dubas, Mount Olive University
Alan Dubinsky, Purdue University
Bob Erffmeyer, University of Wisconsin, Eau Claire
Karen Flaherty, Oklahoma State University
Lucas Forbes, Western Kentucky University

Susan Geringer, California State University, Fresno
Dan Goebel, Northern Arizona University
Larry Goehrig, University of South Alabama
Rajesh Gulati, St. Cloud State University
Alice Gordon Holloway, University of South Alabama
Melodi Guilbault, New Jersey Institute of Technology
Frederick Hong-kit Yim, Hong-Kong Baptist University
Christopher D. Hopkins, Auburn University
Cristal Hunt, University of South Alabama
Mark Johlke, Bradley University
Thomasa Jackson, University of South Alabama
Diane Kirkland, California State University, Long Beach
Andrew Klein, DeVry University
Balaji Krishnan, University of Memphis
David Locander, University of Tennessee at Chatanooga
Mark Leach, University of Wyoming
Britton Leggett, University of South Alabama
Terry Loe, Kennesaw State University
Samuel 'Cy' McCord IV, University of South Alabama
Neda Mossaei, University of South Alabama
James Mullen, Villanova University
Paul Myer, University of Maine
Frank Notturno, Madonna University
Joseph Ouellette, Bryant University
Ossi Pessama, Luleå University of Technology, Sweden
Kathrynn Pounders, University of Texas, Austin
Woodrow D. Richardson, University of Mary Washington
Wendy Ritz, Florida State University–Panama City
Joe Rocereto, Monmouth University
Joe Roman, New Jersey Institute of Technology
C. David Shepherd, Georgia Southern University
Mary Shoemaker, Widener University
G. David Shows, Appalachian State University
J. Gary Smith, Middle Tennessee State University
Mark Somers, New Jersey Institute of Technology
Lei Song, Penn State Abington
Michelle D. Steward, Wake Forest University
Jim Strong, California State University, Stanislaus
Srini Swaminathan, Drexel University
Nabil Tamimi, University of Scranton
Brian Tietje, California Polytechnic State University
Elise Van Zandt, University of South Alabama
Mike Weber, University of Maine
Stacy Wellborn, Springhill College
Vicki West, Texas State University
Jacob Whitmore, University of South Alabama
Scott Widmier, Kennesaw State University
Mike Williams, Oklahoma City University
Mike Wittmann, University of Alabama, Birmingham
Andy Wood, James Madison University

Most important to the initiation and completion of *Sales Force Management* were the members of the John Wiley & Sons, Inc., team who diligently and creatively guided us throughout the various stages of development. These included Lisé Johnson, Judy Howarth, Saravanan Dakshinamurthy, Padmapriya Soundararajan, Aarthi Ramachandran, Venkat Narayanan, and the production team at SPi-Global. Finally, we want to acknowledge our students – past, present, and future – who make our teaching and writing enjoyable and meaningful.

Joseph F. Hair, Jr.
Rolph E. Anderson
Rajiv Mehta
Barry Babin

ABOUT THE AUTHORS

Dr. Joseph F. Hair, Jr., Ph.D.

Dr. Hair is the Director of the Ph.D. Program in Business Administration and Cleverdon Chair of Business, Mitchell College of Business, University of South Alabama. Immediately prior to joining the University of South Alabama, Joe was the Founder and Director of the Kennesaw State University DBA program. Before KSU he was on the faculty of the Ourso College of Business Administration, Louisiana State University, where he held the Copeland Endowed Chair of Marketing. He was a United States Steel Foundation Fellow at the University of Florida, where he earned his Ph.D. in Marketing.

Dr. Hair has been recognized by Clarivate Analytics as being in the top 1% globally of all Business and Economics professors. He was selected for the award based on citations of his research and scholarly accomplishments, which for his career exceed 230,000. He has authored over 80 editions of his books, including *Marketing*, Cengage Learning, 13th edition, 2021; *Multivariate Data Analysis*, Cengage Learning, U.K., 8th edition 2019 (cited 125,000+ times and one of the top five all time social sciences research methods textbooks); *Essentials of Business Research Methods*, Routledge, 4th edition 2020; *Essentials of Marketing Research*, McGraw-Hill, 5th edition 2020; and *A Primer on Partial Least Squares Structural Equation Modeling*, Sage, 2nd edition 2017. He also has published numerous articles in scholarly journals such as the *Journal of Marketing Research*, *Journal of Academy of Marketing Science*, *Organizational Research Methods*, *Journal of Advertising Research*, *European Journal of Management*, *Decision Sciences Journal*, *Journal of Business Research*, *Journal of Long Range Planning*, *Industrial Marketing Management*, *European Journal of Marketing*, *Journal of Retailing*, and others.

Dr. Rolph E. Anderson, Ph.D.

Dr. Rolph Anderson is the Royal H. Gibson, Sr. Chair Professor and former Head (1975–1997) of the Department of Marketing at Drexel University. He earned his Ph.D. from the University of Florida, and his MBA and BA degrees from Michigan State University where he was a member of the varsity basketball team after being selected first team All-State in high school. His primary research and publication areas are personal selling and sales management, customer satisfaction and customer loyalty. He is author or coauthor of over 20 textbooks, including *Multivariate Data Analysis, 8th ed.* – one of the most highly referenced research texts in the social sciences (among top 5 all-time) translated into several languages; *Professional Personal Selling, 3rd ed.*; and

Sales Management: Building Customer Relationships and Partnerships. According to Google Scholar Citations, his research has been cited over 180,000 times in scholarly publications. Dr. Anderson's articles have been widely published in the major journals in his field, including the *Journal of Marketing Research, Journal of Marketing, Journal of Retailing, Journal of the Academy of Marketing Science, MIT Sloan Management Review, Journal of Business Research, European Journal of Marketing, Psychology & Marketing, Business Horizons, Industrial Marketing Management, Journal of Historical Research in Marketing, Journal of Marketing Channels, Journal of Marketing Theory & Practice, Journal of Personal Selling & Sales Management*, and various others. His classic *Journal of Marketing Research* article on "Consumer Dissatisfaction: The Effect of Disconfirmed Expectations on Perceived Product Performance" was one of the pioneering articles in the study of customer satisfaction. He won the national Mu Kappa Tau award in 1988 for the best article published in the *Journal of Personal Selling & Sales Management*. In 1992, Dr. Anderson was selected for the second time by the Drexel College of Business students to receive the Faculty Appreciation Award. He was recipient of the 1995 national "Excellence in Reviewing Award" from the *Journal of Personal Selling & Sales Management*. In 1998, he received the American Marketing Association Sales Special Interest Group inaugural "Excellence in Sales Scholarship Award." For 2000-2001, he received the Drexel University LeBow College of Business "Research Achievement" award. In 2003, he was selected a Distinguished Fellow of the LeBow College Center for Teaching Excellence and received the LeBow College Award for "Academic Leadership in Textbook Publishing." Professor Anderson has served several professional organizations as an officer, including: President, Southeast Institute for Decision Sciences (IDS); President, University of Florida Beta Gamma Sigma Chapter; Board of Directors, American Marketing Association (Philadelphia Chapter); Secretary and Board of Directors, Academy of Marketing Science; Vice President for Programming, American Marketing Association (Philadelphia Chapter); National Council, Institute for Decision Sciences; Board of Directors, Northeast IDS; and Co-Chairman, 61st International American Marketing Association Conference. Dr. Anderson has served and currently serves on the editorial boards of several academic journals. Prior to entering academia, he worked in managerial positions for three Fortune 500 companies, including as New Product Development Manager for the Quaker Oats Company. After active military duty aboard the aircraft carrier U.S.S. Hornet (CVS-12), he remained in the naval reserves and retired as a U.S. Navy Supply Corps Captain (06).

Dr. Rajiv Mehta, Ph.D.

Dr. Rajiv Mehta, who earned his Ph.D. in Marketing from Drexel University in 1994, is a Professor of Marketing at the Martin Tuchman School of Management, New Jersey Institute of Technology. Previously, he served on the faculty of Loyola University New Orleans.

Dr. Mehta's research focuses on the areas of selling and sales management, marketing channels, and global marketing, Japanese Keiretsu, and the cross-border management of International Strategic Distribution Alliances. He is coauthor of four university-level textbooks, including *Personal Selling: Building Customer Relationships and Partnerships, 3rd ed.,* and *Sales Management: Building Customer Relationships and Partnerships.*

Dr. Mehta's research, which has been widely published in major academic journals and presented at national and international academic conferences, has appeared in acclaimed peer reviewed journals, such as *MIT Sloan Management Review, Journal of Business Research, Industrial Marketing Management, Journal of Personal Selling and Sales Management,*

Business Horizons, European Journal of Marketing, International Marketing Review, Journal of Business to Business Marketing, Journal of Business and Industrial Marketing, Journal of Marketing Channels, Journal of Global Marketing, International Journal of Physical Distribution and Logistics Management, Journal of Managerial Issues, Journal of Services Marketing, Management Bibliographies and Reviews, Journal of Shopping Center Research and others.

In 2015, Dr. Mehta received the best paper award for a manuscript entitled *"Empirical Research of Inter-firm Capital Relationship in Yokokai Using IDE Spatial Model,"* which was presented at ICAROB, Oita, Japan. In addition, his coauthored article *"Leadership and Cooperation in Marketing Channels: A Comparative Empirical Analysis of the United States, Finland, and Poland,"* received the award for excellence as the outstanding paper in *International Marketing Review*.

Dr. Mehta received the Martin Tuchman School of Management *Award for Excellence in the Category of Innovative Teaching* in 2018. Additionally, he was bestowed the prestigious *Master Teacher Award* for having demonstrated the highest level of teaching excellence. At New Jersey Institute of Technology, his contributions to teaching were also recognized by the alumni when he has awarded the university-wide *Robert W. Van Houten Award for Teaching Excellence*. While at Loyola University New Orleans, its College of Business Administration chose him three straight years to receive the *Excellence in Research Award*.

Prior to entering academia, Dr. Mehta worked in sales and marketing for a major international manufacturer of steel wire ropes and cables.

Dr. Barry J. Babin, Ph.D.

Dr. Barry J. Babin, Ph.D. (Louisiana State University), is the Morris Lewis Professor and Chair of Marketing at Ole Miss Business School. He has authored well over 100 professional publications with research appearing in the *International Journal of Wine Business Research, Journal of the Academy of Marketing Science, Journal of Marketing, Journal of Retailing, Journal of Business Research, Journal of Consumer Research, European Journal of Marketing*, and many others. His 1994 *JCR* article on utilitarian and hedonic value is one of the most cited papers ever published in JCR (over 6,500 citations). Googlescholar credits his publications with well over 100,000 citations. Barry is Past-President of the Academy of Marketing Science (AMS), Co-Chair of the AMS Board of Governors, the AMS Co-Director of International Programs, and a previous recipient of the AMS Harold W. Berkman Distinguished Service Award. He served as Marketing Section Editor for *JBR* for over 15 years and has won outstanding reviewer awards from multiple journals. He is coauthor of several leading books including *CB: A Consumer Value Framework* (8th edition, 2019), *Multivariate Data Analysis* (8th edition, 2019) and *Exploring Marketing Research* (11th edition, 2018).

CHAPTER 1

Introduction to Sales Force Management and Its Evolving Roles

What Is Sales Force Management?

What an exciting time to be – or anticipate being – a sales manager! Sales force management is one of the most challenging and rewarding of all possible careers today. Few, if any, jobs are more crucial to the ultimate success of a business than sales force management because it shapes and determines the outcome of most interactions with customers.[1] Sales managers are respected marketing professionals who oversee the sales force – the direct income producers who substantially impact the financial health of their organizations. Working together, salespeople and sales managers generate sales revenue for their organizations while carrying out marketing strategies in day-to-day interactions with customers. Unless the sales force is successful, the viable future of the entire company and its employees is in jeopardy.

In present highly competitive markets, sales managers are trying all kinds of new ideas, strategies, tactics, sales channels, and technologies to develop mutually profitable long-run relationships with customers. At the same time, technological innovations, dynamic buyer behavior, rapid changes in the macromarketing environment, and managerial creativity are dramatically affecting the way sales managers understand, prepare for, and accomplish their jobs.[2] Salespeople today, especially in business-to-business (B2B) sales, operate much like "customer consultants" who go beyond focusing only on individual sales transactions to build mutually beneficial long-run relationships and often even symbiotic partnerships with customers. With instant access to company information (latest prices, inventory levels, new products in the pipeline) via their electronic devices (e.g. smartphones, tablets), salespeople have become empowered and increasingly independent of their sales managers. With the widespread availability of electronic devices to access instant information for customers, salespeople are able to function as virtually mobile headquarters for their companies. So, necessarily, the roles of sales force management are correspondingly evolving and expanding.[3] Sales managers are more involved than ever in developing company marketing/sales strategies, employing sales analytics, and ensuring customer satisfaction and loyalty by improving multichannel management relationships (online and off-line) with prospects, customers, and stakeholders. In short, there are continual market changes, challenges, and opportunities for today's and tomorrow's sales managers!

Types, Titles, and Hierarchical Levels of Sales Managers

Depending on the nature of the organization and its managerial philosophy, sales force management activities and titles can vary widely. In some organizations, the sales manager may be little more than a supervisor of the sales force, a kind of "super salesperson" who shows the salespeople how best to do their jobs.[4] In other organizations, the sales manager is the marketing manager in all but position title. Most sales force management activities fit somewhere between these two extremes.

In a national study, sales managers were asked, "If you couldn't use the term 'sales manager', what might you use to describe the job you do?" They gave themselves various titles, including account manager, problem solver, channel manager, business manager, team leader, group psychologist, resource coordinator, sales department administrator, change manager, director of income, contact manager, staff development specialist, trainer/coach, and customer relationship manager.[5] Clearly, sales managers see themselves as wearing a lot of hats and doing everything from traditional leadership and coaching the sales force to taking on new roles in sales channel management and customer relationship management (CRM).

Many not-for-profit organizations also employ salespeople – no matter what their job title – to generate financial support and/or achieve organizational goals, so they also need people to do sales manager type activities. For instance, recruiters for voluntary military service, fundraisers for political parties, institutional development officers, and college admissions representatives are all engaged in various forms of "selling." Not surprisingly, then, selling and sales force management concepts and techniques apply to noncommercial as well as to commercial organizations.

There are various titles and hierarchical levels of sales managers across diverse organizations. Typical position titles and responsibilities of sales managers in business organizations are shown in Table 1.1.

Responsibilities and Duties of Sales Managers

While sales managers' roles are constantly evolving in response to changing market conditions, they still center on traditional sales force management responsibilities and duties. Essentially, sales managers are paid to plan, lead, and control the personal selling activities of their organizations. They carry out these responsibilities and duties within the larger framework of organizational objectives, marketing strategies, and target markets. At the same time, they must continuously monitor and adjust to various changing *macroenvironment* factors (technological, competitive, economic, legal, cultural, and ethical) and the company's *stakeholders* (employees, suppliers, financial community, media, stockholders, special interest groups, governments, and the general public). In sum, sales managers today have an eclectic and increasing challenging job that requires flexibility, adaptability, and ongoing learning. Let's take a closer look at the responsibilities and duties of contemporary sales managers. To facilitate our discussions, Figure 1.1 presents an overall conceptual framework for sales force

TABLE 1.1

Sales Force Management Hierarchies: Titles and Responsibilities

Vice president of sales	This is the highest-level sales executive who, depending on the organization, reports to the vice president of marketing or the company president. The vice president of sales is usually involved in longer run, top-level planning for the company and is directly responsible for sales strategy. In companies with no vice president of marketing, the vice president of sales is responsible for all marketing activities.
National sales manager	This position provides the link between the highest-level company decisions on overall strategy and the line sales managers responsible for carrying out sales plans in their respective regions. Participating in both strategic and tactical planning, the national sales manager provides overall direction on sales operations and conveys top-level decisions and strategies to subordinate sales managers.
Regional, division, or zone sales manager	As the titles indicate, these managers are responsible for line sales activities for successively smaller subdivisions of company sales operations. Starting with the smallest subdivision, zone sales managers report to division sales managers, who, in turn, report to regional sales managers.
District, branch, or field sales manager	These are the first-level line sales managers responsible for handling day-to-day activities of salespeople. Usually, the titles "district," "branch," and "field" indicate successively smaller territorial responsibilities.
Sales supervisor	This more experienced salesperson is responsible for providing general guidance and advice to a few salespeople in a given branch or field territory.
National account manager (NAM), key account manager (KAM), senior account executive	These are typically top-performing, more senior salespeople who are responsible for handling one or only a few major customers, such as large national and international retail chains (e.g. Wal-Mart, Costco, or Home Depot).
Marketing representative, sales representative, account manager, sales engineer, salesperson	These are only a few of the many titles that different companies use for their front-line salespeople who sell products and services to various customer groups, including consumers, industrial companies, nonprofit institutions, and government agencies.
Assistant sales manager, sales analyst, sales training manager	These titles are representative of the many staff positions needed to support the line functions of sales. Staff people function at every level in the sales organization from corporate headquarters to the smallest branch office and report directly to a line manager. Many have very impressive titles, such as corporate vice president of sales or assistant national sales manager, yet have no line sales force management authority. Usually, staff members in these positions assist in performing various support functions at different levels in the sales organization (e.g. forecasting, planning, promotion, recruiting, training, and sales analysis). Sales staff people often receive opportunities to switch over to line management positions.

management decision-making and indicates the chapter in the book where each component is discussed.

Twenty-First-Century Sales Force Management

Chapters 1–4 will help you understand the overall roles of sales managers (Chapter 1) and salespeople (Chapter 4) while professionally and ethically (Chapter 2) building customer relationships and partnerships (Chapter 3). Specific sales force management responsibilities and duties are discussed in Chapters 5–14, but a short overview is offered at this point to help you anticipate and appreciate what lies ahead.

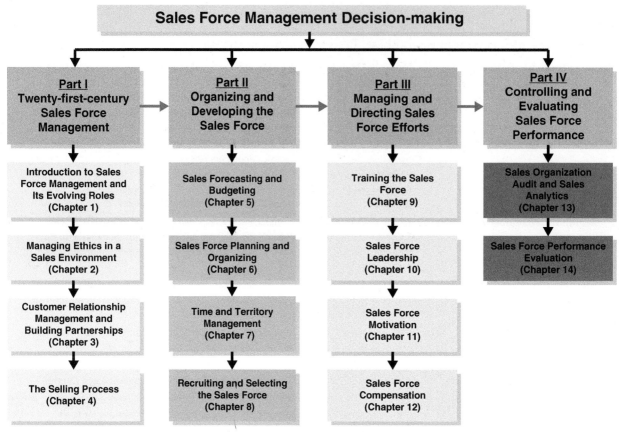

FIGURE 1.1 Responsibilities and duties of sales managers: A conceptual framework.

Organizing and Developing the Sales Force

Sales forecasting and budgeting (Chapter 5) are the cornerstones supporting virtually all sales force management decisions and activities. Sales managers must estimate *market potential* for their industry and *sales potential* for their company before developing a final *sales forecast* on which to base their operational planning and budgeting for their sales force. Savvy sales managers employ both quantitative and qualitative approaches and study the similarities and differences between the two sets of results before deciding on the final sales forecast. Money is needed to implement any sales plan, so preparation of a realistic sales budget is essential. A *sales budget* is simply a financial plan of expenditures needed to achieve the sales forecast and accomplish the organization's sales goals and objectives. The purpose of the sales budget is to ensure that organizational resources are allocated in the most efficient and effective way over the period of the sales forecast. Accurate sales forecasting and budgeting are critical to the success of any organization.

Sales force planning and organizing (Chapter 6) are essential functions of sales managers because they provide guidelines and direction for most sales decisions and activities. As planners, sales managers must set sales goals and objectives, establish sales policies and procedures, devise sales force strategies and tactics, and implement controls to ensure that sales goals and objectives are achieved. Planning requires sales managers to anticipate the possible outcomes and future implications of current decisions, so in many ways, planning is an attempt to prepare for and manage the future. As organizers, sales managers must determine the optimal number of salespeople to hire and the best way to structure the sales force (geographically, by product, by customer type, by activities, or by some combination of these factors). Determining the appropriate number of salespeople and how best to organize them affect several sales force management decision areas, including job descriptions, compensation methods, sales forecasts, quotas, budgets, territory assignments, supervision, motivation, and evaluation of sales force performance. In some companies, the sales manager must also decide whether to substitute external salespeople or *manufacturers' agents/ representatives* (who are not company employees and earn only commissions on their sales) for some or even all members of the direct sales force. Adjustments may be needed in both sales force size and structure in response to changes in marketing strategy or fluctuations of the uncontrollable variables in the marketing environment. In all cases, the overriding purpose in selecting a particular sales organizational structure and size should be to optimize the achievement of sales objectives and goals.

Time and territory management strategies (Chapter 7) help sales managers determine which accounts their salespeople should call on, when, and how often. To effectively allocate sales force efforts, the sales manager must first design sales territories. A *sales territory* is a market segment or group of present and potential customers who usually share some common characteristics relevant to purchasing behavior. Territories should be compared on the basis of sales potential, which, in turn, is used to decide individual *sales quotas* (the motivational targets assigned to the sales force as a whole and to salespeople individually). After sales territories have been determined, management may design a precise *routing* pattern for salespeople to follow in calling on customers. Some sales managers prefer to have the salespeople assume responsibility for efficient scheduling of sales calls and routing themselves, but in either case a predetermined plan should be carried out. Software programs from numerous companies are available to help the scheduling and routing or overall mapping for salespeople. Because few salespeople make optimal use of their most precious resource: time, one of the most important jobs of sales managers is to train and retrain their salespeople in the latest technologies and techniques for improving management of their time and territory.

Recruiting and selecting the sales force (Chapter 8) includes identifying sources of potential sales recruits, methods of reaching them, and strategies for attracting them to apply for a sales job. Once applicants have been recruited, the sales manager must devise a system for measuring applicants against predetermined job requirements. This involves analysis of the numerous tools and techniques available for processing or screening applicants. Finally, the decision to select or reject each applicant must be made. After being hired, new salespeople need to be assimilated or blended smoothly into the sales organization. Included in the assimilation process are an explanation of job responsibilities and managerial expectations, introduction to coworkers, and help for the new salesperson as he or she adjusts socially and psychologically to the organization and sometimes to the community, as well.

Managing and Directing Sales Force Efforts

Traditionally, *training the sales force (Chapter 9)* has focused mainly on selling techniques. But customers today are more knowledgeable and empowered via computer technology than ever. Competition is more intense and customers are demanding more service, so progressive companies have intensified their sales force training and are using the latest telecommunications advances to enhance learning via "real-world"

Because the sales manager's job is so eclectic, it is critical that he or she be trained in an array of activities such as sales forecasting, budgeting, leadership, motivation, compensation, and performance evaluation – essential skills for successful sales force management.

sales practice. Sales managers are also trying to broaden the perspectives of their salespeople by blending sales, marketing, and finance concepts into sales training. This broader-based training not only helps salespeople see how their jobs fit into the overall organization but also prepares them for future responsibilities when they may be promoted to sales or marketing management, and perhaps eventually to top management. Anytime a salesperson receives significantly broader or different responsibilities, it is usually a good idea to consider additional training. In designing a training program, the sales manager must answer several questions: Who should receive the training? Who should do the training? Where, when, and how should the training be accomplished? What should be taught? Sales training programs should seek to help salespeople continually grow in knowledge, selling skills, and customer understanding while reinforcing good attitudes about themselves, their jobs, companies, and customers.

Sales force leadership (Chapter 10) may be thought of as the process of exercising psychological, social, and inspirational influences on individual salespeople and the sales force collectively toward the achievement of organizational objectives, goals, and values. In today's intensely competitive markets, organizations have become flatter and leaner, thereby requiring greater leadership skills at all organizational levels. Supervision, management, and leadership are all related but quite different concepts. Supervision entails performing tasks that deal with monitoring the daily work activities of subordinates. Management is primarily a *learned* process whereby subordinates are guided by formally prescribed duties and procedures toward the achievement of organizational goals. In contrast, leadership is more of an *emotional* process that seeks to inspire salespeople to greater achievements by providing a positive vision of a desired future. Several different theories, concepts, and approaches to effective sales force leadership will be explored, and the individual sales manager must choose those most appropriate for salespeople in different situations.

Sales force motivation (Chapter 11) deals with the set of dynamic interpersonal processes that bring about the initiation, direction, intensity, and persistence of work-related behaviors of salespeople toward the attainment of organizational goals and objectives. Several theories of motivation offer intuitively appealing, but different, explanations for why salespeople exert high levels of effort under varying circumstances to reach their personal and organizational goals. Depending on the situation and the composition of the sales force, sales managers will need to exercise their own individual judgments in deciding which motivation approach applies best.

Sales force compensation (Chapter 12) is widely recognized as the most important and least ambiguous way to spur and guide salesperson performance. It can be viewed as all monetary payments and benefits used to remunerate salespeople. The sales force compensation plan is the "steering wheel" that enables management to directly influence salesperson performance and should reflect the company's goals. While there are a variety of ways to compensate salespeople, most companies use three main methods: (1) *straight salary* – a fixed amount of money at fixed intervals, such as weekly or monthly; (2) *straight commission* – an amount that varies with results, usually sales or profits, and (3) *combination* – a mix of salary and commission. Besides salary and commissions, *salespeople* need to be reimbursed for their sales-related expenses and transportation. *Nonfinancial incentives* not tied directly to individual salesperson performance might include use of a company car, office space, secretarial help, and special company benefits such as life insurance, a retirement plan, and health care. Overall sales force compensation, reimbursement, and indirect incentive plans should be reviewed frequently, and revised when appropriate, to ensure they are continuing to be effective and efficient in producing the results desired.

Controlling and Evaluating Sales Force Performance

Sales organization audit and sales analytics (Chapter 13) is essential to assure the organization's bottom-line goal of improving profitability. Periodically, the entire sales organization should undergo a thorough audit, preferably by an external team of objective experts, to determine the overall effectiveness and efficiency of the sales organization and to make recommendations for improvements. Somewhat like the annual physical that many people take to check on their overall health, the sales organization also needs a checkup on its overall health, because it is such a critical determinant of the well-being of the entire company. Successful sales managers also need to be continually monitoring and actively involved in conducting sales analytics on sales volume, costs, and profitability by product lines, territories, customers, and salespersons, including across sales and marketing functions. An important goal of these analytics is to identify unprofitable market segments and sales operations so that sales managers can take timely corrective action to allocate sales force efforts better and improve overall profitability.

Sales force performance evaluation (Chapter 14) is one of the most important activities for sales managers and their salespeople. Sales force performance must be regularly measured and evaluated to determine commissions and bonuses for salespeople, provide constructive feedback to salespeople, and to make promotion, reassignment, or termination decisions. The overall purpose of performance evaluation, however, is to improve organizational profitability by improving sales force productivity. For effective managerial control and evaluation, standards of performance must be established, then actual performance compared to the predetermined standards, and appropriate corrective action taken to improve performance.

Not to be overlooked in evaluating sales force performance is how well ethical guidelines and standards of social responsibility are being met. A salesperson's reputation for ethical behavior and integrity is one of the most valuable assets he or she can bring to negotiations with prospects and customers. Nothing will destroy the credibility and performance of salespeople faster than the perception by customers that they do not operate in an ethical or socially responsible manner. Most companies understand the importance of ethical behavior and provide written ethical codes and training for all their employees.[6]

Sales Force Management Is Uniquely Challenging

Sales force management has always been a challenging job, but it is more than ever so today because of the greater demands on the job. Sales managers must coordinate and lead the efforts of a unique and diverse group of talented employees, i.e. salespeople, who are often entrepreneurial-type people who like to make their own decisions. Some observers have described sales force management as somewhat like the proverbially frustrating, if not impossible, efforts to "herd cats."[7] Besides the requirement to manage independently minded people who have their own ideas about selling, some salespeople are so successful that they are looked upon by the company's senior management as "superstar" performers. So, these salespeople may be viewed somewhat like outstanding athletes who may have more influence or power over how they handle their unique abilities than do their sales managers. Even beyond these challenging roles, today's sales managers must guide sales force efforts during a time of rapidly advancing technology, evolving customer preferences, intensifying global competition, and a continually changing macromarketing environment that may include fluctuating economic conditions, concerns about resource availability, multichannel global competition, legal and ethical restrictions, cultural diversity within the sales force and among customers, and the oftentimes conflicting interests of various stakeholders internal and external to the organization. Without doubt, sales force management has become one of the most challenging management jobs – one that requires skillful, sensitive handling of many ongoing relationships, including most importantly those with prospects and customers, which is generally called customer relationship management (CRM).

CRM is based on the idea that developing closer relationships with customers is the best way to satisfy customers and achieve purchasing loyalty, which is critical because loyal customers are more profitable than nonloyal customers.[8] CRM usually includes a mixture of strategies, technologies, and activities to collect data and analyze customer–company interactions across multiple contact points (e.g. website, e-mail, podcast, telephone, face-to-face, direct mail, and social media) in order to increase customer satisfaction and customer loyalty that lead to repeat purchases. The potential value of the customer's likely lifetime of purchasing from the company is an important factor in determining the CRM strategies for different customer groups.[9]

Although we discuss CRM in Chapter 3, you might want to visit the websites of companies such as Salesforce.com (www.salesforce.com) and Oracle (www.oracle.com) to gain a greater appreciation of how firms can gain a competitive edge by adopting innovative, "cutting-edge" approaches to manage sales information and serve their customers better.

Salesforce.com (www.salesforce.com) is an example of a company website that advocates attaining a competitive edge by adopting innovative, "cutting-edge" approaches to manage sales information and serve customers better.
Source: https://www.salesforce.com/in/products/what-is-salesforce/?d=cta-brand-learn, April 14, 2020.

Serving as Customer Consultants

In line with their company's CRM orientation, contemporary sales managers are training salespeople to think longer term by striving to build ongoing relationships and, when feasible, mutually profitable partnerships with customers. Salespeople are being asked to go beyond merely "selling" toward "serving" and a role more like customer consultants and business partners. What's more, as companies stress the value of CRM, sales managers and their sales forces are taking on greater roles in carrying out CRM strategies in the selling situation.[10] That means, today's sales managers are responsible for helping their salespeople devise and carry out strategies for building these profitable long-term relationships with customers. At the same time, they also need to skillfully develop their in-house or headquarters relationships by "selling" sales force goals and customer requirements within their own companies to ensure the timely service and technical support their salespeople need to better serve customers. Fortunately, many contemporary senior executives recognize that the whole organization needs to have a customer orientation in order to retain customers and enhance profitability.[11]

Managing the Hybrid Sales Force

For the foreseeable future, sales managers will be under tremendous pressure to adjust to many rapidly changing market forces. Instead of merely directing the field sales force, many sales managers now must oversee salespeople across multiple online and off-line marketing channels and work with diverse types of salespeople, including telesalespeople, telemarketers, e-commerce salespeople, direct mailers, international salespeople, missionary salespeople, technical salespeople, manufacturing representatives, selling agents, and multicultural or international salespeople. To illustrate, one manufacturer of industrial products employs a full-time direct sales force of about 40 salespeople operating across several states. But the company also employs about 70 manufacturers' agents in what it calls "a hybrid sales force approach." Unlike a direct sales force, with annual turnover usually above 20%, manufacturers' agents work solely on commissions and tend to sell in one territory for life. As more emphasis is placed on long-term customer relationships, it's more important than ever to minimize turnover of the salespeople calling on customers so that these relationships are not disrupted. Using manufacturers' agents can oftentimes increase stability in customer relationships.[12] In this era of closer customer relationships and multiple sales channels, hybrid sales forces will likely become more common, and sales managers will need to develop the diverse skills to lead them.

What Qualities Are Needed to Be a Sales Manager?

Exactly what qualities, skills, and attitudes are required to be a successful contemporary sales manager? Sales Management in Action Box 1.1 describes some of the eclectic abilities needed to be a sales manager today.

Box 1.1 | Sales Management in Action 1.1

What It Takes to Be a Sales Manager

First and foremost, sales managers have to be effective leaders and motivators of people. In addition, they must be good decision makers, creative problem solvers, and outstanding communicators. As part of the overall marketing team, they must work closely with other departments and functional areas, helping to coordinate and focus the efforts of product development, manufacturing, market research, and promotion to satisfy customer needs and wants. For example, sales managers may help develop national marketing objectives and strategies with the advertising department, then offer insightful advice on how to tailor these plans to match regional differences, the competitive environment, and customer preferences. Many sales managers use findings from market research to better demonstrate the benefits of company products to their customers while helping generate strong brand support. Based on feedback from customers and monitoring of competitive offerings, sales managers often make recommendations for new or improved products (better functional design, safety enhancements, or user-friendly packaging). Sales managers must spend many hours pouring over financial data to analyze costs and profits by products, customers, territories, and salespeople to decide how best to allocate budgets and human resources to enhance productivity and profitability.

To be successful in sales force management, you have to enjoy challenges and solving problems because you'll be encountering them almost every day. Moreover, you have to be resilient enough not to become discouraged when a customer doesn't buy, resourceful enough to find creative solutions for customer problems, motivated enough to set lofty goals for yourself and the sales team, and then driven enough to surpass them. Most importantly, you have to love working with people of all types within and outside your company because that's the heart of this critical boundary-spanning job. Because sales managers' responsibilities require working closely with customers and with people in nearly all departments of the company while trying to control costs and improve profits, a career in sales force management provides the kind of broad experience and development of skills important to assume senior management responsibilities.[13]

Integrating Sales Force Management and Marketing Management

Sales force management is a specialized set of responsibilities and activities within the larger field of marketing management. In a broad sense, sales managers are really *marketing managers* with the specific task of managing the sales force.[14] Should the link between sales and marketing be closer? Well, in international surveys across a wide range of B2B industries, senior executives have identified sales and marketing integration as one of the organizational changes that would do the most to improve sales force performance.[15] Many experts believe the sales manager heads the most important of all marketing activities – the critical revenue-generating and customer relationship functions – which ultimately determine the success or failure of the overall marketing plan.[16] But without thoroughly understanding the company's goals and marketing strategy, few sales managers can successfully integrate marketing and sales. Let's look at how headquarters marketing and the field sales force support each other.

The Field Sales Force and Headquarters Marketing Support Team

An organization's marketing team usually consists of two basic groups: (1) the field sales force and (2) the headquarters marketing support team. While the field sales force is working with customers out in their sales territories, the headquarters marketing team is providing critical support and service functions. This headquarters support includes contributions from the following areas:

- **Advertising.** Coordinates product or service advertising, often through an outside agency
- **Sales promotion.** Develops brochures, catalogs, direct-mail pieces, and special promotions
- **Sales aids.** Prepares videos, podcasts, product samples or prototypes, flip charts, PowerPoints, and other audiovisual materials for sales presentations
- **Trade shows.** Coordinates arrangements for participation in exhibits and trade shows
- **Product publicity.** Prepares and distributes news releases to various media about new products and services
- **Marketing research.** Collects, analyzes, and interprets data about markets, products, customers, sales, competitors, and other factors
- **Marketing and sales planning.** Assists in the development of marketing and sales objectives, strategies, and tactics
- **Forecasting.** Prepares sales forecasts and predicts market trends
- **Product planning and development.** Helps in planning, developing, and testing new and improved products
- **Market development.** Provides support for deeper penetration of current markets and entering new markets
- **Public relations.** Explains the actions of the sales force to the company's various stakeholders, including employees, the media, special interest groups, suppliers, government agencies, legislators, the financial community, company stockholders, and the general public
- **Internet communications.** Assists with online customer service, website development, and customer databases

Specific responsibilities can vary widely across marketing support teams, and some companies may outsource tasks to external specialists such as advertising agencies, marketing research companies, consulting organizations, and public relations firms. Sales managers need to keep in close touch with these headquarters marketing support people, and also with the outside specialists. Having friendly, cooperative relationships with them can make it easier to obtain timely extra support and services to measurably improve sales force performance.

Yaacov Dagan/Alamy Stock Photo

Salespeople and sales managers work together to generate revenue for their organizations – which often involves CRM activities such as promoting their products at trade shows and conventions.

Integrated Marketing Communication

Another important reason for maintaining cooperation between the field sales force and headquarters marketing support is to improve communication with customers. The coordination of promotional activities (advertising, personal selling, sales promotion, direct marketing, public relations and publicity) with other marketing efforts is called integrated marketing communication (IMC). Many companies today are recognizing that they need to integrate the wide range of promotion mix tools and other marketing efforts in order to communicate effectively and efficiently while presenting a consistent brand image and message to customers. Thus, they're planning and coordinating the total set of marketing communication programs simultaneously, instead of planning each one separately.[17] Since personal selling is the most important and highest cost component of the promotion mix for B2B selling, progressive sales managers and salespeople should work closely with other promotional mix areas in integrating the firm's message to prospects and customers. When implemented

Box 1.2 | Sales Management in Action 1.2

Red Bull's Promotion Strategy

"Red Bull gives you wings" is the slogan of this dominant international energy drink seller. Recognizing that the best way to dominate a market is to create one that doesn't exist, Red Bull (redbull.com) did just that starting back in 1987. When the company started, there didn't seem to be a market for energy drinks and even if there was, how could it be reached with a new, unknown product? Identifying active young people who seek exciting entertainment as a potential target market, Red Bull avoided traditional advertising via television, radio, or newspapers. Instead, they directly reached their target market at colleges, sporting events, coffee shops, concerts, and other places where young people congregate and enjoy fun activities. By providing free samples at these places and events, Red Bull got their target market spreading the word about the product. Thirty years later, Red Bull still successfully uses much the same approach albeit they've been quick to adapt to new technologies and changing preferences for entertaining and exciting events. Red Bull operates more like a media company than an energy drink producer. The company sponsors, creates, and/or is highly visible at exciting events attended by young

people, including extreme sports such as windsurfing, snowboarding, cliff-diving, and freestyle motocross, plus spectacular stunts like the Red Bull Stratos Jump from 128,000 feet above the earth, and music festivals, like Coachella, which runs over two weekends with fans trying to stay awake continuously so as not to miss anything. Red Bull shows up to give the audience wings (energy) to stay awake and keep jamming. Red Bull's presence at events builds brand awareness and generates word-of-mouth advertising online at Facebook, Twitter, YouTube, and via microblogging sites. Red Bull also uses smartphone apps to subtly keep their brand in front of consumers while always focusing on the entertainment, not merely promoting Red Bull. In fact, Red Bull's website doesn't even mention its product. Consumers associate Red Bull with excitement and fun because its consistent, integrated branding is built around thrilling entertainment where spectators need to be highly energized. Red Bull's subtle IMC strategy has worked well for 30 years as it has smoothly adapted to new communication technologies and changes in the entertainment preferences of its youthful target market. All of its promotional messages are built around entertainment and special events that young people love.

properly, IMC can improve the effectiveness of the sales force and increase profitability of the company, as illustrated in Sales Management in Action Box 1.2.

Monitoring and Adapting to the Macroenvironment

Sales managers work within the larger framework of their company's objectives, marketing strategies, and target markets. And they must respond to the concerns of stakeholders, including employees, suppliers, financial community, media, stockholders, special interest groups, government, and the general public. Every corporation has many stakeholders who share a vested interest in its activities, and an increasing number of companies are becoming proactive in dealing with these indirect partners. Large companies, for example, usually have public affairs departments that try to influence government legislation and promote the company to stockholders, the financial community, and the media. Beyond these publics or stakeholders is the larger macroenvironment, which often brings dramatic, unexpected changes in technology, economic conditions, resource availability, competitors, laws, culture, and ethical standards.[18] Sales managers must continuously monitor and adjust to these changing domestic and global variables because they can sharply affect sales.

Successful sales managers need to be alert for new market opportunities as well as threats to existing markets. As the organization's "eyes and ears" in the marketplace, the sales force has a special responsibility to identify opportunities and threats then report them back to headquarters. The sales manager thus operates a kind of early-warning system that, if successful, is invaluable to achieving the organization's short-run and long-run objectives. Organizations usually earn their highest profits by capitalizing on opportunities, not just by solving problems. Early on, Cisco Systems exploited the marketing opportunity to build customer relationships and sales via the Internet while reducing selling costs, as explained in Sales Management in Action Box 1.3.

Megatrends Affecting Sales Force Management

What lies ahead for sales managers? Several inexorable forces or megatrends are and will continue to dramatically impact personal selling and sales force management for the foreseeable future. Sales-related megatrends fall into three major categories – *behavioral, technological*, and *managerial*, as shown in Table 1.2.[19]

Behavioral forces Among the most important megatrends affecting the sales manager's job are changing behavioral forces, which are leading to more expert and demanding buyers, rising customer expectations, globalization of markets, empowerment of customers, and microsegmentation of domestic markets. As customers become increasingly empowered and their purchasing expectations rise, they are becoming more sophisticated in their purchasing decisions and intolerant of poor product quality or service. Both domestic and global competitors remain ever alert to capture customers from companies who are not fully satisfying them, so there is no room for seller complacency in today's intensely competitive markets.

Box 1.3 | Sales Management in Action 1.3

Cisco Systems: Building Customer Relationships via the Internet

Cisco Systems (www.cisco.com) sells the networking products that make the Internet and most corporate intranets work, so naturally it was one of the first companies to use the Web to grow customer relationships. While most other companies were still using the Web primarily as an information channel, Cisco's website became a valuable tool for its salespeople to build customer relationships and make sales. It enabled customers to track the status of their orders and get up-to-date pricing and availability information as well as technical advice, freeing up the salespeople to do what they do best—sell. Cisco's site received hundreds of thousands of hits a month, which translated into millions of dollars in sales and over half its total revenue. Exploiting this channel opportunity ahead of competitors gave Cisco a differential advantage by greatly reducing selling and customer service costs. Instead of spending a lot of time answering customer questions about orders and technical problems, Cisco's salespeople were able to focus on maintaining existing customer relationships and finding new prospects.

TABLE **1.2**

Megatrends Affecting Sales Force Management

Behavioral forces

- More expert and demanding buyers
- Rising customer expectations
- Globalization of markets

- Empowerment of customers
- Microsegmentation of domestic markets

Technological forces

- **Sales force automation**
  - E-mail tracking software
  - Sales intelligence software
  - Sales via AI
  - Web conferencing
  - Productivity apps
  - Document analytics (e.g. PandaDoc)
  - Social media selling (LinkedIn Sales Navigator, Facebook, Instagram)
  - LinkedIn
  - YouTube videos

- **Mobile virtual sales offices**
  - Smartphones and tablets
- **Electronic commerce**
  - Internet
    – Blogs
    – Podcasting
    – Screen sharing
    – WebEx
  - Extranets
  - Intranets

Managerial forces

- **Selling cost reduction efforts**
- **Shift to direct marketing alternatives**
  - Direct mail (catalogs, brochures, and sales letters)
  - Telemarketing
  - Teleselling
  - Personalized e-mail
  - Kiosks
  - Facsimile
  - Social media platforms

- **Shortage of B2B salespeople**
- **Developments in information management**
  - Database marketing
  - Data warehousing
  - Data mining
  - Push technology
- **Professional certification of salespeople**

Technological forces Companies worldwide spend about $4 trillion annually on computer hardware, software, and technology services.[20] Thus, sales managers and their salespeople have their work cut out for them in trying to keep up with the technology their prospects and customers are using. Sales force automation (SFA) is the use of high-tech tools that help salespeople work effectively and efficiently. Sales managers who make skillful and efficient use of swiftly developing SFA technology to increase the productivity of their salespeople in selling to and serving customers are most likely to be successful in the years ahead.[21] To gain a critical understanding of how SFA technologies can augment revenues and increase bottom-line performance, peruse the website of Oracle Corporation (www.oracle.com), a global sales technology solutions provider to clients in the health-care industry.

As seen in Table 1.2, sales managers and salespeople already use a host of SFA innovations. One of the most promising areas of SFA is artificial intelligence (AI). AI is an overall term that covers several different technologies, including machine learning, computer vision, natural language processing, deep learning, and much more. Using an example familiar to most people, AI-powered computer vision systems in self-driving cars and trucks are able to identify obstacles much like humans

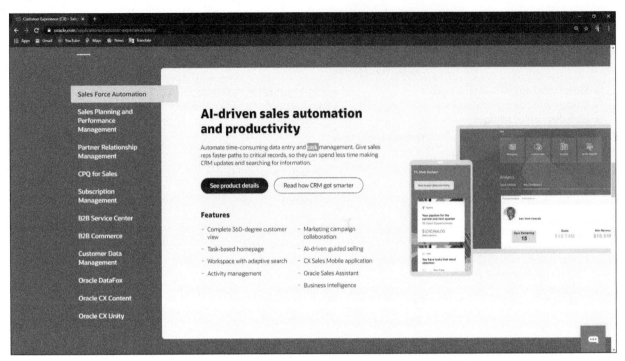

Oracle Corporation (www.oracle.com), a global sales technology solutions provider to clients in the healthcare industry, helps companies implement SFA technologies to increase sales revenues, productivity, and improve bottom-line performance.
Source: https://www.oracle.com/applications/customer-experience/sales/, April 14, 2020.

do and avoid them. On our cellphones, Alexa or Siri understands our spoken questions and can respond with accurate information. A recent national survey shows that 46% of companies are implementing AI systems to increase sales and marketing productivity. Over 80% of the most recent adopters of AI and cognitive technologies say their companies have already achieved benefits and high-performing sales forces are over three times more likely to be outperforming those who do not yet use these technologies.[22] When innovations come along that promise to cut costs and increase efficiency, many companies will adopt them promptly, so sales managers must also adopt them rapidly to keep pace with customers. Instant messaging, for example, is being used by sales teams in different cities around the world to query coworkers and customers anywhere for an instant response without picking up the phone or logging into e-mail. No company can afford to lag behind in adopting technological advances that can increase its effectiveness and efficiency in profitably satisfying customers.

Managerial forces How are sales organizations responding to these relentless behavioral and technological megatrends? As shown in Table 1.2, they're trying various strategies including reducing selling costs, shifting from field selling to direct-marketing alternatives, hiring and developing specialized sales personnel to cope with the shortage of B2B salespeople, requiring salespeople to obtain professional certification to enhance their credibility with customers, and using the latest developments in information management. Sales managers' creativity in promptly responding to evolving behavioral and technological megatrends can give the sales force a significant competitive advantage.

By deploying SFA technology to salespeople and using the latest information management tools, sales managers can increase productivity while reducing sales and marketing costs to improve profitability.

Information management tools Fortunately, sales managers have valuable new data collection and analysis tools that are helping them respond to the domestic and global megatrends affecting the operation of their sales organizations. Among the most widely used of these information management tools are database marketing, data warehousing, data mining, and push technology, all of which are discussed in Chapter 3.

How Well Are Sales Managers Performing?

Sales managers have a challenging job, and they're bound to be criticized by some sales organization members no matter how well they handle their duties. Some of the most common complaints are that sales managers do not take their salespeople's concerns seriously, demand too much paperwork, and often fail to follow up on problems.[23]

Newly selected sales managers may fail to perform well in managerial roles for several reasons: (1) illogical selection of sales managers, (2) inadequate sales force management training programs, (3) lack of a long-run customer relationship orientation in handling sales operations, and (4) insufficient blending of sales, marketing, and financial knowledge.[24]

Illogical Selection of Sales Managers

Through no fault of their own, newly selected sales managers are probably marketing's best example of the Peter Principle: "In a hierarchy, every employee tends to rise to his level of incompetence."[25] Despite articles by marketing scholars and practitioners who stress that a super salesperson does not necessarily make a good sales manager, the reward for a sales rep who does an outstanding selling job for a couple of years or so is often promotion to sales force management – a position for which he or she may be ill-prepared. Ironically, the very skills that enable a person to be an excellent salesperson may inhibit him or her from being a good sales manager. Figure 1.2 shows that as people climb up the managerial staircase, the skills needed to excel change. But at all levels, interpersonal skills are critical to serving effectively as the vital link between the sales force and higher management.

Some sales organizations suffer because the sales manager remains too involved in "doing" instead of managing. Time devoted to determining how to accomplish work through other people is "managing." Time spent on performing activities that subordinates could do is "doing." New sales managers often unconsciously become involved in doing because they feel comfortable in continuing to apply the same skills that earned them promotion to sales force management. Even in small businesses where the size of the sales force restricts the amount of time they can devote to managing, sales managers still should recognize that managerial tasks come first. For example, when sales managers make sales calls on their own, they are not managing. But when they make calls with the salespeople to analyze the latter's presentations, they are performing management duties. Subordinates usually recognize when a manager is doing rather than managing, and few sales managers enhance their own stature with the sales force by preempting salespeople's jobs.

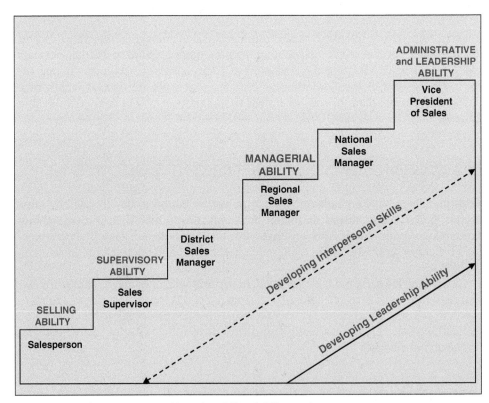

FIGURE 1.2 Sales force management hierarchy: Skill and ability requirements.

Inadequate Sales Force Management Training

Compounding the problem of poor selection criteria for promotion to sales force management is the inadequacy of sales force management training programs. While many companies spend thousands of dollars to train new salespeople, many of these same companies fail to train sales managers adequately. In studies of sales managers from a cross section of 16 industries, fewer than half indicated that their companies provided any sales force management training at all.[26] Even when they do, it often emphasizes company policies and procedures. Seldom is adequate and sound training provided in what constitutes effective management practice or what the holistic role of the successful sales manager should be. As the linchpin between the selling and buying organizations, sales managers are too essential to organizational success to be excluded from managerial training. In fact, over the long run, managerial training for sales managers is even more critical to the organization because many company CEOs come from sales and marketing backgrounds. One recent study found that more than 25% of CEOs worldwide had sales and/or marketing backgrounds.[27]

Lack of a Long-Run Customer Relationship Orientation

Many sales managers still give little more than lip service to developing long-run customer relationships and salespeople pick up on this attitude quickly. Sales managers and salespeople who have a narrow *selling* orientation tend to focus on products and the immediate sale – they emphasize their own needs, not those of customers. In contrast, a customer relationship orientation focuses on the buyer's needs and development of long-term mutually beneficially relationships and partnerships. Hewlett-Packard (www.hp.com), manufacturer of precision electronic devices, puts the customer orientation into practice. Its salespeople, called "field engineers," are encouraged to take the customer's side in any dispute with HP. If sales managers convey even subtly to their salespeople that short-run sales are more important than long-run relationships with customers, customer turnover is likely to be high and this will soon translate into lower sales and profits. Nothing is more important to sales force success than developing and nurturing long-run profitable relationships with customers.

Insufficient Blending of Sales, Marketing, and Financial Knowledge

Marketing and financial knowledge are becoming requirements for sales force management positions in progressive companies. These companies are looking for versatile, well-rounded sales managers who understand and can implement overall marketing strategies and who have strong financial capability. For better sales and marketing coordination, Kraft General Foods (www.kraft.com) gives division sales managers dual reporting responsibilities. Not only do they report directly to a national sales manager, but they also have a direct relationship with the head of the marketing division. The idea is to keep division managers more closely informed about how their particular product lines are being marketing and their relative profitability. Yet, in some companies today, sales managers still are kept in the dark when it comes to sharing marketing and financial information. For example, control reports sent to sales managers often contain only overall sales performance, sales expense, and budget data – not-profit figures, which are too often solely for the eyes of top management. To do their jobs well, sales managers need profit information by customer, product, territory, and other market segments. Otherwise, they will tend to focus on generating the largest sales volume, which may be more unprofitable for the company than smaller, more specialized sales.

Both the field sales and headquarters marketing groups need to appreciate that they are key players on the same team who must cooperate to achieve organization objectives. If either job is viewed as an activity isolated and remote from the other, poor communication and even rivalry can separate the marketing staff and sales force thereby reducing overall company performance. Cross-disciplinary training is one approach to achieving organizational synergism. Some companies periodically bring sales managers into headquarters for training in finance and operations as well as marketing. Broad managerial training in several functional areas can greatly increase the value of sales managers to their companies and help prepare them for promotion to higher management levels.

Developing Sales Managers for the New Millennium

To succeed in the years ahead, sales managers will need to learn fresh roles and reinvent some old ones, including (1) developing closer relationships with online and off-line customers, both domestic and international, and more in-depth understanding of their customers' different businesses, changing needs, and buying patterns; (2) treating salespeople as empowered equals and partnering with them in achieving sales quotas, profitability, and customer satisfaction/loyalty goals; (3) applying flexible motivational skills in working with a multicultural, hybrid sales force of telemarketers, tellsellers, missionary salespeople, direct marketers, manufacturers' agents, field salespeople, international salespeople, online salespeople, and others; (4) keeping up-to-date on the latest technologies affecting buyer–seller relationships and the changing needs and preferences of customers; (5) learning marketing and financial skills in order to better identify potential business opportunities and recommend competitive strategies; (6) working closely with other internal company departments as a member of the total corporate team dedicated to satisfying customers profitably; (7) continually seeking ways to exceed customer expectations and bring *added value* and mutual benefits to the ongoing buyer–seller relationships; and (8) creating a flexible, learning, and adapting environment for all members of the sales and support teams.[28] Table 1.3 contrasts today's sales managers with yesterday's sales managers.

One of the primary goals of our sales force management text is to help current and future sales managers successfully adapt to the inexorable technological, behavioral, and managerial forces that will affect sales forces in the years ahead. The coming chapters provide realistic guidance and learning experiences to help current and future salespeople move into professional sales force management careers in an era of rapid technological advances and evolving multiple sales channels to better serve diverse online and off-line customers – globally as well as domestically.

TABLE **1.3**

Yesterday's versus Today's Sales Manager

Yesterday's sales manager focused on	Today's sales managers focus on
■ Closely monitoring selling interactions between salespeople and customers	■ Developing profitable customer relationships with "win–win" outcomes
■ Short-run objectives – current products, markets, customers, and strategies	■ Monitoring and adjusting to long-run trends, opportunities, and challenges to better serve markets and customers
■ Achieving sales volume and quotas	■ Analyzing profitability by customer types, products, territories, and salespeople
■ Serving as the information conduit between senior management and the sales force with little use of technology other than the telephone	■ Using the latest technologies to effectively and efficiently manage the sales force and carry out CRM activities to achieve customer satisfaction and repeat purchase loyalty
■ Working in sales territories with salespeople with sales managers oftentimes handling their own set of large accounts	■ Developing plans and strategies to achieve organization goals through effective leadership of the sales force
■ Managing field sales activities since marketing was considered the responsibility of senior management at company headquarters	■ Learning marketing and financial skills to identify, assess, and recommend market opportunities and strategies to senior management
■ Accepting detached or even adversarial relationships with other internal company departments, especially those perceived as not being sufficiently responsive to sales force needs	■ Creating positive working relationships with internal company departments as cooperative members of the total corporate team dedicated to fully satisfying customers profitably and earning customer loyalty.
■ Looking for ways to increase sales volume without much concern for profitability	■ Looking for ways to bring mutual *added value* profitably to ongoing buyer–seller relationships
■ Driving the field sales force to achieve their assigned quotas	■ Creating a flexible, learning, and adapting environment for all members of the hybrid sales team across multiple sales channels

Chapter Summary

1. **Summarize the basic responsibilities and evolving roles of sales force management.** Sales managers are instrumental in building relationships with an organization's customers. More specifically, sales managers plan, lead, and control the personal selling activities of the organization. Their basic duties are to prepare sales plans and budgets; set sales goals and objectives; estimate demand and forecast sales; determine the size and structure of the sales force; recruit, select, and train salespeople; determine sales territories, sales quotas, and performance standards; compensate, motivate, and lead the sales force; conduct sales volume, cost and profit analyses; and evaluate sales force performance, including ethical and social conduct.

   Sales managers' responsibilities and titles vary widely depending on the nature of the organization. Most organizations assign traditional duties such as forecasting, planning, budgeting, and profit responsibilities to the sales manager. But, in some, the sales manager is the marketing manager in every way but position title. The sales force management position hierarchy usually starts at the branch level, and moves up through district, zone, division, regional, and national sales manager to vice president of sales in some organizations – with increasing managerial, administrative, and leadership responsibilities at each higher sales force management level.

2. **Demonstrate how sales managers can better integrate their roles with marketing management.** Sales managers are essentially marketing managers with the specific task of managing the sales force in its interactions with prospects and customers. Cooperation between the field sales force and headquarters is extremely important given the trend of IMC and CRM. Many companies today are taking a broader perspective when planning marketing strategies and integrating the total set of communication functions rather than planning each one separately.

3. **Identify and prepare for megatrends that will affect your future in sales force management.** Accelerating megatrends in the marketing environment are making the sales manager's job more complex than ever. These inexorable megatrends include *behavioral, technological,* and *managerial* forces, which are leading to higher customer expectations and buying expertise, globalization and microsegmentation of markets, advances in telecommunications technology, cultural diversity in the sales force and among customers, emphasis on controlling selling costs, and the shortage of qualified B2B salespeople. It is critical that sales managers stay flexible, adaptable, and in a continuous learning mode as they oversee hybrid sales forces in rapidly changing markets.

4. **Evaluate the selection criteria for sales force management and compare them to your present and potential qualifications.** Sales managers in many organizations may not be performing as well as they could due to four major reasons: (1) illogical selection of sales managers, (2) inadequate sales force management training programs, (3) lack of a long-run customer relationship orientation in handling sales operations, and (4) insufficient blending of sales, marketing, and financial knowledge. Unless these four problems in sales manager selection, training, orientation, and integration with marketing are resolved, many newly selected sales managers may not be equipped to handle their expanding responsibilities.

5. **Analyze how the sales manager's job is expanding and what it will mean for your career.** With the empowerment of salespeople through the Internet and SFA, sales force management jobs are shifting more toward CRM while directing a hybrid sales force across multiple sales channels in selling to diverse customers. Sales managers will need more intense training not only in traditional managerial duties but also in blending marketing, finance, and sales perspectives to increase profitability of sales force operations. Only those sales managers who are flexible, adaptable, and continually learning will thrive in the years ahead.

Key Terms

Sales force management	**Customer relationship**	**Integrated marketing**	**Sales force auto-**
Macroenvironment	**management (CRM)**	**communication (IMC)**	**mation (SFA)**
Stakeholders			

Notes

1. Leimbach, M. Sales management as a source of competitive advantage. http://www.wilsonlearning.com/wlw/research-paper/s/sales-mgmt-adv (accessed 30 October 2019); Anderson, R.E., Dubinsky, A.J., and Mehta, R. (2014). *Personal Selling: Building Customer Relationships and Partnerships*, 2–25. Dubuque, I.A: Kendall-Hunt; Ashe-Edmunds, S. Importance of sales management. https://smallbusiness.chron.com/importance-sales-management-65099.html (accessed 29 October 2019); Makela, R. 5 reasons why sales management skills are a top priority. http://www.salesreadinessgroup.com/blog/5-reasons-why-sales-management-skills-are-priority (accessed 29 October 2019).

2. Kimla, N. (2016) Sales analytics and the changing role of sales management. https://salespop.net/sales-management/sales-analytics-role-of-sales-management/ (accessed 21 October 2019); Padelford, L. (2014). 5 ways sales has dramatically changed in 5 years. http://www.business2community.com/sales-management/5-ways-sales-dramatically-changed-5-years-0848036 (accessed 22 October 2019); Anderson, R. (1996). Personal selling and sales management in the new millennium. *Journal of Personal Selling and Sales Management* XVI (Fall): 17–32.

3. Anderson, R.E., Cohen, A.H., Christ, P.F. et al. (2020). Provenance, evolution, and transition of personal selling and sales management to strategic marketing channel management. *Journal of Marketing Channels* (February–March): 28–42; Christ, P.F. and Anderson, R.E. (2011). The impact of technology on evolving roles of salespeople. *Journal of Historical Research in Marketing* 3 (Spring): 173–193.

4. Ruff, R. (2019). Sales managers and the "supersalesperson" syndrome. http://www.linkedin.com/pulse/sales-managers-super-salesperson-syndrome-richard-ruff-1c (accessed 29 October 2019); Rosenbloom, B. and Anderson, R. (1984). The sales manager: Tomorrow's super marketer. *Business Horizons* (March–April): 50–56.

5. Kennan, W. Jr. (1998). The death of the sales manager. *Sales and Marketing Management* 150 (April); Johnstone, K. (2017). Responsibilities of a sales manager: The ultimate guide. http://www.peaksalesrecruiting.com/blog/responsibilities-sales-manager/ (accessed 28 October 2019); Signorelli, B. (2019). 10 Things I wish I knew before becoming a sales manager. https://blog.hubspot.com/sales/things-i-wish-i-knew-before-becoming-a-sales-manager (accessed 30 October 2019).

6. Brooks, J. (2010). Code of ethics for sales professionals. http://customerthink.com/code_of_ethics_for_sales_professionals/; Sales and marketing creed: the international code of ethics for sales and marketing. http://www.smei.org/page/salescode (accessed 30 October 2019); How sales managers can establish ethical behavior in sales teams. https://salesethics.net/blog/how-sales-managers-can-establish-ethical-behavior-in-sales-teams/ (accessed 29 October 2019).

7. Jones, P.M. (2014). Herding cats – Managing sales performance. http://www.philmjones.com/herding-cats-managing-sales-performance/ (accessed 28 October 2019); Rembach, J. Customer experience management is like herding cats. http://www.business2community.com/customer-experience/customer-experience-management-like-herding-cats-0955230 (accessed 28 October 2019).

8. Carpenter, D. Your best asset: What makes customer loyalty so important. http://www.business.com/articles/what-makes-customer-loyalty-so-important/ (accessed 29 October 2019); Swaminathan, S., Anderson, R.E., and Song, L. (2019). Building loyalty in e-commerce: impact of business and customer characteristics. *Journal of Marketing Channels* 25 (Fall): 22–35; Anderson, R.E., Swaminathan, S., and Mehta, R. (2013). How to drive customer satisfaction. *MIT Sloan Management Review* 54 (Summer): 13–15; Anderson, R.E. and Swaminathan, S. (2011). Customer satisfaction and loyalty in e-markets: A PLS path modeling approach. *Journal of Marketing Theory & Practice*) 19 (May): 219–233; Tanner, J.F. Jr., Ahearne, M., Leigh, T.W. et al. (2005). CRM in sales-intensive organizations: a review and future directions. *Journal of Personal Selling & Sales Management*, 25 (Spring): 169–180; Zablah, A.R., Bellenger, D.N., and Johnston, W.J. (2004). An evaluation of divergent perspectives on customer relationship management: towards a common understanding of an emerging phenomenon. *Industrial Marketing Management* 33: 475–489; Srinivasan, S., Anderson, R., and Ponnavolu, K. (2002). Customer loyalty in e-commerce: an exploration of its antecedents and consequences. *Journal of Retailing* 78 (January): 41–50; Grahame, D. (2002). Customer relationship management: in b2c markets, often less is more. *California Management Review* (Spring) 44 (3): 87–104; Seshadri S. and Mishra, R. (2004). Relationship marketing and contract theory. *Industrial Marketing Management* 33: 513–526.

9. Lund, J. (2020). What is CRM and why is it important to your business? http://www.superoffice.com/blog/what-is-crm/ (accessed 30 October 2019); Hawkins, C. (2019). How to create a CRM strategy in 7 steps. https://fitsmallbusiness.com/how-to-create-a-crm-strategy/ (accessed 1 November 2019).

10. Totah, Z. How sales CRM helps increase revenue, improve customer loyalty and more. https://selecthub.com/customer-relationship-management/crm-helps-improve-sales/ (accessed 1 November 2019); Larsen, G. (2019). 15 Sales management software and CRMs used by sales teams. https://blog.insidesales.com/crm/sales-management-software-and-crms/ (accessed 2 November 2019); Hong-kit Yim, F., Anderson, R.E., and Swaminathan, S. (2004). Customer relationship management: its dimensions and effect on customer outcomes. *Journal of Personal Selling & Sales Management* 24 (Fall): 263–278; Boles, J., Brashear, T., Bellenger, D. et al. (2003). Relationship selling behaviors: antecedents and relationship with performance. *Journal of Business & Industrial Marketing* 18 (2–3): 141–162.

11. Jackson, D. (2018). How to build a customer oriented culture from the ground up. http://www.kayako.com/blog/how-to-build-a-customer-oriented-culture-from-the-ground-up/ (accessed 30 October 2019); Gilliland, N. (2019). Five examples of customer centric companies. https://econsultancy.com/examples-customer-centric-companies/ (accessed 30 October 2019); Jaramillo, F., Mulki, J.P., and Marshall, G.W. (2005). A meta-analysis of the relationship between organizational commitment and salesperson job performance: 25 years of research. *Journal of Business Research* 58: 705–714.

12. Cohen, A. (1999). Who needs a sales force, anyway? *Marketing & Sales Management* (February): 13; Adams, B. Independent sales reps: the pros and cons. https://businesstown.com/articles/independent-sales-reps-the-pros-and-cons/ (accessed 3 November 2019).

13. Adapted from various corporate sales recruiting brochures.

14. Rouzies, D., Anderson, E., Kohli, A.K. et al. (2005). Sales and marketing integration: a proposed framework. *Journal of Personal Selling & Sales Management* (Spring) 25 (2): 113–124; Arthur, L. (2017). The relationship between sales and marketing. https://bizfluent.com/about-7523919-relationship-between-sales-marketing.html (accessed 31 October 2019).

15. Rouzies, D., Anderson, E., Kohli, A.K. et al. (2005). Sales and marketing integration: A proposed framework. *Journal of Personal Selling & Sales Management* (Spring) 25 (2): 113–124; Miller, T. G. and Gist, E.P. (2003). *Selling in Turbulence Times*. New York: Accenture-Economist Intelligence Unit Survey; Penner, J. and Hergesell, C. The time is now for tighter sales-marketing integration. http://www.cmo.com/opinion/articles/2018/2/20/why-the-time-is-now-to-integrate-sales-and-marketing-ey.html#gs.dnal3f (accessed 31 October 2019).

16. Thoreson, K. (2019). Sales and marketing management. http://www.business2community.com/sales-management/sales-and-marketing-management-02209729 (accessed 1 November 2019); Sales management importance, sales role in the success of business. https://professortoday.com/importance-sales-management/ (accessed 31 October 2019).

17. Mack, S. How promotional activity is integrated to achieve marketing objectives. https://smallbusiness.chron.com/promotional-activity-integrated-achieve-marketing-objectives-66016.html (accessed 2 November 2019); Kitchen, P. and Schultz, D. (1999). A multi-country comparison of the drive for IMC. *Journal of Advertising Research* 39: 21; Cook, B. (1997). Integrated marketing communications: performing together. *Journal of Advertising Research* 37 (5): 5.

18. McQuerry, L. The importance of using stakeholders to communicate your messages. https://smallbusiness.chron.com/importance-using-stakeholders-communicate-messages-36159.html (accessed 3 November 2019); Sun, L. The role of stakeholders in your business. http://www.businessdictionary.com/article/601/the-role-of-stakeholders-in-your-business/ (accessed 1 November 2019); Jones, E., Brown, S.P., Zoltners, A.A. et al. (2005). The changing environment of selling and sales management. *Journal of Personal Selling & Sales Management* (Spring) 25 (2): 105–112.

19. Adapted and updated from Anderson, R.E. (1996). Personal selling and sales management in the new millennium. *Journal of Personal Selling and Sales Management* 16 (Fall): 17–32.

20. Rosenbaum, E. (2019). Tech spending will near $4 trillion this year. Here's where all the money is going and why. http://www.cnbc.com/2019/04/08/4-trillion-in-tech-spending-in-2019-heres-where-the-money-is-going.html (accessed 2 November 2019); Caputa, P. (2016). Top salespeople are more likely to use these tools than the rest of you. https://blog.hubspot.com/sales/linkedin-state-of-sales-technology-findings (accessed 1 November 2019); Speier, C. and Venkatesh, V. (2002). The hidden minefields in the adoption of sales force automation technologies. *Journal of Marketing* 66 (July): 98–111.

21. Behar, N. How to use technology in sales to improve performance. http://www.salesreadinessgroup.com/blog/how-to-use-technology-in-sales-to-improve-performance (accessed 2 November 2019); 7 types of technologies that will help you get an edge in sales. http://www.tenfold.com/sales-performance/sales-technologies-advantage/ (accessed 3 November 2019); Robinson, L. Jr., Marshall, G.W., and Stamps, M.B. (2004). Sales force use of technology: antecedents to technology acceptance. *Journal of Business Research* 20: 1–9.

22. Gschwandtner, G. (2019) How AI automation will change the state of sales. *Selling Power* (29 May). https://blog.sellingpower.com/gg/sales-technology/ (accessed 2 November 2019); Kaput, M. (2019). Artificial intelligence in sales: what it is, how to use it. http://www.marketingaiinstitute.com/blog/artificial-intelligence-in-sales-what-it-is-how-to-use-it-and-companies-to-demo (accessed 2 November 2019).

23. Zoltners, A.A., Sinha, P., and Lorimer, S.E (2019). Why new sales managers need more training. *Harvard Business Review* (14 March), https://hbr.org/2019/03/why-new-sales-managers-need-more-training (accessed 2 November 2019); Anderson, R., Dubinsky, A., and Mehta, R. (1999). Sales managers: marketing's best example of the Peter principle? *Business Horizons* (January–February): 19–26; Carew, J. (1989). When salespeople evaluate their managers. *Sales & Marketing Management* (March): 24–27; Fisher, D. (2017). The 6 most common reasons why new sales managers fail. http://www.menemshagroup.com/blog/the-six-most-common-reasons-why-sales-managers-fail (accessed 2 November 2019); Werth, J. (2019). Top 10 reasons sales managers fail – and what to do about it. http://www.highprobsell.com/articles/why_sales_managers_fail.html (accessed 2 November 2019).

24. Cowdrey, E. (2014). Basic operational finance for sales managers. http://www.linkedin.com/pulse/20140709133327-46222197-basic-operational-finance-for-sales-managers (accessed 2 November 2019); Åshe-Edmunds, S. The financial information needed by a sales manager. https://work.chron.com/financial-information-needed-sales-manager-20076.html (accessed 2 November 2019);

Hogan, C. (2014) why sales reps should be fluent in finance. http://www.insightsquared.com/blog/why-sales-reps-should-be-fluent-in-finance/ (accessed 2 November 2019).

25. Barrett, S. (2018). The alarming findings about the "Peter principle" and sales managers. http://www.smartcompany.com.au/marketing/sales/alarming-findings-peter-principle-sales-managers/ (accessed 3 November 2019); Anderson, R., Dubinsky, A., and Mehta, R. (1999). Sales managers: marketing's best example of the Peter principle? *Business Horizons* (January–February): 19–26.

26. Zoltners, A.A., Sinha, P., and Lorimer, S.E. (2019). Why new sales managers need more training. *Harvard Business Review* (14 March), https://hbr.org/2019/03/why-new-sales-managers-need-more-training (accessed 2 November 2019); Mehta, R., Anderson, R., and Strong, J. (Summer 1997). An empirical investigation of sales management training for sales managers. *Journal of Personal Selling and Sales Management* 27 (Summer):

53–66; Davis, K.F. (2017). The costly impact of untrained sales managers. https://trainingindustry.com/articles/sales/the-costly-impact-of-untrained-sales-managers/ (accessed 3 November 2019).

27. 10 CEOs who started as sales reps. www.smartwinnr.com/post/top10-ceos-who-started-as-salesreps/ (accessed 3 November 2019); Savitz, E. (2011). The path to becoming a Fortune 500 CEO. http://www.forbes.com/sites/ciocentral/2011/12/05/the-path-to-becoming-a-fortune-500-ceo/#776b2152709b (accessed 3 November 2019); Hedges, N. (2015). From sales rep to CEO: 5 reasons salespeople make great leaders. http://www.inc.com/nick-hedges/from-sales-rep-to-ceo-5-reasons-salespeople-make-great-leaders.html (accessed 2 November 2019).

28. Updated from Anderson, R.E. (1996). Personal selling and sales management in the new millennium. *Journal of Personal Selling and Sales Management* Vol. XVI (Fall): 17–32.

Chapter Review Questions

1. Why and how do you think the sales manager's job will change as we move farther further into the twenty-first century? [LO 5]

2. What domestic and global forces or megatrends are affecting sales managers now and in the foreseeable future? [LO 3]

3. You work for a large machine tool manufacturer and have been recently promoted from the sales force to the position of sales manager in another region. How would you go about ensuring a good working relationship with your salespeople and the headquarters marketing staff? [LO 4]

4. What criteria would you propose for progressive companies to use in selecting salespeople for promotion to sales manager? [LO 4]

5. What kind of training would you provide to new sales managers? What about additional training for more experienced sales managers? [LO 1, 2, 5]

6. If you were the vice president of sales or the national sales manager for a large corporation, what criteria would you use to evaluate the performance of subordinate sales managers? [LO 1, 2, 4]

7. Write a job description for the position of sales manager. What responsibilities and duties do you consider most important? Why? [LO 1]

8. Describe how sales managers can use the latest available technologies to more effectively and efficiently lead and direct the sales force. [LO 3, 5]

9. How might sales managers use the latest technological developments to better satisfy and improve relationships with prospects and customers? [LO 3, 5]

10. Assume that you are the national sales manager for a medium-size company, how will you improve the selection and preparation process for new sales managers? Outline a training process, including specific topics, to provide new sales managers with the knowledge and skills to succeed. [LO 1, 2, 3, 4, 5]

Online Exercise

Use an Internet search engine (e.g. Google or Yahoo) to find three companies that are marketing sales force management training courses. What is the length and cost of each training course? Where is each held – online or off-line? What are the credentials of the people doing the training? What does the training cover that sounds most interesting? Is the focus of the sales training B2B or B2C? Does the training cover customer relationship management? What does the training promise that's new? Based on the online information, which of the training courses would you choose to attend? Explain why?

Role-Play Exercise

Situation

You're a relatively new district sales manager on the east coast for a large consumer products company that sells mainly through wholesalers but also direct to giant chain retailers such as Wal-Mart and Target. Today, you've been invited to be a guest lecturer to talk for an hour to eight newly hired field salespeople who are going through your company's basic sales training program. You've been asked to talk about the company's CRM initiative as it relates to the way field salespeople do their jobs. You want to talk with the salespeople in a down-to-earth, pragmatic way, so that they will grasp what CRM is, why it's so important to the company, and what they can do in their interactions with prospects and customers to further the company-wide CRM initiative.

Role-Play Participants and Assignments

Guest lecturer: District sales manager invited to talk about the company's CRM program and the role of salespeople in implementing it in their interactions with prospects and customers.

Salespeople: Eight people in their twenties with different backgrounds who are just starting their sales careers, so they are likely to have many questions about CRM and their roles.

In-Basket Exercise

You are a district sales manager for a large consumer products company that sells its products largely through wholesalers and directly to a few giant retailers. Your company also has an extranet where business customers can order online. Today, you received an e-mail memorandum from your company's national sales manager saying that the CEO is upset because of poor customer retention rates. Last year, the company lost over 30% of its regular customers through attrition of various kinds. At the same time, promotional costs to attract replacement customers are increasing dramatically, causing profit margins to suffer. The CEO has found this loss of customers and declining profits unacceptable and has demanded that all the company's sales managers start focusing more on customer retention. In addition, he is launching customer relationships training programs for all company managers. Large bonuses will be awarded to those sales managers and their salespeople who can most successfully reduce customer attrition. You have called a sales meeting for all your salespeople to discuss this new initiative by the CEO.

Question

1. What will you tell your sales force? Outline the points that you plan to make to them.

Ethical Dilemma

You're the sales manager for a large chemical company, with reason to suspect that one of your top salespeople isn't always playing by the rules. You know that on occasion Jared has taken friends out to lunch and charged it to the company. At other times, you've caught him conducting personal business on company time with company resources (long-distance telephone calls and charging car mileage to the company for personal business and pleasure). At the end of last year, you discovered that Jared had persuaded one of his best customers to order extra product quantities so he could make his sales quota for the year. In mid-January, that customer returned the excess products for a full refund.

You've overlooked these things in the past because of the large sales volume Jared usually generates in his sales territory. One evening, though, on your way out of the office, you overhear a conversation between Jared and another of your salespeople. Jared comments: "I personally think it's okay to withhold negative information about a product in order to make a big sale, as long as no one can get injured by using the product. Things are getting really tough in our industry, and, if you're going to survive, you've got to do whatever it takes to get a sale!"

Question

1. As Jared's sales manager, what will you do? Should you reprimand him, retrain him, or fire him? Why?

It was a beautiful autumn day in downtown San Diego as the three recently appointed sales managers were enjoying a hearty breakfast in the hotel restaurant. While sipping their second cup of coffee, Juan Carlos Varela, Grace Gallo, and Pam Swenson were discussing the events of the first day in the three-day sales force management seminar Greystone Organics now requires all its new sales managers to attend.

Juan Carlos Varela: I wonder why we spent so much time talking about sales force performance this morning. They're making it sound like sales force success is a big mystery. All that stuff about developing long-term prospects and customer relationships and internal company support is a lot of ivory tower stuff that'll just distract our salespeople and their sales managers. All week I'm running around like a deer on the opening day of hunting season just pushing my salespeople to make their sales quotas. I've got a couple of guys in the office making sales calls by phone on our smaller prospects and customers, and I don't have time to monitor them since I'm out of the office so much. Working with my people in the field and helping them make sales presentations and handle customer complaints keep me from even finding time to do all the paperwork headquarters keeps demanding. And those CRM sales reports we are supposed to review and update each week are no easier to do online than by hand like we have been doing for years. I guess this seminar is supposed to make us more sensitive to our salespeople, prospects, and customers, but I sure don't have much time to worry about subtle things like role perceptions and developing long-term customer relationships. In my opinion, there's only one thing that really matters and that's spelled M-O-N-E-Y. You make the carrot big enough and any donkey will get the job done. And the same goes for customers – you offer products at lower prices than competitors and you've got a sale whether you've got a warm and fuzzy relationship with the customer or not.

Grace Gallo: Yeah, I know what you mean, Juan Carlos. Seems like the sales training manager is trying to impress the big boss by bringing in these glib training whizzes, who probably never carried "the sales bag." They are using fancy terms to tell us what we should be doing and thinking about – besides our pressure-cooker jobs. I'd like to see them try running a sales force. It's a lot easier talking about managing salespeople than actually doing it. Today, the schedule says we're going to discuss "inexorable megatrends in the macromarketing environment" – whatever that string of gobbledygook means. My salespeople know that I'm the only megatrend they have to worry about. If I'm happy, they're happy. They know what they have to do if they want their commissions and bonuses. If they make their quotas, I leave them alone. If they don't, then I come down hard on them. Most of my salespeople would laugh in my face if I told them they had to concentrate more on developing long-term relationships with prospects and customers. I'm not even sure how we would measure it!? In five years, half or more of my salespeople will have moved on, so they are focused on the short term. With salespeople, you're always going to have 20–30% turnover a year because some people just can't cut the mustard in sales, and good salespeople are always been offered jobs by other companies.

Pam Swenson: I have to admit that I'm learning some things I'm going to try when I get back to the office next week. Top management doesn't allow us to match some of the discounts that our competitors are offering, so I know we have to learn to sell on some basis other than price. By focusing on developing closer customer relationships and better service, maybe we can overcome our price disadvantage. I know a lot of salespeople don't think long run because they're opportunists, but maybe I can find a way to reward them for doing a better job in cultivating customer relationships and keeping customers from leaving us for a competitor's latest discount offer. But, like you said, it would be difficult to come up with a good way to measure whether they have done a better job or not. I know that I'm probably going to be at Simpson for the foreseeable future since my kids are just now entering grade school and I don't want to disrupt their lives. So, I've got to figure out a way to keep my profitable loyal customers. Simpson's marketing director told me that the company loses almost 25% of its customers each year, and that it costs about 10 times as much to win new customers as to keep our current ones. She said: "If we could cut back just a little on customer defections each year, our company's profits would soar and we'd probably all get big bonuses." Maybe these trainers can tell us how to get early warnings about coming market trends and how to do this CRM stuff that's supposed to help us keep profitable loyal customers and find new ones. Anyway, I'm willing to listen because I sure don't have all the answers . . . especially since I'm so new to sales force management. That increase in gasoline prices last year caught me off-guard and ran my selling expenses way over budget. If I'd known in advance about the sharp rise in gas prices, I would have had more of my salespeople making telephone calls or sending e-mails to my small customers instead of driving out to their offices.

Grace Gallo: Hey, it's almost 8:00 a.m.! We'd better get over to the seminar room, so we don't make a bad impression by coming in late.

Questions

1. On the basis of the brief conversations between Juan Carlos Varela, Grace Gallo, and Pam Swenson, what kind of sales manager do you think each is? What do you think is the level of performance of the sales force that each

heads? How do you think each will benefit from the sales force management training seminar?

2. If you were a top executive for a company, how would you go about selecting your new sales managers? What specific criteria would you use? How would you determine whether your candidates had the qualities desired?

3. Do you think that outstanding salespeople newly appointed to the position of sales manager need any special training? If so, what should the training cover? Why?

4. Do you think that sales managers can have much impact on the performance of individual salespeople? Specifically, what might new sales managers do to increase the performance of their sales force?

Case prepared by: Terry Loe, Kennesaw State University

| CASE 1.2 | Centroid Computer Corporation: The New Sales Manager |

Centroid Computer Corporation is a Dallas-based manufacturer of personal computers, monitors, interactive terminals, disk drives, and printers. In the last five years, Centroid has expanded into the development of a variety of software as a service (SaaS) packages for small businesses. The firm's growth in the past three years can only be described as explosive as Centroid sales have grown from less than $300 million to over $3 billion. Centroid distributes its products directly. It has an outside sales force of 52 salespeople who call directly on small businesses. It also has an internal sales call center based in Dallas with a little over a hundred representatives pursuing prospects and leads. Most major metropolitan cities have at least one Centroid salesperson assigned, and a few have two. A major responsibility for these salespeople is to convert the leads and prospects generated by the call center into customers. There are four regional sales managers, one national sales manager, and the director of the sales call center.

Six months ago, Alice Champion was promoted to regional sales manager for the southeastern region. Alice grew up in Athens, Georgia, and graduated from the University of Georgia. She spent two years with IBM as a salesperson and then joined Centroid three years ago. Alice is based in Atlanta and has consistently been among the top five salespersons in the company, winning sales awards every year. Alice's new region includes Georgia, Florida, Alabama, Mississippi, Tennessee, North Carolina, and South Carolina. As regional sales

manager, Alice must supervise 14 salespeople in the seven states. She is also permitted to do some personal selling herself, but her primary responsibility is managing the sales force. Since being promoted to sales manager, Alice has spent a great deal of time in the field working with her salespeople. Her years of selling computers have given her many innovative ideas, and she wants to pass along her insights so that all her salespeople can perform better. It has not been uncommon for Alice to spend two or three days per month with each salesperson, showing them the best ways to turn leads and prospects into customers.

Since Alice is such a "super salesperson," her national sales manager finds little need to train her when she is promoted to sales manager. Besides, the company is so busy handling the rapid sales growth that little thought has been given to training needs for sales managers. One of the major reasons they have been promoting outstanding salespeople like Alice to sales manager is that they know these people can teach the sales force "how to sell." In the last couple of months, the national sales manager has received some complaints from salespeople in the southeastern region about Alice spending so much time with them. In fact, they complain that Alice sometimes makes sales presentations to the leads for them. The result, according to these salespeople, is that these new customers are confused as to who is their primary contact.

One of the salespeople complained that she now has a credibility problem with several clients. She stated, "When we made sales calls together, Alice did not allow me to take the lead and handle the call as I normally would. The perception of the prospects was that Alice was not there to help and evaluate me but rather to be there to close the business. Three of my most promising clients asked if Alice was their main point of contact in the future." Other salespeople offered similar comments and even reported that if Alice disapproved of their presentation, she would take over right in the middle in such a manner that "it was clear she was there to teach me a lesson." One salesperson said that Alice's manner was so negative that one of her customers asked: "Was your boss here to help you sell us software or to put you in your place?"

Questions

1. Do you believe Alice is doing a good job in her new sales force management position? Why or why not?

2. Describe the functions Alice should be performing as sales manager. What should the approximate allocation of this time be in performing these functions?

3. Do you believe that Alice's behavior will have a long-term negative effect on those salespeople who have had a problem with her way of field supervision and training? If so, what could Alice do to moderate the situation? How could technology be used here?

4. As the national sales manager, how would you handle this problem with Alice?

5. Do the issues in this case suggest any ethical concerns the national sales manager should consider? If yes, what would be your suggestion as to how to handle them?

Case prepared by: Andy Wood, James Madison University

CHAPTER 2

Managing Ethics in a Sales Environment

LEARNING OBJECTIVES

When you finish this chapter, you should be able to:

1. Define ethics and defend its importance to sales and sales management.
2. Show how salespeople are boundary spanners.
3. Apply a code of ethics to sales and sales force management situations.
4. Apply the criteria for making moral judgments.
5. Create and manage an ethical climate.
6. Observe legal regulations that affect the sales environment.
7. Model good ethical behavior among the sales force.
8. Future developments impacting sales and sales force management ethics.

What Is Business Ethics?

One of the hallmarks of the world's greatest golfers is that they never cheat when playing golf. Jack Nicklaus, Tiger Woods, and Rory McIlroy play golf strictly by the rules and with the greatest respect for their competitors. Why have they never cheated? Clearly, part of the story is in their strong upbringing, which instilled core values of honesty and integrity. Another part of the story, however, is their success.

Let's consider Tiger Woods, who earned the number 1 ranking in golf when he was just 21 years old, and kept that rating for all but a few weeks for over a decade. For years, Tiger was odds-on better than the nearly all his competition. He ranks second in major championships and has as many PGA Tour wins as anybody ever. Maybe when you're that good at a particular sport, you don't need to cheat. Playing the game fairly comes easy when you are so much better than your competitors.

The same is probably true in the world of sales. When you are an effective sales manager for a very successful company, what motivation is there to cheat? But, what happens when you are a struggling sales manager for a struggling company? Perhaps an honest person still may not be tempted to blatantly cheat a customer – in particular, a customer who may be at some disadvantage relative to the salesperson. Sometimes the shades of gray may increase the temptation to cheat. Maybe the sales manager would be tempted to accept or practice behaviors that could somehow be justified as "not really so bad." These might include, for example:

- Misleading customers by not communicating important facts.
- Using guilt tactics such as telling seniors they should have life insurance policies for many relatives.
- Making a product seem more complex and therefore more useful than it really is.
- Using excessive jargon and fine print to make the terms of sale unclear and therefore more favorable.

If your next paycheck is uncertain, might you view some of these acts as acceptable?[1] Should there be different standards for different sales managers?

Perhaps as much as any other legitimate occupation, sales has long been linked with "sleazy" activities. In fact, you might have had personal experiences that confirm this impression. Do salespeople actually deserve this dubious place in society? The answer to this question is not the point of this chapter, because, the past cannot be changed. We can and should, however, learn from the past. This chapter defines key variables that together explain how business ethics and sales management are interrelated. In explaining this connection, we offer advice that enables the sales manager to minimize the likelihood of encouraging a selling environment that encourages unethical sales practices.

Organizational Ethics, Sales, and Sales Force Management

Ethics describes the moral content of behavior. Organizational ethics is the study of how business people in an organization behave when facing a situation with moral consequences. It is easier to think of selling situations *with* moral consequences than to think of situations without them. For instance, whenever salespeople represent a product benefit, they are implicitly saying that the customer can rely on and trust that the promised benefits will indeed result from purchasing and consuming the product. Thus, any situation involving trust also inherently involves business ethics.

Organizational culture consists of the shared values, norms, and artifacts that provide the blueprint for behavior.[2] Within an organization, typically, there are several subcultures associated with different functional areas. The sales force has subgroups as do other organizational groups. Subcultures unify a functional area and the members identify with and share an integrated belief system that influences their behavior. Moreover, subcultures often have values and norms that differ from the overall corporate culture. In fact, the sales subgroup often develops its own subculture that extends beyond individual and organizational boundaries.

Organizational ethics codes and training often do not address the ethical issues and dilemmas faced by sales people in their boundary-spanning role.[3] When this happens, the sales ethics subculture often operates with a different set of ethical issues, values, and norms. The Wells Fargo sales fraud case spanning the years from 2008 to 2015 is a prime example of the potential for the ethics subculture to damage the whole organization's reputation and brand.

The sales subculture is a component of the organizational culture that influences sales force ethical behavior. Sales ethical subcultures are influenced by the organizational structure and culture communicated by top management.[4] Ethical leadership at various management levels should provide directions for all employees, including the sales force, to make ethical day-to-day decisions. But in the final analysis the sales force often develops its own unique ethical subculture. The **sales ethics subculture** is, therefore, understood and recognized in the organization as potentially influencing the decision to comply or not comply with organizational codes of ethics.

Sales management ethics is the specific component of organizational ethics that deals with ethically managing the sales function and the sales force. When a customer and a salesperson communicate with each other in an ethical selling situation, both parties treat each other honestly and there is no attempt by either to take unfair advantage of the other. The sales manager has the special duty of overseeing this process and ensuring the outcome is based on ethical selling practices.

Although some recent business scandals such as the Facebook privacy policy violations and Equifax data breach did not involve salespeople directly, the principles of ethical action in the market place do go beyond the selling environment to the organizational culture. These situations revealed motivations that can easily lead other people to participate in questionable behaviors. In both cases, specific behavior by employees of a company eventually contributed to the harm of others. Were the people involved morally corrupt, or did the system simply encourage morally corrupt behavior?

Within the sales subculture a sales ethics subcompliance culture develops. The sales ethics subcompliance culture is shaped and understood by interactions within the organizational culture. But it is also subject to a phenomena within the sales subculture that can be different, and at times more influential than the organizational culture.[5] In short, the sales ethics subculture is understood and recognized in the organization as potentially influencing the decision to comply or not comply with ethics codes.

It is clear that ethical misconduct can affect company reputation, customer loyalty, and sales performance. With the recognition of the link between sales ethics and company performance, the importance of recruiting and selecting the right candidates has increased. But so has the need for sales ethics training, and ultimately establishing and maintaining a sales ethics subcompliance culture that enhances the likelihood of breaches in the sales code of ethics.

Salespeople Are Boundary Spanners

A boundary spanner is someone who performs their job in the "boundary" between a company and a customer. Salespeople represent the company to the customer and the customer to the company. For example, consider a situation in which a salesperson for an aviation parts supplier is trying to win a contract from Boeing. The salesperson represents their company to Boeing. But the same salesperson represents Boeing to their company. Whenever Boeing asks for information about how the company can satisfy a particular need for parts, the salesperson can face an ethical dilemma. Often the dilemma means weighing telling the truth versus winning business. With either option, however, the salesperson is exposed to the wrath of either their customer or their sales manager should a conflict occur. In this sense, boundary spanners perform their job in a proverbial "no-mans" land, as illustrated in Figure 2.1.

Sales managers have a special role in maintaining an ethical work and sales environment. Their first duty from an ethical perspective is to make sure morally corrupt individuals are not employed by the firm. Second, they must put in place checks on

FIGURE 2.1 Salespeople work in the boundary between the company and the customer.

TABLE 2.1

Sources of Potentially Unfair Advantages and Disadvantages in the Sales Arena

Source of customer vulnerability	Salesperson advantage	Customer disadvantage
Ignorance	Salesperson has superior technological knowledge.	Customer is technologically challenged and cannot understand salesperson.
Naiveté	Salesperson allows room for negotiation in setting prices.	Customer doesn't understand the negotiation process.
Powerlessness	Salesperson works for an exclusive supplier to the customer who is under a contractual obligation to purchase from the supplier.	Customer represents a small online company with few assets and little access to other markets.

any system that encourages or provides an incentive for immoral behavior. Sales managers are also responsible for the way the firm's sales force treats its customers. Thus, management of the sales force and business ethics are very much interrelated – they manage the firm's ethical behavior in the boundary.

Customer Vulnerability

Consider a salesperson working for a financial services firm. Customers in such situations are often *vulnerable*, meaning they are at a disadvantage relative to the company. Most often, the customer disadvantages come in the form of:

- Ignorance – a lack of some vital knowledge, often product knowledge, needed to participate in a fair exchange.
- Naiveté – a lack of experience or the ability to conduct a transaction or negotiate terms of a fair deal.
- Powerlessness – a lack of either competition within a marketplace or sufficient assets with which to be persuasive.

All of the above likely occurred in the Well Fargo sales deception incident.[6] Table 2.1 illustrates these sources of disadvantage.

Several financial services firms have come under scrutiny based on the vulnerability of their customers. One was penalized for creating fake banking accounts and another lost its license to sell securities because it followed unscrupulous sales practices in the sale of annuities to older customers.[7] The financial services customer segment prefers conservative strategies, but salespeople established fake bank accounts and risky annuities by misrepresenting the benefits of these services. These customers were victims of both ignorance and naiveté, and many were charged inappropriate fees or lost much of their life's savings when sold these products.

Did the company have a duty to prevent salespeople from taking advantage of this situation? Or did the salespeople themselves, even if the company overlooked selling to vulnerable customers without adequately informing them of the products they were buying, have a duty to intervene on behalf of the customers? As we shall see later, answers to such questions often are not as clear as they may seem.

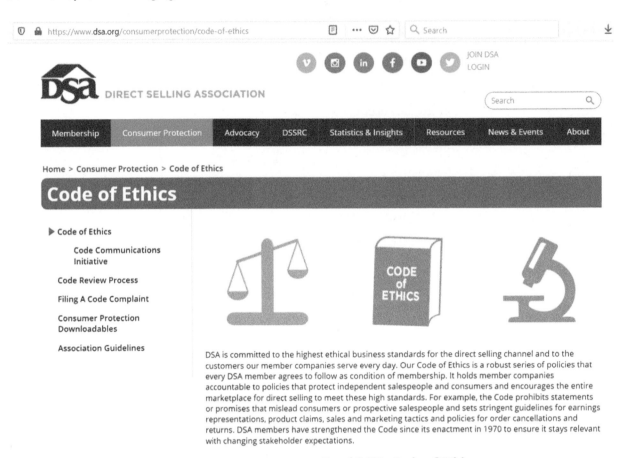

Professional sales organizations frequently adopt a professional code shown here.
Source: https://www.dsa.org/consumerprotection/code-of-ethics, April 14, 2020.

Applying Professional Sales Codes of Ethics

Codes of ethics express the values of a firm by specifying, in writing, specific behaviors that are consistent or inconsistent with those values. Whether codes of ethics are effective is often debated, their mere existence alone does not guarantee a more ethical environment. Codes must not only be adopted, but they must also embody values truly epitomized by top management.[8] How can a sales manager expect a salesperson to conform to a code of behavior the manager openly ignores?

Textbook discussions of ethics can make the topic sound simple. But within the emotion and turmoil of the real-life workplace, making the "right" decision can often be extremely complex. For instance, most people would agree that honesty is an important ethical principle. Consider, however, an otherwise honest salesperson faced with an end of the month quota needing to close one big deal to avoid a severe reprimand for falling short of the number. A customer may ask a question about some benefit such as compatibility of the products being sold. The salesperson, rather than being completely honest about issues related to compatibility, may avoid the issue or become blatantly dishonest to avoid not making the sale and missing the quota. Realize that often the salesperson is facing other ethical dilemmas. Perhaps there are issues concerning providing food for their family, paying for healthcare insurance, or making a house payment to avoid foreclosure. Factors such as these make ethics much more gray than black and white. But ethical codes that spell out specific actions that will not be tolerated under any circumstances may prove helpful in shaping a favorable outcome for all parties involved in the sales transaction.

Some ethics codes are simple and straightforward, relying mostly on the individual's good judgment and character. For example, insurance company Cigna (www .cigna.com) tells employees only that they "will abide by the highest legal and ethical standards without exceptions." Other codes, such as General Dynamics' (www.general dynamics.com) policies for worldwide business conduct, are complex and go on for many pages.[9] Some companies have used creative approaches to providing their employees with ethical guidelines. For example, Texas Instruments (www.ti.com) has an ethics officer who answers employee questions in a weekly electronic news column,[10] and NYNEX Corporation (www.nynex.com) has an ethical "hotline" that receives thousands of calls a year.[11]

Types of Codes of Ethics

There are four basic types of ethical codes:

1. Company codes that define ethical boundaries for employees.
2. Professional codes that define ethical boundaries for occupational groups such as advertisers, marketing researchers, sales representatives, doctors, lawyers, and accountants.
3. Business association codes that define ethical boundaries for people engaged in the same line of business. Examples are codes established by the Direct Selling Association of America and by the American Association of Advertising Agencies.
4. Advisory group codes suggested by government agencies or other special interest groups.

Codes often list employee behaviors that are *not* condoned or accepted by the firm. But since each industry is confronted with somewhat unique ethical situations, the codes vary somewhat. The following list describes behaviors generally prohibited in sales-related codes of ethics:

- Bribes, gifts, kickbacks
- Conflicts of interest
- Illegal political payments
- Violation of laws in general
- Use of insider information
- Violations of secrecy agreements
- Posting inappropriate content on social media
- Submitting false documentation for expense reimbursement
- Moonlighting
- Violation of antitrust laws
- Fraud and deception
- Illegal payments abroad
- Justifying the means based on the anticipated results
- Falsification of sales accounts

Do Codes of Ethics Affect Behavior?

What happens when sales managers work for companies with an effective code of ethics? The "Good and Bad Drug Sellers" box (Sales Management in Action Box 2.1) describing pharmaceutical sales training illustrates how far some sales managers will go to get their sales force to learn the code of ethics. Clearly, such a code does alter the way sales managers view questionable behaviors among the sales force.

Consider two sales managers – one works for a firm with an effective code of ethics and one who works for a firm that does not have a code of ethics. Each discovers a salesperson has intentionally misled a customer about delivery dates in an effort to win a sale. The manager in the firm with a code of ethics will consider the same offense unethical and discipline the employee more severely.[12] When firms have no code the outcome depends entirely on the ethical standards of the sales manager. Moreover, a code of ethics typically does not cover minor issues and, therefore, may not influence outcomes in such situations. For example, a salesperson may not be able to rely on a code of ethics in deciding whether an hour and fifteen-minute lunch break represents unethical behavior.

Companies often engage in discriminatory acts. For instance, airlines treat their high mileage flyers differently than they do other customers. "Diamond" flyers get access to business class lounges in airports and are upgraded to first class on some flights. In addition, when flights have to be rearranged, the best customers are likely to be inconvenienced the least. Is this treatment ethical? The code of ethics should address the extent to which salespeople can go to satisfy the company's best customers.

Ethical Philosophies and Moral Judgments

How can a situation like the one involving financial services sales described above come to be? Were the salespeople acting on their own, or was management so concerned with sales they created a system that rewarded unscrupulous behavior? Part of the answer lies in understanding the everyday moral stress people face when they have to decide between actions that may be beneficial to themselves or even to their families, and actions that are virtuous.[13]

Moral philosophy refers to the systematic ways in which individuals recognize and resolve decisions that include moral content. Many books and articles have been written on this topic alone. Our focus here is on describing how different sales managers, salespeople, channel partners or even customers may behave quite differently when faced with the same ethical situation. Let's look at the concepts of idealism, relativism, and teleology as the basis for different moral philosophies.[14]

Idealism

In moral philosophy, ideals are guidelines individuals apply to ethical and moral decisions. The Golden Rule is considered a widely held moral principle – or moral absolute.[15] Moral absolutes are rules that should always be applied with no exceptions or excuses. But a sales manager may also develop other rules. For instance, some may believe that all customers should be provided with complete and full information. Others may believe "the customer is always right," "salespeople should always be truthful," or a highly idealistic would have a difficult time consciously doing something inconsistent with the terms of a sales contract. Strict idealism is associated with universal standards, meaning they should be applied in all relevant situations regardless of context.

Box 2.1 | Sales Management in Action 2.1

Thomas Northcut/DigitalVision/Getty Images

Good and Bad Drug Sellers

As professional sales jobs go, pharmaceutical selling is considered a glamorous job. Pharmaceutical sales managers have a special duty to ethically manage the sales force, given the obvious implications of selling customers a less than appropriate product. Pharmaceutical salespeople often offer to buy lunch for prospective customers, and sometime set up incentives, such as kickbacks on pharmaceutical sales of opioids.[8] Is this an ethical act? A lunch probably creates no feeling of obligation on the part of potential customers that are healthcare professionals to choose one drug over another more effective drug. But what happens when the gifts become quite large? What if a vacation to Rio is offered instead of lunch? What if substantial incentives are offered, such as the recent opioid incentives?

Abbot Laboratories has a novel approach to instilling proper ethical beliefs and behaviors among its salespeople. Sales and marketing employees are asked to play a videogame involving a virtual salesperson. During the game, the virtual salesperson in the game is confronted with multiple ethical dilemmas, including the opportunity to provide tickets to an event like the Superbowl to a physician from a major medical group. Is this action appropriate? When the Abbot employee chooses incorrectly, the animated salesperson is lit up with about a thousand volts of electrical shock. This is an innovative way to teach ethical standards to the video game generation. Some may question the tactic just as debate rages over videogame violence in general. But the technique speeds up compliance among sales and marketing people.

Sources: Palmer, A., March 30, 2016, Pharmaceutical incentives that work. http://www.incentivemag.com/Strategy/Motivation-Masters/Pharmaceutical-Incentive-Case-Studies-Motivation-Masters/ (accessed June 2019); Sullivan, T., Class action suits over opioid epidemic ramping up, https://www.policymed.com/2017/10/class-action-suits-over-opioid-epidemic-ramping-up.html (accessed May 2019); Anbil, P., April 1, 2019, Pharma's incentive compensation plan landscape. http://www.pharmexec.com/pharmas-incentive-compensation-plan-landscape (accessed June 2019); Cebrzynski, G. (2005). Targeting pharmaceutical reps gives sales a shot in the arm, chains report. *Nation's Restaurant News* (July 25), 12; Kary, T. (2005). Straighten up and fry right. *Psychology Today* 38 (Jan/Feb): 35.

Certainly, there are many, many other principles. Just imagine how such a set of principles might vary with national culture. We would not expect sales managers in South Korea to hold the same set of principles as sales managers in New Zealand. The principles of sales managers in both countries are in general good, they are simply different because of variations in cultural norms.

The merits of each possible principle could be debated, but idealism as a moral philosophy deals more with how people apply these principles than with whether any individual principle itself is universally valid. Idealism is thus a mechanism by which principles become tools for decision-making. It's sometimes called a deontological process, signifying that it is rule-based.

Relativism

"It's all relative." You have probably used this expression thousands of times without giving it much thought. It is another way of saying "It depends." Relativism, as a moral philosophy, is a process by which individuals reach moral decisions based more on the actions they perceive to be acceptable *given a particular situation*. Those who are highly committed to relativism usually reject moral absolutes or imperatives.[16] In this sense, relativism and idealism are competing moral orientations.

Relativism is sometimes called situational ethics, meaning that a behavior acceptable in one situation can be unacceptable in another. Relativism rejects "absolutes" or moral imperatives. Acceptability could be based on the cultural context, for instance. A bribe may be unacceptable in the United States but acceptable in another country. Or it can be based on the social situation. An individual may perceive few social sanctions when illegally downloading a movie from an unauthorized site. But the same person likely would not consider going to a store and shoplifting a flash drive or other storage device containing the same movie.

Teleology

Teleology is a philosophy that defines morality based on the *consequences* of the behavior. It allows some indiscretion based on the argument that the "good" that results is more important than the harm caused. In other words, the end justifies the means. Sales managers sometimes use teleological norms in making decisions.[17]

Moral Judgments

Regardless of your moral philosophy, situations with moral content require you to make a judgment. An ethical dilemma is a situation with alternate courses of action, each having different moral implications. Choices about hiring, firing, and performance evaluations often have moral content, as do many other business decisions. A moral judgment is a person's evaluation of the situation from an ethical perspective. We usually base moral judgments on three criteria[18]:

1. Moral equity is the inherent fairness or justice in a situation.
2. Acceptability describes how culturally or socially acceptable we perceive an action to be.
3. Contractualism is the extent to which an act is consistent with stated or implied contracts and/or laws.

The first criterion – moral equity – spans moral philosophies and comes closest to representing an act's inherent rightness or wrongness. Relativists, on the other hand, are more likely to perform a behavior they view as acceptable. Idealists will have a difficult time with behavior they see as inconsistent with a contract or law. These three dimensions have been used to study salespeople and sales managers across a wide range of business situations from puffery to bribes.[19]

Are Sales People More Unethical Than Anyone Else?

Do salespeople and sales managers deserve the popular perception that they have low moral standards and will do anything to make a sale? Are dishonest people attracted to sales jobs, or do they become dishonest because of the work they do? Or are those involved with sales just like people in other occupations? How do moral philosophies relate to the ethical decisions of sales managers?

Several researchers have examined these issues. Here are some of their findings:

1. Sales managers and salespeople are *not* more likely to engage in unethical practices than are people with other marketing and management jobs.[20]
2. Age is positively related to ethical behavior among sales managers – older sales managers tend to make more ethical decisions.[20]
3. Relatively high levels of relativism are associated with less ethical decision-making among sales managers.[21]
4. Relatively high levels of idealism are associated with a lower likelihood of hiring a controversial job candidate.[22]

Research does not support the popular belief that sales professionals are more unethical than others. Further, findings show that personal characteristics associated with unethical behavior are found across the population in general. In other words, morality lies not in the occupation so much as in the individual, and unethical practices can occur in all jobs and professions.

Potentially Unethical Behaviors

What kinds of selling-related behaviors might be perceived as unethical? Consider the 20 actions listed in Table 2.2.[23] Undergraduate students rated offering a bribe and using expense accounts to pay for personal spending as more serious lapses than misrepresenting intent, price discriminating, and faking a personal relationship. Interestingly, some of the behaviors they rated most severely were those that take advantage of the firm more than the customer, such as padding an expense account or falsely calling in sick.

Developing an exhaustive list of unethical behaviors is likely impossible. But salespeople and managers should view any behavior that unfairly takes advantage of another party in an exchange as a serious breach of ethical conduct. For exchanges to work efficiently, all involved individuals or groups need to treat each other with respect and honesty. If any of the individuals violates the standards of moral conduct, someone is harmed. Therefore, salespeople, sales managers, government officials and even customers must operate with integrity. When the exchange system is efficient and effective, it is the best governance system that exists at that time.

Dealing with Unethical Behavior

Sales managers should not encourage or tolerate sales behaviors inconsistent with professional sales standards or with the moral standards of the firm. But what happens when sales managers must choose between ethics and sales success? While someone

TABLE **2.2**

Potentially Unethical Selling-Related Behaviors

	Behavior	Perceived Seriousness
1.	Offering better prices and terms for customers who buy exclusively from one person.	Not serious
2.	Using customers to get information about competitors' activities.	Not serious
3.	Using shadow prices – attracting customers with lower priced products, then trying to switch them to more expensive products at the sale.	Not serious
4.	Pretending to have a personal or even a romantic interest in a potential customer to close a sale.	Not serious
5.	Misrepresenting the motivation for contacting a customer when the real intent is solely to try and make a sale (e.g. pretending to be conducting research, checking on a previous item sold).	Not serious
6.	Offering a bribe in return for signing a purchase agreement.	Serious
7.	Exaggerating performance of a product offered to customers.	Serious
8.	Disparaging a competitor's products.	Serious
9.	Disparaging a competitor's sales and service people.	Serious
10.	Misleading someone about potential product shortages in an effort to stimulate current sales.	Serious
11.	Using expense account to pay for personal expenses.	Serious
12.	Creating, repeating, or embellishing unsubstantiated rumors reflecting negatively on coworkers or competitors.	Serious
13.	Overstating list prices to give a customer a "refund."	Serious
14.	Misrepresenting the frequency a service should be performed or the quantity of a product that should be used.	Serious
15.	Intentionally misreporting one's work activities to the sales manager.	Serious
16.	Withholding key facts about a product from consumers to keep them uninformed or confuse them.	Serious
17.	A sales manager overlooks payment of bribes by salespeople to increase sales.	Very serious
18.	Padding an expense account.	Very serious
19.	Calling in sick to take a day off when well.	Very serious
20.	Misleading someone about product safety by withholding truthful information.	Very serious

outside the situation might easily condemn a sales manager for looking the other way while a salesperson pays a kickback to gain business, who knows how an individual might behave when faced with the prospect of taking action that may damage job performance?

Research shows that sales managers tend to discipline poor performers more severely than they do more effective salespeople.[24] In other words, when two salespeople have violated the same ethical code, the one with the better sales performance is more likely to escape with little to no reprimand or punishment than the one with the lower sales record. Some sales managers also appear to adjust their disciplinary tactics based on salesperson demographics. For example, given the same violation,

Box 2.2 | Sales Management in Action 2.2

Used, Pre-Owned, Certified, Second Hand?

Car resellers have devoted a lot of resources to transform the image of the "used car" business. Terms like "pre-owned" and "certified program cars" have been coined to avoid any stigma that might be associated with the term "used" car.

Sales managers at auto manufacturers have come under scrutiny for developing and implementing programs selling used automobiles as "Certified Used Cars." In some instances, certified used-car salespeople have been instructed to tout the greater reliability and lower prices of these

vehicles compared to similar offerings by competitors. Unfortunately, research failed to support their claims, and some companies have faced charges for unfair pricing and false advertising. The moral of the story . . . call a duck a duck and a lemon a lemon!

Sources: Montoya, R. (2018). Certified pre-owned cars: A reality check. https://www.edmunds.com/car-buying/certified-pre-owned-cars-a-reality-check.html. (accessed May 2019); Cutler, K.-M. (2005). Certified used car superiority questioned. *Wall Street Journal* 246 (7/12): D1–D3; *Money* (2005). Isn't pre-owned just another word for used? 34: 141.

a sales manager, particularly a male, will tend to discipline a male salesperson more severely than a female salesperson.[25]

An effective sales manager will strive to discipline all salespeople with the same standards. Although unethical selling tactics may benefit firms in the short run, they almost always end up being detrimental in the long run. Good ethical principles and equal standards not only avoid discrimination in disciplinary actions, they also help sales managers avoid litigation by disgruntled employees.

Creating an Ethical Work Climate

What determines a sales manager's or even a salesperson's tolerance for unethical actions among employees? Why do some firms seem to promote selling behaviors that are consistent with high moral standards while others seem to promote pushy techniques that take advantage of sources of consumer vulnerability? The answer is often the result of a salesperson's ethical work climate.

Ethical Work Climate

The organizational climate is the way employees perceive the organizational culture. When the organizational culture is very strong, employees will tend to share the same perceptions.[26] When the culture is not as strong or identifiable, perceptions may vary considerably from one employee to another. The organizational work climate ultimately affects an employee's behavior and often their well-being.

The ethical work climate is a specific aspect of the organizational climate. Specifically, it's the way employees view their work environment on moral dimensions. Ethical climate is a multidimensional concept, with four unique aspects.[27]

Policies and Rules When sales managers and salespeople internalize the policies and rules that govern selling and marketing conduct within the firm, they are more likely to behave ethically.[28] Sometimes, the policies and rules are summarized in a code of ethics. Employee perceptions of the type and severity of sanctions that follow violations of the code of ethics are also related to this dimension.

Trust and Responsibility

The trust and responsibility dimension defines how far people are trusted to behave in a responsible way and are held personally responsible for their actions. Consider a sales manager supervising a dozen outside salespeople. Trust is increased when salespeople are allowed to set their own schedules and are not constantly being monitored. However, this freedom should be accompanied by a sense of responsibility. Salespeople who take advantage of freedom by participating in behaviors such as those in Table 2.2 should be held responsible for their actions. Under conditions like these, the ethical climate dimension of trust and responsibility will be high.

Experiencing trust and responsibility also means carrying out the job responsibly. When employees frequently avoid work or find ways to pass it on to others, they are behaving unethically. Value creation, the reason the company exists, is a primary responsibility of both employees and management. In fact, one of the surest ways of avoiding unethical actions among sales managers and salespeople is to make sure their actions are directed toward maximizing the value provided by the firm's products.

Peer Behavior

Peer behavior, as a dimension of ethical climate, is the extent to which employees view coworkers as having high moral standards. Employees who observe other employees acting in ways that bother them from a moral point of view will perceive the workplace as having a more negative ethical climate and the peer behavior dimension of ethical climate will be reduced.

Bottom-Line Sales Emphasis

Sales emphasis is the extent to which employees feel pressured to prioritize increased sales, profits, margins, or other financial returns over all other concerns. A strong sales emphasis or *bottom-line orientation,* coupled with a control system based on sales quotas, leads to a more negative ethical work climate.[29] When sales

See http://www.realtor.org/mempolweb.nsf/pages/printable2006Code (accessed May 2019) for the full version of the professional real estate agent's code of ethics. Would you expect that this code is widely accepted and observed?

goals are overly aggressive or even unrealistic, closing the sale becomes more important than creating value for customers by providing a product that best matches their needs. Over time, sales managers and salespeople will behave consistently with the compensation system, since it defines which goals are rewarded. The compensation system is a major influence, therefore, in determining the ethical climate of a sales environment.[30]

Managing the Ethical Climate

All four components of ethical work climate dimension can be a tool to help create a positive, healthy ethical work climate. Sales managers should make sure employees are aware of rules and policies and are rewarded and reprimanded based on their actions with no favoritism or bias. They should also be aware of the extent to which they foster a bottom-line orientation.

In addition to increasing performance and creating a more contented, more motivated sales force, a positive ethical climate generates less stress among salespeople.[31] Sales managers and salespeople that internalize policies and rules experience less ambiguity because they are more likely to know how to respond to a given ethical dilemma. When sales managers and salespeople trust each other, they experience less conflict on the job. As a result, sales managers should face fewer problems with turnover.[32]

Promoting an ethical climate is the responsibility of management at all levels of the organization. If top management is unconcerned about ethics in developing strategies, then sales managers are likely to be unconcerned with the way their sales force behaves. Similarly, salespeople are not likely to be concerned with the way they treat customers.[33] In the end, managing the ethical climate should be a top priority for all organizations.

Ethical work climates can be good for business!
Source: https://www.worldsmostethicalcompanies.com/, April 14, 2020.

General Electric (www.ge.com) actively manages its ethical climate. The company has a Vice-President for Corporate Citizenship. This means GE monitors not only its own sales force but also its suppliers to make sure they act consistently with GE values and comply with health, safety, and environmental standards. Moreover, they are looking to the future by exploring the interface between emerging technology and ethical practices.[34] GE is recognized by Dow Jones as a leader in responsible management and is a member of the Dow Jones Sustainability Index (https://www.sustainability-indices.com), a list of more than 400 firms globally that are noted for responsible management practices.

Legal Considerations in the Sales Environment

Domestic and international selling and sales force management activities are regulated by local, state, and federal laws and regulations, as well as by legislation within each country. Some laws are designed to prevent unfair competition, while others protect consumers and society from harmful business practices. This section summarizes the most important U.S. laws and regulations affecting sales and sales management.

Federal Regulation

U.S. legislation regulating business can be divided into two major categories:

1. Laws protecting companies from each other.
2. Laws and policies protecting consumers and society from unfair business practices.

The first category tries to ensure that a competitive marketplace exists. Among many Federal laws regulating business competition, the Robinson–Patman Act, the Sherman Act, and the Clayton Act are the most important. These acts deal with issues including price discrimination, collusion, price fixing, exclusive dealing, restraint of trade, reciprocity, tie-in sales, unordered goods, orders and terms of sale, business descriptions, product descriptions, secret rebates, customer coercion, disparaging competitors' products and services, and business defamation.

Table 2.3 shows major Federal legislation that affects selling and sales management activities directly and indirectly. More recent laws have limited the extent to which sales managers can access customer information using new technologies. For example, the Data Protection Act of 2017, Children's Online Privacy Protection Act (COPPA), the General Data Protection Regulation (GDPR), and the Telephone Record Protection Act are aimed at updating regulation to account for advances in Internet and mobile phone technologies.

General Data Protection Regulation (GDPR) (2018) – EU stated limits on how consumer data can be used and granting consumers right to "disappear" from databases.

Price Discrimination

The Clayton Act prohibits a seller from discriminating on price or terms of sale among different customers when the discrimination has a harmful effect on competition. This practice is known as price discrimination. Clayton makes it unlawful for a buyer to knowingly induce or receive a discriminatory price. Sellers are required to treat similar buyers equally with respect to price and terms of sale.

Section 3 of the Robinson–Patman Act goes even farther by criminalizing behaviors that facilitate discrimination among competing purchasers. Robinson–Patman limits a seller's ability to sell at different prices in different markets, or charge different buyers different prices for the same quality and quantity of goods. However, the act does not make price discrimination necessarily illegal. Price differences or different terms of sale are allowed under two conditions:

1. The price differential is given in good faith to meet a price offered by a competitor.
2. The price differential is based upon cost savings reflecting a difference in the cost of manufacture, sale, or delivery resulting from the differing methods or quantities in which products are sold or delivered.

Price reductions based on volume ordered, close out sales, lower shipping costs, good faith meeting of competition, and lower commissions paid by the seller to its employee salespeople are generally allowable. All these defenses can justify a difference in price or terms of sale. For legal protection, however, sellers should be sure their accounting procedures reflect cost differences that permit the firm to reduce prices or terms of sale to certain customers. Price discrimination laws are particularly applicable to business-to-business sales, although business-to-consumer marketers also could be found culpable in a price discrimination suit.

TABLE 2.3

Key Legislation Affecting Selling and Sales Management

Laws Intended to Regulate Business Competition

Sherman Antitrust Act (1890) – prohibits (a) "monopolies or attempts to monopolize" and (b) "contracts, combinations, or conspiracies in restraint of trade" in interstate and foreign commerce.

Federal Trade Commission Act (1914) – established the FTC as a body of specialists with broad powers to investigate and issue cease-and-desist orders to enforce Section 5, which declares "unfair methods of competition in commerce are unlawful."

Clayton Act (1914) – supplements the Sherman Act by prohibiting certain specific practices (certain types of price discrimination, tying clauses, exclusive dealing, inter-corporate stockholdings, and interlocking directorates) "where the effect . . .. may be to substantially lessen competition or tend to create a monopoly in any line of commerce"; provides that corporate officials violating the law can be held individually responsible.

Robinson–Patman Act (1936) – amends the Clayton Act by strengthening the prohibition of price discrimination (subject to certain defenses); provides the FTC with the right to establish limits on quantity discounts, to forbid brokerage allowances except to independent brokers, and to prohibit promotional allowances, services or facilities except where made available to all "on proportionately equal terms."

Wheeler–Lea Act (1938) – amends the FTC Act; prohibits unfair and deceptive acts and practices regardless of whether competition is injured.

Lanham Trademark Act (1946) – regulates brands and trademarks.

Consumer Goods Pricing Act (1975) – repeals Federal "fair-trade laws" and state laws allowing manufacturers to set retail prices.

FTC Improvement Act (1980) – enables the Senate and House of Representatives to exercise joint veto power over FTC trade regulations, and limits FTC power to regulate unfairness issues.

Laws Deregulating Specific Industries

- Natural Gas Policy Act (1978)
- Airline Deregulation Act (1978)
- Motor Carrier Act (1980)
- Staggers Rail Act (1980)
- Depository Institutions Act (1981)
- Telecommunications Act (1996)

(Continued)

> **TABLE 2.3**
>
> ## Key Legislation Affecting Selling and Sales Management (*Continued*)
>
> ### Laws Intended to Protect Consumers
>
> *Pure Food and Drug Act (1906)* – regulates labeling of food and drugs and prohibits manufacture or marketing of adulterated food or drugs. Amended in 1938 by Food, Drug, and Cosmetics Act.
>
> *Meat Inspection Act (1906)* – regulates meatpacking houses and provides for federal inspection of meats.
>
> *Textile Labeling Laws* – require the manufacturer to indicate what their product is made of:
>
> - Wood Products Labeling Act (1939)
> - Fur Products Labeling Act (1951)
> - Flammable Fabrics Act (1953)
> - Textile Fiber Products Identification Act.
>
> *Automobile Information Disclosure Act (1958)* – prohibits car dealers from inflating the factory price of new cars.
>
> *Kefauver–Harris Drug Amendments (1962)* – requires (a) that drugs be labeled with their generic names, (b) that new drugs be pretested, and (c) that new drugs get approval of Food and Drug Administration before being marketed.
>
> *Fair Packaging and Labeling Act (1966)* – provides for the regulation of the packaging and labeling of consumer goods. Requires manufacturers to state what the package contains, who made it, and how much it contains. The act allows industries to voluntarily adopt uniform packaging standards.
>
> *National Traffic and Motor Vehicle Safety Act (1966)* – provides for safety standards for tires and automobiles.
>
> *Fair Packaging and Labeling Act (1966)* – the "truth in packaging" law that regulates packaging and labeling to disclose name and address of manufacturer or distributor, and information about the quality of contents.
>
> *Child Protection Act (1966)* – bans sale of hazardous toys and other unsafe articles. Amended in 1969 to include articles that pose electrical, mechanical, or thermal hazards.
>
> *Federal Cigarette Labeling and Advertising Acts (1967, 1971)* – requires manufacturers to label cigarettes with written health warnings (1967); prohibits tobacco advertising on radio or television (1971).
>
> *Consumer Credit Protection Act (1968)* – "Truth in lending" law that requires lenders to state the true costs of a credit transaction, outlaws the use of actual or threatened violence in collecting loans, and restricts the amount of garnishments.
>
> *Fair Credit Reporting Act (1970)* – ensures that a consumer's credit report will contain only accurate, relevant, and recent information and will be confidential unless requested for an appropriate reason by a proper party.
>
> *National Environmental Policy Act (1970)* – established the Environmental Protection Agency to deal with various types of pollution and organizations that create pollution.
>
> *Consumer Product Safety Act (1972)* – established the Consumer Product Safety Commission and authorizes it to set safety standards for consumer products as well as exact penalties for failure to uphold the standards.
>
> *Consumer Goods Pricing Act (1975)* – prohibits the use of price maintenance agreements among manufacturers and resellers in interstate commerce.
>
> *Magnuson–Moss Warranty/FTC Improvement Act (1975)* – authorizes the FTC to determine rules concerning consumer warranties and provides for consumer access to means of redress, such as the "class action" suit. Also expands FTC regulatory powers over unfair or deceptive acts or practices.
>
> *Equal Credit Opportunity Act (1975, 1977)* – prohibits discrimination in a credit transaction because of sex and marital status (1975), and race, national origin, religion, age, or receipt of public assistance (1977).
>
> *Fair Debt Collection Practice Act (1978)* – makes it illegal to harass or abuse any person and make false statements or use unfair methods when collecting a debt.
>
> *Nutrition Label and Education Act (1990)* – requires food manufacturers and processors to provide detailed information on the labeling of most foods.
>
> *Children's Television Act (1990)* – limits the advertising shown during children's television programs to no more than 10.5 minutes per hour on weekends and not more than 12 minutes per hour on weekdays.
>
> *Americans with Disabilities Act (1991)* – protects the rights of people with disabilities by making it illegal to discriminate against them in public accommodations, transportation, and telecommunications.
>
> *Brady Law (1993)* – imposes a five-day waiting period and a background check before a purchaser can receive a gun.

The terms listed below describe different behaviors associated with discrimination in the marketplace:

Collusion. Competitors who conspire to set prices, agree to divide territories on a noncompetitive basis, or join together to act to the detriment of another competitor, are practicing illegal collusion.

Price Fixing. Competitors who conspire to set or maintain uniform prices and profit margins are fixing prices. Informally exchanging price information with competitors, or discussing pricing policies at trade association meetings, has been found illegal by the courts.

Exclusive Dealing. Agreements in which a manufacturer or wholesaler grants one dealer exclusive rights to sell a product in a certain trading area or insists that the dealer not carry competing lines are illegal under the Clayton Act.

Restraint of Trade. Under the Sherman and Clayton Acts, competitors colluding to divide a market into noncompetitive territories or to restrict competition in a market are in restraint of trade. Nor can dealers be required to refrain from selling competitors' products as a condition of receiving the right to sell the manufacturer's product. However, a unilateral refusal to deal with a price-cutter is not illegal so long as there is no effort on the manufacturer's part to raise or maintain prices in doing so.

Reciprocity. Selecting only suppliers who will also purchase from the buyer – "You buy from me and I'll buy from you" – can be considered illegal. The Federal Trade Commission took nearly a year to investigate the competitive practices of American Standard Company, a manufacturer of plumbing, heating, and air conditioning products. American had a director of sales coordination whose job was to coordinate its reciprocal trade agreements. Beyond this, American kept its funds in banks whose borrowers were involved in building projects utilizing American Standard products. These practices are prohibited by Section 5 of the Federal Trade Commission Act, so American Standard (https://www.americanstandard-us.com/about/company-info) agreed to stop such activities and even eliminated the position of sales coordinator. Most buyers and salespeople believe reciprocity should be illegal.

Tie-in Sales. Purchasers cannot be forced to buy an unwanted item or items in return for being allowed to purchase a product in heavy demand.

Unordered Goods. Section 5 of the FTC Act prohibits companies from shipping unordered goods or shipping larger amounts than ordered hoping the buyer will pay for them.

Orders and Terms of Sale. The FTC Act makes selling substitute goods different from those ordered, intentionally misrepresenting delivery dates, failing to actually fill an order, and not filling an order in a reasonable time illegal. Terms of sale or conditions of sales offer cannot be misrepresented. Key terms of sale include warranties and guarantees, the ability of the buyer to cancel a contract or obtain a refund, and important facts in a credit or financing transaction.

Business Descriptions. Salespeople must never misrepresent the company's financial strength, length of time in business, reputation, or facts concerning its plant, equipment, or facilities.

Product Descriptions. Salespeople must not misrepresent the method by which a product is produced. For example, it is illegal to state that a product is "custom-made" or "tailor-made" when it is ready-made. Furthermore, no statements can be legally made about "proven" claims unless scientific or empirical evidence has been obtained to establish their truth.

Customer Coercion. Coercing a customer into a sale can be illegal when sales practice places undo pressure, intimidation, or fear on the buyer. This includes practices such as badgering a customer with repeated sales calls.

Business Defamation. Hundreds of company and manufacturing agents have been sued for making slanderous statements about a company resulting in financial damages, lost customers, unemployment, or lost sales. For example, a competitor to Starbucks can't say that Starbuck's coffee tastes like swill without some means of supporting the statement. Customers can bring private lawsuits, and also the Federal Trade Commission is empowered to impose a cease-and-desist order or injunction on companies that engage in unfair or deceptive practices through their salespeople. Business defamation includes the following offenses:

1. *Business slander* – when an unfair and untrue oral statement is made about a competitor, the statement becomes actionable when it is communicated to a third party and can be interpreted as damaging the reputation of the competitor or the personal reputation of an individual in that business.
2. *Business libel* – when an unfair and untrue statement is made about a competitor in writing (usually a letter, sales literature, advertisement, or company brochure), the statement becomes actionable when it is communicated to a third party and can be interpreted as damaging the competitors' reputation or the personal reputation of an individual in that business.
3. *Product disparagement* – false or deceptive comparisons or distorted claims are made concerning a competitor's product, services, or property.
4. *Unfair competition* – injury to a competitor can result from the false advertising of one's own product, misrepresentation of the qualities or characteristics of the product, or related unfair or deceptive trade practices.

False statements made by a salesperson during or after the sales presentation can be especially troublesome. The law treats the kinds of statements listed below as defamatory. A company or defamed individual does not have to prove actual damages to successfully win a verdict. All that needs be proved is that the statement is untrue. Types of statements considered personally defamatory are as follows:

- Untrue statements insinuating that a competitor engages in illegal or unfair business practices.
- Untrue statements insinuating that a competitor fails to live up to contractual obligations and responsibilities.
- Untrue statements regarding a competitor's financial condition.
- Untrue statements insinuating that a principal in the competitor's business is incompetent, of poor moral character, unreliable, or dishonest.

A company's, salesperson's, or sales manager's reputation for integrity and high ethical standards in dealing with all people at all times is an invaluable attribute for long-run business success. Nearly all customers prefer to do business with a company whose representatives can be trusted to be ethical and honest in all their negotiations.

International Regulation of Sales

International sellers must cope with three different sets of laws restricting their operations. First, U.S. laws sometimes forbid U.S. companies to trade with foreign countries. For example, the U.S. government imposed an embargo on trade with Vietnam in 1975 that wasn't lifted until 1994[35] and a trade embargo has been in force with Cuba since the early 1960s. Most recently, trade embargoes have been placed against Iran and North Korea.

Second, multinational firms also must obey the laws of any country in which they operates, even though these may differ sharply from U.S. laws. Many times, foreign laws are less stringent, allowing sale of products banned in the United States or openly permitting bribery. Considering what U.S. law considers bribes, for instance, Germany holds such payments legal and tax deductible as long as they are made outside Germany. Quite a few countries, including Cambodia, Pakistan, Yemen, Morocco, and Nigeria have lax standards regarding bribery, while Switzerland, Australia, Singapore, the United States, and Britain have the most stringent.[36] Consider how these differences affect the ethics of a sales situation. While bribery may be more acceptable and consistent with the law in Pakistan, the moral equity may be unchanged. Reflect on the ethical philosophies from the beginning of the chapter. Does greater acceptability and consistency with the law necessarily make a bribe fair or just to all parties involved?

On the other hand, foreign laws are sometimes *more* restrictive. For example, restrictions against false and misleading advertising in Europe are often more stringent than in the United States. Thus, a U.S. firm that wants to supplement its sales efforts in France with television promotion has to carefully design its advertising to ensure that it complies with local laws.

Finally, multinational firms are subject to international laws that are enforced across national boundaries. Both the United Nations and the European Union are standardizing commercial codes, such as privacy, environmental, and product safety standards, binding on all companies that do business in those countries. The European Union General Data Protection Regulation (GDPR) Act is a good example of a law that enforces standards across national boundaries.

Personal Selling

International salespeople will find a wide variety of business practices as they travel across countries and cultures. But sales managers should also be aware that different ethical standards exist from culture to culture. The inter-relationships between cultural elements and ethical climate vary as well. A positive ethical climate, for instance, is associated with higher performance among U.S. salespeople. But increased ethical climate is not associated with performance for Mexican salespeople.[37]

Why is this difference important for sales managers? Sales managers have a duty to protect the salespeople under their direction, as well as the reputation of the firm. Although certain practices may be acceptable, legal, and even expected in other cultures, the sales manager should caution salespeople to avoid practices that are unethical at home. Once a company establishes ethical standards, those standards should be observed in all cultures, even if they impact performance. While sales managers train salespeople to adapt to other cultures, adaptations should not permit salespersons to act inconsistently with company values.

State and Local Regulation

Among the most important state and local laws and ordinances designed to regulate selling activities are the Uniform Commercial Code, and the Green River Ordinances. The Uniform Commercial Code is a set of guidelines adopted by most states that set forth the rules of contracts and the law pertaining to sales. The code regulates the performance of goods, sellers' warranties, and the maximum allowable rates of interest and carrying charges. Court actions under this code usually concern buyers' claims that salespeople misrepresented the goods or made promises that were not kept. In defending itself, sales organizations must be able to provide the court with substantiating sales documentation, including contracts, letters of agreement, and similar documentation.

Green River Ordinances, which were originally passed in Green River, Wyoming, in 1933, are local ordinances requiring nonresidents to obtain a license from city authorities to sell goods or services direct to consumers in that vicinity. Adopted by most metropolitan areas, the laws tend to discourage many companies from trying to distribute their products and services door-to-door on a national basis.

Cooling Off Rules are closely connected to the Green River Ordinances and requires door-to-door salespeople to give written notice to customers placing orders of $25 or more that they can cancel their purchase within three days. This FTC ruling came after years of complaints about high-pressure tactics in selling magazines, jewelry, encyclopedias, cosmetics, and other merchandise house-to-house.

Model Good Ethical Behavior Among the Sales Force

Few topics discussed in this book are more complex than ethics. Sales managers and salespeople might be tempted to follow simple rules like "always obey the law." There are times, however, when legal actions may be unethical, and illegal actions can be ethical. For instance, a pharmaceutical rep may be tempted to disproportionately leave samples with physicians who administer care to populations containing high proportions of illegal immigrants. Many people may consider this ethical since these people could not obtain the medicine otherwise. However, the practice could be illegal. Also, consider how inadequate simple rules could become when the sales manager is responsible for salespeople operating in different countries – each with a different set of laws and a different culture. For example, some countries have strict rules concerning the types of behaviors that women should exhibit. Something as simple as a dress code may violate cultural norms in some cultures.

With this in mind, a sales manager often experiences ethical stress in the form of ambiguity or conflict. Ambiguity means the sales manager simply does not know what to do in a given situation. Conflict means the sales manager is torn between multiple courses of action, each with different moral implications for the people involved. We next present advice for trying to maintain a positive ethical climate. Ultimately, this is the best way to deal with ethical stress.

Understanding Ethics

Marketing is occasionally criticized for failing to adequately train employees before "turning them loose" on customers. Sales managers have many sales practices to teach professional salespeople before they can carry out their individual jobs. Indeed, ethics training may not seem to be a very high priority. But if the firm has strong ethical values and compliance culture, then ethics training is essential. Even if the salesperson already believes he or she knows the difference between right and wrong, training can increase sensitivity to ethical issues and make the salesperson more aware of potential ethical implications. Awareness is an essential part of morally virtuous behavior. This is particularly true since organizational ethics influences brand attitudes and ultimately sales.[38]

Salespeople reach ethical maturity when they place moral treatment of others ahead of short-term personal gains. Interestingly, as we saw above, age is one of the strongest causal factors of ethical actions. Older managers generally behave more ethically than younger sales managers.[39] But older employees are not always more honest,

Example item	Strongly Disagree	Disagree	Neutral	Agree	Strongly Agree
Trust/responsibility: Employees are held accountable for their actions	☐	☐	☐	☐	☐
Peer behavior: Employees here sometimes perform unethical acts	☐	☐	☐	☐	☐
Policies and rules Employees are reminded of company policies regarding fair treatment	☐	☐	☐	☐	☐
Sales emphasis Employees here are strongly encouraged to "up-sell" customers	☐	☐	☐	☐	☐

FIGURE 2.2 Sample items for measuring the ethical climate as perceived by employees.

dependable, and fair than younger employees. Each person exhibits a set of values that shape personal ethical standards. Individuals tend to become more ethical, however, with the wisdom of experience and age.

Measuring the Ethical Climate

A reduction in the ethical climate could signal problems. Fortunately, managers can monitor the ethical climate, for instance with surveys. Figure 2.2 shows some items that capture the dimensions of ethical climate. By measuring multiple dimensions, the sales manager may be able to diagnose particular areas needing attention. For example, if the score on rules/policies drops, the sales manager may consider holding training sessions that clearly outline ethics policies and the implications of violating these policies. Likewise, if salespeople begin to sense a climate increasingly typified by a bottom line sales orientation, sales managers may wish to reconsider the motivational tactics they use to shape job performance.

Leading by Example

A positive, healthy, and moral ethical work climate begins at the top. Likewise, salespeople should realize the people they supervise look to them in forming expectations of their own moral behavior. If the sales manager fails to treat salespeople honestly, fairly, and equally, salespeople are likely to have a low regard for fair, equitable, and honest treatment of customers, suppliers, channel partners, or even coworkers. Similarly, sales managers must thoroughly know and practice the company code of ethics (assuming one exists) if they expect salespeople to follow it.

Sales Manager Ethics Checklist

What is a sales manager to do, given the complexity of ethical behavior? How can you be sure you recognize situations and actions that may violate ethical standards?

TABLE **2.4**

Sales Manager's Ethical Checklist

Briefly describe the decision you face:

Use the following questions to analyze the situation:

1. Will the action I take diminish the value of the product we are selling?

   ☐ YES

   ☐ NO

2. Will the action I take result in inequitable or disrespectful treatment of a salesperson?

   ☐ YES

   ☐ NO

3. Will this action place a greater emphasis on sales or profits than on the ethical treatment of the customer?

   ☐ YES

   ☐ NO

4. Will the action take unfair advantage of vulnerabilities among customers, suppliers, employees, or shareholders?

   ☐ YES

   ☐ NO

5. Will my action, either intentionally or unintentionally, motivate a salesperson to treat someone unethically?

   ☐ YES

   ☐ NO

6. Would I be comfortable telling my children about the way I acted in this situation?

   ☐ YES

   ☐ NO

Table 2.4 provides a sample ethical checklist tailored specifically to the sales manager's job. Try to avoid situations leading to "yes" answers to the questions:

Future Developments Impacting Sales Ethics

Digital technologies are disrupting established sales practices, including ethics. Sales managers and salespeople have to coexist and evolve with the development of artificial intelligence (AI), blockchain systems, and related emerging technologies. AI algorithms and software bots are intended to "think" like humans and make decisions, including decisions that have ethical ramifications. Just as Amazon and Netflix use machine learning to scan data and make movie recommendations, AI will monitor management and sales behavior and make judgments based on formalized codes of ethics. Machines trained by humans will have enhanced cognitive skills enabling them to recall stored data exactly, and provide specific guidelines on what and how to perform tasks, as well as when these guidelines have not been followed.[40]

Blockchain systems are efficient processes executed in blocks or immutable chains of information. The processes extract and process information from databases based on specific rules. Control of the blockchain process is distributed, with each block of data added to the next making the record chronological and permanent. As a result, there is no single point of failure or ability to change "history" to suit one individual's needs because no single person has access to all the stored data. These processes will track products from point of production to consumption, geo-targeted sales and advertising campaigns, price optimization, and ethical practices in the workplace as well as in sales territories. The result will be AI oversight and compliance assessment not only for sales and marketing strategies, but also ethical practices and decisions.[41]

Chapter Summary

1. **Define ethics and defend its importance to sales and sales management.** Business ethics determines how companies resolve dilemmas with moral consequences. Sales managers cannot escape dealing with these types of ethical dilemmas and should make sure customers' vulnerabilities in the exchange are not exploited.

2. **Show how salespeople are boundary spanners.** Salespeople are considered boundary spanners because they work in the "boundary" between customers and the organization. As such, they perform actions that link the customer to the firm. In this position, the salesperson often faces an ethical dilemma involving the fair treatment of customers, the organization or both.

3. **Apply a code of ethics to sales and sales force management situations.** A code of ethics expresses the values of a firm by specifying in writing specific behaviors that are consistent or inconsistent with those values. Their effectiveness is a debated topic since the mere existence of a code does not guarantee a more ethical environment. Codes must not only be adopted, but top management must truly epitomize the values they embody. A sales manager cannot expect salespeople to conform to a code of behavior the manager openly behaves with inconsistently. There are four basic types of ethical codes: (1) company codes that define ethical boundaries for employees; (2) professional codes that define ethical boundaries for occupational groups such advertisers, marketing researchers, sales representatives, doctors, lawyers, accountants, etc.; (3) business association codes that define ethical boundaries for people engaged in the same line of business; and (4) advisory group codes suggested by government agencies or other special interests groups. Each industry is confronted with unique ethical issues and must adapt its code to meet the situation.

4. **Apply the criteria for making moral judgments.** Every person has a particular ethical philosophy. Idealism is a philosophy in which we judge actions against some applicable, universal standard, or guiding principle. Relativism is a philosophy in which we judge the acceptability of actions in the context of some situation. Teleology is the philosophy that the end justifies the means. Three dimensions of moral judgments are (1) moral equity, the fairness of justness of some behavior, (2) acceptability, or the way we judge socially or culturally consistency of behavior is judged, and (3) contractualism, or whether an act violates written or implied policies, contracts, or laws.

5. **Create and manage an ethical climate.** An ethical climate is the way employees view their work environment on moral dimensions. Four dimensions of ethical climate are policies and rules, trust/responsibility, peer behavior, and a bottom line sales orientation. In particular, a strong bottom-line orientation placing emphasis on making the numbers no matter what is responsible for motivating unethical actions. The sales manager can work toward a more positive ethical climate by emphasizing four workplace outcomes: (1) employees should have a knowledge of and understand ethics, (2) management should measure the ethical climate and use the measure to diagnose potential problems, (3) managers should lead by example, and (4) managers should use an ethics checklist to avoid making incorrect decisions when faced with ethical dilemmas.

6. **Observe legal regulations that affect the sales environment.** Observation of legal regulations begins with knowledge. Many legal regulations that affect the sales environment were summarized in the chapter. Key regulatory acts include the Sherman anti-trust act, the child protection act, and recent privacy legislation. These regulations are largely intended to make sure that a competitive marketplace is maintained or to protect populations perceived as vulnerable. Thus, sales managers must be aware of the key legal regulations that are relevant in their respective industries, as well as in the countries in which their employer sells products and/or services.

7. **Model good ethical behavior among the sales force.** Sales managers have many things to teach professional salespeople before they can carry out their individual jobs. Ethics training may not seem to be a high priority, but if the organization has strong ethical values, then ethics training is essential. Even if the salespeople already believe they know the difference between right and wrong, training increases ethical sensitivity and makes salespeople more aware of potential ethical implications. A positive, healthy, and moral ethical work climate begins at the top. If the sales manager does not treat salespeople honestly and fairly, they are likely to have a low regard for equitable and honest treatment of customers, suppliers, channel partners or even coworkers. Similarly, sales managers must thoroughly know and practice the company code of ethics (assuming one exists) if they expect salespeople to follow it.

8. **Future developments impacting sales and sales force management ethics.** Digital technologies are disrupting established sales and sales force management practices, including ethics. Sales managers and salespeople will have to coexist and evolve with artificial intelligence (AI), blockchain systems, and related emerging technologies. AI systems trained by humans will have enhanced cognitive skills enabling them to recall stored data exactly, provide specific guidelines on what and how to perform tasks, and monitor whether the guidelines were followed. Blockchain processes will track products from point of production to consumption, geo-targeted sales and advertising campaigns, price optimization, and ethical practices in the workplace. The result will be AI oversight and compliance assessment not only for sales and marketing strategies, but also ethical practices and decisions in general.

Key Terms

Organizational ethics	Sales management ethics	Boundary spanner	Moral philosophy
Organizational culture	Sales ethics subcompliance culture	Vulnerable	Ideals
Sales subculture		Codes of ethics	Deontological

Relativism	**Acceptability**	**Trust and responsibility**	**Cooling off rules**
Situational ethics	**Contractualism**	**Peer behavior**	**Ethical stress**
Teleology	**Organizational climate**	**Sales emphasis**	**Ethical maturity**
Ethical dilemma	**ethical work climate**	**Price discrimination**	**Artificial intelligence (AI)**
Moral judgment	**Ethical work climate**	**Uniform commercial code**	**Blockchain systems**
Moral equity	**Policies and rules**	**Green river ordinances**	

Notes

1. Adapted from: Goulston, M. (2005). *Tiger Woods doesn't cheat: How to be ethical and profitable. Sales and Service Excellence*, 2004 July 10; Shades of gray, *Sales & Marketing Management*, 156 (November), 26; Diez J. What made Tiger Woods great—and can again. *Golf Digest* (accessed February 2020); Tiger in prime played best golf ever. www.ESPN.com (accessed February 2020).

2. Ferrell, O.C., Fraedrich, J., and Ferrell, L. (2015). *Business Ethics: Ethical Decision-making and Cases*. 10th ed. New York: Houghton Mifflin Company.

3. Bush, V., Bush, A., Oakley, J., and Cicala, J. (2017). The sales profession as a subculture: implications for ethical decision making. *Journal of Business Ethics* 142 (3): 549–565.

4. Ibid.

5. Weber, J. and Wasieleski, D. (2013). Corporate ethics and compliance programs: a report, analysis and critique. *Journal of Business Ethics* 112 (4): 609–626; Rick, S. and Jasny, R. (2018). The compliance index model: Mitigating compliance risks by applying PLS-SEM to measure the perceived effectiveness of compliance programs. In: *Partial Least Squares Structural Equation Modeling* (eds. N.K. Avkiran and C.M. Ringle) (Vol. 267, pp. 125–170). https://doi.org/10.1007/978-3-319-71691-6_5 (accessed February 2020); and MacLean, T. L. and Behnam, M. (2010). The dangers of decoupling: the relationship between compliance programs, legitimacy perceptions, and institutionalized misconduct. *Academy of Management Journal* 53(6): 1499–1520. https://doi.org/10.5465/amj.2010.57319198 (accessed February 2020).

6. Flitter, E. and Cowley S. (2019 March 9). Wells Fargo says its culture has changed. Some employees disagree. https://www.nytimes.com/2019/03/09/business/wells-fargo-sales-culture.html (accessed July 2019); Egan, M. (2018 September 7) The two-year Wells Fargo horror story just won't end, *CNN Business*. https://money.cnn.com/2018/09/07/news/companies/wells-fargo-scandal-two-years/index.html (accessed June 2019); CEO Says Wells Fargo has transformed after scandals; Lawmakers are skeptical, *NPR*, 2019 March 12. https://www.npr.org/2019/03/12/702501160/ceo-says-wells-fargo-has-transformed-after-scandals-lawmakers-are-skeptical (accessed June 2019).

7. Ibid; Duska, R.F. (2004). Ethical issues with annuities: some situations for reflection. *Journal of Financial Service Professionals* 58 (September): 38–42.

8. Only ethical marketing will stand the test of time. https://www.entrepreneur.com/article/290891 (accessed June 2019); Akaah, I. P. and Riordan, E.A. (1989). Judgments of marketing professionals about ethical issues in marketing research. *Journal of Marketing Research* 26 (February): 112–120.

9. We pride ourselves on our responsible and ethical practices. https://www.gd.com/responsibility/commitment-to-ethics (accessed May 2019); Baker, R. (1993). An evaluation of the ethics program at general dynamics. *Journal of Business Ethics* 12: 165–177.

10. Accountability at Texas instruments. http://www.ti.com/corp/docs/csr/2012/corpgov/ethics/accountability.shtml (accessed May 2019); Larick, K. (1992). The crisis in business management. *Fortune* 20: 176.

11. Guyer, S. Case study for creating the NYNEX privacy principles. https://www.ntia.doc.gov/page/chapter-6-corporate-experiences-privacy-self-regulation (accessed June 2019); Gaines, S. (1994). Handling out halos. *Business Ethics* (March–April): 21.

12. Deconinck, J. (2005). The influence of ethical control systems and moral intensity on sales managers' ethical perceptions and behavioral intentions. *Marketing Management Journal* 15 (Fall): 123–131.

13. Lieber, R. We went to a steak dinner annuity pitch. The salesman wasn't pleased, *The New York Times*. https://www.nytimes.com/2018/11/30/your-money/retirement-annuities-steak-dinner.html (accessed May 2019); Schultz, E., and Opdyke, J. (2002). At Annuity University Agents learn how to pitch to seniors. *Wall Street Journal* (July 2): B1.

14. Knowles, P., and Singhapakdi, A. (2000). Distinguishing sales professionals from their marketing counterparts: an empirical inquiry. *Marketing Management Journal* 10(2): 41–53.

15. Hayden, B. (2016). Why the golden rule must be practiced in business, *Entrepreneur Magazine*. https://www.entrepreneur.com/article/281387; Vitel, S., Rallapalli, K., and Singhapakdi, A. (1993). Marketing norms: the influence of personal moral philosophies and organizational ethical culture. *Journal of the Academy of Marketing Science* 21 (Fall): 331–337.

16. Lee, Y., Heinze, T., and Donoho, C. (2018). An international study of culture, gender, and moral ideology on sales ethics evaluations: How should educators respond? *Journal of Marketing Education*. https://journals.sagepub.com/doi/10.1177/0273475318755492 (accessed May 2019); Sivadas, E., Kleiser, S., Kellaris, J. (2003). Moral philosophy, ethical evaluations, and sales manager hiring practices. *Journal of Personal Selling & Sales Management* 23: (Winter 2002–2003): 7–21.

17. Forsey, C. (2018). How to practice ethical decision making at work, *Hubspot Blog*. https://blog.hubspot.com/marketing/ethical-decision-making (accessed May 2019); Why ethics are still essential

in management (2016). https://online.se.edu/articles/mba/why-ethics-are-still-essential-in-management.aspx, Menguc, B. (1998). Organizational consequences, marketing ethics and salesperson supervision: further empirical evidence. *Journal of Business Ethics* 17 (March): 333–352.

18. Noh, Y. and Jung, M. (2013). A study of moral judgment and ethical decision making and ethical dilemmas experienced in practice by nursing student. *Journal of Korea Academia-Industrial Cooperation Society* 14 (6), 2915–2925; Robin, D., Reidenbach, E., and Babin, B.J. (1997). The nature, measurement and stability of ethical judgments in the workplace. *Psychological Reports* 80: 563–580.

19. Ibid, Robin, Reidenbach, and Babin.

20. Cadogan, J., Lee, N., Tarkiaainen, A., and Sundqvist, S. (2009). Sales manager and sales team determinants of salesperson ethical behavior. *European Journal of Marketing* 43 (7,8): 907–993; Barnett, T., Bass, K., and Brown, G. et al. (1998). The moral philosophy of sales managers and its influence on ethical decision making. *Journal of Personal Selling and Sales Management* 18 (Spring): 1–17. Dubinsky, A.J., Nataraajan, R., and Huang, W.-Y. (2004). The influence of moral philosophy on retail salespeople's ethical perceptions. *The Journal of Consumer Affairs* 38 (2): 297.

21. Fatima, Z., and Azam, K. (2016). Sales force control system and ethical behaviour: a review based article. *Asian Journal of Marketing* 10: 1–7; Bass et al. (1998); Román, S. and Munuera, J.-L. (2005). Determinants and consequences of ethical behaviour: an empirical study of salespeople. *European Journal of Marketing* 39 (5/6): 473–495.

22. Lee, Y., Heinze, T., and Donoho, C. (2018). An international study of culture, gender, and moral ideology on sales ethics evaluations: How should educators respond? *Journal of Marketing Education.* https://journals.sagepub.com/doi/10.1177/0273475318755492 (accessed May 2019); and Sivadas et al. (2003).

23. Lee, Y., Heinze, T., and Donoho, C. (2018). An international study of culture, gender, and moral ideology on sales ethics evaluations: how should educators respond? *Journal of Marketing Education.* https://journals.sagepub.com/doi/10.1177/0273475318755492 (accessed May 2019); and Sivadas et al. (2003).

24. McConnachie, C. (2019) Unethical sales practices that will damage your brand. https://www.salesforcesearch.com/blog/4-unethical-sales-practices-will-damage-brand/ (accessed May 2019); Sparks, J.R. and Johlke, M. (1996). Factors influencing student perceptions of unethical behavior by personal salespeople: an experimental investigation. *Journal of Business Ethics* 15: 871–887.

25. Why some employees get away with unethical conduct and others do not, (2016). *Insurance Journal.* https://www.insurancejournal.com/news/national/2016/04/13/405023.htm (accessed June 2019); Bellizzi, J.A. (2006). Disciplining top performing unethical salespeople: Examining the moderating effects of ethical seriousness and consequences. *Psychology & Marketing* 23 (February): 181–201.

26. Bellizi, J.A. and Hasty, R.D. (2002). Supervising unethical sales force behavior: Do men and women managers discipline men and women subordinates uniformly? *Journal of Business Ethics* 40 (October): 155–166.

27. Victoria, B., Bush, A.J., Oakley, J., and Cicala, J.E. (2017). The sales profession as a subculture: implications for ethical decision making. *Journal of Business Ethics* 142 (3): 549–565.

28. Babin, B.J., Boles, J.S., and Robin, D.P. (2000). Representing the perceived ethical work climate among marketing employees. *Journal of the Academy of Marketing Science* 28 (Summer): 345–359.

29. Schwepker, C.H. Jr. and Hartline, M.D. (2005). Managing the ethical climate of customer-contact service employees. *Journal of Service Research*, 7 (May): 377–397.

30. Schwepker, C.H. and Good, D.J. (2005). The impact of sales quotas on moral judgment in the financial services industry. *Journal of Services Marketing* 13 (1): 35–58.

31. Román, S. and Munuera, J.L. (2005). Determinants and consequences of ethical behaviour: an empirical study of salespeople. *European Journal of Marketing* 39 (5): 473–495.

32. Babin et al. (2000); Schwepker and Hartline (2005).

33. Mulki, J.P., Jaramillo, F., and Locander, W.B. (2006). Effects of ethical climate and supervisory trust on salesperson's job attitudes and intentions to quit. *Journal of Personal Selling & Sales Management* 26 (Winter): 19–26.

34. Weeks, W.A., Loe, T.W., Chonko, L.R. et al. (2006). Cognitive moral development and the impact of perceived organizational ethical climate on the search for sales force excellence: a cross-cultural study. *Journal of Personal Selling and Sales Management* 26 (Spring): 205–217.

35. Klein, E. and Pratt, K. Helping or hacking? Engineers and ethicists must work together on brain-computer interface technology. https://www.ge.com/reports/helping-hacking-engineers-ethicists-must-work-together-brain-computer-interface-technology/ (accessed February 2020); Gunther, M. (2004). Money and morals at GE. *Fortune* 150 (11/15): 176–182.

36. Clinton lifts ban on trade with Vietnam, *Wall Street Journal*, February 4, 1994, p. A12.

37. 20 countries where bribery in business is common. https://www.worldatlas.com/articles/20-countries-where-bribery-in-business-is-common-practice.html (accessed May 2019); Singapore remains a graft-free haven. *Straits Times*, April 9, 1996, p. 3.96.

38. Weeks et al. (2006).

39. Ferrell, O.C., Harrison, D., Ferrell, L. (2019). Business ethics, corporate social responsibility, and brand attitudes: an exploratory study. *Journal of Business Research* 95: 491–501.

40. Román and Munuera (2005).

41. Singh, J., Flaherty, K., Sohi, R.S., et al. (2019) Sales profession and professionals in the age of digitization and artificial intelligence technologies: concepts, priorities, and questions. *Journal of Personal Selling & Sales Management* 39 (1): 2–22. doi: https://doi.org/10.1080/08853134.2018.1557525 (accessed February 2020).

Chapter Review Questions

1. Define business ethics. [LO 1]

2. Why are salespeople considered boundary spanners? [LO 2]

3. Describe why business ethics is such an important topic in sales force management. [LO 1]

4. Why is it important to understand the sales ethics subculture? [LO 1]

5. Define vulnerability in a business context. Provide an example for each scenario below:
   a. Salesperson is vulnerable to a customer based on a knowledge deficit.
   b. A customer is vulnerable to a salesperson based on naiveté.
   c. A sales manager is vulnerable to a salesperson based on a power discrepancy.
   d. A customer is vulnerable to a salesperson based on a power discrepancy. [LO 1, 3]

6. A sales manager sends a salesperson to Latin American country noted for corruption in business to try and close a deal to supply parts to a heavy equipment manufacturer. The salesperson will only be able to close the deal if a bribe (a new BMW) is provided to a buyer from the manufacturer. How would you resolve this decision? Based on your decision, would you say your moral philosophy leans more toward idealism or relativism?

How would a person with the other moral philosophy resolve the situation? [LO 4]

7. List and define each dimension of moral judgment. [LO 4]

8. List at least 10 salesperson behaviors that would generally be considered unethical. [LO 5]

9. What is the Clayton Act? [LO 6]

10. When is price discrimination considered legal? [LO 6]

11. Define ethical climate. List two local companies that you are somewhat familiar with. What do you think the ethical climate is like in these companies? [LO 5]

12. If your university was a workplace, what would the ethical climate be in terms of each of its four dimensions? [LO 5]

13. What is ethical stress? How can ethical stress be resolved in the workplace? [LO 7]

14. Do you believe that the common negative perception of salesperson ethics is fact or fiction? [LO 1]

15. Question for Thought: Consider the material in the chapter describing the sales manager and the salesperson's role as a boundary spanner. Do you believe the boundary spanning nature of selling is responsible for the bad reputation of salespeople? [LO 2]

Online Exercises

1. The Direct Selling Association posts its code of ethics at the following website: http://www.dsa.org/ethics/code/. Log onto the website and review the code. Is the code useful as a decision-making guide for sales managers and sales people? Prepare a list of positive characteristics of the code and a list of vague areas.

2. Use a search engine such as ask.com or google.com to find some company or industry codes of ethics. Do these codes of ethics appear more consistent with idealism or relativism? Do you think the codes are effective?

Role-Play Exercise

A sales manager receives a call from a customer. The customer is concerned because the company salesperson has not made a call to her business in over 10 weeks. As a result, she is out of stock on some critical items causing her own production to become inefficient. When the sales manager confronts the rep about this action, he does not deny the story. Instead, he insists he was acting consistent with company policy that places a high value on maximizing shareholder wealth. His quotas are tied to this goal and he believes that providing sales and service support to small customers undermines his effort to obtain sales from better customers. Assume you were the sales manager, how would you react to the salesperson? What tools or knowledge might assist you in resolving the dilemma?

In-Basket Exercise

You are a district sales manager for an electronics firm that markets to industrial users, and you have recently been receiving complaints from customers about late deliveries. It appears that, on occasion, several of your salespeople promised customers certain delivery dates without checking with the product and shipping departments. As a result, the products reached the customers a day or two after the promised delivery date. When you confronted your sales-people with this issue, they claimed, "Everyone in the indus-try does it," and said, "The competition is getting so intense that we have to do it to compete." Moreover, your salespeople told you that an "on-time delivery" is more of an exception that the rule for the industry.

Questions

1. Should anything be done in this situation? Why or why not?

2. Would developing a code of ethics that includes the issue of "over promising" effectively deal with the situation? Why or why not?

3. How would you develop a code of ethics for your company a situation like this?

4. How would you enforce the code?

Ethical Dilemma

Tawania Williams sells copiers and other office equipment for Centroid Business Supplies and Equipment. She is hav-ing an excellent year and wants to win the incentive trip the company gives to the top salesperson each year. It is the last quarter of the year and Tawania learns the sales for another salesperson are higher than hers. She also learns the other salesperson is misrepresenting product and service benefits in his sales message but the sales manager appears to be over-looking this. What should Tawania do?

Consider a sales manager working for a small manufac-turing firm. A salesperson in the field phones with a problem.

Yesterday he committed to a deal to provide products to a retail chain operating in three states with two dozen stores. Today, he can close a deal with a nation-wide retailer with over 100 stores, but he wonders whether his firm can supply enough products to fulfill both customers' demands. The sales manager knows the answer to this question. There is no way the company can fulfill the deal signed yesterday and meet the demands of the larger retailer. So the sales manager is con-sidering whether to have the salesperson mislead the smaller retailer while diverting deliveries to the larger retailer. What should the sales manager do?

Vita Soup: Role-Play Exercise

As American as apple pie, the Vita Soup Company comes close to being a household tradition. Started over 100 years ago, the company has weathered several economic storms and managed to stay afloat despite considerable changes in con-sumer lifestyles, distribution channel alternatives, and man-ufacturing technology. The company is currently confronted many challenges, but the one creating chaos within the sales organization is a proposed new code of ethics. Last year a new marketing director from a much larger firm was hired to grow sales and distribution. At his previous employer they had a formal, widely circulated code of ethics, with specific sections relating to the sales division. In contrast, Vita Soup is family owned and managed, has never had any serious or even small

ethical violations, and has no formal code of ethics. The sales manager and the 22 sales people are happy with the current situation. The marketing director says no matter what size the company is, how it is owned, how long it has been operating, or whether it has ever had ethical issues, there should be a formal code of ethics and specific provisions for the sales orga-nization. The participants and assignments are as follows:

James Reed, Marketing Director, argues for a formal code of ethics.

Charles Hebert, Sales Manager, supports the current situ-ation and argues a formal code of ethics in not needed for Vita Soup.

Johnson Industrial: Advancing Production in the Modern World

Johnson Industrial recently celebrated its 70th year of business. Johnson produces high-quality, custom-tooled machine parts/components by hand. In its 70 year history, Johnson Industrial gained a reputation for superior quality and exacting workmanship, so for decades, manufacturers in need of exacting prototypes went to Johnson Industrial.

Throughout its history, Johnson Industrial has worked closely with several profitable industries, including the auto industry in producing robotic parts for production equipment. Johnson's mastery at custom work made them a respected industry leader, however the world is moving towards replicable mass production, and Johnson, being the industry leader in custom parts, must expand its competencies towards mass production if it wants to continue to compete.

Jerod Smith has been a successful commission sales rep for Johnson Industrial for 11 years. He has extensive connections with many varied Original Equipment Manufacturers (OEMs). Because of Johnson Industrial's expertise with custom components, they frequently make prototypes for these OEMs that are later mass produced by outside manufacturers. Prior to moving to these components towards mass production, Johnson Industrial perfects the tolerances and passes them, along with specification sheets (spec sheets), to mass producers with expertise in Computer Numerical Control (CNC) lathes. CNC lathes are specialized milling equipment that allow for the transfer of coding between computers (or thumb drives) and the lathe for the production of components requiring precise milling and exacting tolerances. While their processes are separate, both Johnson Industrial and the various CNC manufacturers they partner with are both required to get products to market. Jerod's customers are satisfied with Jerod's reputation, and that of Johnson Industrial — neither Jerod nor Johnson Industrial has ever let them down, however Jerod's job had just changed from pushing custom components to pushing custom components *and* their subsequent mass production.

The management of Johnson Industrial is intent on remaining competitive in the future. As the robotics world moves away from limited, specialized manufacturing towards mass production, it has become evident that exacting duplication of custom parts is not attainable without a new standard of quality control measurement. Mass producers of components have for years, relied on ISO9001 (International Standards Organization) protocol to navigate their quality control (QC) processes. ISO9001 is essentially an internationally accepted system of documenting a manufacturer's quality control procedures via an outside audit. This gives OEMs an accurate view into the QC process of the production manufacturers, and thereby a sense of security in selecting viable manufacturers. While this was not an issue when Johnson was making one-off components, if Johnson wanted to move to mass production, ISO9001 approval was absolutely critical.

Three months ago, Jerod approached a long-time customer, Bob Chaney at Plaxton Robotics, to bid on a component. Bob Chaney, the Purchasing manager at Plaxton, was familiar with and appreciated Johnson Industrial's high standards. Bob told Jerod that he was seriously considering one of Johnson's competitors with a solid history of CNC manufacturing to take one of Johnson's prototype components and mass produce it, as they have done multiple times in the past. Jerod, wanting to capture the mass production business of a long-time customer, told Bob that Johnson Industrial could handle the mass production, as they have already made the move to CNC production, when in truth, they were still in the exploratory research stages.

Bob, having worked successfully with Jerod over the years, had no reason to doubt him, and took Jerod at his word — Bob gave Jerod the 10,000 piece component order. Elated, Jerod took the order. With a brand new house and a baby on the way, Jerod was thrilled to get the business.

Johnson Industrial moved ahead with Plaxton's production, however they used injection-molds instead of CNCs, which yielded small, yet critical flaws in the tolerances–consistent precision in the components was lacking, rendering them useless. Jerod tried to have production QC 100% of the components, but it was slow, costly, and inefficient. "QC-ing" 100% of the components ate up any profits Johnson hoped to reap. The more inconsistencies came up, the more Jerod tried to hide the problem. Management at Johnson had hit its limit; too much money had been wasted.

It was clear that Johnson Industrial had to invest in CNC technology, or partner with a CNC expert and give up the commissions related to mass production.

Questions

1. Briefly describe all of the issues described by this case.

2. For each issue in question one, please rate its importance on the following scale:

Unimportant						Very Important
	1	2	3	4	5	6	7

3. What signs did Johnson Industrial and Jerod ignore that led them to their current situation? Could this problem have been anticipated?

4. What systems could Johnson Industrial have put in place that would have eased their change from custom production to mass production?

5. Could a code of ethics or Mission Statement featuring ethics, well publicized within Johnson Industrial, have averted their current dilemma?

   a. If you answered "yes," please give an example of what information should have been internally publicized.

   b. Should this code of ethics or Mission Statement be accessible to internal and external customers?

6. What advice do you have for Jerod in his current situation? Please back up your advice with logic and reason.

7. Is this more of an ethics issue or more of a manufacturing issue?

Case prepared by: Diane Kirkland, California State University, Long Beach.

CASE 2.2 | J&R Company: Unethical Sales Practices

Tom Peterson is an industrial sales rep for J&R Company, a large company in the pipe, valve, and fitting industry. J&R Company sells to customers with facilities in which gases or liquids are moved from one place to another in the manufacturing process. Tom returned to his office after visiting a large potential customer in the paper and pulp industry. During his drive, Tom made a decision to call his weekly golf partner Sam McNeil, a popular technical blogger for Tom's industry. Tom planned to ask Sam to write a blog about his company's new product and the two largest companies that Tom believed would soon sign a contract with J&R to purchase the product. Sam had already written several positive online reviews about J&R. Tom could ask Sam to just note the new product in his reviews of the company, which may end up on the first page of a potential buyer's online search.

J&R Company had developed a new valve system that they believed would reduce spills and leaks in customers' manufacturing facilities. However, the product was slow to take off in the market. While J&R's system reduced leaks by 0.4% (0.5% with the additional purchase of an extended service contract), Tom believed that those reports significantly underestimated the value of the system. With the on-site support of a J&R technician, Tom believed that greater efficiencies could be obtained. Tom would discuss his idea of a customer technician with his manager should the customers see a benefit and decide to buy.

Valve leak detection systems had become very popular in manufacturing facilities in recent years. Tom sensed that the product was slow-moving on the market because companies felt the leak detection systems were more cost-effective than purchasing a completely new valve system and stopping production while the new system was installed.

Earlier in the day Tom visited one of his company's largest prospective customers, Biddle Inc., a major pulp and paper company. Tom told Biddle Inc. that one of Biddle's closest competitors was going to soon begin using J&R's new valve system. While Biddle Inc.'s competitor had not yet signed a contract or committed to J&R, Tom felt they soon would come around and agree to purchase the system as well as the extended service contract.

Tom offered Biddle Inc. a low price on the initial system. He knew the initial system would be obsolete in the next year as the company refined the system and decreased the spill/leakage rate significantly. But Tom felt that if Biddle Inc. agreed to buy the initial system that they would see how well the product performed and naturally upgrade to the refined system once it was placed on the market.

Tom explained to Biddle Inc. that the new system substantially reduced the risk of leaks and spills, which slow down production and are costly. Tom built his sales presentation around the costs of leaks or spills across all industries. He mentioned several times in his sales presentation that the purchase of the extended service contract would offer Biddle Inc. a 20% reduction in the spill rate, as compared to just the purchase of the new valve system.

Tom hoped that if Sam, his golfing partner, would help him with digital promotion for J&R's new valve system that the product might start to pick up some momentum on the market. He planned to use coverage of the story as an additional lever to close the deals with Biddle Inc. and their competitor. While neither potential customer had committed, and both frankly told Tom that they had serious reservations about the new product, Tom thought a product review published in a respected trade publication would offer the product the credibility it needed to jump-start sales. In any case, Sam owed Tom a favor.

If the valve system did not do well in the market in the next quarter, J&R had made clear the company would be forced to downsize their sales force. The company had an extended line of products and services, and while senior management hoped their new valve system would become a flagship product for the company, management would not sacrifice the reputation of their other products in attempts to force a lackluster product to market.

Tom has worked for J&R for 10 years. Nevertheless, he felt his job was vulnerable. He had shifted his sales emphasis entirely to the new valve system, giving up territory and smaller customers who purchased other products and services from the company. In Tom's city, industrial sales positions were very limited. With two children, one in high school, and the other in middle school, and a wife with a secure position at a large law firm in the area, Tom did not welcome the prospects of job change. He had to find a way to make the new valve system a marketplace success.

Questions

1. Briefly describe the issues raised in the case.

2. For each issue you listed in the first question, rate how important you believe each issue is on the following scale:

Unimportant						Very Important
1	2	3	4	5	6	7

3. How could a company code of ethics aid Tom in his decisions? What are some examples of what the company code of ethics might contain to assist sales reps in similar situations?

4. What risk might J&R be exposed to based on Tom's actions?

5. What questions might Tom have asked himself during this situation to determine whether or not his actions are ethical?

6. Recommend a course of action Tom might have taken, and support your recommendations.

This case prepared by: Dr. Wendy Ritz, Florida State University, Panama City and Dr. Michelle Steward, Wake Forest University

CHAPTER 3

Customer Relationship Management (CRM) and Building Partnerships

What Is CRM?

Customer relationship management (CRM) is an essential sales management tool. CRM's roots have been around for many years. As long ago as the 1960s, Reader's Digest kept files on over 10,000,000 customers that were segmented into three groups based on the likelihood of their responding to promotional appeals. The system answered the question: "If a customer is sent a new book to review, how likely will they be to respond by purchasing the book and buying others?" One group was highly likely to respond, another group responded only with more prodding, and a third group was highly unlikely to respond. While primitive by today's standards, this example captures the basic notion of CRM.[1]

CRM includes a wide variety of business solutions for handling customer-related information. Thus, finding a universally accepted definition of CRM is difficult.[2] Here, we focus on CRM from a sales and sales force management perspective. In this context, CRM is a systematic integration of information technology and human resources designed to provide maximum value to customers and to obtain maximum value from customers for the company.[3] In other words, a CRM system helps salespeople match customers with the goods and services that are best for them, and in doing so, leveraging company resources into higher sales and profits. Today, more than ever, CRM depends on data. The ability to record, store, and analyze data about customers provides the fuel for successful CRM. Indeed, companies adopting CRM programs often, but not always, experience higher business performance. When CRM fails, the problem is seldom in the technology and more often in the human element, as we will see.

As the name implies, CRM deals with managing relationships. Thus, just as people have different relationships with other people, businesses also have different relationships with different customers. CRM is sometimes referred to as relationship marketing. So before explaining CRM systems, let's consider the nature of relationships between selling approaches and customers.

Relationship Orientation and CRM

Businesses approach customers in different ways. We can summarize almost all of the ways into a few types, as shown in Figure 3.1.

Mass Marketing—the same product for the entire market

Differentiated Marketing—different products for each customer group

Niche Marketing—a single unique
product for a single customer group

One-to-One Marketing—a unique
product for each customer

FIGURE 3.1 Relationships between businesses and customers.

Mass Marketing

When we think of marketing, many people think of mass marketing first. Mass marketing is a way of dealing with customers by offering the same product to the entire market. In other words, all customers get almost the same treatment. The company may make small variations in the products sold, but the main concern is efficiency in production and distribution. Mass marketing evokes images of large factories with high-volume assembly lines. You may have heard the expression attributed to Henry Ford "the customer can have any color car he wants, as long as it's black!"

Mass marketing focuses on efficiently distributing a firm's products to many consumers. As a result, the orientation is maximizing market share, while at the same time minimizing costs by allocating them across sales to large numbers of people. Sales managers typically serve a large number of customers with a limited sales force. Marketing expenses are generally minimal and the sales effort becomes routinized. Salespeople generally possess greater expertise in their products than customer knowledge when a firm has a mass marketing orientation. Mass marketing is used much less often today than through much of the twentieth century, but many firms selling commodity-type goods or services still operate as mass marketers.

Differentiated Marketing

Differentiated marketing is selling to different groups of customers by offering a unique product for each group. Many consumer-goods firms use differentiated marketing. For example, Coca-Cola has products for traditional cola lovers, cola lovers with concerns about calories, energy drinks, products without caffeine, and even products for different types of water lovers! Coke also sells different products for institutional customers and individual consumers. A large portion of Coca-Cola's business lies in the B2B side where they sell different beverage packages to different institutional customers. For example, Delta Airlines purchases different products and services than does McDonald's hamburgers.

Differentiated marketing requires a more customized sales effort and greater attention to customer research than does mass marketing. Sales managers must decide, for example, whether to assign salespeople based on customer similarities or product similarities, or whether the same salespeople calling on customers purchasing large amounts should also call on smaller customers. CRM influences these decisions, as we will see later.

Niche Marketing

Niche marketing offers a specialized product or a small range of products to an individual customer segment with specialized needs. For instance, some insurance companies focus on providing insurance for specific circumstances. AFLAC (www.aflac.com) sells supplementary disability insurance for people who are unable to work. Salespeople for niche marketers must be very knowledgeable about the needs of the niche market the company serves.

One-to-One Marketing

One-to-one marketing, as the name implies, matches individual products with individual customers. This way of dealing with customers takes differentiated or niche marketing to the extreme. The result is a product personalized for each customer in some way.[4] Many textbook publishers customize textbooks for individual courses at different universities. Perhaps some of your textbooks contain material and/or pictures depicting things specific to your school. If so, chances are the publisher has agreed to produce a special version of the book for use only at your university. This is an example of one-to-one marketing.

Casinos often develop specific promotional appeals to individual customers based on information collected when the customer swipes his or her "players" card at various locations within the casino. Casino managers then know the types of food the customer enjoys, the games the customer plays, and the time of day, week, or month the customer visits the casino – information that helps them customize a product for each customer who merits such specialized attention. This type of customization doesn't work with all customers. But giving your best customers this kind of attention can be a wise strategy.

Successful one-to-one marketing requires detailed knowledge of customers. A custom homebuilder, for example, relies on the customer to provide all the details desired in the home. A mobile home manufacturer, obviously not a one-to-one marketer, provides customers very little opportunity to choose features. Custom homebuilders add features based on feedback customers provide directly. But manufacturers of many other types of products rely on technology to gather detailed customer information and feed it directly into the design of a customized product. Sales Management in Action Box 3.1 describes one way to accomplish such a task.

CRM systems contain integrated data systems that greatly facilitate one-to-one marketing compared to previous times. At the consumer level (B2C), customer data allows that customer to easily customize clothing, bicycles, hotel stays, etc., so that the end-result is truly a co-created consumption experience.[5] By co-creation, we mean that both the company and the consumer provide resources into the production and consumption of a product offering. On the B2B side, data exchanges allow customized solutions. Waste management, for example, provides customers with mobile applications that push data to the company that allow tailored solutions to individual customers by providing specialized delivery times and truck types based on a customer's specific waste needs.[6] Effective data systems are the key to success in customizing and co-creating value.

Using Information to Meet Customer Needs

Many companies that previously practiced mass marketing are moving quickly toward differentiated marketing – and sometimes even one-to-one marketing. Through the middle of the twentieth century, television viewing in the United States was dominated by three national networks, each offering a single programming option for the entire viewing audience. Networks have now diversified and offer many programming options for different customer segments. Most of the major networks own differentiated news channels (MSNBC, Fox News, CNN, Fox Business) and sports channels (ESPN, ESPN2, ESPN-Classic, etc.). Sky Network (www.sky.uk) operates many different cable options. Streaming services like Netflix allow individualized solutions for customers to watch what they want when they want to watch it.

Even supermarket giants such as Tesco (www.tesco.uk.com) and Sainsbury's (www.sainsburys.co.uk) are adopting some one-to-one marketing practices. Tesco, for example, sends its entire market traditional flyers with weekly specials. But it also sends flyers with over 5,000,000 different variations, each tailored for a specific customer bascd on his or her buying patterns.

How can a company try to match up 5,000,000 different promotional products with 5,000,000 individual customers? With technology! Companies like Unica (www.unica. com) offer software that tracks individual customer activities and ties those activities to targeted communications. The information is gathered through scanner data or online cookies. Industrial customers, in particular, are realizing that allowing a firm to have access to your cookies can be a win–win situation. In this way, information that salespeople used to collect in the field can be replaced or complemented by data gathered easily and inexpensively using technology.[7]

Production Versus Marketing Orientation

Production and marketing orientations are complementary ways to look at business. The industrial revolution enabled businesses to manufacture in high volumes efficiently and at lower costs, which is the essence of a production orientation. Companies with this outlook focus on processes that facilitate large-scale, efficient, and economic production. They need little customer research because they do not change their products to fit the demands of any particular market.[8] Instead, production-oriented firms continuously work to make the production and supply chains more efficient to deliver products to customers while incurring minimal costs.

Table 3.1 illustrates the similarities between mass marketing and a production orientation. Sales managers in mass marketing firms concentrate on moving large quantities of products through traditional distribution channels that allow for economical shipping, such as trucking and railroad freight. Sales practices rely heavily on price promotions such as trade allowances and discounts, because the products often are seen as somewhat interchangeable.

The production orientation dominated industry in the United States and other developed economies through the mid-twentieth century. Indeed, the production orientation helped the Allies win World War II as factories turned out large quantities of B-17s, P-47s, Sherman tanks, and Liberty ships at a pace unmatched before. Production capacity more than satisfied the demand for basic goods. But eventually businesses had to do more than just sell whatever they could make.

The answer emerged from a new way of doing business called market orientation. With this approach companies focus more on making what they can sell.[9] Market-oriented firms seek success in a competitive marketplace by focusing on providing value for customers. This means knowledge of consumers must be shared through all areas of the firm. Sales managers play an important role not only in carrying outbound communications to customers but also in steering inbound communications that flow from customers back through various organizational levels within a company. When a firm becomes market-oriented, these communications can end up altering the design and production of products as well as promotion and distribution strategies.

Market-oriented firms are customer-centric – customers are the heart of the business process. These firms focus on customer value, which is the net positive worth resulting from participation in exchanges. Differentiated marketers and one-to-one marketers follow market orientation, since their products must closely match consumer desires or a competitor will move in to better meet the demand. General Electric is often credited with developing the concept of a marketing orientation in the early 1960s. GE emphasized the critical role played by customer research prior to launching new products. This was a revolutionary concept in the mid-twentieth century.

Salespeople can be more or less customer-oriented. Sales-oriented salespeople are motivated to maximize sales from each contact even if a product does not best match customer needs and desires. But customer-oriented salespeople are motivated

TABLE 3.1

Production Orientation to Market Orientation in the Twentieth Century

1900–1940	1941–1945	1946–1959	1960–1990	1991–beyond
Industrial capacity increases—the production orientation is born.	Industrial capacity reaches its highest productivity in war time.	The economy is strong, but firms can make more than can be sold.	Better marketing research techniques allow more input from consumers prior to making key marketing decisions—the marketing orientation is born.	Firms become more customer-centric as many firms move from transactional exchange to relational exchange—the marketing orientation leads to CRM.

primarily to match customers with products that best meet their needs. Research generally supports the idea that positive outcomes come from both firm market orientation and salesperson consumer orientation.[10] The positive outcomes include better customer service and improved performance.[11] These developments are summarized in Table 3.1.

CRM and Repeat Business

CRM is based on the premise that companies interact with customers more than one time and in more than one way. Businesses that assume contact will be made with each customer seldom or only one time are much less motivated to provide excellent service than those that assume they will be in touch with customers many times over an extended period. The extra motivation is based on the likelihood of repeat business.

A touchpoint is a situation in which the customer and the company come together either personally or virtually. For example, a touchpoint occurs when a salesperson calls on a customer at his or her place of business; when a customer phones the business for sales assistance or service; when a customer posts a message on a website or complains on a customer blog; when an individual accesses the company's website on their smartphone or other mobile device, or when an individual checks prices or availability on an iPhone or a wearable device like an iWatch; and even when the customer hears a radio advertisement for the company. With CRM, touchpoints become critical parts of the service delivery process.

Perhaps the most critical touchpoint is at the point of exchange. A sales exchange is the act of trading economic resources (usually money) for a specific set of benefits offered by a company. Marketing facilitates exchange, and salespeople play the key functional role in conducting exchanges for the organization.

Transactional View

One view of exchange is that each and every interaction with a customer is a unique and independent event. Companies that consistently follow this view are practicing transactional selling. Here, the salesperson is concerned most with winning business from a particular exchange touchpoint.

Transactional selling is at the low end of the relational involvement continuum (see Table 3.2). The exchange environment is characterized by short-term customer needs.

TABLE 3.2

Contrasting Types of Exchange Relationships

Event	Nature of exchange relationship		
	Transactional →	Relational →	Partnership
Exchange environment	Competitive	Cooperative	Collaborative
Timing of contact	Periodic sales calls	Frequent contact – near daily	Intensive contact – dedicated sales associate(s)
Service level	Good	Very good	Intensive
Trust	Moderate	High	Complete
Interdependence	Low	High	Extreme – vertical integration possible
Sales pattern	Independent	Renewing contract	Ongoing contract
Governance	Market forces	Contract	Relational

Sales reps make periodic sales calls, with high-volume customers receiving more frequent visits than low-volume customers. Buyers and sellers remain independent and each transaction is conducted as if it were a new event. Thus, the relationship may last only as long as necessary to negotiate the sales transaction. There is no long-term commitment or loyalty, and little value is assigned to understanding long-run buyer needs and expectations or to satisfying customers.

Transactional selling is often more adversarial than cooperative. Price becomes a key consideration – neither the salesperson nor the customer is looking for much beyond the immediate transaction, and issues like service after the sale are relatively less important. Thus, the most common way to increase value is to lower price.

Although buyers and sellers participate in transactional exchanges many times over a period of years, they negotiate prices and other terms each time an exchange takes place. Interpersonal trust may develop over time, but the transactional exchange does not require high trust levels. If customers have a bad experience, they simply exclude the company from the consideration set next time.

Selling firms with this orientation generally have to touch large numbers of customers to generate business. In this sense, risk is reduced because the selling firm is less dependent on any one or small number of customers.

Relational Selling

The cost of attracting new customers typically is significantly higher than the cost of reselling to current customers. When salespeople use past customers as leads to future business, they have performed a basic function of relational selling. In relational exchange, both buyer and seller recognize that each transaction is one in a series of purchase agreements. Thus, relational selling is more customer-centric than transactional exchanges.

With relational selling, the exchange environment is characterized by a spirit of cooperation between buyer and seller. Firms seek to develop profitable, ongoing relationships with customers by delivering high value that creates a sense of loyalty. In fact, loyal customers frequently become a company's best unpaid salespeople by referring other prospects and spreading positive "word-of-mouth" messages.

Sales managers must be committed to providing very good to exceptional service. This relatively high customer-service level is influential in customer retention. Customer retention is the percentage of customers who repeatedly purchase products from the selling firm. Any relationship, whether social or business, requires regular attention and nurturing if it is to survive. Poorly served or neglected customers are likely to start looking for alternate suppliers. Thus, relational exchange relationships are characterized by frequent, even daily, contacts between the sales force and the customer as well as using online interactions that enable the seller to monitor various aspects of the buyer's business, such as inventory levels and reorder points.

Relational exchange has a longer-term focus than transactional exchange. As a result, salespeople can develop cost-effective, high-value ties that generate repeated transactions. These relationships require higher levels of trust, since the switching costs are increased due to greater dependence. Consider a computer manufacturer that purchases processor chips via transactional exchange relationships. Over time the company will use many different suppliers. If on any given occasion a supplier is unable to fill an order, the company can probably quickly go to one of that firm's competitors and strike up another arm's-length deal, but it may have to pay a higher price.

Relational exchanges should result in "win–win" sales solutions. Sales managers emphasize the importance of understanding customer needs and requirements. This corporate knowledge must be communicated to the sales people in the field. CRM provides a more high-tech approach to staying in touch with customers. The Sales Management in Action 3.1 provides some insight into this process for a new pharmaceutical rep. The overall objective is to achieve both customer satisfaction and loyalty by providing superior value through reliable customer service and support activities.

Box 3.1 | Sales Management in Action 3.1

Merck Goes High Tech

Jane Smart is about to begin teaching a sales training class for new hires at Merck. She has been a sales manager for 20 years and is reflecting on how things have changed. She tells the class about her first sales calls to physicians' offices. Each new sales call was a nerve-racking experience. She had no information from previous reps about the types of products each doctor was likely to respond positively to, no knowledge of who the key people in the office were or how to actually get access to the physician, and no clue about the demeanor of the physician and whether she would be greeted warmly or rudely or be thrown out of the office because of something another rep had done. She quickly learned that taking notes following a sales call was essential to making the next call more effective.

The class will add a couple of dozen people to the more than 90,000 pharmaceutical reps selling drugs across the United States. In contrast to Jane Smart's early experiences, each rep will receive sophisticated training, including a detailed history of each existing account. This history will be instantly available from cloud databases that store information about physicians, regulations, clinical drug trials, and potential competing products. The system is the result of a partnership between Microsoft and Accenture to produce a product especially for Merck sales reps. Following each sales call, reps enter notes about what happened, and the information is integrated into the system, enabling each rep to use time more effectively, managing customers with a combination of technology and personal attention. Although the selling process is more complicated than when she began, Jane realizes new Merck reps will be more productive and get more out of the limited time each has with a customer. How things have changed![12]

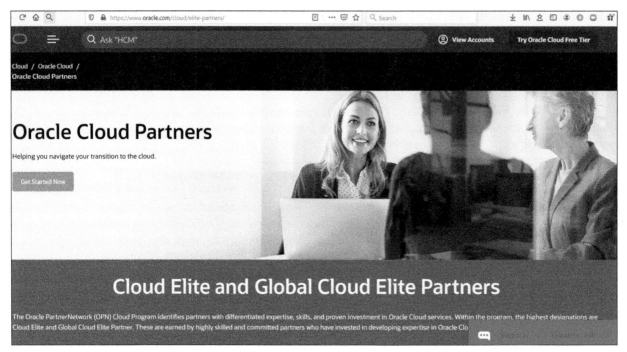

Oracle touts its strategic partnerships.
Source: https://www.oracle.com/cloud/elite-partners/, April 14, 2020.

Strategic Partnerships

In relational exchanges, the buying and selling firms are so closely intertwined they sometimes become partners. This type of exchange environment is a strategic partnership. Strategic partnerships arise when the goals, strategies, and resources of buyers and sellers are so interconnected they develop an integrated, symbiotic relationship while retaining their independent identities.[13]

To use a romantic analogy, transactional selling is like the "dating stage," relationship selling is like "going steady," and a strategic partnership is more like a marriage except that strategic business partners do not fully merge and become a single company.

Strategic partnerships and other inter-firm collaborative arrangements are commonplace in today's global economy. As companies increasingly specialize, they are moving away from rigid, control-based structures and adopting more flexible, relationship-based partnering arrangements that capitalize on the relative strengths of each partner. In fact, many companies have re-engineered their business processes to create coalitions and partnerships with their customers' companies, thus developing tightly interwoven and interdependent value chains.

Strategic partnerships are at the opposite end of the exchange continuum from transactional exchanges. They are based more on inter-organizational *collaboration* than on arm's-length aggressive bargaining and are not viewed as competitive. In fact, in the spirit of co-creation, decision-making often is collaborative and firms share managerial resources and expertise when solving key strategic and tactical issues. Companies that skillfully establish strategic partnering agreements can shore up weaknesses and capitalize on strengths together, thereby making both partners stronger.[14]

Strategic partnerships result in continuous, recurring exchanges. This requires frequent communication, relationship openness, information sharing, joint problem solving, strategic integration, and mutual learning. Strategic partnerships also exhibit high levels of collaboration among partners, equality, shared vision, benefits and goals, and high levels of trust.

Mutual loyalty occurs in successful strategic partnerships when both buyer and seller are committed to each other and avoid behaviors that may damage the relationship. Sun Microsystems, now a part of Oracle (www.sun.com/www.oracle.com), is an example of a firm that developed strategic partnerships. Sun has strong brand identity and is known as a key technology provider that manufactures server hardware, workstations, and storage devices. Oracle's specialty provides Sun's systems with data management capabilities. Prior to Sun's acquisition, Sun and Oracle worked closely together, and together they worked closely with customers, with the result being comprehensive, tailored solutions. Sun, Oracle, and the customers worked together as partners, not as competitors.

Companies that rely on strategic partnerships may actually reduce the need for salespeople. Sales managers then oversee reps that function as employees of the buyer's firm. In this way, the reps acquire the detailed knowledge needed to maintain healthy relationships with their customers, and much information including sales histories, sales forecasts, and even market research results are shared between firms – often in real time.

Strategic partnerships often result in vertical integration. Vertical integration is a pattern of controlling and perhaps acquiring assets and resources at different levels of the marketing channel. It enables the manufacturer to tightly control production and distribution processes, creating value for the customer. The increased control means customer needs are more precisely met.

Bridgestone Tire Company (www.bridgestone-firestone.com) creates strategic partnerships with customers. Bridgestone even manages inventories for customers, eliminating their need to place orders. Thus, sales reps don't need to call on dealers for routine order taking. In addition, Bridgestone controls many aspects of the distribution channel. It owns its own fleet of trucks and has a customized delivery system that allows it to offer 24-hour delivery. Bridgestone also owns manufacturing assets including rubber farms. All these steps help Bridgestone provide value for customers.

Mechanisms That Govern Exchanges

All types of exchanges involve some type of governance. Governance is the mechanism that helps ensure the exchange is fair to all parties involved. As shown in Table 3.2, transactional exchanges are controlled by market forces, relational exchanges are governed by contracts, and strategic partnerships are governed by a mechanism known as relational governance.

Market forces are the simplest because they don't require any artificial mechanism. If a firm has a problem with the other firm in the exchange, it looks for another supplier it believes will treat it more fairly. Contracts are more complicated and specify the legal obligations of buyers and sellers. Fair exchange proceeds so long as each party lives up to its obligations. If either falls short, the other can take legal action.

Formal contracts can also be prepared that place specific limits on how each party can behave in an exchange setting. If either the buyer or the seller violates the terms of the contract, there are specified penalties. If the firm refuses to comply with the penalties, legal action is likely.

Relational governance includes arrangements for sharing information and tasks between the buying and selling firm but does not include specific obligations for each party. Written statement of commitment between buyer and seller, but relational governance allows greater flexibility than a contractual governance structure.

	Strongly Disagree	Disagree	Neutral	Agree	Strongly Agree
The distributor has not kept some promises that were made when we began the relationship	1	2	3	4	5
The distributor has ignored some aspects of the contract that were designed to increase our ability to reach and service customers.	1	2	3	4	5
The distributor has interpreted terms of the contract in [its] favor at our expense.	1	2	3	4	5
The distributor has coerced us unfairly in order to gain concessions.	1	2	3	4	5
The distributor has violated contractual terms.	1	2	3	4	5

FIGURE 3.2 Measuring opportunism in a relational exchange environment.

In all relationships, sometimes, one party takes advantage of the other. When this occurs, the firm has behaved in an opportunistic manner. Figure 3.2 shows survey scale items that measure whether a customer believes a supplier has behaved opportunistically.[15] Generally, written agreements and greater trust result in less opportunism. But when a selling situation is characterized by high ambiguity, relational-based governance creates a high degree of opportunistic behavior.[16] For example, cross-cultural exchanges include considerable amounts of ambiguity due to cultural uncertainties and unfamiliarity with legal systems, regulations, and infrastructures.[17] In these situations, many opportunities exist for one firm to take advantage of another.

For instance, consider a company that supplies combustion engine parts including regulators, release valves, and water pumps to original equipment manufacturers (OEM). The company's largest customer is John Deere (www.johndeere.com), which competes with Caterpillar (www.cat.com). Suppose a sales rep that works for the company with a relationship with John Deere later develops a relationship with Caterpillar representatives and has the opportunity to sell them large numbers of water pumps. But if the company does so, it will be unable to meet the needs of John Deere. How should a sales manager react upon learning of this situation?

It depends on the type of exchange relationship the company has with John Deere. If the relationships are market exchanges, the company would be free to move its business to Caterpillar with no fear of legal problems with John Deere for behaving opportunistically. But it must realize John Deere will have reservations about future business with the company.

If the relationship between the company and John Deere is relational, there would be a legal obligation for the company to live up to the contract terms. In other words, if the contract specifies that 1000 water pumps must be delivered each month, then the company must deliver this quantity or face legal problems. This type of arrangement should discourage opportunistic behavior, at least for the length of the contract.

If the relationship between the company and John Deere is based on an ongoing contract, the relational governance for opportunism is altered somewhat. When the company acts opportunistically, it risks losing the John Deere contract. Under a strategic partnership, however, mutual benefit is tied to performance. In other words, when one company performs well, the other is rewarded. Thus, the company is less likely to behave opportunistically if doing so lowers the partner's performance.

CRM, Customer Loyalty and Lifetime Value

CRM makes sense particularly when a firm expects to do business with its customers repeatedly over an extended period of time. Thus, companies succeed by offering superior value to customers over repeated sales exchanges. In return customers become more valuable to the firm. The focus is not on value from a single transaction, but on the mutual value resulting from relational exchanges extending over an extended period of time.

Customer Loyalty

Loyal customers are like money in the bank, because they will continue to purchase and provide revenue in the future. Customer loyalty is a function of two components – customer share and customer commitment.

The behavioral component of customer loyalty is customer share.[18] Customer share is the proportion of resources a customer spends with one among a set of competing suppliers. For example, if Walgreens (www.walgreens.com) purchases generic heart medicine from a supplier of generic drugs such as Currax Pharmaceuticals (www.currax.com), customer share is the amount Walgreens purchases from Currax compared to the amount it purchases from Currax's competitors. If Walgreens purchases half from Currax and half from other generic suppliers, customer share is 50%. Thus, as Currax becomes more and more an exclusive supplier to Walgreens, customer share increases. High customer share is an important component of true loyalty. Customer share is a tangible component of the value of a customer because it is based on actual behavior.

The second component of customer loyalty is intangible and based on emotion. Customer commitment is the bond between a customer and a sales firm that builds up over time as a customer continues to have rewarding sales exchanges with a supplier. Trust develops, as do comfort and favorable emotions.

Part of the commitment is toward the firm and part toward the sales rep or other company representatives. Thus, one consideration for a sales manager in reassigning reps is the amount of commitment customers may feel toward the current reps. High commitment builds switching costs, since the customer feels less comfortable with and has a more difficult time understanding a new rep or supplier. Customer commitment, although less tangible than customer share, is very real.

Computing the Value of a Customer

CRM implies that firms should manage different customers differently. Valuable customers deserve special treatment. "Diamond" flyers with Delta Airlines are identified by recording information in a database each time they access the company website, whether by laptop, by smartphone, or in person. These loyal customers have membership in the Sky Club where complimentary food and drink is available, preferred seating on flights where they receive more complimentary food and drink, and also a higher degree of service. While infrequent flyers may not view things the same way, the special treatment is worthwhile because Diamond flyers provide a disproportionate amount of revenue based on their frequent flying behavior.

Thus, with CRM the company can determine how much a customer is truly worth. Customer lifetime value is the monetary amount representing the worth of a customer to a firm over the foreseeable life of a relationship. Let's look at some different approaches for determining customer lifetime value (CLV).

Consider a firm that takes a transactional view of customers. It assumes each exchange is a unique and independent event. Therefore, the life of a relationship is one sale. In this case, we can think of the value of each customer as:

$$CLV_1 = (R_1 - C_1)$$

The CLV for customer 1 is the amount of revenue generated by this particular sale (R) less the costs associated with selling to and serving this customer (C).

Relational exchange and strategic partnerships are based on the idea that repeated transactions with customers will result from sales efforts. Thus, we adjust the basic equation to reflect this notion:

$$CLV_i = \sum_{t=1}^{p}(R_t - C_t)$$

where

CLV = the lifetime value of customer i
t = the time period
p = the total number of time periods of the relationship
R = the revenue gained from the customer in the time period
C = the cost of the sales and service effort directed at the customer in the time period t

Knowing the value of a customer is critical within CRM. For example, a firm can determine how much should be spent to acquire a new customer. If the costs of acquiring the customer are high relative to the estimated CLV, those resources might be better spent elsewhere. In this way, CLV enables the firm to estimate the potential return on investment in any given customer. Similarly, we can see that loyalty pays off in the form of higher CLV. As a firm acquires more and more loyal customers, it will expect better financial performance. In fact, if we sum the CLV values for all current and future customers for a given firm, we have an estimate of total customer equity.

With CRM we can use CLV to identify customers with more desirable characteristics. These customers may have higher CLV values or they may not be as price sensitive as other customers – making each exchange more profitable. In fact, a company may be tempted to implement a pricing strategy in which less price-sensitive customers are charged higher prices than other customers. Even Coca-Cola has considered such a move by creating vending machines that automatically adjust prices based on the temperature. Customers purchasing in hot weather would be asked to pay more than customers approaching the vending machine in cool weather. Research on this topic, based on CLV concepts, demonstrates that customers are actually more valuable when prices are increased in several small increments rather than all at once.[19]

One might argue that the CLV formula could be modified to reflect factors such as money's time-value. More distant revenues and costs could be discounted. However, both costs and revenues would be discounted at the same arguable rate, with the net effect being very little compared to the added complexity of the formula. Thus, we leave formulas with time-value discounts for the readers to explore on their own.

However, one could also argue that CLV summative formula should take into account less direct consequences of relational exchange. Truly committed customers become advocates for the firms they truly appreciate. Thus, committed customers become sales agents by spreading positive (negative if the experience is bad) word-of-mouth and by providing referrals. If a firm can obtain data that would project a monetary

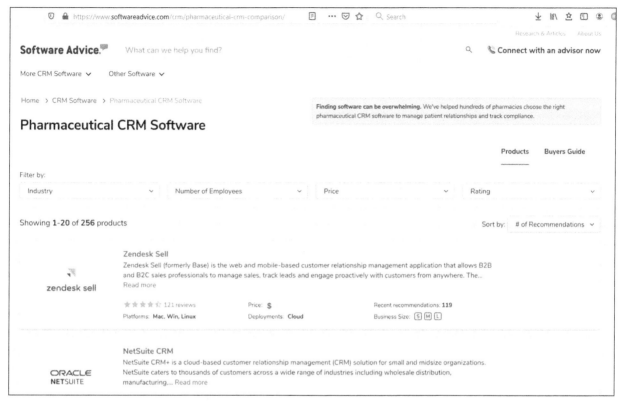

Pharmaceutical CRM tools are big business!
Source: https://www.softwareadvice.com/crm/pharmaceutical-crm-comparison/, April 14, 2020.

value on customers' advocacy behaviors, it should be added to the CLV equation to improve accuracy.

Risks of Relational Selling

Relational selling and strategic partnerships clearly have advantages. As we mentioned earlier, most businesses find selling to existing customers less expensive than selling to new customers. It is also easier to predict the future because long-term commitments ensure future business for the company.

These advantages do not come without a price. Relational selling can increase the firm's dependence on its partners. Consider the case of an auto parts supplier forming a strategic partnership with Ford Motor Company. The partnership requires the company to divert over 75% of its production capacity to satisfying the demand from Ford. The fortunes of this firm now become heavily dependent on Ford. If Ford does well, so will the supplier. In contrast, if the auto parts supplier avoids the partnership and instead sells auto parts to various wholesalers throughout North and South America, its fortunes are not likely to be hurt if one of its many customers falls on hard times. Therefore, relational selling increases risk when either the buying or selling firm is small relative to the other firm.

Firms may also alter their way of doing business to better satisfy a relational or strategic partner. For example, a relational partner may demand some type of automated self-service communication system that allows them to process orders without the intervention of the selling firm's employees. An automated system can be costly and may require changing other company procedures. As a result, the company could lose flexibility and be less able to capitalize on future business opportunities with new customers. Sales managers need to be careful not to commit to a change for the sake of one customer that will affect the way business is done with other good customers.

Another danger is companies that form relationships and strategic partnerships with a few large customers may become complacent with current customer(s) and grow less creative. They may not see opportunities to extend their business to new customers or into new business areas. In contrast, sales managers taking a transactional view are constantly looking for new business opportunities.

CRM and the Selling Process

Although CRM stands for customer relationship *management*, the "M" may just as easily represent *marketing*. The goal of CRM is generating higher profits from customers by providing more value. A CRM system greatly facilitates exchange between a customer and the selling firm, and therefore it is a marketing system. CRM's roots are in marketing and the technologies designed to better communicate with customers.

Nintendo (www.nintendo.com) applies a CRM approach in managing key market segments. For instance, it views college students as a key customer group. Nintendo not only maintains a database of information about customers, much of it acquired through product registration information, but it also provides websites where customers go to obtain product knowledge that enhances satisfaction and value from gaming experiences. The websites can also record customer activities to provide more information about gamers. With this information, Nintendo can offer complementary products and services. For instance, Nintendo reps are targeting college campuses to organize virtual dog shows, extremely popular among customers of *Nintendogs*, an electronic dog design game. Students enter their dogs in a show and other students vote to identify the "best in show." All the while, Nintendo reps gather information from customers that will lead to even more opportunities to extend this concept into more value opportunities among this customer segment.[20] Nintendo also launched Nintendogs and Cats, to make sure lover of virtual cats also were contacted. Nintendo is also eyeing a smartphone launch as a way of getting more Chinese consumers engaging with the brand, potentially through mobile game, and as a way of gathering potentially valuable customer data.

CRM and Sales

The salesperson's role changes across different business orientations. With a production orientation, the salesperson may be primarily an order taker. The products are essentially homogeneous across all customers as are ancillary services that accompany product purchase. With a customer orientation, the salesperson becomes much more involved with each customer. CRM requires the salesperson to have greater knowledge of customers and generally provides greater flexibility in making decisions that enhance customer satisfaction. In addition, many mundane tasks are performed automatically through electronic tracking and/or communication devices. This frees up the sales team for more important tasks. Thus, with CRM the salesperson becomes a value manager, managing the benefit customers obtain from exchanges.

The Salesperson and Managing Customers

Marketing strategy is one of the ways firms go about creating value. The salesperson plays a key role in this process. Although value is often used in everyday language as a synonym for low price, this view is far too narrow. Value is an individual's selective perception of the worth of some activity, object, or idea. The consumer creates this perception by weighing all costs, both monetary and non-monetary. The great thing about providing customers with value is that it is the single best way to provide value for the firm.

With CRM, the salesperson does more than just create sales.[21] The salesperson has four important goals, all of which help create value for the customer:

1. The salesperson gathers important data about the customer and the market.
2. The salesperson identifies the types of data needed to provide the customer with better service.
3. The salesperson provides input into how the CRM system should utilize data to create value for the customer.
4. The salesperson manages the relationship between the firm and the customers to whom the salesperson is assigned.

A CRM approach means the salesperson is responsible for balancing high tech processes against high touch approaches that personalize service offerings. Salespeople spend more time with individual customers who are relatively valuable to the firm compared to those customers who are less loyal, and therefore less valuable. The intimate knowledge developed through the high-touch process enables the salesperson to accomplish the four tasks outlined above. Thus, sales managers must create environments enabling salespeople to spend significantly more time with customers. The Sales Management in Action 3.2 discusses how this can be a successful strategy.

Box 3.2 | Sales Management in Action 3.2

High Tech – High Touch at HP

N.Z.Photography/Shutterstock.com

Box 3.2 | Continued

While technology can allow customers to perform some traditional selling tasks through self-service, only a human being can create the positive emotions that lead to strong, long-lasting commitment. Indeed, when a salesperson takes advantage of technology, his or her performance improves.

Hewlett Packard (HP – www.hp.com) underwent a successful turnaround in response to data showing that HP salespeople spent only slightly more than 30% of their time with customers. The rest was spent dealing with internal HP matters or in transit. True relational selling became difficult as salespeople failed to spend enough time with individual customers, even the very best customers, to develop a deep understanding of their businesses. HP reorganized and reduced the size of the sales force. But the new organizational structure freed reps from red tape and changed the reward system in a way that enabled salespeople to focus on their best customers. As a result, HP reps became as intimately involved in their best customers' business as were employees of those businesses themselves. The bottom line: by increasing customer contact so that salespeople spend about half of their time with customers, HP increased profits as a reward for the value the salespeople created.[22]

In a later chapter, we discuss time and territory management and the way salespeople are traditionally assigned to customers. In examining the different views of exchange relationships from transactional to strategic partnerships, management must make crucial decisions about how to assign customers to salespeople. Some factors may be more important than geography or convenience.

Product Portfolios

A product portfolio is the set of products (goods and services) a salesperson is responsible for selling. For instance, Novartis (www.novartis.com) sells a portfolio of well over 100 medicines in the United States alone; and they sell medicine in over 150 countries.[23] Like most drug companies, the portfolio includes both branded and generic products. A salesperson might be responsible for selling the entire portfolio or just some subset. For a pharmaceutical firm, some sales managers might oversee only branded medications, while others oversee salespeople responsible only for generic products; some may be assigned to a specific drug group or disease, such as diabetic or cardiology issues. The key is a salesperson's responsibility is to sell a portfolio of products to customers within some defined segment. By narrowing down the range of products a salesperson is responsible for, the sales manager has organized the selling effort based on product knowledge. Therefore, the customers in these segments can be better served.

Customer Portfolios

With CRM, sales managers are more interested in having their salespeople know customers than products. Thus, salesperson responsibilities are more likely to be arranged by customer portfolios. Customer portfolios are sets of customers that have something in common. Instead of assigning salespeople based upon product characteristics, as might be the case in a generic, branded product assignment, the manager assigns salespeople based on customer characteristics. Pharmaceutical salespeople may be assigned to customer groups defined by areas of medical specialties such as pediatrics or cardiology. Or they might be assigned to private physician groups, institutional medical facilities or even specific health plans. Thus, if a salesperson calls only on physician groups, he or she develops an in-depth knowledge of factors that contribute to success in that particular business environment.

IBM has a sales force numbering over 12,000 employees that is organized based upon specific industries rather than product characteristics or territories.[24] As a result, the IBM product development division focuses on developing industry-specific products. It has financial industry solutions, medical industry solutions, education industry solutions, and so on. The more intimate knowledge enables salespeople to generate more value for customers.

Cross-selling and up-selling also become easier using customer portfolios rather than product portfolios.[25] A customer's past behavior is the single best indicator of future purchasing behavior. When salespeople are assigned to small numbers of similar customers, they become very familiar with past behavior. In addition, if the firm adopts CRM systems, it can integrate information about previous purchasing behavior into its decision support systems. Customer portfolio assignments enable salespeople to empathize with the customers' problems and quickly suggest solutions. This not only increases sales, but also, more importantly, the customer realizes greater value, strengthening the relationship even further.

CRM and Production

CRM systems can be either analytical or operational.[26] Analytical CRM focuses on aggregating customer information in a digital database, enabling the company to better identify target markets and opportunities for cross-selling. In contrast, operational CRM is more focused on using information to improve internal efficiencies. Information about a transaction with a customer is stored in a decision support system that schedules logistical and production operations. One of the advantages of automating certain sales and service operations using a digital interface is that information the customer enters is also automatically used to adjust schedules. These adjustments are made with no incremental cost to the firm.

Consider companies like Bridgestone or Michelin. Both companies are sales leaders in the tire business, both in B2C and B2B markets. Increasingly, new car models are made with unique specifications for tires – meaning the number of different types of tires that must be produced has increased dramatically. Without CRM, a production manager might have to carefully devise a production schedule calling for certain models of tires to be produced on certain days of the month. With CRM the production manager doesn't worry about this decision. Information from customer orders is automatically fed into a decision support system and production schedules are determined just in time. In other words, the number and types of tires produced is based on real-time sales information. CRM integration is one of the keys to CRM success.

Using Technology in CRM

Companies adopting CRM cannot avoid high-technology solutions. CRM on any large scale is impossible without digital storage and processing of large quantities of data that all functional areas of the firm can share. Considering the salesperson is the direct agent interacting with customers, the sales manager as a supervisor is responsible for managing many inputs into this system. Indeed, when CRM fails, some aspect of technology or the use of the technology is almost always responsible. Thus, the sales manager must be familiar with basic CRM technology components.

Web Technologies and CRM

Although CRM's roots are older than the widespread adoption of the Internet, Web-based technologies have contributed a great deal to the design and effectiveness of CRM systems. A primary role played by the Internet in CRM implementation is to allow the sharing of information between buying and selling firms. This takes place in several ways.

E-mail is useful in managing customer contact information and becomes critical in customer service efforts. Many leads are generated from e-mails. E-mail also helps with push technology, which uses data stored about a particular customer or customer group to send information and promotional material at a time when the data suggests the customer will be interested in a purchase. The customer does not initiate the sales contact. Rather, an automated system invites the customer into a sales transaction.

E-mail used to be a relatively safe, reliable communication vehicle. Today, with the siege of spam e-mails and hackers, firms use protective systems to curtail the volume of junk messages. Unfortunately, network spam filters sometimes identify e-mail from legitimate businesses as spam, based on issues that are difficult to control. For example, as a company sends e-mails to more undeliverable addresses, its chances of getting put on a spam list increase. In fact, the more e-mail a company sends in general, the greater the chance of the mail being identified as spam. As a result, bulk e-mail communication, while still a widely applied tool, has become less reliable and firms are looking for solutions to these technology problems.

One solution is for salespeople to closely monitor the customer list and identify each customer as a valid address. This means firms must make sure their customer lists are constantly updated and verified by salespeople – which can be difficult. Another partial solution is to send e-mails that are going out to groups of customers in small batches. Deliverability describes the proportion of e-mail sent that is successfully delivered to the intended recipient. But even with a 96% success rate, 4% of communications are not delivered as expected. Certainly, every undelivered communication could lead to lost business or lower customer satisfaction.

Integrated Web Solutions

When firms take a relational approach or become strategic partners, they may avoid e-mail for key communications. Instead, they use the Internet to develop an integrated Web-based database. How does this work? Well, if you've taken an online course you probably submitted completed assignments by depositing them into an Internet drop box. Your instructor receives your assignment without using e-mail. An integrated information system works in much the same way. Information is stored online in ways that give the strategic partner secure access. Some of the information becomes integrated into the strategic partner's decision support system, particularly when dealing with issues like inventory systems. This type of communication is more reliable than e-mail.

The challenge for the CRM system is to take information from the various touch-points and integrate them into relevant databases that act as a single information system. Figure 3.3 illustrates the process of integrating information from these touch-points including customers phoning a call center,[27] salespeople recording information from a sales call using a mobile device, customers sending an e-mail to a service center or leaving a response at the company's website, and an inventory system recording stock rates. All this information is stored in cloud-based systems such as salesforce.com (www.salesforce.com), where the Web service helps integrate the information and transforms the content so sales managers, salespeople, and other employees can access what they need on any type of electronic device.

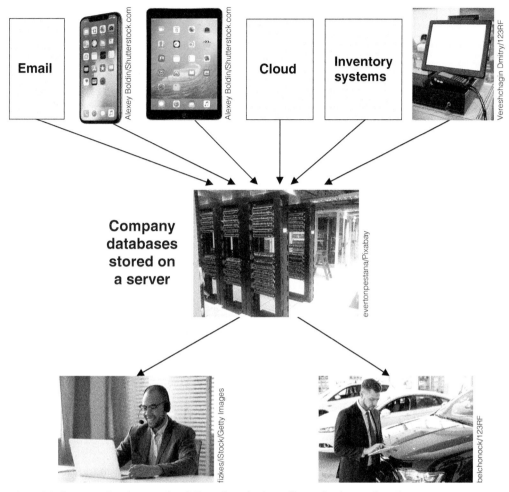

FIGURE 3.3 Customer data integrated and disseminated using online technology and services.

Marketing Automation and CRM

Technology does not stand still. The first industrial revolution mechanized many processes that ultimately replaced large quantities of manual labor with skilled machine operators. Some say we are living in the "fourth industrial revolution."[28] Data systems feed communications technologies and artificial intelligence (AI) enabling machines, as with the first industrial revolution, to do work humans previously did. AI refers to cognitive-like functions such as problem solving and learning that are performed by computer systems. Machine learning is a closely related term that can be defined as the ability for computer systems to take actions without being specifically programed to perform that action. We interact with such systems everyday now. Get in your car for the morning commute, and your smartphone likely tells you where you are going (it's learned from previous behavior) and can put the best route to take into its navigation system (deciding the way and replacing a human action).

Machine learning and AI have affected all the stages of the selling process from prospecting through follow-up. Prospecting e-mails can be automatically triggered based on data gathered from cookies and other tacit data. AI systems can help sales managers predict customer objections before the objections are voiced by the customer.

Follow-up service can be made more efficient through data-driven scheduling, tailoring the timing and content of follow-up calls based on data fed into AI. No wonder more and more firms are adopting marketing automation. Salesforce.com estimates that nearly 6 in 10 high-performing marketing organizations employ a marketing automation platform.[29] Marketing automation means routine marketing functions can be performed by digital and mechanical systems instead of human beings.

AI and machine learning applications are at the heart of marketing automation and they are transforming CRM as well. The following list summarizes the ways in which the transformation is taking place:[30]

1. Better data integrity – machine learning processes are taking the place of manual data entry.
2. Better data ingestion – software like Callminer (see www.callminer.com) captures and codes all communication with individual customers. Data subsequently enhances salesperson effectiveness.
3. Sentiment analysis facilitation – reviews and posts on social media are gathered as data and interpreted to gauge sentiment as pro or con.
4. Predictive lead scoring – potential and current customers can be more accurately scored.
5. Account-specific recommendations provided – the output suggests to salespeople what actions to take with a specific customer and why to take those actions. The result is more trusted relationship.

Sales Force Automation

Marketing and sales, as discussed previously, should work together. Consequently, part of the marketing automation process deals specifically with the sales function – sales force automation (SFA). Like marketing automation in general, SFA is an integrated system of computer software and hardware that performs routine selling and management functions formerly performed by independent and often manual processes. An integrated SFA system ties together some or all the following functions:

1. Expense reports
2. Presentation software
3. Sales call scheduling (contact management)
4. Call (touchpoint) logging
5. Territory management
6. Proposal generation
7. Order entry
8. Data entry
9. Team selling materials
10. Access to sales data, including social media
11. Sales analytics, tracking, and forecasting
12. E-mail and text drafts
13. Lead prioritization

All information recorded by the SFA system is integrated into other CRM systems. Thus, salespeople *must* use the SFA tools, or the company will be operating with inaccurate information or no information at all. In fact, getting salespeople to actually adopt SFA procedures is among the most difficult steps in implementing CRM presenting a challenge for sales managers to overcome. Salespeople mistakenly believe SFA means salespeople will no longer be needed, which isn't the case at all. When effective, SFA adoption frees salespeople to spend more time actually selling rather than performing routine tasks.

An effective SFA program is really a way of making salespeople more productive. Although salespeople may feel taking the time to enter information into an SFA system would be better spent actually selling to customers, in reality the system enables them to be more certain that each sales call will actually produce sales. By carrying company data with them on a mobile device, salespeople have the information they need in the right place – wherever they are! Research on sales forces using SFA is mixed. Although job performance does seem to improve with SFA, salespeople also report more rather than less stress on the job as they go through growing pains in learning and using new technologies.[31] Sales managers can facilitate adoption of SFA systems by working with sales people to be receptive to change, and by providing training as needed on the value of effective SFA. Increasingly, SFA systems eliminate manual data entry. E-mail and other communications logs, phone calls, text messages, blogs, social media, and content from presentations can be automatically recorded and accessed.

Salespeople already use a host of SFA innovations, including mobile notebook laptops or iPads, electronic data interchange, videoconferencing, multifunction mobile phones, satellite pagers, voice mail, and electronic mail to increase their productivity. SFA tools provide many benefits for resourceful and creative sales managers and salespeople. But the use of artificial intelligence (AI) in SFA has changed other aspects of sales and sales management as well, from reactive to proactive, and from instinct-driven to insight and data-driven. Over 60% of the managerial respondents in one study indicated their companies were generating more revenue by using sales technologies.[32]

A complete list of the benefits of SFA would be difficult to compile. However, here are some:[33]

- Ease of spotting opportunities based on the information available through the SFA system.
- Increased ability to monitor, coach, and mentor salespeople.
- Greater ability to assess, analyze, and react to results of sales calls.
- More efficient allocation of sales resources.
- More accurate data recording.
- More accurate sales predictions.[34]

Increasingly, robots supported by AI perform routine selling functions. Pepper, a Japanese robot (there are thousands of Peppers produced by a company called Softbank), performs routine service functions, such as staffing hotel check-in, and simple sales functions. The robotic salesperson epitomizes machine learning and SFA, and supposedly understands and reacts to human emotion. But, does the robot replace salespeople or make the sales function more efficient by freeing resources to deal with more intricate and profitable types of selling? Will customers warm up to or react negatively to Pepper, or similar robots? Those are questions that will be answered with more certainty in the coming years.

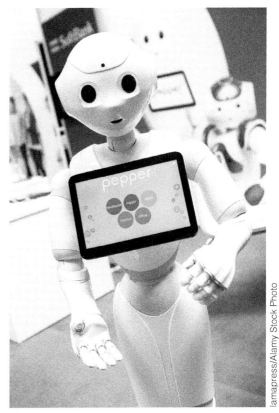

lamapress/Alamy Stock Photo

There also is a WSJ article "SoftBank Robot Pepper Sells Out in a Minute from June 22, 2015 with a photo.

Box 3.3 | Sales Management in Action 3.3

SFA Sells

SFA represents a core business at salesforce.com. Salesforce.com claims a 28% increase in sales through cloud-based automation of routine selling functions (see https://www.salesforce.com/products/sales-cloud/overview/). Automated systems allow less room for routine activities to fall through the cracks and get overlooked. Follow-ups, reminders, and even cold calls become functions relegated to machines and software rather than human salespeople. According to salesforce.com, automated systems:

- Empower salespeople by allowing them time to focus on important functions and providing them with timelier (real-time) and more actionable data.
- Deliver a more personalized experience as systems tailor messages to the specific characteristics and preferences of customers.
- Provide greater flexibility to adjust strategies in a timely manner.

However, firms should not expect SFA to be a panacea. Salespeople may fear it initially as the perception may develop that automation means less need for human agents. Therefore, it is critical to get staff buy-in during the adoption of automated systems.

CRM Hardware

Mobile devices, laptops, and servers are all important CRM technological components. But CRM is more than hardware, and it benefits from technological breakthroughs. CRM has given the sales manager a new terminology, not just new hardware.

Database marketing is a computerized process for analyzing customer databases in a way that enables more effective selling by tailoring product and promotional offerings to a specific customer's sales patterns. Database marketing is the starting point for a CRM system. The sheer size a single database can be amazing. Ford Motor Company (www.ford.com) has 50 million names in its customer database. Citicorp has (www.citicorp.com) 30 million, Kimberly Clark (www.kimberly-clark.com) 10 million, and Kraft General Foods (www.kraft.com) 2.5 million customer records. General Motors (www.gm.com) has 12 million GM credit card holders in a database yielding detailed data on customer buying habits. For each name in the database, the companies have an average of 20 separate pieces of information. Detailed customer information can be translated into effective strategies for field salespeople.

A **data warehouse** is an electronic storage center containing data records from diverse information systems that are shared across all functional departments. American Airlines (www.aa.com) gathers customer information from all its customer touch points. Data collected includes demographics, take-off points and destinations, prices paid, and hotel accommodations. When customers call, e-mail, or connect to the American Airlines website, they are immediately recognized and classified as to their relative profitability to AA. Then, on the basis of their past purchase preferences, they are offered a customized package that might include recommendations for hotels, car rentals, and vacation packages in addition to flight options. Data such as cookies from customers browsing behavior also feeds the data warehouse.

Data analytics involves exploratory statistical analysis of data in the data warehouse. The objective is to identify relationships that enable customers to be targeted more accurately. Multivariate statistical tools such as cluster analysis, discriminant analysis, multiple regression, and automatic interaction detection analysis help with data analytics. For instance, data analytic techniques discovered a relationship between diaper sales and beer purchases. This finding was explained by the fact that fathers often buy beer when sent to the store to buy baby diapers. So, displaying beer near the diaper aisle can increase sales of both products. But, is this an optimal decision? Perhaps overall sales decrease because customers stroll through less of a store and make fewer impulse purchases. Auchan (www.auchan.fr) and TESCO (www.tesco.uk.com), two of the largest retailers in the world, among many others, use data analytics to develop merchandising plans.

Harrah's Entertainment, Inc. has individual profiles of millions of customers. The models include ages, gender, zip codes, amount of time spent gambling, and how much the person has won or lost. Analyses of these data enable Harrah's to target individuals with special offers, like getaway weekends and gourmet restaurant meals, to attract them back to the casinos to gamble more. Sophisticated modeling of customers has enabled Harrah's to average 22% growth for the past five years, while its stock price has tripled.[35] Resourceful sales managers make use of these systematically designed and implemented database technologies to help salespeople develop long-term, personalized, and profitable relationships with each of their customers.

CRM Software

The real heart of CRM technology is the software. Software makes information stored in a CRM system useful by allowing sales managers to act with greater intelligence than they could otherwise. When CRM software converts information into data that can be used in solving a sales manager's problem, we have CRM Intelligence. Here we review a few software applications to illustrate types of products available.

The CRM industry is a multibillion-dollar entity with numerous vendors. Perhaps the best known companies are Siebel Systems (www.oracle.com/siebel/index.html), Salesforce.com (www.salesforce.com), SAP (www.sap.com), and Hubspot (www.hubspot.com). Table 3.3 provides a list of application software vendors.

What should sales managers look for in a CRM software system? Certainly, no one size fits all CRM applications. A few things sales managers should consider before recommending a particular CRM application includes the following.[36]

1. Flexible Sales Effectiveness Processes. Sales managers should develop sales processes that salespeople in different areas and selling different portfolios can apply.

TABLE 3.3

CRM Software Application Vendors and Characteristics

Application type	Company	Relative strength	Leading industries
Data quality and integration	Firstlogic (www.firstlogic.com)	High customer satisfaction,	Financial services, retailing,
marketing automation	Aprimo (www.aprimo.com)	functionality	pharmaceuticals, media/entertainment
SFA	Salesforce.com (www.salesforce.com)	Reputation	Financial services, communications
Large Enterprises	Siebel Systems (www.siebel.com)	Functionality	Professional services, public sector
Small/medium firms	Hubspot (www.hubspot.com)	Easy startup (free trial)	Marketing (retail, sales, service)
Small businesses	Maximizer Software (www.maximizer.com)	Customer satisfaction	Real estate, manufacturing

2. Easy Coaching. Make step by step advice available for salespeople in the field.
3. Easy Data Access. All salespeople should enter data accurately and in a timely fashion so they can work with accurate data in the field. Data entry should be made easy, which more and more, means the data entry is automated.
4. Advanced Analytics. The system should analyze current sales performance along with past performance data. The result should provide diagnostic information so a salesperson can spot and correct potential problems.

Potential customers today often turn to the Web for information about products they want to buy. Current customers who have a problem are likely to first go to the company website to find help. Records of this activity can be useful to the sales manager. One aspect of CRM software that helps in this conversion is click-stream analysis.

Click-stream analysis draws conclusions based on the path a customer takes while navigating the company website. In other words, to identify and classify sales prospects, the software uses information about which pages a customer clicked through and how long he or she spent on each. A customer who reads product specifications in some detail is a hotter sales prospect than one who doesn't even click through to this information. The software may automatically send out e-mail responses to leads who provide an e-mail address but who do not appear very engaged with the company or its products based on the click-through analysis. Customers showing a more promising pattern of "clicks" may be placed on a list with the recommendation that a company representative phone them. Google analytics provides a fairly easy interface to display the browsing behavior of specific website users. The software provides a report identifying the most promising prospects for a face-to-face sales call.

CRM Successes and Failures

Despite CRM's popularity, its adoption is no guarantee of success. Some estimates suggest that over half the firms that try CRM are unhappy with the results.[37] CRM systems are not for everybody. For example, it won't benefit firms using a transactional approach because they treat all exchanges as independent. Thus, tracking information about customers isn't consistent with their approach.

CRM is also not for firms whose customers won't realize added value from the benefits provided by the CRM process. For instance, some B2B firms now sell significant portions of their inventories through reverse auctions, particularly when the economy is weak. A reverse auction is a process in which buyers have sellers compete for a sale based exclusively on price. Thus, the margins for the seller are competitively reduced. When price competition dominates a market, CRM may not be advantageous.

Factors Contributing to Success/Failure. The promise of complete information integration that CRM offers is undeniably a good thing. Like many aspects of business, CRM fails, when it does, not because the idea is bad, but because implementing it creates many difficult hurdles. Table 3.4 lists some factors contributing to success or failure of CRM implementation.[38]

CRM is successful only when the people who work for the business truly believe the benefits will be worth the added expense and effort. This begins with the CEO or top management. If top management is often heard disparaging the CRM system, how can they expect other employees to support CRM applications?

Sales managers and sales staff often resist CRM applications. They believe that tasks like entering electronic notes into the CRM software isn't worth the trouble, or that their time is better spent selling than entering data into a laptop or smartphone. If information about customers is available through the company's information system,

TABLE **3.4**

Success or Failure in CRM Implementation

	Factor	Effective	Ineffective
1	Top management gives its support.	Top managers believe in CRM and are truly customer oriented.	Top managers have doubts about the technology, or lack customer orientation.
2	Sales managers and sales force buy in to CRM.	Sales managers and salespeople share top management's enthusiasm and religiously follow CRM procedures.	Sales managers or salespeople fail to see how the added complexities of CRM will enhance their job performance – or they see CRM as a threat.
3	CRM system does not fit the firm's situation.	CRM system matches the focus and size of the organization.	CRM either too elaborate or too simple for firm's needs.
4	Confidence in CRM vendor	Everyone has faith in the added value that the system provides.	People doubt the system will really enhance value for anybody.
5	Training	Training is adequate and ongoing.	Training is looked at as expensive and of relatively little value.
6	A well-defined sales process	Sales process is widely known and practiced.	No identifiable sales process exists.
7	Expectations	Sales managers have realistic expectations for what a CRM system can do for them.	Sales managers believe CRM is the answer to all prayers.

the salesperson may also feel less job security. Sales managers can overcome this problem by convincing employees they will benefit from CRM. For example, a CRM system should allow salespeople to spend more time with more profitable customers. As a result, each salesperson should sell more and collect higher bonuses and/or commissions, but salespeople must be convinced of this. The fact that all areas of the firm must buy into CRM means that CRM should always be a cross-functional effort.

Firms should select a CRM vendor carefully. Different software products have features making them more or less suitable to different types of organizations. Systems that are difficult to use lead to disgruntled employees who dread having to deal with CRM. As a result, they become less cooperative in following its procedures. Only careful research can ensure that the CRM solution fits the particular company. When the company has checked out alternate vendors to validate its choice, employees are more likely to have confidence in the system.

Training also is critical. The CRM vendor should provide ongoing training on how to apply CRM and why it's important. But, the firm should also make its own training available to employees who feel they cannot adequately perform the CRM tasks.

Neither CRM nor the SFA components replace sales force management or selling processes. These high-tech components merely enhance the activities of sales managers and salespeople. The sales process also extends beyond salespeople. Hitachi (www.hitachi.com) data systems recently increased sales effectiveness by implementing a new sales process through training sessions for salespeople, service techs, sales managers, and top management.[39] Not only did the process improve sales and customer satisfaction, it also helped increase compliance with CRM maintenance procedures. The sales process helps make sure companies are truly both *high tech* and *high touch*.

Finally, CRM implementation may fail because top management has "pie in the sky" expectations. CRM is not a panacea. Expectations for sales increases should be realistic. Also, given that CRM is a long-term oriented system, management should not expect benefits to occur too soon. Management may feel the CRM system is ineffective because sales increased only 20% in five years when the goal was an unrealistic 40%. If the goal had been 15%, they may feel quite different. Thus, CRM vendors should help establish realistic expectations for what CRM can do.

Chapter Summary

1. **Master the different ways companies deal with customers.** CRM is a systematic integration of information, technology, and human resources all oriented toward (a) providing maximum value to customers and (b) maximizing the value obtained from customers. A *production*-oriented sales manager focuses a sales force on selling products. A *customer*-oriented sales manager, more typical of a marketing-oriented firm, focuses a sales force on providing value by filling a customer's needs. The greater use of information and knowledge of customers that comes with a CRM program is vital to understanding how best to provide a customer with value.

   A firm that practices *transactional* selling treats each and every interaction with a customer as a unique and independent event. In a transactional view, loyalty is not necessary. In a *relational* view, each exchange between a salesperson and a customer is but one in a series. The customer is seen as a customer for life, not a customer for today. In a third option, the company views each customer as a *strategic partner*. Strategic partners are generally considered loyal to one another.

2. **Build customer relationships that lead to repeat business.** CRM is based on the premise that companies interact with customers more than one time and in more than one way. Businesses that assume each customer will be contacted one time are less motivated to provide excellent service than those that assume they will contact customers many times over an extended period. The extra motivation is based on the likelihood of repeat business.

   A CRM system should be both high tech and high touch. The salesperson should use information technology, including CRM-related hardware and software, to serve the customer better, not as a replacement for true service to the customer. Good customers deserve personal attention. While technology can help personalize products, regular contact with the customer is necessary to help build the bond that represents true commitment. The combination of high tech and high touch helps create value for the customer. Sales managers must realize that CRM technology and systems are not a replacement for a true sales process.

3. **Relate customer loyalty to customer lifetime value.** True customer loyalty exists when the customer exhibits both high customer share and high customer commitment. Customer commitment represents the bonding, or affective attachment, between a customer and a sales firm. Loyalty contributes to customer lifetime value by guaranteeing a larger stream of sales over the lifetime of a relationship and through the fact that a loyal customer serves as an advocate for the firm. Commitment means that the customer will stick with the selling firm even if others are offering similar products for a lower price. Committed customers also work like salespeople in spreading positive word of mouth about the firm.

   CRM makes the most sense when a firm expects to do business with a customer repeatedly over an extended period of time. Thus, companies succeed by offering superior value to customers over repeated sales exchanges. In return, customers become more valuable to the firm. Loyal customers are like money in the bank because they will continue to purchase into the future. Customer loyalty is a function of two components – customer share and customer commitment. The behavioral component of customer loyalty is *customer share*, the proportion of resources a customer spends with one among a set of competing suppliers. In a CRM framework, a firm can determine how much it should spend to acquire a new customer. If the costs of acquiring the customer are high relative to the estimated CLV, those resources might be better spent elsewhere.

4. **Apply CRM to the selling process.** An effective CRM system uses physical devices like smartphones, tablets, notebook computers, servers, and other types of communication and storage devices. In addition, many companies specialize in software allowing all the information gathered in these communications to be harvested and stored in a data warehouse. The integration of this information, making it available to employees throughout the firm, is a key function of CRM technology. Companies must match the right CRM system to the particular characteristics of the firm. Software products in particular specialize in firms of certain sizes and in certain industries. The risk of CRM failure from choosing the wrong product is real. So, time and effort invested in getting the CRM technology right is well spent.

5. **Use technology successfully in CRM programs.** Table 3.4 summarizes factors that contribute to the success or failure of CRM implementation; these factors suggest that CRM is not merely a technology issue. If the technology is right, but the human element is lacking, CRM will fail. Thus, implementing CRM requires getting buy-in from all members of the organization – from the top through entry level sales personnel.

6. **Marketing Automation and CRM.** Artificial intelligence and machine learning enable marketing automation in general, and SFA more specifically, to replace repetitive human actions with digitized or mechanized solutions. The results is more accurate and more rich data that yield better sales predictions at the individual-customer level. Automation affects all levels of the sales process from prospecting to follow-up, and, automation has made CRM systems better. Many routine functions including e-mail marketing and call scheduling have become automated. Data integrity and data analytics are critical to the success of a CRM system. The end-result is better firm–customer relationships through applied CRM technology.

Key Terms

CRM	Customer-oriented	Relational governance	Deliverability
Mass marketing	salesperson	Opportunistic behavior	Artificial intelligence (AI)
Differentiated	Touchpoint	Customer share	Machine learning
marketing	sales exchange	Customer commitment	Marketing automation
Niche marketing	Transactional selling	Customer lifetime value	Sales force automation
One-to-one marketing	Relational exchange	Value	(SFA)
Production orientation	Customer retention	Product portfolio	Database marketing
Market orientation	Strategic partnerships	Customer portfolios	CRM Intelligence
Customer centric	Mutual loyalty	Analytical CRM	Click-stream analysis
Customer value	Vertical integration	Operational CRM	
Sales-oriented	Governance	Push technology	

Notes

1. Bennett, E. (2006). CRM before there was CRM. *Baseline* 46 (July): 49.

2. Payne, A. and Frow, P. (2005). A strategic framework for customer relationship management. *Journal of Marketing* 69 (October): 167–176.

3. Reinartz, W., Kraft, M., Hoyer, W.D. (2004). The customer relationship management process: its measurement and impact on performance. *Journal of Marketing Research* 41 (August): 293–305.

4. Peppers, D. and Martha, R. (1999). *The One-to-One Fieldbook: The Complete Toolkit for Implementing a 1 to 1 Marketing Program*. London: Piakus.

5. Aluri, A., Price, B.S., and McIntyre, N.H. (2019). Using machine learning to cocreate value through dyamic customer engagment in a brand loyalty program. *Journal of Hospitality & Tourism Research* 43: 78–100.

6. Pagel, A. (2019). CRM at waste management. https://www.streetdirectory.com/travel_guide/136652/enterprise_information_systems/crm_system_issues__crm_in_waste_management.html (accessed 11 August 2019).

7. Taken from the following sources: Shermach, K. (2006). Growing acceptance of cookies. *Sales and Marketing Management* 158 (September): 20. Britt, B. (2006). Customized publishing on the rise. *Marketing* (10/18): 15.

8. Church, R. (1999). New perspectives on the history of products, firms, marketing and consumers in Britain and the United States in the nineteenth century. *Economic History Review* 52 (3): 405–435.

9. Ibid.

10. Jones, E., Paul, B., and Peter, D. (2003). Firm market orientation and salesperson customer orientation: interpersonal and intrapersonal influences on customer service and retention in business-to-business buyer-seller relationships. *Journal of Business Research* 56: 323–340.

11. Rust, R.T., Katherine, L., and Das, N. (2005). *Customer Equity Management*. Upper Saddle River, NJ: Prentice Hall.

12. Adapted from Myron, D. (2004). Pharmaceutical firms find a spoonful of CRM helps the sales pitch go down. *CRM Magazine* 8 (May): 14–17. *Medical Marketing & Media*, (2004). Update, 39 (7): 9; https://www.merck.com/index.html (accessed August 2019), Riley, G. Merck plans restructuring after beating estimates. https://www.bloomberg.com/news/articles/2019-04-30/merck-plans-restructuring-after-beating-estimates-as-drugs-grow (accessed August 2019).

13. de Man, A.-P. (2013). *Alliances: An Executive Guide to Designing Successful Strategic Partnerships*, New York: Wiley; Eli, J., Lawrence, B.C., and Roberts, J.A. (2003) Creating a partnership-oriented, knowledge creation culture in strategic sales alliances: a conceptual framework. *Journal of Business & Industrial Marketing* 18, 4/5: 336–352; and Rich, M.K. (2003) Requirements for successful marketing alliances. *Journal of Business & Industrial Marketing* 18, 4/5: 447–456.

14. Yaprak, A., Cavusgil, S. T., and Kandemir, D. (2006). Alliance orientation: conceptualization, measurement and impact on market performance. *Journal of the Academy of Marketing Science*, 34 (Summer): 324–340.

15. Cavusgil, T., Deligonul, S., and Zhang, C. (2004). Curbing foreign distributor opportunism: an examination of trust, contracts, and the legal environment in international channel relationships. *Journal of International Marketing*, 12 (2): 7–27.

16. Yikuan, L. and Cavusgil, S. T. (2006). Enhancing alliance performance: the effects of contractual-based versus relational-based governance. *Journal of Business Research*, 59 (August): 896–905.

17. Carson, S.J., Madhok, A., and Wu, T. (2006). Uncertainty, opportunism, and governance: the effects of volatility and ambiguity on formal and relational contracting. *Academy of Management Journal* 49 (May): 1058–1077.

18. Babin, B.J. and Attaway, J. (2000). Atmospheric affect as a tool for creating value and gaining share of customer. *Journal of Business Research* 49: 91–99.

19. How to increase Customer Lifetime Value (CLV). Pay more now, get more later (2018). https://www.shopify.com/enterprise/increase-customer-lifetime-value-clv (accessed May 2019).

20. Precision Marketing. (2005). Nintendo Tours Universities to Push Pet Game, 18 (12/9): 2.

21. Landry, T.D., Todd, J.A., and Aaron, A. (2005). A compendium of sales-related literature in customer relationship management processes and technologies with managerial implications. *Journal of Personal Selling and Sales Management* 25 (Summer): 231–251.

22. Ahearn, M., Narasimhan, S., and Luke, W. (2004). Effect of technology on sales performance: progressing from technology acceptance to technology usage and consequence. *Journal of Personal Selling and Sales Management* 24 (Fall): 297–310; Tam, P.-W. (2006). Hurd's big challenge at HP: overhauling corporate sales. *Wall Street Journal* (April 3): A1.

23. How many medications does novartis manufacture? https://sunrisehouse.com/research/pharmaceutical-industry/novartis/ (accessed May 2019).

24. LaMonica, M. (2005). IBM to beef up sales staff. News.com, (March 24), http://news.com.com/IBM%20to%20beef%20up%20software%20sales%20staff/2100-1012_3-5634664.html (accessed August 2019).

25. Big Commerce Essentials. (2018). What is the difference between upselling and cross-selling? https://www.bigcommerce.com/ecommerce-answers/what-difference-between-upselling-and-cross-selling/ (accessed May 2019).

26. Pushkala, R., Wittmann, C.M., and Nancy, A.R. (2006). Leveraging CRM for sales: the role of organizational capabilities in successful CRM implementation. *Journal of Personal Selling and Sales Management* 26 (Winter): 39–53.

27. Shah, J.R. and Murtaza, M.B. (2005). Effective customer relationship management through Web services. *Journal of Computer Information Systems* (Fall): 98–109.

28. Jelinick, R., Michael, A., John, M. (2006). A longitudinal examination of individual, organizational and contextual factors on sales technology adoption and job performance. *Journal of Marketing, Theory and Practice*, 14 (Winter): 7–23.

29. Salesforce.com (2019). *Marketing Automation and Your CRM: Better Together*. White paper.

30. Fatemi, F. (2019). 5 ways AI is transforming CRMs. *Forbes*. https://www.forbes.com/sites/falonfatemi/2019/08/10/5-ways-artificial-intelligence-is-transforming-crms/#e9e766e53546 (accessed August 21, 2019).

31. Rangarajan, D., Eli, J., and Wynne, C. (2005). Impact of sales force automation on technology-related stress, effort, and technology usage among salespeople. *Industrial Marketing Management* 34 (May): 345–354. Jelinick et al. (2006).

32. https://www.saleshacker.com/sales-tools/ (accessed August 2019).

33. Beasty, C. (2006). How sales teams should use CRM. *CRM* (February): 30–34.

34. Bohanec, M., Borstnar, M.K., and Robnik-Sikonja, M. (2017). Explaining machine learning models in sales predictions. *Expert Systems with Applications* 71: 416–428.

35. Baker, S. (2006). Math will rock your world. *Business Week* (23 January), 54–62.

36. CRM Magazine, Replicate your sales success: clone your salespeople. https://www.questia.com/magazine/1G1-151051865/replicate-sales-success-clone-your-star-salespeople (accessed 21 August 2019).

37. Thomas, D. (2003). Firms are unhappy with CRM. *Computer Weekly* (23 January).

38. See for example, Jayachandran, S., Sharma, S., Kaufman, P. (2005). The role of relational information processes and technology use in customer relationship management. *Journal of Marketing*, 69 (October): 177–192; IOMA (2002). *A look at why CRM fails and how you can prevent it*. 2 (February): 1–14; Trailor and Dickie (2006).

39. Cummings, B. (2006). Proving the sales process. *Sales and Marketing Management*, 158 (June): 15.

Chapter Review Questions

1. Define CRM. What are the two key goals of CRM? [LO 1]

2. How would a sales manager's approach in motivating a sales force differ based on the way the company approaches customers. [LO 1]

3. Define a relational view to exchange relationships and a transactional view to exchange relationships. [LO 1]

4. Use the Internet to find a list of the 10 most successful companies in two different industries. Do you think the firms are generally more production or market oriented? Do you think they tend to emphasize a transactional or relational approach to customers? Discuss in terms of the role of CRM in a company with either a production or market orientation. [LO 1]

5. What does it mean for a company to be customer centric? [LO 2]

6. Would a company that views its customers as strategic partners tend to have a larger or smaller sales force than a similar sized company with a more transactional view of customers? Explain. [LO 2]

7. What is meant by the term opportunistic behavior in the context of an exchange relationship? [LO 3]

8. What are some risks associated with relational selling (including strategic partnerships)? [LO 3]

9. What is the difference between a customer portfolio and product portfolio approach from a sales manager's perspective? [LO 4]

10. What are four things a sales manager should look for when choosing a CRM vendor? [LO 4]

11. List and briefly explain factors associated with an unsuccessful CRM implementation. [LO 5]

12. Use the list of CRM success/failure factors to describe how a pharmaceutical firm might implement a CRM system. [LO 5]

13. In what ways is AI transforming CRM? [LO 6]

14. List functions that SFA allows to be automated. Do you think that SFA will help make sales managers and salespeople more or less friendly toward CRM adoption (explain your answer)? [LO6]

Online Exercise

Go to the website at: www.1000ventures.com/business_guide/mbs_mini_spartnerships.html and review the articles, case studies, and slide shows on developing strategic partnerships.

How does the material enhance your understanding of this "cutting-edge" business philosophy?

Role-Play Exercise

Capital Wireless

Capital Wireless invested thousands of dollars last year in a new SFA system. It has all the latest technology and the sales rep for the SFA vendor promised account closing ratios would double and customer satisfaction increase substantially. The system has been in place and operational for about eight months but there are lots of problems. The sales force had three one-hour training sessions and the sales manager has suggested more. Unfortunately, most of the sales force do not see the value of the system and after entering the basic customer profile data pretty much ignore the system, saying they know their customers and do not need a computerized system. The vendor and the company CEO are taking a hard line and plan to just fire all the sales people who will not use the system. On the other hand, the sales manager says firing

these salespeople is unrealistic and will create serious problems. But other than additional training the sales manager has not yet offered any further ideas.

Role-Play Participants and Assignments

Alvin Burns, CEO, argues to just get rid of the salespeople who will not use the SFA system. They paid a lot for it and the need for it is clear. After all, it is the job of the salespeople to do what the company says, and not complying with company guidelines is grounds for dismissal.

Sheri Ahuja, Sales Manager, wants to find another way to solve the problem. She poses and justifies several alternatives to firing salespeople, at least a large number. She is concerned the CEO will say the other alternatives will take too long so she needs to be prepared to defend her plans.

In-Basket Exercise

Zenon is an oil-field service company that specializes in well cementing and acid and hydraulic fracturing treatments. The oil industry typically goes through boom and bust cycles, often attributed to the price of a barrel of oil. During boom times, the demand far outstrips the supply of services for the entire industry. In fact, the sales manager has urged salespeople to avoid commitments to some customers and be more selective in seeking future business. One possible solution

is to implement a CRM system to make the sales force more efficient in serving current customers and to more effectively target future customers.

1. Prepare an e-mail to your boss encouraging the adoption of a CRM program for Zenon.
2. In your e-mail be sure to outline how CRM has the potential to improve customer service and increase repeat business.

Ethical Dilemma

Drexel Pharmaceuticals manufactures and sells several generic drugs designed to treat high blood pressure, arthritis, and other diseases. The company has a positive relationship with many of its patients who learn about its medications and other current issues from its website and newsletter that have the latest developments on new medical research and

treatments as well as general health and fitness materials. Drexel was recently acquired by an investment banking group that also owns another company that sells hydrotherapy spas and hot tubs. The sales manager from the spa company has asked to use the e-mail and regular mail lists to promote their products. What should Drexel Pharmaceuticals do?

CASE 3.1 Briley Transport: A CRM Solution – Or Not?

Hotshot transportation is a unique freight system where goods are hauled in an expedited fashion, and no industry matches the need for expedition like the offshore oil industry. The Gulf of Mexico is home to over 4 000 production platforms and working drilling rigs. *Production platforms* process petrochemicals that are shipped to the mainland in underground pipelines. *Drilling rigs* are practicing the art of speculation, searching out potential resources. Both production platforms and drilling rigs function at enormous costs. The oil companies actually rent large machines that process and search for oil, costing them an average of half-a-million dollars a day. Under such circumstances, stopping work for a single day because of a broken part can be a disaster. It is a situation where the part is needed urgently, so money is no object.

With problems, often come opportunities. Such was the case for Jim Briley, who started his business with a single truck and a vision. Jim parked his truck in front of the Shell Oil Company dock one day in Morgan City, Louisiana and told the yard man there he would take any part anywhere and in record time. The yard man didn't have any work at the time, so Jim said he'd wait. He stayed there for five weeks, living out of his truck, when finally, the day came. Port Hardware heard of Jim and had a package to be delivered to the Port Fourchon dock, 95 miles away on not the best of roads. Jim got that part to the dock in one hour and ten minutes. Hasty calculations meant Jim definitely broke some speed limits. When asked about his speed, Jim said, "you said not to waste time."

Jim prospered in the salty world of the Oil Patch. After five years, he had thirty trucks, ranging from pickups to a couple of tractor-trailer rigs. Jim's client base includes every independent oil company and several major petroleum companies. His proud brand mantra was "Any Time, Any Where;" and it was Jim's answer when a client asked for his hours and delivery area.

With three route managers, 40 employees, and a dozen emergency independents on call when needed, Jim is rolling. But he's also in trouble. Jim's problem is his customer resource management system (CRM) exists on index cards and an Excel spreadsheet. He spends hours during his day lining up *runs*, updating delivery whereabouts, and making sure he has transportation for the next client. It's a job that won't fix itself, and, he needs relief.

One day he finds what appears to be a solution while looking at a CRM routing system built for the delivery of milk. Harvest Software had a package complete with an app that would enable dairy farmers to request milk pickup on demand. Customers would type in the weight of milk, and the dairy processor would automatically process a ticket to go pick up the milk. On the business side the manager could see their entire fleet in real time via GPS devices activated through the trucker's phones. The phone app contained other data including each truck's gross weight and its estimated carrying capacity. Jim looked upon this system as the perfect solution to his problem, including the sales module. He bought it on sight, with assurances it would work in his situation. He gave it to his three route managers, got his old system transferred to the new system, sent out instructions to his customers, and then left for a long-deserved week vacation.

Jim was back in four days. The first issues came to him in a call after the second day. Drivers were running late. Trucks were not showing up on the system. The problems stemmed from the fact that the route system was built around a system of *timed pickups*, not an emergency one. When customers ordered a pickup immediately, the system *automatically set it* to a two-hour pickup time frame. In his career, Jim never let a client wait more than 30 minutes before dispatch. Trying to have a delivery item picked up in less than two hours caused problems in the system. Because of these kinds of problems, most customers ditched the app and phoned their old contacts, meaning services were taking place outside the system. One major client canceled their delivery when the system proved difficult and used Jim's competitor instead. On the manager side, the software didn't effectively work because it relied on an integration between the phone app and the phones' GPS technology. However, one third of drivers used iPhones, a third used Samsung phones, and the rest used LG or other brands. Thus, the software worked only on a portion of the delivery drivers' phones. Compounding this problem, at least one third of drivers never installed the app on their phone and continued to communicate through voice alone.

Jim has hired you to come in and make sense of this mess. He wants honest answers as to why everything went wrong.

Questions

1. What mistakes did Jim make in purchasing a CRM system?
2. Given the situation Jim is in now, what recommendations would you give Jim in handling the situation?
3. What are proper steps to installing and implementing a CRM system?

Case prepared by: G. David Shows, Appalachian State University

---

CASE 3.2　TC's Bookings: CRM

Tony Charles owns TC's Bookings, an independent booking agency servicing four states – Wisconsin, Illinois, Indiana, and Michigan. These four states include large metro areas like Chicago, Detroit, Milwaukee, and Indianapolis, as well as a number of university towns. This is a part-time business Tony operates as a way of pursuing two of his passions – music and marketing – in order to supplement his income as a marketing professor. It also allows him to apply many of the marketing principles and skills he has studied, practiced, and taught for many years. Tony is successful in this part-time role because he manages four salespeople – one for each state in which he operates. However, the way the industry has changed over the last decade, he has had to change how the company does business as well as its structure.

TC's Bookings represents its clients to music venues. The clients are 19 bands (ranging from 3 to 6 members) and 10 acoustic duos. All of the musicians focus on classic rock, but some of the bands also play the blues, country, or folk music as well. Two of the duos specialize in traditional Irish folk music, as well as classic rock. Most of the songs the bands play are commercial hits ranging from the 1960s to the 1990s. These include hits from such stars as Led Zeppelin, The Rolling Stones, The Beatles, Aerosmith, and Bad Company to name a few. Eight of the bands create and perform their own original songs.

Booking agents serve as a liaison between the client (the bands) and the music venues (customers). Some agents represent only the bands, while others represent only the venues. The difference relates to how the agent gets paid. If working for the bands, the booking agent is basically a sales representative responsible for getting maximum pay for the bands and gets paid a percentage, usually 10–15% of the price of the gig. If working for the venue, the booking agent plays the role of a purchasing agent responsible for negotiating the lowest price. In this situation, he or she may be paid a percentage or a flat fee per show or may be on a retainer to the venue. TC's Bookings, aside from the 29 musical groups, also represents six venues. In dealings between his clients and these two venues, Tony tries to reach a fair compromise for both parties by substituting some of the pay for the bands with more shows at these venues. This keeps both the bands and the venues satisfied. The venues are Tony's customers and he markets his bands to them. Venues include bars, restaurants, nightclubs, casinos, and, in the summertime, local festivals. Basically, anyone who hires live music can be a customer for TC's Bookings.

TC's maintains an extensive database on the venues that offer live music in the four states it serves. He'd like to say "all of the venues" but the fact of the matter is live music is a very dynamic industry. Venues such as bars, nightclubs, and restaurants go out of business all the time, while new ones crop up seemingly out of thin air. If a venue hits a slump it might decide to go to a less expensive form of entertainment, such as a DJ or karaoke. Both of these forms of entertainment cost about half the price of a live band and, depending on the venue, can be a viable alternative. In fact, most venues the company deals with will offer a "karaoke night" to satisfy those "wannabe" rock stars. They may also offer a "DJ night" for the younger crowd that wants to dance to the "thump, thump" beat of electronic or techno dance music, and "live music nights" for those customers who really enjoy watching and listening to musicians perform. If the venue's business slows down, the first thing to go is the live entertainment as the club will likely substitute DJs or karaoke for the band, thereby cutting its cost of entertainment in half.

The database consists of the following information on each customer:

- Venue name
- Address
- Contact (the decision-maker; usually the owner, but sometimes a manager or another booking agent)
- Best time to contact
- Phone number and e-mail address
- Which days the venue has live music
- Size of the bands the venue is looking for
- Genre(s) of music the venue hires
- Venue's budget
- How far in advance the venue books musicians (some book one month, some three months, and some six months in advance)
- When the venue does bookings (some book continuously and others book three months in the course of two to three days)
- Whether the venue books one-nighters or weekends
- Whether the venue has its own Public Address System or the band must supply one (the former situation is rare but is very appealing to a band. Setting up and tearing down a PA could take 30–45 minutes before and after a show)
- Whether the venue has a strong regular crowd or is expecting the band to promote and bring lots of customers
- Any other peculiarities about the stage or the venue like the size of the stage, size of the venue, and whether the band needs to play "quieter" or volume-controlled

TC's also maintains a database on its bands. This database includes the band's name, website, members, phone numbers, e-mail addresses, genre(s) of music, song list, which parts of Southeastern Michigan the band prefers to play, a schedule of the band's gigs, dates the band has blocked off as "not available," acceptable minimum price the band is willing to play for, photos, logos, and songs that are used in the band's demo.

TC's Bookings is a full-service agency, booking not only shows or "gigs" for the bands, but also creating their promotional packages or "kits" as well. The kits usually include a biography of the band and its members, a group photo as well as individual photos, a song list, and a demo. The demo usually has 4–5 songs the band has recorded live or in a studio. But some bands want an entire CD marketed as a demo, or perhaps an entire set (usually 10–12 songs) that was recorded live at one of its shows.

Over the years, these "physical" promotional kits have transitioned to EPKs (electronic promotional kits), which are e-mailed to the venues. Truth be told, these venues are bombarded with 10, 15, and sometimes 20 bands a week, all leaving behind promotional kits. The number of EPKs increased substantially, and oftentimes the buyer didn't have the time to look at each kit as it came in. As a result, the kits piled up on shelves, desks, or even the floor in an office, and were never looked at. It was all a waste of money. And while EPKs were a less-expensive method, technological advances in websites, e-mail, social media, and sites such as YouTube provided more convenience to Tony, his clients, and his buyers.

These days, TC's can embed links to YouTube videos and MP3 recordings of the band and attach a "one-sheet" of the bio and band photo to an e-mail and send it to the buyer. The buyer, in turn, can open the e-mail, see, hear, and read the information in a matter of minutes and make a decision on whether it wants to book the group.

As technology changed the way the music and videos were presented to the venues, it also changed the relationship between buyer and seller. There was less need for personal sales calls, as there was no promotional kit to drop off. The relationship became increasingly electronic with more e-mail and texts being utilized. The reduction in cost and time from not having to visit the venues has often enabled Tony to reduce the number of sales reps from four to two by combining Wisconsin and Illinois under one rep, and Michigan and Indiana under the other. This change, which occurred three years ago, coincided with the purchase of a CRM system that enabled the reps to stay in close contact with current venues, as well utilize a planned approach to attract new venues. Overall, today the company is far more efficient and profitable.

TC's Bookings also recently made the decision to eliminate its website and to utilize Facebook, Twitter, and Instagram in its place. The website features the bands, a description of each, and their schedules. Customers are directed to the website through TC's business contact information, which is included in each promotional kit, and a label that goes onto each demo and through e-mail correspondence. This change mirrored what Tony saw happening with both his bands and his venues. Social media represented a more proactive approach to promoting the bands to the venues and the venues to its customers. Instead of waiting for people to come to the website, Tony decided to reach out to his customers on social media sites where they are spending most of their time.

TC's Bookings has done very well in building and maintaining relationships with its customers. But there are still many venues to which the door is closed to the agency. And while Tony realizes the agency cannot serve every venue, the industry is dynamic and customers today may be out of business tomorrow. Therefore, the agency must always be seeking to establish new relationships as well as trying to enhance the relationships that already exist.

Questions

1. Evaluate the changes the company has made in recent years.

2. Are there other methods of maintaining and enhancing customer relationships the company is missing?

3. How might you use these methods?

Case prepared by: Frank Notturno, Madonna University

The Selling Process[1]

Unless you're a tremendous athlete with a chance to turn professional, or a super talented entertainer who may become the next American Idol, you're probably going to start your career after college making an average salary, receiving annual raises about matching inflation, and working hard for many years or decades trying to climb the corporate ladder. Of course, other college graduates in your company will be doing the same thing, and only a few will be able to climb very high up the ladder. You may be the one to make it, and we hope you are! But how would you like to learn about another career opportunity that will give you a great chance to make a six figure income in your twenties, plus many other exceptional benefits, while having the gratifying job of helping people solve their problems?

If you start in professional selling after college, you'll likely be able to receive these opportunities and benefits at an early age. What's more, after only a few years as a successful salesperson, at most companies you're eligible for promotion into multiple career paths, including sales force management, marketing management, and high level professional selling, that is, national or key account executive positions with only one or two major customers such as Procter & Gamble (www.pg.com) or DuPont (www.dupont.com). Nearly all sales managers began their sales careers in selling, so we're going to take a close look at professional selling in this chapter to help you understand the exciting things ahead for you in your first sales job.

Updating the Roles of Salespeople

Be honest now, what are your impressions of salespeople? Do you picture the flamboyant caricatures of salespeople in television shows, or Willy Loman in the play, *Death of a Salesman*? Do you visualize salespeople going door-to-door to sell encyclopedias, cosmetics, or life insurance? If so, you have a real awakening ahead as you learn about contemporary business-to-business salespeople.

Stereotypical "door-to-door" salespeople have essentially been replaced by various forms of direct marketing including e-mails, e-commerce websites, teleselling, catalogs, and sales letters. College graduates who enter sales today are most likely to be calling on professional buyers working for manufacturers, producers, retailers, wholesalers, distributors, government agencies, and various not-for-profit institutions. With access to various online and off-line sources to gather information and compare offerings before buying, customers have become empowered. They expect greater value at lower prices while demanding better service.

At the same time, salespeople themselves are empowered by technology, and increasingly independent of their sales managers. No matter where they are, salespeople have instant access to all the information they and their customers need via computer laptops or multi-function cell phones. They can serve prospects and customers much like trusted consultants or business partners. Present-day salespeople are also developing a new level of professionalism and sensitivity to customer concerns, as they face diverse and sophisticated buyers whose expectations continually rise.

Customer Relationship Management

We've seen in earlier chapters that salespeople are essential in providing added value for customers while creatively managing the buyer–seller interface. Salespeople generally have the greatest influence in reducing customer defection, and their efforts largely determine the effectiveness of CRM strategies aimed at creating customer loyalty.[2] Thus, in their boundary spanner roles, salespeople must continuously keep in touch with customer expectations, organizational goals, and changes in the macromarketing environment. Top performing salespeople are not focused on merely mastering the critical seven steps of the selling process discussed below. They also are heavily involved in customer relationship management for their companies.[3] To appreciate the differences between yesterday's and today's salespeople, see Table 4.1.

TABLE 4.1

Contrasting Yesterday's and Today's Salespeople

Yesterday's Salesperson	Today's Salesperson
Was product oriented	Is customer oriented
Focused on *selling* customers	Focuses on *serving* customers
Did little sales call planning	Develops sales call strategy to achieve specific objectives
Made sales pitches without listening much to customers	Listens to and communicates meaningfully with customers
Stressed product features and price in sales presentations	Stresses customer benefits and service in sales presentations
Often used manipulative selling techniques	Tries to help customers solve their problems
Sought to make immediate sales and achieve quotas	Seeks to develop mutually beneficial long-term relationships with customers
Disappeared after the sale was made until the next sales call	Follows up with customers to provide service and ensure satisfaction leading to customer loyalty
Worked largely alone and had little interest in understanding customers' problems	Works as a member of a team of specialists to serve customers

Source: Adapted from Anderson, R.E., Dubinsky, A.J., and Mehta, R. (2007). *Personal Selling: Building Customer Relationships and Partnerships*, 2nd ed., 10. Boston: Houghton Mifflin.

Opportunities in Selling and Sales Management

According to the Occupational Outlook Handbook of the Bureau of Labor Statistics, the median annual salary for sales managers as of May 2018 was $124,220 with the top ten percent of sales manager earning $208,000 or more. Demand for sales managers remains high as projected growth for sales managers is at least 5% annually between 2018 and 2028[4] Because salespeople often earn more than their sales managers, a recent trend among some companies is to increase compensation for sales managers by providing them with commissions or bonuses on the sales and/or profits earned by their salespeople.[5] Salespeople and sales managers in high demand sales areas, such as emerging technologies, are often in short supply, so they may receive substantial signing or hiring bonuses.[6]

Unlike most jobs, where annual raises are low and often only partially offset cost of living increases or are determined by a superior's subjective performance evaluation, the sales profession offers salaries, commissions, bonuses, sales contest prizes, and relatively objective performance evaluations. In addition, salespeople may receive many "perks," including expense accounts, club memberships, company credit cards, automobiles, cell phones, and tablet or laptop computers. Beyond tangible rewards, high performing salespeople also enjoy a high degree of recognition within their companies. At some companies, top performing salespeople are invited to special meetings with the CEO to discuss organizational issues. Other benefits of a sales career include consistently high demand, job freedom and independence, the adventure of interacting with new prospects and buying situations, personal satisfaction in doing a job that contributes directly to the welfare of one's company and the economy, plus excellent promotion opportunities. Because they interact with and know customers best, successful salespeople are among the employees most likely to be promoted into senior management positions. Many chief executive officers, including Howard Schultz of Starbucks (www.starbucks.com), Warren Buffet of Berkshire Hathaway (www.berkshirehathaway.com), William Weldon of Johnson & Johnson (www.jnj.com), Samuel Palmisano of IBM (www.ibm.com), Anne Mulcahy of Xerox (www.xerox.com), and Mark Cuban – billionaire entrepreneur and "Shark" television personality – began their careers as sales representatives.[7] As direct revenue generators, salespeople guided by their sales managers are critical to the well-being of their companies. Unless its products and services are profitably sold, a company cannot stay in business long and its employees will lose their jobs. Thus, in many ways, the success of every business depends on the success of its salespeople.

Careers for Different Types of Individuals

No particular cultural background, ethnic group, gender, age, physical appearance, or personality ensures success in selling to diverse customer types. Studies have long found that sales effectiveness is most related to the degree of similarity between the customer and salesperson[8] – such as age, gender, personality, and thought patterns.[9] As a result, many sales managers try to match their salespeople with similar customer types.[10] It follows then that women and minorities may be especially effective salespeople when calling on female and minority customers, particularly if they are alike in other characteristics relevant to the buying situation.

Everyone Sells Something

Robert Louis Stevenson, the great novelist, once said: "Everybody lives by selling something." Tens of millions of salespeople are working in all types of profit-oriented and not-for-profit organizations selling products, services, and ideas. But what Stevenson recognized is that all of us, whether we earn our living in sales or not, must engage in persuasive two-way communication to convince (sell) others in various situations at different times about various things. For example, when you graduate from college or university, even if you're not applying for a sales job, you'll still need to "sell" potential employers on hiring *you*, rather than someone else with similar credentials who may apply for the job. In other situations, you may want to "sell" someone on voting for your favorite political candidate, attending your alma mater, allowing you to take an exam early, giving you a day off work, donating to a charitable organization, or loaning you money. Learning the principles of selling will improve anyone's chances for success in all these situations and in virtually every career. Jay Leno, long-time former host of "The Tonight Show," planned from early childhood to become a salesperson, and he attributes much of his success as a standup comedian and in-demand corporate speaker to his knowledge of selling techniques.[11]

The good news for most of us is that, although some people may have more natural ability than others, selling is not an art or innate talent but a discipline that most people can learn how to do. There's a specific selling process to learn and all you need is a disciplined, organized approach to carry it out. If you have that, you'll outperform others who don't understand the process nearly every time.[12]

What Salespeople Do: The Stages of the Selling Process

Although there are diverse types of customers, products, services, and sales situations, there are only seven basic interacting, overlapping stages that form the selling process (SP). Here they are, in order:

1. Prospecting and qualifying
2. Planning the sales call (preapproach)
3. Approaching the prospect
4. Making the sales presentation and demonstration
5. Negotiating sales resistance or objections
6. Confirming and closing the sale
7. Following up and servicing the account[13]

Continuous Cycle or Wheel of Selling

The seven stages of the SP are best depicted as a continuous cycle or wheel of overlapping stages, as shown in Figure 4.1. Once the wheel of selling is set in motion, it continues to rotate from one stage to the next. Thus, it's easy to see that stage seven isn't really the end of the cycle but rather a new beginning, because the salesperson's follow-up and service activities can generate repeat sales or purchases of new products and services as customer needs grow. The wheel is not a rigid mechanism that can't be stopped, changed, or reversed if necessary. Sometimes, the salesperson may need to skip over, redesign, or return to a previous stage in the SP when an initial approach or turn of the wheel fails to work. Sensitivity and flexibility in responding to feedback from customers about their needs and wants is critical for the salesperson to make the most effective and efficient use of the SP process. As seen in Figure 4.1, the wheel's center axle is comprised of prospects and customers. Without them, the wheel would have nothing around which to revolve. Let's discuss each of the seven stages in the SP.

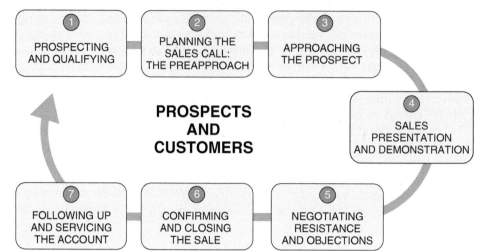

FIGURE 4.1 The selling process: Wheel of selling
Source: From Anderson, R.E., Dubinsky, A.J., and Mehta, R. (2007). *Personal Selling: Building Customer Relationships and Partnerships*, 2nd ed., 101. Boston: Houghton Mifflin.

Prospecting and Qualifying

Customers are continually leaving for various reasons, whether death, bankruptcy, relocation, or switching to other suppliers. From 10 to 30% of the company's current customers leave each year.[14] To increase or even maintain sales volume, salespeople must continually search for potential new customers, called *prospects*. Prospecting requires salespeople to first obtain *leads*. A lead is basically the name and address or telephone number of a person or organization that may have a need for the company's products or services. Before considering a *lead* to be a valid prospect, the salesperson must qualify it in terms of *need or want*, *authority to buy*, *money to buy*, and *eligibility to buy* (e.g. salespeople who call on wholesalers cannot bypass them to sell directly to retailers without disrupting channel relationships). One way to remember these four qualifiers is the acronym "NAME," which consists of the first initial of each prospecting stage. When companies or individuals pass all four of these screens, they become prospects for a sales call. Many salespeople consider prospects their "pot of gold nuggets" from which they can draw when sales slow-down, and most spend more time on prospecting than on any other selling activity. Various random-lead and selective-lead searching methods for finding new organization or individual prospects are presented in Table 4.2.

Planning the Sales Call (Preapproach)

In the preapproach or planning stage, salespeople carry out seven basic steps as outlined in Table 4.3. An effective way to prepare the prospect for the first sales contact is called "seeding." With this technique, the salesperson mails pertinent news articles to the potential buyer over several weeks thereby establishing a kind of "pen-pal" relationship before calling to ask for an appointment. Prospects do not want their time wasted, so salespeople must learn to "sell" the sales call. A step beyond "seeding" is a technique called "prenotification" in which the salesperson makes a telephone call or sends a letter, text message, e-mail, or fax to request permission to send sales materials and pique the prospect's interest in scheduling the face-to-face sales call.

Before developing a sales call strategy, it's especially important to gather detailed information about the prospect and the buying situation. As Table 4.4 shows, selective

TABLE **4.2**

Looking for New Prospects

Random-Lead Searching Methods	
Door-to-door canvassing of organizations	Advertising (print, broadcast, or online)
Territory blitz of organizations	Websites, social media
Cold calls on organizations	Electronic mail (e-mail)

Selective-Lead Searching Methods	
Direct sources	**Indirect sources**
Networking through friends, neighbors, colleagues, and acquaintances	Postal or electronic sales letters, oftentimes with attachments
Personal observation	Trade shows, fairs, and exhibitions
Spotters, or "bird dogs"	Professional seminars and conferences
Current satisfied customers and former customers	Contests or lotteries for prospects to enter for a chance to win a product or service
Endless chain (obtaining referrals from prospects and customers)	Free gift offers that entice prospects to listen to a sales presentation
Centers of influence (joining social or business groups to meet potential prospects)	Unsolicited inquiries sent to prospects
Surveys	Telemarketing
Internet (World Wide Web)	
Sales associates and professional sales organizations	
Company records, directories, mailing lists, newsletters	

Source: Adapted from Anderson, R.E., Dubinsky, A.J., and Mehta, R. (2007). *Personal Selling: Building Customer Relationships and Partnerships*, 2nd ed., 105. Boston: Houghton Mifflin.

Box 4.1 | Sales Management in Action 4.1

Former Field Salespeople Recruited for Telemarketing

Sales managers at DuPont (www.dupont.com), the chemical giant, have a unique approach to prospecting and supporting the field sales force. Former field salespeople are recruited as telemarketing reps to identify "hot prospects" for the Dupont field sales force, answer customers' technical questions, help resolve distribution problems, and even sell some products. Having knowledgeable former field salespeople make the initial telephone contact with potential customers has sharply increased the conversion rate of leads to prospects to customers. More than 50% of the leads passed on to the field sales force by these sales-savvy telemarketers become DuPont customers.

information sources may include trade associations, chambers of commerce, credit bureaus, mailing list companies, government and public libraries, investment firms, business websites, and numerous Internet search engines, such as Google (www .google.com) or Bing (www.bing.com). For instance, visit the website of the Thomas Register of American Manufacturers (www.thomasnet.com), which is widely used by B2B salespeople because it provides a wealth of information for planning sales calls on

The more information salespeople have regarding a prospect, the better prepared they will be to handle any situation during a sales call.

TABLE 4.3

Seven Steps in Preapproach Planning

1. Prepare the prospect for the initial sales call (for example, by using the "seeding" technique).

2. "Sell" the sales call appointment to the prospect through "prenotification."

3. Gather and analyze information about the prospect.

4. Conduct a Problems and Needs Assessment for the prospect.

5. Identify the product *Features*, *Advantages*, and *Benefits* likely to be of most interest to the prospect, with major focus on the benefits.

6. Select the best sales presentation and demonstration strategy for the prospect.

7. Plan and rehearse your approach to the prospect.

Source: Adapted from Anderson, R.E., Dubinsky, A.J., and Mehta, R. (2007). *Personal Selling: Building Customer Relationships and Partnerships*, 2nd ed., 139. Boston: Houghton Mifflin.

---

manufacturers (Figure 4.2). One of the most direct ways to obtain information is a low-profile preliminary call at the prospect's business location. While there, salespeople can talk to receptionists or other employees, gather company brochures and materials, and simply observe the way the business operates. Such efforts should be low-key, diplomatic, and gracious, though, to avoid the impression of spying or snooping. Oftentimes, you can simply ask the business prospect's permission to visit and gather basic

TABLE 4.4

Selective Electronic Sources of Information

Name	Type of information	Website
Thomas Register of American Manufacturers	American manufacturers based on product classifications	www.thomasnet.com
Yellow Pages	Information on more than 10 million businesses	www.yellowpages.com
Fortune Magazine	Fortune 500 firms	www.fortune.com
Forbes Magazine	Forbes 500 firms	www.forbes.com
Inc. Magazine	*Inc.* magazine fastest-growing small firms	www.inc.com
U. S. Census Bureau	Information on industrial activity	www.census.gov/cir/www/
Dun & Bradstreet	Information on small and large firms	www.dnb.com/us/
Moody's Industrial Manuals	Data on over 10,000 corporations	www.moodys.com/cust/default.asp
Hoover's Online	Information on small and large businesses	www.hoovers.com
ABI-Inform	Data on industries, companies, products, and current business topics from 550 publications	www.proquest.com
Standard & Poor's	Detailed balance sheet and income statement information for more than 5,000 firms	www.standardandpoors.com
Industry Data Sources	Trade association reports, government publications, and industry studies by brokerage firms on 65 major industries	www.virtualpet.com/industry/data/data.htm
Economic Information Systems	Data on over 400,000 organizations	www.fisher.lib.virginia.edu

Source: Adapted from Anderson, R.E., Dubinsky, A.J., and Mehta, R. (2007). *Personal Selling: Building Customer Relationships and Partnerships*, 2nd ed., 148. Boston: Houghton Mifflin.

information about product or service needs, so you can develop appropriate problem solutions for a later sales call.

Approaching the Prospect

Salespeople make their critical, often long-lasting, impressions in the approach stage. As you see in Table 4.5, several methods for approaching the prospect can succeed, ranging from a referral by a mutual acquaintance to beginning an immediate product demonstration upon first interacting with the prospect. For example, while walking or driving to a prospect's office, a salesperson may call the prospect and say something like: "Hi John, I'm calling you on our new Celestial 3000 smartphone. How's the sound coming through? I think you'll like the smartphone's exciting new features and unique benefits for your salespeople. You can see for yourself in just a few minutes when I'll be knocking on your door for our appointment."

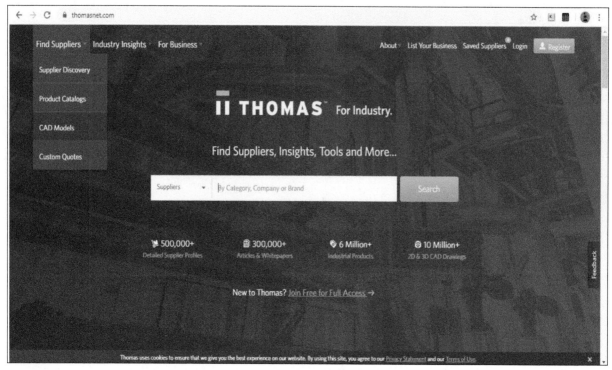

FIGURE 4.2 Salespeople can find a wealth of information for planning sales calls from various sources, such as trade associations, chambers of commerce, or the website of the *Thomas Register of American Manufacturers*.

Source: Thomas Publishing Company, April 14, 2020.

TABLE 4.5

Strategies for Approaching Prospects

Nonproduct-Related Approaches	
Mutual acquaintance or reference	Mention the name of a respected mutual acquaintance who has referred the prospect to you.
Self-introduction	Smoothly and professionally greet the prospect.
Free gift or sample	Offer a free gift, sample, or luncheon invitation.
Memorable or dramatic act	Do something memorable or even dramatic in a positive way to demonstrate key product benefits.
Piquing-Interest Approaches	
Customer benefit	Offer the customer a desired benefit immediately.
Curiosity	Offer the prospect a potential benefit that appeals to the prospect's curiosity.
Consumer-Directed Approaches	
Compliment or praise	Subtly but sincerely compliment the prospect.
Survey	Ask permission to obtain information about whether the prospect might need your product, and how soon.
Question	Involve the prospect in two-way communication early on by asking a question.
Product-Related Approaches	
Product or ingredient	Show the customer the product or a model of the product.
Product demonstration	Begin demonstrating the product upon first interacting with the prospect.

Source: Adapted from Anderson, R.E., Dubinsky, A.J., and Mehta, R. (2007). *Personal Selling: Building Customer Relationships and Partnerships*, 2nd ed., 157. Boston: Houghton Mifflin.

Whatever the approach, successful salespeople must tailor it to each prospect. Successful salespeople often set a *primary objective* (targeted outcome), a *minimal objective* (lowest acceptable outcome), and an *optimal objective* (best possible outcome) before approaching the prospect. It's a good idea to use "*SMART*" steps to set objectives[15]:

- *Specific:* Establish a specific, major objective for the sales call.
- *Measurable:* Ensure that your major objective is measurable or quantifiable – for example, a certain number of units or dollar sales volume.
- *Achievable:* Make sure the goals you set are realistic and achievable.
- *Relational:* Always try to further a positive long-term relationship with the prospect whether you achieve your major objective on this sales call or not.
- *Temporal:* If you can, establish with the prospect a specific timeframe for achieving the major objective. For instance, arrange for trial use of the product or service for a designated time period, with the prospect's purchase decision to follow.

Ultimately, most sales calls should achieve one or more of three overall objectives:

1. *Generate sales* – sell particular products or services to target customers on designated sales calls.
2. *Develop the market* – lay the groundwork for generating new business by educating customers, gaining visibility, and developing relationships with prospective buyers.
3. *Protect the market* – learn competitors' strategies and tactics and protect relationships with current customers to keep them satisfied and loyal.

Making the Sales Presentation and Demonstration

Persuasive communication is at the heart of the selling process, and the sales presentation/demonstration is the critical center stage or "show time" for salespeople. After asking the customer qualifying questions to uncover specific needs, the salesperson presents the products and services that will best satisfy those needs; highlights their features, advantages, and benefits; and stimulates desire for the offerings with a skillful demonstration. Prospects are primarily interested in the benefits being offered them. Product features and advantages are important only if they can be tied directly to a specific benefit the prospect is seeking. For instance, pointing out a flat screen monitor feature when demonstrating a new desktop computer does not mean much to a prospect unless the salesperson explains the related benefits of taking up less desk space, reducing eye strain, and increasing employee productivity.

Success in this stage requires development of carefully tailored and practiced strategies, including a convincing product demonstration. It's been said that a picture is worth a thousand words, and a demonstration is worth a thousand pictures. One successful sales representative used to carry a hammer and a plate of his company's unbreakable glass with him to demonstrate its strength. One day, instead of hitting the glass with the hammer himself, he let the prospect do it. From that time one, his sales soared as he continued to let customers swing the hammer. Salespeople should always try to get the prospect involved in demonstrating the product or "trying it out," to enable them to gain confidence in using it. A "dog and pony show," no matter how elaborate, seldom succeeds because prospects usually see its focus as "selling" instead of "solving" their problems.

Salespeople who use skillful questioning and reactive listening while prospects describe their needs can often adjust their sales presentation and demonstration "on the fly" to provide the best customer solutions. Various sales presentations strategies

TABLE 4.6

Sales Presentation Strategies

Strategy	Approach	Advantage or disadvantage
Stimulus-response	Salesperson asks a series of positive leading questions.	Customer develops habit of answering "yes," which may lead to a positive response to the closing question. Can appear manipulative to sophisticated prospects.
Formula	Salesperson leads the prospect through the mental states of buying (AIDA: attention, interest, desire, and action).	Prospect is led toward purchase action one step at a time, as the prospect participates in the interview. May come across as too mechanical and rehearsed to win prospect's trust and confidence.
Need satisfaction	Salesperson tries to find the prospect's dominant but often latent buying needs; skillful listening, questioning, and use of certain image-producing words will help the salesperson uncover the critical needs to be satisfied if the sale is to be won.	Salesperson listens and responds to the prospect while "leading" the prospect to buy; the salesperson learns dominant buyer needs and motivations. Salesperson must not overlook possible latent needs of prospect that are not articulated.
Consultative problem solving	Salesperson carefully listens and asks probing questions to more fully understand the prospect's problems and specific needs and then recommends the best alternative solutions.	Through the parties working together to understand and solve problems, the salesperson forges a trustful, consultative relationship with the prospect. Salesperson and buyer negotiations focus on a "win-win" outcome and a long-run relationship.
Depth selling	Salesperson employs a skillful mix of several sales presentation methods.	A customized mix of the best features of all of the strategies that draws on most of their advantages. Depth selling requires exceptional salesperson skill and experience.
Team selling	Salesperson, in concert with other company personnel, sells the product/service benefits and avoids intra-group conflicts by promoting harmony, identifying and catering to the needs of each interest group.	Team selling involves counterparts from both the buyer and seller organizations interacting and cooperating to find solutions to problems. Salesperson serves as coordinator of the buyer–seller team interactions.

Source: Adapted from Anderson, R.E., Dubinsky, A.J., and Mehta, R. (2007). *Personal Selling: Building Customer Relationships and Partnerships*, 2nd ed., 197. Boston: Houghton Mifflin.

are presented in Table 4.6, but most professional business-to-business salespeople find the consultative problem-solving strategy to be most effective, along with tactics that anticipate likely interactions between buyer and seller. Like an actor or athlete, the salesperson needs to diligently practice the sales presentation with a sales associate or friend. Some salespeople enroll in sales presentation training programs offered by companies, such as Effective Presentations (www.effectivepresentations.com), to further develop their selling proficiency (Figure 4.3).

Adaptive Versus Canned Sales Presentations

Traditional salespeople tend to make relatively standard sales presentations that don't vary much from one prospect to another. Top performing salespeople try instead to adapt each presentation to the particular prospect and selling situation.[16] Salespeople who modify their presentations in accordance with specific prospect or customer needs and behaviors are more effective than those who do not.[17] This may seem obvious, but only salespeople who are predisposed to adjust their sales presentation to the

FIGURE 4.3 Salespeople can enroll in training programs offered by companies such as Effective Presentations to augment their sales presentation expertise.

Source: https://www.effectivepresentations.com/corporate/sales-training/, April 14, 2020.

customer are likely to do so during the sales call.[18] Successful salespeople regularly practice adapting their sales presentation to different customer types and sales situations, and they stay alert to prospect's verbal and nonverbal feedback during the presentation. For example, if the purchasing manager for Hertz (www.hertz.com) shows more interest in safety than gas mileage, then an observant salesperson for General Motors (www.gm.com) can quickly adapt the sales presentation by emphasizing the safety benefits of GM cars. Although adaptive selling is generally best, canned (or programmed) selling can be appropriate for some types of prospects, selling situations, and salespeople. In fact, the most effective sales presentations often blend the canned and adaptive approaches.[19] Many professional salespeople use programmed multimedia to present general information efficiently and effectively and to enliven their sales presentations. While the multimedia presentation is being presented, salespeople are able to closely observe the prospect's reaction and accordingly better adapt later stages of the sales presentation. To gauge how adaptive you are as a salesperson, take the test in Table 4.7.

Negotiating Sales Resistance or Buyer Objections

Even after an effective sales presentation and demonstration, most prospects and customers are not ready to sign a purchase agreement. Instead, they're likely to ask more questions and put up resistance to making the purchase. However, you shouldn't be discouraged by prospect resistance or objections. Experienced salespeople know the sale doesn't really begin until the prospect says "No." Usually, objections are simply a request for more information so that the prospect can justify a purchase decision.

> ### TABLE 4.7
>
> ## How Adaptive Are You in Dealing with Prospects and Customers?
>
> *Assume you're a B2B salesperson, and assign one of the five levels of agreement or disagreement to each of the following 15 statements to determine how adaptive you are or would be in dealing with a prospect or a customer;*
>
> | Strongly Agree | Agree | Neither Agree nor Disagree | Disagree | Strongly Disagree |
> |:---:|:---:|:---:|:---:|:---:|
> | 5 | 4 | 3 | 2 | 1 |
>
> 1. Each customer requires a somewhat different approach.
> 2. When my sales approach is not working well, I try another approach.
> 3. It's important to experiment with different sales approaches.
> 4. Salespeople need to be flexible in the selling approach they use with different customers.
> 5. Most buyers can be dealt with in different ways.
> 6. My approach tends to change from one customer to the next.
> 7. In sales calls, I often use a variety of selling approaches.
> 8. Salespeople should know and practice different sales approaches.
> 9. When the customer or situation calls for it, I alter my sales presentation appropriately.
> 10. My general approach is to tailor my sales presentation to the customer.
> 11. Being sensitive to the needs of customers and reading nonverbal clues is critical in making a sales presentation.
> 12. Most times, I am able to adapt my presentation style to the specific buyer.
> 13. My sales style adjusts from situation to situation and customer to customer.
> 14. Understanding one's customers and their changing needs is critical in sales.
> 15. Whenever necessary, I'm able to confidently change my planned presentation to a customer.
>
> **DIRECTIONS:** Add your scores for the 15 questions. A score of 60 or higher indicates that your adaptability tends to be strong; a score of 45 or less indicates that your adaptability may be weak and could benefit from some changes.

Salespeople can use various negotiating techniques to achieve "win–win" agreements.

Nestor Rizhniak/Shutterstock.com

Before making a sales call, it's always a good idea to anticipate prospect objections and prepare appropriate responses to win the sale.

Sales resistance can consist of either valid or invalid objections, and salespeople need to recognize each type in negotiating with prospects or customers. Table 4.8 summarizes various forms of common valid and invalid objections that you're likely to encounter in your selling efforts. It's generally futile for salespeople to try to negotiate invalid or hidden objections.

TABLE 4.8

Types of Valid and Invalid Objections

	Valid objections
Product objections	• Product characteristics and benefits are perceived as less than desired by the prospect. • The proposed product is not superior to the product currently being used. • Product characteristics and benefits are not competitive.
Price objections	• Price is too high for the perceived value offered. • Price isn't competitive. • Price exceeds the prospect's budget limitations. • Discounts are inadequate. • Payment terms are out-of-line.
Promotion objections	• Cooperative advertising is insufficient. • Free display merchandise is not offered. • No "push money" is provided for reseller salespeople. • No advertising support is offered.
Distribution objections	• Delivery lead time is too long. • Minimum order size requirements are unacceptable. • Delivery arrangements are inadequate. • Questions regarding who pays transportation costs. • The salesperson's company is unwilling to provide consignment sales. • Inadequate damage and return goods policy. • Prospect's fear of being overstocked.
Capital objections	• Required investment outlays are too high. • Customer credit rating is too low to obtain favorable interest rate for capital fund loans. • The prospect company's capital budget has not yet been approved. • Customer has cash flow problems, so is currently unable to buy capital goods.
Source objections	• Source company's reputation is poor. • Buyer prefers a local supplier. • Buyer wants to do business with a national company. • Lingering concerns over past problems in doing business with the seller. • Buyer prefers to stick to the status quo in supplier relationships. • Vendor has a reputation for manufacturing low-quality products. • Vendor is known to be unethical.
Needs objections	• Buyer has no need for the seller's product or service. • Buyer is satisfied with the products currently being purchased.
	Invalid objections
Latent objections	• Buyer usually purchases from an old friend or the source desired by his boss. • Prospect does not have the authority to make the purchase but is embarrassed to let salesperson know this. • Prospect resents the salesperson making an unannounced visit. • Prospect simply doesn't like the salesperson or his or her company and doesn't want to start a business relationship.

(Continued)

TABLE 4.8

Types of Valid and Invalid Objections (*Continued*)

	Valid objections

Stalling objections	• To put-off the salesperson for the time being or get him to leave and perhaps not return, the prospect says something like:
	  • "Thanks for coming in, we'll get back to you if we decide to consider purchasing your products."
	  • "Purchasing decisions are made by a buying committee, so I'll let you know if the committee decides to consider your company as a supplier."

Time objections	• Prospect says he has to prepare for a meeting. • Prospect claims he needs time to assess the purchase specifications and requirements. • Prospect says he is just too busy to meet with the salesperson.
Unethical objections	• Prospect does not want to do business with salespeople from a particular demographic background or psychographic orientation. • Prospect makes unwelcome sexual overtures to the salesperson. • Prospect solicits bribes or kickbacks from the salesperson.

Source: From Anderson, R.E., Dubinsky, A.J., and Mehta, R. (2007). *Personal Selling: Building Customer Relationships and Partnerships*, 2nd ed. (Boston: Houghton Mifflin): 218–219. Used with permission of Rajiv Mehta.

There are too many specific techniques for negotiating buyer objections to discuss in this overview (see Table 4.9), but a couple deserve special mention. One especially useful technique is called "Feel, Felt, Found." To illustrate, if a prospect says: "This new copier is too complicated for me to operate," the salesperson can respond: "I know just how you *feel*, I *felt* the same way when I first saw it, but I've *found* that you need to concern yourself with only five buttons to do over 90% of the operations."

Another surprisingly useful technique is called "boomerang" or turning an objection into a reason for buying. For example, assume an automobile dealership is considering buying new garage doors for its large repair facility, and the manager says: "Your garage door is slower and noisier going up and down than all your competitors'

TABLE 4.9

Specific Techniques for Negotiating Buyer Objections

Put-off strategies	Provide proof strategies
• I'm coming to that • Pass-off	• Case history • Demonstration • Propose trial use

Denial strategies	Switch focus strategies
• Indirect denial • Direct denial	• Alternative product • Feel, felt, found • Comparison or contrast • Answer with a question

Offset strategies	
• Boomerang • Compensation or counterbalance	• Agree and neutralize • Humor

Source: From Rolph E. Anderson, Alan J. Dubinsky, and Rajiv Mehta, *Personal Selling: Building Customer Relationships and Partnerships*, 2nd ed. (Boston: Houghton Mifflin, 2007): 231. Used with permission of Rajiv Mehta.

doors." In response, the salesperson might say: "Yes, our 'safety first' brand door is the slowest and nosiest for a good reason. Our safety engineers learned that most accidents with heavy garage doors are the result of their coming down too fast and too quietly, so all our doors were redesigned to come down more slowly and to make a loud noise in doing so. No one has been injured by our 'safety first' doors since we began selling them six months ago."

To learn more about closing sales and improve their sales closing performance ratio, sales managers can enroll their salespeople in skill improvement workshops offered by companies, such as Sales Force Search (www.salesforcesearch.com) as shown in Figure 4.4.

Confirming and Closing the Sale

For most salespeople, a successful close is the exciting high point in the selling process. Like scoring the winning goal in a game, it's the exhilarating reward for which the salesperson has worked so hard. Skillful salespeople learn a variety of closing techniques, as set forth in Table 4.10, to help prospects make decisions in the buying process.

One of the most *straight-forward* closing approaches, when the salesperson and the prospect seem to be in agreement, is to simply ask: "Shall we write up the order?" but the close need not be that blatant. Often, the salesperson can accomplish the same result with a subtler *assumptive close* question, such as "When do you need the product delivered?" Another concern for many new salespeople is determining *when* to try to close the sale. There's no single best time. The close can happen at any time during the sales process – in the first few minutes of the first sales call, or in the last few seconds of the sixth. An old axiom for salespeople is to recite your ABCs (that is, "always be

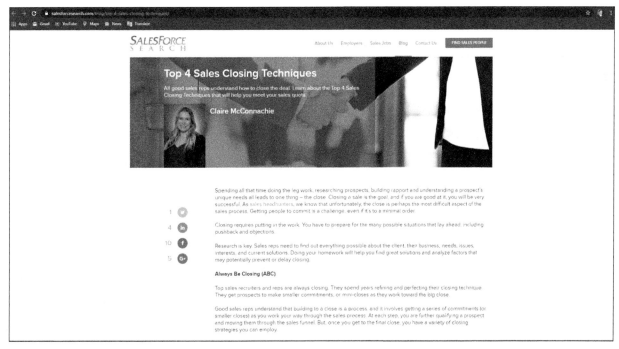

FIGURE 4.4 Sales managers can enroll their salespeople in special skill improvement workshops offered by companies, such as Sales Force Search, to further augment their closing expertise.

Source: https://www.salesforcesearch.com/blog/top-4-sales-closing-techniques/, April 14, 2020.

> **TABLE 4.10**

Types of Closes

Closing technique	Explanation
Clarification closes	
Assumptive close	Assume that the purchase decision has already been made so that the prospect feels compelled to buy.
Choice close	Offer the prospect alternative products from which to choose.
Success story close	Tell a story about a customer with a similar problem who solved it by buying the product. Alternatively, provide satisfied customers' written or verbal testimonies supporting the product. Especially effective are endorsements from people well known and respected by the prospect.
Contingent close	Elicit the prospect's agreement to buy if the salesperson can demonstrate the benefits promised.
Counterbalance close	Offset an undeniable objection by balancing it with an important buying benefit.
Boomerang close	Turn an objection around so that it becomes a reason for buying.
Future order close	If a prospect does not have a current need, but may have one in the future, the salesperson can ask for a commitment from the prospect to purchase at a future time.
If/when close	Asking the prospect to provide a clarification as to *when* an order will be placed, as opposed to *if* an order will be placed.
Probability close	Although seemingly comparable to the if/when close described above, the probability closing technique asks the prospect to assign a quantified likelihood of signing a sales contract in the near future.
Suggestion close	Gets the prospect to accept the advice offered without giving it a great deal of thought. A salesperson could suggest that the many customers who have purchased the product have reported high levels of satisfaction, thereby suggesting that the prospect should purchase it.
Psychological closes	
Stimulus-response close	Use a sequence of leading questions to make it easier for the prospect to say yes when finally asked for the order.
Minor points close	Secure favorable decisions on several minor points, leading to eventual purchase of the product.
Standing room only (SRO) close	Suggest that the opportunity to buy is brief because demand is high and the product is in short supply.
Impending event close	Warn the prospect about some upcoming event that makes it more advantageous to buy now.
Advantage close	This variation of the impending event close emphasizes the specific advantages of making a timely decision, while still stressing a sense of immediacy.
Puppy dog close	Let the prospect use the product for a while and, as with a puppy, an emotional attachment may develop, leading to a purchase.
Compliment close	Praise prospects for raising interesting and intelligent questions to flatter their egos and lead them to sign the sales order.
Reserve advantage close	In this slight variation of the advantage close described above, salespeople identify a number of merits for purchasing a product, but save a few to use if the prospect exhibits resistance yet again.
Dependency close	Used to break the "choke-hold" that a competing firm has over a prospect's business by suggesting that the prospect needs an alternative supplier to reduce the risk of being dependent on one supplier.
Straightforward closes	
Ask-for-the-order close	Ask for the order directly or indirectly.
Order form close	While asking the prospect a series of questions, start filling out basic information on the contract or order form.

TABLE **4.10**

Types of Closes (*Continued*)

Closing technique	Explanation
Straightforward closes (*Continued*)	
Summary close	Summarize the advantages and disadvantages of buying the product before asking for the order.
Repeated-yes close	This variation of the summary close requires a salesperson to pose several leading questions to which the prospect has little choice but to respond in an affirmative manner.
Benefits close	Also a variation of the summary close, it requires the salesperson to identify and present a synopsis of the various salient benefits that the sales solution offers.
Action close	The salesperson simply hands the prospect a pen along with the contract, and frequently the prospect, almost by reflex, will sign.
Negotiation close	Both the buyer and the salesperson negotiate a compromise, thus ensuring a "win-win" agreement.
Technology close	The salesperson more impactfully and effectively summarizes key value-added benefits for the prospect by using technologies such as PowerPoint, Excel, or other multi-media tools.
Concession closes	
Special deal close	Offer a special incentive to encourage the prospect to buy now.
No-risk close	Agree to take the product back and refund the customer's money if the product doesn't prove satisfactory.
Management close	When salespeople do not have the authority to make the prospect's requested commitments or concessions, they can elicit the assistance of a senior sales manager who has the authority to make the necessary decisions to close the sale.
Takeaway close	Used as an emotional fear appeal to cause anxiety that the prospect may lose out on a special deal or incentive. A salesperson could suggest that the special offer to provide an ancillary product or service free of charge is available only for another week, thereby evoking an immediate purchase.
Lost-sale closes	
Turnover close	Turn the prospect over to another salesperson with a fresh approach or a better chance to make the sale.
Pretend-to-leave close	Start to walk away, and then "remember" another benefit or special offer after the prospect has relaxed his or her defenses.
Ask-for-help close	When the sale seems lost, apologize for not being able to satisfy the prospect and ask what it would have taken to secure the sale. Then offer that.

Source: From Anderson, R.E., Dubinsky, A.J., and Mehta, R. (2007). *Personal Selling: Building Customer Relationships and Partnerships*, 2nd ed. (Boston: Houghton Mifflin): 258–260. Used with permission of Rajiv Mehta.

closing"), which advocates making "trial closes" throughout your interaction with the prospect. Trial closes are simply attempts to test the prospect's *readiness to buy*. Examples include statements like: "Do you think this product will meet your needs?" or "So, what do you think about that benefit?"

A *puppy dog close* can be especially effective because it simply lets the prospect use the product for a while and, as with a puppy, an emotional attachment may develop, leading to a purchase. Even when the sale seems lost, salespeople still can use the *ask-for-help close*. Simply apologize for not being able to satisfy the prospect and ask what it would have taken to secure the sale. When the prospect answers, offer that.

Nonverbal trial closes can also be effective. Even a small physical act such as moving the order form and pen in front of prospects may generate a reflex action to pick up the pen and sign the order. Most salespeople also learn to read and closely observe prospect body language to spot an opportune time to try a close. Some verbal and non-verbal signals indicating it's time for a trial close are presented in Table 4.11.

Following Up and Servicing the Account

After making the sale, top salespeople don't disappear. Instead, they maintain close contact with the customer to handle any complaints (see Table 4.12 for basic guide-lines in handling customer complaints) and to provide customer service such as

---

TABLE 4.11

Trial Closing Signals

Verbal signals

When the prospect asks
- about product price, delivery, installation, or service.
- about any special discounts, deals, or special incentives to buy.
- a hypothetical question about buying: "If I do decide to buy . . ."
- who else has bought the product.
- what other customers think about the product.
- whether a special feature is included or available.
- whether the product can accomplish a particular task.
- the salesperson's opinion about one product version versus another.
- what method of payment is acceptable.

When the prospect says
- something positive about the product.
- that he or she has always wanted some special product feature.

When the salesperson
- successfully answers one of the prospect's objections.
- asks whether the prospect has any more questions and the prospect says no or is silent.

Nonverbal signals

When the prospect
- begins closely studying and handling the product.
- tests or tries out the product.
- seems pleased by the product's performance or by some product feature.
- looks more relaxed.
- becomes more friendly.
- increases eye contact with the salesperson.
- looks over the order form or picks up the pen the salesperson has handed the prospect.
- nods in agreement or leans toward the salesperson.
- begins to listen more intently to the salesperson.
- lends the salesperson a pen.
- picks up, fondles, smells, tastes, or closely studies the product.
- unconsciously reaches for a checkbook or wallet.

When the salesperson
- finishes the sales presentation.
- completes a successful product demonstration.
- hands the order form and a pen to the prospect.

Source: From Rolph E. Anderson, Alan J. Dubinsky, and Rajiv Mehta, *Personal Selling: Building Customer Relationships and Partnerships*, 2nd ed. (Boston: Houghton Mifflin, 2007): 254. Used with permission of Rajiv Mehta.

Salespeople should be looking for verbal and nonverbal signals from customers that indicate it's time to close a sale.

TABLE 4.12

Basic Guidelines for Handling Customer Complaints

- Anticipate customer complaints and try to resolve them before the customer expresses them.
- Listen closely and patiently to customers' complaints without interrupting.
- Never belittle a customer's complaint. Few customers actually complain, and those who do are a valuable source of feedback and information that can help improve the quality of your product and service.
- Encourage customers to talk and fully express their feelings so that they can vent their emotions.
- Don't argue with customers or take their complaints personally. You gain nothing by making a customer angry, and there is no surer way to do so than to argue over the customer's version of the complaint.
- Record the facts as the customer sees them. If you take the complaint over the telephone, let him or her know that you are carefully recording the facts without passing judgment.
- Reassure customers that you hear and understand their complaints accurately by verbally repeating the information as you record it. This repetition reassures customers about your accuracy and interest. Asking non-threatening and nonjudgmental questions to clarify their various points can also help them to know that they are communicating successfully.
- Empathize with customers and try to see the situation from their point of view.
- Don't make excuses for service problems or criticize your firm's service personnel.
- Ask customers how they would like to have their complaint resolved instead of volunteering what you're going to do. Customers may have quite different expectations about how to solve their problem, and you may offer the wrong solution or much more than they expect. By asking customers what they want, you'll give them power to meet their expectations and not overdo it in making your amends.
- Resolve problems promptly and fairly, even if that means the sale will become unprofitable because their life-time value in repeat purchases from your company is most important.
- Thank customers for voicing the complaint. Welcome them as people who care enough to try to help you improve your products and services.
- Follow up to ensure that customer complaints have been resolved to their satisfaction.
- Keep records on all customer complaints and their outcomes so that, through analysis, you can spot patterns of problems.

Source: From Anderson, R.E., Dubinsky, A.J., and Mehta, R. (2007). *Personal Selling: Building Customer Relationships and Partnerships*, 2nd ed. (Boston: Houghton Mifflin): 307. Used with permission of Rajiv Mehta.

installation, repair, or credit approvals. It's far easier – and much less costly – to keep present customers satisfied than to search out and acquire new customers. Fully satisfied customers are the ones most likely to become loyal repeat buyers thereby cutting costs for the company in various ways.[20] They are generally easier to work with and satisfy because your relationship has reached a high level of understanding about what the customer expects. In addition, loyal customers will often buy additional products and refer you to other excellent prospects, so you can reduce expenditures on promotion to attract new prospects. Over their lifetimes, they can be worth up to ten times as much to a business as the average customer.[21] Companies as diverse as Pizza Hut (www.pizzahut.com), Home Depot (www.homedepot.com), and General Motors (www.gm.com) are working not only to satisfy customers but also to keep their loyalty. Starbucks estimates that the lifetime value of its loyal customers is over $14,000. The Cadillac (www.cadillac.com) division of General Motors reports $332,000, and Lexus (www.lexus.com) calculates over $600,000.[22] Frequent and comprehensive follow-up is a primary means of retaining long-run, satisfied, loyal, and profitable customers . . . and of keeping the *selling process wheel* revolving.

Applying CRM to the Selling Process

Empowering Salespeople for CRM

As their companies' frontline representatives, salespeople are the ultimate customer relationship builders. In recent years, their roles have shifted from merely selling goods and services to building and maintaining long-term mutually profitable relationships with valued customers. Yet, despite their expanding responsibilities for CRM, most salespeople have not been sufficiently trained or empowered by their companies to perform effectively and efficiently in this challenging new role. Even sales managers may not have a CRM attitude toward serving customers. To see how customer oriented you are, assume that you are a salesperson or sales manager for a company selling B2B, then honestly answer the questions in Table 4.13.

Kotler and Armstrong define CRM as "the overall process of building and maintaining profitable customer relationships by delivering superior customer value and satisfaction."[23] CRM has been called an inevitable – literally relentless – movement because it represents the way customers want to be served, and offers a more effective and efficient way of conducting business.[24] Many companies are developing complex CRM strategies that integrate sales force automation (SFA), data warehousing, data mining, push technology, and other tools to more fully understand and serve their most valuable customers. For example, KeyCorp (www.keycorp.net) achieved a return of over 350% by collecting customer profiles, interests, activities, and goals on its website then designing strategies to cross-sell products via direct mail, teleselling, and the Internet.[25] It is critical for sales managers to empower salespeople by enabling them to promptly address customer needs and negotiate mutually satisfying agreements with them. In practice, empowerment should seek to strengthen the flexibility, self-confidence, authority, and effectiveness of salespeople as they try to fully satisfy customers and achieve CRM objectives. One important way to empower salespeople is to give them more financial flexibility to commit company resources in serving customers – promptly approving reimbursements for unsatisfactory products, negotiating price discounts, providing purchase incentives, and resolving customer complaints. By being able to make on-the-spot decisions, salespeople can enhance their image and competence with customers, and thereby feel more psychologically empowered and motivated for CRM.[26]

> **TABLE 4.13**

Are You B2B Customer Oriented or Not?

Determine how customer oriented you are by responding to the statements below, using the following scale:

Strongly Agree	Agree	Neither Agree nor Disagree	Disagree Strongly	Disagree
5	4	3	2	1

1. Most of my customers have relatively standard needs, so I generally use a canned sales presentation on most sales calls.
2. Listening to customers first is more important than making my sales presentation, so that I can fully understand their needs and wants.
3. In answering a customer's questions, I always try to be as honest as possible, or as they say in court I tell "the whole truth and nothing but the truth."
4. To best help solve a customer's problems, I will sometimes recommend a competitor's product or service.
5. Occasionally, I gently disagree with customers in order to help them choose the product and/or service that best solves their problem.
6. It's important for me to make sure that customer expectations for my company's product or service are accurate.
7. When customers complain, I ask them how they would like their complaint resolved then I do this for them as promptly as possible.
8. It's very important that I make sure that my customers are fully satisfied with their purchases with me so they will become my loyal repeat buyers.
9. Being honest, I admit that I sometimes try to persuade customers to buy a higher quantity or different version of a product in order to achieve my sales quota or increase my commission.
10. In selling, it's important to determine a customer's personality in order to know just how and when to apply buying pressure to make the sale.
11. Unless asked, I don't try to help customers decide which product to buy because that's their job, not mine.
12. If a customer doesn't ask about a particular product weakness, I don't think it's my job to mention it.
13. It's probably best to not disclose a weakness in your product or service unless a customer specifically asks about it.
14. If a customer asks for something that will require special effort on my part, I sometimes say that what they asking for is beyond my control even if it's not.
15. I don't let customers assume anything that's incorrect because that misunderstanding might jeopardize the relationship of professional trust that I want to build with the customer.

DIRECTIONS: The higher your score for items 2 through 8, plus 15, the more customer oriented you are. Total scores of 36 or higher on these items indicate a relatively strong customer orientation; a score of lower than 36 may indicate that your customer orientation is not as strong as it probably needs to be for optimal long run success in B2B sales. The lower your score for item 1 plus items 10 through 14, the more customer oriented you are. Total scores of 14 or less on these items indicate a strong customer orientation.

In sum, managers can foster a CRM orientation among salespeople by increasing their feelings of empowerment, releasing managerial power and control of resources to salespeople, providing continual empowerment and CRM training, keeping recognition and reward systems current with organizational goals, and eliminating barriers in the organizational structure and work environment that affect empowerment of both salespeople and customers.[27]

CRM Training and Rewards

In order to develop the empowerment and customer relationship building skills needed for effective CRM, salespeople need appropriate training programs. They must be trained and rewarded for proactively taking initiatives that build customer relationships. Customer expectations for products and services have been continually rising for decades, indicating that they are infinitely elastic.[28] Therefore, CRM training for salespeople must be ongoing to keep up with the increasingly higher-level buying experience and relationship expectations of customers. Salespeople need to be empowered to make on-the-spot decisions that respond to customer requests. Delaying responses because managerial approval is required visibly undercuts the salesperson's power before customers and can hurt his or her CRM dedication and performance.

Traditional sales quota systems for motivating, evaluating, and rewarding the sales force need updating to include tangible goals and rewards for cultivation and retention of key customers through empowered CRM activities. To achieve this, salespeople ought to have access to profit figures by different market segments – information that some managements still are reluctant to share. Finally, in designing reward systems, perceived managerial fairness or evenhandedness is essential for maintaining highly motivated, satisfied, and committed CRM salespeople.

Chapter Summary

1. **Evaluate the benefits and opportunities available in a sales career.** Among the many benefits available to salespeople are high earnings potential from salaries, commissions, and bonuses; various "perks," and interaction with senior management. Other benefits of a sales career include consistently high demand, job freedom and independence, the adventure of interacting with new prospects and buying situations, and personal satisfaction in doing a job that contributes directly to the welfare of one's company and the economy. In addition, after performing successfully for a few years, salespeople are usually given opportunities for promotion into sales force management or marketing management or to become a national account manager for one or two major customers.

2. **Compare and contrast today's sales professional with yesterday's.** Yesterday's salespeople were largely product oriented, focusing on selling, did little sales call planning, made sales pitches without listening much to customers, stressed product features and price, often used manipulative techniques, worked largely alone, showed little interest in understanding customers' problems, and usually disappeared after the sale was made until the next sales call. By contrast, today's professional salespeople are customer oriented, focused on serving customers, develop sales call strategies with specific objectives for each sales call, listen to and communicate meaningfully with customers, stress customer benefits and service, try to help customers solve their problems, follow-up with customers to ensure full satisfaction leading to customer loyalty, and work as coordinator of a team of specialists to best serve customers.

3. **Describe the seven stages in the selling process (SP).** The SP is depicted as a revolving wheel of seven overlapping, interacting stages. *Stage 1* is prospecting and qualifying that involves finding organizational leads and qualifying them on the basis of four criteria: *Stage 2* is planning the sales call or the preapproach. Here, the salesperson obtains detailed information from diverse print and electronic sources about the prospect and the buying situation, then develops a strategy for a favorable reception. *Stage 3* is approaching the prospect, and it can include various strategies ranging from a referral from a mutual acquaintance to a customer benefit approach. *Stage 4* is making the Sales presentation and demonstration. There are various sales presentation options but the *consultative problem solving* is most widely used by business-to-business salespeople. *Stage 5* is negotiating sales resistance or objections. There are numerous techniques to handle objections and the savvy salesperson will anticipate and prepare in advance for them. *Stage 6* is confirming and closing the sale which is the ultimate moment that the salesperson has worked so hard

to reach. There are many types of closes ranging from directly "asking for the order" to the "puppy dog" close where the prospect is allowed to try the product out for a period before making a purchase decision. *Stage 7* is following up and serving the account after the purchase. This stage is critical in ensuring customer satisfaction and retention.

4. **Use various searching methods for finding new prospects.** *Random-lead searching methods* for prospects include door-to-door canvassing, a territory blitz, cold calls, general e-mails, advertising through print and broadcast media, and websites. *Selective-lead searching methods* include *direct sources* (i.e. pre-targeted organizations or people) and *indirect sources* where organizations or people must identify themselves by responding.

5. **Apply several sales presentation strategies.** The most important sales presentation strategy for business-to-business salespeople is *consultative problem solving* where the salesperson carefully listens and asks probing questions to more fully understand the prospect's problems and specific needs before recommending the best alternative solutions. By working together with prospects to understand and solve problems, the salesperson forges a trustful, consultative relationship focused on a "win–win" outcome and a long-run customer relationship.

6. **Overcome prospect objections and resistance through negotiation.** Negotiating prospect objections or resistance is an essential skill for today's salesperson. Objections should not be feared as they are usually pleas for more information in order to justify a purchase. Although there are many types of prospect objections, negotiation strategies can be categorized under five headings: *put-off, denial, offset, provide proof,* and *switch focus.*

7. **Demonstrate closing techniques from each of five closing categories.** There are many closing techniques but they can be divided into five basic categories, as follows: (a) clarification, (b) psychological, (c) straightforward, (d) concession, and (e) lost-sale.

8. **Explain how to empower salespeople for CRM roles.** Empowerment of salespeople can strengthen their flexibility, self-confidence, authority, and effectiveness in striving to fully satisfy customers and achieve CRM objectives. An important way to empower salespeople is to give them more financial flexibility to commit company resources in serving customers, e.g. approving reimbursements for unsatisfactory products, negotiating price discounts, providing purchase incentives, and resolving customer complaints.

Key Terms

Wheel of selling	**SMART objectives**	**Objection**	**Trial close**
Prospecting	**Adaptive selling**	**Valid objections**	**Follow-up**
Preapproach	**Canned (or programmed)**	**Invalid objections**	
Approach	**selling**	**Close**	

Notes

1. Some of the material in this chapter has been adapted and updated from Anderson, R., Dubinsky, A., and Mehta, R. (2007). *Personal Selling: Building Customer Relationships and Partnerships.* Boston: Houghton Mifflin.

2. Johnson, J.T., Barksdale, H.C., and Boles, J.S. (2001). The strategic role of the salesperson in reducing customer defection in business relationships. *Journal of Personal Selling & Sales Management* 21 (Spring): 123–124; Bhasin, H. (3 February 2020).

How to reduce customer defection and bring down defection rate? http://www.google.com/search?client=firefox-b-1-d&q=reducing+customer+defections+by+crm (accessed 13 February 2020); Hanif, M., Hafeez, S., and Riuz, A. (2010). Factors affecting customer satisfaction. *International Research Journal of Finance and Economics* 60: 44–52.

3. Yim, F.H., Anderson, R.E., and Swaminathan, S. (2004). Customer relationship management: its dimensions and effect on customer outcomes. *Journal of Personal Selling and Sales Management* 24 (Fall): 263–278; Kunsman, T. (29 May 2018). Why relationship selling is still one of the most important tactics salespeople need to master. http://www.google.com/search?client=firefox-b-1-d&q=salespeople+and+customer+relationship+management (accessed 8 November 2019); Howard, M. 17 CRM stats that sales professionals need to know. http://www.google.com/search?client=firefox-b-1-d&q=crm+and+salespeople (accessed 8 November 2019).

4. Occupational Outlook Handbook, Bureau of Labor Statistics. (4 September 2019) http://www.bls.gov/ooh/management/sales-managers.htm (accessed 9 November 2019); https://money.usnews.com/careers/best-jobs/sales-manager (accessed 9 November 2019).

5. Rose, D. What is the right sales manager commission percentage? https://cygnalgroup.com/sales-manager-commission-percentage/ (accessed 8 November 2019); Hamel, G. What percent of profits should I pay my sales manager? https://smallbusiness.chron.com/percentage-profits-should-pay-sales-manager-37264.html (accessed 7 November 2019); Sandilands, T. (21 November 2018) Sales manager commission structure. https://bizfluent.com/info-8608270-difference-pay-incentives-pay-performance.html (accessed 10 November 2019); 2019 sales compensation trends survey executive summary. http://www.alexandergroup.com/insights/2019-sales-compensation-trends-survey-executive-summary/ (accessed 10 November 2019).

6. Bennett, J. (2005). Selling technology can be a taxing task and top salespeople are tough to find. *Wall Street Journal* (April 5): B7; Corcodilos, N. What you need to know about signing bonuses. http://www.cmo.com/opinion/articles/2017/2/3/what-you-need-to-know-about-signing-bonuses.html#gs.fd6f0f (accessed 11 November 2019); Heathfield, S.M. (30 April 2019). Why might an employer pay a signing bonus? http://www.thebalancecareers.com/signing-bonus-1918264 (accessed 12 November 2019).

7. Top 10 CEOs who started in sales. http://www.smartwinnr.com/post/top10-ceos-who-started-as-salesreps/ (accessed 10 November 2019); Anderson, R., Alan Dubinsky, A., and Mehta, R. (2014). *Personal Selling: Building Customer Relationships and Partnerships*, 3rd ed., 20–25. Dubuque, Iowa: Kendall Hunt.

8. Evans, F.B. (1963). Selling as a dyadic relationship—a new approach. *American Behavioral Scientist* 6 (May): 76–79. Other supporting studies include Gadel, M.S. (1964). Concentration by salesmen on congenial prospects. *Journal of Marketing* 28 (April): 64–66; Woodside, A.G. and Davenport, J.W., Jr. (1974). The effect of salesman similarity and expertise on consumer purchasing behavior. *Journal of Marketing Research* 11 (May): 198–202; Riordan, E.A., Oliver, R.L., and Donnelly, J.H. (1977). The unsold prospect: dyadic and attitudinal determinants. *Journal of Marketing Research* 14 (November): 530–537; Crosby, L.A., Evans, K.R., and Cowles, D. (1990). Relationship quality in services selling: an interpersonal influence perspective. *Journal of Marketing* 54 (July): 68–81.

9. Lichtenthal, D.J. and Tellefsen, T. (2001). Toward a theory of business buyer–seller similarity. *Journal of Personal Selling and Sales Management* 21 (Winter): 1–14.

10. Greenberg, H.M. and Greenberg, J. (1980). Job matching for better sales performance. *Harvard Business Review* (September–October): 128–133; Zimmer, R.J. and Hugstad, P.S. (1981). A contingency approach to specializing industrial sales force. *Journal of Personal Selling and Sales Management* 1 (Spring/Summer): 27–35.

11. Jay Leno's Secrets of Sales Success. https://blog.sellingpower.com/gg/2014/01/jay-lenos-secrets-to-sales-success-.html (accessed 11 July 2020).

12. "Thriving on order," *INC.* (December 1989): 49.

13. For an alternative view of the seven-step selling process, see Moncrief, W.C. and Marshall, G.W. (2005). The evolution of the seven steps of selling. *Industrial Marketing Management* 34: 13–22.

14. Anderson, R. and Srini Srinivasan, S. (2003). Make profits soar with the 8Cs of customer loyalty. *LeBow Business Knowledge* (June): 2.

15. Stephan, D. (28 November 2018) How to set SMART sales goals https://about.crunchbase.com/blog/how-to-set-smart-sales-goals/ (accessed 12 November 2019).

16. Vecchio, S.D., Zemanek, J., McIntyre, R., and Claxton, R. (2004). Updating the adaptive selling behaviors: tactics to keep and tactics to discard. *Journal of Marketing Management* 2: 859–876; Weitz, B., Sujan, H., and Sujan, M. (1986). Knowledge, motivation, and adaptive behavior: a framework for improving selling effectiveness. *Journal of Marketing* (October): 174–191; Bhasin, H. (12 March 2018). Adaptive selling & how to use it for sales. http://www.marketing91.com/adaptive-selling-how-to-use-it-for-sales/ (accessed 10 November 2019); McCandless, K. (22 November 2017) What is adaptive selling strategy and how it can save the sales industry. https://lab.getapp.com/what-is-adaptive-selling/ (accessed 11 November 2019).

17. Blume, J. (8 January 2018). How to make the ultimate sales presentation. http://www.brightcarbon.com/blog/make-ultimate-sales-presentation/ (accessed 10 November 2019; Goolsby, J.R., Lagace, R.L., and Broom, M.L. (1992). Psychological adaptiveness and sales performance. *Journal of Personal Selling and Sales Management* 12 (Spring): 51–66.

18. Porter, S.S and Inks, L.W. (2000). Cognitive complexity and salesperson adaptability: an exploratory investigation. *Journal of Personal Selling and Sales Management* 20 (Winter): 15–21.

19. Jolson, M.A. (1989). Canned adaptiveness: a new direction for modern salesmanship. *Business Horizons* 32 (January–February): 7–12; Jolson, M.A. (1975). The underestimated potential of the canned sales presentation. *Journal of Marketing* 30(1): 75–78.

20. Reichheld F. and Sasser, E., Jr. (1995). Why satisfied customers defect. *Harvard Business Review* (November–December): 88; Reichheld, F.F. Markey, R.G., Jr., and Hopton, C. (2000). The

loyalty effect—the relationship between loyalty and profits. *European Business Journal*: 134–139.

21. Anderson, R., Dubinsky, A., and Mehta, R. (2007). *Personal Selling: Building Customer Relationships and Partnerships*, 2nd ed., 19. Boston: Houghton Mifflin.

22. Desjardins, J. (28 January 2016). This is the lifetime value of a Starbucks customer. http://www.businessinsider.com/lifetime-value-of-a-starbucks-customer-2016-1 (accessed 8 November 2019); Lexus delighting customer after the sale to keep them coming back (26 November 2016) http://www.zabanga.us/customer-relationships/real-dzr.html (accessed 9 November 2019); Leith, M. (September–October 2010). The lifetime value of a loyal customer. http://www.childcareexchange.com/catalog/product/the-lifetime-value-of-a-loyal-customer/5019530/ (accessed 9 November 2019); Heskett, J.L., Jones, T.O., Loveman, G.W. (1994). Putting the service-profit chain to work. *Harvard Business Review* (March–April):165–166; Healt, R.P. (1997) Loyalty for sale: everybody's doing frequency marketing—but only a few companies are doing it well. *Marketing Tools* (July): 65; Cooper, K.C. (2002). The relational enterprise. *Customer Relationship Management* (July): 42–45: Customer lifetime value (CLV) and how to calculate it (15 January 2019). http://www.crazyegg.com/blog/customer-lifetime-value/ (accessed 11 November 2019).

23. Kotler, P. and Armstrong, G. (2017). *Principles of Marketing*, 13th ed. Hoboken, NJ: Pearson.

24. Peppers, D. and Rogers, M. (2017). *Managing Customer Relationships: A Strategic Framework*, 3rd ed. Hoboken, NJ: John Wiley & Sons; Grunert, J. (14 August 2018). Don't manage customer relationships, build them. https://medium.com/@jeannegrunert/dont-manage-customer-relationships-build-them-9f0aff6b98bc (accessed 11 November 2019).

25. Peppers, D. and Rogers, M. (2017). *Managing Customer Relationships: A Strategic Framework*, 3rd ed. Hoboken, NJ: John Wiley &Sons; Jantsch, J. The incredibly logical way to manage customer relationships. https://ducttapemarketing.com/the-incredibly-logical-way-to-manage-customer-relationships/ (accessed 11 November 2019).

26. Anderson, R.E. and Huang, W. (2006). Empowering salespeople: personal, managerial, and organizational perspectives. *Psychology and Marketing* 23 (February): 139–159; Yim, F.H.K., Swaminathan, S., and Anderson, R. (2015). Empowering salespeople: Does it work? Marketing dynamism & sustainability: things change, things stay the same: *Proceedings of the Academy of Marketing Science* (2015). http://www.google.com/search?client=firefox-b-1d&q=empowering+salespeoplel+by+r.e.+anderson+et+alSalespeople (accessed 11 November 2019); Matthews, L.M. (2015). Why empowering salespeople is a double-edged sword. Doctoral Dissertation, Coles College of Business, Kennesaw State University.

27. Zikmund, W.G., McLeod, R. Jr., and Gilbert, F.W. (2003). Customer relationship management: integrating marketing strategy and information technology. New York: Wiley; Chamberlain, N. (25 August 2017). The three biggest barriers to sales. https://medium.com/multiplier-magazine/the-three-biggest-barriers-to-sales-ee39961c55d2 (accessed 10 November 2019); Askari, F. (6 June 2016) 11 barriers to sales and how to solve them. https://blog.strategic-ic.co.uk/inbound-sales-barriers (accessed 10 November 2019); Boaze, S. The six most common barriers to sales success. http://www.streetdirectory.com/travel_guide/1374/business_and_finance/the_six_most_common_barriers_to_sales_success.html (accessed 10 November 2019).

28. Anderson, R. (1996). Personal selling and sales management in the new millennium. *Journal of Personal Selling and Sales Management* 16 (Fall): 17–32; Lesonsky, R. (10 April 2019). Customer services expectations are rising: is your business keeping up? http://www.forbes.com/sites/allbusiness/2019/04/10/customer-service-expectations/#74dfef4414e5 (accessed 12 November 2019); Peppers, D. (January 2016). The rising tide of customer expectations. http://www.ttec.com/articles/rising-tide-customer-expectations (accessed 12 November 2019).

Chapter Review Questions

1. Why do you think so many successful CEOs of top companies have come up through sales? [LO 1]
2. What qualities do you think are needed by top performing salespeople of today and tomorrow? [LO 2]
3. Describe the seven stages in the professional selling process (SP). Why are they depicted as a revolving wheel? [LO 3, 4, 5, 6, 7]
4. Salespeople spend more time on prospecting than on any other of the seven stages in the SP. Why do you think this is so? [LO 4]
5. Describe the different sales presentation strategies, including the advantages and disadvantages associated with each. [LO 5]
6. How should salespeople view "buyer objections and resistance"? [LO 6]
7. Identify the five basic techniques for handling buyer objections and provide examples of each. [LO 6]
8. What is a "trial close"? Give some examples of trial closes. When should they be used? [LO 5, 7]
9. Name and explain as many closing strategies as you can. [LO 7]
10. Why should salespeople be empowered in their dealings with prospects and customers? [LO 8]

Online Exercise

1. You have been appointed to work as a U.S. sales representative for AIRBUS (www.airbus.com), which has just developed the A350-1000, a start-of-the-art carbon-composite airliner, that comfortably carries over 400 passengers for 18+ hour flights. Conduct a Web-based search for detailed information about the airline industry. More specifically, to help you plan the sales call and make your approach successful, find the following information:

   - The addresses and locations of the headquarters of the major companies in the airline industry (passenger airlines and cargo carriers)

   - The sales, market share, profits, and size of each of the major competitors
   - The regions of the United States and of the world where they operate
   - What type of aircraft they currently use
   - The names, addresses, e-mail addresses, telephone numbers, and purchasing managers for all of the airlines and cargo carriers

Role-Play Exercise

Handling Customer Complaints

Situation

Alex Webster, a sales representative for Tectron Scientific Software (TSS) Corporation, recently sold an expensive new software program to a new account, the Biology Department of the University of Western Pennsylvania. A week after the software was installed, Alex called the department chairperson, Dr. Kim Feng, to see how the program was working out.

Role Play Participants and Assignments

Dr. Kim Feng – Graduate students have complained that the TSS software is not working right, and they suspect there are some errors in the software program. Dr. Feng can't tolerate any bugs in the software, which is being used for high-precision work under a National Science Foundation research grant. Due to time pressures to complete this research, Dr. Feng wants Alex to pick up this software and refund the purchase price, so the department can buy a competitor's product.

Alex Webster – What should he say to Dr. Feng? How could he have prevented the problem in the first place?

In-basket Exercise

You have recently been promoted to district sales manager. You now have responsibility for the performance of 30 salespeople who call on industrial distributors in Pennsylvania, New Jersey, and Delaware who sell mainly to independently owned hardware stores and franchises. Perhaps because you recently earned an MBA degree in Marketing, your national sales manager has asked you to develop a program to empower the company's field salespeople in carrying out the CEO's mandate for a total sales force customer relationship management (CRM) program to retain profitable business customers. Prepare a bulleted outline or executive summary of your proposed sales force empowerment program to submit to the national sales manager.

Ethical Dilemma

Clive Farley sells multi-function machines that print, copy, scan, and fax. On Friday night, he's preparing his sales presentation and demonstration prior to making the third sales call on a medium-size manufacturer who has asked for a product demonstration this coming Monday morning. Clive knows that his company's machine is very slow compared to competitors in making copies on both sides of the paper. Although many companies are trying to save copying costs by using both sides of the paper, Clive doubts that his prospect will ask for a demonstration of this feature nor is it likely to come up in their discussions. So, Clive is thinking that he should avoid mentioning or doing any demonstration of two-sided copying because his machine is about 10–15% less expensive than the competitors and is equally good on all other features. He fears that a direct comparison of his machine with competitors on two-sided copying will probably cost him the sale. What would you advise Clive to do?

CASE 4.1 — Micronix-Digital: Negotiation Strategies that Work

Janeen Mena, a senior sales rep for Micronix-Digital – a large semiconductor manufacturer – is negotiating with the chief buyer for China Changhong Computers (CCC). The buyer, Lawrence McCann, a long-time employee of CCC now nearing retirement, is such an aggressive, greedy bargainer that most salespeople hate to negotiate with him. He views each sales negotiation as a contest to be won, so he won't agree to sign a contract unless he feels that he's gotten the best of the supplier. Salespeople who do agree to the usual "seller lose–buyer win" agreement with Mr. McCann usually try to salvage a little profit on the contract by cutting some corners, usually on product quality or service. But this strategy often leads to dissatisfaction by CCC, so Mr. McCann usually moves on to another supplier for the next contract. The CCC account could be very valuable since its annual purchases of semiconductors exceed $6 million and are steadily increasing by about 5% a year. Mr. McCann, however, makes sales to CCC very dicey by insisting on squeezing out most of the profit margin and then switching suppliers if performance is less than fully satisfactory. Mr. McCann's assistant, Lester Bates, seems to be much more reasonable, but he doesn't say much in negotiations since McCann always dominates. Most of the sales reps who call on CCC seem to be looking forward to the day when Mr. McCann retires because they often subtly ask receptionists about his retirement plans.

Mr. McCann has just demanded that Janeen give him a whopping 20% discount on all CCC purchases – or, as he bluntly states, "I won't be buying anything from Micronix-Digital." If the 20% discount is provided, Mr. McCann promises to give Micronix-Digital all of CCC's semiconductor business this year. Janeen knows her company can't make any profit if she agrees to a 20% discount, and she's quite sure no other semiconductor supplier will offer such a large discount. While Mr. McCann continues talking, Janeen wonders how to respond to his demand.

Questions

1. Is it worthwhile for Janeen to negotiate with Mr. McCann when his demands are so unreasonable – and unprofitable if she agrees to the 20% discount? Explain.

2. Should Janeen do like most salespeople who "win" orders from Mr. McCann – simply cut back on product quality and/or service and be relatively unresponsive to complaints, so that her company can make a little profit? If she follows this strategy, Janeen realizes that she probably won't get any orders from Mr. McCann next year, and it may hurt her company's reputation – not only with CCC, but with other companies through negative word of mouth.

3. Janeen wants to keep CCC as a customer because it could become a valued account when Mr. McCann retires. So she's thinking about calling her sales manager to ask if she can offer the 20% discount and accept a loss on the contract in order to keep the customer relationship going with CCC. As her sales manager, what advice would you give Janeen?

4. What role, if any, does customer relationship management play when dealing with difficult buyers like Mr. McCann?

Case prepared by: Woodrow D. Richardson, University of Mary Washington

CASE 4.2 — Dasseaux Pharmaceuticals: Relationship Versus Transactional Selling

Dasseaux Pharmaceuticals is a French-owned firm that entered the U.S. market about five years ago. The company markets over-the-counter ophthalmic products east of the Mississippi River using two separate sales groups. One of the sales groups concentrates its efforts on independently owned retail drugstores and cooperatives, such as Good Neighbor Pharmacy, while the other much smaller group focuses on selling to chain drug stores such as Walgreen's and CVS Caremark, as well as to grocery chains, such as Kroger and Publix. The primary promotional thrust of Dasseaux Pharmaceuticals is on trade advertising to create brand awareness with pharmacists at independent drugstores and chains, as well as purchasing agents for large drugstore and grocery chains. They also provide point-of-purchase display materials and offer co-op advertising programs. The retail price of their products is competitive with similar products available in the market. But the retail margin for drugstores is a little higher than on other brands typically sold in the stores. Package design and color are contemporary, and product quality meets or exceeds competitive offerings.

Along with providing an extensive array of in-store promotional materials, Dasseaux Pharmaceuticals relies on the pharmacists to recommend its products. The success of this strategy depends a lot on how effective salespeople are when communicating to the pharmacists the fact that margins and therefore profits are higher with Dasseaux products.

Questions

1. Is a relationship selling approach or transactional selling approach best in this situation? Would the same approach work for independent and chain drugstores, or should a different selling approach be used? Justify your recommendation.

2. How would the method of prospecting differ between the independent drugstores and the chain drugstores?

Case prepared by: Balaji Krishnan, University of Memphis

CHAPTER 5

Sales Forecasting and Budgeting

Forecasting is important to almost all marketing organizations. Without a short-term forecast, sales managers would not have a logical basis for assigning workloads or deciding when and where to concentrate the sales effort. Without a long-term forecast, sales managers would not know how many salespeople the firm will need or how many should be promoted to a sales management position. The mere fact that a forecast has to be done admits that uncertainty exists in the process. In other words, forecasting is important, but the art and science of forecasting is imperfect, and every forecast possesses a degree of accuracy.

In many industries, managers still determine sales forecasts by comparing this year's sales with last year's sales for the same time period. But consider how much information is not included with this approach. For companies, such as Toyota, Eli Lilly Pharmaceuticals, and IBM, a simple prediction will be useful only when conditions like economic trends and consumer tastes remain unchanged. How likely are these conditions to remain unchanged? In the pharmaceutical industry, predicting demand for a new drug depends on variables like how many people are likely to contract a certain disease, the life expectancy of someone with the disease, and even the likelihood of getting Food and Drug Administration's (FDA) approval. Thus, forecasting is not only important, but it is also often complex. This chapter provides an overview of the topic of sales forecasting.

LEARNING OBJECTIVES

When you finish this chapter, you should be able to:

1. Relate sales forecasting to operational planning.
2. Know the most popular quantitative and qualitative sales forecasting tools.
3. Evaluate the various sales forecasting techniques.
4. Identify the purpose and benefits of sales budgets.
5. Prepare an annual sales budget.

Sales Forecasting and Its Relationship to Operational Planning

The Weather Channel may not provide the most exciting programming on television. But more U.S. viewers tune in to the Weather Channel at some time during the week than they do to practically all other topical cable networks. Why? People need to plan and organize their day, and the Weather Channel's local weather forecasts tell them what type of clothing to wear, and whether taking an umbrella is a good idea. A quick trip to the Weather Channel website (http://www.weather.com) or a check of the Weather Channel App can also be helpful when deciding what activities to choose for an upcoming weekend, or a trip abroad. Weather forecasts make planning and organizing family activities much easier.

Sales forecasts work in much the same way. Many operational and strategic decisions are much riskier without a sales forecast. A sales forecast is a prediction of the future market potential for a specific product or service or for a salesperson or sales group. Simply put, a sales forecast sets sales expectations for a given time period. And just like the weather forecast, an incorrect sales forecast may result in some stormy times ahead.

Companies sometimes develop strategic plans while paying little or no attention to forecasting, which is a bit like getting in a car without navigation. The odds are better you'll end up in a pleasant place if you start out with some idea of how far away and in what direction a pleasant place might be. A forecast provides the "how far" by estimating the amount of sales possible in a given situation and it also gives the direction by indicating what types of products customers are likely to want. Just as the navigation app on a smartphone tells you the directions to a particular location, and estimates the time it will take to get there, sales forecasts and plans identify alternative strategies and identify likely goals for a product's, salesperson's, or a company's sales.

Sales managers are much more likely to arrive at a pleasant outcome if they begin with valid data about the marketplace. Sales forecasts provide an assessment of both market and sales potentials. Market potential is a quantitative estimate, in either physical or monetary units, of the total sales for a product (or service) within a specified market. Sales potential is the portion of market potential that one among a set of competing firms can reasonably expect to obtain.

Sales managers use market and sales information in making critical operational decisions, such as setting logical and realistic sales goals for different sales territories and individual salespeople. Sales goals of this type are sometimes known as sales quotas. Sales managers should use this term with some caution, however, because salespeople often interpret *quota* to mean, "Do this or else!"

Forecasting is important for giant multinational corporations as well as small entrepreneurial firms. The forecast of sales potential becomes a starting point for sales and marketing planning, production scheduling, cash flow projections, financial planning, capital investment, procurement, inventory management, human resource planning, and budgeting. For example, before developing a production schedule, a company must know how much of their products will be sold. The production schedule, in turn, determines how much material the company will order and how much labor will be scheduled for the period. Sales managers must know their operating budget before they can determine how many new salespeople to hire.

Accurate sales forecasts are also important for avoiding unfavorable inventory situations. The purchasing department schedules purchases of supplies and raw materials according to sales forecasts. A large inventory of unsold goods piles up when the forecast is too high. Plant shutdowns, employee layoffs, and deteriorating raw materials can soon follow. On the other hand, a sales forecast that *underestimates* demand causes stockouts. Sales are lost as a result, and customers may be lost permanently as they are forced to seek products elsewhere. Table 5.1 summarizes the impact of erroneous sales forecasts on planning in various functional areas.

A typical time period for sales forecasts is one year. The following is an example of using a sales forecast to calculate how many salespeople are needed for an upcoming year. For our example, the sales potential approach will be used. Suppose a company expected $500,000 in annual sales. Over time, the sales managers have learned a typical salesperson can sell $50,000 per year and that 10% of the sales force will quit

TABLE **5.1**

Impact of Erroneous Sales Forecasts

Functional Area	Forecast	
	Too High	**Too Low**
Production	Excess output, unsold products	Inadequate output to meet customer demand
Inventory	Overstock	Understock
Finance	Idle cash	Cash shortage
Promotion	Wasted expenditures	Insufficient expenditures to cover the market
Distribution	Costly, insufficient to sell excess products	Inadequate to reach market
Pricing	Reductions to sell excess products	Price increases to allocate scarce products
Sales force	Too many salespeople, high selling costs	Too few salespeople, market not covered
Customer relations	Money wasted on unneeded activities, resulting in lower profits	Unsatisfactory due to out-of-stock products
Profits	Lower unit profits since expenses are high	Lower total profits because market not covered

during the year. One method of determining the number of salespeople needed is as follows:

$$NSP = \left(\frac{SalesPotential}{Sales\_per\_SP}\right) \times (1 + TO) = \left(\frac{\$500,000}{\$50,000 \bigg/ SP}\right) \times (1 + .1) = 10 \times 1.1 = 11$$

where

NSP = number of salespeople
Sales per SP = sales per salesperson
TO = turnover

Sales and Operational Planning (S&OP)

More and more firms are realizing how important sales are to operational planning. Many have adopted a formal sales and operational planning process (S&OP). An S&OP is an organized process that uses sales inputs to forecast business for future periods of varying length. Sales inputs come in the form of archived customer data, data on market conditions, and salesperson and sales management judgment. The S&OP then adjusts planning parameters (purchasing, labor schedules, and capital requirements) based on the forecast.

Figure 5.1 illustrates how an S&OP works.[1] The sales team starts with data from various sales records, such as order or shipment data, which helps them develop an initial sales forecast. Managers from various functional areas – including marketing,

| Analyze sales records | Develop a preliminary forecast | Have managers review forecast & adjust | Build a sales plan around the forecast | Make adjustments to operating plans |

FIGURE 5.1 Sales and operational planning process.

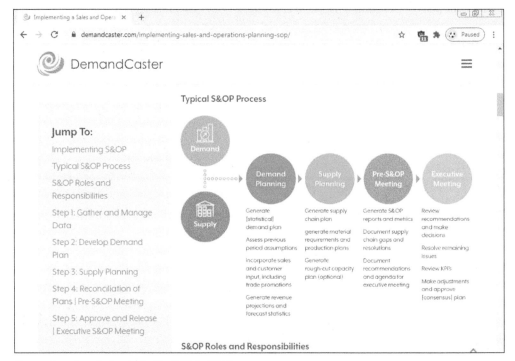

Companies rely on technologies like SAP for S&OP.
Source: https://www.demandcaster.com/implementing-sales-and-operations-planning-sop/.

sales, production, and finance – review the preliminary forecast and suggest any necessary adjustments. For example, a marketing manager may possess knowledge from a market research report that suggests some change from the previous period. The team then builds a sales plan around the resulting forecast. The plan includes operational parameters and potential trigger points for various contingencies. A contingency in this sense refers to events that are conceivable, but less likely than those based directly on the forecast. For example, a resort hotel may build in a plan to shift sales efforts away from vacationers and more toward business meetings if vacation bookings are not materializing as expected. This event may even be tied to a long-range seasonal weather forecast. In the end, operational actions and adjustments are driven by this plan.

Manufacturing, marketing, procurement, customer service, and sales all improve with an effective S&OP.[2] Successful S&OP programs improve efforts to fulfill customer purchases, customer retention, and gross margin. Five characteristics that help make S&OP programs successful include[3]:

1. *Supportive people* – All managerial levels must support the S&OP process and the resulting plans. Each department in the firm also must cooperate and respect the process.
2. *Process* – Regular meetings are important in developing a successful operational plan. The process also includes metrics and sales analytics to measure progress and provide benchmarks.
3. *Appropriate technology* – Market intelligence and other key information is integrated into a decision support system that automates some decisions with machine learning and provides reports that assist in further planning. Companies must maintain sufficient technological sophistication to ensure an efficient S&OP process.
4. *Strategy* – Effective strategy goes beyond finance and should align supply and inventories with demand. The strategy should also make continuous improvement possible and integrate customer data and sales analytics to highlight exactly where the company can create value.
5. *Performance measures* – Firms do not know how well they are doing unless they measure outcomes. Managers should derive metrics from the firm's goals, monitor progress to assess the plan's effectiveness, and include feedback in subsequent S&OP processes.

S&OP can extend beyond the walls of the firm, since the task of integrating data systems and planning processes often needs to include suppliers and downstream customers too. Delta Air Lines (www.delta.com) invested over $1 billion in a data analytics system that interconnected multiple databases to help it forecast sales for given routes, labor demand, fuel purchases, and baggage-moving demands.[4]

Estimating Consumer Demand

Sales managers estimate consumer market potentials from basic economic data. Analysts provide basic estimates of Buying Power/Potential (BP) by assessing product sales within a region given the region's specific population and income, all expressed as a percentage of regional sales potential for a product. To give an idea of how buying power is assessed, consider the market for business jets. In the United States, over 21,000 business jets are legally registered. Thus, there is one business jet for approximately every 16,000 U.S. citizens. In contrast, Brazil is the second leading nation in terms of number of business jets with over 1500 registered. That means one jet for every 135,000 people. The same ratio in China is more like 1 to every 3 million people. Thus, a firm selling business jets would look at the United States as the market with the greatest buying power. Sales analytics software like Mindtickle (www.mindtickle. com) facilitates such calculations within a given industry that enable a firm to adopt a degree of readiness based on the forecasted value of a potential customer.

Estimating Industrial Demand

Two approaches show how firms estimate industrial demand. One relies on the government's Standard Industrial Classification (SIC) – a uniform numbering system for categorizing nearly all industries according to their particular product or operation. The second approach involves surveys of buyer intentions, conducted by sales force personnel, the in-house marketing research staff, or an outside research agency.

Standardized Classification Systems The *Standard Industrial Classification Manual* was the previously used approach to estimate industrial demand based on information published by the U.S. Office of Management and Budget (OMB). The U.S. Department of Labor provides codes classifying all industries into several divisions, identifying industry and product subgroups with increasing specificity by up to seven digits. With that information, sales managers could classify current and potential customers with a standardized classification system and more easily locate prospective new customers, determine market potentials, and improve the accuracy of their sales forecasts.

Today, the North American Industrial Classification System (NAICS) has replaced the original SIC. Canada, Mexico, and the United States created this system for categorizing firms. The NAICS system was formally adopted with the 2002 Economic Census and the publication of the *2002 U.S. NAICS Manual*. NAICS codes can be accessed online through the U.S. Census Bureau (www.census.gov) and greatly facilitate statistical comparisons across industries.[5] An NAICS code exists for nearly 1200 different industries. Table 5.2 illustrates how the NAICS uses a numerical system for identifying industries in an increasingly specific manner. The guide to industry NAICS codes can be accessed at: https://www.census.gov/cgi-bin/sssd/naics/naicsrch?chart=2020.

TABLE **5.2**		
Sample NAICS Codes		
	Industry Description	**NAICS Code**
	Transportation	
		481
	Scheduled Air Service	48111
	Scheduled Freight Air Service	481112
	Scheduled Passenger Air Service	481111
	Wholesalers	
		424
	Pharmaceutical Wholesalers	424210
	Wine Wholesalers	424820
	Technical or Scientific Services	
		541
	Management Consulting Services	5416
	Sales Management Consulting Services	541613

IM_photo/Shutterstock.com

albertus engbers/123RF

marctran/123 RF

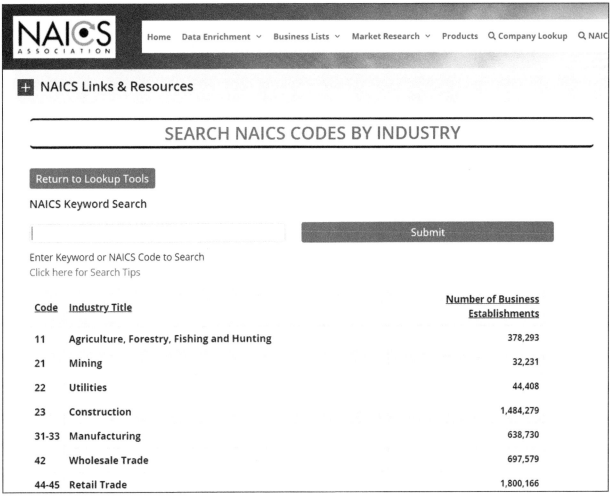

Looking up NAICS codes is easy.\
Source: https://www.naics.com/search-naics-codes-by-industry/, accessed April 4, 2020.

The North American Product Classification System (NAPCS) focuses on consumer products and service industries. The NAPCS works in much the same way as the NAICS.[6]

Once you find the NAICS designation for a targeted industry, you can identify firms in that industry using sources including the *U.S. Census of Manufacturers*, the *U.S. Survey of Manufacturers*, the *U.S. Industrial Outlook*, and *County Business Patterns*. Websites such as https://www.naics.com/company-lookup-tool/ also assist in identifying companies within an industry.

Buyer Intentions The second approach surveys potential industrial customers, such as those identified via a NAICS classification, to measure their purchase intentions – the likelihood they will actually purchase a given product. A company can send questionnaires to prospective customers within selected NAICS codes to measure purchase intentions over a given forecast period. Response rates (whether responses come by e-mail, online platforms like Qualtrics, or other electronic transmission format) are usually sufficiently high to estimate market potential accurately, particularly when executed by a professional marketing research company. We discuss surveys of buyer intentions in more detail in the next section.

Forecasting Approaches and Techniques

Managers can develop forecasts with either the breakdown approach or the build-up approach. The breakdown approach starts with a forecast of general economic conditions, typically projected gross national product (GNP) in constant dollars, along with projections of consumer and wholesale price indexes, interest rates, unemployment levels, and federal government expenditures. An industry forecast, company forecast, and product forecasts follow in succession. The "top-down" steps in developing a sales forecast using the breakdown approach are as follows:

1. Forecast general economic conditions.
2. Estimate the industry's total market potential for a product category.
3. Determine the share of this market the company currently holds and is likely to retain in view of competitive efforts.
4. Forecast sales of the product.
5. Use the sales forecast for operational planning and budgeting.

A model of the breakdown approach is shown in Figure 5.2.

The build-up approach is based on *primary research*, which is new data collected for the specific purpose at hand – in this case, a specific forecast for a specific company. The research either surveys individual salespeople about what they expect to sell in a future time period, or it asks customers about their purchase intentions. Managers then sum the individual estimates to provide a sales forecast.

Industrial buyers are generally cooperative, and it is sometimes possible to achieve a survey response rate of 50% or higher. Consumers are usually less cooperative. When

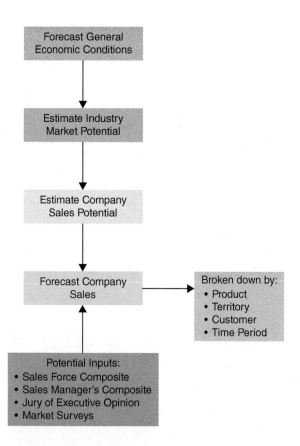

FIGURE 5.2 Sales fore-
casting model.

a representative random sample is impossible or impractical, firms rely on nonprobability sampling techniques. The response rate with these is usually sufficiently high to develop a good estimate of the potential market. When using nonprobability samples, however, firms need to closely examine profiles of respondents to assess their relative representativeness.

Because no consensus exists on which approach is better, some companies prefer to use both the breakdown and the build-up approach to increase their confidence in the sales forecast. In general, the breakdown approach is less expensive because aggregate, publicly distributed forecasts from secondary sources provide the basis for decision-making. Secondary sources such as university libraries, policy agencies, and the federal government make many forecasts available to the public, often free of charge and sometimes through the Internet. But there are also many commercial sources of information such as Salesforce.com and Dun and Bradstreet (dnb.com). The breakdown approach is particularly useful and reliable when forecasting for periods of six months or longer. The build-up approach becomes more attractive as the time frame gets shorter. Primary data collection can be tailored specifically for the company, and for the particular time frame of interest.

We classify the more common sales forecasting techniques as either quantitative or nonquantitative, as shown in Figure 5.3. The nonquantitative methods rely primarily on judgment or opinion, whereas the quantitative methods use statistical techniques with varying degrees of complexity.

Nonquantitative Forecasting Techniques

Many companies use several methods to compare sales projections before settling on a particular sales forecast. Nonquantitative forecasting techniques are often called *subjective forecasts*, because they're based on knowledgeable people's opinions instead of being analytically derived. Results range from very good to poor, but in some cases, subjective forecasts are superior to expensive, sophisticated, quantitative techniques. Nonquantitative forecasts are popular and can be a practical alternative to quantitative approaches. Two major types of nonquantitative forecasts are judgment methods and counting methods.

Nonquantitative

◇ **Judgment methods**
- Jury of executive opinion
- Sales force composite

◇ **Counting methods**
- Survey of customers' buying intentions
- Test marketing

Quantitative

◇ **Time-series methods**
- Moving averages
- Exponential smoothing
- Trend analysis using ARIMA

◇ **Causal or association methods**
- Correlation–regression
- Econometric models
- Input–output models

FIGURE 5.3 Classification of sales forecasting approaches.

Judgment Methods The simplest judgment method is the naïve forecast. It assumes, naively, that the next period's sales will be the same as they were in the previous period, and that an extrapolation of the last period's sales will give an acceptable estimate of the next period's sales. This method provides some initial insight, but other judgment methods are typically more accurate.

The jury of executive opinion method asks key managers within the company for their best estimate of sales in a given planning horizon and combines the results to develop the forecast. Some managers may support their opinions with facts, while others may rely on intuition alone. The consensus is generally better than any single person's opinion.

The jury of executive opinion can be done quickly and easily. In industries characterized by rapid changes, it may be the best forecasting approach because it's flexible and fast. It's also often less expensive than other methods.

But the executive opinion method has several disadvantages. Since it's based on opinions and not facts, it can be unscientific and little better than a guess. Second, the technique diverts top managers from other tasks that may be more important, and often they are not in touch with developments in local markets anyway. For example, could we expect the CIO or CFO to know about future sales in a particular market? Despite these disadvantages, smaller companies often use the jury of executive opinion method.

The sales force composite method is similar, but it asks the *sales force* for their best estimates of sales in the planning horizon. Managers evaluate and adjust each salesperson's estimate before combining them to form an overall forecast. A list of the advantages of this approach is as follows:

- Assigns forecasting responsibility to those held responsible for making the sales
- Uses specialized knowledge of salespeople in the field
- Helps salespeople accept sales quotas assigned to them because they participate in developing forecasts
- Yields results that are often more reliable and accurate because a larger number of knowledgeable individuals contribute to them
- Enables estimates to be prepared by products, customers, and territories so a final, detailed forecast is readily available

Here are the disadvantages of the sales force composite method:

- Relies on input from salespeople who are not trained in forecasting; so forecasts are often too optimistic or too pessimistic
- Allows a salesperson to deliberately underestimate their forecast so quotas can be more easily reached
- Yields forecasts based on present rather than future conditions, because salespeople often lack the perspective for future planning
- Requires a considerable amount of sales force time that otherwise could be spent in the field attracting new customers
- Relies on salespeople who may not be interested in forecasting and, as a result, put little effort into sales predictions

Counting Methods Forecasting approaches that tabulate responses to questions on surveys or count the numbers of buyers or purchases are called counting methods. Two types of counting methods are surveys of customer buying intentions and test marketing.

Surveys of buying intentions sample customers and ask about their intentions to buy various products over a specified period. Managers then combine the responses into one forecast, generally by products, customers, and territories. This method of forecasting is particularly useful for companies selling industrial products, because their customers are easily identified and few in number, able to estimate their purchasing requirements well in advance of ordering, and highly likely to follow through on buying intentions. Some advantages of using surveys of buying intentions are as follows:

- The actual product users determine the forecasts.
- Forecasts are relatively fast and inexpensive when only a small number of customers are surveyed.
- Research gives the sales forecaster a good prediction of customers' buying intentions and some of the subjective reasoning behind their answers.
- Research gives the forecaster a viable forecasting basis when others may be inadequate or impossible to use, such as when there is no historical data.

The disadvantages are as follows:

- Surveys can be expensive and time-consuming in markets with a large number of customers who are not easily located.
- Buyer intentions can be inaccurate, since what people say they're going to buy and what they actually buy can differ.
- Forecasts depend on the judgment and cooperation of the product users, but some of the users may be uncooperative or uninformed.
- Buying intentions, especially for industrial products, often are subject to multiple effects because the demand for industrial products is derived from the demand for consumer products.

Estimating sales for a new product is the most difficult type of forecast since no historical sales data is available. A new product's sales forecast is particularly difficult when the new product is very different from the company's current product mix. A popular forecasting method for consumer-packaged goods products is a type of counting method called test marketing. Test marketing is like a full-dress rehearsal performed to a limited audience. Actual sales results from a limited market test project consumer reactions in general before expanding to regional and national markets. By carefully selecting a few representative market areas, marketing managers can observe the impact on sales of various combinations of the marketing mix and use measures of market share in these small markets to forecast the total market. For example, if Samsung (www.samsung.com) achieves a 10% market share in the test markets for a new Galaxy smartphone, it will assume it can achieve approximately this share in the expanded market.

Mobile phone manufacturers such as Samsung and Apple, as well as other third-party providers, have mobile marketing apps that match services to customers' smart phones via Bluetooth. The objective of these apps is to identify smartphone users' interest in downloadable wallpapers, mobile coupons, video clips, and other mobile content. Apps like these facilitate test marketing of downloadable products.

Some managers believe that test marketing takes too long (often a year or more), costs too much, and reveals too much to competitors who often monitor the test markets and may even attempt to disrupt the test or distort results. But in recent years these limitations have been mostly overcome with online test marketing, particularly in consumer marketing. To minimize the likelihood of competitors observing field tests, some companies use laboratory testing of products instead of field tests. Laboratory methods ask a panel of customers to evaluate different marketing mix combinations and choose a particular product. Laboratory tests provide more privacy, lower costs, and quicker answers than traditional test marketing does, particularly when the tests can be carried out online.

Quantitative Forecasting Techniques

User-friendly statistical software enables sales managers to develop forecasts that only trained statisticians used to do, and to "crunch the numbers" with numerous quantitative sales forecasting techniques. Two broad categories of methods are time-series analyses and causal or association methods.

Time-Series Methods Time-series techniques use historical data to predict future sales. We'll discuss three types: moving averages, exponential smoothing, and ARIMA. When using time-series methods, forecasters look for the following four factors:

1. *Trends* – Upward or downward movements in a time series as a result of basic developments in population, technology, or capital formation.
2. *Periodic movements* – Consistent patterns of sales changes in a given period, such as a year, generally called *seasonal variations*. Snow skis and boats are examples of products that have seasonal patterns.
3. *Cyclical movements* – Wave-like movements of sales that are longer in duration than a year and often irregular in occurrence, such as business recessions. The housing market is characterized by cyclical fluctuations.
4. *Erratic movements* – One-time specific events – such as wars, strikes, snowstorms, hurricanes, fires, and floods – that are not predictable.

All these factors can affect sales forecasts. Time-series methods attempt to separate their impact from random variations and identify true trends in data.

Moving Averages Forecasts developed using a moving average predict future sales as a mathematical function of sales in recent time periods. The statistical approach is based on an average of several months' sales, where the high and low values are made less extreme. As the forecasters add each new period's sales data to the average, they remove from the total the data from the oldest period. They compute a new average for each period, and the new average is the moving average. Consider a sales manager trying to project sales for the year 2021. Data is available showing the total sales obtained in each year from 2010 through 2020. One method of forecasting is to predict 2021 sales will be the same as sales in 2020. Alternatively, the sales manager could base the forecast on one of the other years' results or take an average of all the data. The moving average provides a compromise between these approaches by assuming the information from the most recent years' sales performance is more likely to reflect the current situation than is data from many years ago.

Table 5.3 illustrates predictions made using the moving average and several other methods. The data are from years 2005 through 2020. The forecasted sales are for years 2011 and 2019. The "Simple average" column simply takes the mean of the previous years' sales. So, the prediction for 2011 (1158 units) was based on data from 2005 to 2010. The prediction for 2021 is based on sales data from 2005 through 2020. The three-year moving averages use the average of only the most recent three years. Thus, the 2021 forecast is based only on sales data from the years 2020, 2019, and 2018. Similarly, the five-year moving average is based on an average from 2016 through 2020.

Notice in this example the forecasts are not equally accurate. The 2011 simple average forecast proved more accurate than either the 3- or 5-year forecast. Sales for this company seem particularly volatile. When this is the case, an average containing more data, rather than less, is likely to be more accurate. But for firms experiencing growth or a decline in sales, the moving averages will generally be more accurate. For instance, three-month moving averages are generally used to predict sales technology products in a given month.

TABLE **5.3**

Time-Series Forecasts Using Several Average Methods

Year	Actual Sales (Units)	Simple Average	3-year Moving Average	5-year Moving Average	Exponential Smoothing
2005	1500				
2006	750				
2007	1250				
2008	800				
2009	1750				
2010	900				
2011	1400	**1158**	**1150**	**1090**	**1167**
2012	750				
2013	900				
2014	1125				
2015	900				
2016	1000				
2017	500				
2018	650				
2019	1150				
2020	850				
2021	TBD	**1011**	**883**	**830**	**917**

Exponential Smoothing Like the moving average, exponential smoothing is useful in spotting trends. Exponential smoothing is a type of moving average that represents the weighted sum of all past numbers in a time series, with the heaviest weight placed on the most recent data. Exponential smoothing modifies the moving-average method by systematically stressing recent sales results while de-emphasizing older sales data. Exponential smoothing overcomes a significant disadvantage of the moving average. That is, the moving average does *not* adjust for recency in sales trends. Instead, the forecasting equation for exponential smoothing more heavily weights the more recent data points. Thus, for example, if a three-year weighted average is used, the forecast (*FC*) for 2021 can be computed as follows:

$$FC_{2021} = \frac{1}{6}(Sales_{2018}) + \frac{1}{3}(Sales_{2019}) + \frac{1}{2}(Sales_{2020})$$

Notice that the most recent year (2020) is weighted with the largest of the three numbers representing weights (1/2). The most distant data year, 2018, is weighted the smallest (1/6).

Using data from Table 5.3, this yields a prediction of 917 units for 2021, which we compute as follows:

$$FC_{2021} = \frac{1}{6}(Sales_{2018}) + \frac{1}{3}(Sales_{2019}) + \frac{1}{2}(Sales_{2020}) = \frac{1}{6}(650) + \frac{1}{3}(1150) + \frac{1}{2}(850)$$

$$FC_{2021} = 917 \text{ units}$$

In 2011, the exponential smoothing forecast was the most accurate. Perhaps the same will be true for 2021.

Sophisticated algorithms exist to help determine the weighting scheme that is most accurate in a given situation. Exponential smoothing is particularly appropriate in industries experiencing high growth and can also reflect seasonality in forecasts for short period. Exponential smoothing and moving averages are increasingly being used by sales managers because many easy-to-use point-and-click options are available in standard software packages. With these software packages, sales managers need not even enter a formula – they simply select the years to be included, and the software does the rest.

Other Trend Analyses Managers can use many other statistical approaches to prepare forecasts using trends over time. Simple regression predicts sales for a period using time as an independent variable. An ARIMA (autoregressive integrated moving average) model is a sophisticated forecasting approach based on the moving average concept. The model incorporates information about trends by spotting patterns in the fluctuations in data. The exact process for conducting an ARIMA forecast is beyond the scope of this text. However, ARIMA models have been useful in predicting many types of sales, from predicting the demand for tourism to the sale of mountain bikes and smartphones.

Causal/Association Methods Instead of predicting directly on the basis of judgment or historical data, causal/association methods attempt to identify the factors affecting sales and to determine the nature of the relationship between them. Causal, or associative, methods include correlation–regression analysis, econometric models, and input–output models.

Correlation analysis is a statistical approach analyzing the way variables are related to one another, or *move together*, in some way. A correlation coefficient is a measure of how much two variables are related to one another. Correlations alone do not imply cause and effect. Regression analysis, which you may be familiar with, is a statistical approach to predicting a dependent variable such as sales, using one or more independent variables, such as advertising expenditures. Regression analysis can examine whether a change in sales is associated with a change in advertising expenditures or a change in labor costs. Managers often use scatter diagrams with correlation and regression analyses. A scatter diagram plots one variable against another to see if there is a pattern in the way one variable varies with another. Predictor variables, independent or X variables, are displayed along the horizontal axis of the graph. The variable being predicted is the dependent, or Y variable, and appears on the vertical axis. Figure 5.4 shows a typical scatter diagram. Notice how the plotted points in this example tend to line up. Such an alignment indicates the two variables are related because the plotted dots tend to follow a line.

$$Y = -701.2 + 39.0X \qquad R^2 = 0.85, \ F_{1,13} = 73.8, \ p < 0.0001$$

Simple Regression The relationship between two variables is shown by fitting a straight line to plotted points. We can use visual inspection to draw the line with a ruler, but this may not be the most reliable approach, because different analysts may put the line in slightly different places. Simple regression finds the best-fitting line mathematically using the least squares estimation formula for a straight line:

$$Y = a + bX,$$

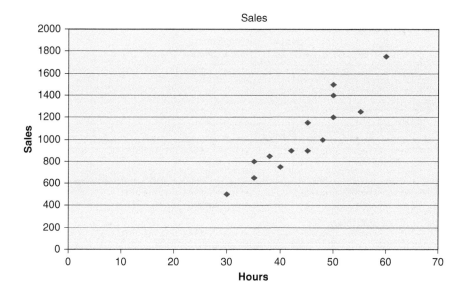

FIGURE 5.4 A scatter plot of sales against labor expenditures.

where *a* is the *intercept* (intersecting with the vertical axis) and *b* is the *slope* of the trend line. The least squares method estimates coefficients (*a*, *b*) by mathematically minimizing the squared differences between actual plotted sales and the values predicted by the regression line.

A trend analysis can provide a quantitative forecast. In a trend analysis forecasting sales, the dependent variable is sales, and the independent variable is time. If such a model produced an estimated regression equation of $Y = 33.5 + 10.5X$, we could predict sales for any year by inserting the desired time period for X. We can derive year 5 sales, for example, by multiplying 5 by the slope (trend) coefficient of 10.5 and adding the constant term (intercept) of 33.5. The result is a forecast of 86.

Multiple Regression Regression analysis can use many kinds of independent variables to produce a forecast. In Figure 5.4, sales (dependent variable) are forecasted with labor hours (independent variable). If a salesperson works 50 hours, the regression model predicts $1249 in sales. The model explains a significant portion of sales, as evidenced by the statistical significance value ($p < 0.0001$), meaning that labor hours explain a significant portion of the variability in sales. Another way of looking at this is by knowing labor hours, we can predict sales with some accuracy.

Simple regression describes the relationship between a single independent variable and a single dependent variable. In our example, *time* (labor hours) is the independent variable and *sales* is the dependent variable. More realistically, sales are probably associated with several independent variables (advertising expenditures, number of sales calls, prices, or interest rates). Multiple regression is a tool for forecasting a single dependent variable like sales using more than one independent variable simultaneously. Software programs such as Excel, SPSS (an IBM product), and SAS JMP, simplify forecasting by performing the mathematical calculations needed to estimate a multiple regression model. The results show the strength of relationships between the independent variables and the single dependent variable. We can make forecasts using multiple regression for any given quantitative values

Model Summary

Model	R	R Square	Adjusted R Square	Std. Error of the Estimate
1	.990[a]	.979	.974	204.31553

a. Predictors: (Constant), Number of Salespersons, Advertsing, Price

ANOVA[b]

Model		Sum of Squares	df	Mean Square	F	Sig.
1	Regression	21932369	3	7310789.625	175.130	.000[a]
	Residual	459193.2	11	41744.836		
	Total	22391562	14			

a. Predictors: (Constant), Number of Salespersons, Advertsing, Price

b. Dependent Variable: Sales

Coefficients[a]

Model		Unstandardized Coefficients		Standardized Coefficients		
		B	Std. Error	Beta	t	Sig.
1	(Constant)	1916.341	1081.924		1.771	.104
	Advertising	8.656	.722	.773	11.985	.000
	Price	−4.740	2.013	−177	−2.354	.038
	Number of Salespersons	132.198	32.698	.219	4.043	.002

a. Dependent Variable: Sales

FIGURE 5.5 Multiple regression of sales and three independent variables.

of the independent variables. The software packages also greatly enhance graphical presentations of forecasts.

As an example, EMCO sells mobile telecommunications equipment and has 15 years of data in its data cloud storage. The single dependent variable is sales, and three independent variables are advertising, price, and number of salespeople. The output from the SPSS multiple regression appears in Figure 5.5. Like simple regression, SPSS produces coefficient estimates that represent the relationship between each independent variable and the dependent variable, annual sales. Using the constant term (Y intercept) of 1916.341 and the unstandardized coefficients (weightings) for the three variables = 8.656, −4.740, and 132.198, we derive this forecasting equation:

$$Y = 1916.341 + 8.656\,X_1 + -4.740\,X_2 + 132.198\,X_3$$

where

Y = annual sales
X_1 = advertising expenditures
X_2 = price
X_3 = number of salespersons.

We can generate a forecast for any values of the independent variables. Suppose the independent variables take on the following values:

- $X_1 = 10$ ($100,000 in advertising)
- $X_2 = 100
- $X_3 = 5$ salespeople

Then, substituting these values into the regression equation yields the following result:

$$Y = 1916.3 + 8.656(10) - 4.740(100) + 132.20(5)$$
$$Y = 1916.3 + 86.56 - 474.0 + 661 = 2189.9$$

The equation indicates that annual sales increase as advertising expenditures and number of salespersons increase. The sign of the coefficient for X_2 (price) is negative, which indicates that as we lower price, sales increase. A *multiple R* of 0.990 is a correlation coefficient reflecting the degree of association between the dependent variable and the three independent variables. The *multiple R-square*, also called the coefficient of determination, indicates the percentage (97.9%) of total variation in Y (sales) explained by the three independent variables (X_1, advertising; X_2, price; and X_3, number of salespersons).

The *standard error of the estimate* is a measure of the accuracy of the prediction. That is, it is the range of error around the sales forecast. The standard error 204.316 means there is a 68% chance (one standard deviation) that actual dollar sales will be within ±204.316 of any forecast made with our derived equation. A model F statistic also demonstrates that a significant (significance level < 0.000) portion of the variance in sales is explained by the three independent variables.

We can analyze forecasting quality by computing standard errors for the coefficients for our three independent variables. These error coefficients show the expected dispersion (or scatter) around the coefficient estimates. *F-values* indicate that all three independent variables are highly significant in forecasting sales. Thus, advertising expenditures and number of salespersons are key variables in understanding and predicting sales from period to period. Similarly, price is important too; and as we expected, lower prices are associated with higher sales.

When using multiple regression for forecasting purposes, the model R^2 is an important diagnostic tool for estimating the accuracy of prediction. R^2 values range from 0 to 1. A value of one means that 100% of the variance in the dependent variable is explained by the set of independent variables – in this case, the forecast would be exact. Conversely, if the R^2 is 0, the independent variables do not enable us to predict with any accuracy. In other words, we may as well use a wild guess. In practice, R^2 values below 0.2 suggest poor forecasting ability. Values between 0.2 and 0.5 indicate modest predictive power, values above 0.5 to 0.75 indicate good predictive power, and values above 0.75 indicate excellent predictive power. Thus, the equation in our example shows very high predictive power.

Econometric Models Econometric models are based on a series of regression equations. The number of equations can range from 1 to 1000 or more. These models have been developed to trace economic conditions in the United States by industry, and their objective is to capture, in the form of equations, complex interrelationships among the factors affecting either the total economy or industry and/or company sales. For example, consumer spending is related to disposable income and interest rates, while fixed capital spending is explained by the past value of capital, interest rates,

Box 5.1 | Sales Management in Action 5.1

How Many Drugs Can Be Sold?

New product development is very important in the pharmaceutical industry. Not only does new product development ensure the health of the firm, but also the quality of life and even the survival of many consumers depends on continued advancement in pharmaceutical products. For a host of reasons, however, accurate sales forecasts for any given drug, in particular a new drug, are complicated by many uncertainties. Not the least of these is that an entirely separate forecasting process is likely needed to predict the timing of release of the new drug. Even once the product has been refined, FDA approval can take years. In addition, new therapeutic treatments may make the drug obsolete. Competition from generic drug companies also affects sales, making up a dynamic but growing market that has grown about 20% a year in recent years.

Managers in the pharmaceutical industry are constantly trying to improve their sales forecasts. Multiple regression enables them to consider information about the lifestyles of market segments, aspects of the approval process, and even information about competing companies, among other things. In addition, online and cloud technology enables firms to harvest, from the "information market," data they might not otherwise have found. Eli Lilly and other pharmaceutical companies are using these approaches to forecast which developmental products are most likely to win FDA approval. Information may also include insights into potential consumer reactions. In either event, pharmaceutical forecasts that take into account more information than simple trends from the big data explosion will achieve greater accuracy in their forecasts.

Sources: Adapted from 10 Best Anti-Aging Products and Wrinkle Creams of 2019 (2019). https://www.goodhouse-keeping.com/beauty-products/g723/anti-aging-skin-awards/ (accessed September 2019); Kamal, R., Cox, C., and McDermott, D. (2019). Recent and forecasted trends in prescription drug spending. Kaiser Foundation Health System Tracker, https://www.healthsystemtracker.org/chart-collection/recent-forecasted-trends-prescription-drug-spending/ (accessed September 2019); and Ostrover, S. (2005). Employing information markets to achieve truly collaborative sales forecasting. *Journal of Business Forecasting* 9–12.

and economic activity. Another purpose of such models is to predict the future. Large corporations such as General Motors, General Electric, Amazon, and IBM develop their own econometric models, but off-the-shelf data analytics packages are increasingly available for medium sized and even smaller companies. Econometric models require specialized expertise to develop but there are third party vendors that can access company and industry data to prepare these types of forecasts. Regression approaches offer a less expensive alternative for firms with fewer resources. But data analytics predictive models are increasingly being used by more companies to develop overall forecasts as well as company sales forecasts.

Input–Output Models Input–output models are complex systems showing the amount of input required from each industry for a specified output of another industry. This type of model takes time to develop and is relatively more expensive, but generally provides good intermediate and long-range forecasts for industries such as metals, energy utilities, and automobiles. Due to the difficulty of building large input–output model, this type of forecasting typically is outsourced to specialized experts.

Evaluating Forecasting Approaches

Quantitative sales forecasting techniques use a variety of sophisticated mathematics and statistics. Some of the techniques are expensive, time-consuming, and require considerable forecaster expertise. In fact, using a complex forecasting technique is no promise of predictive accuracy. Companies with limited historical data or in rapidly changing markets often have to use less-sophisticated techniques.

Nonquantitative techniques have been criticized for their lack of consistency. But with the more widespread availability of user-friendly software and historical data, their use is increasing. In selecting a forecasting method, sales managers should consider several criteria:

- *Comprehensibility* – Sales managers must understand the basic methods of developing forecasts. This understanding provides confidence in the estimates of different approaches. It's harder to be confident when using highly complicated quantitative techniques. If only statisticians can understand the way the estimates are derived, sales executives and other decision makers will not trust the results as much as they would a process they at least partially understand.
- *Accuracy* – A forecasting method must provide results that are sufficiently accurate for the purpose desired. Most forecasts contain inaccuracies but still furnish valuable information for managerial decision-making. A projection within 10% accuracy is considered acceptable by many sales forecasters. In fact, S&OP programs generally are based on an outcome forecasted under pessimistic conditions and one under optimistic conditions. Thus, a forecast is actually a range of values instead of one number.
- *Timeliness* – The forecasting method must generate forecasts in time for managers to use them. Complex quantitative techniques or surveys can require weeks to deliver a forecast. Thus, sales managers who need answers quickly may resort to faster but potentially less accurate estimates.
- *Quality and quantity of information* – Any forecasting method is limited by the amount and quality of information available to the organization. In forecasting as in other areas, "garbage" input leads to "garbage" output (GIGO).
- *Qualified personnel* – Experts can give opinions on qualitative techniques like the jury of executives' opinions or the Delphi method. The Delphi method polls a small panel of experts concerning future events. Unlike the jury of executive opinion, these experts are generally from outside the firm and often from closely related industries. Once the company has collected the experts' opinions, an analyst summarizes the results in a report. Thus, companies such as Samsung, Huawei, or Xiaomi might use the Delphi technique to estimate the effect of the Apple iPhone (or iWatch) on the demand for their own products. The specialists in this case might be top executives at media, entertainment, and telecommunications companies. But other trained specialists may be needed for some advanced quantitative forecasting approaches. Sales managers hiring people to consult on the sales forecast must be sure that consultants are fully qualified for the job.
- *Flexibility* – Managers continually monitor actual sales for any deviations from forecast that may indicate the need for revised sales forecasting tools. Their sales forecasting methods should be flexible enough to adapt to changing conditions.
- *Costs/Benefits* – The benefits from forecasting must more than offset the costs of generating the sales forecast. And if the cost of an incorrect forecast is high, then sales managers should spare little expense in deriving an accurate forecast.

Once again, forecasters should use more than one method so they can compare the results of several techniques. More and more, forecasts are provided by artificial intelligence platforms such as Salesforce.com's Einstein. Those platforms make use of various simulation and statistical models to provide projections. The bottom line is that managers should examine forecasts from several sources and hopefully, the various models will converge to provide more precision and accuracy. In much the same way, hurricane forecasters rely on more than one forecast model in trying to make their own decisions on where a hurricane might go. Finally, it's good to examine several "what-if" scenarios that incorporate all the bad assumptions as well as all the good ones.

When the sales manager has an acceptable sales forecast, the next area of concern is to obtain sufficient funds (i.e. a budget) to execute the sales strategy. Our next discussion topic, therefore, is sales budget planning.

Sales Budget Planning

Sales managers must decide either what level of sales they can obtain with a given budget, or what level of expenditures they will need to reach forecasted sales. A sales budget is a financial sales plan outlining how to allocate resources and selling efforts to achieve the sales forecast. Sales forecasts and sales budgets are interdependent planning tools that require close coordination with other marketing activities. If a sales budget is inadequate, the sales forecast will be accurate only by pure chance. When the importance of a forecast increases, so does the sales budget.

Sales budgets are used in planning, coordinating, and controlling selling activities. Sales managers should appreciate the significance and value of sales budgets in the overall planning and administration of a sales territory.

The Planning Function

Sales managers must translate department goals and objectives into actionable tasks. Each task is associated with an estimated cost. Budgeting, therefore, is an operational planning process expressed in financial terms. The budget provides a guide for action toward achieving the organization's objectives.

Budgets exist for different planning horizons. A long-range budget may require a forecast for five years or more. Typically, a one-year operational budget includes a forecast for the upcoming 12 months. Short-range budgets may cover periods of six months or less. A quarterly budget is commonly required. Thus, firms should have both long- and short-range budgets.

For a smooth transition from one period to another, some sales budgets overlap – that is, a 12-month budget might include a three-month overlap period at the beginning and end of the year, so the actual budget plan covers 18 months. Other sales organizations operate on a continuous budget by projecting a month or a quarter ahead as each month or quarter ends. This procedure forces sales managers to continuously revise and update the budget in response to external and internal opportunities and problems.

The Coordinating Function

Sales budgets must be closely integrated with budgets for other marketing functions. Personal selling is only one element in the promotional mix, and promotion is only one element in the marketing mix. We can't develop distribution plans, for example, until we know the amount of products that must be distributed. This number depends on the sales forecast, which is part of the budget. The sales budget should reflect a well-thought-out allocation of resources and efforts designed to meet goals and objectives.

TABLE **5.4**

Budget Variances

	VARIANCES			
	Budget	**Actual**	**Favorable**	**Unfavorable**
Sales: Expense;	$715,000	$733,000	$18,000	
▪ **Direct Selling**	384,000	375,900	8,000	
▪ **Sales Promotion**	107,250	117,328		$10,078
▪ **Advertising**	87,000	93,281		6,281
▪ **Administrative**	44,500	43,617	883	
Total Expenses	$622,750	$630,126		7,376
Profits (before taxes)	$ 92,250	$102,874	$10,624	

The Controlling Function

The control function of a sales budget is to evaluate actual results against sales budget expectations. Differences between them are budget variances. Favorable variances reflect a positive budget outcome, such as lower actual costs than were anticipated to produce a forecasted amount of sales. In this case, the sales manager might reduce future budgets in an effort to maintain accuracy. Unfavorable variances are the result of actual costs that are higher than anticipated costs and require corrective action. If the firm cannot avoid the higher costs in future periods, a budget adjustment is needed.

An illustration of budget variances is shown in Table 5.4. You can see that unfavorable variances are easy to identify. Sales managers are responsible for determining why actual promotional and advertising expenses exceeded budgeted amounts. This doesn't mean managers should always avoid unfavorable expense variances. For example, actual sales may also be higher in the same period that expenses are higher than expected. Notice in the table that sales are $18,000 more than budgeted or forecast. Thus, as long as expenses are proportionately higher or less, the higher expenses are likely justified. Using the budget variances approach enables a sales manager to more quickly spot potential problems or to better plan for unexpected developments such as higher-than-expected sales.

Preparing the Annual Sales Budget

Preparing the annual sales budget is often considered one of the most tedious and unrewarding jobs the sales manager does. Yet managers should view the sales budget instead as an opportunity for profit planning, and for obtaining the resources needed to achieve projected sales. Budgets benefit the sales department in the following ways:

- Ensure a systematic approach to allocation resources.
- Develop the sales manager's knowledge of profitable resource utilization.
- Create awareness of the necessity of coordinating selling efforts with other divisions of the company.
- Establish standards for measuring the performance of the sales organization.
- Obtain input from all areas of the company in the profit-planning process.

Most sales organizations have specified procedures and timetables for developing the sales budget. The following sections describe a typical set of steps.

Step 1: Review and Analyze the Situation

Beginning with the last budget period's variances, *where, when, and how much* were the deviations from planned performance, and *who* was responsible? Review of past budget performance helps the sales manager avoid variances in the coming period. Changes in the current budget period, such as introduction of new products, marketing mix adjustments, or developments in the uncontrollable marketing environment, must be anticipated and worked into the sales budget. Here are some common line items in sales budgets:

- *Salaries* – for salespeople, administrative support, sales supervisors, and managers
- *Direct selling expenses* – travel, lodging, food, and entertainment
- *Commissions and bonuses*
- *Benefit package* – social security, medical insurance, retirement contributions, and stock options
- *Office expenses* – mailing, telephone, office supplies, miscellaneous
- *Promotional materials* – selling aids, premiums, contest awards, product samples, catalogs, price lists, and so on
- *Advertising*

Step 2: Communicate Sales Goals and Objectives

All management levels must be fully informed about sales goals and objectives, including their relative priorities, to ensure everyone is developing their budgets using the same assumptions and general guidelines. Encourage participation of all supervisors and managers in the budget process so that, having been a part of its development, they will accept responsibility for the budget and enthusiastically implement it.

Step 3: Identify Specific Market Opportunities and Problems

Sales managers and salespeople should use budget resources to pursue specific market opportunities as well as deal with problems. This enables them to respond in a timely manner.

Step 4: Develop a Preliminary Allocation of Resources

Initially, assign resources to particular activities, customers, products, and territories. Later, you can make revisions in the initial sales budget. But make all budgets as realistic as possible at each development stage to maximize their favorable impact on the organization. When you accomplish budget goals through a cooperative team effort, you create a feeling of organizational confidence. Instead of emphasizing punishment for failure to stay within budgets, sales managers should stress rewards and public commendations for staying within budgets, thereby encouraging positive attitudes toward budget goals and pride in their achievement.

Step 5: Prepare a Budget Presentation

All organizational divisions clamor for an increased allocation of funds. Unless sales managers can justify each line item in their budgets on the basis of its profit contribution, the item will be ripe for higher management to cut. Succinct, well-reasoned written and oral budget presentations are worth the preparation they require. They're even more effective when supported by alternate budget scenarios that are easy to develop with spreadsheet software.

Step 6: Implement the Budget and Provide Periodic Feedback

Although salespeople can be trained to be more budget conscious and provide early warning of budget overruns, the sales manager must ensure that sales revenue and cost ratios remain within reasonable budget limits. Sales managers might consider a monthly or quarterly sales budget and control chart (illustrated in Table 5.5) to monitor budget variances and make timely corrective actions. They can post this on the company website or automatically distribute it via the company intranet.

Budget preparation is easier and more systematic today because many software packages are available to facilitate the process. For example, the IBM sales and support environment solution integrates existing customer and research information across the firm, so it's available in real time for budgeting as well as for other selling objectives. SAP (www.sap.com) also offers an integrated sales budgeting option in its enterprise software platform. These two alternatives are more complex, but you can find many options that are available off the shelf by using a search engine and entering the keywords "sales budget software."

TABLE 5.5

Monthly Sales Budget

	January			February		
Line Items	Budget	Actual	Variance	Budget	Actual	Variance
Sales Expenses						
▪ Salaries						
▪ Commissions						
▪ Bonuses						
▪ Social Security						
▪ Medical Insurance						
▪ Retirement						
Travel						
▪ Food						
▪ Lodging						
▪ Entertainment						
Office Expenses						
▪ Mail						
▪ Telephone						
▪ Miscellaneous						
Promotion						
▪ Samples						
▪ Premiums						
▪ Technology						
Advertising						

Box 5.2 | Sales Management in Action 5.2

Big Predictions??

Not all forecasts are directed specifically toward some company's sales and not all expert predictions are correct. Check out these *infamous* forecasts by technology, Internet, and social media experts:

- Marty Cooper, inventor of the first popular portable cell phone said, "cellular phones will absolutely not replace land-line phones."
- Time magazine predicted in 1966: "Remote shopping, while entirely feasible, will flop!"
- Steve Ballmer predicted in 2006, "there is no way the iPhone is going to get any significant market share."
- Social media guru Andrew Green predicted in 2008 that Mahalo, the human search engine, will overtake Google's market share.

- And also, that the majority of text creation will come from speech recognition (why am I typing this?)
- In the first decade of the 2000s, auto experts widely speculated that all autos will be self-driving by 2016.

Obviously, forecast accuracy depends on a host of events that cannot be anticipated. Thus, its best to rely on multiple sources as even one source, though an expert, can be very misguided.

Sources: https://www.businessinsider.com/11-hilariously-wrong-internet-predictions-2013-11#robert-metcalfe-the-inventor-of-ethernet-wrote-an-article-for-infoworld-in-december-1995-in-which-he-predicted-i-predict-the-internet-will-soon-go-spectacularly-supernova-and-in-1996-catastrophically-collapse-2. https://www.forbes.com/sites/robertszczerba/2015/01/05/15-worst-tech-predictions-of-all-time/#35928fc61299 (accessed September 2019).

Chapter Summary

1. **Relate sales forecasting to operational planning.** Planning is the most basic function that sales managers do because it creates the essential framework for all other decision making. Organizing, sales forecasting, and budgeting are all integral parts of the planning process. A sales forecast is the cornerstone of all operational planning, and the sales budget represents the conversion of the sales forecast into meaningful financial terms. If a sales budget is inadequate, the sales forecast probably will not be met, and the overall sales plan may not be accomplished. An effective, flexible organizational structure is necessary to achieving sales force goals and objectives, and to efficiently using the allocated budget.

   If a sales forecast is too high, it can lead to excessive production, unsold products, excess inventory, idle cash, wasteful promotion expenditures, price reductions, too many salespeople, and lower unit profits. Conversely, if a sales forecast is too low, it may cause inadequate output to meet customer demand, understock, cash shortages, insufficient promotional expenditures to cover the market, price increases, too few salespeople, out-of-stocks, dissatisfied customers, and lower total profits.

2. **Use the most popular quantitative and qualitative sales forecasting tools.** Qualitative forecasting tools still play an important role for many sales managers. But by using computers and user-friendly statistical software, sales managers can apply numerous quantitative sales forecasting methods. Thus, sales managers can serve the managerial role of data analyst in using

sophisticated forecasting tools, without having to become adept in statistical procedures.

3. **Evaluate the various sales forecasting techniques.** When considering the use of a particular sales forecasting method, sales managers should compare the method to alternative methods with respect to comprehensibility, accuracy, timeliness, availability of information, qualified personnel required, flexibility, and cost-benefit trade-offs. Several approaches often are used so the results can be compared and a more accurate forecast prepared.

4. **Identify the purpose and benefits of sales budgets.** A sales budget puts the sales forecast into dollar terms by serving as the financial sales plan outlining how resources and selling efforts should be allocated to achieve the sales forecast. Sales budgets can provide several benefits, such as (1) improve morale, (2) provide direction and focus for organizational efforts, (3) improve cooperation and coordination, (4) develop individual and collective standards for measuring performance, and (5) increase sales organization flexibility.

5. **Prepare an annual sales budget.** The steps in systematic budget planning are (1) review and analyze the situation, (2) communicate sales goals and objectives, (3) identify specific market opportunities and problems, (4) develop a preliminary allocation of resources, (5) prepare a budget presentation, and (6) implement the budget and provide periodic feedback.

Key Terms

Sales forecast	NAICS (North American	Sales force composite	methods
Market potential	Industrial Classifi-	Counting methods	Correlation analysis
Sales potential	cation System)	Surveys of buying	Correlation coefficient
Quotas	North American	intentions	Regression analysis
Sales and operational	Product Classification	Test marketing	Scatter diagram
planning process	System (NAPCS)	Time-series technique	Trend analysis
(S&OP)	Purchase intentions	Moving average	Multiple regression
Contingency	Breakdown approach	Exponential	Econometric models
Buying Power/	Build-up approach	smoothing	Input–output models
Potential (BP)	Nonquantitative	ARIMA (autoregressive	Sales budget
Standard Industrial	forecasting techniques	integrated moving	Budgeting
Classification	Naïve forecast	average)	Budget variances
(SIC)	Jury of executive opinion	Causal/association	

Notes

1. Whisenant, C. (2006). The politics of forecasting in sales and operations planning. *Journal of Business Forecasting* 25: 17–19.

2. Muzumdar, M. and Fontanella, J. (2006). The secrets to S&OP success. *Supply Chain Management Review*: 34–41.

3. Ibid.

4. Tillet, S. and Shwartz, J. (2001). Delta syncs data, ops. *Internet Week*: 1–2.

5. https://www.census.gov/eos/www/naics/ (accessed September 2019).

6. https://www.census.gov/eos/www/napcs/ (accessed September 2019).

Chapter Review Questions

1. What assumptions might a sales manager make (sometimes subconsciously) about the marketplace in preparing the annual plan? How would you ensure that these assumptions are valid? [LO1, LO5]

2. Do you think the role of the sales manager in sales planning, organizing, forecasting, and budgeting will become less or more important with the ever-growing power of computer technology, software sophistication, and AI? Explain. [LO2]

3. What erroneous assumptions do you think Apple Computer executives may have made in devising their strategic plans over the past decade? [LO1]

4. Using the sales potential approach, how many salespeople will be needed if the company sales forecast is $22 million, annual sales volume productivity for the average salesperson is $400,000, and the anticipated annual rate of sales force turnover is 25%? [LO2]

5. Which of the forecasting techniques do you feel are most appropriate for small business operations? Which for a large corporation? Which for nonprofit organizations, such as museums or public libraries? [LO3]

6. Assume that you are an entrepreneur who owns a small machine tool company with 14 employees. Describe the kind of problems you will encounter if your sales forecast for the coming year turns out to be 25% too high. Describe the scenario if your sales forecast turns out to be 25% too low. [LO1, LO5]

7. Go to a business reference source for the North American Industrial System Classification Manual (likehttps://www.naics.com/search/). Choose an industry of interest to you. Then sequentially follow an NAICS code all the way through to seven digits. Write down the increasingly detailed descriptions that accompany each additional NAICS classification. Step by step, explain how you can use this information to identify potential customers. [LO 1]

8. Go to the Cisco Systems case study of developing its Sales Web Portal at https://www.google.com/search?source=hp&ei=z6iCXfjQB6Ob_QbrsqGYDQ&q=Cisco+sales+forecasting&oq=Cisco+sales+

forecasting&gs_l=psy-ab.3. . .1889.8798. .10376. . . 0.0. .0.179.2286.14j9. . . . . .0. . . .1. .gws-wiz. . .. . . . 0i131j0j0i131i70i250j0i10j0i22i30j0i22i10i30j0i13 j0i13i30j33i160.T0jZvr1heGk&ved=0ahUKEwi49M mir9vkAhWjTd8KHWtZCNMQ4dUDCAs&uact=5. Review how the sales portal facilitates sales forecasting and improves productivity. What problems might Cisco Systems have with its approach? [LO1, LO4]

9. Consider the following data:

Year	Sales
2011	900
2012	1400
2013	1750
2014	1900
2015	1700
2016	1500
2017	2000
2018	1950
2019	2250
2020	2300

Suppose you wished to forecast sales for 2021. Which time-series forecasting method would you suggest as appropriate for this data? Compute the forecast using a simple average, a three-year weighted average, a five-year weighted average, and a five-year exponentially smoothed weighted average. Suppose actual sales for 2021 were 2500. Which forecasting technique is most accurate in this case? [LO3]

10. Consider a consumer goods company introducing a new product. The sales manager argues for a conservative forecast, meaning that care should be taken not to overestimate sales for the first six months of the product's life. What is the danger in making too conservative an estimate? Assuming an equally inaccurate forecast, is it better to underestimate or overestimate demand? [LO5]

11. What are the key purposes and benefits of sales budgets? [LO4, LO5]

Online Exercise

Use a search engine such as Bing or Google to search for sales forecasting software on the Internet. Locate at least three different software packages, each from a different company. Read the overviews of each product. If possible, also find the price. Would you recommend any of these for a small, start-up business that supplies industrial products to CAT-scan manufacturers?

Role-Play Exercise

Sales Forecasting

Situation

Toni King is a sales manager for a restaurant supply firm and receives an annual sales forecast from the home office each year. Top management expects Toni to use this forecast to establish sales quotas for each salesperson in the territory. The forecast is a simple, five-year moving average. Management takes the forecasted sales amount and then adds 5% to "stretch" the goals and motivate the sales force. Each year, as sales manager, Toni is pressured to eliminate sales people who do not meet their goals. Personally, Toni is considering establishing her own goals based on a five-year exponential smoothing forecast – with no stretch. Toni is unsure how top management would perceive this move. However, she feels such a forecast would be both more accurate and more equitable to the sales force.

Role-Play Participants and Assignments

Toni King Assume you are Toni. Do you believe a moving average or an exponential smoothing forecast would be more accurate in a restaurant-related business? Do you consider stretch goals ethical? Playing the role of Toni, consider your options and decide what to do – will you go along with the company policy, or establish your own goals and risk conflict with your superiors?

In-Basket Exercise

You are a sales manager for a consumer goods company that has just launched a new product. Although all the staff members are extremely excited about its potential, after only a few months on the market the product is generating disappointing responses from buyers. One of your salespeople recently heard a major wholesaler, serving over five hundred supermarkets, say: "We've had this product three months, and it's not moving, so we're going to yank it from the stores!"

Questions

1. What possible factors may be contributing to this situation?
2. What steps can you take to ensure a more accurate forecast for a new product?

Ethical Dilemma

Forecasting is one task that presents ethical dilemmas for sales managers. Consider a sales manager faced with endorsing a forecast for a new high-tech radio frequency identification (RFID) tracking device being developed by the company. We'll call the sales manager Abby. Abby has asked an outside firm to present a sales forecast for the new product. The forecast is rosy, suggesting enough demand to warrant the hiring of about ten new salespeople. Abby is very excited about the prospects for this new product and plans a meeting with top management to present the plan for hiring additional salespeople. The meeting goes well, and Abby is given authority to expand the sales force immediately. Three salespeople are hired within the week, with plans for more.

A few weeks after the presentation, Abby reads an article about the business cycle. Many forecasters believe managers must take the business cycle into account when making predictions about high-ticket items because inevitable peaks in the health of the economy are followed every few years by a period of decline. The article predicts an upcoming decline. Abby also reads in a trade magazine that a competing firm with even more resources is developing a similar RFID device. After going back and reading the commissioned forecast report, Abby realizes the outside firm has not taken either of these pieces of information into consideration. If either is true, the forecast almost certainly overstates sales for the RFID tracking device.

Abby now faces the dilemma of either informing management that the forecast may be wrong, and the product will not live up to sales expectations, or trying to take corrective action that could include layoffs. Either of these courses could deal a blow to Abby's career, and many questions enter her mind: "Maybe the business cycle doesn't exist? Maybe the other company won't be able to get the product to market quickly? Or maybe other companies are secretly working on the product as well?"

What is Abby's best course of action from this point?

| CASE 5.1 | **AKAMAI Corporation: Developing Sales Forecasts** |

AKAMAI Corporation is a diversified producer of performance chemicals for the petroleum industry. Performance chemicals are designed to meet rigid specifications to enhance the performance of a variety of end-use products. AKAMAI also produces plastics and aluminum products. The company is organized into three groups – Chemicals, Plastics, and Aluminum.

To maintain growth AKAMAI manages its various groups with the goal of maintaining a healthy mix of businesses in different life-cycle stages. New products must be in the pipeline either in development or commercial introduction ready to replace declining ones. Equally important is managing growing and mature products to extend their life cycle and maximize cash flow to support new product development which will require substantial investment. The Chemicals Group has experienced dramatic growth and changing market conditions in the last three years, and AKAMAI has recently replaced the Vice-President of that group. Because of the importance of this group to overall corporate growth and profits, sales forecasts must be accurate.

The Chemicals Group is managed by Gabriel Perez, and is organized into three operating divisions – industrial intermediates, made up of polymers and detergents, specialty chemicals, and bromine. The three divisions are managed by separate general managers that have product managers reporting to them. Total polymer intermediates sales reached 62 billion U.K. pounds in 2020, and 2021 sales are expected to exceed 75 billion U.K. pounds. This will be almost a 40% increase over a two-year period. The market for detergent intermediates, on the other hand, is mature and stable. The market has become increasingly competitive, with an annual growth of only about 3%. But AKAMAI is a leading competitor and has recently been gaining in market share.

The Specialty Chemicals Division is made up of a diverse product mix. The performance polymers market is the primary revenue-producing unit and is highly dependent on market conditions for crude oil. Agricultural chemicals are a growth market too but also are dependent on the crude oil market. The pharmaceuticals market is growing, and the company has a strong market position as the only domestic producer of the active ingredient for one of the best selling over-the-counter analgesics.

The performance of the Bromine Division is expected to be very good. The AKAMAI sales force has been successful in securing some major new accounts. The success has been achieved based on AKAMAI's favorable reputation as a quality producer of industrial chemicals and from an aggressive sales effort.

In the past, sales forecasts were prepared by the general manager of each division based on a percentage increase determined by the VP of the Chemicals Group. In approaching this task for the first time, new Group VP Perez believes improvements are necessary in the sales forecasting method. Because market conditions for each division are diverse, Perez believes different methods of forecasting should be considered for each of the three divisions.

Group VP Perez began his market analyses with a review of sales data for each division. The Industrial Intermediates Division represents about 54% of sales, specialty chemicals about 39%, and bromine the remaining 7%. Perez also examined sales data by year for each division to track market trends. Exhibit 5.1 summarizes the sales of the Industrial Intermediates Division by quarter for a 10-year period from 2011 to 2020.

Relevant sales data for the Specialty Chemicals Division was available only for a six-year period because the division is relatively new and experiences somewhat unstable market conditions. Quarterly sales data are provided in Exhibit 5.2 for 2015 through 2020.

The Bromine Division is entering its third year in operation, so little sales history is available. Perez has therefore asked for input from the sales force as well as industry data from trade publications. Following is a summary of the sales and market conditions prepared for each division.

Case Exhibit 5.1

Industrial Intermediates Division: Sales Summary										
Quarter	2011	2012	2013	2014	2015	2016	2017	2018	2019	2020
1	54.2	55.2	56.0	59.9	63.4	65.2	68.3	68.2	71.4	79.8
2	53.2	56.1	59.0	61.6	63.8	67.4	71.2	73.1	88.7	100.2
3	54.2	56.1	58.1	59.0	62.5	64.1	67.5	74.1	87.4	95.8
4	53.5	55.2	57.1	59.6	59.9	63.4	66.8	73.2	73.7	84.4
Total	215.1	220.6	230.2	240.1	249.6	260.1	273.8	288.6	321.2	360.2

Case Exhibit 5.2

Specialty Chemicals Division: Sales Summary

Quarter	2015	2016	2017	2018	2019	2020
1	11.0	15.0	22.7	29.6	34.9	43.3
2	14.0	15.1	23.8	31.3	41.7	52.7
3	11.5	16.3	20.7	31.5	40.3	50.7
4	13.5	14.2	21.9	32.2	36.6	45.2
Total	50.0	60.6	89.1	124.6	153.5	191.9

Industrial Intermediates Division

- Recent increase in sales and market share for polymers
- Large number of competitors
- Many customers
- Strong, stable, mature market for detergent intermediaries
- No foreseeable significant market changes for detergents
- Extensive historical sales data
- Represents 54% of sales

Specialty Chemicals Division

- Growth market
- Uncertain market conditions
- Highly dependent on crude oil market
- Represents 39% of sales

Bromine Division

- New market
- No historical sales data

- Only a few key customers
- Small sales force
- Need for accurate forecast by product line
- Limited number of products
- Few competitors

Questions

1. What recommendations would you give Mr. Perez to develop more precise sales forecasts?
2. What forecasting methods would you use for each division and why?
3. Prepare a sales forecast for the Specialty Chemicals Division and justify your results.
4. What additional information would enable you to develop a more precise forecast for the Industrial Intermediates Division? Which method would you use?

Case prepared by: Christopher D. Hopkins, Auburn University

| CASE 5.2 | **Global Container Corporation: Creative Sales Forecasting** |

Global Container (GC) is a large manufacturer of plastic containers for a variety of liquids, from beverages to industrial fluids. GC's products are marketed worldwide through a well-established channel of distribution. Recently Maiko Sakane, Director of New Product Development for GC, returned from a vacation in the Bahamas with what she thought was a great new product idea. After a week of lying on the beach and watching the sights, Maiko discovered something interesting about snorkelers. Most of them bring their snorkeling equipment to the beach in a rather haphazard way. Either they attempt to carry their masks, fins, gauges, and so on loosely – often dropping several of the items into the sand – or they put everything into a mesh bag. The divers' gear is a bit disorganized in the mesh bag, but the carrier appears to work well. The only problem is finding a place to put the bag once the gear is removed.

Maiko believes there is unfulfilled need in the marketplace for a product that will help snorkelers carry their gear onto the beach. Therefore, she created the "Snork-All," a lightweight plastic device that easily carries a diver's fins, mask, knife, various gauges, an underwater camera, and related equipment. The Snork-All could easily snap on to any belt or bathing suit the diver is wearing. Being an expert in plastics, Maiko believes this product represents an opportunity for GC to diversify its product line and expand into new markets.

Once back in the states, Maiko presented her new product idea to a somewhat disenchanted CEO and senior management team. Several of the management team liked the idea, and so did the sales manager and other salespeople. But management was uncertain about what action to take since the company's previous experience was in an entirely different industry. The major concerns of management were the potential sales of the proposed new product. Without any knowledge of total market potential, and ultimately a sales forecast for Snork-All, GC management resisted backing the idea. While Maiko is a brilliant idea person, her expertise in marketing planning and forecasting is limited, particularly regarding the snorkel/scuba customer. She believes her Snork-All concept has great potential, but she needs solid evidence so that she may approach GC management again with her idea. She knows she will need to contact various teams within the company to inquire if they can provide her with information regarding their customers. Much internal data has been collected, but with this new marketing venture, the team suggests that mining through big data (including inside and outside sources) would be appropriate to determine the demographics and psychographics of this new target market, as well as the preferences of the consumer in this market niche, and the potential for sales in this potential market.

Questions

1. How would you estimate the total market potential for Snork-All? What kind of historical data might help with this project?

2. How would you estimate GC's sales potential for Snork-All? Which team(s) from GC should be involved in developing the sales estimate?

3. What type of forecasting methods might work best in developing a sales forecast for Snork-All?

4. How would you determine if Snork-All is the best label for the new product?

5. How would social media information aid Maiko in better understanding the snorkel/scuba customer?

Case prepared by: Susan Geringer, California State University, Fresno

CHAPTER 6

Sales Force Planning and Organizing

Purpose and Levels of Organizational Planning

Planning creates the essential framework for all other decision making. Without well-thought-out plans, getting anything accomplished efficiently and effectively is difficult, especially in larger companies. Effective sales managers are usually good planners.

Why Should Sales Managers Plan?

Planning requires sales managers to anticipate the possible outcomes and future implications of current decisions; thus, planning is an attempt to manage the future. In fact, a succinct definition of planning is "making decisions today to create a desired tomorrow."

Some sales managers argue the marketplace changes too fast for planning to be of much value. These managers are fooling themselves, because without a plan to provide direction, decision-making tends to be merely reactive, especially in even in rapidly changing markets. For example, sales managers who recruit and select a sales force without planning are likely to find themselves continually underhiring, overhiring, and firing employees. Similarly, sales managers who organize, train, motivate, or evaluate salespeople without a plan are likely to be frequently reorganizing, retraining, and suffering poor morale and high sales force turnover.

Sales managers make decisions in an environment where change is continuous – whether in competitive, technological, political, economic, or social arenas. Planning minimizes environmental shocks such as energy price increases, raw materials or component parts shortages, or major changes in tax laws. If sales managers don't anticipate marketplace changes, they'll be caught up in a whiplash decision-making process where they are batted back and forth by a rapidly changing marketing environment. Instead, they must ensure that salespeople collaborate with customers to create solutions neither would have been able to put together by themselves.

Planning has several potential benefits for the sales manager. First, morale improves when the entire sales organization actively participates in the planning process. Second, planning provides direction and focus for organizational efforts. Third, it improves cooperation and coordination of sales force efforts. Fourth, planning helps develop individual and collective standards that can be used to measure sales force performance, and deviations identified in time to take corrective action. Fifth, planning increases the sales organization's flexibility in dealing with unexpected developments.

Levels of Organizational Planning

Every manager should plan, and more effective planners tend to be more effective managers. At the top, CEOs, boards of directors, presidents, and vice presidents spend more time planning than do middle managers. Similarly, middle managers spend more time planning than do supervisory level people. Top management focuses on strategic planning for the company, while middle managers – such as regional and district sales managers – spend most of their planning time on shorter-run tactical plans. Table 6.1 illustrates types of planning at different levels in the organization.

As planners and administrators, sales managers must (1) define goals and objectives, (2) set policies, (3) establish procedures, (4) devise strategies, (5) direct tactics, and (6) develop and enforce controls. Our discussion now focuses on these essential planning and administrative roles.

Goals and Objectives Effective sales-department planning requires communication of clear-cut goals and objectives to all organizational members involved in planning. Goals are general, long-range destinations. In contrast, objectives are specific results desired within a designated time frame – usually the period covered by the annual sales plan. One sales goal for IBM (www.ibm.com) is to be recognized as the most service-oriented sales force in its industry. In fact, sales executives at IBM think the company's best advertisement declares simply: "IBM means service." Objectives for most companies are expressed in terms of annual sales volume targets or quotas, market share, return on assets managed (ROAM), earnings per share of common stock, inventory turnover, back orders, accounts receivable, or employee turnover.[1] Without clearly communicated goals and objectives, sales efforts may not be synergistic with those of other departments and can even be conflicting.

TABLE 6.1

Planning at Different Levels of Management

Type	Participants	Focus
Strategic planning	CEO, board of directors, president, senior VPs	Company mission, vision, goals, primary strategies, and overall budgeting
Tactical planning	General sales manager and director of marketing quarterly plans, policies	Departmental, yearly, and procedures, and budgets
Monthly and weekly planning	Regional sales managers	Branch plans and budgets
Daily planning	Sales supervisors and sales reps	Unit plans and budget

Policies and Procedures Predetermined approaches for handling routine matters or reoccurring situations are called policies. For example, there should be a policy regarding product returns, trade-ins, warranty, and credit terms when customers purchase new products. Policies enable sales managers to avoid answering the same questions over and over, and to focus on more important decision-making such as strategic sales planning.

Detailed descriptions of specific steps for carrying out actions are called procedures. For example, when offering a refund on a defective product, salespeople should follow a clear-cut series of steps to ensure the transaction is handled correctly.

Strategies and Tactics A strategy is an overall program of action (ways) for using resources to achieve value-creating goals or objectives. Tactics are day-to-day actions that make up the strategic plan. One example of a sales strategy is Honeywell's (www. honeywell.com) decision to concentrate its field sales force in smaller cities to compete against other manufacturers whose resources are located in larger cities. Special sales presentation formats to approach different customer categories are examples of sales tactics.

Controls For effective control, sales managers must develop performance standards so they can compare actual performance to predetermined standards. If there are gaps between actual and planned results, the sales manager has two options: (1) increase sales efforts to accomplish the plan, or (2) revise the sales plan to conform to a new "reality" in the marketplace. The appropriate course of action depends on the reasons for the gap. In analyzing the situation, the sales manager needs to consider the following: Were planning assumptions used in preparing the sales forecast and performance objectives realistic? Have there been major strategic or tactical changes by competitors? Have customer tastes or preferences changed? Are product quality, price, and service satisfactory? Are advertising, social media, promotions, and other support activities effective? Are salespeople properly trained and motivated? Is the sales force optimally organized? Only after sorting through the myriad possibilities can the sales manager decide which approach to use to realign planned and actual sales performance.

Sales Management Planning Process

Sales management planning is never completed and requires several sequential steps. The process never comes to an end because it is really continuous. As soon as the first plan is prepared, something has changed in the marketing environment – perhaps a competitor's actions – that calls for an adjustment in the original plan. Planning enables a sales manager to be proactive rather than reactive.

When beginning the planning process, sales managers should consider six basic questions:

Diagnosis: Where are we now?
Prognosis: Where are we headed if no changes are made?
Objectives: Where should we be headed?
Strategy: What is the best way to get there?
Tactics: What actions need to be taken by whom, and when?
Control: What measures must be monitored so we know how we're doing?

Let's examine the flowchart in Figure 6.1 as we discuss each of the stages in the sales management planning process.

FIGURE 6.1 The sales management planning process.

Analyze the Situation

The planning process begins with an analysis of where the organization is today and where it is headed if no changes are made. Managers learn this by reviewing the organization's past performance, judging its progress compared to the competition, and reviewing its success in accomplishing objectives and goals. Here are some key variables to study in the situation analysis:

- *Market characteristics* – number and types of potential buyers, their demographic and behavioral profiles, their attitudes and buying patterns, and their servicing needs.
- *Competition* – number and types of competitors, their strengths and weaknesses, their products, prices, and brands, market shares, characteristics, and sales trends for each competitive brand.
- *Sales, cost, and profit data for current and recent years* – by product, market, territory, and time period.
- *Benefits offered as perceived by potential customers* – products, brand names, prices, packages, and service.
- *Promotional mix* – personal selling, advertising, social media, sales promotion, publicity programs, and particularly emerging digital marketing strategies.
- *Distribution systems* – channels of distribution, channel partners, storage and transportation facilities, and intensity of distribution.

Sales managers and others engaged in the planning process at any level need to monitor internal and external events that directly or indirectly affect the organization. It is particularly important to match the organization's strengths and weaknesses against the opportunities and threats facing it. By building on strengths and shoring up weaknesses, the organization puts itself in a good position to counter market challenges and exploit opportunities. Understanding comparative strengths and weaknesses is essential for survival and growth, but management must be aware of emerging marketplace trends. General Electric (www.ge.com) relies on its sales portal to assemble information for use in sales planning. The portal accesses multiple databases simultaneously to obtain everything from sales tracking and customer data to parts pricing, production schedules, and external data from news and trade industry RSS feeds. Using sales analytics techniques, the portal dynamically assembles personalized "portlets," such as a customized view of industry news, customer profiles and sales performance year-to-date, and presents them in a unified way. The result is less time spent preparing for sales calls and more time spent face-to-face making sales and building partnerships.[2] Salesforce.com's enterprise software called Einstein can automate much of the process by integrating data into an AI system.

Set Goals and Objectives

Organizations usually have multiple goals and objectives. In many cases, especially in smaller companies, goals are often vague or inadequately defined. For example, "We want to become one of the best in the industry" is virtually impossible to evaluate. Without a clear understanding of what "one of the best" means, the goal is not very meaningful.

All units and employees in an organization should understand overall goals and objectives, as well as individual goals and objectives. One way to improve development of goals and objectives is by using interactive sales force automation (SFA) applications. For example, companies like Salesforce.com sell Interactive Sales Manager (ISM) packages that have many sales force automation applications. The applications make a salesperson's goals and expectations easier to confirm, and then managers can prepare plans that serve sales territories and accounts to best meet goals and expectations. The ISM tool tracks performance against plans, current activity, and future commitments, and even identifies mentoring opportunities.[3] Sales Management in Action Box 6.1 illustrates this point further.

Box 6.1 | Sales Management in Action 6.1

Using SFA Systems to Monitor and Plan

Technology is changing nearly all aspects of sales and sales management. Planning and monitoring used to be handled by referring to information on index cards filed in boxes. Today, sales force automation (SFA) programs have made these processes much easier and more effective for many sales managers. Salespeople previously had to do the best they could in developing ways to implement company strategies. Today SFA systems help salespersons to plan activities in a way that makes their behavior more consistent with company desires. During the sales call, the SFA system also provides more of the information the salesperson needs to accomplish key goals. For example, a pharmaceutical salesperson might make only one sales call (detail) per year to rural physicians. The frequency of sales calls and the information that should be conveyed during the visit are all provided by the SFA system.

Additionally, the SFA system enables the sales manager to track progress toward key goals in real time. When a salesperson is lagging on some goal, or emphasizing nonproductive accounts too much, the sales manager doesn't have to wait for a paper report to take corrective action. Instead, the real-time data in the SFA provides the guidance needed to nip many problems in the bud.

Sources: Sales force automation, *Business Jargons.* https://businessjargons.com/sales-force-automation.html (accessed August 2019); The automator, *Pharmaceutical Executive* 27 (February 2007), pp. 36–40; What does the sales force do? *Builder's Merchant Journal,* October 2006, p. 35, and SFA. http://www.businesscreatorpro.com/articles/sales_force_automation_sfa.php (accessed August 2019).

Goals and objectives must be spelled out explicitly and in order of priority. They also must be consistent, particularly between different company divisions and departments. Sample goals and objectives for a national sales manager in large office supply manufacturer might include the examples listed in Table 6.2.

TABLE 6.2

Sample Goals and Objectives for a National Sales Manager

Goals	Objectives
▪ Implement a sales analytics platform to provide data to identify sales opportunities	▪ Select a sales analytics platform in next three months
▪ Expand our market coverage over the next five years to include all of nation's primary metropolitan statistical areas	▪ Reduce customer complaints by 10% next year
▪ Reduce sales force turnover to below the industry average over the next five years	▪ Increase the number of new customer accounts by 20% in the next six months
▪ Implement a new sales training program	▪ Increase sales by 15% next year

We discuss individual salesperson goals and objectives in Chapter 14 – Sales Force Performance Evaluation.

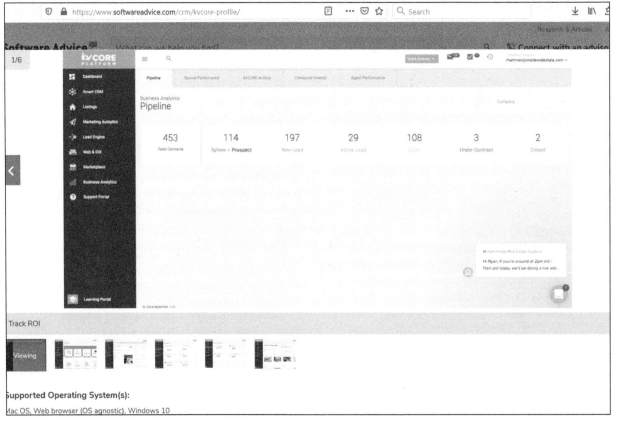

Sales force automation is big business these days as the right software is critical to success.
Source: https://www.softwareadvice.com/crm/kvcore-profile/, April 14, 2020.

Determine Market Potential and Forecast Sales

After managers and salespeople have agreed on goals and objectives, the next step in the planning process is to assess market potential – the maximum possible sales for an entire industry, and sales potential – the maximum possible sales for a company. Market and sales potentials are typically estimated for a specified period of time based on favorable assumptions about the marketing environment and marketing expenditures. Some sales managers, however, prefer to develop separate (1) optimistic, (2) expected, and (3) pessimistic assumptions for market and sales potential using different possible scenarios.

Market capacity refers to the units the market will absorb if the product or service is free. Since market potential assumes a competitive pricing structure, the market potential number will always be less than market capacity. Potentials developed for an organization are generally grouped for planning purposes, for example, in geographic or customer terms such as sales territories. Thus, sales managers know where sales potential is highest and can better allocate the sales force and set sales quotas. Estimates of customer potential also help in scheduling sales calls and implementing promotional support.

Market potential determination starts with the study of present customers and their characteristics. For example, characteristics might include what is the customer's place of purchase, method of purchase, type of payment, product size, and usage rate. Sales managers can then access sales analytics tools to estimate usage rates if the current product is modified for existing customers or repositioned for potential new customers. Finally, market potential is estimated for new products and services. Analysis of market potential leads to the development of more realistic sales forecasts for the next quarter or year.

Sales forecasts predict future sales for a specified period as part of marketing and sales plans based on a set of assumptions about the marketing environment. Since an accurate sales forecast is essential to the success of an organization, most firms are constantly seeking more reliable sales forecasting methods. Sales forecasting can be quite complex and sometimes utilize sophisticated mathematical models. Some firms have established separate departments specializing in sales forecasting, but many firms rely on off-the-shelf packages available with CRM systems. For small- and medium-sized firms, IBM (www.ibm.com) and its channel partners provide free sales planning solutions on topics such as: defining market opportunities, targeting the most attractive market segments, identifying appropriate sales coverage, and assigning sales responsibilities during each step of the sales cycle, from demand generation to postsale support.[4]

Develop Strategies

After organizational objectives have been determined and sales forecasts developed, the next step is to determine the best way to achieve the targets. Strategy planning is the process of setting overall objectives, allocating resources, and developing broad courses of action. Strategic decisions give the organization a plan of action to serve customers better, take advantage of competitors' weaknesses, and capitalize on the firm's strengths.

Growth Strategies

Figure 6.2 depicts four types of growth strategies. Market penetration focuses on increasing sales of current products in current markets by more intensive marketing efforts. As an example, Aflac recently refocused its marketing effort by allocating more

	Current Products	New Products
Current Markets	Market Penetration	Product Development
New Markets	Market Development	Diversification

FIGURE 6.2 Growth strategies for sales management.

resources to sales. The hope was to get salespeople to spend more time in the organizations where Aflac's core product, supplemental disability insurance, is sold. In this way, Aflac might capitalize on the name recognition created through advertising, by educating employees on the actual product that Aflac sells.

Market development seeks to open up new markets for current products. To illustrate, the Cross Pen Company (cross.com) continues to enjoy good earnings growth because it has concentrated on developing an upscale market among corporations (beyond the traditional retail consumer market) for its high-quality pens as special gifts for customers and awards for employees.

Product development creates new or improved products for current markets by adding new sizes, models with new features, alternative quality versions, or creative new alternatives to satisfy the same basic needs. For example, farmers are increasingly using biogenetics and hydroponics for applications formerly involving chemical fertilizers and pesticides. Biogenetics is the breeding of strains of plants that are resistant to pests and diseases, thus eliminating the need for pesticides or herbicides. Hydroponics is the science of growing plants indoors in a controlled environment that requires no herbicides, pesticides, or fertilizers. New products from biogenetics and hydroponics offer many exciting growth opportunities.

Above the sales management level, two other growth strategies are to diversify by purchasing new businesses or product lines, and to obtain ownership or control over different levels of distribution channels. For example, the Firestone Division of Bridgestone Tires integrated forward through ownership of its retail outlets in the United States, while Holiday Inns, a division of InterContinental Hotels Group (IHG), integrated backward into manufacturing by acquiring carpet mills and furniture plants.

Business Portfolio Approach Two major growth concepts are the strategic business unit and the market share/market growth matrix. Strategic business units (SBUs) are logical divisions of major businesses within multiple product companies. SBUs are evaluated on the basis of their profit and growth potential just as if they were stand-alone companies. SBUs have several characteristics: (1) distinct mission, (2) separate management, (3) unique customer segments, (4) their own competitors, and (5) planning that is largely independent of other units in the company. Many of the largest U.S. manufacturing corporations apply the SBU concept as an organizational approach. For example, Campbell Soup Co. set up multiple SBUs, including: Soups, Beverages, Pet Foods, Frozen Foods, Fresh Produce, Main Meals, Snacks, Grocery, and Food Service. The SBUs manage a diversified range of brands including Prego, Lance, and Pepperidge Farm.

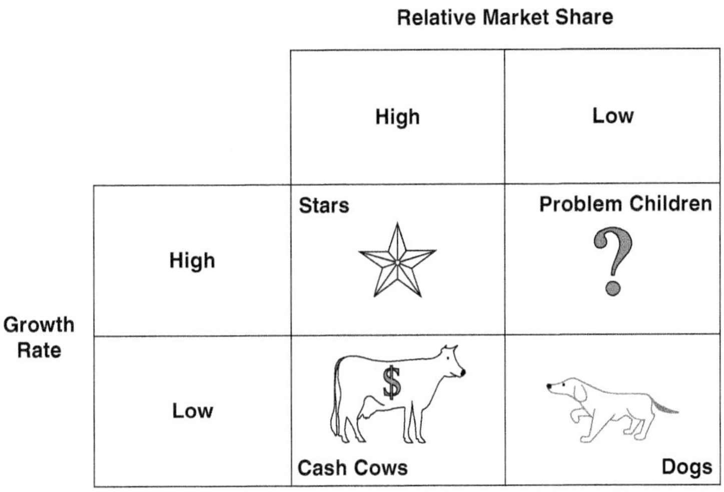

Relative Market Share

FIGURE 6.3 The BCG growth/market share matrix.

In evaluating the strategic business units of a company, the most popular approach is the business portfolio matrix. This method segments the company's activities into groups of well-defined businesses for which distinct strategies are developed. The most widely used is Boston Consulting Group's (BCG) growth-share matrix, which plots market share on the horizontal axis and market growth potential on the vertical axis. It evaluates a company's businesses on the basis of market share and market growth, and then puts them in one of four quadrants labeled cash cows, stars, dogs, or problem children (also referred to as question marks), as shown in Figure 6.3.

Strategies based on the four quadrants suggest the following:

- Stars produce large amounts of cash because of high market share, but stars consume large amounts of cash because of high growth. If stars maintain or extend market share, they become cash cows.
- Cash Cows are leaders in mature markets and produce much more cash than they consume. Companies "milk" business units so they can invest cash in other products or services. For example, the cash might be used to turn problem children into stars.
- Problem Children are growing rapidly and consume large amounts of cash. Also known as "question marks," they have the potential to increase market share and become stars. But if they do not increase market share, they may become dogs.
- Dogs have low market share and low growth rates. They do not consume much cash but also do not produce any. These business units are likely to be sold.

Stakeholders Marketing planning and strategy must consider an organization's relationship with all stakeholder publics, not just customers. Government – whether federal, state, or local – can change a company's structure, pass laws, issue regulations, and become either a customer or a competitor of the organization. Government actions have ranged from the Product Safety Commission demanding numerous product recalls, to the Food and Drug Administration banning sale of certain products as possible cancer-causing agents, to the Department of Agriculture providing subsidies to tobacco growers at the same time as the Department of Health and Human Services campaigns against cigarette smoking. Special-interest groups battle either for or against handgun-control, nuclear power plants, and tax reform, while the general public protests wasteful government spending. Company employees demand higher wages and better working conditions. Stockholders vote against extravagant executive salaries and benefits or commercial dealings with governments that violate human rights. The financial community provides either easy or tight credit terms. Suppliers make decisions on allocation of scarce commodities. Investigative reporters for the independent print and broadcast media expose legal, moral, and ethical violations by business – whether they are misleading advertising claims, faulty product designs, or insider stock trading. Each of these stakeholders influences sales force operations for better or worse. Thus, managers must consider each in planning overall marketing strategy and tactics.

After the overall strategy has been decided, the planning process incorporates more detailed activities – tactics. Tactics focus on implementation of the strategic plan and are really the functional sub-plans that underlie and accomplish the strategy plan. Tactical action plans identify what needs to be done, who is responsible, what resources are needed, and what benefits are expected. Sales Management in Action Box 6.2 on teamwork illustrates one approach. Figure 6.4 shows a sample action plan.

Allocate Resources and Develop Budgets

Given detailed subplans and tactics, sales managers must allocate resources – money, people, materials, equipment, and time – to carry out the plans. Budgets are the formal expression of managerial support. The sales budget is the expected expenditures required to achieve projected sales revenues. It must support the sales forecast. If budgeted resources are inadequate, the entire plan – including the sales forecast – must be scaled down. As pointed out in Chapter 5, budgets coordinate and control company resources during the period covered by the sales forecast.

Box 6.2 | Sales Management in Action 6.2

Developing Successful Cross-Functional Teams

Comprehensive sales plans will often need cooperation from many camps if they are to be implemented successfully. Some companies have turned to cross-functional teams (CFTs) and charged them with implementing an action plan aimed at accomplishing major sales and marketing objectives. The cross-functional team involves marketing, innovation, data analytics, engineering, research, and financial personnel. A CFT can better ensure that all issues involved in a sales contract are covered with sufficient expertise. But CFTs are not always effective. Here are some guidelines to make a CFT work:

1. Spread the work around to avoid bottlenecks. Each member of the CFT should be charged with approximately the same amount of responsibility. If someone on the CFT does not have

responsibility, then perhaps they don't belong on the team.

2. Provide quantitative success goals. Each member of the team should have access to sale analytics tools and realistic benchmarks to assess progress.

3. Celebrate success. When goals are met, the entire CFT should be recognized for achievement. This is time to celebrate!

Cross-functional teams can be a good solution in a CRM environment. Like most tools, however, they do not apply to every action plan.

Sources: Westland, J. 6 tips for developing cross functional teams. https://www.projectmanager.com/blog/6-tips-developing-cross-functional-teams (accessed August 2019); 18 reasons why you should build cross-functional teams. https://www.workzone.com/blog/cross-functional-teams/ (accessed August 2019); and Antonucci, D. and Kono, K. (2006). High energy: Sustain the momentum of your cross-functional team. *Marketing Management* 14–16.

Tactical Action Plan

Velop Manufacturing Co.

Eastern Region

Goal: To call on 200 new accounts during the first quarter of fiscal year 2021.

Strategy/Tactics:
- Develop list of potential new accounts.
- Contract with telemarketing firm to prescreen list to determine likely prospects.
- Assign prescreened prospects to sales force by territory.
- Hold a training workshop to make sure all salespeople know what background material to develop on prospects, and where to obtain it.
- Develop timetables and quotas for each salesperson.

Responsibility: Sales Manager, Eastern Region

Start Date: October 1, 2020

Completion Date: December 31, 2020

Resources Needed: $38,000 to develop list and contract with telemarketing firm.

Benefits:
- Ensures new accounts are called upon.
- Facilitates achieving projected 5% increase in sales for FY 2021.

FIGURE 6.4 Sample action plan.

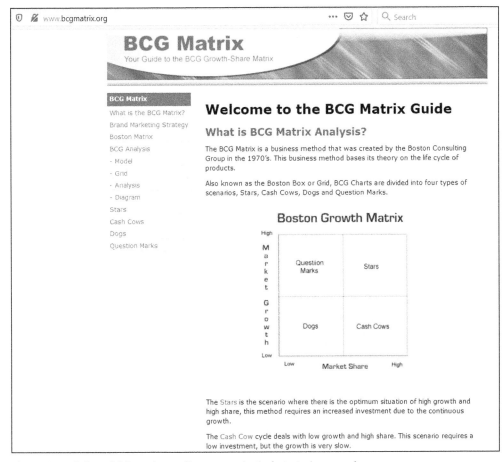

The BCG Matrix is useful for understanding an organization's strategic approach.

Source: www.bcgmatrix.org, April 14, 2020.

Implement the Plan

Goals, objectives, strategies, and tactics need to be communicated throughout the organization. Upper-level management wants to be sure departmental plans are consistent with overall corporate objectives. Sales managers often use "management by objectives" (MBO) to involve subordinates in planning and budgeting, since subordinates are more likely to accept and carry out plans if they're involved in their preparation. A program evaluation and review technique (PERT) network is commonly used for planning and scheduling. PERT diagrams specify a project's critical path – the sequence of tasks to be completed, the time to complete each activity, and the responsible individuals. In most instances, sales managers create this scheduling tool through a Web-based portal for increased control, access to information, and dissemination of ongoing progress reports.

Regardless of the approach, it is essential to ensure project progress is closely monitored. Some companies assign full-time project coordinators to follow-up with those responsible for completing each task. Because the planning process is based on many assumptions about the external environment, changes or modifications may be necessary at various points in the implementation stage. Sales managers that anticipate the unexpected can adjust plans and implementation quickly.

Evaluate and Control

A sound planning process requires a built-in monitoring device for management evaluation and control. The device should include regular measurements to check progress toward specific objectives and signal deviations in time to take corrective actions and get back on track. Whenever possible, managers should quantify measurements.

Performance Standards and Measures In Table 6.3, we show three types of performance standards and relate them to eight performance measures. One measure of performance is comparisons to industry averages. Of course, when the total industry is performing poorly, it is small consolation to be doing just as well as the average company. Another type of standard is past performance, which can indicate favorable or unfavorable trends. Probably, the most important standards are managerial expectations, because they are based on the organization's objectives, forecasts, and budgetary support. Even if sales exceed past performance and industry norms, management will view failure to meet expectations negatively.

These performance measures are unlikely to all be used in any specific situation. But managers do need multiple measures to adequately monitor and control progress toward achieving goals and objectives.

Each of these standards reflects the organization's internal measures. But two *external* measures may be even more critical to the organization's long-run survival: customer satisfaction and societal satisfaction. Indicators of customer satisfaction or dissatisfaction include purchase frequencies and quantities, repurchase rates, brand or store loyalty, customer satisfaction rankings, social media postings, blogs and wikis, customer perceptions of product quality and service, number of customer complaints, and overall organizational reputation. Societal satisfaction is more difficult to measure or even set standards for, because societal expectations for all levels of performance seem to rise continually and quicker as a result of social media platforms and the 24-hour news cycle. Nevertheless, an organization can track areas most likely to affect societal perceptions, such as product safety and quality standards, equal employment and promotion opportunities, nondiscriminatory treatment of customers and suppliers, promotional truthfulness and disclosure, energy conservation, and

TABLE **6.3**

Performance Standards and Performance Measures for Sales Managers

Performance Measures	Performance Standard		
	Industry Averages	Past Performance	Managerial Expectations
Sales volume	Trade publications	Sales records	Sales forecast
	Annual reports		
New accounts	Trade publications	Sales records	MBO contract
Selling costs	Trade publications	Sales records	Budgeted costs
Sales force turnover	Trade publications	Personnel records	MBO contract
Market share	Trade publications	Marketing Dept.	Forecast
Profit margins	Trade publications	Accounting Dept.	Pro forma statement
	Annual reports		
Customer service	Trade publications	Complaint records	MBO contract
	Customer surveys	Products returned	
		Number of service calls	
Website resources	Trade publications	Cloud storage	Marketing plans
	Customer surveys	Sales analytics	

environmental policies. Remaining alert and responsive to government initiatives and public interest groups helps organizations satisfy societal expectations.

By establishing standards, organizations can regularly compare the gap between actual performance and benchmarks to ensure timely corrective action. Unless performance is continuously monitored, planning is likely a waste of resources.

Causes of Unsuccessful Planning

Some plans are poorly prepared, filed away, and not looked at again until next year's plan is due. This kind of planning doesn't represent much real planning and is a big waste of time and resources. Merely "going through the planning motions" is probably not much better than having no plan at all.

Many organizations devote substantial time and effort to the planning process. They also use computer simulations and quantitative analytics to improve the process. Despite the serious commitment and sophisticated effort, however, unsuccessful plans are too often the outcome. Poor results are not limited to small or new companies. Global corporations have had drastic planning failures, too, as witnessed by the failure of Nokia and Blackberry mobile phones, and both Texas Instruments and AT&T in personal computers. Probably the most universal cause of unsuccessful planning is making one or more erroneous assumptions in each stage of the planning process. To illustrate, Texaco, Inc., an American oil subsidiary of Chevron Corporation, decided to stop exploring for oil and to concentrate on refining and distributing oil products. Management's erroneous assumption was that there would be a cheap, plentiful supply of oil for the foreseeable future. In planning, management *must* make assumptions about the future, so it's important for the assumptions to be systematically considered. Let's consider two planning tools.

Dialectic Planning

One approach to examining the validity of assumptions in a forecast is called dialectic planning. This approach calls for making a new set of assumptions – sometimes directly opposite – and reevaluating all previous planning decisions. Plans are rigorously challenged at every step and a second plan with different assumptions is prepared. Forcing management to come up with a different second plan enables them to view the planning process from two contrasting views and reduces the chance of mistakes. With two alternative plans, however, management uncertainty may increase, sometimes resulting in delayed decision-making or a compromise that produces undesirable results.

Contingency Planning

Another tool used to reduce the risk of future problems is contingency planning. A contingency plan is a back-up plan to the one adopted and will be executed only if events occur beyond the control of the major plan. For example, electrical systems in many hospitals have "redundancy" or "back-up" systems in case the primary system fails. Contingency planning is expensive and time-consuming, but its value has been proven many times. Sales managers must therefore anticipate and prepare for an unlikely turn of events, or an emergency, when preparing plans.

Organizing the Sales Force

A proper organizational structure is necessary to effectively implement the sales manager's plan. Organizational structure determines how well activities are coordinated in serving customers profitably, and how quickly the organization can adapt to changes in the marketing environment. The purpose of the sales organization is to facilitate the accomplishment of marketing and sales objectives by (1) shortening the time a sales manager needs to evaluate and respond to changing market needs, (2) arranging activities efficiently, and (3) establishing and maintaining open channels of communication with customers, salespeople, support staff, and concerned stakeholders. No sales organization can remain stagnant and expect long-run success. The success of companies such as Coca-Cola, Microsoft, Apple, and Alphabet can be partially attributed to their continuously adapting organizational structures to market conditions.

Types of Organizations

Depending on its objectives, an organization can be structured in many ways. But most are one of three types: line, line and staff, or functional. A variation of these three is the matrix organization. Management can modify these structures as needed to decentralize or to organize by product, customer, function, territory, or a combination. In addition, all organizations have an informal network.

Line Organization A line organization is the simplest design and the one most often used by smaller firms. It typically consists of only a few managers who have authority over specific functional areas of the business, such as production, finance, or sales. A line organization is shown in Figure 6.5. When a firm is small and managers interact frequently, line organizations are efficient and flexible. But as firms grow, line organizations are much less effective because decision-making is slower and managers have too many responsibilities.

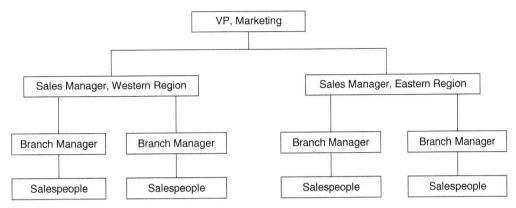

FIGURE 6.5 Line organization for marketing and sales.

Line-and-Staff Organization A line-and-staff organization creates more functional areas and adds staff assistants to complete specialized support activities, such as marketing research or sales forecasting. A vice president of marketing or a sales manager heads the department. Staff people provide specialized skills for the sales manager and enable them to spend more time working with salespeople. Line managers have direct authority over the operations of the organization, while staff managers only make recommendations or assist line managers. An example of a line-and-staff organization is provided in Figure 6.6.

Functional Organization In functional organizations, staff specialists have line authority, as shown in Figure 6.7. The sales manager directs salespeople through district managers, but the director of sales training also has authority over the sales force for training, as does the manager of technical services. In functional structures, managers are highly qualified specialists whose job is to make sure their function is accomplished. This type of organization creates many conflicts for salespeople, who must react to several bosses.

Matrix Organizations Matrix organizations are typical in industries confronted with rapid technological changes and the need to quickly develop new products or services. Traditional organizations are designed around functions while matrix organizations revolve

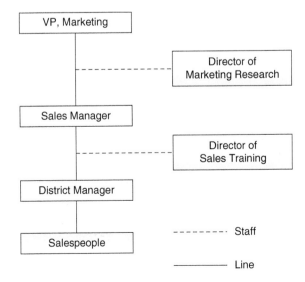

FIGURE 6.6 Line-and-staff organization.

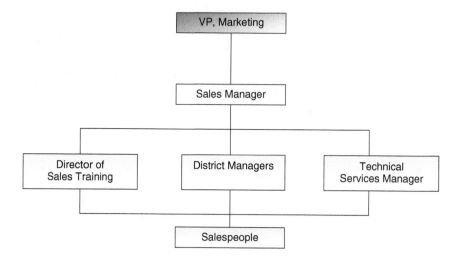

FIGURE 6.7 Functional organization.

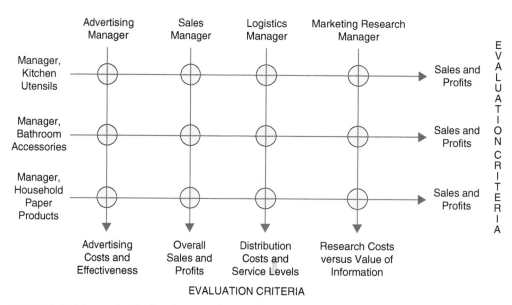

FIGURE 6.8 Matrix organization focusing on products or projects.

around projects. The firm's efforts focus on a specific project and the functional areas are integrated into the project structure. Figure 6.8 shows a matrix organization in which the focus is on specific products and projects. While the functional aspects are still present, they are secondary. Project managers head a team of individuals from different functional areas and have responsibility for coordinating these functions toward project completion. Individual team members still have a functional superior such as the sales manager, but they also report to their project managers. Matrix organizations are much easier to implement today as a result of enterprise software platforms. These platforms facilitate management overview of all activities, streamline processes, and empower employees.[5]

Matrix organizations encourage teamwork to maximize individual contributions. They view team leaders as coordinators of efforts rather than as bosses. Matrix organizations are most effective when projects or products are unique, team members have the expertise and skills needed, the project covers a limited time period, and speed and creativity are important, as is cost. Companies as diverse as Shell Oil (www.shell.com), Kraft

Foods (www.kraft.com), IBM (www.ibm.com), Alcoa Aluminum (www.alcoa.com), and Westinghouse (www.westinghouse.com) have made effective use of matrix organizations. Matrix organizations are flexible, develop employee skills, encourage cooperation between departments, as well as motivating and challenging employees to do their best.

Informal Organization In spite of organizational structures, the informal organizational structure is the network by which things often get done. Healthy organizations are dynamic and self-adjusting and find the most efficient methods to accomplish objectives, without regard to how the objectives are supposed to be achieved. Employees adapt to the way the organization actually works rather than to the way the organization structure indicates it should. Real power and authority in an organization may belong to a strong staff manager or junior line manager who works with weaker or less competent senior managers. The way an organization really functions is eventually reflected in the organization structure, but the actual chains of authority can take a long time, perhaps years, to develop.

Types of Sales Department Organizations

Sales organization efforts center on products, markets, and functions. These elements are blended together differently by various industries and companies in the same industry. Sales departments have traditionally been organized into five basic types: geographic, product, function, market, or some combination of the four. Let's look briefly at each one.

Geographic Organizations Geographic sales organizations are most common. But they often are used in combination with product-, function-, or market-oriented structures. Some examples of geographic organizations are banks with suburban branches, magazine publishers with regional editions, hotel chains with regional divisions, or companies with international and domestic sales divisions. A sales manager has authority over a specific geographic area and several salespeople assigned a separate part of the territory report to him or her.

Geographic organization has advantages and disadvantages. Advantages come from a decentralized line authority structure ensuring flexibility in adapting to needs, problems, buying patterns, service requirements, and competitive conditions in the regional markets. Disadvantages include the overhead costs of management as more levels of geographic executives are created and problems in coordinating total company sales efforts when several sales divisions operate with considerable autonomy. Lack of functional specialists can also be a problem, since territorial managers are expected to operate as "Jacks-of-all-trades" and handle advertising, sales analysis, billing, credit, and collection in addition to managing the sales force. Figure 6.9 shows a geographic sales organization.

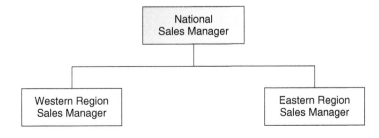

FIGURE 6.9 Geographic sales organization.

Product-Oriented Organizations Product structured sales organizations are useful when product lines are complex or distinct and require increased individualized attention. Under this setup, products compete among themselves for profit, market share, and company resources. Procter and Gamble (www.pg.com), one of the world's most successful consumer products companies, uses a product-oriented structure. Competition among P&G products, sometimes sold to overlapping market segments, is encouraged.

Disadvantages of product structures are the additional expense – increased specialization usually requires additional management – and the possible irritation of customers who lose time because more than one salesperson from the same company calls on them for different products. Also, multiple-salespeople calls tend to confuse the image of the seller. Figure 6.10 shows a sales force organized by product.

Function-Oriented Organizations Function-oriented sales organizations are structured by major functions, such as development of new accounts or maintenance of current customers. This structure offers specialization and efficiency in performing selling activities, and is best for companies selling only a few or very similar products to relatively few customer types. Generally, it is used by medium to large companies that can afford for salespeople to focus on a small number of activities.

A common problem among growing companies is motivating salespeople to call on potential new accounts. They are reluctant to call on new accounts because a different set of sales skills is required than selling to existing customers. Assigning these two functions to separate sales groups would be an appropriate use of the functional organization. Unlike a pure line-and-staff organization, in function-oriented structures specialists have line authority over salespeople. Figure 6.11 depicts a sales department organized by function.

The cost effectiveness of a function-oriented organization is questionable. Small companies seldom find it practical to have such a high degree of specialization. In large organizations, however, it's difficult to coordinate functions throughout the sales department because of the size of the sales force. Furthermore, when several functional specialists have line authority over salespeople, as shown in Figure 6.7, conflicts are likely among the function managers, as well as confusion and frustration in the sales force.

FIGURE 6.10 Product sales organization.

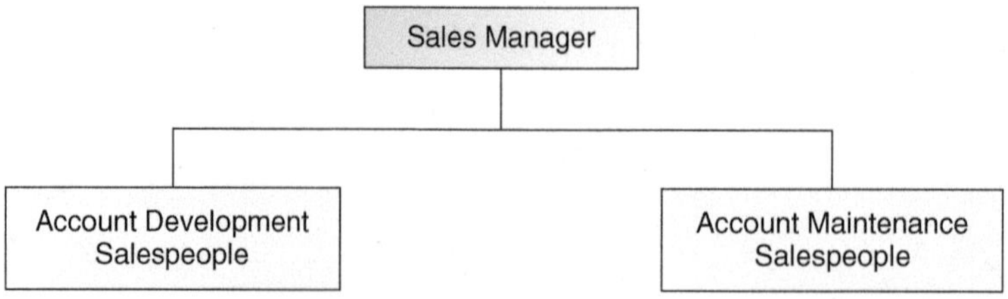

FIGURE 6.11 Functional sales organization.

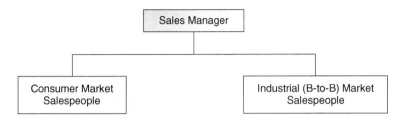

FIGURE 6.12 Customer/market sales organization.

Customer/Market-Oriented Organizations Customer/market-oriented sales organizations are appropriate for companies whose products are purchased in multiple combinations by several customer types with unique needs. Aircraft manufacturers such as Boeing (www.boeing.com) and Lockheed-Martin (www .lockheedmartin.com) have different marketing efforts for government, military, and commercial markets. Similarly, electric utilities separate their markets into residential and commercial accounts. Figure 6.12 shows a customer/market sales organization.

As we discussed in Chapter 3, CRM is more effective when salespeople are organized by market or type of customer. Customers are frequently classified by industry, channel of distribution, or importance of the account (national or local). A market-oriented sales structure can often more successfully reach different industries with unique needs. But the other two classifications – distribution channels and account size – are less obvious. Organization by distribution channel is appropriate when a company sells through several competing channels that use different pricing strategies such as drugstores, supermarkets, and discount stores. Under these conditions, it may be advantageous to create separate sales units for each channel to reduce customer complaints and divided salesperson loyalties. The organization structure for IBM is customer/market oriented because salespeople typically specialize in serving a customer type in a single industry. The objective of this approach is for salespeople to better understand, through specialization, how customers/markets purchase and use their products and services. Salespeople are then more effective in building long-term relationships with customers.

Many companies use a variation of customer/market-oriented structures called key account selling. Key accounts are high-volume, important customers that require added attention from the sales organization. This type of organization is based on the 80—20 rule that says a large percentage of a firm's sales (80%) come from a relatively small number of accounts (20%). Organization by national or key accounts is appropriate when a company's customers centralize buying at national or regional offices. Companies such as Gillette (www.gillette.com) prefer a customer-focused sales structure to give special attention to large accounts. Key account organization also avoids duplication of sales efforts because only one salesperson calls on a particular customer. With the trend in business toward concentrated industries, large customers, centralized purchasing, and fewer new markets to enter with existing products, ensuring the satisfaction of the largest and most important customers is becoming a critical concern. Thus, many sales organizations are transitioning to organizing by customers/markets because it enables them to create competitive advantages and achieve superior financial performance.[6]

Market-oriented structures overcome some limitations of product structures, but still have disadvantages. Market-oriented structures result in expensive overlapping of territorial sales coverage when customers are geographically dispersed. Higher overhead from added layers of management and increased compensation for salespeople who represent a full line of products also adds cost. Overall, however, market-oriented sales organizations match the problem-solving approach of today's consultative sales reps.

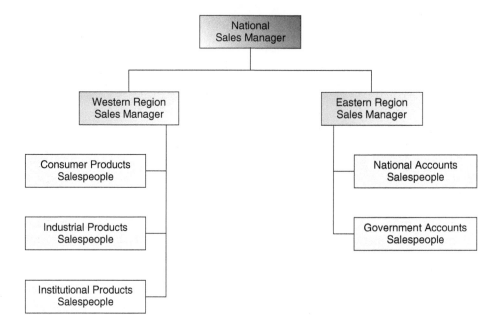

FIGURE 6.13 Combination sales organization – organized by geography, products, and customers.

Combination Combinations of basic types of sales organizations are not uncommon. Figure 6.13 depicts a sales force organized by territories, products, *and* markets. Many companies use a combination structure for the sales organization as they grow in size and complexity. Kraft Foods (www.kraft.com) and DuPont (https://www.dupont.com) are successfully using a combination sales structure. Similarly, Coca-Cola (www.coca-cola.com) uses a product-by-market structure. For many years, Coca-Cola was produced as a single product made according to a secret formula and sold at one retail price. However, with the demand for sugar-free soft drinks, bottled and flavored waters, large bottles, and new flavors, Coca-Cola began marketing a range of sizes, prices, and new products to specific market segments.

Team Selling

Decisions occur at many levels in medium and larger sized businesses. A single salesperson seldom knows enough about all products and services to close the sale at all the various levels. At the same time, customer expectations are escalating, and many companies are looking for ways to reorganize traditional sales functions and processes. To increase the likelihood of closing sales and to deliver superior value consistently under today's highly competitive conditions, companies increasingly are relying on team selling. Team selling relies on several individuals in an organization to sell products and services to all relevant decision-makers. The goal of team selling is to develop long-term, mutually beneficial relationships among people, products, and companies.[7]

Team selling is often used by firms that have a key account or customer/market-oriented sales organization. Reasons for adopting a team selling approach are that information needs of customers are large, a number of people are involved in the decision to buy, the potential sale is large for the selling or buying company or both, and the complexity of the products or services is high and therefore beyond a single individual's capabilities.[8] Selling teams frequently include individuals from diverse functional areas such as operations, finance, R&D, marketing, and sometimes even the CEO. In fact, an increasing number of companies have offices located in or near the customer's facilities. One of the best examples of this concept is the large number of companies that have set up offices in Bentonville, Arkansas to sell to WalMart (www. walmartstores.com). Procter & Gamble, for instance, has a team of 200 people who work solely on the Wal-Mart account.[9]

Guidelines for Developing Sales Organizations

Sales organizations that are well designed encourage effectiveness, efficiency, intra-organizational cooperation, customer loyalty, and profitability. All new sales reps should be given a copy of the organizational manual, which includes the organizational chart and describes the duties of each job and reporting relationships. There is no perfect sales organization, but here are suggestions for developing a sound sales organization:

- *A market-oriented approach* – recognize the customer as the organization's reason for being, and design the organization with a customer-centric approach.
- *An approach designed around sales activities* – we cannot ignore the people who will perform the work. Sales organizations should be designed to accomplish major sales activities, such as sales planning, sales development, sales analytics, and customer service. In practice, it may be necessary to adapt an organization to take advantage of human strengths or to work around weaknesses.
- *Defined areas of authority and responsibility* – clearly communicate individual responsibility and allocate sufficient authority to accomplish work assigned. For example, if branch sales managers are given sales quotas, they should be able to select their sales members and allocate their efforts.
- *A reasonable span of control* – in addition to handling administrative responsibilities, sales managers must be able to control the sales force adequately through frequent contact. While there is no magic number of people a manager can control, keep the number at ten or fewer, depending on the abilities of the sales manager and salesperson, as well as the challenges encountered.
- *Flexibility* – an organization needs to be flexible enough to survive stress, such as sales declines or the loss of key personnel. Enhance flexibility by ensuring a trained replacement is ready to move into any position and by using staff specialists to give the manager more time for other tasks.
- *Coordination and balance* – sales managers should not allow any unit or individual to have excessive influence on operations. Ensure coordination and balance in all relationships involving sales and marketing, as well as other functional areas of the business.
- *Access to Data and Sales Analytics* – the sales organization should be designed to take advantage of customer and market data and sales analytics technology, and must be continuously evolving as new data and innovations become available.

Not every possible sales organizational form can be listed here. Sales Management in Action Box 6.3 provides an interesting idea to add creativity to the sales organization.

Size of the Sales Force

The size of the sales force is an important consideration in managing it. Some companies may have too many salespeople and need to reduce the size of their sales force;

Box 6.3 | Sales Management in Action 6.3

Going Outside the Organization for Creative Ideas

Big firms are seldom as creative as small and medium-sized firms. Corporate culture is often a good thing. But a strong culture can also create a climate where all employees think and act the same way. Some innovative companies involved in sales and marketing actually go outside in search of innovative ideas. One CEO has recruited people who come from all walks of life and have expertise in quite different areas from the immediate task. For example, an "idea generator" might be pulled from working behind the bar to sit in on a planning team for the day. A bartender is likely to generate thoughts the Sales Manager would never come up with alone. Similarly, a mechanic

and a mom might be recruited to assist in developing new automotive sales approaches. The key to making the "Going Outside" method effective is these people are from outside the organization and are not restricted by the corporate culture existing on the inside. The CEO or sales manager who adopts this approach can avoid what has often been a major sales bias of the past – emphasizing conformity over creativity.

Sources: Rooney, J. (2006). Tapping the brilliance of ad-hoc experts. *Advertising Age* 4: 18; Mayer, D. and Greenberg, H. (2006). What makes a good salesman. *Harvard Business Review* (July–August): 164–71; and John G. Agno blog, Looking outside for executives. https://coachingtip.blogs.com/coaching_tip/2006/02/looking_outside.html (accessed August 2019).

others may have too few salespeople and need to increase. The number of salespeople in a company directly influences the nature of sales planning, as does the type of salespeople. Companies must consider not only the optimal number of salespeople, but also the number of inside sales reps versus outside sales reps. Other issues that affect the size of the sales force include productivity of salespeople, turnover, and company strategies such as increasing market share or cutting costs. Sales managers generally welcome increases in the size of the sales force. But they usually oppose decreasing sales force size, even when necessary, because they fear giving competitors a differential advantage.

Several methods are available to determine the optimum sales force size, including equalized workload, incremental productivity, and sales potential. Each has strengths and weaknesses, as we will see next.

Equalized Workload   In the equalized-workload method, each salesperson is assigned a set of customer accounts that demand about the same total sales time and effort. The assumption of this approach is that the total workload in covering the market consists of three factors: customer size, sales volume potential, and travel time. There are six steps in the workload calculation:

1. *Classify present and prospective customers according to sales potential.* For example, there are 500 total customers (present and potential) classified by sales volume potential:

   > Class A (large) = 100 accounts
   > Class B (medium) = 180 accounts
   > Class C (small) = 220 accounts

2. *Estimate the length of time per sales call and desired call frequency for each customer class.* Assume both present and potential customers require the same time per sales call and the same sales call frequency.

Class A: 30 minutes/call × 150 calls/year = 75 hours/year
Class B: 20 minutes/call × 210 calls/year = 70 hours/year
Class C: 15 minutes/call × 160 calls/year = 40 hours/year

3. *Compute the total work necessary to cover the market.*

Class A: 100 accounts × 75 hours/year = 7500 hours/year
Class B: 180 accounts × 70 hours/year = 12,600 hours/year
Class C: 220 accounts × 40 hours/year = <u>8800</u> hours/year
Total = 28,900 hours/year

4. *Calculate the total work time available per salesperson.* Assume a sales manager specifies that salespeople work 40 hours per week, 45 weeks per year (allowing 7 weeks for vacations, holidays, illness, and the like). Thus, each salesperson has the following hours available each year.

40 hours/week × 45 weeks = 1800 hours/year

5. *Divide the total work time available per salesperson by sales task.* Assume management requires salespeople to apportion their time in this manner.

Selling tasks: 55% = 990 hours
Nonselling tasks: 20% = 360 hours
Traveling: 25% = 450 hours
Total 100% = 1800 hours

6. *Determine the total number of salespeople required.* Divide the total market workload by the total selling time available per salesperson.

Salespeople needed = 28,900 hours

= 29.2990 hours

Assuming the company now has 20 salespeople, it should hire nine new people to equalize the workload.

Despite its apparent simplicity, the workload method requires up-to-date and accurate input data. Estimating the number of potential customers and the ideal frequency of calls can be especially difficult. Furthermore, the approach does not consider the cost–profit ratio associated with a sales call and the cost of increasing the size of the sales force. Nevertheless, it provides valuable input to decision-making when combined with managerial judgment.

Incremental Productivity The incremental-productivity method is based on economic marginal analysis theory. It assumes the sales force should be increased until profits added by the salesperson hired last equal the costs of employing that salesperson. Managers must compare the costs of training a new salesperson, his or her salary, and selling expenses with the marginal revenue generated by that salesperson. In short, marginal revenue equals marginal cost in the ideal size sales force.

To illustrate this method, consider a company whose total sales volume varies directly with the number of salespeople in the field. Costs of goods sold remain constant at 70% of sales. All company salespeople receive a straight salary of $25,000 yearly plus commissions of 5% of total sales volume. Also, each salesperson receives $1000 per month for travel expenses. Currently, there are 32 members of the sales force, and the sales manager wants to determine whether to add more. To make this decision, the managers must first estimate the increases in sales volume, costs of goods sold, and gross margin from the addition of each salesperson.

Salesperson #	Sales volume ($) −	Cost of goods ($) =	Gross margin ($)
33	300,000	210,000	90,000
34	225,000	157,500	67,500
35	150,000	105,000	45,000
36	75,000	52,500	22,500

Next, the sales manager calculates the net profit contribution with the addition of each salesperson, as below:

Salesperson #	Gross margin ($) −	Salaries ($) +	Commissions ($) +	Total expenses ($)	Net profit contribution ($)
33	90,000 −	25,000 +	15,000 +	12,000	= 38,000
34	67,500 −	25,000 +	11,250 +	12,000	= 19,250
35	45,000 −	25,000 +	7,500 +	12,000	= 500
36	22,500 −	25,000 +	3,750 +	12,000	= −18,250

The incremental analysis shows it would pay to add three more salespeople but not four. While the third salesperson (#35) would add $500 of marginal revenue, the net profit contribution of the fourth (#36) would be a negative $18,250.

Limitations of this approach include lack of cost data in most organizations, the assumption of no increase in efficiency as new salespeople become more experienced, and not including the effect of territorial assignment on the marginal revenue produced by new salespeople. Nevertheless, the incremental productivity concept can help sales managers think pragmatically about sales force size, even if the relationship between marginal cost and revenue is imprecise.

Sales Potential The sales potential approach to determining sales force size starts with the sales manager's assumption of what the average sales representative will achieve in terms of annual sales volume. Divide the total sales forecast for the year by this figure to obtain the number of salespeople needed. In equation form, the relationship is:

$$N = \frac{S \times (1+T)}{P}$$

where

N = number of salespeople needed
S = annual sales forecast for the company
P = estimated sales productivity of the average salesperson
T = estimated percentage of annual sales force turnover

For example, if the company sales forecast is $10 million, annual sales volume productivity for the average salesperson is $500,000, and the anticipated annual rate of sales force turnover is 20%, the calculation is:

$$N = \frac{\$10,000,000 \times 1.20}{\$500,000} = 24$$

Twenty-four salespeople are needed.

In using the sales potential approach, the sales manager must consider several limitations. First, a sufficient lead time is needed for formal training and field experience before new salespeople reach average productivity. Second, since all salespeople are not equally productive, we must account for the relative quality of each salesperson hired. Third, the sales manager must estimate resignations, retirements, and promotions in estimating sales force turnover. Finally, any adjustments in the sales forecast will require changes in the size of the sales force.

Instead of relying on just one method to determine sales force size, sales managers will probably employ all three approaches to see how closely they coincide before making the final decision.

Manufacturer's Representatives One relatively low-risk way to increase the sales force is to use manufacturers' representatives. Entrepreneurial, independent salespeople who sell products for several noncompeting companies, manufacturers' reps usually become specialists in certain markets before starting their own sales operations. Many companies use manufacturers' reps to do specialized selling or to increase call frequencies on certain customers. In the frozen foods market, Quaker Oats (www .quakeroats.com), a Division of PepsiCo, Inc., believes manufacturers' reps enable the company to increase call frequencies on supermarkets so in-store stocks are replenished at least weekly. Along with providing specialized selling experience and expertise, a fixed cost-to-sales ratio, and rapid penetration of new markets, reps may also bring problems. They sometimes are reluctant to handle customer service problems, to go to training, or to allow control over their sales activities. Moreover, they tend to emphasize major product lines where minimal selling is necessary. Finally, their time with customers is divided because they also sell other manufacturer's products.

Small companies often start out using agents to sell their products instead of spending their limited resources on maintaining their own sales force. Manufacturers' reps offer a way to minimize selling costs so more funds can be allocated to new product development, sales forecasting, and pricing. Thus, manufacturers' reps can be a substantial benefit to companies they represent.

Developing a High-Quality Sales Organization

The overall quality of the sales organization is contingent on effective organization in general. The sales manager should consider the following practical guidelines in developing and managing the sales organization.

- *Develop the sales organization around data generated by a sales portal.* Capturing accurate and timely data that generates insights from sales analytics will provide a foundation for an optimal sales organization.
- *Be sure authority equals responsibility.* Salespeople find it difficult to perform effectively without the authority to make necessary decisions.
- *Put salespeople where they fit best.* Consider geography and personality types and compare aptitude for inside and outside positions or national and local accounts.
- *Be willing to delegate.* The task of the sales manager is to accomplish objectives through the efforts of the sales force.
- *Be more than just an efficiency expert.* Do not ignore qualitative considerations while focusing on quantitative issues. The human element must be considered.
- *Hold sales force personnel accountable for what they do.* This is the basic means of maintaining control.
- *Be flexible.* An organization structure effective today may not be the best for tomorrow. The sales force organization must be open to new ideas.

- *Know what needs to be done.* Sales force organizations should be directed toward accomplishing sales goals.
- *Organize the sales force to avoid unequal workloads.* Inequitable distribution of work for salespeople creates satisfaction and reduces productivity.

These guidelines should result in a highly productive sales force. A well-thought-out and carefully developed sales organization can be invaluable to salespeople, customers, and the company. But the really critical part of any sales organization is the quality of its people.[10]

Chapter Summary

1. **Understand the purpose and levels of organizational planning.** Planning creates the essential framework for all other decision-making. It requires sales managers to anticipate the possible outcomes and future implications of current decisions. Thus, planning is an attempt to manage the future.

   Every manager should plan, and more effective planners tend to be more effective managers. Top management focuses on strategic planning for the company, while middle managers – such as regional and district sales managers – spend most of their planning time on shorter-run tactical plans. As planners and administrators, sales managers must (1) define goals and objectives, (2) set policies, (3) establish procedures, (4) devise strategies, (5) direct tactics, and (6) develop and enforce controls.

2. **Apply the sales planning process including strategic and tactical sales planning.** Sales planning is the primary function of sales managers because the sales plan provides basic guidelines and direction for all other sales decisions and activities. In their role as planners and administrators, sales managers must set goals and objectives establish sales policies and procedures, devise strategies and tactics, and implement controls to ensure that goals and objectives are achieved. Prior to beginning the planning process, sales managers should think through the six-stage process of diagnosis, prognosis, objectives, strategy, tactics, and control. The actual steps involved in the sales planning process are (1) analyze the situation, (2) set goals and objectives, (3) determine market potential, (4) forecast sales, (5) select strategies, (6) develop detailed activities, (7) allocate necessary resources (budgeting), (8) implement the plan, and (9) control the plan.

   Strategic sales planning is the process of setting the sales organization's overall objectives, allocating total resources, and outlining broad courses of action. Strategic decisions give the organization a total plan of action to serve customers better, to take advantage of competitors' weaknesses, and to capitalize on the firm's strengths. Tactical sales plans are the functional subplans that underlie and accomplish the overall strategic plan. Tactical action plans identify what needs to be done, who is responsible, what resources are needed, and what benefits are expected. It has been said that strategic sales planning is what generals do while tactical sales planning is what soldiers do.

3. **Avoid unsuccessful sales planning.** The major cause of unsuccessful sales planning is likely the number of unchallenged and often erroneous assumptions made in each stage of the planning process. Dialectic and contingency planning can help overcome the inherent problems of underlying assumptions in sales planning. Another reason for planning failures is the

perfunctory approach often followed in the planning process whereby the plan is simply filed away after preparation, without having much impact on actual operations.

4. **Describe different ways to organize the sales force, including calculating its optimal size.** Most sales forces can be organized in four different ways: (1) by geography, (2) by function, (3) by market or customer type, or (4) by a combination of two or more of the preceding. Many sales organizations also are supplemented by manufacturers' agents or reps. Optimal sales force size is estimated using three different approaches: (1) equalized workload method, (2) incremental productivity, or (3) sales potential. Probably the easiest approach to apply in developing the sales organization is the sales potential approach, which requires only an annual sales forecast, estimated sales productivity of the average salesperson, and an estimate of anticipated annual sales force turnover. But it is often the most risky. The best decision is based on comparing the results of all three approaches, and then selecting the optimum size.

Key Terms

Diagnosis	**Strategy**	**Contingency**	**Sales budget**
Prognosis	**Tactics**	**planning**	
Objectives	**Dialectic planning**	**Sales forecast**	

Notes

1. www.ibm.com (accessed August 2019).

2. General Electric Sales and Marketing Portal. http://www.geautomation.com/smp (accessed August 2019), General electric power. https://www.ge.com/power/about/suppliers (accessed August 2019).

3. www.salesforce.com Connect to your customers in a whole new way with the world's #1 CRM platform. https://www.salesforce.com/# (accessed August 2019).

4. www.ibm.com; and Trusted platforms for today's digital transformation. https://www.redbooks.ibm.com/?lnk=ushpv18ct10 (accessed August 2019).

5. Matrix organizational structure: advantages, disadvantages & examples. https://study.com/academy/lesson/matrix-organizational-structure-advantages-disadvantages-examples.html (accessed August 2019).

6. 4 Important differences between key accounts and sales. https://kapta.com/key-account-management/4-important-differences-between-key-accounts-and-sales/ (accessed August 2019); and Jones, E., Dixon, A.L., Chonko, L. and Cannon, J. (2005) Key accounts and team selling: A review, framework, and research agenda. *Journal of Personal Selling and Sales Management* 25: 181–198.

7. How to create a team selling approach that wins more deals. https://blog.hubspot.com/sales/team-selling-approach (accessed August 2019); and Menguc, B. and Barker, T. (2005) Re-examining field sales unit performance: Insights from the resource-based view and dynamic capabilities perspective. *European Journal of Marketing* 39: 885–909.

8. Best practices for successful team selling, sales training connection. http://salestrainingconnection.com/2013/10/06/team-selling-8-best-practices/ (accessed August 2019); and Jones, E., Dixon, A.L. Chonko, L. et al. (2005) Key accounts and team selling: A review, framework, and research agenda. *Journal of Personal Selling and Sales Management* 25: 181–198.

9. WalMart new selling strategies that can help drive more sales. https://www.sellerapp.com/blog/walmart-selling-strategies/ and https://corporate.walmart.com (accessed August 2019).

10. Ashley, C. 10 Tips to build a top-notch sales organization. https://www.wrike.com/blog/10-tips-build-top-notch-sales-organization/ (accessed August 2019); and Salesforce.com: A cloud-based customer relationship management solution. https://www.salesforce.com/form/sem/sales-software/?d=70130000002E07a&nc=7010M000000jBAn&DCMP=KNC-Google&ef_id=EAIaIQobChMI2N3xoPH94wIVTuDICh2qOQUCEAAYBCAAEgJecPD_BwE:G:s&s_kwcid=AL!4604!3!185426944022!b!!g!!%2Bsales%20%2Bmanagement&&gclid=EAIaIQobChMI2N3xoPH94wIVTuDICh2qOQUCEAAYBCAAEgJecPD_BwE (accessed August 2019).

Chapter Review Questions

1. What assumptions might a sales manager make (sometimes subconsciously) about the marketplace in preparing the annual plan? How would you ensure that these assumptions are valid? [LO 1]

2. Do you think the role of the sales manager in sales planning, organizing, forecasting, and budgeting will become less or more important with the ever-growing power of computers and software sophistication? Explain. [LO 1]

3. What are the potential benefits of sales management planning? [LO 2]

4. What are the essential planning and administrative roles of the sales manager? [LO 2]

5. What is the difference between a sales strategy and a sales tactic? Give recent examples of each using a source like the *WSJ*. [LO 2]

6. What are three types of performance standards relevant for sales managers? When is each type particularly appropriate? [LO 2]

7. What are the biggest sources of unsuccessful sales planning? [LO 3]

8. When is organizing departments by distribution channel appropriate? [LO 4]

9. If a sales firm has 200 "A" customers and 200 "B" customers, and each sales call to an "A" consumer takes 1 hour and each sales call to a "B" consumer takes 2 hours, the firm expects 75 sales calls per year to "A" customers and 100 sales calls per year to "B" customers. The salespeople spend 20% of their time on nonselling tasks and 25% of their time traveling from sales call to sales call. How big of a sales force is needed? [LO 5]

It's Up to You

Suppose you were asked to advise a family-owned farm equipment company in Iowa on their sales management practices. The company has been successful for many decades without any formal organizational structure or any real effort at sales planning. Different family members tell "Uncle Ted" where they are off to each day and somehow the company has managed to survive and make a decent living for everybody in the company. However, you believe some type of formal planning is needed to optimize their sales performance. You are asked to make a short presentation to the family with your recommendations. What would you do to convince them that formal planning and organizing would be a good thing for the company. Develop a short PowerPoint slide show that you would use to accomplish this task. It's really up to you!

Online Exercise

Think of three companies where you would like to get a sales job. List them and describe the business that each is in. Use Internet resources to see what each company is doing with time management and their sales force. What type of time management system would you recommend for each company? Have they selected the best type of time management training approach?

Role-Play Exercise

Role Play: Denman Business Forms

For many years Denman has been a leader in manufacturing and selling business forms and related products directly to industrial users. The last 10 years could be characterized as a "change" decade for this industry. The current situation facing Denman can be summarized as follows:

- Demand for business forms has declined in recent years because of increased affordability and usage of desktop publishing.
- Denman's market share has been steadily shrinking for the past five years.

- Future growth in sales and profits is not expected to come from business form sales.
- The sales force has little autonomy or authority, and training historically has been in areas such as order taking and inventory control.
- Denman has three major product lines – business forms, office supplies, and office equipment – and sales reps sell only one product line so they can specialize, even though each customer gets sales calls from three separate Denman sales reps.

Role-Play Participants and Assignments

Rick Andrews, CEO and owner, is in his mid-50s and argues the entire problem is at the sales level. They must be out of touch with what's happening with their customers and they need to work harder.

Patrick Schul, recently hired Sales Manager with ten years experience at Cisco, says they have a loyal sales force and need to be careful what actions they take. While the situation they are facing is difficult, he believes more information is needed to make the right decision.

In-Basket Exercise

You are a sales manager for a consumer goods company that has just launched a new product. Although all the staff members are extremely excited about its potential, after only a few months on the market the product is generating disappointing responses from buyers. One of your salespeople recently heard a major wholesaler, serving over 500 supermarkets, say: "We've had this product three months, and it's not moving, so we're going to yank it from the stores!"

Consider the following: How do you respond to this? What do you tell your salespeople? What tools are available to help you in the rather gloomy situation?

Prepare a list of things you will discuss in a meeting with your salespeople to deal with this issue.

Ethical Dilemma

Bruce is a branch sales manager in a traditional line-organization. He decides to assign the sales force based on products rather than geographic territories. His thinking is that this will increase the perceived expertise of the sales force. However, his supervisor approaches him upon hearing of the plan. "The problem is that you will end up assigning some salespeople predominantly cash cows, others are getting problem children, while still others are assigned only stars." Bruce replies that he has thought of this and assigned only the most experienced salespeople to stars and the least experienced people to problem children. Some of the salespeople have begun to complain to Bruce after only a few months of the plan.

Questions

1. Does this situation present any moral dilemmas for Bruce or his supervisor? Explain.

2. Can any moral issue be resolved without scrapping Bruce's organizational plan completely?

CASE 6.1   PlayMart Toyz: Building a Sales Organization

It was December of 2020, and Pam Siira found herself contemplative and somewhat detached. On the outside, she was able to join her new husband and friends in the celebration of the holiday season. But inside, her mind was working nonstop – organizing, planning and strategizing. She had accepted a challenging, yet exciting new role that was to begin the first week of January and was responsible for achieving a major objective.

In November, Pam accepted an offer to be Senior Vice-President of Sales for PlayMart Toyz. Siira previously had a working relationship with PlayMart, having sold the company's famous water guns and dart guns for ten years, but she was never an employee of the company. As an independent manufacturers' representative, Siira represented several toy manufacturers, along with PlayMart. Now, she was working solely for PlayMart as an executive reporting to the owner and she had the responsibility of doubling sales to $100 million over the next five years.

The change in employment status required Siira to organize her thoughts and efforts a bit differently. She was no longer "independent" in the sense of working for herself. She was now responsible to a company that had invested its future in her, and her new role focused on managing the other North America PlayMart sales reps. This would involve hiring and firing when necessary, training them properly, troubleshooting any issues along the way, motivating them to give maximum effort to reach objectives and evaluating their efforts. This was going to be a change from what she was used to but Pam felt ready for the challenge!

Aside from the new role and status, Pam was also considering how to reorganize PlayMart's sales organization. While toy sales have been steadily growing in the United States, retail toy stores have been faltering at an alarming rate as consumers shifted to online purchasing. For years, the sales organization consisted of 50 independent sales representatives working on a commission basis. Each representative received a 3% commission of total dollar sales volume and was placed according to geographic territories based on potential sales volume. In more dense areas like the northeast there were two or more PlayMart reps in a particular state, while in the plains region one rep handled several states. The goal was for each sales rep to be able to earn a worthwhile commission in the area that he or she covered.

Online shopping, however, was forcing many specialty retail toy stores out of business. Toys-R-Us and KB Toys were both "key accounts" for PlayMart, however KB struggled and was forced to close over 800 of its 1324 stores nationwide, and was ultimately purchased by Toys-R-Us. This purchase, however, was not enough to save Toys-R-Us, which ultimately closed its doors in 2018. The same effect was true for mass merchandisers such as K-Mart, which was also a key account for PlayMart. K-Mart, at its peak, had 2323 stores, but was down to 200 by 2018. Some of PlayMart's smaller key accounts were also affected as Shopko went out of business in 2019 and Sam's Club closed 63 of its stores to focus more on its online business. The reduction in the number of stores selling PlayMart Toyz called to question the need for so many sales reps, and what the best territory alignment would be.

PlayMart Toyz has regional offices in Bentonville, Arkansas where the company's lone "key store account," Wal-Mart, has its headquarters, and Chicago, Illinois where K-Mart is located. Wal-Mart, the largest store retailer, continues to do a healthy store business and has developed a strong online presence as well, however, a decision needed to be made on the Chicago office. Pam needs to determine whether to move the second regional office to Seattle, Washington where the company's "key online account," Amazon, is located. Amazon has disrupted so many industries in becoming the largest online retailer in the world and is primed to become PlayMart's largest customer. Other smaller key accounts include Meijer, Kohl's, Target, JC Penney, and Costco. The rest of the customer base includes regional drug outlets, regional chains, pool and spa chains, and toy distributors.

The PlayMart Toyz product line started with large water guns that kids could be seen "blasting" streams of water at each other during the hot summer months. Sales of this product are highly seasonal and skewed toward warmer climates. Over the years, the company has added products that would provide balanced sales throughout the year and would reach different age groups. For example, dart guns, young girl's makeup kits, and play horse action figures are items that are sold year round. Mobiles, soft crib toys, and musical toys are targeted to infants and toddlers and are also year round. And sporting goods such as pogo sticks and foam balls are targeted to children in their formative years and are slightly skewed toward the summer months. Products are all manufactured in China according to PlayMart Toyz specifications and are shipped to the United States and Canada.

PlayMart is well established in major retail chains so much of the sales rep's job was really one of inventory management. Each sales rep monitored inventory at the chain level and was responsible to make sure:

- the chain's yearly forecast is accurate
- actual sales are on par with historical data
- current inventory levels are sufficient to handle demand
- the proper amount of new shipments are in-transit
- the proper amount of product is on order

Traditionally, the bottom line for the chain was to have product available on each store's shelf when customers came looking. Being out of stock on a particular item meant the store failed to properly satisfy customers and ran the risk of sending that customer to a competing chain. The PlayMart rep's job was to work together in partnership with each chain to make sure this did not happen. This relationship was changing however for two reasons. First, each year more customers were moving to online shopping, making forecasting difficult, so the issue became one of having too much product on the shelves that wasn't being sold. Many of these chains adapted to the situation by adding an online presence so that their customers had a choice of purchasing online and in-store; more product stayed in the warehouse where online orders were fulfilled, and less made it out to the store shelves. Second, automated reordering and tracking software enabled the chains to better track their sales, place orders, and track the movement of those orders from the warehouse in China to their own. This reduced the reliance on the salesperson. Salespeople were still needed to handle any issues and to sell promotions, but this reduced interaction meant fewer salespeople were needed, and these salespeople were responsible for more accounts and developing new business.

Another issue facing the toy industry is the seasonality of certain items. The toy industry has two seasons: summer and the holidays. Planning and strategizing for summer occurs in June/July. It is at this time that decisions are made as to what will be needed for spring/summer of the following year. Orders must be placed, product manufactured and shipped, product received and sorted at the chain's distribution center, and then finally shipped to the stores and placed on the shelves. The entire process is repeated in December/January for the next year's fall season with merchandise being shipped in June. Basically, PlayMart needs to plan one year in advance.

It is at these times that the sales representative needs to be working together with the chain to make sure enough product is planned for shipment and that it will be delivered on time. Failure to do this accurately results in product arriving too late, having too much product at the end of the season, or having to order another shipment from China, which may not arrive in time causing additional problems. The first situation results in missing the rush as customers come in waves when the season starts but drizzle out afterwards. If a retailer doesn't have what the customers want when they want it, customers will look elsewhere. The second situation forces the retailer to discount heavily to unload product. This eats into profits. The last situation can be a problem as someone has to absorb the cost of reordering and potentially marking down the product. This last expense usually falls in the shoulders of the manufacturer and can be very expensive. The occurrence of any of these situations can sour one of the partners, so the harmony of the relationship depends on these partners getting it right the first time!

Siira knows most salespeople are motivated by money and they might be interested in encouraging a customer to overorder so to increase sales volume and the amount of the commission check. Some, she knows, might be motivated to keep the customer happy and will stay silent when the chain underorders, even though they know it will leave the company out of stock early in the selling season. Consequently, Siira has been wondering how she can get her salespeople to work together with the chains to plan properly for the good of both parties in the relationship.

The remainder of the sales rep's job is to find and cultivate new business. This has become very difficult with the decline of store retailing. It becomes more of an issue of finding new markets. One new market to explore is the online retailers, some toy-specific and some general merchandise, that are cropping up on the Internet. Another is pool and spa retailers, both store and online, that sell water guns and other water-related toys. Four years ago, PlayMart made a concerted effort to enter this market and achieved some success, but there is clearly room to grow. The one issue here is the pool and spa market is highly seasonal in some parts of the country. Siira realizes developing these two new markets will be important to reaching the objective. That means she has to develop a strategy for determining how to approach and get sold into these markets. Once the strategy is developed, she has to develop an incentive plan to motivate the PlayMart reps to implement the strategy.

So as Pam Siira was celebrating the holidays and relocating her office in December 2020 all of these issues regarding her new job were rolling around in her head:

- How many sales reps does the company need?
- Should the company employ an online sales force and a store sales force?
- What should the territory alignment be?
- How can the company improve its planning with its customers so that PlayMart Toyz can maintain a harmonious relationship with all its customers?
- What new markets would be best to pursue? Which ones will allow the company to grow the fastest?
- What new strategies can she employ over the next five years to achieve the 100% increase in sales that the company has set forth as her objective?

Questions

1. Should PlayMart Toyz reduce the size and alignment of the sales force?
2. Should Siira close the Chicago office and move it to Seattle?
3. Should the company employ an online sales force, along with a store sales force?
4. What other markets could PlayMart pursue to reach its objective?
5. Outline a plan for how PlayMart Toyz' sales force should be configured. Address size and alignment, combined or separate online/store, independent/corporate, and office location in your plan.

Case prepared by: Frank Notturno, Madonna University

CASE 6.2 Modern Century Dental Supply, Inc.

Dental practices regularly place orders for disposable products such as gloves, masks, bibs, and chair covers. There are several well-known suppliers such as Pearson, Henry Schein, and Patterson. But there are numerous other smaller dental supply companies that try to sell to local dental practices within a 100-mile radius. These smaller suppliers offer their products at a lower price to compete with well-known supply companies. Dental practices usually place orders for the disposable products every three or six months. The amount of orders is based on the number of patients who are being seen in the office and the available space to store the supplies.

Modern Century Dental Supply, Inc. is owned by two friends, Brad and Jeff. They manufacture high-quality dental supplies in the United States and offer their products at a low price but still higher than the larger, well-known dental supply companies. As a result, their profit margin is low and unfortunately their annual sales is low as well. If their sales volume was higher, it could have compensated for the low margin, but their company hasn't grown much since starting three years ago.

Brad and Jeff have been calling local practices and those within driving distance from their warehouse to grow their sales. They offer dental practices the price matching option with their current suppliers for the first order in order to show them the quality of their products. Dentists who purchased from Jeff and Brad for the first time, at the price-matched price, love the quality of the Modern Century Dental Supplies, but were not willing to continue ordering from them due to higher prices.

Jeff and Brad decided to start selling online and introduce their company to dental practices all over the United States. In order to do so, they utilized the power of social media in combination with their paid advertising. They advertised on Facebook, Instagram, and Twitter but even six months after implementing the social media plan their sales have not improved much. Brad started talking to a few dentists who were their customers, and discussed their new sales strategy. About half of the dentists commented they barely have time to sign in to their social media accounts, while the other half never even had any social media accounts. They did confirm, however, that in many of the practices the back

office managers are the ones who make these purchases. Brad and Jeff decided to advertise heavily on social media to target and hopefully capture more sales from dental offices where practice managers are making the purchases. They also hired two additional sales employees to make cold calls and call on practices that prefer to speak to a sales person and meet them face-to-face.

Direct-to-customer sales revenue increased by 5% within six months of hiring the two new salespersons. During the same time period, online revenue increased by 15%. The owners need to decide which selling strategy is best for their company. They also are considering whether selling fewer products will reduce their manufacturing costs and generate more revenue, or if selling a broader line of products is best.

Questions

1. What should the two entrepreneurs do first to decide how to expand their business?

2. What topics should their sales plan include?

3. What other selling strategies could be employed?

4. Considering recent successes in direct versus online sales, what is the best decision to geographically expand Modern Century Dental Supply, Inc.?

Case prepared by: Neda Mossaei, University of South Alabama

CHAPTER 7

Time and Territory Management

Improving Sales Productivity

George likes to unwind and reward himself during the middle of the week by taking a leisurely two-hour, or so, lunch on Wednesdays. He feels this helps motivate him to work for the rest of the week. On Fridays, after working hard all week making sales calls and providing customer service, George usually takes the afternoon off to play golf. Although he has convinced himself these habits actually help his productivity by keeping him motivated, it's more likely they are "time traps" that can seriously diminish George's performance as well as the efforts of the whole sales team.

Time and territory management strategies help sales managers determine which accounts are called on, when, how often, as well as how much time is spent on sales account activities versus other sales tasks. Rising fuel prices have had a domino effect, increasing the prices of many other products and services – and sales costs have consistently increased. While it varies by industry and geography, the average outside sales call costs almost $600, a figure that can be as much as $3000 for some high-tech firms. Managers are therefore searching for less expensive ways to sell products and services. For instance, electronic channels such as social media, digital marketing, telemarketing, Internet, intranets, and extranets are increasingly being used to perform many steps in the selling process. As a result, many traditional sales forces have become hybrids, relying on these electronic channels to support field salespeople.[1] Simultaneously, managers are equipping their salespeople with laptop computers, mobile phones, iPads, cloud-based systems to access information produced by sales analytics, and similar technology enabling them to access websites, blogs, wikis, podcasts, webinars, real-time inventory and delivery information, and other support mechanisms. Along with these technological innovations, there is renewed emphasis on better training for salespeople to help them use technology to improve time and territory management.

Technology enables salespeople to become increasingly independent from sales managers. But time and territory management will continue to be among the sales manager's most important roles.

LEARNING OBJECTIVES

When you finish this chapter, you should be able to:

1. Describe the basic reasons for establishing sales territories.
2. Apply procedures for setting up sales territories.
3. Evaluate when and why to revise sales territories.
4. Apply the concepts of self-management to sales and sales management.
5. Use the techniques of scheduling and routing for sales success.

Establishing Sales Territories

One of the most important tasks in time and territory management is effective development of sales territories in combination with assignment of salespeople to territories. A sales territory is usually a specific geographic area that contains present and potential customers and is assigned to a particular salesperson. Because the total market of most companies is usually too large to manage efficiently, territories help the sales manager in directing, evaluating, and controlling the sales force. Assigning sales territories also helps the sales manager achieve a match between salesperson skills, sales efforts, and sales opportunities.

Most companies establish territories on a geographic basis. Customers and prospects are grouped so the salesperson serving the accounts can call on them as conveniently and economically as possible. But geographic considerations are only the initial focus. Companies determine their markets primarily based on the number of customers and their purchasing power, not on square miles.

Reasons for Sales Territories

Sales territories facilitate planning and controlling selling activities. But sales managers have other reasons for developing them.

Enhance Market Coverage Sales calls should be planned as efficiently as possible to ensure proper coverage of current and potential customers. Coverage is more thorough when each salesperson is assigned to a well-designed sales territory rather than when all salespeople are allowed to sell anywhere. A sales territory should not be so large that the salesperson spends a great deal of time traveling, or has time to call on only a few of the best customers. On the other hand, a sales territory should not be so small that the salesperson is calling on customers too often. Sales territories should be big enough to represent a reasonable workload but small enough to ensure the salesperson can visit all potential customers as often as needed.

Minimize Selling Costs Inflation affects the price of food, lodging, and transportation – and selling costs. Sales managers must design cost effective territories by eliminating or minimizing overnight travel and by finding alternate methods of reaching customers. Alternatives to face-to-face interaction with customers include digital marketing, teleconferencing, social media, e-mail and text messaging, and inside sales reps. These options enable salespeople to work from office or home, thereby reducing travel, hotel, and dining expenses.

Strengthen Customer Relations Efficient territories enable salespeople to spend more time with present and potential customers and less time on the road. The more salespeople learn about their customers by spending time with them, the better they understand customers' problems and the more comfortable their relationship becomes – until it evolves into a partnership. Sales territories facilitate regularly scheduled sales calls on customers. Regular contact with prospects or infrequent buyers via alternative methods can turn infrequent buyers into more frequent buyers, and prospects into customers.

Build a More Effective Sales Force Well-designed sales territories motivate sales-people, improve morale, increase interest, and build a more effective sales force. When salespeople are assigned a territory and given responsibility for it, they become the manager of the territory. Clearly defined responsibility is a powerful motivator for many people, and when territories are distributed equitably among the salespeople, with specific accounts assigned to each, fewer conflicts arise about which accounts belong to each salesperson and why.

Better Evaluate Sales Assigning salespeople to specific geographic areas improves performance evaluations because salespeople can be assessed on their performance compared with the territory's potential. Historical databases enable sales managers to access past information and compare it with current performance in each terri-tory. By examining sales performance territory by territory, sales managers can identify changing market conditions and make needed adjustments in sales tactics. Assigning salespeople a specific geographic area facilitates efficient routing, establishes a strong customer base by building rapport with each customer, and helps determine the best call frequency for each customer.

Coordinate Selling with Other Marketing Functions Well-designed sales ter-ritories enable management to better perform other marketing functions. Sales and cost analysis is easier on a territory basis than for the entire market. Market research and sales analytics on a territory basis are also more effective for setting sales quotas and expense budgets. If salespeople are able to help customers launch advertising and media campaigns, distribute point-of-purchase displays, sell channel partners on cooperative marketing communications strategies, or perform other work related to sales promotions and social media, the results often are better when work is managed on a territory-by-territory basis rather than for the market as a whole. Finally, if the company uses inside sales reps to support the field sales force, territory assignments enable them to pinpoint whose territory the customer or potential customer is in, rather than just randomly assigning a salesperson to the account. In this way, sales-people can respond to customers more quickly and effectively.

Reasons for Not Having Sales Territories

Despite the advantages, geographic sales territories are not needed in all situations. For example, small companies with only a few people selling in a local market do not need territories. Assigning sales territories in this case would only slow decision-making by sales managers. Territory assignments generally become necessary only as the sales force increases in size.

Individuals may not be assigned sales territories when sales coverage is far below the sales potential of the market – that is, when there is more than enough business for every salesperson. This is often the case for small companies; those selling products most everyone needs (such as insurance), and those introducing a new product. Not assigning sales territories in such situations, however, could mean a potential segment of the market is neglected, thereby inviting competition to enter the market. If this is the case, the firm should hire additional sales people as soon as possible.

Other reasons have been used to justify not establishing territories. For example, sales territories may not be needed when sales are made primarily on the basis of social contacts or personal friendships, or if territories will have to be revised in the near future, thereby likely resulting in disagreement among the salespeople.

CRM and Sales Territories

As we discussed in Chapter 3, companies that have adopted a CRM perspective see benefits in assigning territories based on customer characteristics rather than geography. Thus, a tire manufacturer may assign one sales manager to deal with all U.S. OEM customers, while another may be assigned responsibility for a single retailer such as Walmart. The principle here is that the enhanced knowledge that comes when a salesperson deals only with very similar customers more than compensates for any additional costs arising from an inefficient geographic assignment. Thus, in this situation, geography is not the primary factor in assigning responsibilities for customers.

Trust between customers and sales reps is critical with CRM. Thus, the frequency of contact needed between a customer and a salesperson is another important factor in making assignments. Pfizer, Inc. (www.pfizer.com) found maintaining high levels of trust with traditional territory management practices were very difficult. The solution the firm adopted was to use part-time reps to call on customers located in rural areas or not designated as "best" customers. The "best" customers were assigned full-time reps.

Box 7.1 | Sales Management in Action 7.1

Cisco's Web Portal Improves Sales Productivity

Salespeople are much more successful if they have complete and up-to-date customer information. Cisco Systems has more than 40,000 salespeople and hundreds local offices worldwide, as well as numerous regional and corporate headquarters employees. To increase sales productivity, Cisco wanted a new sales management tool to help salespeople work more efficiently and spend more time with customers. One problem was that reps were spending a lot of time identifying high-volume customers. Another was that the reps' daily status reports did not have relevant, real-time, customer information to help them develop close customer relationships. The solution was the E-Sales Web portal initiative, which created Web-based information-sharing tools.

E-Sales included a portal with a collection of sales information and forecasting applications in a single location and a single format, to help salespeople work more effectively and efficiently. Personalized alerts, reports based on user type, sales projections based on realistic customer opportunities, and other specialized features were designed to meet the needs of the sales, finance, marketing, production planning, and executive divisions. One feature was the *My Bookings Reports* for salespeople that deliver near real-time information (every 15 minutes) about customer orders. The *My News* application provides daily information about customers, market issues, competitor activity, and the latest Cisco sales-related information. Another option is *Personalized Customer Alerts* that notify account managers of time-sensitive customer information requiring a salesperson's immediate attention, such as order status, warranty expiration dates, end-of-sale announcements, and so forth. The *Sales Territory* application uses account and geographic data to track sales activities by salesperson and territory. Both qualitative and quantitative assessments using data analytics taken from E-Sales portals demonstrate its value in improving salesperson productivity and improving sales forecasting.[2]

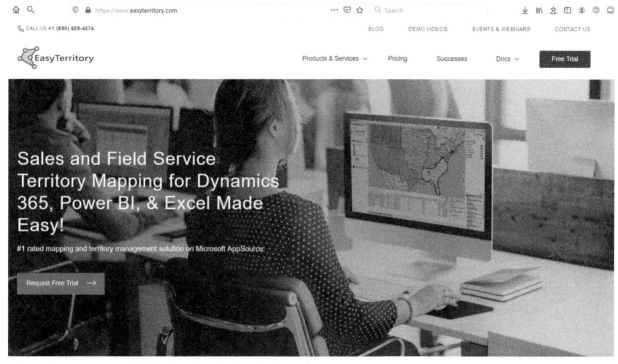

Sales territory management is helped greatly today by technology.
Source: www.easyterritory.com, April 14, 2020.

Setting Up Sales Territories

Whether a company is setting up geographic sales territories for the first time or revising ones that already exist, the same procedure applies: (1) select a geographic control unit, (2) conduct an account analysis, (3) develop a salesperson workload analysis, (4) combine geographic control units into territories, and (5) assign salespeople to territories. All of these steps are executed based on the information obtained from the company's data analytics capabilities.

Selecting a Geographic Control Unit

The starting point in developing territories is selecting a geographic control unit. Units most often used are states, counties, zip-code areas, cities, metropolitan statistical areas, trading areas, and major accounts, or a combination of these. Control units should be as small as possible for two reasons. First, smaller units help management pinpoint the geographic location and/or customer sales potential. Second, small geographic areas make adjusting territories much easier. One salesperson's territory can be increased and another's reduced, and adjustments are easier if the control unit is smaller – for example, a county rather than a state.

Political units (state, county, or city) are often used as geographic control units because census data and other market information for the geographic areas are available. Political units and market factors such as buying habits and patterns of trade flow also serve as geographic control units. For example, sales territories can be based on a trading area that lies within county lines. This makes data for a particular trading area easy to collect.

States Firms sometimes use state boundaries to develop territories, especially in the early stages of territory development. A state may be an adequate control unit for companies with a small sales force covering the market selectively rather than intensively. States as territory boundaries also work well for companies seeking nationwide distribution for the first time. In fact, in these situations salespeople may be assigned to territories that consist of more than one state. This typically is temporary until the market develops, at which time the firm switches to smaller control units.

State sales territories are simple, convenient, and inexpensive. But not many companies use them. Customers from one state often cross boundaries into another state to do their purchasing. For example, hundreds of thousands of shoppers a year cross from New York into northern New Jersey to make their purchases because shopping malls are centrally located and easy to get to, there is less traffic, and New Jersey has a lower sales tax. In the other direction, the tourist appeal of New York City and its diversity of goods and services attract millions of shoppers from around the country, and indeed around the world.

Another reason for not using states as territories is some states are just too large. Most companies would need more than one person to handle California or Texas. If one person did cover California, another salesperson would have to cover a dozen or more Rocky Mountain states to have a territory equal to California in sales potential. Finally, a state may simply be too large and diverse in market potential for management to control or evaluate salesperson performance.

Counties and Zip Codes Counties are much smaller units than states and better for dividing territories. There are over 3000 counties in the United States but only 50 states. Territories with approximately equal sales potential are easier to develop in smaller control units.

Counties as control units offer several other advantages. Counties typically are the smallest units for which government data are available. Many government, commercial, and private sources report market data (such as population, retail sales, income, employment, and manufacturing information) by county. Also, counties are usually small enough so that management can better identify problems. Finally, the small size of counties makes shifting salespeople from one territory to another easier because fewer customers are affected.

Counties have some of the same drawbacks as states. Not all counties are similar in size, sales potential, or ease of market coverage. Some may be too large for practical use as control units. For example, Cook County (Chicago) may require several salespeople to cover the market adequately. In such cases, a company may divide a county into several territories, so the control unit is smaller than a county.

Territories based on zip codes are flexible and typically reflect the economic and demographic characteristics of individual areas, whereas political subdivisions, such as states and counties, do not. D&B – Dun's Market Identifiers® (DMI) is a directory file produced by D&B, Inc. that contains basic company data, executive names and titles, corporate linkages, DUNS® (Data Universal Numbering System) Numbers, organization status, and other marketing information on over 300 million businesses globally, including public, private, and government organizations. Dun & Bradstreet also produces other databases available on DIALOG, including D&B Duns Financial Records PlusTM. Non-U.S. businesses can be found in several D&B files accessed via the DIA-LOG Database Catalogue. In designing territories, sales managers can use this directory to pinpoint companies by geographic area.

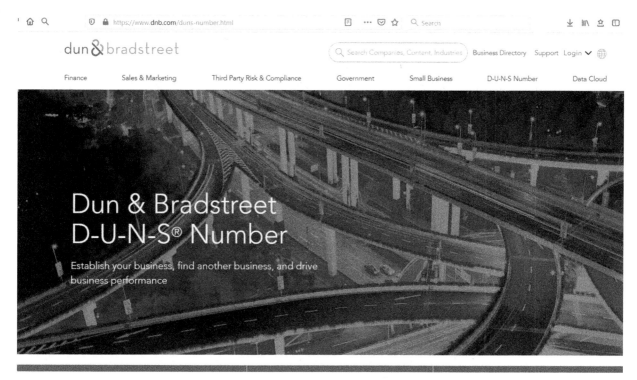

The Dun and Bradsheet identifier system.
Source: www.dnb.com/duns-number.html, April 14, 2020.

Cities and Metropolitan Areas Metropolitan statistical areas (MSAs) often serve as territories instead of cities. MSAs are boundaries that include the major city as well as the surrounding suburban and satellite cities. Each MSA must have at least:

- One city with 50,000 inhabitants or more, or
- A census-defined urbanized area of at least 50,000 inhabitants and a total MSA population of at least 100,000 (75,000 in New England)

Some MSAs are considered a core-based statistical area (CBSA). A CBSA is a U.S. geographic area consisting of one or more counties (or equivalents) anchored by an urban center of at least 10,000 people plus adjacent counties that are socioeconomically tied to the urban center by commuting. The large concentration of population, retail, industry, and income in MSAs and CBSAs is a justification firms use to choose them as control units for territories.

Trading Areas Another possible control unit for establishing sales territories is the trading area. A trading area is a geographic region that consists of a city and the surrounding areas that serve as the dominant retail or wholesale center for the region. Trading areas are a logical control unit, since they are based on the natural flow of goods and services rather than on political or economic boundaries. Firms that sell through channel partners often use trading areas as a control unit.

Customers in one trading area typically do not go outside their boundaries to buy merchandise, nor will a customer from outside enter the trading area to purchase products. This is not always the case, however, because sometimes trading areas overlap, and buyers in the overlapping areas make purchases in one or both areas.

A trading area as a geographic control unit has several advantages. Since trading areas are based on economic considerations, they are representative of customer buying habits and patterns of trade. Trading areas also facilitate planning and control. For example, the same salesperson usually calls on all wholesalers in a trading area. Thus, the likelihood salespeople will steal each other's accounts is minimized.

Several disadvantages are associated with using trading areas as control units. Two of the main problems are defining trading areas and obtaining statistical information to use in forecasting the sales potential in each area. The difficulty of defining trading areas has been reduced by companies such as Rand-McNally (www.randmcnally .com/), which specializes in fleet telematics that improve fleet management with GPS tracking, and publishes maps of the United States delineating several hundred trading areas. Another company is BizReport, which publishes *Sales & Marketing Management* magazine as well as maps associated with trading areas. As an example, one report provides consumer market information by counties, while another shows industrial market data on a county-by-county basis. Companies can reduce limitations in available statistical data by adapting the dimensions of the trading areas to the counties included. While county market information may not fit the trading area exactly, it often is the best and most readily available data.

Conducting an Account Analysis

After a company selects a geographic control unit, the next step is to audit each geographic unit. The purpose of the audit is to identify customers and prospects and determine the sales potential of each account.

Accounts must first be identified by name. Many sources containing this information are available. For example, *Spokeo.com* (a search engine that organizes white pages listings, public records, and social network information into profiles to find people) is one source for identifying individuals quickly. Another source is Dun and Bradstreet, which has a list of millions of U.S. businesses. This service can, for example, tell sales reps how many doctors are in any city in the United States, complete with names, mailing addresses, and phone numbers. Other sources for identifying customers include internal company records of past sales; trade directories; professional association membership lists; directories of corporations; publishers of mailing lists; trade books and periodicals; chambers of commerce; federal, state, and local governments; and personal observation by the salesperson. Today almost all of this information is available electronically, either directly or from third-part data aggregators, so it can quickly be stored for analysis in the firm's database.

After potential accounts have been identified, the next step is to estimate the total sales potential for all accounts in each geographic control unit, using one of the methods discussed in Chapter 5. Then determine how much of this total the company can expect to get. Estimated sales potential for a company in a particular territory is often a judgment call based on the company's existing sales in that territory, the level of competition, any differential advantages enjoyed by the company or its competitors, and the relationship with current accounts.

Sales managers forecast sales potential in a territory using big data, data analytics, and other statistical techniques. Firms can store and organize the information they gather about potential and existing accounts in a variety of ways: name, zip code, account size, purchase frequency, or primary business. Once the information is obtained, organized and stored, often with cloud-based storage providers, the company can retrieve the information in seconds in whatever form or basis of analysis they need, such as estimated sales potential based on predetermined criteria. Sales managers often classify accounts based on annual buying potential in order to determine appropriate sales call patterns.

Developing a Salesperson Workload Analysis

The third step in setting up sales territories is to develop a salesperson workload analysis, an estimate of the time and effort required to cover each geographic control unit. The estimate is based on an analysis of the number of accounts to be called on, the frequency of the calls, typical length of each call, the travel time needed, considering traffic issues, and the nonselling time required. The outcome of a workload analysis is a sales call pattern for each geographic control unit.

Several factors affect the number of accounts reps can call on in each geographic control unit. One is the length of time required to call on each account. This in turn is influenced by the number of people to be seen during each call, the amount of account servicing needed, and the length of waiting time. The sales manager can find information about these factors from company records or by talking with salespeople. Nonselling time also must be included in a workload analysis. Nonselling activities include preparing for sales calls as well as processing orders and servicing accounts after the sale.

Another factor affecting the number of accounts a rep can call on is travel time between accounts. Travel time will vary considerably from one region to another depending on transportation, traffic congestion, weather conditions, and the density of present and potential accounts. The objective of workload analysis is to minimize travel time and thereby increase the number of accounts reps can visit and/or the frequency of sales calls. Fortunately, there are a number of traffic congestion apps today, such as Google maps and Waze that enable salespeople to identify the fastest route between customers by avoiding traffic backups.

The frequency of sales calls is influenced by a number of factors. Accounts generally are divided into several groups according to sales potential and assigned to a category – often A, B, or C. For example, accounts with potential annual sales of over $1 million would be called on most frequently and placed into group A; accounts with potential sales of $250,000–$1 million would be put into group B and called on less frequently; and finally group C accounts, with potential annual sales under $250,000, would receive the lowest number of sales calls. Other factors influencing call frequency are the nature of the product, the level of competition, and estimates of a seller's ability to win the business. For example, supermarkets purchasing canned food products require frequent calls because of the high inventory turnover rate, whereas a private high school purchasing textbooks requires only two or three calls a year. Of course, if there is strong competition within the market, more frequent sales calls may be needed.

An alternative to the analytical rigor of mathematical models is the portfolio analysis approach presented in Figure 7.1. This method classifies accounts into one of four types based on competition and opportunity, and each account type merits different sales call frequencies.[3] Segment 1 (top left) represents what most companies call key accounts. Segment 2 (top right) is considered a potential customer or prospect. Segment 3 (lower left) is a stable account, and Segment 4 (lower right) represents a weak account. Although the portfolio analysis approach is logical and easy to use, it is somewhat limited by having only four account categories.

Competitive Assessment

		Strong	Weak
Account Opportunity	**High**	Attractiveness: Accounts are very attractive, offer high opportunity, and sales organization has strong position. Call Strategy: Frequent sales calls.	Attractiveness: Accounts are potentially attractive based on high opportunity, but sales organization has weak position. Call Strategy: Frequent sales calls to strengthen position.
	Low	Attractiveness: Accounts are somewhat attractive since sales organization has strong position, but future opportunity is limited. Call Strategy: Moderate frequency to maintain current position.	Attractiveness: Accounts are very unattractive since they offer low opportunity and sales organization has weak position. Call Strategy: Minimal sales calls and migrate personal sales calls to telephone or Internet.

FIGURE 7.1 Account analysis.

Combining Geographic Control Units into Sales Territories

Up to this point the sales manager has been working with the geographic control unit initially selected for setting up sales territories. Whether the unit is a state, county, MSA, or some other geographic area, the sales manager is now ready to consider grouping adjacent control units into territories of roughly equal sales potential. Numerous territory mapping software packages are available to align territories quickly and equitably. One of these packages is described in the Sales Management in Action Box 7.2.

Box 7.2 | Sales Management in Action 7.2

Sales Territory Alignment and Optimization

Since each sale often costs as much as $1500 or more, the sales force is one of the most expensive human resource investments for many companies. As a result, companies have turned to Sales Force Automation (SFA), Customer Relationship Management (CRM), enhanced sales training, and account management programs to increase sales force productivity. While all these approaches can produce benefits, sales territory alignment often increases productivity and sales at a relatively lower cost.

Sales territories are most often based on geographic considerations. When they are out of balance, some areas with high potential can be underserved while other areas are saturated. Similarly, too much effort may be devoted to low-potential customers. Sales and service people need to spend more time seeing and listening to customers, and less time driving.

Oracle Sales Cloud offer a number of territory management and sales analytics services that improve sales force performance by optimizing the shape and content of territories. In combination, they are designed to minimize travel time, balance sales opportunities, and maximize returns. Oracle Sales Cloud, along with other vendors, leverages available information and company criteria with sophisticated data analytics to develop optimal sales territory solutions.

Source: https://www.oracle.com/webfolder/technetwork/tutorials/tutorial/cloud/r13/wn/r13-sales-wn.htm (accessed February 2020).

Sometimes territories have equal sales potential, but each territory has its own level of coverage difficulty, such as poor highways. With almost any realignment, sales managers will have to make compromises, because some territories may have higher sales potential than others. Territories with unequal sales potential are not necessarily bad. Salespeople vary in ability and experience as well as initiative, and some can be assigned heavier workloads than others. Sales managers should assign the best salespeople to territories with high sales potential, and newer or less effective salespeople to the second- and third-ranking territories. Some further adjustment in sales quotas and commission levels may be necessary, depending on the relative sales potential of a specific area and the types of selling or non-selling tasks required.

Assigning Salespeople to Territories

Once the sales manager has devised an optimal territory alignment, the next task is to assign salespeople to territories. Salespeople vary in physical condition, as well as ability, initiative, and effectiveness. A reasonable and desirable workload for one may overload another and frustrate another. In addition, interactions of an individual salesperson with customers and prospects may be affected by factors such as customer characteristics, market traditions, and social influences. Thus, a salesperson may be outstanding in one territory and less effective in another, even though sales potential and workload for the two territories are similar.

In assigning sales personnel to territories, managers should rank them according to relative ability. When assessing a salesperson's relative ability, look at factors such as product and industry knowledge, energy level, persuasiveness, and verbal ability. All good salespeople rate high on these factors, though some are better than others. What ultimately determines the salesperson's assignment to a territory, however, is his or her potential sales effectiveness within that territory. To judge a salesperson's effectiveness within a territory, the sales manager must look at the salesperson's physical, social, and cultural characteristics and compare them to those of prospects and customers in the territory. For instance, a salesperson raised on a farm in Iowa is likely to be more effective with rural clients than with urban customers because he or she would most likely share the same values as the rural clients. The goal in matching salespeople to territories in this manner is to maximize the territory's sales potential by making the salesperson comfortable with the territory and the customers comfortable with the salesperson.

Revising Sales Territories

Firms consider revising established territories for two major reasons. When a firm is just starting in business, territories are not designed very precisely. Often, the firm is unaware of problems in covering a territory, and sometimes the territory's sales potential and workload is over- or underestimated. But as the company grows and gains in experience, the sales manager recognizes where territory revision is needed. In other situations, territories may become outdated because of changing market conditions or other factors beyond management control.

Before making revisions, the sales manager should determine whether the problems with the original alignment are due to poor territory design, market changes, or problems in other areas. For example, if the territory alignment problem is caused by the compensation plan or training program, then it would likely be a mistake to revise sales territories. Generally, however, appropriate redesign of sales territories will have a positive impact on the bottom line.

Signs Indicating the Need for Territorial Revisions

As a company grows, it usually needs a larger sales force to cover the market adequately. If the company does not hire additional salespeople, the sales force is likely to only skim-the-cream in the territory instead of covering it intensely. If sales managers have not estimated territorial sales potential accurately, sales performance may be misleading. Also, morale problems will emerge if there are wide variations among salespeople in territory potential.

Territories may also need revision when sales potential has been overestimated or changes have occurred. Sometimes, a territory may be too small for even a good salesperson to earn an adequate income. Overlapping territories are another reason for revision. This problem usually occurs when territories are split, and it can cause a tremendous amount of dissatisfaction in the sales force. Salespeople are reluctant to have their territories divided because that generally means they must hand over accounts they have built up and nurtured. The thought that another salesperson is reaping the benefits of their hard work can lead to bitterness. The organization should correct this problem in a way that will benefit the existing rep and the new rep. No one should be unfairly penalized in a territorial revision. Overlap should be minimized or eliminated for other reasons, too. For example, overlapping territories usually mean higher traveling costs and wasted selling time, which increases overall selling expenses and reduces profitability.

Territory revisions may be necessary when one salesperson jumps into another salesperson's territory in search of business. This is an unethical practice, and it will cause substantial problems within the sales force unless dealt with quickly. Territory jumping is usually a sign salespeople are not developing their territory satisfactorily. If salespeople are doing a good job covering their own market but contiguous markets have more potential, reps may be unable to resist the temptation to enter adjacent markets. But it can also indicate sales potential in one territory is greater than in another. If territories have been designed properly, there should be no need for jumping. Before making territory realignments, however, the sales manager should evaluate whether closer supervision or the refusal to pay commissions on orders outside a rep's territory is a better solution to the problem.

Territory jumping may also be a sign of poor management. Some salespeople are interested only in quick and easy sales. Instead of developing their own territories, they will jump into another area unless management stops them. Unless quickly halted, territory jumping often leads to higher costs, selling inefficiencies, bitterness, and low morale in the sales force.

Impact of Territory Revision on Salespeople

Salespeople dislike change because of the uncertainty that accompanies it. Management must decide whether it is preferable to avoid territory revisions for fear of damaging morale, or to revise the territories to correct problems. When territories are reduced, salespeople often face a reduction in potential income and the loss of key accounts developed over years. The result is likely to be low morale. Therefore, before making revisions, salespeople should be consulted for suggestions that might avoid or reduce other problems.

Compensation adjustments sometimes can avoid morale problems. Salespeople whose territory is being reduced need to be shown that a smaller territory can be covered more intensely, thereby offering a higher sales volume for the same (or lower) travel time. Most firms talk with sales reps before making a change but make no salary adjustments until the territory develops. The problem here is that developing the territory may take some time, and the salesperson's income may suffer in the meantime. During this transition period, additional compensation or increased commissions may be needed to maintain morale and loyalty.

One approach to compensating salespeople during the transition period is to guarantee the previous level of income. For example, a sales rep covering the entire state of Texas may be earning an excellent commission, even though he or she is only skimming the territory. The sales rep will probably resist the idea of having the territory split in two in order to get better coverage. Thus, the company may guarantee the salesperson's level of commission until he or she has had reasonable time to penetrate the smaller territory and achieve a satisfactory commission level. While this approach may maintain morale and loyalty, it also can reduce the salesperson's aggressiveness in gaining new accounts. Another solution is to compromise. For example, if the transition period is three years, the company guarantees a portion of the salesperson's income but the guaranteed portion declines in the last two years. As the salary guarantee declines, the salesperson's incentive to develop the territory to its full potential increases.

Self-Management

Few jobs allow, or require, more self-management than personal selling. This is particularly true as technology enables salespeople to cover their territories from mobile virtual offices. Instead of fighting what may seem like a loss of control over the sales force, sales managers must recognize that more self-management gives them additional time to spend on other managerial tasks.

Sales managers must make sure salespeople understand self-management is more difficult than getting direct feedback and motivation. But salespeople increasingly must decide what, how, and when to do their sales tasks. Most field salespeople set their daily agenda, sales call objectives, and even performance standards. Empowering salespeople enables them to serve prospects and customers faster and better. A tool such as Oracle CRM OnDemand can improve sales productivity by helping salespeople manage their activities more efficiently. They can quickly and easily create to-do lists, schedule activities and appointments, and track priorities and due dates. By streamlining these and other administrative tasks, salespeople have more time to focus on what they are paid to do – sell![4]

How Salespeople Spend Their Time

Effective and efficient use of time is critical to successful performance for both sales managers and salespeople. Many sales managers spend too much time in the field because they feel most comfortable using the same skills that earned them promotion to sales manager. When managers make sales calls on their own, they are "doing" (as opposed to managing), because this is work salespeople could and likely should perform. Time devoted instead to determining how to accomplish work through other people is managing. Sales managers who make sales calls with their salespeople to observe, analyze, and coach them in improving their presentations are performing managerial duties. The difference between a skillful sales manager and a mere "doer" can make a substantial impact on the success of sales force efforts.

Salespeople who work for firms such as Cisco, General Electric, and IBM spend a large proportion of their time gathering information about potential customers,

TABLE 7.1

Activities of Salespeople

Sales	Communication	Relationship	Team	CRM/Database
- Setting appointments	- E-mail - Internet	- Website - Work with channel partners	- Conferencing - Mentoring	- Collect data
- Preparing sales appeals	- Voice mail - Mobile phone	- Helping customers	- Selling - Coordinate sales support	- Enter data
- Obtain customer background	- Websites - Maintain/develop virtual office	- Call on CEOs		- Update files
- Use technology for presentations	- Conferencing	- Build rapport with buying center		
- Share technology with customers	- Provide technical information			
- Adaptive and consultative selling	- Practice presentation skills	- Build trust - Network		
- Call planning	- Training to update skills	- Work with others within their company		
- Responding to referrals				
- Identify key accounts				
- Listen				
- Ask questions				
- Assess nonverbal communications				
- Traveling				

planning sales call activities, working with other departments, and servicing existing customers. Indeed, it is difficult to identify all the activities salespeople perform, but the list in Table 7.1 summarizes the main types.[5]

Table 7.2 shows the typical ways outside salespeople spend their time. You may have thought outside salespeople spend most of their time selling, but in fact about two-thirds of it is spent traveling, waiting, or doing administrative tasks.

Whether salespeople spend a quarter or a third of their time in face-to-face selling can have a tremendous impact on their sales effectiveness and efficiency. For example, assume the typical salesperson works 40 hours per week and takes a two-week annual vacation. That leaves just 500 hours a year ($40 \times 50 \times 0.25 = 500$) for face-to-face selling for salespeople who devote 25% of their time to selling. Salespeople whose efficiency allows them to devote 33% of their time to face-to-face selling spend 660 hours a year ($40 \times 50 \times 0.333 = 660$), or 160 hours more. Given these assumptions, how much is an hour of the salesperson's time worth at different earning levels? For someone earning $50,000 a year, each hour of selling time costs $100 if only 25% of working time is spent in face-to-face selling, but that cost drops to $76 an hour if selling time is increased

---

TABLE 7.2

How Salespeople Spend Their Time

Activity	Percentage
Prospecting	15
With customers	15
Administrative tasks	35
Service calls	5
Waiting/traveling	30
Total	100%

TABLE 7.3

Dollar Cost of an Hour of a Salesperson's Selling Time

	Approximate cost of an hour of salesperson time	
Earnings	Salespeople who spend 25% of their time in face-to-face selling (500 hours per year)	Salespeople who spend 33% of their time in face-to-face selling (660 hours per year)
$ 20,000	$ 40	$ 30
30,000	60	45
40,000	80	61
50,000	100	76
60,000	120	91
70,000	140	106
80,00	160	121
90,000	180	136
$100,000	$200	$152

to 33%, as depicted in Table 7.3. Thus, finding ways to increase face-to-face selling time yields a substantial payoff in efficiency.

Salespeople can increase interactions with prospects and customers by using combinations of selling aids such as Web conferencing, e-mailing, telephone contacts, and faxing. If a sales rep can increase interactions by 20%, it seems reasonable that sales volume might also increase by 20%. Thus, an increasingly important role for sales managers is coaching salespeople on how to be successful self-managers. Some of the most important concepts to teach salespeople in helping them manage their activities are: (1) finding an optimal combination of effectiveness and efficiency, (2) calculating the return on time invested (ROTI), and (3) setting priorities for objectives and activities. Let's briefly discuss each of these.

Achieving Effectiveness and Efficiency   A basic concept sales managers need to convey to salespeople is that successful territory management depends on an optimal combination of effectiveness and efficiency. Effectiveness is results-oriented and focuses on achieving sales goals, while efficiency is cost-oriented and focuses on making the best possible use of the salesperson's time and efforts. Together, the two equal selling success:

$$E_1 \left(\textbf{Effectiveness} \right) + E_2 \left(\textbf{Efficiency} \right) = S_1 \left(\textbf{Selling Success} \right)$$

Measuring Return on Time Invested ROTI, or return on time invested, is a financial concept that helps salespeople spend their time more profitably with prospects and customers. Return can be measured in various ways, such as dollar sales to a customer, profits on a certain product category, or new customers won. ROTI is the designated return divided by the hours spent achieving it. For example, if a salesperson spends 60 hours in preparing a sales call, making a sales presentation, and providing service to a customer who orders $90,000 worth of products, that salesperson's ROTI is $90,000 divided by 60 or $1500. Another salesperson that invests 30 hours of time to make a sale of $25,000 has an ROTI of $833.

To determine their ROTI for different activities, customers, and products, salespeople need to keep accurate hourly records. Although this may sound like tedious record keeping, it takes only a few minutes a day to record this information. Moreover, personal digital assistants and similar devices can store the information as well as the software to provide real-time updates for sales call planning.

Setting Priorities Setting priorities is essential. Salespeople who don't set priorities often work on relatively minor tasks first because they are the easiest to complete and thus provide a feeling of accomplishment. But this may not be the best use of their time. Priorities should relate to specific objectives to be accomplished over a certain time period, such as a year, a quarter, a month, a week, and even each day. Once managers have determined selling objectives, they should rank them according to their importance and assign dates for completion to each one. Top performing salespeople always set priorities in their work based on Parkinson's Law and the concentration principle.

Parkinson's Law Parkinson's Law says that work tends to expand to fill the time allotted for its completion. For instance, if salespeople have eight hours to write a sales proposal, it will probably take that much time to complete the task. But if salespeople have only four hours, they will somehow manage to complete the proposal within that time frame.

Concentration Principle Often called the "80–20 rule," the concentration principle states that most of a salesperson's sales, costs, and profits come from a relatively small proportion of customers and products. Global firms such as GE, Xerox, IBM, Dell, and Cisco sell their products in many countries, but a small number of countries account for a very high proportion of their sales. The same is true for smaller firms, but in their case the principle suggests a small number of companies will account for a high proportion of sales.

New Sales Manager Roles

Sales force automation and salesperson empowerment are dramatically changing selling. Today, salespeople are able to access customer data 24/7, obtain training by virtual Web conferencing or webinars, increasingly supported by virtual reality (VR) and artificial intelligence (AI), and can communicate with virtually anyone via e-mail, phone, or texting. Thus, the sales manager's former roles as communications conduit, data analyst, information disseminator, and hands-on manager are changing. Increasingly, the emphasis is moving from one-to-one coaching and motivation of field salespeople to re-organizing, training, motivating, and providing support and resources for a hybrid sales force comprised of various types of electronic contacts as well as field salespeople. With increasing empowerment, salespeople are reporting to higher management levels. Many companies have increased the range of control for district sales managers and eliminated lower level sales managers. Overall, the sales manager's job is evolving toward being a channel manager – overseeing a hybrid sales force operating in diverse electronic and field channels and managing channel partner relationships.

To succeed, sales managers need to (1) build closer relationships with customers to better understand their businesses, (2) work in coordinated teams with other departments in their companies to satisfy customers, (3) treat salespeople as partners, (4) improve marketing skills, including direct marketing and e-commerce, to spot potential business opportunities, (5) develop improved motivational skills, and (6) become partners with salespeople and channel members to achieve goals. No other managers will need more eclectic or adaptable skills than sales managers.

Customer Reviews of Performance

Many customers are conducting annual performance reviews of their suppliers and deciding which ones to keep or drop. To avoid unpleasant surprises, sales managers and salespeople should proactively ask for annual performance review meetings with customers. Obtaining regular feedback from customers is one of the most effective ways to keep from losing touch with customers. Among the primary reasons customers switch suppliers is a new supplier offers a better deal, or the sales rep failed to maintain regular contact.

Time Management and Routing

After sales managers have established sales territories and assigned salespeople to them, they should turn their attention to scheduling and routing the sales force within territories. Scheduling and routing are vital in order to keep productivity high and sales costs low. Unfortunately, many companies ignore these tasks. Salespeople often are told either to call on as many accounts as possible or to call only on accounts where the potential is above a specified level.

Some companies do not take the time to route or schedule a salesperson, especially if the salesperson's sales figures are good. A good record can be misleading, however, because even if sales are high, the cost of the sales may also be high. One salesperson may be spending more time and money than necessary on overnight sales calls or wasting time on the road by taking inefficient routes. Another salesperson could be spending too much money entertaining clients or even entertaining the wrong clients. In order to accomplish sales objectives set for the sales force and each individual territory, the sales manager must ensure proper routing and scheduling of each sales rep.

Managing Salesperson Time

Salespeople must be good time managers because this is one of the best ways to improve territory coverage. Think of the salesperson's use of time as a resource-allocation problem, whose solution is to eliminate wasted time, increase efficiency, and maximize productivity. Some examples of time allocation problems are: (1) deciding which accounts to call on; (2) dividing time between selling and paperwork; (3) allocating time between present customers, prospective customers, and service calls; and (4) allocating time to spend with demanding customers or new prospects.

Salespeople must be good time managers to control these problems and maximize time spent interacting with prospects and customers. How can salespeople maximize their productive time? An important first step is to avoid time traps.

Avoid Time Traps Good time use requires that salespeople recognize and avoid "time traps" that can erode their effectiveness (see Table 7.4). Calling on unqualified or unprofitable prospects, failing to prioritize their work, making poor use of waiting time, and not breaking up large, long-range projects into currently manageable pieces are a few of the many time traps that sales reps can easily fall into. Reps also need a system or procedure to help them plan how to use their time effectively (several are described below). Different selling situations will require different approaches to time management. The sales manager must work with the salespeople to develop an effective time management procedure.

Allocate Time In allocating time, salespeople need to first decide on the principal tasks or activities they need to do, and then determine the amount of time to allocate to each. Although sales tasks vary widely, we can classify them into five general areas: waiting and traveling, doing face-to-face selling, making service calls, clearing administrative tasks, and prospecting. A simple way to determine how much time a salesperson is spending on each of the basic sales activities is to ask the salesperson carry out an activity analysis for several representative days – usually five to ten. The analysis should include different days of the week as well as days in different parts of the territory. After the salesperson records time use for several days on an activity analysis

---

TABLE 7.4

Common Time Traps

Calling on unqualified or unprofitable prospects	Failing to prioritize work
Insufficiently planning each day's activities	Procrastinating on major projects, resulting in redundant preparation and paperwork
Making poor territorial routing and travel plans	Inefficiently handling paperwork and keeping disorganized records
Taking long lunch hours and too many coffee breaks	Failing to break up huge, long-range projects into small, currently manageable tasks
Making poor use of waiting time between appointments	Ending workdays early, especially on Friday afternoons
Spending too much time entertaining prospects and customers	Failing to insulate oneself from interruptions or sales calls or while doing paperwork
Not using modern telecommunications equipment such as a cellular phone, pager, facsimile, and laptop computer	Conducting unnecessary meetings, visits, and phone calls
Doing tasks that could be delegated to a staff person or to automated equipment	Neglecting customer service until a small problem becomes a large one that takes more time to resolve

Sales Rep: Ermanno Eaffuso Date: May 8, 2020	
Territory: Atlanta, GA Day: Wednesday	
Call 1: 9:00 a.m. Phil Piper at Centroid Wireless in Suwanee Travel: 20 min. Reorder; try to sell new products	Wait: 10 min. Contact: 35 min.
Call 2: 10:00 a.m. Carolyn Crawford, BTW Co. in Lawrenceville New prospect, just opened last month	Travel: 20 min. Wait: 5 min. Contact: 75 min.
Call 3: 12:00 Luncheon presentation with A&R industries in Lawrenceville, Group of 17, including VP Marketing	Travel: 10 min. Wait: 20 min. Contact: 60 min.
Call 4: 1:30 p.m. Bob Joyce at ACME Associates in Alpharetta Service visit, explain new Web portal	Travel: 30 min. Wait: 10 min. Contact: 35 min.
Call 5: 2:30 a.m. Sid Green at Pinnacle Industries in Sandy Springs. Reorder and service visit.	Travel: 15 min. Wait: 10 min. Contact: 30 min.
Call 6: 3:30 p.m. Laura Smith at Smith and Co. in Roswell New prospect; found website using search engine	Travel: 25 min. Wait: 15 min. Contact: 40 min.
To office: 35 minutes travel	
Administrative work: 1 hr. 15 minutes	

FIGURE 7.2 Daily activity analysis report.

sheet such as that shown in Figure 7.2, the sales manager works with the salesperson to increase the amount of time spent on productive activities.

Set Weekly and Daily Goals The sales manager and the salesperson should work together to develop a weekly action plan. Weekly sales goals set targets for planned days, number of sales calls, number of demonstrations, and type of customer coverage. The sales call plan can set the course of action for the week as well as for each day. Figure 7.3 is a typical sales call planning sheet. Reps can prepare a custom planning format using Excel, or one of many off-the-shelf versions available with standard CRM systems.

Probably the most important aspect of sales call planning is identifying the type of customer coverage. Ranking customers by the volume of business and profit generated enables salespeople to focus on important accounts and minimize time spent with relatively unimportant ones (see Figure 7.4).

In addition to sales call planning, salespeople must also allocate time to selling and nonselling activities. Selling and servicing activities should be planned for the time of day when customers and prospects are available. To the extent possible, nonselling activities – traveling, waiting, and handling administrative work – should be done in nonprime hours, when customers are not available.

Manage Time During Sales Calls A frequently neglected aspect of time management for salespeople is how they manage their time *during* sales calls. Studies show the amount of time salespeople spend with customers does not influence performance, unless it is quality time spent with customers. Instead, sales success is related

Sales Rep: Lisa Cummings	Week ending: September 6, 2021
Territory: Los Angeles, CA	
Planned Itinerary	Completed Itinerary
Number of sales calls ___	Number of sales calls ___
Number of demonstrations ___	Number of demonstrations ___
Number of A account calls ___	Number of A account calls ___
Number of B account calls ___	Number of B account calls ___
Number of C account calls ___	Number of C account calls ___

Detailed Sales Itinerary

Company	Location	Rating	Purpose
Jasmin WiFi	Bel Air	A	Reorder
Linklines Mobile	Santa Monica	B	Sell new product
GIGA News	Glendale	C	Prospect
Apple Store	Burbank	A	Reorder
Verizon Wireless	Pasadena	A	Explain new Web portal

FIGURE 7.3 Sales call plan.

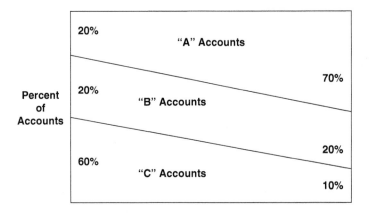

FIGURE 7.4 Customers based on sales volume and profitability.

more to what takes place during the customer–salesperson interaction. Therefore, just spending extra time with customers does not always lead to additional sales. Customers are more appreciative and more likely to develop partnerships with salespeople when sales calls are efficient rather than long.

Evaluate Ideally, as the week progresses, salespeople keep records on planned and actual activities, and constantly monitor their use of time. But at the end of the week, they meet with the sales manager to review the week's activities. Together the rep and manager measure efficiency in selling activities from the sales call plan and evaluate time devoted to nonselling activities. In this manner, they can quickly detect time-allocation problems and take corrective actions. Both parties should monitor time usage over time, so they can identify trends and make any needed changes to improve efficiency and productivity.

Routing One of the most valuable tools for time management is the planning of efficient routes to cover a territory. Territorial routing is devising a travel plan or pattern to use when making sales calls. Routing systems may be complex, but we can develop a basic pattern by finding accounts on a map and then identifying the optimal sequence and fastest route for visiting them. Time wasted on the road is often due to simple things like having poor directions and getting lost. Salespeople who get lost run the risk of being late for an appointment, and few customers will tolerate tardiness. Indeed, some customers refuse to see latecomers. At a minimum, being late is unprofessional and makes closing the sale more difficult.

During initial training, the sales rep and sales manager usually do the routing together. After training, routing becomes the primary responsibility of the salesperson. Routing is not a difficult task for most salespeople, especially if they are familiar with the territory. But poor routing often makes the difference between closing the sale and losing it. A properly designed routing system has three primary advantages:

1. **Reduced travel time and selling costs.** Perhaps the greatest advantage of routing plans is reduced travel time and selling costs, giving salespeople more productive time to spend with customers. The main objective is to eliminate backtracking and nonselling time in completing sales calls. Studies show that as much as one-third of the field salesperson's daily working time is spent traveling. Thus, the typical sales rep spends three to four months of the year on the road. Obviously, anything that can reduce travel time and increase the salesperson's productive selling time is highly desirable.

2. **Improved territory coverage.** A routing plan also improves territory coverage. Detailed information about the number and location of customers, methods of transportation available within a territory, and call frequencies are essential in developing a routing plan that ensures orderly, thorough coverage of the market.

3. **Improved communication.** If the sales manager knows where salespeople are, it is easier to offer last-minute information or instructions. While email and mobile phones generally provide instant communications, other means of contact based on a routing plan can be useful. A well-designed routing plan not only improves communication, but it also helps the sales manager monitor individual salespeople.

The major disadvantage of routing is it reduces the salespersons' initiative and places him or her in a pattern that can become inflexible. Many sales executives believe the field salesperson is best able to determine the order in which to call on customers, and how long to stay. Many times a prospect can be won over with just a little more time and effort – something a formalized routing plan may not allow. Also, in changing market conditions, a strict routing plan prevents salespeople from making changes to adapt to new situations. These disadvantages are reduced by CRM systems that enable continuous updating of routing patterns. After a sale is completed, the salesperson can contact the next customer to reconfirm their appointment or adjust the routing pattern.

Routing is recommended for all companies with a field sales force, but flexibility in implementing it is important. For instance, a firm entering a new area may not know the number and location of potential customers, so a strict routing schedule is impractical. In this situation, routing plans must structure sales calls that are flexible enough to allow reps to pursue previously unknown prospects. Also, high caliber salespeople and independent salespeople such as manufacturers' reps require a more flexible routing approach than other types of salespeople. These individuals resist a fixed routing schedule that restricts their ability to adapt to situations.

The extent to which firms use routing depends on two issues: the nature of the product and the nature of the job. If the product requires regular calls and frequent servicing, routing is definitely necessary. Driver-salespeople who sell soft drinks, tobacco, and grocery items are usually routed. In fact, routing is so important to these salespeople that an irregular call often leads to losing the account.

The nature of the sales job also determines whether routing is desirable. Routing is definitely needed if the job is routine. But situations requiring creative selling techniques and a high-caliber sales force need a more flexible routing schedule. Finally, established companies are more likely to use a routing plan than new companies just entering a geographic area.

Time Management for Sales Managers

Just as salespeople need to make effective use of their time, sales managers also need to manage their time. The approach is similar for both. The sales manager identifies tasks that must be carried out and allocates time appropriately. Sales management tasks differ from company to company. Some sales managers manage a group of salespeople and also personally handle a sales territory. Others may sell to a small number of major accounts while managing the sales force, and still others only manage the sales force.

Sales managers must set daily and weekly objectives. They should make an itinerary of things they need to accomplish in a particular week and rank them in order of importance. Examples might include setting up salesperson recruiting visits to two universities, working out the details for a training program for new salespeople, hiring a training consultant to present a motivational seminar to the sales force, and evaluating sales call reports for individual salespeople.

As the week progresses, sales managers, like salespeople, need to review and evaluate their performance to determine how successful they have been in accomplishing their objectives. If they haven't completed their planned tasks, then the sales managers should examine their planned time allocation and make necessary adjustments. To successfully plan and control the activities of the sales force in achieving sales goals and objectives, the sales manager first must be an effective and efficient manager of his or her own time.

Chapter Summary

1. **Describe the basic reasons for establishing sales territories.** Escalating costs of making personal sales calls have spurred sales managers to seek more efficient and effective means of reaching customers. Sales managers are achieving these goals through time and territory management and by adopting new technology. The six basic reasons for establishing sales territories are to: (1) enhance market coverage, (2) keep selling costs at a minimum, (3) strengthen customer relations, (4) building a more effective sales force, (5) better evaluate the sales force, and (6) coordinate selling with other marketing functions. A CRM program may help determine the way salespeople are assigned to customers.

2. **Apply procedures for setting up sales territories.** In brief, the procedures for setting up sales territories are: (1) select a geographic control unit, (2) conduct an account analysis, (3) develop a salesperson workload analysis,

(4) combine geographic control units into sales territories, and (5) assign sales personnel to territories.

3. **Evaluate when and why to revise sales territories.** Sales territories are often revised when relatively new companies initially over- or underestimate territorial sales potential and the required salesperson workload. In other cases, the original territorial design may become outdated because of changed market conditions. Overlapping territories are still another reason for revision. Territory revision can be damaging to sales force morale unless it is carefully thought-out beforehand, with input from the salespeople. When a territory is reduced, the salesperson assigned there may suffer a sharp reduction in income and the loss of key accounts developed over many years. One solution is to guarantee some portion of the salesperson's income for a year or two until the salesperson can develop his or her new, smaller territory. In any sales territory revision, sensitive and savvy sales managers will seek out and fully consider the advice of the affected salespeople before implemented the change. Oftentimes, some reasonable compromise can be reached that will not adversely affect sales force morale.

4. **Apply the concept of self-management to sales and sales management.** Few jobs allow or require more self-management than personal selling, especially now as technology enables salespeople to cover their territories from mobile virtual offices. Instead of fighting what may seem like a loss of control over the sales force, sales managers should recognize that rep self-management gives them additional time to spend on other managerial tasks. Most field salespeople set their daily agenda, sales call objectives, and even performance standards. But they also must monitor their performance and take corrective actions. Empowering salespeople enables them to serve prospects and customers faster and better.

5. **Use the techniques of scheduling and routing for sales success.** More efficient sales call planning and routing within each salesperson's territory can significantly save time, reduce costs, and improve overall profitability. Salespeople typically spend up to one-third of their time traveling to and from prospects and customers. More efficient time and territory management enables salespeople to make more frequent sales calls on current customers, call on more new prospects, and spend more time developing customer relationships through customer service – all of which should lead to more sales, greater customer loyalty, and higher profits. Numerous mathematical models have been designed to develop routing plans so salespeople maximize their selling time and minimize travel costs. Sales managers use many of these tools to design and update sales territories and routing plans.

Key Terms

Time and territory management	metropolitan statistical area (MSA)	salesperson workload analysis	return on time invested (ROTI)
sales territory	core-based statistical area	Effectiveness	Parkinson's Law
D&B – Dun's Market Identifiers® (DMI)	trading area	Efficiency	concentration principle
			Territorial routing

Notes

1. The Hybrid Sales Channel, https://www3.greatamerica.com/hybrid-business-model (accessed August 2019); Lehman, J. (2006). *The Sales Manager's Mentor.* Mentor Press LLC, Seattle, Washington, 2006; Anderson, R. (1996). Personal selling and sales management in the new millennium. *Journal of Personal Selling and Sales Management* 4 (Fall): 17–32.

2. Cisco Employees by the Numbers. https://www.cisco.com/c/dam/en_us/about/ac227/csr2009/pdfs/CSR_09_Employees_Demographics.pdf (accessed August 2019); 5 Surprising Statistics About Cisco's Channel Strategy. https://www.crn.com/slide-shows/networking/300081194/5-surprising-statistics-about-ciscos-channel-strategy.htm (accessed August 2019); Web-based sales portal provides central point for sales information, forecasting, and management applications. https://www.cisco.com/c/en/us/about/cisco-on-cisco/business-it/web-sales-portal-web.html (accessed August 2019); Cisco on Cisco, https://www.cisco.com/c/en/us/solutions/cisco-on-cisco.html (accessed August 2019).

3. Pulles, N.J., Schiele, H., Veldman, J., and Hüttinger, L. (2016). The impact of customer attractiveness and supplier satisfaction on becoming a preferred customer. *Industrial Marketing Management* 54: 129–140; La Rocca, A., Caruana, A., and Snehota, I. (2012). Measuring customer attractiveness. *Industrial Marketing Management* 41(8): 1241–1248; Schiele, H., Calvi, R., and Gibbert, M. (2012). Customer attractiveness, supplier satisfaction and preferred customer status: Introduction, definitions and an overarching framework. *Industrial Marketing Management* 41(8): 1178–1185; Dubinsky, A. and Ingram, T. (1984). A portfolio approach to account profitability. *Industrial Marketing Management* 13: 33–41; Laforge, R.W., Young, C.E., and Curtis Hamm, B. (1983). Increasing sales call productivity through improved sales call allocation strategies. *Journal of Personal Selling & Sales Management* 54–61.

4. Oracle CRM On Demand, http://www.oracle.com/us/products/applications/crmondemand/index.html (accessed August 2019).

5. Hain, J., Rutherford, B., and Hair, J. (2019). A taxonomy for financial services selling. *Journal of Personal Selling and Sales Management* 39(1): 172–188; Marshall, G., Moncrief, W., and Lassk, F. (1999). The current state of sales force activities. *Industrial Marketing Management January*: 87–98.

Chapter Review Questions

1. Why is it necessary to establish sales territories that are approximately equal in sales potential? [LO 1]

2. Why is it important to match the right salesperson with the right territory? [LO 1]

3. How might a company adopting a strong CRM focus assign sales reps to customers in a way unlike a company without such a focus? [LO 2]

4. What is a salesperson workload analysis report? [LO 3]

5. How should you, the sales manager, be using the latest technology? [LO 3]

6. Describe the Sales Call Grid Analysis Approach to managing sales people. [LO 3]

7. What are some time traps that you personally tend to fall into? What could you do to avoid these time traps? [LO 4]

8. Is it important for a salesperson to be worried about time management during a sales call? Why or why not? [LO 5]

Online Exercise

Think of three companies where you would like to get a sales job. Describe the business that each is in. Use Internet resources to see what each company is doing with time management and the sales force. What type of time management system would you recommend for each company? Has each selected the best type of time management training approach?

Role-Play Exercises

Role Play: Datacor Software

Datacor Software, Inc. (DSI) is a small computer software company located in Lexington, Massachusetts, that develops and market innovative software packages. The company has several managing partners who founded the company. DSI has experienced rapid growth since its formation in 2006, but sales have not reached expectations. The main product is called HURRY-SELL. It was designed to enable sales organization to train sales reps at their own pace and also at a reasonable cost. The primary method of selling is telemarketing to end users and dealers in the United States and Canada. DSI's sales force is organized geographically, so that each of five sales reps has sole responsibility for a defined territory. Reps work from home and sell to end users almost entirely by phone but are expected to visit dealer-account purchasing executives at least twice a year. As the sales manager says, "Dealers are in a position to move a lot of product. Therefore, I do not want reps to be strangers to these companies. There is no substitute for personal contact." Based on the less than expected sales performance, the partners need to brainstorm how to better understand why sales are not what they should be.

Role-Play Participants and Assignments

Karen Tutor, one of the founding partners, argues the entire problem is at the sales level. The company has set up territories and they should be working.

Carlos Rodriguez, another partner, suggests centralizing the telemarketing activities in Lexington.

Sara Kakutani, recently hired Sales Manager with 10 years of experience at IBM, says they need to look at how the salespeople are using their time. She also suggests trying to find out whether sales reps truly know what is expected of them.

In-Basket Exercise

You were recently promoted to sales manager of one of your company's most productive regions. After several weeks on the job you are becoming concerned about Brad, one of your veteran salespeople. Although he is quite successful as a salesperson, Brad seems to have a problem dealing with time. On several occasions you received reports from him that read "Chicago Monday, Detroit Tuesday, Chicago Wednesday." Moreover, his paperwork is late — if he turns it in at all. When you question Brad about these issues, he replies: "I just want to hit the road and sell. I don't have time for all this paperwork! Plus, I've always had the impression it's sales volume that counts with this company. In sixteen years with the company, I've always surpassed my quota!"

1. Prepare a memo explaining to Brad why his behavior is unacceptable and how it is affecting other salespeople.

2. Prepare an email explaining the situation to your boss. Suggest a possible solution and ask her advice on how to deal with this situation.

Ethical Dilemma

Establishing Boundaries for Sales Territories

You have recently received complaints from several of your salespeople concerning one of your newer reps. Although this person is familiar with the assigned sales territories, he has gone into an adjacent sales territory several times to make a sale. He recently landed a new account you have been trying to get for years. When you question him about leaving his territory to make a sale, he claims the prospect was a "referral from a new, important client," who asked him "to call on a friend of his across town."

1. How would you handle this situation without insulting the new client or the territory-jumping salesperson?

2. What do you tell the salespeople in the territory that is being invaded by the new sales rep?

3. Are there alternatives regarding realignment of sales territories?

| CASE 7.1 | Insurance Group for Manufacturers: Territory Management |

Ashley Roberts is a sales manager for the Insurance Group for Manufacturers (IGM). IGM specializes in providing a variety of policies to limit various types of manufacturer's liabilities. IGM provides supplemental insurance and covers "gaps" in insurance coverage of traditional policies. Traditional policy limits are often lower for manufacturers than for other industries such as retailing due to the additional safety risks in a manufacturing environment. For example, IGM has a policy that covers worker's medical costs, should they be injured on the job, above and beyond traditional policy limits. Another IGM policy provides employees with additional coverage when dealing with an extended sick leave. IGM offers over a dozen additional policies for manufacturer's employees. The additional cost of the insurance is typically split between the employer and the employee. Some manufacturers pay none of the cost and some pay all of the cost.

IGM currently operates in 15 mid-western states. For most of the salespeople state boundaries are the geographic territory control units. In a few instances, however, the states are divided into two or even three territories. The divisions are based on account and workload analyses that indicate divisions smaller than states to balance the sales potential between territories. In one case, however, two states were combined into a single territory. IGM has decided to expand operations into five additional southern states: Alabama, Georgia, Florida, Mississippi, and Tennessee. Ainsley Sharp has learned that territory sales potential is derived from the number of manufacturing employees. Ainsley first goes to www.census.gov to find the number of people employed in manufacturing in each state. She searches the U.S. Statistical Abstract after clicking on the "Survey/Programs," "Annual Survey of Manufacturers (ASM)," "Data," "ASM Tables," and "Annual Survey of Manufacturers: Tables." This document, reported in Excel® format shows the number of employees and payroll by state. The number of employees for each of the five states are listed below:

• Alabama	–	234,803
• Georgia	–	351,951
• Florida	–	270,180
• Mississippi	–	130,537
• Tennessee	–	308,966

While the type of manufacturing differs throughout the states, Ainsley has learned sales potential depends largely on the number of employees. She next uses *Dun's Market Identifiers*® to identify the specific manufacturers in each state using the DIALOG database. Access to this database gives her an immediate electronic file containing the names, addresses, officers, and number of employees among other data. The distribution of manufacturers and number of employees in each state identifies two patterns. First, the largest concentration of manufacturers in the five state areas is near Atlanta, Georgia. Moreover, there is about equal sales potential in the Atlanta metropolitan area compared to the rest of the State of Georgia. Second, there is a higher concentration of manufacturing in Memphis, Tennessee than in other areas of the five southern states, except for Atlanta. But in comparison the Memphis area manufacturers are not as large as those in the Atlanta area. Finally, the potential in the remaining states is fairly evenly distributed across the states.

In terms of workload with each account, insurance sales require a large time commitment in the early life of each account. Thereafter, there should be steady, periodic calls on accounts to ensure proper maintenance. With regard to travel, there is much less travel for a salesperson operating in the Atlanta area due to the concentration of manufacturers. But the potential of the largest accounts in the Atlanta area will require more time per account. This additional time will be required not only acquire the accounts initially, but also for maintaining the accounts as well. The larger the number of employees at each new account, the more likely there would be claims, and thus salespersons will have to gather information and verify more information related to claims from the accounts. Otherwise, the workload among the other states would be expected to be pretty evenly balanced with the exception of Mississippi, which in general has smaller accounts. Every other state had some larger accounts in larger cities such as Miami, Birmingham, Nashville, and Memphis.

Questions

1. States are used as the geographic control unit by IGM. What are the advantages of using states? Disadvantages?

2. What should be Ainsley Sharp's goal in determining territories in the new, five state markets?

3. How would you assign territories if you were Ainsley Sharp?

4. Since the data in the Annual Survey of Manufacturers are based on a report that is a few years old, what other more recent sources could Sharp use to ensure her decisions are current?

Case prepared by: Samuel 'Cy' McCord IV, University of South Alabama, and Stacy Wellborn, Springhill College

CASE 7.2 — TechSales & Services, Inc.: Responding to Rapid Growth

TechSales & Services, Inc. (TSS) is a sales software company located in Palo Alto, California. TSS sells sales force automation software to niche markets as an "add-on" to larger more well-known companies selling branded CRM packages. TSS's best-selling product is designed for companies selling medical devices and supplies to the healthcare industry. It's major competitive advantages are the ability to recognize words and phrases associated with the medical and healthcare industry in most major languages (English, French, German, Spanish, and Italian) and the user-friendly interface it has developed with companies selling contact information for prospects likely to be interested in purchasing healthcare equipment and supplies. TSS has several other innovative software products that appear to have significant market potential and should be ready to introduce in the next 12–18 months. The owners of the company are Rex Sanford, a former Microsoft software engineer, who has been developing the products, Hassan Raiyani, a wealthy entrepreneur who has been funding the business, and Ginny Miller, a former Cisco sales representative, that has been handling most of the sales management responsibilities.

TSS has experienced rapid growth since it was founded in 2016, but sales have not yet reached expectations. Average annual sales have been increasing slowly and are now about 4250 units a year worldwide. The owners are not sure why sales have not grown as anticipated. When the company was formed, they hired a consultant from Stanford University to develop a business plan and his projections estimated sales would reach 11,000 units after three years.

TechSales & Services, Inc. has used three primary methods to sell. One is telemarketing directly to users in economically developed countries, mostly North America, South America, European Union, and Australia. The objective of the telemarketing strategy was to maintain as much control as possible over the distribution and sales of products. The second method was to establish distributor relationships with local companies operating in the various geographic territories. A third method of selling was via both the company's website and social media platforms, which sometimes involved direct purchasing via downloads and other times requires one of the telemarketers to work with the customer.

Business Plan Sales Projections in Units

	Projection Year				
	2016	**2017**	**2018**	**2019**	**2020**
Optimistic	10,000	15,000	22,000	37,000	46,000
Likely	7,000	11,000	16,000	23,000	34,000
Pessimistic	4,000	9,000	11,000	18,000	28,000

Substantial growth was anticipated after 2018 based on market awareness and new products.

The TSS sales force was organized geographically into territories so that each of the four sales reps has sole responsibility for a defined territory. With the exception of distributors and Internet sales, reps are expected to sell TSS products via telephone and mail. Sales reps are generally fluent in the languages of their geographic areas in all regions except the European Union because of the number of different languages spoken there. In addition to telemarketing activities, sales reps are expected to visit major distributors at least twice a year to build relationships and provide training on recent developments and future plans. The philosophy of senior management is personal contact with distributors is important to ensure their full support in selling TSS products.

TSS Organization Chart

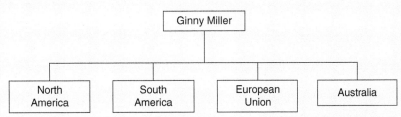

TSS's owners decided to retain the consultant who had prepared the original business plan to work with them to better understand why sales had not developed as expected. After reviewing the situation, the consultant noted the following:

- The current organizational approach is working relatively well except in the European Union. The multiple languages are creating a problem. Because of the potential of this market it may need to be divided into several smaller markets, perhaps on a country-by-country basis.

- Telemarketing activities are both outbound and inbound. Outbound is working better than inbound but both have problems. The inbound telemarketing calls are generated by advertisements in trade journals, booths at trade shows, social media platforms, and by TSS's website. There is a toll-free number for the sales rep in each of the four territories. The consultant suggests that perhaps inbound telemarketing activities need to be centralized and handled out of the home office in Palo Alto, or outsourced to another company that could provide 24/7 coverage. Further, because of the many languages involved it may be necessary to have more than one company handle the telemarketing, but this could cause problems as well.

- Sales reps are expected to sell to distributors located in their geographic territory. The distributors are often small and carry a wide assortment of software packages. Sales reps have been given little support in selling to distributors. In three of the geographic territories the accounts were the result of distributors contacting TSS about distribution possibilities. Channel conflicts have resulted in numerous situations where telemarketers and distributors have argued about who should get the commission on a particular sale. These conflicts are complicated by the fact that some inquiries originate from the website and it is not clear whether the telemarketer or distributor should get the credit. The consultant recommended that the strategy in accepting distributors needed to be closely studied. Distributors must be highly motivated, well supported by training and technical consultation, and aggressive in contacting potential customers and providing feedback to TSS management. In addition, reps need to make more frequent contact with distributors and be given more direction on how to effectively work with distributors.

- In reviewing the four sales territories the consultant and management concluded the current arrangement needs reconsideration. The geographic areas are large and difficult to adequately service, and the potential differs substantially. TSS attempted to become a global company to quickly and needs to consider a more focused strategy in the areas with greatest potential. This is particularly important where sales reps are expected to establish personal relationships with distributors.

- The sales reps are typically young (ages 27–35), college graduates, and enthusiastic about working for the company. But a couple of problems have emerged. The two top sales reps are highly motivated by money. It appears that some of the leads generated by dealers were taken by the sales reps and classified as Internet-originated, but this has been difficult to trace. Another problem is time management. The reps have had difficulty balancing their efforts on telemarketing and distributor visits, and with the differences in time zones for the European Union and Australian reps there often is a problem in responding to inquiries in a timely manner. The consultant suggested outsourcing the telemarketing activities either to a central location in the United States that operated 24/7 or to remote locations in the appropriate time zones.

Questions

1. Which of the consultant's recommendations should be implemented, and if more than one is accepted, what is the highest priority and why?

2. Should TSS divide the European Union into several territories? If yes, what factors should be considered in making this decision?

3. If the sales reps responsibilities are divided so they handle contacts only with distributors, will this help resolve the time management problems? Explain.

4. Should the two top sales reps that appear to be stealing customers from distributors be fired? Or how should this be handled by TSS?

Case prepared by: Bob Erffmeyer, University of Wisconsin, Eau Claire

CHAPTER 8

Recruiting and Selecting the Sales Force

Importance of Recruiting and Selection

Sales force recruitment and selection are among the most important responsibilities of the sales manager, because to most customers and prospects the salespeople *are* the company. What salespeople say, how they handle themselves, and how they react in face-to-face interactions with customers definitely influence the sales success of the company.

Most companies recruit new people in response to business expansion or increased sales. But sales turnover also is a major catalyst to sales force recruitment. The average turnover rate for all industry groups is just under 20% (that is, about 20% of all workers leave their jobs each year), but in some industries employee turnover averages almost 100%. With that level of turnover each year, a company must hire a new employee for every employee currently working for the organization. For salespeople in the United States, the annual turnover rate is about 35%.

What are the typical reasons salespeople leave? Among the most often reported reasons is an incompetent sales manager or company management in general. Other reasons include company expectations for salespeople are too high (e.g., sales quotas) and the compensation is inadequate. Medical sales professionals have a much lower turnover rate than other industries. But they have the highest percentage of salespeople constantly searching for other sales opportunities, due to the difficulty in accessing physicians and customers in general, the volatility of the industry, and unrealistic job performance expectations.[1]

High turnover rates are expensive to a company for a host of reasons. Every job takes some time to learn. During the learning period, most new salespeople do not produce enough revenue to pay their salary. For the average salesperson, it takes about five months to reach meaningful productivity levels. Turnover also affects customer sales and retention. Customers used to dealing with their previous sales rep may take their business elsewhere or follow up with the former sales rep once he or she is settled with a new company. As a result, companies must also cover the expense of replacing lost customers with new ones.

Because of the critical importance of recruiting and the company-wide effects of salesperson turnover, sales managers should have an effective and well-planned system for finding and selecting sales personnel. Its value is even more important when the cost of replacing salespeople is considered. Direct costs, such as maintaining recruiting teams and placing recruiting advertisements, as well as indirect costs like employee time, amount to thousands of dollars for recruiting and selecting new salespeople.

Managing employee turnover and retention requires a lot of effort and time. To be effective sales managers must be flexible, knowledgeable, and empathetic toward their salespeople, particularly top performers. Indeed, matching a competitive offer to keep a top performer can sometimes be a good idea. Sales leaders need to use flexibility and empathy when addressing employee concerns and issues, and respond quickly when the need arises. If sales force turnover is too high, sales managers must examine internal forces such as the sales culture, organizational instability, and territory alignment, as well as external forces like market adjustments due to economic challenges and competitor strategies.

Ineffective recruitment can force companies to hire people who do not meet their needs because not enough qualified applicants apply. Hiring the wrong person can cost a company many thousands of dollars a year in training, salary, benefits, and lost productivity. But if recruitment and selection of salespeople is executed properly, companies can reduce the cost of selecting and developing new salespeople, and they can be productive much faster.[2]

In this chapter we will cover methods for sales rep recruitment and selection. Our focus is on "how to do it" from the sales manager's perspective, but the information will also help you to know what is expected when you apply for a sales position.

What Is Recruitment?

Recruitment is finding potential job applicants, telling them about the company, and getting them to apply. Recruitment should not simply generate applicants. It should find applicants who are *potentially good employees* and motivate them to apply. The entire sales organization ultimately depends on a successful recruiting approach.

Recruiting should be an ongoing activity at all companies. Unfortunately, many sales managers start recruiting only after someone leaves. One of the problems of waiting until you actually need someone is that it limits the pool of candidates you can screen, interview, and ultimately consider hiring. Managers who constantly recruit have a useful backlog of prescreened candidates from which to choose. A second problem of waiting to recruit until you have an opening is that you can fall prey to a sense of desperation. The result of desperation is often hiring someone too quickly without proper screening. Finally, companies lose sales opportunities to the competition during the hiring process when no one is covering the territory.

Many sales managers have little training in recruitment. As a result, they do not know the best sources to find qualified candidates. They may explore the few they know, but sources change quickly in this era of social media so they may overlook the best source. In addition to not being trained in recruitment, sales managers also are not properly trained in interviewing techniques or screening, and do not know how to conduct background checks on candidates. This can only result in bad hires.

Laws and regulations play a major role in recruitment. Sales managers must be familiar with laws that limit questions asked on applications or in interviews. For example, asking about a candidate's personal life, which may hold clues to his or her integrity, stability, or work ethic, is illegal. A human resources (HR) person often accompanies recruiters on college campus recruiting trips as one way of making sure the laws and regulations governing recruiting are followed.

The Recruitment Process

No single set of applicant characteristics or abilities can tell you as a sales manager which recruits to hire for sales positions. Different types of sales positions call for performing different activities and therefore different skills. So you must assess each recruit's characteristics and abilities to determine whether that person is likely to do well in a particular sales position.

To ensure new recruits have the aptitude necessary to be successful in a particular type of sales job, it's best to follow systematic procedures in the recruitment process. The steps in this process are shown in Figure 8.1.

Newly established firms or divisions go through each of the steps. Existing firms should have completed the first three steps – conduct a job analysis, prepare a job description, and identify sales job qualifications – but many do not. This is one reason many firms are ineffective in recruitment and selection and suffer turnover problems. Firms that have written job descriptions and qualifications need to review them from time to time to ensure they accurately represent the current scope and activities of sales positions.

Job Analysis

Before a company can search for a salesperson, it must know something about the sales job to be filled. To improve the process, the firm should conduct a job analysis to identify the duties, requirements, responsibilities, and conditions of the job. A proper job analysis has these steps:

1. Analyze the environment in which the salesperson is to work. For example:
   - What is the competition the salesperson faces?
   - What kinds of customers will be contacted, and what problems do they have?

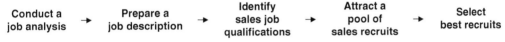

FIGURE 8.1 The recruitment process.

Salesperson recruiting is an important topic across many industries.
Source: https://www.entrepreneur.com/article/290342, April 14, 2020.

- What knowledge, skills, and potential are needed for this position?
- What products and services will the salesperson be selling?

2. Determine duties and responsibilities expected from the salesperson. Obtain information about these from:
   - Salespeople
   - Channel partners, if any
   - Customers
   - The sales manager and
   - Other marketing executives, including the advertising manager, marketing services manager, distribution manager, marketing research director, and credit manager.

3. Spend time making calls with several salespeople, observing and recording the job tasks as they are actually performed. Do this for different types of customers and over a representative period of time.

Preparing a Job Description

The result of a formal job analysis is a job description, probably the single most important tool used in managing the sales force. The job description explains to job applicants and current sales personnel what the duties and responsibilities of the sales position are, what skills are needed on the job, and on what basis the new employee will be evaluated. Since it will be used in recruiting, selecting, training, compensating, and evaluating the sales force, the job description should be in writing so that everyone can refer to it when needed.

Job descriptions help managers not only to supervise and motivate, but also to determine whether each salesperson has a reasonable workload. Most companies provide an overview of their job descriptions online. To see examples, type the key words "cisco sales representative job description" and a company name into a search engine. For example, Cisco Systems lists current job descriptions at the following website: https://www.indeed.com/q-Cisco-Sales-Representative-jobs.html. Two excellent websites to obtain information on sales job descriptions are www.Indeed.com and www.Glassdoor.com.

Since the job description is used in evaluating the salesperson's performance, and even in terminating poorly performing employees, many of the tasks must be stated in quantitative terms. For example, the number and frequency of sales calls by type of customer, the number and types of reports to be turned in, and the number of sales promotion displays to be set up should all be included. In addition, since many tasks compete for the salesperson's time, the job description should specify the job's priorities. Most companies review the job description with sales candidates during the initial interview. If this is done properly, candidates then know exactly what is expected of them before they accept the job. They can also ask specific questions about each of the tasks included in the job description.

Sales industry experts say quite a few job descriptions are so brief and ambiguously written they are of little use in the hiring process. Thus, it is important to be specific in preparing job descriptions. Table 8.1 includes a checklist for developing a job description. It is organized into six major categories: sales activities, servicing functions, territory management, sales promotion, executive activities, and goodwill.

Developing a Set of Job Qualifications

The duties and responsibilities in the job description should be converted into a set of job qualifications recruits have to perform satisfactorily on the sales job. Determining

TABLE 8.1

Checklist for Preparing a Sales Job Description

Sales activities
- Make regular calls
- Sell the product or product line
- Handle questions and objections
- Check stock; identify possible product uses
- Interpret sales points or products to customers
- Estimate customer's potential needs
- Emphasize quality
- Explain company policy on price, delivery, and credit
- Get the order

Servicing functions
- Install the product or display
- Report product weaknesses and complaints
- Handle adjustments, returns, and allowances
- Handle requests for credit
- Handle special orders
- Establish priorities
- Analyze local conditions for customer

Account/territory management
- Arrange route for best coverage
- Maintain sales portfolios, samples, kits, etc.
- Establish and maintain customer database
- Balance effort with customers against the potential volume

Sales promotion
- Develop new prospects and accounts
- Distribute company, product, and industry information
- Make calls with customer's salespeople
- Train personnel of channel partners, etc.
- Present survey reports, layouts, and proposals

Executive activities
- Develop monthly and weekly work plan
- Each night make a daily work plan for the next day
- Organize field activity for minimum travel and maximum calls
- Prepare and submit special reports on trends and competition
- Prepare and submit statistical data requested by home office
- Investigate lost sales and reason for loss
- Prepare reports on developments, trends, new objectives, and new ways to meet objectives
- Attend sales meetings
- Build a prospect list
- Collect overdue accounts; report on faulty accounts
- Collect credit information
- Analyze work plans to determine which goals were not met and why

Goodwill
- Counsel customers on their problems
- Build relationships with channel partners
- Maintain loyalty and respect for the company
- Attend sales meetings held by customers

these qualifications is probably the most difficult aspect of the entire recruitment process. One reason is the manager is dealing with people, and thus many subjective and complex characteristics come into play. Qualifications such as education and experience are included in the job description, thus making good candidates easier to identify initially. But most firms also try to identify personality traits that presumably make better salespersons, such as self-confidence, aggressiveness, and gregariousness. For example, a T-Mobile Wireless Sales Representative (https://www.t-mobile.com/careers/meet-our-teams/sales) is expected to have the following qualifications: *age 18+, regular work attendance, above average interpersonal and communication skills, a desire to excel personally and financially – wireless experience a plus*. Current information on T-Mobile sales jobs as well as other sales positions can be found on the Indeed.com and Glassdoor.com websites.

Personality Traits Although many studies have attempted to determine which qualifications are most important for a sales position, none has developed an ideal list. Table 8.2 shows the critical characteristics sought by a *Fortune 500* company. Using a 10-point scale, the company evaluates candidates on college campuses in terms of these characteristics, and only those who score 7.0 or higher are invited to follow-up interviews at the company.

Qualifications By knowing what the job consists of, the sales manager understands the qualifications a person should have to fill the position. Overqualified people generally are not happy in a position that offers little challenge. On the other hand, people in over their head usually do not succeed. In determining the type of person best suited for a sales position, sales managers should keep in mind the following characteristics of selling jobs:

- *Travel, sometimes overnight.* Many sales positions require some kind of travel, often overnight. People who are to be successful in sales must have no major reservations about travel or overnight trips.

TABLE 8.2

Critical Characteristics and Behaviors of Sales Recruits

Intelligence	Demonstrates in verbal expression, depth of response, analytical thought process.
Decisiveness	When asked, makes definite choices, lets you know where he or she stands on issues, is not tentative.
Energy and enthusiasm	Is animated, positive, spontaneous, fast-paced.
Results orientation	Gets to the point, emphasizes achievement; responses are relevant to interview objectives.
Maturity	Shows poise, self-confidence, and maturity in dress, general demeanor, and degree of relaxation.
Assertiveness	Takes charge, is forceful, convincing, and persuasive.
Sensitivity	Is sincere, friendly, tactful, responsive, and not aloof.
Openness	Responses are not canned and superficial.
Tough-mindedness	Discusses persons and events critically; doesn't allow emotions to cloud perceptions.

- *Supervision.* Few sales jobs involve close supervision. The salesperson is in the field, traveling from one account to another, and may have contact with the home office or sales manager only every two or three days. Salespersons are for the most part their own boss, determining what time to get up in the morning and start work and what time to go home. To be successful, a salesperson must be a self-starter and have a great deal of self-discipline.
- *Little work experience.* People who enter sales generally have little or no work experience. Therefore, their success on the job is very hard to predict. Equally difficult is matching the job description to the individual with no track record.
- *High turnover.* As a result of the above conditions, high employee turnover is typical in sales. Many people change from sales job to sales job, while others exit the sales profession altogether after only a short period of time.

Job qualifications should identify the characteristics and abilities a person must have to meet the requirements of the sales position. For example, a prospective salesperson might need any or all of the following qualifications: two years of college, at least four years of work experience, ability to make decisions under stress, specific product knowledge, technology literacy, a car, and the ability to travel.

Since recruits with *all* the most important qualifications are seldom found, managers must decide which are the most important and what trade-offs they consider acceptable. For instance, can enthusiasm and high ambition substitute for relatively poor verbal skills? The answer to such questions depends on the sales job and the extent to which the recruit can be trained to overcome weaknesses.

There is no one method for every company to use in determining the qualifications of sales recruits. The logical starting point, however, is the job description. If the sales position requires technical or analytical skills, then specific educational background or work experience may be necessary. Technology companies, for example, often hire salespeople with technical backgrounds in engineering or computer science. Also, sales positions with limited supervision may necessitate hiring mature, experienced persons. For example, Automatic Data Processing (ADP) hires only experienced salespeople with the skills and confidence to manage their own sales territories and exceed quota, and who are not afraid to work hard.

Models for Success Companies that have been in business for several years often analyze personal histories of present and past salespeople to determine job qualifications. Comparing the characteristics of good, average, and poor salespeople suggests traits that predict success in a sales career with the company. To conduct this analysis, firms store the information in their sales recruitment database and apply data analytics hiring models to differentiate high performers from low performers. Predictive models examine historical hiring and success histories that incorporate the unique characteristics of salespeople who failed or were fired, as well as the successful ones. The candidate profiles are used to enhance recruitment, selection, and hiring decisions.

Sales managers rely on analytical hiring models because they improve the manager's ability to recruit and ultimately select qualified individuals. But equally important, they help validate selection criteria, and validation is required by government regulations on equal employment opportunity in hiring. Some companies might use an outside organization such as a consulting firm specializing in personnel services, or a similar but noncompeting firm, to develop job qualifications. But for many companies, the best approach is to complete most, if not all, of the recruitment, selection, and hiring tasks themselves.

Attracting a Pool of Applicants

The next step in the recruitment and selection process is attracting a pool of applicants for the sales position. Companies need to continuously identify, locate, and attract salespeople. Candidates who apply become the pool from which new salespeople are chosen. The quality of this pool predicts future successes or problems encountered by the sales force.

The importance of starting with a large pool of applicants cannot be overemphasized. If there are too few applicants, the probability is high a person with inferior selling abilities will be hired. When a firm processes large numbers of applicants, the recruiting program serves as an automatic screening system. But sales managers must be careful not to screen out good candidates. The interview process is only one screening device. Others are the recruiting sources used, such as the colleges visited or the websites and newspapers where ads are placed. An advertisement in the *Wall Street Journal,* for example, will attract a different type of recruit than an ad on Monster.com, Indeed.com, or Ziprecruiter.com.

Recruiting is not equally important in all firms. The quality of salespeople needed, the rate of turnover expected, and a company's financial position and reputation are just a few of the factors that account for the difference. For example, Apple, Microsoft, and Google will attract much higher quality sales applicants based on their reputation. When higher-caliber salespeople are needed, managers must screen more applicants before finding someone who meets the hiring specifications. At firms that experience high turnover, recruiting must be continuous. Financially strong companies typically have traveling recruiting teams, whereas weaker firms may rely heavily on online websites.

Sources of Salespeople

There are many places to find recruits. Managers need to analyze potential sources to determine which produce the best recruits for the sales position to be filled. Then they should maintain a continuing relationship with these sources, even during periods when no hiring is being done. Good sources are hard to find, and goodwill must be established between the firm and the source to ensure good recruits in the future.

Some firms use only one source while others use several. The most frequently used sources are persons within the company, competitors, noncompeting companies, educational institutions, websites such as LinkedIn.com, Glassdoor.com, Indeed.com, Ziprecruiter.com, and Monster.com, as well as employment agencies.

Persons Within the Company

Companies often recruit salespeople from other departments, such as production or engineering, as well as from the nonselling section of the sales department. These people are familiar with company policies and the technical aspects of the product itself. The chances of finding good salespeople within the company are excellent because sales managers know the people and can assess their sales potential. In fact, many firms turn to nonsales personnel within the company as their first source of new sales recruits.

Hiring people from within the company can lift morale because a transfer to sales is often viewed as a promotion. But transferring outstanding workers from the plant or office into the sales department does not guarantee success. In some cases, hostility can arise among plant and office supervisors, who feel their personnel are being taken by the sales department. Recommendations from the present sales force and sales executives usually yield better internal prospects than those of other employees, because the people in sales understand the needed qualifications. It is better to hire candidates with selling skills instead of just shuffling employees from other departments.[3]

Competitors

Salespeople recruited from competitors are trained, have experience selling similar products to similar markets, and should be ready to sell almost immediately. But usually a premium must be paid to attract them from their present jobs. Some sales managers are reluctant to hire competitors' salespeople because the practice is sometimes viewed as unethical. But is trying to lure away a competitor's employees really different from attempting to take a competitor's customers or market share? No. Recruiting a competitor's employees out of revenge, however, is unethical. Likewise, ethical issues arise when newly hired salespeople use valuable proprietary information from their former employer to look good on the new job. Hiring a competitor's reps may also pose legal questions if they have signed a noncompete or nonsolicitation agreement with their former employer. Courts today generally do not support noncompete agreements since they can hinder someone's ability to earn a livelihood. Nonsolicitation agreements, on the other hand, are more easily enforced, because the salesperson has agreed not to contact customers acquired while with the former company.

Recruiting competitors' salespeople may bring other problems. Although they are highly trained and know the market and product very well, it is often hard for them to unlearn old practices. Also, they may not be compatible with the culture of the new organization and management. Finally, recruits from competitors usually are expected to switch their customers to the new business. But if they are unable to do so, their new employer may be disappointed.

We can evaluate the risk of incurring these problems by asking one question: Why is the person leaving their present employer? A satisfactory answer often clears up doubts and identifies a valuable employee. The difficulty arises, however, in determining the real answer. Often it's almost impossible to determine why someone is looking for another job. Good sales managers must be able to accurately evaluate the information they get.

Noncompeting Companies

Noncompeting firms can provide a good source of trained and experienced salespeople, especially if they are selling similar products or selling to the same market. Even though some recruits may be unfamiliar with the recruiting firm's product line, they do have selling experience and require less training.

Companies that are either vendors or customers of the recruiting firm are also an excellent source of candidates. Recruits from these sources have some knowledge of the company from having sold to or purchased from it, and their familiarity reduces the time it takes to make them productive. Another advantage of recruits from these sources is they are already familiar with the industry.

Educational Institutions

High schools, adult evening classes, business colleges, vocational schools, junior colleges, and universities are all sources of sales recruits. Large firms usually are successful in recruiting from universities, but small firms tend to be more successful in recruiting from smaller educational institutions or other sources.

While most college graduates lack specific sales experience, they have the education and perspective many employers seek in potential sales representatives. College graduates tend to adapt more easily than experienced personnel and have not developed any loyalties to a firm or an industry. They usually have acquired social skills, are more mature than persons of the same age without college training, and can think logically and express themselves reasonably well. In addition, many colleges and universities organize career fairs so their students can meet prospective employers, and increasingly student internships provide opportunities for students to meet and interact with companies seeking salespeople.

Companies recruiting from campuses have found that students from universities with specialized sales programs like Kennesaw State University (www.kennesaw.edu) in Atlanta, Georgia and Illinois State University (www.ilstu.edu) in Normal, Illinois, have a much lower turnover rate than those from other programs. Some universities even have more specific sales programs such as the pharmaceutical sales program at the University of Southern Mississippi (www.usm.edu). Sales organizations increasingly focus their campus recruiting efforts on students that graduate from specialized sales programs.

A problem in recruiting from college campuses is the unfavorable image some students have of sales. Recruiters report some college students accept sales positions only after they have been turned down for other jobs or rejected by law schools or medical schools. In spite of these problems, educational institutions remain a good source of sales recruits.[4]

Advertisements

Classified advertisements in newspapers, trade journals, and on Internet websites are another source of recruits. The *Wall Street Journal, U.S.A. Today,* and various trade journals are used in recruiting for high-caliber sales and sales force management positions. Local newspapers may be used to recruit for lower-level sales positions, but other sources are increasingly used.

While advertisements reach a large audience, the caliber of applicants is often second-rate. This places a burden on those doing the initial screening. Managers can also increase the quality of applicants recruited by advertisements by carefully selecting the media and describing the job qualifications specifically in the ad. To be effective, a recruiting ad must attract attention and have credibility. Include the following elements to ensure an ad's effectiveness: company name, product, territory, hiring qualifications, compensation plan, expense plan, and fringe benefits, and how to contact the employer.

Online Recruiting

Many companies use the Internet to recruit for sales positions. Two of the most frequently used online recruiting sites are Linkedin (www.linkedin.com) and monster. com (www.monster.com). LinkedIn is a business and employment-oriented service that operates via websites and mobile apps. Monster.com is a recruitment and human resources database that posts job listings from companies like Coca-Cola, Bank of America, Procter & Gamble, and General Electric. The website has thousands of resumes at any given time – about 12% of these postings are for sales and marketing positions. JobWeb (www.jobweb.org) sponsored by the National Association of Colleges and Employers and Facebook (facebook.com) are two other popular recruitment sites. Finally, individuals interested in a sales position can use Google.com, Bing.com, or another online search engine to find sales opportunities or sales recruitment sources.

Most sites offer both job and resume postings, as well as keyword searches and searches by state, locality, industry, company, or title. Sites like www.careerbuilder.com, www.monster.com, www.jobs4sales.com, and similar job boards are increasingly popular, but recruiters need to go to the specific pages and departments on these sites that drill down to find applicants interested in sales. Even better is to use websites specifically tailored to the sales profession, like www.saleshead.com.

An important advantage of online recruitment sources is their low cost compared to other recruitment methods. Other advantages include access to more people and a broader selection of applicants, the ability to target the type of people needed, access to people with a technical background who know computers, convenience, quicker response and turnaround, and ease of use. Recruiting online can also have its disadvantages. For example, some companies are concerned about the high volume of resumes they might receive from the Internet and their limited resources to review them.

Want a job in sales?
Source: www.salesjobs.com, April 14, 2020.

Employment Agencies and Professional Recruiters

Third-party employment agencies and professional recruiters are among the best and the worst sources. Often the quality of results depends on the relationship between the agency or recruiter and the sales manager. So sales managers should select the agency or recruiter carefully and develop a good working relationship. The third-party must clearly understand both the job description and the qualifications for the sales position to be filled.

In recent years, employment agencies and recruiters have steadily improved and expanded their services. They now screen candidates so that in-house recruiters can spend more time with the most highly qualified prospects. Many employment agencies provide a full array of services for recruiting, from searching for candidates to screening, interviewing, and recommending the best candidate.

Tradeshows and Conferences

Companies can sponsor a booth at an industry tradeshow or conference. Individuals who contact companies at these sources are generally interested in your company and familiar with its products and services. If they lack knowledge about your company, this is an informal way to communicate the nature of your company and the advantages of working there. Sponsors can obtain a list of individuals preregistered for the conference and contact them ahead of time, and definitely afterward if they are not able to contact them at the conference or tradeshow. There are even tradeshows and conferences that focus on sales positions, such as inbound.com, dreamforce.com, Sales 3.0, and Rainmaker.com.

Factors to Consider in Evaluating Sources

Recruiting differs substantially from company to company. The following summarizes the major factors to consider when deciding which recruiting sources to use:

- *Nature of the product.* A highly technical product requires an experienced, knowledgeable person. The firm may look at persons in its own production department, experienced persons from other companies, or candidates with specific educational backgrounds.
- *Nature of the market.* Experienced salespeople may be needed to deal with well-informed purchasing agents or with high-level executives.
- *Policy on promoting from within.* If this policy is the rule, recruiters know where to look first.
- *Sales training provided by the company.* A company that has its own sales training program can recruit inexperienced people. But if a salesperson needs to be productive quickly, it may be necessary to seek experienced recruits.
- *Personnel needs of the company.* If the company is seeking career salespeople, then MBA graduates may not be appropriate recruits, since many aspire to higher management positions.
- *Sources of successful recruits in the past.* Past sources can be used again as long as there have been no changes in the sales position.
- *Recruiting budget.* A small budget means a firm must limit its sources.
- *Legal considerations.* Civil rights laws and other regulations must be considered when a firm is deciding on sources of recruits.

Recruiters know top-rated candidates can come from any source, and they must be careful not to overlook sources because of a few poor experiences in the past. With the cost of recruiting increasing in recent years, it is still important to be selective. Sales managers must constantly analyze sources and devote time to those that are most productive, while ensuring EEOC guidelines are met.

The Sales Force Selection Process

The recruiting process produces a pool of applicants from which to choose. The selection process involves choosing candidates that best meet the qualifications and have the greatest aptitude for the job. Numerous tools, techniques, and procedures can aid the selection process. For instance, applications or brief phone interviews help initially screen out candidates. In-depth interviews and tests, such as sales aptitude or psychological tests, provide further information for final candidate selection. Reference checking adds third-party comments to the selection process. None of these should be used alone. Each is designed to collect different information.

Steps in the salesperson selection process are shown in Figure 8.2. Depending on the size of the company, the number of salespeople needed, and the importance of the position to be filled, the steps will vary from company to company. For example, sales recruits for some companies may have to pass a psychological or intelligence test before being invited to an in-depth interview. Other companies may not check a candidate's references until just before an offer is made, and still others may not require employment tests at all. While successful selection of sales applicants does not require that all steps be completed, the more steps completed, the higher the probability of selecting successful salespeople.

Hiring successful candidates usually results in increased sales. But hiring the wrong person can cost a company thousands of dollars a year for training, salary, benefits, and lost sales. To avoid these losses, many companies are using technological advances such as employment tests and analytical predictive models in the selection process. Sales managers must remember, though, that selection tools and techniques are merely aids to sound executive judgment that can only eliminate obviously unqualified candidates and identify the more competent.

Initial Screening

The purpose of the initial screening is to eliminate undesirable recruits as soon as possible. Initial screening may start with an application form or resume, a screening interview, a review of the candidate's Facebook page and other online sources of information, or some type of brief test. No matter which tool is used, the shorter it is, the more it will reduce costs. But it must not be so brief that it screens out good candidates. Today, many companies conduct initial screenings online. When applications are completed and resumes uploaded, key qualifications stored in the company database are

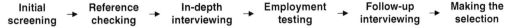

FIGURE 8.2 Steps in the sales force selection process.

Note: Applicants may be rejected at any one of these steps.

automatically screened by software that ranks applicants and provides a list of the most qualified individuals, who are then scheduled for an interview, increasingly with no real person being involved – just the computer software.

Application Forms Application forms and resumes are the most widely used screening tools. An application form is an easy means of collecting the information necessary for determining an applicant's qualifications. That usually includes name, contact information, position applied for, educational background, work experience, military service, involvement in social organizations, outside interests and activities, and personal references. Other important questions on an application form relate directly to the sales position for which the application is applying. For example:

- Why do you want this job?
- Why do you want to change jobs?
- What minimum income do you require?
- Are you willing to travel?
- Are you willing to be transferred?
- What do you want to be doing five years from now? Ten years from now?
- Are you willing to use your car for business?

Application forms differ from company to company. On all forms, however, it is illegal to include questions that are not related to the job, such as age, race, national origin, marital status, or disabilities. Applications forms are more useful as screening devices than resumes since they can address specific information that may not be included on a resume.

Another important function of application forms is to help sales managers prepare for personal interviews with sales candidates. By reviewing the application before the interview, sales managers can get an initial impression of the applicant and prepare a list of questions to ask during the interview. Specific considerations are:

- Appearance of the application.
- Missing information – Are there blank spots or shortcuts that seem inconsistent with the rest of the application? Ask about these during the interview.
- Indications of instability – Does the history include more than three jobs in five years, any job held for less than one year, more than two colleges, and the like?
- Reason for job change.
- Career progression – Do the job changes represent a growth in income and responsibility?

Past behavior patterns revealed in application forms are useful predictors of future behavior, and therefore are important for screening applicants. Table 8.3 summarizes how to use application information in selection.

Companies can use weighted application forms to help them distinguish between good and poor salespeople. These forms place more importance on such items as years of selling experience, employment length, career objectives, or educational level. Thus, managers can consider only applicants who rate higher than an established minimum number of points on these items and reject those who fail to reach the cutoff point. Of course, weighted application forms must be validated for each sales position in the firm so they reflect the unique requirements of the sales position. Also, managers should periodically reevaluate the validity of the weights because the importance of an item may change over time.

> **TABLE 8.3**
>
> ## Application Items that Predict Performance and Turnover
>
> | Indicators of higher performance | Indicators of lower turnover |
> |---|---|
> | • *Employment:* Currently employed at time of hiring.
• *Prior Sales Experience:* Selling experience at most recent job.
• *Knowledge of Job Requirements:* Has an understanding of the selling position.
• *Recruitment Source:* Recruited through the use of newspaper or Internet advertising rather than through unsolicited applications.
• *Residential Moves:* Has made fewer residential moves.
• *Education:* Has a bachelor's degree. | • *Career Aspirations:* More interested in a career sales position than using the selling job as a stepping-stone position.
• *Employment:* Currently employed at time of hiring.
• *Prior Sales Experience:* Selling experience at most recent job, but less overall sales experience.
• *Employment Length:* Has spent more time at their most recent job. |

Initial Screening Interviews and Tests Almost all companies make use of initial screening interviews or tests. Usually conducted in person or over the telephone, the interviews or tests typically last from 20 to 30 minutes and generally are given by assistant human resource managers, assistant sales managers, or sales personnel. Interviews a recruiter conducts on campus with college students, for instance, are initial screening interviews. Each recruiter talks with eight or ten students a day and selects the best ones to invite back for in-depth interviews.

Automated Screening Techniques Both human resource officers and sales managers are increasingly using automated telephone and computer screening devices to screen job applicants. Some employers, for instance, require candidates to pass computerized screening tests measuring honesty, personality, and other traits. Candidates are instructed to questions using a computer or a mobile device so response delays and inconsistent answers can be identified, and a score is calculated. Those who pass are granted an in-person interview.

Automated screening procedures speed the gathering and analysis of data from applicants. Automated devices never forget to ask a question and always ask questions the same way each time. Interestingly, people often give more truthful answers to machines than to human interviewers. Many companies using computer interviewing have found it is an effective tool for streamlining the employee selection process and reducing employee turnover, while capturing data for use in future hiring and employee development.

Computer screening has disadvantages. Some opponents fear electronic "profiling" will exclude those who do not fall within the desired response range, even though a person might have the skills the company really needs. Computers cannot recognize fuzzy or superficial answers, and it can be difficult to ask interviewees to elaborate on an initial response. Automated screening software also cannot ask follow-up questions of interviewees who provide unexpected leads. Finally, in selecting screening software, companies should inquire specifically about the criteria that will be applied to select or reject candidates.

Online Profiles Online profiles are increasingly being used to screen candidates for sales positions. More than 70% of employers use social media to screen applicants, and almost half will not hire an individual who does not have an online presence. Individuals need to constantly monitor any public online information employers can access and make sure it is positive, or at least neutral.[5] Current employers have been known to search online sites of their employees and upon finding unacceptable behavior have disciplined them, and in some cases even terminated employees. Even if you already have your "dream job" you need to think about the future when monitoring and updating your online profile, since individuals in their 20s are projected to have about ten different employers in their working lifetime. The problem is what is acceptable today could easily change tomorrow. Remember too the judge and jury on decisions about acceptable and unacceptable behavior will not be your friends. Employers will clearly have different standards than your friends.

When employers search online for information on sales candidates, they are not necessarily looking for something negative. In fact, staff individuals with no knowledge of the applicant or outside agencies typically conduct the online searches based on criteria specified by the employer. Facebook, Instagram, and Twitter are among the social media sites most often examined, but other public sites can be easily accessed by employers. When the searches are conducted postings that create problems include any indication of excessive drinking, drug usage, photos of questionable activities, comments that are racist or appear to discriminate against protected groups, and any indication of illegal or inappropriate behavior.

Checking References A company cannot be sure it has all the needed information about an applicant until it has thoroughly checked references. Reference checking is a screening tool that enables a company to obtain information from former and current bosses, coworkers, clients, and other professionals. One survey indicated almost 60% of companies have found incorrect information on resumes.[6] Education is the area to check most closely for misrepresentation. Sales managers will need, therefore, to thoroughly check references and verify critical information at some point during the selection process before the final interview and selection takes place.

References from teachers and former employers are generally more helpful than other types. Teachers can give an indication of intelligence, work habits, and personality traits. Former employers can be used to find out why the person left the job and how well he or she got along with others. The question "Would you rehire the applicant again if you had the chance?" tends to bring out accurate responses. Sales managers should also not overlook references from an applicant's current clients, if the candidate is an experienced salesperson. These references provide valuable clues about a candidate's selling style and whether the candidate will fit in with the company's culture.

In general, however, the quality of reference checks is questionable. Contacting the names supplied by a candidate is often a waste of time, because it is unlikely serious problems will be uncovered or the applicant would not have given those names. Fearful of lawsuits, former employers are also careful not to divulge anything about an employee other than the dates the employee worked for the company. To increase the chances of getting more information, many sales managers have candidates sign a waiver that releases their former employers from liability and agrees to let the sales manager contact additional references. If the references still will not give any information about the candidate, sales managers should ask the candidate to help. If the candidate refuses or cannot come up with other references, then they probably do not have anyone that will give them a good recommendation.

Many firms try to talk with people who know the applicant but were not listed on the application form as a reference. For reference checking to be a useful selection tool, the sales manager must be resourceful and pursue leads that are not directly given. For instance, a bit of sleuthing can find people willing to give references who may have worked with the candidate or who were their clients. While reference checking can be a frustrating and laborious process, many sales managers have found that even if only one significant fact is uncovered, it usually makes the effort worthwhile.

Standard Company Reviews In addition to checking references, company policy at many firms requires standard reviews on all applicants as a condition of employment. These may include physical examinations, drug tests, and background checks, usually conducted by someone in the human resources department rather than the sales manager. Since many of these reviews or investigations are covered in some aspect by law, they should be used with caution. Further, it may be illegal to conduct some of these investigative reviews until the company has made a job offer to the candidate in question.

- *Physical examinations.* Many sales jobs require a degree of physical activity and stamina, and therefore poor physical condition may hinder a salesperson's job performance. When sales jobs require strenuous activity, many companies insist on a thorough medical examination for all sales recruits. But physical exams or access to medical records is possible only after an offer has been made.
- *Drug tests.* Drug testing programs are used frequently in industry. Proponents of drug testing claim that it leads to a safer and more productive work environment. Critics argue that drug testing violates constitutional protection against unreasonable search and seizure and invades the individual's privacy. They also contend that screening is an attempt by employers to regulate workers' behavior off the job and the results may be used as a tool for harassment. Opponents also raise doubts about the validity of the most widely used tests, because they are subject to high error rates. Thus, innocent persons may be falsely classified as drug abusers. As with physical exams, drug tests can be legally administered only after the company makes a job offer contingent upon a negative test result.
- *Background checks.* Many companies also conduct background checks to give them more information about a candidate. Common types include checking the applicant's workers' compensation, credit, driving, and criminal records. These checks raise legal questions, however, and may violate anti-discrimination laws such as the *Americans with Disabilities Act* and the *Civil Rights Act of 1964*. Companies that base hiring decisions on these checks must demonstrate the information they obtain is related to the job.

In-Depth Interviewing

The in-depth interview is the most used and least scientific of the various tools for selecting employees. A salesperson is seldom hired without a face-to-face in-depth interview. In fact, three or four interviews are typically conducted with the most desirable candidates. No other selection tool can take the place of getting to know the applicant personally. To better understand the interviewing process, search for the Cisco Systems website using the keywords "Cisco Systems, interviewing".

In-depth interviews help companies determine whether a person is right for the job. They bring out personal characteristics that no other selection tool can reveal. The interview also serves as a two-way channel of communication because both the company and the applicant can ask questions and learn about each other. Questions asked during an interview should be aimed at finding out certain things: Is the candidate qualified for the job? Does the candidate really want the job? Will this sales job help the candidate fulfill personal goals? Will the candidate find this sales position challenging enough? These questions, like those on the application form, examine the applicant's past behavior, experiences, and motivation.

When candidates have prior sales experience, in-depth interviews can be used to clarify their previous selling environment. This information shows whether the candidate's past experience fits the job at hand. For example, an experienced candidate who was successful under a short sales cycle where sales are made daily may not be happy in an environment where the sales cycle may take years, such as with commercial airliners. Examples of information you can obtain from an in-depth interview of experienced salespeople are shown in Table 8.4.

Sales managers use different approaches to obtain useful information, depending on their own personality, training, and work experience. Table 8.5 provides an example of an interview guide.

Types of In-Depth Interviews Interviews differ depending on the number of questions that are prepared in advance and the extent to which the interviewer guides the conversation. Some are highly structured interviews. Others are informal and unstructured.

In the structured interview, the recruiter asks each candidate the same set of standardized questions designed to determine the applicant's fitness for a sales position. Since structured interviews don't probe candidates for in-depth information, they are more often used as an initial screening tool. They are particularly useful for inexperienced interviewers, since they guide the interview and ensure that all factors relevant to the candidate's qualifications are covered.

TABLE 8.4

Interviewing Candidates with Prior Sales Experience

- **Was the candidate a *salesperson* or an *account manager*?** Candidates responsible for obtaining new customers are different from those responsible for servicing current customers.
- **What is the source and quality of candidate's past sales leads?** There are substantial differences between selling to customers when qualified and highly developed leads are provided versus. selling to prospects where either no or unqualified leads are furnished.
- **What is the length of the sales cycle the candidate has been successful with?** Salespeople who thrive on long sales cycles are generally very different from those successful in short cycles.
- **What is the level the candidate has been selling to?** Is the candidate used to dealing with channel partners or with presidents and CEOs, and how will this fit in with the sales environment of the offered job?
- **What compensation plan does the candidate succeed under?** Was the candidate successful under a salary plan in which none or very little of the compensation was at-risk or under a commission plan in which most or all compensation was at-risk? Candidates who thrive under a commission-only plan may not feel motivated under a base salary plan. On the other hand, candidates compensated almost totally on base salary may regard the commission-only plan as too risky.
- **Has the candidate worked alone or as a team member?** Some salespeople work most effectively as members of a group, and others work best on their own. If the job requires a lot of interaction with other members of a sales team, then the candidate should be able to contribute to a team-selling environment.
- **Why does the candidate want to change sales positions?** The true reason may be hard to get at, but sales managers should determine why candidates want to leave their current sales position and if the terms of the offered job will be appealing. For instance, if the salesperson wants to leave because he or she is dissatisfied with their present income, will the job offered provide the necessary increase? Likewise, if the salesperson was passed over for promotion, does the job offered provide career advancement?

> **TABLE 8.5**
>
> ## Approaches Interviewers Use to Obtain Useful Information
>
> 1. Build a rapport quickly.
> 2. Structure the interview so that the interviewee clearly understands what is expected.
> 3. Elicit desired behavior by not showing disapproval or disagreement, by using humor, by showing sympathy and understanding, and by interrupting infrequently only for clarification or redirection.
> 4. Use probing, open-ended questions and avoid yes-or-no questions.
>   Examples of typical open-ended questions are:
>   - Tell me about . . .
>   - What did you like . . .
>   - How would you compare . . .
>   - Why did you decide to do that . . .
>   - Tell me about the people . . .
>   - How did you find that experience . . .
>   - How would you describe . . .
>   - How did you feel about . . .
>   - What were the differences . . .
>   Examples of probing techniques are reflection, paraphrasing, and phrases such as:
>   - How so . . .
>   - Because . . .
>   - In what respect . . .
> 5. Ask candidates whether they have any questions.

Unstructured interviews are informal and nondirected, except for perhaps the general topics to cover. The goal of an unstructured interview is to get the candidate to talk freely on a variety of topics. Frequently the recruiter begins the interview by saying to the candidate, "Tell me about yourself," or by asking questions such as "Why did you decide to interview with our company?" Examples of some probing questions used in unstructured interviews are presented in Table 8.6.

Several problems are associated with unstructured interviews. One is they do not provide answers to standard questions the interviewer can compare with other

> **TABLE 8.6**
>
> ## Typical Probing Questions Asked in Unstructured Interviews
>
> *Questions that determine whether a candidate is self-motivated:*
> - "What is the single most important thing that you want to accomplish that a sales position will enable you to accomplish?"
> - "What personal goals have you set for yourself for the next year?"
>
> *Questions that identify candidates who will work on their own to improve themselves:*
> - "What is one thing you really do well? How did you learn that skill?"
> - "What is the last book you read or seminar you attended? What have you done as a result?"
> - "Describe your favorite coach or instructor. What did you learn from that person?"
> - "What is the latest investment you've made in yourself?"
>
> *Questions that determine the candidate's pattern for winning or recovering from loss:*
> - "Describe you earliest successes."
> - "When did you first realize you were a winner?"
> - "Describe your most competitive endeavor. How did you do?"
> - "What was your last failure? How did you recover? What did you do to turn things around?"

Box 8.1 | Sales Management in Action 8.1

One sales manager asks the following probing question: "I need to get five thousand new customers on my mobile phone network next week. What would you do to get these customers on the network? You have 30 minutes to tell me." This type of unstructured, probing interview enables the manager to observe candidates' personalities and eliminate canned responses. And because they routinely hire reps for new, undefined markets, the company looks for candidates who can think quickly and offer innovative solutions.

Do you think this is an effective way to interview candidates?

candidates' responses or with the company's past experiences. Also, it is possible to spend considerable time on relatively unimportant topics. But experts say this technique is the best for probing an individual's personality and for gaining insights into the candidate's attitudes and opinions.

To administer and interpret unstructured interviews, interviewers must be well trained. Unfortunately, sales managers for many firms have had relatively little experience as interviewers, and few have ever had special training in interviewing techniques. Therefore, many firms use a combination of structured and unstructured approaches, usually referred to as a semistructured interview. In semistructured interviews, the interviewer has a preplanned list of questions but allows time for interaction and discussion. This approach is flexible and can be tailored to meet the needs of different candidates as well as different interviewers.

Applicants' Responsibility in an Interview Applicants should prepare for interviews by learning about the company and trying to anticipate questions that may be asked. This task is very easy today because almost all companies have websites that are easily accessed. For some sales positions it may be helpful to practice answers ahead of time. After all, applicants are "selling" themselves to the interviewer, and the objective is to make a favorable impression. A review of Table 8.6 will suggest some of the questions that applicants should be prepared to answer. And just as companies make recruiting and selection a serious process, so also should candidates be shrewd job seekers. Applicants should consider whether the job is a good fit with their background, skills, and temperament, determine whether the organization's approach to getting work done matches their own, and assess whether the job and organization offer opportunities for professional growth and advancement.

During the interview, applicants should ask questions to help them decide whether they want the position if it is offered to them. Table 8.7 lists questions candidates typically ask in the interview. While all the questions are important, some are more important than others, and applicants should choose ahead of time the most important questions to ask if the questioning period is short. Sales managers also need to be prepared to answer questions on these topics.

The types of questions applicants ask also provide clues for the sales manager about their values, aspirations and goals, technology capabilities, sales skills, as well as knowledge and abilities. Candidates who ask only "what's-in-it-for-me" questions about salary, benefits, vacation policies, and promotability, or those who ask only "filler" questions, such as when the company was founded or how many employees there are, show little insight, initiative, or creativity. Applicants who ask absolutely no questions are suggesting they are not interested in the job, unless all of their questions have already been answered. On the other hand, good candidates ask questions that

---

TABLE 8.7

Questions Typically Asked by Candidates During Interviews

- Where are the entry-level positions? (Start at the division level)
- What are these positions?
- How is the training conducted? How long? Formal or informal?
- What percentage of the job will require travel?
- What is the likelihood of relocation?
- What are the starting salaries for a particular position?
- What kind of technology support does the company provide?
- What is the typical career path of each position?
- How long will it take?
- What is the selection process like?
- What is the compensation package?
- What are the benefits?
- How am I evaluated for promotion?
- What are your selection criteria, or what do you look for most in a candidate?
- Does your company encourage furthering one's education?
- How would you describe the culture of the company?
- What criteria make someone successful in sales at your company?
- Are employees required to assume responsibilities beyond the written job description?
- What proportion of the time spent with customers is face-to-face versus remotely via mobile devices?
- What kind of social media strategies does the company undertake to support salespeople?

---

help them gain a more accurate picture of what it takes to be a success in the job and at the company.

Sales recruits often successfully pass screening interviews as well as resume reviews and application forms. The in-depth personal interview is much more challenging, however, and many have difficulty with it. Table 8.8 lists negative factors that frequently lead to rejection of applicants during employment interviews. Sales applicants should be aware of these and avoid them whenever possible.

Employment Testing

Employment tests are an objective way to measure traits or characteristics of applicants for sales positions and to increase the chances of selecting good salespeople. They can identify traits and qualifications, such as intelligence, aptitude, and personality that other selection tools cannot measure. Another reason for using employment tests relates to the high cost of training and hiring the sales force. A selection tool that can reduce sales force turnover and increase sales productivity is definitely desirable. Tests also provide a basis for interviewing. Questionable points noted in the test results may be probed more deeply during the interview. There are six basic tests used in selecting sales personnel:

- *Intelligence tests.* Intelligence tests measure a salesperson's general cognitive ability or intelligence as an indicator of future job performance. While not used as frequently as other tests in sales force selection, intelligence tests can often be an effective tool for selecting salespeople.
- *Knowledge tests.* Knowledge tests measure what the applicant knows about a particular product, service, market, and the like.

TABLE **8.8**

Factors Identified During the Employment Interview that Frequently Lead to Rejection

1. Poor appearance	2. Failure to ask questions about the job
3. Overbearing, overaggressive, conceited attitude	4. Little sense of humor
5. Inability to express self clearly; poor voice, diction, grammar	6. Sloppy, poorly prepared application
7. Lack of career planning; no purpose or goals	8. Evidence of merely shopping around for a job
9. Lack of interest and enthusiasm; a passive indifferent manner	10. Desires job for short time only
11. Lack of confidence and poise; nervousness	12. Lack of knowledge in field of specialization
13. Failure to participate in extracurricular activities	14. No interest in company or industry
15. Overemphasis on money, interest in "best dollar" offer	16. Emphasis on whom the applicant knows
17. Poor scholastic record	18. Unwillingness to relocate, if necessary
19. Unwillingness to start at the bottom; the expectation of too much too soon	20. Cynical attitude
21. Evasiveness; failure to be clear about unfavorable factors in record	22. Low moral standards
23. Lack of tact	24. Laziness
25. Lack of maturity	26. Intolerance; strong prejudice
27. Lack of courtesy	28. Narrow interests
29. Condemnation of past employers	30. Evidence of wasted time
31. Lack of social understanding	32. Poor handling of personal finances
33. Marked dislike for hard work	34. No interest in community activities
35. Lack of vitality	36. Inability to take criticism
37. Failure to make eye contact with interviewer	38. Lack of appreciation of the value of experience
39. Weak handshake	40. Radical ideas
41. Indecision	42. Tardiness to interview without good reason
43. Indefinite responses to questions	44. Failure to express appreciation for interviewer's time

- *Sales aptitude tests.* Sales aptitude tests measure a person's innate or acquired social skills and selling know-how as well as tact and diplomacy.
- *Vocational interest tests.* Vocational interest tests assume that a person is going to be more effective and stable if he or she has a strong interest in selling. They're more likely to be administered to high-school or college students as a means of assessing career potential.
- *Attitude and lifestyle tests.* Attitude and lifestyle tests assess honesty and identify drug abusers. Typical test items include questions that ask how often the applicant drinks alcoholic beverages, whether the applicant daydreams, and how the applicant feels about drug abuse. They also include indirect questions about habits and attitudes of friends.
- *Personality tests.* Personality tests measure the behavioral traits the interviewer believes are necessary for success in selling, such as assertiveness, initiative, and extroversion. They are being used more often by sales organizations as valid forms with proven results have emerged.

Personality traits measured in a typical assessment profile are listed in Table 8.9. Tests measuring personality profiles should be designed to meet the needs of a particular job. Sales managers should first identify factors related to job success at their company. Next collect information on tests that are valid and reliable measures of the

> **TABLE 8.9**
>
> **Typical Personality Traits Assessed Using Tests**
>
> - **Trust**
> - **Sensitivity**
> - **Assertiveness**
> - **Intuition**
> - **Motivation**
> - **Emotional intensity**
> - **Exaggeration**

factors, or purchase appropriate standardized tests. Since tests can have a cultural bias and may discriminate against certain groups, their use must be continually monitored. Also, a test may be a valid predictor for one type of sales job but not for all. Companies should keep records, therefore, showing that the tests and questions are relevant to the job and are not screening out a large proportion of women or minorities.

Advantages and Disadvantages of Testing Pre-employment tests are one of the most controversial tools used in the selection process. The need for application forms, reference checks, and personal interviews is seldom disputed, but there are differences of opinion about whether tests are necessary in the hiring of salespeople. Questions about the legality of testing have increased the controversy surrounding its use as a screening tool. But test data has proven useful to management in selecting sales applicants likely to be high performers. Considering the fact that hiring mistakes can cost companies $200,000 or more, any tool that helps firms make the right selection decision is welcome.

Opponents of employment tests say tests are not as objective and scientific as they are purported to be. Savvy test-takers can often figure out the "right" or "wrong" answers to questions. Further, critics question the methodology used to develop tests. For instance, most test consultants profile a client's top sales performers and then match test results against their personality traits. But salesperson success can be influenced by factors other than personality, such as having the best territory or the longest tenure. The result is potentially successful salespeople may be screened out because they do not fit the stereotype.

Another problem is many managers use tests as the only or most important hiring decision factor. Recruits may look good on the basis of interviews, application forms, and reference checks. But if their test scores are low, they may not be considered further. If the score is somewhat below the acceptable level, and the candidate looks favorable on other criteria, applicants should probably be retested. Thus, test scores should not be the sole criterion used in making hiring decisions. Rather they should be one of several factors considered.

Tests are often misunderstood and misused, causing many sales managers to conclude they are of little value as a screening tool. For example, management sometimes believes the highest score on the test indicates the best prospect. But all applicants who score above the minimum level should be judged equally qualified for the job.

Follow-Up Interviewing

Sales managers seldom decide which candidate to hire after only one in-depth personal interview. Strong candidates often go through several interviews with more than one interviewer. Candidates who rate favorable after the in-depth interview and score in the acceptable range on employment tests are asked to come back for follow-up interviews with other members of the sales team, such as other sales managers, division managers, and sales reps. Like the in-depth interview, these follow-up interviews can either be structured or unstructured, or a combination of both, depending upon the interviewer's style and the objectives of the interview.

Making the Selection

When all other steps have been completed in the selection process, the sales manager must decide whether or not to hire each applicant. The manager reviews everything known about a particular applicant from screening, reference checks, interviews, and tests. The next step is to match the applicant's goals and ambitions against present and future opportunities, challenges, and other types of rewards offered by the job and the company.

Selection tools used in sales force selection are only aids to executive judgment. They can eliminate the obviously unqualified candidates and generally spot the more competent individuals. But since many recruits fall between these extremes, the tools can only suggest which ones will be more successful in sales. Thus, executive judgment is relied on heavily in the final selection of salespeople.

While judgment is often necessary in making a selection, sales managers should avoid letting emotion or intuition cloud the decision. Inexperienced sales managers often hire a candidate because he or she interviewed well, they "hit it off," or the manager put too much emphasis on the candidate's physical appearance. Some managers even boast of being able to decide whether to hire a sales rep after the first five minutes of the interview.

While the sales manager's intuition does matter, seasoned sales executives know that hiring completely on intuition or emotion can prove disastrous. If the manager has any uneasy feelings about top candidates, they should be called back for another interview, and additional reference checking or testing should be done. If a company follows the logical sequence of a well-planned recruiting and selection system, the executive's intuitions will soon be transformed into objective criteria that can help compare applicants and make decisions among them.

A decision to hire is followed by a formal offer, with no unspecified details or surprises. The terms should be in writing for the protection of both the recruit and the firm. Many companies require that all new salespeople sign contracts containing important job-related information. Table 8.10 emphasizes some key points for sales managers to cover when making a formal offer to a candidate.

Box 8.2 | Sales Management in Action 8.2

Selecting Salespeople for Overseas Assignments

A growing concern of many U.S. corporations is selecting qualified salespeople for global markets. As U.S. companies go overseas to sell their products, they soon realize how different the selling environment and the markets are from those in the United States. Differences in ethnic compositions, religious orientations, social class, cultural values, and education definitely complicate the sales force selection process for multinational corporations. Sales force recruitment for multinational companies is different. Therefore, salesperson selection criteria are ranked different for overseas markets than for US markets. For example, education, cultural adaptation skills, social class, religion, and ethnicity are more important in hiring sales people for overseas assignments. Differences in the selling environments and cultures make the use of standardized selection criteria questionable when salespeople are being selected for overseas markets.

TABLE **8.10**

Key Points to Cover When Hiring a Salesperson

Duties of the Salesperson

- Exercise best efforts in representing the company and its products or services.
- Make no representations, warranties, or commitments binding the company without the company's prior consent. Salespeople will be personally liable and required to reimburse the company in the event they exceed this authority.
- Forward all field inquiries or complaints in the field to the company immediately.
- Work full-time for the company without any sideline. Do not represent or form a competing business.
- Personally solicit the product and do not hire an associate to represent the company without prior written approval.
- Maintain minimum general and automobile liability coverage.
- Attend sales meetings, both local and national.
- Call on accounts periodically, service accounts, and maintain accurate selling records and lead sheets.
- Assist in any collection efforts requested by the company.
- Promise to protect all trade secrets, customer lists, and other forms of confidential information acquired while working for the company.
- Outside activities reflect not only on the salesperson, but also on the company. The company expects sales people will interact with online websites, including social media platforms. Posting of inappropriate content that reflects negatively on the company may influence an employee's job status.

Compensation

1. *Salary:*
   - Specify the amount and when it is payable.
2. *Draw:*
   - Specify whether it is applied against commission.
   - Specify the amount and when it is payable.
   - Clarify that the company can stop the draw at any time without prior notice when commission earnings do not exceed the draw.
   - Specify that the sales rep is personally liable for repayment when draw exceeds commission earnings and the rep resigns or is fired from his or her job.
   - State that the company has the right to sell off draw and reduce the amount of commission owed on termination of the employment relationship.
3. *Bonus and Quotas:*
   - Specify whether the bonus is enforceable by contract.
   - Specify the amount and when it is payable.
   - Identify and clarify any quotas that must be achieved to receive compensation of any type.
   - Specify that pro rata bonuses will not be given in the event the salesperson resigns or is fired prior to the date the bonus will be paid.
   - Avoid basing the bonus on a determination of profits, because this may give the salesperson the right to inspect the company's books and records.
4. *Commission:*
   - Specify the commission rate and when it is payable.
   - Avoid guaranteed shipping arrangements.
   - Specify split-commission policies if working in a team-oriented environment.
   - Specify all deductions from commissions and how and when they are computed, such as for returns, freight charges, unauthorized price concessions given by the salesperson, billing and advertising discounts, collection charges, failure of the customer to pay.
   - Specify commission for large orders, special customers, off-price goods, and reorders.
5. *Expenses:*
   - Specify the kinds and amount of expenses that are reimbursable.
   - Specify the kind of documentation the salesperson must supply in order to receive reimbursement.

(Continued)

TABLE 8.10

Key Points to Cover When Hiring a Salesperson (*Continued*)

Territory
- Identify how the salesperson's territory or customers are determined (by geographic boundaries, industry or customer group, functional group, etc.)
- Clarify whether the sales rep has exclusive or nonexclusive territorial rights.
- Be sure to discuss all house accounts and document these in writing.
- Determine how products sold in one territory and shipped in another will affect your split-commission policy.
- Clarify whether the salesperson can sell in other territories or to other groups of customers not solicited by other sales-people, such as at trade shows?
- If exclusive territorial rights are not involved, ensure that the salesperson will not receive commission for orders not actually solicited by him or her.

Length of Employment Relationship
- Specify date employment is to begin.
- Specify length of employment and whether employment is at will (the salesperson can be fired any time) or for a definite term, say, two years.
- If employment is at will, specify whether notice is required. If so, say how far in advance it must be sent for the termination to be effective, and by what means (certified or regular mail).
- Never give assurances of job security if you are hiring a salesperson at will.
- If employment is for a definite term, say whether the contract is renewable under the same terms and conditions after the expiration of the original term, and whether notice must be sent to confirm this.
- Peg employment to a minimum sales quota, if applicable.

Termination of Employment
- Clarify when commissions stop; upon termination, upon shipment of order, upon shipment with a cutoff date to eliminate the problem of reorders.
- Avoid severance compensation arrangements.
- Specify when a final accounting will be made.
- Limit the right of the salesperson to sue for commissions within a specified period.
- Specify the prompt return of all samples, customer lists, orders, field information, with a penalty if not complied with.
- Include a restrictive covenant for additional protection in writing.

If a chosen candidate seems to have a lot of reservations about the job, sales managers should not attempt persuasion. Applicants that are too hesitant are not likely to give the company their best efforts.

Sales Force Socialization

Once you've completed the process of recruiting and selecting the new salesperson, it's time to integrate that person into the organization. Sales force socialization is the proper introduction of the recruit to company practices, procedures, and philosophy and the social aspects of the job. The process actually begins when the potential sales candidate reads recruiting literature about the firm and attends the first interview with company representatives. Socialization is crucial in achieving a return on the sizable investment made during the recruiting and selection process. The effective development of job skills, the adoption of appropriate role behaviors and organization values, and adaptation to the work group and its norms can influence a recruit's motivation, job satisfaction, and performance. With large numbers of women and minorities entering the workplace as entry-level salespersons, the socialization process takes on an increasingly critical role in the future success of the firm.

Recruiting, selection, and training all play an important part in the socialization process. The most important benefits of a formal sales force socialization program include greater job satisfaction, increased employee commitment, greater job involvement, improved chance for survival of new salespeople, and the new hire's better understanding of his or her role in the company.

Sales force socialization can also contribute to person-organization fit. Person-organization fit, or POF, describes how consistent a salesperson's beliefs and value system are with those of the organization for which he or she works. POF has many positive job outcomes including higher job satisfaction, lower stress, and a lower likelihood of turnover.[7]

Sales managers have a greater impact on new salespeople and improve the culture of the sales organization more successfully. Socialization should be implemented in organized programs rather than creating a unique socialization experience for each new hire. If done properly, socialization programs have a greater impact on new salespeople and are more successful in improving the culture of the sales organization. A formal socialization program is a common learning experience all recruits go through that removes newcomers from their normal work setting and offers guidelines about the sequence and timing of progression in the organization. Socialization programs also offer close contact with experienced salespeople in the organization and provide social support from other members of the sales organization that reinforces the newcomer's identity. Thus, socialization is a critical part of the hiring process.

There are two types of socialization. The first is initial socialization. This preliminary exposure to the firm begins with the recruiting and selection process and ends with the initial orientation of the salesperson to the firm's procedures and policies. The second type, extended socialization, makes new salespeople feel they are an integral part of the company. This is achieved by exposing new recruits to the corporate culture (values, philosophy, group norms, different work groups, corporate officers, and so on) and helping them adapting to the new culture in as short a period of time as possible.

Initial Socialization

Initial socialization occurs during recruiting, selecting, and introductory training.

Recruiting Most firms begin the socialization process by sending the sales candidate recruiting literature that details the company's philosophy and the role of the salesperson in the organization. Today, many companies post recruiting material online, as do other organizations such as Indeed.com, CareerBuilders.com, and Glassdoor.com. Interested sales job seekers can browse through descriptions of jobs available and information about the hiring company's culture.

Selection The interview process can give both the candidate and the recruiter some idea of how the new salesperson will respond to the socialization efforts of the company. For example, sales representatives may be expected to dress conservatively. By conforming to this pattern, the recruiter signals the company's expectations to the recruit. In addition, this image may yield clues about the organization's philosophy and the structure of the company.

Many firms also schedule multiple interviews at all levels of the company and in other functional departments. The purpose is not only to get multiple opinions about how well the recruit will respond to socialization efforts but also to expose candidates to the organization's culture. For example, IBM requires five or six interviews for sales recruits in an effort to find those who will be successful in the IBM culture.

Professional recruiting brochures and lengthy interview processes are typical of many large and medium-sized firms. But small firms may not be able to afford the expense of such high-quality recruiting materials. When smaller firms recruit salespeople, the firm's owner is often involved in the interviewing process. Thus, the candidate can get firsthand information about the owner's philosophy of running the business and the role of the sales force. Likewise, the owner may discern whether the candidate fits the characteristics the firm is seeking.

Introductory Training After successfully completing the recruiting and selection process, the new recruit has some notion of the firm's corporate philosophy and the nature of the sales position. Some companies prepare detailed human resources manuals covering the company's history, product line, organization, job descriptions, and various compensation and benefit packages. By receiving such a manual before they report for work, new salespeople can quickly find answers for many of their questions concerning the company's procedures and policies.

When the salesperson reports to work for the first time, immediate placement into a selling situation in the field may result in improper socialization. New recruits should report first to the home or regional office so they can be properly informed about the job, company procedures, policies, and so forth. Recruits should also be encouraged to ask questions about information in the human resources manual or other materials given to them prior to reporting to work.

While at the home office, sales recruits should be exposed to the actual operations of the firm. Payroll procedures, expense accounts, office procedures and policies, and routine items such as parking and dining facilities should be explained by members of the human resources department or sales training staff, or by the sales manager.

Extended Socialization

Extended socialization programs include long-term training, job rotation, and corporate social activities. The focus of extended socialization is building *esprit de corps* and camaraderie in the sales organization.

Long-term Training Many large companies use long-term training programs to educate salespeople about the firm's products, customers, and competitors and to ensure the new recruits are properly socialized. A number of companies train sales recruits for as long as six-months before they are assigned to their own territory. This extended training includes classroom lectures, independent study, a sales simulation, role-playing, and time spent in the field with experienced sales professionals. All these efforts are undertaken to ensure superior product knowledge and an understanding of the market and customers.

Companies that engage in extended socialization programs are seeking consistent adherence to company practices, procedures, and philosophy. In addition, they want to assist new salespeople in acquiring a high level of job skills and an understanding of appropriate role behaviors and work-group values. This standardization of values, behavior norms, and philosophy helps produce consistent sales performance results, because salespeople become highly motivated team players.

There is, however, a negative side to this type of extended socialization. Some recruits may resent being asked to "fit the mold" and may leave the firm. Through proper selection methods and accurate presentation of company expectations, managers can screen such individuals out before company resources are expended in training them.

Job Rotation Both large and small firms use job rotation as a way to expose sales trainees to the corporate culture. Not only do the recruits learn how different departments work, but they also make social contacts and are exposed to the overall organization. This broad exposure to the firm early in their sales career helps instill a sense of belonging and camaraderie in recruits.

Corporate Social Activity Many firms recognize the value of informal ways of socializing new employees. Company picnics, sports teams, and sales meetings all provide an opportunity for the new salesperson to interact with experienced salespersons, sales managers, and company executives in a non-threatening environment. In these types of settings, the new employee can ask questions and observe how everyone fits into the social structure of the firm. Often the recruit's spouse or significant other is included in the activity. This helps affirm the role of the new employee's partner in the successful performance of the sales job. The main problem with these kinds of activities is usually the distance between a salesperson's territory and corporate headquarters.

Corporate social activity aimed at socialization need not be elaborate or expensive. Hallway conversations and softball teams can be effective means of socializing the new salesperson. Each of these methods facilitates the major purpose – building *esprit de corps* within the sales organization.

Chapter Summary

1. **Follow the steps in the sales force recruitment process.** Because of the critical importance of recruiting, sales managers should have an effective system for finding and selecting sales personnel. To ensure new recruits have the aptitude necessary to be successful in a particular type of sales job, sales managers should follow the steps in the recruitment process. These steps include (1) conducting a job analysis, (2) preparing a job description, (3) identifying sales job qualifications, (4) attracting a pool of sales recruits, and (5) evaluating and selecting the best recruit available. Before a company can search for a particular type of salesperson, it must know something about the sales job to be filled. This is determined through conducting a job analysis and developing a job description. The job description clarifies exactly what the duties and responsibilities of the sales position are, and on what basis the new employee will be evaluated. Since a job description is used in recruiting, selecting, training, compensating, and evaluating the sales force, the description should be in writing. The duties and responsibilities set forth in the job description should be converted into a set of job qualifications. Job qualifications should specifically spell out the characteristics and abilities a person must have in order to carry out the requirements of the sales position, such as education, previous experience, decision-making ability, product knowledge, transportation, ability to travel, and computer literacy.

2. **Identify sources of sales applicants.** Companies use several sources to find qualified applicants. The search can begin within the company by surveying the sales force for possible recruits and then seeking individuals from other departments. Some of the external sources include competitive and noncompetitive firms, educational institutions, advertisements, and employment agencies. A relatively new source of sales candidates is through online career

centers. Recruiters must recognize that top-rated candidates can come from any source. However, with the increasing costs of recruiting, sales managers must be careful to devote their time to the most productive sources.

3. **Follow the steps in the sales force selection process.** Selecting good applicants is an extremely important and challenging task for the sales manager. The salesperson selection process involves choosing the candidates who best meet the qualifications and have the greatest aptitude for the job. The general steps in the salesperson selection process include (1) initial screening, (2) reference checking, (3) in-depth interviewing, (4) employment testing, (5) follow-up interviewing, and (6) making the selection. In selecting salespeople, several tools are used to screen and eliminate undesirable recruits. Initial screening may start with an application form or résumé, a screening interview, or some type of brief test. Application forms, as well as résumés, are the most widely used screening tools and are easy means of collecting the information necessary for determining an applicant's qualifications, such as educational background, work experience, and personal references. An important function of application forms is to help sales managers prepare for personal interviews with candidates for sales positions. Almost all companies make use of initial screening interviews or tests.

4. **Apply the criteria used to make the final selection decision.** When all other steps have been completed in the selection process, the sales manager must decide whether or not to hire each applicant. The company reviews everything known about a particular applicant gathered from screening, reference checks, interviews, and tests. The applicant's goals and ambitions are matched against present and future opportunities, challenges, and other types of rewards offered by the job and the company. While selection tools and techniques can eliminate the obviously unqualified candidates and generally spot the more competent individuals, some amount of judgment is typically used to make the final selection decision.

5. **Implement the sales force socialization process.** Once the process of recruiting and selection is complete, the new salesperson must be integrated into the sales force. Socialization involves the formal introduction of the recruit to company practices, procedures, and philosophy as well as the social aspects of the job. Effective development of job skills, adoption of appropriate role behaviors and organization values, and adaptation to the work group and its norms can influence a recruit's motivation, job satisfaction, and performance. There are two levels in the socialization process. Initial socialization occurs during the recruiting, selection, and introductory training processes. Extended socialization is accomplished through long-term training, job rotation, and corporate social activities.

Key Terms

Recruitment	Selection process	In-depth interview	Socialization
Recruitment process	Initial screening	Structured interview	Person-organization
Job analysis	Weighted application	Unstructured interviews	fit, or POF
Job description	forms	Semistructured interview	Initial socialization
Job qualifications	Reference checking	Employment tests	Extended socialization

Notes

1. Anthony, C. (2017). Why is turnover so high in B2B sales? https://www.linkedin.com/pulse/why-turnover-so-high-b2b-sales-anthony-chaine/ (accessed February 2020).

2. Bleeke, N. (12 July 2017). The good, bad, and ugly of sales rep turnover. https://www.salesproinsider.com/good-bad-ugly-sales-rep-turnover/ (accessed February 2020).

3. Prater, M. 10 Essential selling skills every sales rep needs in 2019. https://blog.hubspot.com/sales/10-essential-selling-skills-2014-infographic (February 2020).

4. Shineman, E. 5 Secrets for recruiting sales talent right out of college. https://www.salesgenomix.com/college-sales-recruiting-secrets/ (accessed February 2020).

5. Online Screening Sources: Press Release. Number of employers using social media to screen candidates at all-time high, finds latest careerbuilder study, June 15, 2017, CareerBuilder.com. http://press.careerbuilder.com/2017-06-15-Number-of-Employers-Using-Social-Media-to-Screen-Candidates-at-All-Time-High-Finds-Latest-CareerBuilder-Study (accessed February 2020); and Saige, D, *Keep it clean: Social media screenings gain in popularity*, 7 October 2018.: https://www.businessnewsdaily.com/2377-social-media-hiring.html (accessed February 2020).

6. Career Builder. Fifty-eight percent of employers have caught a lie on a resume, according to a new careerbuilder survey. https://www.careerbuilder.com/share/aboutus/pressreleasesdetail.aspx?sd=8%2F7%2F2014&id=pr837&ed=12%2F31%2F2014 (accessed February 2020).

7. Hiring a new employee: Person-organizational fit and why it's important (11 June 2018). http://www.4pointconsulting.com/blog/2018/06/11/hiring-a-new-employee-person-organizational-fit-and-why-its-important/ (accessed February 2020).

Chapter Review Questions

1. What are the steps involved in the recruiting process? [LO 1]

2. Why should sales managers conduct job analyses before recruiting salespeople? [LO 1]

3. How is the job description used in managing the sales force? [LO 1]

4. What factors should sales managers consider when deciding which recruitment source to use? Explain. [LO 2]

5. Why should sales managers develop a set of job qualifications? Is this a difficult process? Explain. [LO 3]

6. Discuss the benefits of screening tools to the selection process. How might screening tools help control the cost of salesperson selection? [LO 4]

7. What is socialization? When does it occur? Why is socialization of new salespersons important to the culture of the sales organization? [LO 5]

8. What is POF? How does socialization contribute to POF? What do you think tends to happen when an employee experiences low levels of POF? [LO 5]

Online Exercise

United Parcel Service (UPS) emphasizes diversity, in its recruiting efforts. Go to: https://pressroom.ups.com/pressroom/ContentDetailsViewer.page?ConceptType=PressReleases&id=1500902414450-249. Compare UPS's diversity efforts with those of two other companies at which you are interested in getting a sales job. Which has the best diversity program and why?

Discussion Questions

You have just finished a series of interviews with a person who you feel is an excellent candidate for your open sales position. She has a 3.4 grade-point average and a marketing degree. The candidate has excellent communication skills, held a part-time sales job throughout college to help pay for school, and was an officer in the sales fraternity on campus. She will definitely make a great entry-level salesperson at your company. Your only concern is that another company will offer her a job before you do! Before any candidate is offered a job, your company requires that a few of the applicant's references be checked. During the process, you discover that your ideal candidate lied on her résumé and application. She was never an officer in the sales fraternity; she was only a member.

1. Given the difficulty in finding excellent candidates, what do you do with this person?

2. Would your decision change if you also find out this candidate has several speeding tickets?

3. Prepare an email for the human resources department to support hiring this individual.

Role-Play Exercise

Determining the Ethics of a Candidate

Even the sleaziest rep can look like a saint in an interview. So how can you tell if a rep is ethical before you make the job offer? There's no foolproof method, but human resources experts say sales and marketing executives need to probe candidates for important characteristics – self-discipline, honesty, openness, self-respect, level-headedness, and a mix of aggressiveness and empathy. One way to uncover these qualities is by posing hypothetical dilemmas to potential hires. One global management and human resources consulting firm based in the United States uses the combined responses from the following scenarios asked during an interview to determine an overall pattern of ethics, or lack thereof, in job candidates.

- A few months after joining the company your colleagues tell you about a credit card that gives 20% cash refunds at certain restaurants. Easy money, especially if you're just beginning to establish a territory. Since the company encourages entertaining, the salespeople reason, why not take clients to those restaurants and pocket the refunds? It won't cost the company any money. Do you join in?

- After speaking with a sales manager at a competitor's trade show booth, you spot a hard copy from the competitor's database listing 100 qualified leads from the show. You can slip it into your briefcase easily, and no one will see. What do you do?

- After meeting with a customer you discover a competitor has lowballed your offer by 15%. This competitor has a reputation for offering products at the lowest possible price, but failing to provide an acceptable level of service. Do you warn the customer, attempting to push him toward your offer, or walk away from the business, hoping he'll find out for himself and choose your company in the future?

- The standard rate for your product is $15,000. After negotiations with an important customer you discover the company can realistically only afford $13,000. A few weeks later you receive the purchasing order with the original $15,000 price. You receive a 5% commission on the total dollar value of the deal. Do you correct the customer's mistake, or allow the company to be billed for $15,000, hoping the error is never discovered?

- You're on a sales call and a key customer from a *Fortune 500* company says she won't buy from you unless you match a competitor's offer. The competitor's offer includes a 10-day trip to Hawaii for the customer and her husband. What do you do?

In evaluating the responses, concern arises if the answers suggest a salesperson will do anything to make a sale – especially in ways that may jeopardize the company's reputation. For example, a rep who would not hesitate to steal the competitor's list of qualified leads or match a potentially questionable offer by a competitor to send a client on an exotic trip. An ethical rep would also warn a customer about the competitor who offers products at a low price, but skimps on service. Further, ethical salespeople would raise the issue of the 20% credit card with his or her management before proceeding. Last, in the case of the billing mistake, ethical reps will correct the error immediately to preserve the relationship of trust with the client.[2] The role-play participants and assignments are:

Debbie Stuart. This sales rep argues these practices are unacceptable.

Shane Williams. This sales rep argues these are standard practices in the industry and should be OK.

Ethical Dilemma

Playing the Recruiting Game

Your company uses a two-person team approach to recruit sales applicants. When visiting college campuses, two sales managers sit in on the initial employment interview and individually evaluate the applicant. You have been paired with a very successful veteran sales manager. After several interviews you noticed that he always brings up sports, in particular, golfing, during the interview. At first you assumed the sports questions were a form of "ice breaker" and a good way to build rapport with the college recruits. You've come to realize, however, that your partner rates applicants poorly if they are not avid golfers and/or sports enthusiasts. This is particularly upsetting to you since several of the recruits you evaluated very highly were rejected by the veteran sales manager. You feel that you really don't want to question his ability as a recruiter. However, you are concerned that if your evaluations of the recruits are continually different from those of the successful veteran, your own career may be jeopardized.

What do you do? If you confront the veteran sales manager, could there be any negative outcomes? Any positive ones? Are any legal ramifications possible as a result of the veteran sales manager's actions?

| CASE 8.1 | Vector Marketing Corporation: Recruiting and Selecting College Students |

Vector Marketing Corporation, headquartered in Olean, NY, is the North American distributor of CUTCO Cutlery. Both Vector Marketing Corporation and CUTCO Cutlery Corporation are wholly owned subsidiaries of the CUTCO Corporation, founded in 1949. CUTCO Cutlery are high-quality products manufactured by CUTCO Cutlery Corporation in Olean, NY. The product line features kitchen knives, carving knives and forks, gourmet cookware, kitchen utensils, selected hunting and fishing knives, as well as garden tools.

Vector divides North America into seven major selling zones (six in the United States, and one in Canada), with approximately 300+ year-round sales offices, called District Offices, and an additional 350+ summer offices, called Branch Offices. Annual sales total over $210 million, which is more than 25% growth in four years. The growth of Vector is attributed to the outstanding quality of CUTCO products, managerial leadership, and an outstanding sales force comprised mainly of college students who sell CUTCO full-time during the summer and part-time during the school year.

Sales representatives demonstrate CUTCO Cutlery under the direction of local office sales managers. All Vector sales representatives and office sales managers are independent sales contractors working primarily on a sales commission basis. Vector offers a base pay program for all representatives to ensure that they are paid for a sales demonstration even if the customer does not purchase any CUTCO. The representative receives whichever amount is higher at the end of each week – the base pay for appointments, or the commission. Salespeople develop sales leads almost entirely from referrals and make appointments via telephone. There is no "cold-calling" or "door-to-door" solicitation.

Vector salespeople participate in a highly recognized sales training program. Basic product and sales training is conducted at the local office level in individual and small-group live sessions along with virtual training with webinars, blogs, and skill building videos. In addition to the initial onboarding and sales training, advanced training is provided on selling and communication skills. Further training is offered at regional sales meetings and conferences along with individualized coaching-for-success throughout the year. Salespeople

are trained to follow Vector's sales approach that is based on 'showing' rather than 'selling' – which alleviates the customers' pressure to buy and the representatives' pressure to sell.

Advancement within Vector is based solely on effort and performance. Sales representatives can advance to the top sales representative level of Field Sales Manager. During this past year, the average income of the top high-level sales representatives was $11,500/year and the top 100 performers earned over $105,000/year (students typically work full-time during the summer and part-time during the school year). More than just the potential to earn income, sales representatives are emphatic that their experience with Vector has built the skills necessary for professional success. These "Skills for Life" include communication, self-confidence, time management, public speaking, goal setting, and customer service. Since college students are the dominant majority of the sales force, Vector has established a scholarship program as an incentive for outstanding sales performance, awarding $40,000 in college scholarships annually.

An extensive customer service program is designed to support the sales force's efforts with the customer. CUTCO products are backed with a forever satisfaction guarantee. Prompt order processing and shipping enable customers to receive CUTCO within 7–10 days of the in-home demonstration. In the event of any questions about the order, a toll-free number and online chat are available for customers. An additional benefit of the customer service program is to give the salesperson added confidence in the product they sell, as well as to enhance Vector's image as a reputable company. Vector also adheres to the Code of Ethics established by the Direct Selling Association as part of its customer service effort.

Substantial effort is focused on selecting, training, and equipping the sales force with the sales support programs needed to successfully sell CUTCO. Public relations and advertising expenses for CUTCO products are relatively small because the products are mainly demonstrated and sold in customer homes or online with a customer. The sales representative's job is to show CUTCO products – in person or virtually – and help the customer find the perfect set that fits their needs. Getting the word out to customers is done via the word-of-mouth referral system utilized by the sales force. Vector does, however, use Web advertising plus direct mail to recruit salespeople along with a personal referral program for the existing sales force. Additional marketing tools include a direct mail catalog that is sent as a service to existing CUTCO owners. If a sales rep is still active in the business, they are eligible to receive a commission on any sales that are made through the catalog to their previous customers. Managers also receive a commission on any sales made from the catalog in the geographic area of their office. In addition, CUTCO has a website (www.cutco.com) to provide information and communication for consumers.

A comprehensive sales incentive support program provides motivation for, and recognition of, sales achievements by the Vector sales representatives and field sales managers. Incentives range from cash bonuses and prizes, to a travel incentive program for trips to locations such as Italy and Hawaii, recently. In addition, all conferences and sales meetings include a great deal of emphasis on recognition and sales awards for the sales reps and managers.

Vector is part of a growing number of firms that are selling directly to consumers in their homes. Direct selling is an important and unique retail channel because of the way in which products and services are marketed to customers. Instead of relying on traditional retail outlets or online marketplaces, direct selling companies utilize a salesforce of millions of independent sales consultants who directly interact with and sell to consumers. With over 60 million sales representatives worldwide contributing over $114 billion in sales, it goes without saying that the direct selling channel plays a major role in the global economy. Used by top global brands as well as smaller, entrepreneurial companies, direct selling is a go-to-market strategy that, in this age of social networking, can be more effective than traditional advertising or securing shelf space in brick-and-mortar retail outlets. Direct selling isn't only about getting great products into consumers' hands. It is also a pathway enabling entrepreneurial individuals to work independently to build a business with low start-up and overhead costs and flexible work hours. In this era of the gig economy, a large and growing sector of the population are attracted to these flexible and independent worker relationships that characterize the direct selling retail channel.

The rapid success of Vector can be traced to the company's basic founding principle, which is "to be successful we must first help others to succeed." An expanding, committed sales force selling a superior product is essential to Vector's continued success. Meet Jim Stitt, President and CEO of CUTCO Corporation, experience the companies' culture and core values, and take a tour of the manufacturing facility at https://www.youtube.com/watch?v=j1OLjSnKbb4&t=4s.

Questions

1. What are some of the challenges to managing a sales force consisting mainly of college students?

2. Develop a profile of the ideal candidate you would select for the Vector sales position.

3. What could management do to increase the number of students that apply for a sales job with Vector Marketing?

Case prepared by: Michael Williams, Oklahoma City University

| CASE 8.2 | **S.A. Jaguar Nuclear Operating Power Plant: Improving Recruitment and Selection** |

S.A. Jaguar Nuclear Operating Power Plant (Jaguar Power), in operation since 2013, is a 3-unit, 24-hour baseload nuclear power plant. The plant is in a rural town home to 4500 residents. A junior college and two universities are located 12–15 miles away from the plant. Jaguar Power supplies 25% of the state's electric power generation – 831 MW of energy from Units 1 and 2 and 947 MW from Unit 3. The plant has been a mainstay in the community and operates as a self-contained city with 823 employees at varying levels of experience and exposure to the control tower and the nuclear fission process. Jaguar Power's design is a pressurized water reactor (PWR) Westinghouse design, with original construction costs of $3.2 billion in 2001.

The plant's current operating budget of $438 million has a major economic impact on the town. The United States Nuclear Regulatory Commission (NCR) heavily regulates the industry and requires each plant to conduct safety training, assessments, and a series of reviews and tests during annual shutdowns for maintenance. During these mandatory shutdowns, two of Jaguar Power's three units are taken offline for refueling, new staff onboarding, training, and review of all human performance (HP) errors identified.

At a recent Human Resources and Training Department meeting, a goal was set to increase recruitment of prospective trainees by 17% in the next year. Due to the type of operations at Jaguar Power and the skill level required, Vice President of Human Resources, Kellie Singer, and her team have had a difficult time recruiting and retaining employees. After repeated job fairs, hosted lunch and learns, and signing bonuses, their bad luck is persisting. It appeared no one wanted to work at Jaguar Power, especially the junior engineers and veterans they desperately sought to attract. Despite all recent efforts, only 20–30 recruits attended the Open Job Fair. Most of the attendees were not qualified due to several factors. This has made it difficult for Kellie and her team to decrease the 12% turnover rate in the new hires brought on two years earlier, as well as make progress on meeting higher recruiting goals.

As initial efforts directed toward addressing these concerns, management felt it was imperative employees perform community service hours, and that a steady pipeline for recruits be established between the organization and the local colleges and universities. With such huge efforts directed toward being a positive presence in the community, it baffled Kellie that there were so few people interested in working for an organization like Jaguar Power. It was equally concerning that so few would remain for any significant period of time after being hired or promoted internally. To be successful at performing her job duties, she desperately needed to find answers to these conundrums!

Because of the critical importance of recruiting and the company-wide effects of turnover, managers at Jaguar Power need to implement a new mechanism for increasing their applicant pool as well as selecting employees. Kellie, along with the board of directors, decided to restructure their recruiting and selection strategy. Kellie and her team agreed that adding job listings on Internet job boards and websites, such as Indeed.com, should increase their applicant pool. They posted job descriptions and qualifications in electronic format online as the first phase of this project. The number of resumes increased substantially, but the review of each application was consuming a lot of the HR team's time, which in turn, increased the amount of overtime current employees needed to handle other HR-related tasks.

Applicants at Jaguar Power must be thoroughly reviewed before selection due to the high-risk nature of the job. The job criteria, personnel psychological testing, and an in-depth background check are all required before an interview is scheduled. All of these steps during the selection process are time-consuming and require a great deal of checks-and-balances from multiple HR and administrative personnel to ensure that all hiring procedures have been conducted. Now that recruiting is automated, HR is hoping to utilize these Web-based features within the selection process as well. The Web-based application is still requiring more time from HR,

but the network it has provided in finding qualified applicants also has increased. Kellie believes the initial implementation of electronic selection processes has helped solve the original issue of the small applicant pool, but now she must research how this technology can be utilized more efficiently to reduce the overtime while still processing all the applications as well as improving the quality of applicants being identified for in-person interviews. Ineffective recruitment can cause a ripple effect throughout the organization. Hiring an unqualified person is costly, but if the recruitment and selection of employees is properly executed, companies can reduce the selection and development costs and the organization can become productive much faster.

Jaguar Power's sales team is a vital component of the plant's success. Kellie's team determined they also needed to hire energy wholesale traders, nuclear physicists, and plant support staff. To conserve staff time, remove selection bias, and improve the quality of their applicant pool, Kellie decided to employ artificial intelligence (AI) to aid them in the process. Applications would be screened using software programed to rank applicants based on the ability of keywords in their resume matching key qualifications placed in the company's database. Also, virtual reality simulators will be utilized to give potential workers a "realistic experience" of the conditions under which they will be working, as well as train current employees in an effort to decrease training injuries.

Utilizing information from HR and her department's recruiting efforts, as well as conducting an internal review, Kellie distributed surveys and conducted in-person interviews with applicants and employees from the past two years. As a result, she was able to unearth practices that suggested why the turnover percentage was so high. But applicants had discovered a way to minimize the likelihood of AI weeding out their application. Several of the previous applicants admitted to placing keywords from the job description, that did not easily fit into describing their previous job duties, into the footer of their resume. Those words were typed in white font as to not be easily detected by the human eye but read by AI. Also, while performing community service hours, employees had been talking with students about the great pay but lack of consistent warm water in the showers, unsafe work conditions, confined spaces, baby boomers who do not communicate to the younger workers, and even unhealthy food served in the on-site café. Review of the internal promotion process revealed department transfers were based on the recommendation of subordinates and not the department supervisors. The combination of poorly executed internal practices and current employees' willingness to share their dissatisfaction of the work environment with members of their strongest source of future applicants must be corrected immediately.

Kellie decided to conduct a meeting with her staff to address her findings. You will be present at the meeting and below are the questions she will pose. With the knowledge you have acquired from reading this chapter, what would your response be?

Questions

1. Jaguar Power is having a difficult time recruiting and selecting applicants, so they switch to using Web-based job applications. Now they are having a difficult time processing all of the applicants and weeding out the initial unqualified individuals. Natural Language Processing (NLP) is a subfield of AI, which analyzes and processes large amounts of data. It provides a computerized linguistic function by "reading" the data and extracting critical information programmed to help make decisions. How can NLP reduce the manual effort and time constraints currently impacting the HR department?

2. The job requirements are high-risk due to the nature of this type of job. The selection process requires specific criteria, such as psychological testing and in-depth background checks. This is a very time-consuming and labor-intensive process for both the HR personnel and the applicant. How can technology enhance the accuracy while reducing human intervention during the selection process?

3. The training required to retain employees is specific and high-risk. How can Virtual Reality (VR) provide trainers and trainees a realistic, consistent, and measurable program? How is this likely to impact retention?

Case prepared by: Alice Gordon Holloway, University of South Alabama, Cristal Hunt, University of South Alabama, and Elise Van Zandt, University of South Alabama

CHAPTER 9

Training the Sales Force

YouTube, Social Media, Blogs, Wikis, Podcasts, and More

YouTube, social media, blogs, wikis, podcasts, and similar digital media are increasingly the way companies communicate, both with customers and employees. The same communication technologies are now mainstream in sales training. Dynamic databases such as external and internal wikis and blogs, podcasts, smartphones, personal assistants, wearable devices, and online internal company help sites are just some of the access channels sales managers and salespeople use, not just to keep in touch but also to get the most out of sales training opportunities.

With this technology salespeople can access "take-it-anytime" sales instructions. Much of this "on-demand" help is in the form of modules – short five-to-ten-minute recorded content focusing on a particular message or discussion topic. Blogs and content downloads do more than provide immediate access to needed information; they stimulate curiosity and motivate people to enroll in formal training that might not have been pursued in the past. Online delivery also reinforces concepts and provides insights into what is working and what needs improvement. Within the coming years, more and more training will involve augmented reality (AR), which means media can project instructional images and/or messages onto what the salesperson actually encounters. Rapidly and continuously emerging methods of training salespeople, extending traditional approaches, are the focus of this chapter.

> **LEARNING OBJECTIVES**
> When you finish this chapter, you should be able to:
> 1. Explain the importance and benefits of sales training programs.
> 2. Follow the steps in developing and implementing sales training programs.
> 3. Apply different instructional methods for training.
> 4. Prepare, motivate, and reinforce trainees.
> 5. Evaluate training programs.
> 6. Meet the sales training challenges of global companies.

Importance of Sales Training

Developing effective sales training programs is one of the most important parts of a sales manager's job. Technology has made customers more knowledgeable than ever before, and they now demand more quality and better service from sales interactions. In addition, more purchasing options and increased global competition have created new challenges. Sales reps must be able to call on CEOs of multi-billion-dollar corporations, sell to national and global accounts, and use consultative selling approaches, not just peddle products. An organization's sales training influences the partnerships it builds with customers and supply chain members and ultimately the success of the organization.

Sales training takes human inputs – salespeople – and develops them into successful, productive members of a sales and marketing team. It is a long-term, ongoing process facilitating the continual growth and productivity of salespeople and channel partners. With effective training, salespeople continually grow in knowledge, skills, and selling techniques, and develop good attitudes about their jobs, companies, and customers. Thus, sales training includes both formal and informal programs designed for sales force and channel member development to achieve the overall, long-run goals of the organization.

Cisco Systems (www.cisco.com) understands the importance of training its own sales force as well as supply chain partners. According to Cisco's Senior VP of World-wide Channels, in the past the company determined how to train its sales force and then adapted those methods to its supply chain partners. Now it looks at both its own needs and those of its partners in developing training concepts and delivery vehicles that work for both. Cisco believes a partner-focused approach is important to future growth and is expanding its Partner E-Learning portal.[1]

Benefits of Sales Force Training

The long-term objective of sales training is customer loyalty and increased profits. Sales training teaches effective ways to plan, sell, serve customers, and implement company procedures. Through sales training, management also hopes to improve customer relations, reduce sales force turnover, and achieve better sales force control. Immediate benefits of sales training include faster development of the sales force, because they don't have to learn as much through their own experience, greater role clarity and job

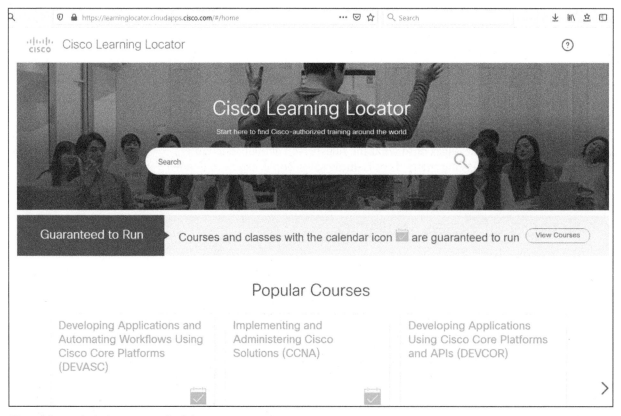

Cisco understands the importance of training.
Source: https://learninglocator.cloudapps.cisco.com/#/home, April 14, 2020.

TABLE **9.1**

Benefits of Training Programs

Training program inputs	Anticipated changes	Long-run outputs
• Initial training • Continuous training	• Faster development • Better role clarity • Improved morale • Higher job satisfaction	• More sales force control • Better customer relations • Lower turnover • Increased sales • Higher company profits

satisfaction, and improved morale because training makes sales reps more successful. These benefits are summarized in Table 9.1.

Keys to Sales Training Success

U.S. companies spend about $175 billion annually on training, and 10% of that focuses on sales training. The average salesperson receives about 35 hours of training per year. But not many companies actually measure the return on investment (ROI) for their training, resulting in billions of wasted training dollars. Why does so much training go to waste?

Much of the squandered training money goes to programs that are not necessary, or the programs focus on problems that cannot be solved through training. Sales managers often request courses without assessing their employees' training needs. Further, managers frequently neglect to reinforce newly acquired skills. Other training programs are so poorly designed their failure is guaranteed, and few companies evaluate their training programs or measure the ROI for training.[2]

So how can sales managers make sales training a meaningful learning experience and achieve the intended goals and objectives? Several keys to success facilitate both planning and implementing sales training programs and provide a checklist for developing effective sales training programs (see Table 9.2). When sales managers are

TABLE **9.2**

10 Key Ingredients for Sales Training Success

Sales training should . . .
1. Conduct a training needs assessment first
2. Link training to desired goals
3. Cover topics identified in needs assessment
4. Be delivered by skilled, professional trainers
5. Have measurable sales performance outcomes
6. Be engaging and interactive
7. Use the correct delivery method
8. Include real-world, practical story-telling examples
9. Be cost effective and measure ROI
10. Endorsed and embraced by senior management

Sources: O' Brien, J. 5 Steps to improve sales performance. https://fowmedia.com/5-steps-sales-training-success/ (accessed August 2019); Drive success through sales training with these three conversations. https://www.integritysolutions.com/salestrainingconversations?gclid=CjwKCAjw_MnmBRAoEiwAPRRWW9GLFWxYNSEuLFhb-vrJLW-RYAlQLGTIgH2psIGYCtKNGvV7yUaOxOhoCuyEQAvD_BwE (accessed August 2019); Keys to successful selling for the first-time sales rep. https://blog.hubspot.com/sales/keys-to-successful-selling-for-the-first-time-sales-rep (accessed February 2020).

considering implementation of a training program, they can use these success keys to evaluate the program's merit. These attributes should be considered when developing any sales training program.

Developing and Implementing Sales Training

Your goal as a sales manager is to design and implement training based on the skills and experiences of your salespeople and other supply chain partners. This means first identifying the gaps between sales force and channel partner skills and the firm's objectives, and then developing training programs to fill these gaps. Sales training programs often weed out individuals who slipped through the recruitment and selection process but are not actually fit for the job. In this sense, sales training is an investment in a salesperson with the hope of continued productivity. Usually, however, training programs identify the skills needed and then develop those skills.

Sales training programs are a challenge to design. As the checklist in Table 9.3 shows, there are many questions to answer in the design process. The questions can

---

TABLE **9.3**

Checklist for Developing Sales Training Programs

Performance needs analysis:
- Why do you think your sales force and/or channel partners need training?
- What is the problem?
- Why is it happening?
- What should be happening instead?
- What factors help or hinder performance?
- What improvements do you expect from the trainees?
- What improvements do you hope for in the organization?

Training needs analysis:
- Who will attend the training?
- What are the training objectives?
- What topics will be taught?
- How will training be presented?
- Who will present it?
- What do salespeople and channel partners already know about the topic?
- What should they be able to do afterward?
- How will success be determined and measured?

Feasibility analysis:
- Is the training solution practical?
- Does the training have management support?
- What is the budget?
- What are the technical requirements?
- How long will the training take?
- How many people will attend?

Sources: Adapted from Lehman, J. (2013). *The Sales Manager's Mentor*. Seattle, Washington: Mentor Press LLC; Drive success through sales training with these three conversations. https://www.integritysolutions.com/sales trainingconversations?gclid=CjwKCAjw_MnmBRAoEiwAPRRWW9GLFWxYNSEuLFhbvrJLW-RYAlQLGTIgH2ps IGYCtKNGvV7yUaOxOhoCuyEQAvD_BwE (accessed February 2020); and Kurlan, D. 5 Steps to improve sales performance. https://fowmedia.com/5-steps-sales-training-success/ (accessed February 2020).

Box 9.1 | Sales Management in Action 9.1

Ensuring Success for Newly Recruited University Graduates

After completing a masters program in physics at Creighton University in Omaha, Nebraska, Jeff Gross spent a year doing research and teaching undergraduates, but felt something was missing from his professional life. He longed for more interaction with people, and he found the perfect match when he accepted a job with JCI (Johnson Controls, Inc., https://www.johnsoncontrols.com).

The company was looking for recent college graduates with engineering backgrounds who wanted to get into sales but had not sold anything before. "It couldn't have been more perfect," says Gross. What came next was a bit of a shock. When building construction rates began increasing, JCI wanted to put more focus on sales. The company also needed consistency, and it decided to start by hiring green salespeople and molding them through an intensive sales training program. Gross, along with other rookie salespeople, spent the first six months learning about the marketplace, how to sell products, and how best to interact with customers.

When designing the rookie sales training program, JCI decided to take a gradual approach so trainees would have the chance to apply what they learned. The six-month program covered company orientation, product knowledge, information about the installation business and estimating skills, on-the-job training with experienced field engineers and sales managers, sales skills development, relationship-building, and a mentoring stint with an assigned sales engineer. By the end of the program, trainees had to prove they could sell on their own. To avoid sending any of the new reps out unprepared, the firm designed the last session as a sales simulation program. The new salespeople not only had to make presentations to judges and mock customers, but also had to do it in front of their peers.

As Gross finished the training program, he felt a sense of accomplishment. Going out into the field alone, he was confident he could do the job well. While the training had taken six months to complete, he was confident he was ready to apply what he had learned. Developing the skills and qualities necessary to become a successful salesperson or sales manager requires a lot of practice. Sales managers must develop the proper training program to assist their people in practicing to become the best salespeople they can be.

Sources: Johnson Controls brings innovative technologies to data centers. https://www.johnsoncontrols.com/media-center/news/press-releases/2019/02/11/johnson-controls-brings-innovative-technologies-to-data-centers (accessed February 2020); Careers. https://www.johnsoncontrols.com/careers/why-johnson-controls (accessed February 2020); and Johnson Controls Salesforce https://www.salesforce.com/ap/customer-success-stories/johnson-controls/ (accessed February 2020).

help make sure the training program is designed around the ten key ingredients of success listed in Table 9.2. For instance, the questions can help design a program that is relevant by attacking a genuine and important problem identified in the needs assessment. Focusing on the questions also should lead to customized training for a specific company's sales force. Finally, a training feasibility analysis addresses the importance of cost effectiveness. Using these two checklists will help the sales manager avoid training blunders.

Sales Training Development Process

Whether you are designing initial or continuing sales training programs, several planning decisions must be made. The sales training development process, shown in Figure 9.1, lists the major decision areas. We examine each of these areas in the following sections.

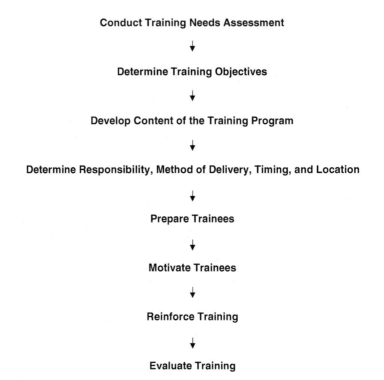

FIGURE 9.1 Sales training development process.

In developing training programs, sales managers all too often do little planning. The sales development process provides a way of avoiding the lack-of-planning mistake. Other mistakes include boring content, or content that oversimplifies the selling situation, using trainers that are not effective communicators, or overwhelming trainees by trying to teach too much in single training sessions. Common training mistakes and their remedies are listed in Table 9.4.

Conduct a Training Needs Assessment

The first step in designing an effective sales training program is to conduct a training needs assessment. Managers should review trainees' backgrounds and experiences to identify gaps between their qualifications and the required job activities. The pharmaceutical company Pfizer (https://www.pfizer.com), for example, surveys salespeople and their managers to determine where salespeople need help. When the surveys are returned, salespeople meet with their managers and determine what training they should take. Managers then develop training programs with customized curriculums based on the developmental needs of each salesperson.[3]

Determine Training Objectives

The next step in designing an effective sales training program is to state your objectives in realistic, measurable terms and include a specific time period. Make notes to use later in evaluating the program's effectiveness.

The key to achieving successful results from training is to focus on performance objectives rather than learning objectives. In other words, what the sales force *does*

| | TABLE **9.4** | |

Common Sales Training Mistakes and Avoidance Strategies

Training mistake	Mistake avoidance action strategy
Lack of planning	• Use checklists in Tables 9.2 and 9.3.
No perceived reason or benefit for training in the minds of the participants	When announcing or beginning a training session, tell participants: • Purpose of training. • How they will benefit. • How they will use it.
Boring content and approach	• Make sure trainers are well prepared. • Customize the content to the audience. • Use personal illustrations to maintain interest. • Use appropriate technology to deliver content.
Unenthusiastic trainer	Keep a positive attitude toward the training; it will spread among the trainees.
Lack of involvement by trainees	Build involvement into the sessions by including role-plays, question and answer sessions, discussion and brainstorming, written activities, watching recorded sales approaches, and games.
Insufficient instructions on how to apply material in the field that is learned in training	Have trainees write a list of action steps they will practice when they finish training at the end of each session or module.
No encouragement, recognition, or approval	Encourage, recognize, approve, and congratulate participation during training.
Lack of follow-up or measurement	• Set performance objectives before training begins and determine how it will be measured. • Include electronic methods such as podcasts to reinforce learning. • Reward trainees when they apply concepts in the fields they learned in training. • Schedule a follow-up session to discuss success stories. • Use success stories as examples in future training sessions.

Source: Adapted from Stritch, E. Common sales training mistakes to avoid. https://www.rainsalestraining.com/blog/common-sales-training-mistakes-to-avoid (accessed May 2019); Williams, B. The most common sales training mistake. https://blog.thebrevetgroup.com/common-sales-training-mistake (accessed May 2019); and Grimse, R. 3 deadly sales training mistakes (and how to fix them). https://www.thebrevetgroup.com/3-deadly-sales-training-mistakes/ (accessed August 2019).

with its newly learned skills should be more important than how much they *know*. Concentrate your objectives on changing or improving a salesperson's behavior.

Prepare specific goals and objectives, and share them with salespeople. For instance, the objective of initial sales training (described below) is usually to assimilate new salespeople into the organization and develop them into top producers. A specific performance objective might be to train new salespeople to meet a quota of *selling at least 75% of what experienced salespeople sell by the end of their first year on the job.*

A primary objective of many training programs is to teach the sales force and channel members how to be more productive. Productivity usually increases with experience. But if sales training can substitute for some of the needed experience, reps can reach higher productivity levels sooner. Sales training not only helps to increase productivity faster but higher productivity also reduces sales force turnover, which lowers hiring and training costs.

Another objective of sales training is to instill pride and demonstrate the importance of the selling function to the individual salesperson, the firm, and to the customer. To achieve high morale, a key to success, the sales force must realize the importance of the role they play in introducing innovations to markets, conveying information to customers, facilitating value from consumption of goods and services, serving as a channel of communication between the company and its markets, and – most important for a marketing-oriented sales organization – solving problems for customers. The overriding philosophy is that professional salespeople are advisers or consultants that create value; they are not mere product pushers. Table 9.5 contrasts the two types of salespeople.

Training programs should also stress the idea that a professional salesperson must continually seek self-improvement. For example, trainees should be taught that it pays to be up to date on selling techniques, new products, new uses for old products, technology to support higher productivity, and upcoming changes and emerging problems in their industry.

Determine Training Program Content

Sales managers choose from two broad types of sales training programs. One is an initial sales training program, designed for newly hired salespeople, which is comprehensive and usually lasts three to six months. A second type is a continuing sales training program for experienced salespeople. Continuing sales training is shorter and more intensive in its coverage of specialized topics relative to initial sales training programs.

TABLE **9.5**

New Versus Old Salesperson Concepts

Sales adviser or consultant	Product pusher
Develops a long-term relationship with clients.	Is interested in making an immediate sale. Shows little concern for the long term.
Identifies the client's problems and suggests solutions.	Emphasizes a particular product's benefits regardless of a client's needs.
Depends on providing helpful information and service to secure business.	Uses high pressure, sometimes unethical, tactics to close a sale.
Often works as a member of a team of specialists who co-create value for customers.	Works alone and has little special product knowledge.
Follows through to ensure customer satisfaction.	Often neglects to follow-up.
Works closely with headquarters marketing support staff.	Ignores headquarters marketing people; thinks they are a nuisance or hindrance to field sales.
Wants to participate in training to enhance selling and relationship building skills.	Does not want to participate in training, and thinks they already know all there is to know about selling.

The scope of initial sales training programs is usually broad because it must cover all aspects of the new salesperson's job, including eight basic elements:

1. company knowledge,
2. product knowledge,
3. knowledge of competitors and the overall industry,
4. customer and market knowledge,
5. selling skills knowledge,
6. technology-based skills, including social media practices,
7. sales portal features and operations, including cloud storage, and
8. sales analytics resources and capabilities.

Company Knowledge New recruits must learn about the company's policies in general – including things such as company benefits, office protocol, payment methods, expense accounts, social media usage, codes of ethics, and communication channels – as well as about specific selling policies. Trainees need to know policies covering selling practices, such as how many sales calls to make per day, email and social media policies, how to handle returns, and how to submit orders. Company knowledge is not hard to teach. Lectures are useful for explaining policies, procedures, and the rationale for them, and specific documentation for these should be accessible electronically in the company's cloud storage. Once the program has covered these issues, training should quickly move on to prevent boredom and loss of enthusiasm.

Product Knowledge Trainees should not only study the company's products and how customers use them, but they must also learn how to solve customers' problems better than anyone else. Consequently, to be successful, trainees also need to learn about and use *competitors'* products. Key topics related to product knowledge that trainers should discuss with salespeople during product training are listed in Table 9.6.

Knowledge of Competitors and the Industry Sales trainees should know about industry trends and competitor tactics, and almost as much about competitors' products and services as they know about their own. Knowledge of competitors' offerings enables the salesperson to compare brands, highlight advantages of the firm's

---

TABLE 9.6

Essential Product Training Topics

- What is the product?
- Why do people buy it?
- Who participates in the buying process?
- How do I find and qualify buyers?
- How do I differentiate the product (its advantages)?
- Who are the major competitors?
- What are strengths and weaknesses of our product and competitors' products?
- What are the product's price and terms of sale?
- What, if anything, is unique about the way a customer uses the product?
- What is the product's availability?
- How long will the product take to arrive?
- What does the company do to support my sales efforts?
- How does the company communicate with its stakeholders, including social media strategies?
- Who do I contact to get answers to my questions?

products, overcome customer objections, and make sure the customer gets the most valuable outcome possible.

Customer and Market Knowledge Today's customers are more knowledgeable and have greater expectations than before. Sales channels, once a relatively simple path between manufacturer and customer with a few distributor relationships, are now a complex maze, many times with multiple sales channels. Product cycles are shorter, and technology has modified almost every aspect of sales and supply chain management. For instance, in the software industry, sales channels may include not only manufacturer's salespeople, but also system integrators, computer resellers, and consultants that offer the product in a sale or select a competitor's product instead.

As a result, effective sales training must go beyond the basics. It no longer is enough to teach salespeople to overcome customer objections. They must be trained to create strategic relationships with customers. Table 9.7 highlights important sales training topics designed to improve partnerships with channel partners and customers.

Selling Skills Knowledge Sales trainees must learn the selling process as well as selling techniques to apply in different situations. The basic steps of the selling process are (1) prospecting, (2) planning the call, (3) approaching the prospect, (4) making the sales presentation, (5) meeting objections, (6) closing the sale, and (7) following up.

TABLE 9.7

Training to Build Partnerships

The following skills help trainees develop customer knowledge:

- *Understand the company's products thoroughly.* Customers expect salespeople and channel partners to know how the products they sell are made, packaged, shipped, installed, operated, and so on. In short, how will the product solve their problem, and how is it different from the competitor's solution?
- *Penetrate customers' buying organizations.* Sales reps must know how to find and communicate with decision-makers in customers' organizations. They must understand and create relationships across customer functions – such as technical, operations, and finance.
- *Know the customers' markets.* Successful partnerships are created when salespeople and channel partners understand relationships customers have with *their* customers.
- *Relate to customers' requirements.* Sales reps must know customers' requirements, such as delivery and inventory control, and how to best meet them.
- *Make professional sales calls.* Training programs must emphasize the importance of listening, which has overtaken presenting in importance.
- *Become team coordinators.* Salespeople must participate in or be aware of all communications that take place between the company and the customer.
- *Stay in close contact with customers.* Making a sale is only the first step in a long relationship with the customer.
- *Become an expert in using the sales portal and sales analytics resources.* These tools are absolutely essential for effective selling, time management, and sales planning.

Sources: Adapted from Lehman, J. (2013). *The Sales Manager's Mentor.* Seattle, Washington: Mentor Press LLC; Drive success through sales training with these three conversations. https://www.integritysolutions.com/salestrain ingconversations?gclid=CjwKCAjw_MnmBRAoEiwAPRRWW9GLFWxYNSEuLFhbvrJLW-RYAlQLGTIgH2psIGY-CtKNGvV7yUaOxOhoCuyEQAvD_BwE (accessed May 2019); and Kurlan, D. 5 Steps to improve sales performance. https://fowmedia.com/5-steps-sales-training-success/ (accessed August 2019).

New salespeople are often provided a list of prospects to get started. In training, they learn how experienced salespeople identify and qualify their own prospects. New salespeople also learn how to use analytics to prospect electronically. Trainees then learn how to plan sales calls on qualified prospects, and how to gather information so they can answer the following questions: What are the objectives of the sales call? What are the customer's needs? How can my company's products satisfy these needs? How do my competitors' products satisfy the customer's needs? What objections might be raised, and how can I handle them? What kinds of presentation or support materials will I need? Answers to these questions help tailor the sales presentation to the prospect – the next step in the selling process.

Since salespeople often have only one opportunity in front of the customer, a large part of sales training is devoted to presentation skills. Training should address skills like establishing rapport, presenting the product's benefits, identifying buying signals of customers, handling customer objections, and using trial closes. Training on presentation skills also includes basics such as vocal inflection and tone of voice, eye contact, hand and arm gestures, and listening skills. Presentation skills are often taught through role-play, which we discuss later in the chapter.

Trainees learn the sale is not complete once they've obtained an order. A good salesperson follows up the sale to make sure he or she has answered all questions, the product arrived at the specified time and in good condition, and the customer is satisfied. Follow-up reassures the customer that he or she made a wise decision and builds customer loyalty, which can substantially increase future sales. Finally, follow-up often generates sales of complementary items or referrals of new prospects.

Technology Training Recall from Chapter 3, Sales Force Automation (SFA) and CRM require salespeople and sales managers to engage with information technologies. New sales reps need to know how to use the software, what information they are required to maintain electronically about their customers and sales calls, what reports are expected, how to protect data, and how to use equipment and applications such as online portals, websites, and particularly social media platforms, which enhance the automated sales environment. As discussed previously, sales reps that travel need to learn how to use digital assistants, mobile phone apps, and related online tools to transmit data and communicate with individuals at other locations.

For every dollar spent on technology, sales managers should budget at least two to three times that amount for training. SFA adoption may actually reduce salesperson effectiveness and efficiency when not supported by adequate training and support.[4] Content developed for and presented in sales training programs can improve sales force productivity and help an organization accomplish its objectives. But when planning technology training sales managers must anticipate that problems can surface during training programs and be prepared to deal with those problems.

Making Training Delivery Decisions

After you have defined the training needs of the sales force, set objectives, and determined the content of the training program, you are ready to make training delivery decisions. Who will conduct the training, will it be for individuals or a group, what method will be used to deliver it, and where and when will training take place are important decisions to be made.

Determine Responsibility for Training

Because trainers often both develop and deliver training program, managers must decide who will conduct the training in the early stages of designing any training. Depending on the situation, responsibility for training can belong to line executives, staff trainers, or outside training specialists.

Line Sales Executives Whether the company is large or small, line executives (sales managers, senior sales representatives, field supervisors, and division managers) often train new as well as experienced salespeople. Line sales executives are usually highly respected, and their messages tend to carry more authority than those of staff executives or outside training specialists. They are also in a better position to evaluate each trainee's ability and performance than administrators who do not participate in the training.

Even if line executives are not entirely responsible for training, they should always participate in planning and selecting training situations. Sales executives are most familiar with the needs of the entire sales force and the selling resources of the firm, and they can effectively design such programs.[5]

Staff Trainers Staff trainers are either members of personnel, production, or office management teams; or they are company employees hired specifically to conduct sales training programs. People from elsewhere in the organization are best used in combination with other trainers, such as line sales executives or outside specialists.

If a company chooses to use staff trainers, often the best strategy is to maintain a training department. Staff trainers have the time and teaching skills necessary for sales training, and can also develop training programs for channel members, to teach them how to sell the firm's products effectively.

Staff trainers hired specifically for training purposes may have disadvantages. To some extent they lack control over trainees, who often do not look up to them as they do to line sales executives. Management support of the sales trainer can help overcome this problem. Another problem is the cost of hiring and maintaining staff trainers is high. Depending on qualifications, the trainer's salary can be $100,000 or more per year.

Outside Training Specialists Outside training specialists help small businesses that cannot afford to have their own sales training departments. They also help large companies by implementing refresher training programs and special-purpose sessions. Outside training specialists offer flexibility because they can conduct the entire training program or handle only the particular part a firm needs the most. Because their livelihood depends on the satisfaction of their clients, outside trainers usually are knowledgeable, interesting, and inspiring in conducting sales training.

Before hiring outside training specialists, sales managers should make sure they not only have excellent presentation and communication skills, but also the sales background and practical knowledge – and therefore the credibility – that only real-world experience can provide. The trainer should also understand the company's sales problems, terminology, and sales cycle. Finally, outside trainers should go on sales calls with a few reps and also interview a few customers to determine what salespeople need to do to get and keep their business.

Many companies have found hiring outside training firms is a useful way of providing consistent training to sales reps. American Express (www.americanexpress.com)

has partnered with outside training groups to sell its products, from credit cards to travel services to traveler's checks. The company used to have 100-plus training programs and the salespeople were selling differently all over the world. Now salespeople undergo competency-based assessment tests to determine what training is needed. Then they participate in numerous sales training programs designed to meet their specific needs and taught at locations around the world.[6] One of the biggest advantages of outside training specialists is that they offer fresher and more innovative perspectives than internal trainers because their perspective is not restricted by a single firm's worldview (i.e., ". . . the way we do it here at XYZ . . .").

Select Group or Individual Training

Group training methods usually work well for formal training programs, and individual training methods work well for informal training programs (especially field training). For example, lectures and role playing are usually effective with groups of trainees in a formal sales training program, whereas personal conferences, on-the-job training, and online modules are better for individual trainees once they are in the field.

Most firms want trainees to go through formal group training before they go into the field. But some firms – for example, many insurance companies – use field training and selling first to see whether the trainee's selling ability justifies the cost of formal training. In most situations, both group and individual training methods are needed. For example, new hires may attend initial training sessions as a group and then return to their home office for on-the-job training where they are paired with more experienced salespeople. More group training can follow, particular when a topic is delivered efficiently to groups. But self-directed online modules are also made available to teach them additional skills and update them on company developments. Online modules are often used to introduce new technology, and to remind and update employees about cybersecurity threats, workplace harassment issues, and similar topics.

Instructional methods for group or individual training are listed in Table 9.8. Of course, some methods are effective for both group and individual training. For example, video presentations can show examples of sales methods during a group training session, or individual salespeople can view them during spare time.

TABLE 9.8

Individual Versus Group Instructional Methods

Group instructional methods:	Individual instructional methods:
Lectures	On-the-job training and mentoring
Literature (manuals, workbooks)	Personal conferences and coaching
Group discussion	Online modules (video/audio)
Conferencing/e-learning	E-learning
Simulation games	Computer-based training, games,
Demonstrations	Podcasts, wikis, etc.
Role playing	Computer-based training, games
	Literature (manuals, workbooks, electronic message boards, etc.)

Choosing Instructional Methods

There are many methods of training, some that sales managers have used for many years and others that have emerged more recently. We summarize the major instructional methods in this section.

Traditional Training Methods

Lectures Lectures can present more information to a larger number of trainees in a shorter period of time relative to many other teaching methods. Also, lectures are an efficient way to present technical data or information that requires a large amount of time to write out. Lecturing in sales training programs should be limited, however, because lectures often do not generate active participation. Plan lectures thoughtfully and keep sessions short, interrupting them with other activities.

Literature Good manuals or workbooks serve as study guides and should be accessible online. The materials contain outlines of the presentations made throughout the training program, lists of related reading materials, learning objectives for each training session, and thought-provoking questions, cases, and problems. Other useful materials are company bulletins, sales and product handbooks, and technical and trade publications.

Group Discussions In the simplest form of group discussion, the trainer leads and stimulates engagement and participation by trainees. Case studies are a good tool for stimulating group discussion. Trainees are given access to cases to study ahead of time, and then the trainer leads a class discussion to analyze and solve the problems in the case. Group discussions also can take place via online chat rooms, which are particularly useful when training is being delivered to people over a wide range of geographic locations.

Role Playing If experience is the best teacher, then a good role-playing session is the next best teacher, because role playing is learning by doing. In role playing, the trainee tries to sell a product to a hypothetical prospect (usually played by the trainer or another trainee). Role playing can help trainees learn to handle unforeseen developments that often arise in selling situations. It also gives the trainer a chance to work with trainees on voice, poise, mannerisms, speech, and movements. All in all, role-playing impresses on trainees that, in a selling situation, knowing what to do is one thing, but doing it is another.

Simulation Games Simulation games can aid in learning by allowing the trainees to assume the roles of decision-makers either in their own or customers' organizations. In the simulations, participants make decisions about the timing and size of orders, territory assignments, sales forecasts, advertising, pricing, and similar tasks. Trainees then receive feedback on the outcomes of their decisions. Simulation games generate enthusiasm through competitive game playing, aid trainees in developing skills to correctly perceive key factors that influence customer decisions and show the uses and value of planning techniques. Simulations also can be fun and force trainees to become actively engaged in the learning process.

Simulation games have a few disadvantages. First, they're time-consuming: it usually takes three to four hours for trainees to generate decisions, and several rounds of decisions are needed to complete a simulation. Also, because simulation games are preprogrammed computer packages, decisions that are novel or unique seldom receive the payoff they deserve. Thus, simulations seldom reward creative thinking.

Demonstrations Demonstrations can be a powerful instructional method because learners tend to retain more information if they can actually see a product in use or a service being delivered. Even more powerful are demonstrations that allow hands-on or active participation. Trainees learning how to use sales force automation software, for example, can experiment with the same computer and communications accessories they'll actually use on the job. Examples in such demonstrations should reflect real-world situations the sales rep will experience.

On-the-Job Training On-the-job training (sometimes referred to as buddy-system or suitcase training) is an individual instructional method in which an experienced salesperson is assigned to a trainee to teach them about the job and how to sell. In this situation, an experienced salesperson typically go on sales calls made by a trainee, and later the two evaluate and analyze the call. The major advantage is trainees can learn firsthand how actual sales calls are conducted. But for on-the-job training to be effective, the experienced salesperson must be highly qualified to train and influence the trainee. An important disadvantage of on-the-job training is that it is very time-consuming and costly for both people.

Mentoring typically pairs a new or inexperienced sales rep with a sales manager or executive, or a more experienced senior sales rep. Salespeople often learn the basics of selling by traveling with more than one sales manager, spending a week or more with each of them. This enables reps to identify the strengths and weaknesses of each manager, and eventually create their own style. Other mentoring programs may last for a year or more and can serve to groom high-potential candidates for managerial positions. Spending time with a sales manager gives the sales rep experience in thinking about executive decisions.[7]

Personal Conferences Managers and trainers often hesitate to use personal conferences because they assume learning cannot take place in an unstructured situation. However, experience has shown that the personal conference can be a very effective learning tool, and it can establish good rapport between the trainee and the sales executive or trainer. But the trainer must be careful to avoid idle chitchat during conference time.

Audiotapes Thousands of audiotape programs are available in podcast form that can assist salespeople in anything from selling skills to personal development. Many companies develop or purchase low-cost audiocassette tapes to give salespeople regular refresher courses on precall planning, presentations, product offerings, and a variety of other topics. Examples of tape topics include discussions of product features for new products, competitor strategies, economic developments, new sales approaches, and so forth. Companies believe audiotapes are a worthwhile method of sales training because they use unproductive driving time for training and professional development.

DVDs In a group setting, DVDs serve a function similar to conferencing. Outside consultants and senior management can prerecord training with audio and video messages. DVDs also minimize travel and time-loss expenses because the firm can easily mail them to remote sales offices for training seminars.

Disadvantages of DVDs, similar to group conferences, are the interaction is one-way, from presenter to trainee, and they are impersonal. Since viewers cannot ask the trainer questions, a sales manager or other knowledgeable individual should be available to answer queries. One note of caution: DVD lectures should be used sparingly. While they are effective on a limited basis, a full day of this type of training would be very boring and not likely to be effective in meeting training objectives.

Technology-Based Training Technology-based training, or TBT, is training that uses any type of technology as the primary delivery method. TBT-based teaching methods have the advantage of using technology to deliver on-demand, just-in-time training. Technology-based training reduces the time and cost it takes to train salespeople and works well when all participants need to be brought up to the same level before further group training. While still an effective training approach, TBT is being replaced by Internet-based approaches.[8]

Conferencing Conferencing is any training in which participants at different locations interact electronically via telephones, satellite, or the Internet. It can take several forms, including videoconferencing and audioconferencing. Most conferencing today accesses online platforms such as Zoom.com, Skype, Go-to-Meeting, and so forth. Conferencing links remote locations (sales offices) to the home office or another facility via the Internet.

In online conferencing, the most popular approach used by participants is a computer, smartphone, or other digital device to communicate with others via the Internet. With *screen sharing*, participants see whatever is on the presenter's screen and respond via their keyboard. Voice communication without video is also possible, through either a traditional telephone or Voice over Internet Protocol (VoIP), although sometimes text chat is used instead of voice. A webinar, a variation on Web conferencing, is a seminar or web conference conducted over the Internet. In contrast to a Webcast, which transmits information in one direction only, a webinar is designed to be interactive between the presenter and audience. It is live and conveys information according to an agenda, with a starting and ending time. In some cases, the presenter speaks over a telephone line, pointing out information being presented on screen, and the audience responds over the telephone, preferably a speakerphone. But almost all platforms include both speaking and visual capabilities.

Conferencing is an effective training approach. Pretest and posttest scores of trainees show no significant difference in learning when trainees take courses via videoconferencing or with an in-class instructor. Research shows the tasks that occur most frequently in educational settings – giving and receiving information, asking questions, exchanging opinions, and problem-solving – are done just as effectively using online platforms as in face-to-face meetings.[9]

E-Learning E-learning is a broad term that refers to computer-enhanced learning, although it is often extended to include the use of mobile technologies. E-learning may include the use of Web-based teaching materials and hypermedia in general, multimedia CD-ROMs or websites, discussion boards, collaborative software, blogs, computer-aided assessment, animation, simulations, games, learning management software, electronic voting systems, and so on. Sometimes managers use a combination of more than one method.

E-learning is also broader than the term online learning, which is purely Web-based learning. E-learning often involves conferencing and distance learning, but it also works in conjunction with face-to-face teaching, in which the term blended learning is used. The term m-learning refers to training through mobile technologies.

Among the e-learning methods most heavily reliant on technology are RSS feeds, blogs, podcasts, and wikis. RSS is a format typically associated with syndicated news and content of news-like sites, including Wired.com and many personal blogs. RSS feeds are not just for news. RSS news aggregators help salespeople keep up with their favorite blogs by checking their RSS feeds and displaying new items from each of them. Google, Facebook, and Twitter do not support RSS feeds, but YouTube, Reddit, Squarespace, WordPress, and many other sites do.

Wikis are another e-learning sales training technique. A wiki enables contributors to create and update documents collectively, usually with no review, using a Web browser. Wikis are a simple, easy-to-use user-maintained database for creating and searching information. Most general-purpose wikis are open to the public without the need to register any user account. Many edits, however, can be made in real-time and appear almost instantaneously online. Company-maintained wikis, such as those used for sales training, are located on private servers and require user authentication before readers can edit or sometimes even read the pages.

E-learning has been the greatest change in training to occur in recent years. Salespeople can now be trained anywhere, anytime, whether through a laptop or mobile phone, or in a car, train, or airplane. The main reasons for e-learning's popularity are the convenience and cost-effectiveness compared to traveling for a training session in a hotel conference room.[10]

Intranet Businesses that want sales training available over the Internet can set up programs on their own internal intranets. An intranet uses Internet and Web technologies but is accessible only to the company's reps and others, such as supply chain members, who are given permission to access the system. Intranet-based training programs generally have more audio and video capabilities than Internet-based programs, though access can be slower and more limited based on connection speeds.

Salespeople at Sun Microsystems (www.sun.com), for example, log onto a centralized server and access a browser that steps them through intranet-delivered sales training programs. With thousands of channel members and salespeople, it would take Sun more than a year to effectively train everyone each time a new product is introduced. With its intranet-based training system, salespeople and channel members can effectively sell a new product line in three months or less.[11]

The president of The Training Clinic in Seal Beach, California (http://thetraining-clinic.com) says some things still can't be taught online: "For interpersonal skills, classroom learning usually works better." The classroom offers feedback from instructors and peers, which is crucial to the learning process. What often works best is training first in the classroom and then incorporating e-learning to reinforce. E-learning is more efficient and effective when people can first meet face-to-face.[12]

Location of Training

Centralized training programs usually include organized training schools, periodic conventions, or seminars held in a central location such as the home office. In smaller firms, where sales territories often are in close proximity to the home office, it's convenient and logical for training activities to be centralized. Organizations that hire large numbers of salespeople each year also typically use centralized training. An advantage is that trainees can quickly get acquainted with each other, top managers, and key home-office personnel. Beyond this, many experts believe removing trainees from the distractions of their daily work and home life is conducive to learning. The major disadvantages of centralized training are the substantial expense and organizational effort it requires.

Decentralized training can include office instruction, use of experienced salespeople, on-the-job training, podcasts, blogs, webinars, and other e-learning approaches. It therefore usually takes place while trainees are actually working in the field, giving them a chance to learn and be productive at the same time, and avoiding the cost of supporting nonproductive trainees while they are trained in centralized programs. Also, the branch manager or an assistant is usually responsible for decentralized training, enabling sales managers to directly evaluate the trainees.

Timing of Training Programs

Although training should be a continual process, management must still decide when to emphasize it. Most managers believe no one should be placed in the field until he or she is trained to sell, with a thorough knowledge of the product, company, customers, competitors, and selling techniques. The other philosophy is to evaluate the new salesperson's desire and ability to sell before spending money and time on actual training. This philosophy places recruits in the field with minimal information about selling and evaluates them on the basis of how well they do, considering their lack of actual training.

Insisting that salespeople be thoroughly trained before they enter the field means they should become top sales producers quicker. But this takes time, can be expensive, and may lower the new salesperson's morale and enthusiasm because he or she may resent feeling nonproductive for the length of time it takes to become thoroughly knowledgeable. The strategy of placing new salespeople in the field first and then training them can weed out people not suited for selling. Also, people selected for training learn more quickly and easily when they have had previous selling experience. Companies can lose customers or create ill will, however, by sending untrained salespeople into the field. Read about one such dilemma in the Sales Management in Action Box 9.1.

Box 9.2 | Sales Management in Action 9.2

The Small Business Sales Manager: *Training on a Shoestring*

Bob Randall had a big problem. In the past two years, sales had nearly tripled at the small printing business that he founded six years ago. Business at Topnotch Press had now expanded from a small graphic design shop to a full-service printing house offering commercial design and printing. Randall had carved a niche for his business providing design and printing services to most of the city's larger retailers and printing menus and signs for local restaurants.

Randall hired two new reps he felt were talented enough to become top sellers. Jill Tompkins was a business major with good grades and was active in several collegiate clubs while holding down a job as a waitress at several area restaurants. Randall hoped her previous restaurant jobs would provide her with some immediate sales contacts. Joe Rothfield, on the other hand, was a graphics design major who had an internship at another local printing shop, although not in the sales area. Although he had no business background, Randall felt he had a firm grasp on the printing business and could make the transition

easily. In the interviews Randall had conducted with the two new hires, he got the impression they were both aggressive and determined enough to make it in sales.

Without any formal training program in place, Randall sent both Tompkins and Rothfield into the field almost immediately with only three days of orientation. Tompkins and Rothfield visited with Topnotch's full-time rep and were quickly taught about the paper products and printing methods available, the design services offered, how to write orders, and what types of services they were expected to provide customers. They were also given a list of retailers and restaurants that inquired about the company's printing services within the last six months, but who had not been followed up on. A new large retail center was also near completion on the north side of town that offered possible new business.

It was now three months to the day that Tompkins and Rothfield had started, and neither one of them had landed any substantial accounts. After going on several calls with them Randall realized the salespeople did not understand the selling process and were still very "green." Both Tompkins and Rothfield were becoming noticeably frustrated and Randall overheard them both contemplating giving up. Randall did not want to lose these new reps because he knew they had potential. They just needed to learn some selling skills, how to determine customer needs, how to analyze their competitors, and some negotiation skills. Randall knew that training was the answer, but

he did not have anyone in-house who had the skills or the time to do it, let alone put a training agenda together.

What methods of training might work for Randall to help his new reps learn important selling skills while not taking them away from their jobs for too long? What topics should be included in the training? How can Randall prevent these problems in the future?

Preparing, Motivating, and Coaching Trainees

While planning how, when, and where training will occur, sales managers often overlook the importance of thoroughly preparing their salespeople for training, motivating trainees to learn, and then following up with them after training. Let's look at some successful strategies for filling these needs.

Preparing Trainees for Training

People look for and anticipate learning experiences only when they see a need for them. If trainees do not understand why they are being trained and what benefit they will receive from it, chances are the training will not be effective.

One of the most effective means of increasing the positive results of sales training is for managers to prepare their salespeople ahead of time. A pretraining briefing tells participants the training's purpose and objectives, why they were selected to attend, and the business need the sales training hopes to meet. By setting goals in advance of training, the sales manager can make sure trainees are more tuned in during the training sessions and thinking about ways to apply their new skills afterward. By endorsing the training program, sales managers exert more influence on whether the training accomplishes its goals than anything a trainer can do during the training. If it's a particularly important sales topic, a member of senior management can kick off the training to enhance its credibility and confirm corporate support. In addition, asking several questions ahead of time, as shown in Table 9.9, can help sales managers and trainers determine whether trainees are ready for the training.

The trainer may also want to give participants a *pretest* to measure how much they know about the training topic and to provide a preview of the content so they come ready to learn. Comparing pretest scores to *posttest* evaluations at the end of training will reveal how much trainees have absorbed.

Motivating Trainees During Training

If trainees aren't motivated during the training session, then learning will not take place. So how do sales managers and trainers get salespeople motivated for learning? One way is by encouraging student involvement and minimizing lectures. Most sales

TABLE 9.9

Prequalifying Participants for Training

If the sales trainee disagrees with any of these statements, they are likely not ready for the training program.

Check "disagree" or "agree" to the following statements:

	Disagree	Agree
My sales manager is knowledgeable about the training we need.		
The training topics focus on issues that will help me improve my skills.		
This training will help me be a better salesperson.		
I am looking forward to learning more about this training topic.		
I can see how I can apply what we will learn in this training.		
My sales manager did a good job of explaining how the training will help me.		
There are ways the training could help the sales force.		
What I learn in this training is likely to count on my performance appraisals.		
My sales manager wants us to learn skills and knowledge covered by the training.		
After this training, I will have more tools to use in communicating with my customers.		

training programs succeed by balancing a small amount of lecture with activities that get trainees engaged in the program, such as group discussions and role playing. Since salespeople often thrive on being in the spotlight, have trainees present some of the material to the rest of the class. Another way is to ask questions. This approach not only engages trainees, it also generates feedback on learning, understanding, and misunderstanding. Involvement and interaction are necessary for in-person training as well as e-learning approaches.

Another important factor is the training environment. Sales training must feel like a safe environment, so trainees are at ease trying different selling techniques during group activities and role playing. Some people are hesitant to role-play in front of their peers, especially if the group is critical or if an individual feels he or she is not up to speed on certain skills. Having management present may also stifle a trainee's participation. Table 9.10 summarizes ways trainers can motivate salespeople to learn during training sessions.

Conducting Post-Training Reinforcement

Just as they need pretraining preparation, trainees also need follow-up on the skills and concepts they learned during training. Coaching is defined here as informal, give-and-take discussions between sales managers and salespeople for the purpose of reinforcing training concepts, solving selling problems, and improving basic selling skills. The sales manager always needs to monitor how the training is going. The last thing you want is to implement selling tools and then not reinforce or use them.[13] Requirements for effective coaching are shown in Table 9.11.

> **TABLE 9.10**

Motivating Trainees During Training

- *Use positive reinforcement.* Reward trainees for learning through positive body language and words of encouragement.
- *Use active training formats and variety.* In addition to lectures, use other learning methods such as discussions, demonstrations, role playing, visuals, games, and simulations.
- *Encourage social interaction.* Social interaction is a strong motivator. Include interaction and group discussions and problem-solving exercises.
- *Facilitate expertise sharing.* Ask trainees to share their specialized skills, knowledge, experiences, or "secrets to success" with the rest of the class.
- *Include realistic examples and situations.* Trainees will pick up skills faster and achieve better results if they get a chance to apply ideas and techniques that mirror their real world.
- *Establish a safe environment for learning.* Eliminate fear in the training environment. Trainees might develop a list of rules to follow during the training session, such as "No criticism," "No interruptions," and "Everything said is confidential."
- *Encourage self-evaluation.* Self-evaluation is an excellent motivator. Trainees can evaluate their progress during training with self-graded quizzes or "learning scorecards."
- *Recognize early success.* Include activities trainees can learn quickly and be rewarded for before presenting the more difficult ones.
- *Include sufficient practice.* Encourage trainees to practice their new skills on the job by scheduling follow-up evaluations.
- *Encourage goal setting.* Have trainees make a list of post-training goals or ways to use their newly acquired skills after training is completed. Schedule a follow-up meeting with trainees to measure their success.

Sources: Adapted from Lehman, J. (2013). *The Sales Manager's Mentor.* Seattle, Washington: Mentor Press LLC; Drive success through sales training with these three conversations. https://www.integritysolutions.com/salestrainingconversations?gclid=CjwKCAjw_MnmBRAoEiwAPRRWW9GLFWxYN SEuLFhbvrJLW-RYAlQLGTIgH2psIGYCtKNGvV7yUaOxOhoCuyEQAvD_BwE (accessed February 2020); and Kurlan, D. 5 Steps to improve sales performance. https://fowmedia.com/5-steps-sales-training-success/ (accessed February 2020).

> **TABLE 9.11**

Requirements for Effective Coaching

1. Coaches and salespeople must trust one another.	The actions of the coach tell salespeople if they can be trusted. Do you expect your salespeople to do as you say or as you do? Always keep your word to your sales team, and avoid competing with them. Encourage open communication to show your salespeople they can confide in you.
2. Salespeople must respect the coach's expertise and ability.	If salespeople are to accept instructions from coaches, they must have faith in their direction. Learning is a lifelong process. Good coaches stay informed, keep their skills sharp, and are never too experienced or knowledgeable to learn something new.
3. Salespeople must want to learn, grow, and change.	Positive, self-motivated salespeople are more receptive to good coaching than negative people – and are more likely to put it to good use. When you hire your next salesperson, consider attitude over experience. Experience is helpful, but teaching new skills is often easier than changing a person's thinking.
4. Coaches should have excellent teaching skills, particularly questioning and listening.	To teach effectively, coaches must present material so salespeople can absorb it easily. They also must be good at asking questions and listening. Provide the sales team with a nonthreatening learning environment. Mistakes are often the best teachers – let your salespeople know that it's okay to make mistakes as long as they learn from them.
5. Coaches should be empathetic	Coaching should never be given without remembering what it is like to be in the salesperson's shoes. Being empathetic with the salesperson is one of the best ways to ensure the salesperson is empathetic with the customer.

Sources: Adapted from What are the necessary conditions for coaching to be effective? https://www.wjmassoc.com/coaching/what-are-the-necessary-conditions-for-coaching-to-be-effective/ (accessed February 2020); Fukuda, M. The 5 essentials to effective coaching. https://www.entrepreneur.com/article/292877 (accessed February 2020); and Bacharach, Y. 5 Essential skills for successful coaching. https://www.inc.com/yael-bacharach/five-essential-skills-for-successful-coaching.html (accessed February 2020).

Evaluating Training Programs

Once you've carried out a sales training program, it's essential to evaluate its effectiveness and determine how well you've met your overall objectives and specific goals for the program.

Table 9.12 illustrates a four-level method to gauge effectiveness. First, the *reaction* level method measures trainees' attitudes and feelings toward the training program. Second, evaluation at the *learning* level assesses how well the trainees learned basic principles, facts, and so on, during the training program. (This requires testing trainees before and after training.) Third, *behavior*-level evaluation measures changes in behavior as a result of the training. Are trainees using their new attitudes, knowledge, and skills on the job? Questionnaires from supervisors, subordinates, and even customers can provide answers. These assessments are often subjective, however, because of personal relationships that often develop during training. Finally, at the *results* level we measure changes in performance. Plot salespeople's performance before and after training and compare the results against training program objectives.[14]

To evaluate new-hire sales trainees, many companies follow the four levels evaluation model presented in Table 9.12. The first two levels – reaction and learning – are measured in the classroom. For example, in a test of product knowledge, trainees could be given a time limit to respond to a checklist of attributes. Further evaluation of learning comes from the trainees' managers, who score reps on their presentation skills, sales skills, and product knowledge. For level three, trainers conduct follow-up interviews to measure how well reps apply their new attitudes, knowledge, and skills on the job. At the fourth level of evaluation, which measures the effect training has on the company, sales managers who have new hires working for them meet in focus groups to discuss relevant issues. While the evidence gained in this approach may be more anecdotal than scientific, experiences with this approach have demonstrated the value.[15]

Figure 9.2 is an example of an evaluation form that could be given to trainees to assess their reactions to the sales training program (Level 1). The trainers' sample evaluation form in Figure 9.3 assesses trainees' changes in attitudes and behaviors as a result of a sales training concentrating on selling skills (Level 3).

TABLE 9.12

Training Evaluation Methods

Levels	Measures	Methods
Reactions	Attitudes, feelings, and satisfaction with the training program	Surveys, comment sheets, and exit interviews are used to evaluate the training experience.
Learning	Principles, facts, concepts, and techniques learned	Trainer administers tests before and after the training program.
Behavior	Changes in behavior as a result of training	Trainer observes and/or surveys trainees and managers after the training program.
Results	Changes in performance, both individual and company-wide	Managers measure change in sales, profits, costs, customer relations, and so forth.

Sources: Adapted from Ashraf, M.A. and Honeycutt, E.D. (2012). Measuring sales training effectiveness at the behavior and results levels using self- and supervisor evaluations. *Marketing Intelligence and Planning* 30 (3): 324–338; Tan, K. and Newman, E. (2013). The evaluation of sales force training in retail organizations: A test of Kirkpatrick's four-level model. *International Journal of Management* 30 (2): 692–703; and Tan, K. and Newman, E. (2012). Sales force training evaluation. *Journal of Business & Economic Research* 10 (2): 105–109.

	Strongly Disagree	Disagree	Neutral	Agree	Strongly Agree
The instructor was well prepared.	☐	☐	☐	☐	☐
The material was relevant to my needs.	☐	☐	☐	☐	☐
The objectives of the training program were made clear.	☐	☐	☐	☐	☐
Visual aids were used effectively.	☐	☐	☐	☐	☐

FIGURE 9.2 Training program evaluation form – Evaluating reactions.

CONFIDENTIAL

Date _____

Salesperson _____   Sales Manager _____

Date report discussed with salesperson _____

4 *Excellent* – skills have been effectively mastered
3 *Satisfactory* – salesperson has shown improvement skills
2 *Unsatisfactory* – salesperson may need follow-up training for these skills
1 *Poor* – Further training and follow-up is required for this skill
0 *Not applicable*

Please circle the number that most closely represents your feelings.

1. *Prospecting*

New lead generation	4	3	2	1	0
Lead qualification	4	3	2	1	0
Follow-up of leads	4	3	2	1	0

2. *Call Preparation*

Determining sales call objectives	4	3	2	1	0
Prospect needs analysis	4	3	2	1	0
Competitor analysis	4	3	2	1	0
Gathering of secondary data	4	3	2	1	0

3. *Approach*

Rapport with customers	4	3	2	1	0
Use of approach methods	4	3	2	1	0

4. *Presentation Skills*

Use of sales presentation strategies	4	3	2	1	0

5. *Handling Objections*

Use of methods to deal with customer objectives	4	3	2	1	0

6. *Closing*

Use of closing techniques	4	3	2	1	0
Increase in new business	4	3	2	1	0
Increase in repeat business	4	3	2	1	0

7. *Follow-up*

Use of follow-up with customers	4	3	2	1	0
Post-sale customer satisfaction	4	3	2	1	0

FIGURE 9.3 Field evaluation and career development report – Evaluating learning.

Some firms specialize in producing better sales coaching.
Source: https://www.rainsalestraining.com/solutions/sales-coaching, April 14, 2020.

Top-level managers are demanding concrete evidence that training is achieving its goals of changing behavior on the job (Level 3 evaluation) and contributing to the bottom line (Level 4 evaluation). Technology has also made it easier to gather data necessary to evaluate training efforts, and research has shown evaluation using the four-level approach outlined here is effective.[16]

Continuous Training Programs

We've focused thus far on initial sales training programs. But sales managers also must develop continuous training. Two types of continuous training – refresher training and retraining – help upgrade the present sales force. The third – managerial training – focuses on sales managers, who need to maintain and sharpen their skills so they can remain effective and efficient. Continuous training conveys information about changes in the company's policies, products, marketing strategies, and the like, helping the sales force understand and adapt to changes quickly.

Refresher Training

Nothing is constant except change, and few places is this truer than in selling.

The purpose of refresher training is to help salespeople do their jobs better by keeping them abreast of changes in technology, products, markets, and company objectives.

Refresher training reinforces the customer-driven approach that characterizes many companies. As customers become more sophisticated and knowledgeable in their buying strategies, salespeople need to be equally sophisticated in their selling strategies. Refresher training and education therefore become even more important.

Some types of refresher training that can help salespeople grow and succeed at their jobs are presented in Table 9.13.

Managers can plan refresher training for either individuals or groups. The nature of the salesperson's deficiencies determines which is most appropriate. Table 9.14 shows a checklist of ways to overcome deficiencies and upgrade the sales force.

TABLE 9.13

Refresher Training Topics

Training aspect	Goal
Basic skills	Learn how to qualify, greet, negotiate, present, and close.
Research	Increase confidence and preparedness by learning how to use available resources and how to find information about customers' and competitors' products or services.
Listening skills	Learn to ask questions and *listen* to answers.
Interpersonal skills	Learn to read and assess body language and intonation, as well as how to control and adjust one's own actions to match that of the customer.
Team selling	Learn to think like a team player and work with other departments in the company to be more effective in satisfying customer needs.
Motivation	Understand what motivates and demotivates sales reps and how it affects their work.
Positive thinking	Learn how to and turn negative thoughts into positive ones – even the best reps go through slumps.
Self-esteem	Learn to quickly recover from rejection.
Alternate disciplines	Take training courses from other departments in the company, such as marketing and customer service, to become more knowledgeable and a better team player.
Technology	Learn how to use digital assistants, mobile phones, iPads, blogs, wikis, SFA, the sales portal and cloud storage, and other support technologies.

TABLE 9.14

Checklist for Upgrading the Sales Force

Individual training
- On-the-job coaching by sales supervisor
- Courses for self-instruction prepared by the training department (example: podcasts on recent developments)
- Commercial self-instruction courses (example: webinars on selling skills)
- Attendance at workshops, clinics, or seminars
- Courses at local schools for special skills (accounting, computer science, drafting, design, etc.)
- Coaching by senior salesperson (example: goes with trainee to watch sales presentation)

Group training
- Sales meetings
- Presentation by specialists in the firm (engineer, accountant, purchasing agent, etc.)
- Presentations by other salespeople (example: how they landed a good account)
- Workshops and seminars developed by the firm's training department
- Commercial training aids (example: podcasts or webinars on selling skills, motivation, and other topics)
- Subscriptions and RSS feeds to:
  - Journals or magazines devoted to sales, sales force management, or marketing
  - Journals relating to the industries of key accounts
  - General business magazines (*Business Week, Dun's Review, Forbes, Nation's Business*, etc.)
  - National news magazines (*U.S. News & World Report, Newsweek*, etc.)
  - Business newspapers (*The Wall Street Journal, The New York Times*, etc.)

Retraining

When a salesperson's job requirements change because the company has added new products or services, revised sales territories, or upgraded sales force automation or CRM technology, retraining is needed. Designing retraining programs includes the following steps:

1. *Determine which aspects of the new job are the most important.* Cover all the bases but know what is most essential and teach that first.
2. *Determine which aspects of the new job are the most difficult.* Some new information can be learned quickly; some takes longer. Devote more time to difficult areas of a new position or responsibility.
3. *Determine which aspects of the new job are the most prevalent.* Emphasize tasks the salesperson will do most often or spend more time on.

In designing retraining programs, sales managers should also include ways to foster positive attitudes toward the job, other salespeople, and the participants themselves. Salespeople who are satisfied with their jobs and the organization make a more loyal and productive sales force. Often sales managers face the added challenge of dissolving resistance to retraining. Established salespeople may feel that management is trying to change them, and some will resist anything that hints of change. Sales managers should support the retraining wholeheartedly once the salespeople are back on the job.

Like initial and continuous training, retraining must include topics like adaptive skills, coping skills, problem-solving, and improvisation to help salespeople grow and respond to change. Topics like self-assessment, self-direction, self-monitoring, and self-reinforcement are necessary to achieve the self-management required in today's selling environment. Thus, sales managers must view training from the perspective of life-long learning and growth.

Managerial Training

Just like salespeople, sales managers must also participate in training programs to ensure that they are aware of new developments. Managerial training should cover all aspects of the sales manager's job, not just the training function. The purpose of the programs is to introduce new approaches to organization, planning, motivation, compensation, supervision, evaluation, and control over the areas the sales manager is responsible for. Managerial training is usually sponsored by the company itself or by professional associations, universities, training companies, or private consultants.

Managerial training should also be provided for new sales managers making the transition from personal selling or another position into management. Salespeople, in particular, often have difficulty making a successful transition into sales management, but research has shown that sales management training remains one of the most neglected areas in sales training. Research suggests that fewer than half of companies surveyed provide new sales managers with formal training. Instead, sales management training consists primarily of informal, on-the-job coaching by superiors or peers. Many of the companies that do provide formal sales management training delay it until the sales managers have been promoted to senior-level sales management positions. But a sales force will have difficulty performing at the highest levels while its sales manager is learning on the job through trial-and-error.

Sales Training Challenges for Global Companies

While most of the sales skills taught to U.S. salespeople can be translated into other countries, differences across cultures do need to be accounted for in training. For example, notions of time differ from country to country, as well as protocols and formalities. Even colors can convey meaning to certain cultures. Printed materials presented to Chinese trainees, for example, should be in black and white, since colors have such great significance to the Chinese. Also, the way people learn differs from culture to culture. U.S. trainees, for instance, are results-oriented and tend to focus on the end result during training. On the other hand, in other countries trainers use deductive logic, emphasizing the process and how to get to the end. Sales training programs for global companies need to be tailored to different cultures and concepts, allowing salespeople to learn in a familiar environment.

When designing sales training programs for global companies, sales managers must determine the type and amount of training. Figure 9.4 suggests one approach to making these decisions.[17]

The more similar the culture, the less important is training in cultural knowledge. When executives have extensive cultural experiences, they also need less training in negotiating with or managing individuals with similar language and historical backgrounds. But sales executives with limited cultural experience, particularly those confronted with very different cultures, will need extensive knowledge of differences before they begin selling to, managing, or negotiating with people from very different cultures and languages. They also will need training in adaptability skills so they can assess cultural encounters and deal with them quickly and effectively. Read about ways to ensure the success of global sales training in Sales Management in Action Box 9.3.

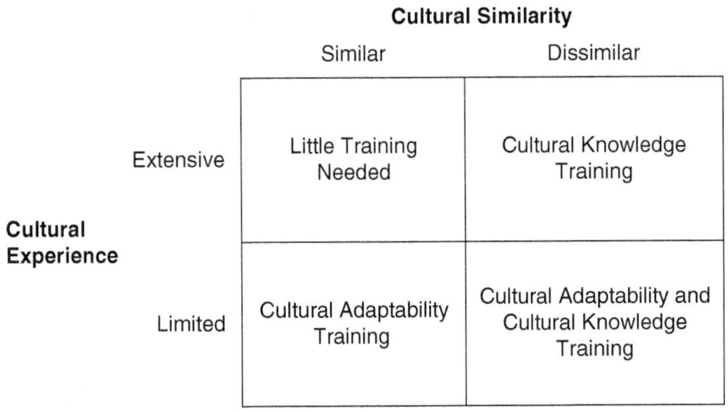

	Cultural Similarity	
	Similar	Dissimilar
Extensive	Little Training Needed	Cultural Knowledge Training
Limited	Cultural Adaptability Training	Cultural Adaptability and Cultural Knowledge Training

Cultural Experience (row label applied to Extensive / Limited)

FIGURE 9.4 Determining when cultural training is needed.

Box 9.3 | Sales Management in Action 9.3

Making Sales Training Friendly to Other Cultures

Global competition has increased to a level never seen before and the global marketplace is becoming increasingly crowded. Salespeople and sales managers in this environment need to know the products they are selling and how best to sell them. In a word, they need training. Below is a list of ways sales managers can better provide training to their increasingly diverse staff.

- *Include international members on the training design team.* People already familiar with the culture of the trainees can design better training.
- *Thoroughly research the culture of the host country.* Read about the host country's culture and politics beforehand. If possible, spend some time in the country with the salespeople to get a better idea of how culture affects the selling process.
- *Offer English classes.* If the training class will be conducted in English, teach some English before

and during training to individuals who have language difficulties. This will help these trainees deal with the vocabulary presented in class and assist in their translating information correctly and quickly enough to keep up with the instructor.

- *Avoid idioms, jargon, slang, and humor in class.* This information often does not translate readily to other cultures.
- *Be sensitive to nonverbal language.* Body language and facial expressions provide subtle messages regarding the level of understanding and learning that is taking place.
- *Schedule a question-and-answer session during a class break or after class.* In some cultures, it is rude to interrupt by asking questions during training. Other cultures consider volunteering a way of bragging.
- *Include managers and others given foreign assignments in training.* All individuals sent abroad need training if the assignment is new to them, not just salespeople.[18]

Chapter Summary

1. **Explain the importance and benefits of sales training programs.** Developing an effective sales training program is increasingly becoming a critical part of the sales manager's job. Customers are more knowledgeable than ever before, competition is stronger, and customers are demanding more quality and service from sales interactions. With the rapidly rising costs of training and the many high-technology products, sales training is gaining more respect among upper-level executives. Sales training programs should seek to continually help salespeople grow in knowledge, selling habits, and selling techniques and develop good attitudes about themselves and their jobs, companies, and customers.

2. **Follow the steps in developing and implementing sales training programs.** Sales training design should be based on the requirements of the company and on the skills and experience of the company's salespeople. Therefore, the design process should begin with a needs assessment to determine the gap between what the sales force knows and what they should know. Once these gaps in learning are determined, then specific performance objectives can be set and the content of the training program developed. Training program delivery decisions include who will train, what method will be used to train, where training will occur, and when training will occur. Trainees should be prepared before training, motivated during training, and new skills reinforced after training. Every well-designed training program also includes an evaluation to determine if the program's objectives have been met.

3. **Apply different instructional methods for training.** Companies must decide whether to conduct training individually or in a group setting. Usually,

group training methods are used in formal training programs, and individual training methods are used in informal training programs (specifically, in field training). There are many methods of training. Lectures, group discussions, role playing, demonstrations, simulation games, intranet-based training, and technology-based training have all been used for many years and are considered traditional methods. Online conferencing, online cloud-based resources, and e-learning are emerging techniques.

4. **Prepare, motivate, and reinforce trainees.** If trainees don't understand why they are being trained and what benefit they will receive from it, chances are the training will not be effective. A pretraining briefing can tell participants the training's purpose and objectives, why they were selected to attend, and what business need the sales manager hopes to meet. Once training begins, student involvement should be encouraged, and lectures kept to a minimum. The trainer should also ask questions to get trainees to provide feedback. Additionally, the training environment should be considered "safe" so that trainees feel at ease trying different selling techniques during group activities and role playing. Post-training reinforcement through coaching is critical for learning to persist. Coaching generally involves informal, give-and-take discussions between sales managers and salespeople with the purpose of reinforcing sales training concepts, solving selling problems, and improving basic selling skills.

5. **Evaluate training programs.** There are four levels of evaluation used to gauge the effectiveness of a training program. First, at the *reaction* level the trainees' attitudes and feelings toward the training program are measured. Second, evaluation at the *learning* level assesses how well the trainees learned basic principles, facts, and so on, during the training program. Third, *behavior*-level evaluation measures changes in behavior as a result of the training. Finally, at the *results* level changes in performance are measured by plotting salespeople's performance before and after training and comparing the results against training program objectives.

6. **Meet the sales training challenges of global companies.** While many of the sales skills taught to U.S. salespeople can be translated into other countries, there are differences across cultures that need to be accounted for in training. Differences include notions of time, protocols, formalities, how people learn, and even such things as color. Ways to enhance success during multicultural sales training include increased planning by the trainer, research into each country's politics, economics, and culture, integrating local examples into the training material and discussion, including international members on the design team, avoiding unfamiliar terms and humor, paying attention to nonverbal cues, using visuals, and providing question-and-answer sessions.

Key Terms

Augmented reality (AR)
Sales training
Sales training development process
Training needs assessment
performance
objectives
learning objectives
Initial sales training program

Continuing sales training program
Training delivery decisions
Group training methods
Individual training methods
Role playing
Mentoring
Technology-based training

Conferencing
online conferencing
webinar
E-learning
online learning
blended learning
m-learning
RSS
wiki
Intranet

Centralized training programs
Decentralized training
Pretraining briefing
Coaching
Refresher training
Retraining
Managerial training

Notes

1. Stop at Cisco to propel your career forward. https://www.net-comlearning.com/cisco-training/?advid=1220&gclid=Cj0KC Qjwn8_mBRCLARIsAKxi0GJSWERRbyPs8zIMObtwHUI3s-P1Ku56SKJtOQtEFqECzGxhbkP-5hPMaAhcPEALw_wcB (accessed May 2019).

2. Lehman, J. (2013). *The Sales Manager's Mentor*. Seattle, Washington: Mentor Press LLC; Drive success through sales training with these three conversations. https://www.integritysolutions.com/salestrainingconversations?gclid=CjwKCAjw_MnmBRAoE iwAPRRWW9GLFWxYNSEuLFhbvrJLW-RYAlQLGTIgH2p sIGYCtKNGvV7yUaOxOhoCuyEQAvD_BwE (accessed May 2019); and Kurlan, D. 5 Steps to improve sales performance. https://fowmedia.com/5-steps-sales-training-success/ (accessed May 2019).

3. Sales training at Pfizer. https://www.pfizer.com/search/site/sales%20training (accessed May 2019).

4. Babu, J.M., Chad, M., Lee, S. et al. (2014). Salesperson competitive intelligence and performance: The role of product knowledge and sales force automation usage. *Industrial Marketing Management* 43 (1): 136–145; and Ahearne, M., Jelinek, R. and Rapp, A. (2005). Moving beyond the direct effect of SFA adoption on salesperson performance: Training and support as key moderating factors. *Industrial Marketing Management* 34: 379–388.

5. Brooks, M. The benefits of a selling sales manager leading your team. https://www.salesgravy.com/sales-articles/sales-leadership/the-benefits-of-a-selling-sales-manager-leading-your-team.html (accessed May 2019).

6. American Express Training. https://www.americanexpress.com/en-us/business/trends-and-insights/keywords/employee-training/ (accessed May 2019).

7. Lehman, J. (2013). *The Sales Manager's Mentor*. Seattle, Washington: Mentor Press LLC; Drive success through sales training with these three conversations. https://www.integritysolutions.com/salestrainingconversations?gclid=CjwKCAjw_MnmBRAoE iwAPRRWW9GLFWxYNSEuLFhbvrJLW-RYAlQLGTIgH2p sIGYCtKNGvV7yUaOxOhoCuyEQAvD_BwE (accessed May 2019); and Kurlan, D. 5 Steps to improve sales performance. https://fowmedia.com/5-steps-sales-training-success/ (accessed May 2019).

8. Saurabh, G. and Robert, B. (2012). Research note—An investigation of the appropriation of technology-mediated training methods incorporating enactive and collaborative learning. *Information Systems Research* 24 (2): 201–497. https://pubsonline.informs.org/doi/abs/10.1287/isre.1120.0433

9. Sun, Y.S. and Jin, N.C. (2014). Do organizations spend wisely on employees? Effects of training and development investments on learning and innovation in organizations. *Journal of Organizational Behavior* 35 (3): 393–412.

10. Lindsey, F. and Andrew, C.H. (2014). Training the millennial generation: Implications for organizational climate. *Journal of Organizational Learning and Leadership* 12 (1): 47–60.

11. Sun Microsystems, Online SUN Microsystems Certified Training & eLearning Courses. https://www.trainup.com/SUN-Microsystems-Certified-Training/Online/2559 (accessed May 2019).

12. The Training Clinic. https://thetrainingclinic.com (accessed May 2019).

13. Tan, K. and Newman, E. (2012). Sales force training evaluation. *Journal of Business & Economics Research* 10 (2): 105–109.

14. Felicia, L., Tom, I., Florian, K. et al. (2013). The future of sales training: Challenges and related research questions. *Journal of Personal Selling and Sales Management* 32 (1): 141–154.

15. Sun, Y.S. and Jin, N.C. (2014). Do organizations spend wisely on employees? Effects of training and development investments on learning and innovation in organizations. *Journal of Organizational Behavior* 35 (3): 393–412.

16. Tan, K. and Newman, E. (2012). Sales force training evaluation. *Journal of Business & Economics Research* 10 (2): 105–109.

17. Widmier, S. and Hair, J. (2007) Enhancing global sales skills through executive education programs. *Journal of Executive Education* 6 (1).

18. Grohmann, A. and Kauffeld, S. (2013). Evaluating training programs: Development and correlates of the Questionnaire for Professional Training Evaluation. *International Journal of Training and Development* 17 (2): 135–155; Attia, A.M, Honeycutt, E.D. and Jantan, M.A. (2008). Global sales training: In search of antecedent, mediating and consequence variables. *Industrial Marketing Management* 37 (2): 181–190; and Wilson, J.P. (2014). *International Human Resource Development: Learning, Education and Training for Individuals and Organisations* (3rd ed.), *Development and Learning in Organizations: An International Journal* 28 (2), https://www.emeraldinsight.com/doi/full/10.1108/DLO-02-2014-0010.

Chapter Review Questions

1. Why should sales training and sales force development be thought of as a long-term, ongoing process?

2. "Good salespeople are born, not made." Agree or disagree?

3. What are some of the benefits a company can expect from a well-developed sales training program? Do these benefits outweigh the costs? Why or why not?

4. Why is the design and implementation of sales training programs such a critical task for sales managers? Briefly

discuss the planning decisions that must be made by sales managers in designing sales training programs.

5. Discuss the basic elements that all initial sales training programs must cover. Are these elements any different from elements of continuous training programs?

6. What are some of the problems that can arise when delegating the responsibility of the sales training program to line executives? To staff trainers? To outside training specialists?

7. How is technology impacting sales training? What benefits can sales managers realize by using e-learning methods?

8. Why is pretraining preparation and post-training reinforcement so critical to the success of a sales training program? What are some things a trainer could do to make the sales training class more motivational?

9. A pharmaceutical sales firm adopts a new SFA system that tracks customer sales calls, notes, and samples. What recommendations would you make when planning the training for this program?

Online Exercise

Visit the Cisco Systems (www.cisco.com) website. Insert the key words sales training in the search option and see what you find. Prepare a brief report on the two training topics you found the most interesting.

You are sales manager for a large consumer goods company and have just finished your best recruiting and selection process in years. You hired six great people from college campuses around the country, and you believe a couple of them have the potential to be top salespeople.

This morning you received a surprising memo from the sales trainer. She reports that your superstar recruits are doing poorly in training. In fact, they have consistently finished last on the exams. They seem uninterested in the training and have indicated that since the trainer has "never been in the field, there's no point listening to her!" She has labeled your top recruits "know-it-alls" who won't respond to sales training.

1. Do you believe a problem like this is more the fault of the trainer or the recruits?

2. What aspects from the chapter may help to resolve the conflict and result in more effective training results?

Role-Play Exercise

Sal is a sales manager for a multinational footwear company specializing in casual and athletic shoes. Traditionally, training has been limited to break out sessions at the bi-annual sales conference held in Kansas City each year. But increasingly, production has moved from Korea to China and India. The company now has sales operations in 25 countries in four continents. Sal argues with Tom, the VP of Marketing, that the traditional sales conference is inadequate given the new global focus in both production and sales. Tom argues "training is training!" It doesn't matter where the people are when they get trained and any sales rep worth their salt doesn't need to be *retrained* more than once every two years! Sal walks away determined to revamp the sales training program to make her division and the company more successful.

1. What should Sal consider when she is deciding how to respond to Tom's opinions?

2. Prepare a slide show with no more than eight slides that focuses on reasons why the current sales approach may be inadequate.

Ethical Dilemma

Teaching Appropriate Material in a Sales Training Course

You were recently hired as a sales representative for a large financial-services organization. You will be responsible for finding individuals interested in investments and convincing them that your company is the best choice for help in managing a financial portfolio. Before going into the field, you are participating in a training program. Your sales trainer is doing a good job of teaching financial management, consumer behavior, and corporate culture. Occasionally, however, he injects personal bias into the program. For example, in an informal way he told the class that, in a competitive market like financial services "Not acknowledging the strengths of your competitors can be helpful if a client is naive." Also, several times he stated ". . . the best place to look for new clients is in the obituary column of a newspaper. People who have recently lost a family member are excellent prospects to call on because they usually receive large sums of money after someone dies."

Questions

1. What is your initial response to such advice? Even if such suggestions work, should they be included in a training program?

2. At the end of the training, trainees normally fill out a short questionnaire with a spot for comments. Do you think anybody would comment on these statements? Would they likely be positive or negative comments?

CASE 9.1   Hops Distributors, Inc.

James Williams is the sales manager for Hops Distributors, Inc. in Kansas City, Kansas. The company is a local beer distributor and carries one of the top national brands, a number of imports, and several local craft brews. Hops has approximately 500 accounts in each of its sales territories. Hops is facing increasing competition from other local distributors and the increasing popularity of wine and bourbon. In the past, salespeople were divided into three groups based on the customers they served. The four categories of customers include: (1) high-volume accounts – over 200 cases per week; (2) moderate volume accounts – 100 to 200 cases per week; (3) low-volume accounts – over 10 but less than 100 cases per week; (4) ultralow volume accounts – 10 or fewer cases per week. One group of sales representatives only called on the first category (high volume), a second group called on moderate volume accounts, and the third group focused on the remaining two groups of accounts (low and ultralow).

Over the last few years, salespeople have been called on to help the delivery drivers when they call in sick, forget to load enough product, or simply don't do what was promised to the customer. This approach of splitting time doing sales as well as some deliveries and merchandising work has been a source of many problems.

Recently, the top managers in the organization have decided to make several significant changes. First, salespeople will no longer do any deliveries. The delivery employees will be more accountable and responsible for fulfilling orders as sold by the salesperson. This will allow salespeople to focus more on selling. Second, while the commission structure will stay the same, there will be a new focus on increasing sales volume and profit margins.

The management group has created a sales contest that rewards salespeople who are able to increase overall sales volume and increase margins. Salespeople who meet these two criteria will earn an additional $5,000,00 per quarter. Those that do not meet these criteria will receive $0 from the sales contest.

When James first learned that his salespeople would no longer have to deal with deliveries and would be spending more time selling, he was excited. He also thought, at first, that the sales contest would be a great source of motivation. However, after some thought he has several concerns.

First, in a competitive market, how can salespeople both increase revenue and margins? Second, do they currently have the right organizational structure given the changes top management is implementing? Third, what kind of training needs to take place to make sure this strategy is a success? Finally, what could happen if the sales contest does not work?

Questions

1. Evaluate the pros and cons of Hops' new strategy.

2. What are the potential issues created by these changes?

3. What are some potential training needs for salespeople to be able to operate in this new environment?

4. Evaluate the sales contest. Will it be effective? Why or why not? Does the contest create additional training needs?

Case prepared by: Mike Wittmann, The University of Alabama at Birmingham

Midwest Auto Parts, Inc.: Training Using Artificial Intelligence

CASE 9.2

The engine electrical equipment industry is almost a $25-billion-dollar-a-year industry. In recent years competition from U.S. companies has increased, but the industry clearly is facing strong competition from abroad, particularly Japan and South Korea. The engine electrical equipment industry is divided into three main segments. Original equipment parts are supplied domestically to Ford, General Motors, and Chrysler. Companies supplying these parts are called OEM's. The second segment is called the after-market or replacement parts segment. After-market parts are supplied to wholesalers and retailers of auto parts to be sold to repair automobiles after they have left the factory. The third segment is called the non-automotive segment – it supplies parts for engines other than automobiles.

Midwest Auto Parts, Inc. sells to two of these segments: the OEM parts segment and the aftermarket parts segment. Midwest Auto Parts, Inc. has been in business for over 40 years and has manufacturing plants in the United States, Canada, and Mexico. Sales are coordinated by a National Sales Director and ten regional sales representatives. The regional sales reps line up independent manufacturer's reps who actually do the selling. The manufacturers' reps are paid on a commission basis and generally carry products of several non-competing companies.

In the last few years the regional sales reps have had a lot of trouble recruiting and keeping manufacturers' reps. In the past they simply signed them up and they usually stayed with Midwest Auto Parts. But several years ago the industry leader, Premier Motor Products, Inc. started taking away their best reps. The National Sales Director could not understand why the reps were leaving their company and going to Premier Motor Products. The Director assumed that their commission schedule for reps was very competitive. The Director knew it was important to identify why their sales reps were leaving. The cost of hiring and training new reps is time consuming and very expensive for the company. The Director recently ran into one of Midwest Auto Parts former reps and asked him why he quit. He said the reason was that Premier Motor Products offered him a sales training class and an extensive sales support package. The former rep indicated the sales training class was especially helpful because it provided useful information on generating new prospects and minimizing problems with current customers through greater service.

After talking with the former rep, the sales director from Midwest began exploring some training programs. One of the programs the Director found was called Virtual Simulation, an artificial intelligent (AI) program designed using virtual reality (VR). This program makes requests for merchandise based upon the trainee's interactions. After testing this program and other training methods with a small group of sales representatives, the Director found that utilizing AI and VR has improved employee retention, especially when the training identifies ways that employees can use their new knowledge to advance their careers. In addition, employee surveys have shown that opportunities to develop personal attributes and career advancement are major reasons why employees remain in their current job.

The sales-support package utilized by Premier Motor Products included information on the following:

- Industry sales by region and state
- Industry sales by customer type
- Industry sales by product line
- A sales portal with simple instructions on how to apply sales analytics to identify sales opportunities

In addition, the package included access to Salesforce.com data and analytics services, and, general information about the target market by state.

Market Size by State

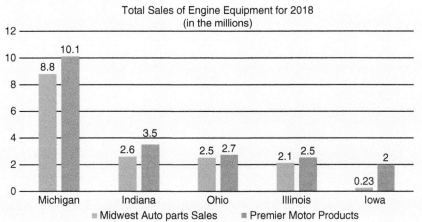

Total Sales of Engine Equipment for 2018
(in the millions)

*Information based on numbers gathered from Inc. Facts

There is not a market size for Virginia, North Dakota, Massachusetts, Rhode Island, or West Virginia. Engine electrical equipment industry has yet to reach out to these states and offer their services to those markets.

Questions

1. What can Midwest Auto Parts, Inc. do to keep its reps from quitting, and going to work for Premier Motor Products?

2. How could the sales rep use the information provided in the traditional sales support package? Which would be more beneficial to companies; the traditional sales support package, using artificial intelligence designed with virtual reality, or integrating both?

3. What kinds of topics should be emphasized in a training program for a company like Midwest Auto Parts, Inc.?

4. What strategy should Midwest Auto Parts, Inc. install to increase market share and/or expand to other areas that they are not a power in electrical equipment parts sales?

5. Would it benefit Midwest Auto Parts, Inc. to become more automated? Should they include more artificial intelligence-based support packages to help the company expand and increase sales and market share, and potentially decrease training?

Case prepared by: Larry Goehrig, University of South Alabama, and Thomasa Jackson, University of South Alabama

CHAPTER 10

Sales Force Leadership

In the preceding chapters, we've talked about organizing and developing the sales force. We now turn our attention to the activities that take center stage in managing and directing the sales force once we've carefully recruited, selected, and trained salespeople. The first and perhaps most important of these is leadership.

Some well-known researchers have questioned whether leadership really has any observable effect on organizational effectiveness.[1] They argue that because it's so difficult to identify, or even define what an effective leader is, we often work from rather romanticized ideas. However, leadership qualities and behaviors have been shown to have a big impact on organizational results.[2] One well-known example is Steve Jobs, who left Apple – the company he co-founded – when he could not convince the CEO John Sculley and the majority of board members about his strategy for Apple. Jobs, however, did convince several key Apple employees to follow him out of the company to create NeXT, then later Pixar which produced the first 3D computer animated film, *Toy Story*, and several others. Jobs later returned to Apple as CEO when it merged with NeXT and by extraordinary leadership he revived Apple from near bankruptcy into one of the most successful companies in the world. Using the advertising slogan "Think Different," his visionary leadership brought about dynamic changes in several industries via innovative products, including: iMac, iTunes, iPod, Apple Stores, iPhone, App Store, and iPad. Although Jobs' technical abilities were limited, he was a brilliant marketer in touch with consumer wants, and the inspirational leader needed to turn Apple into an exciting company with imaginative new technological products and passionately loyal customers. His obsessive perfectionism about product quality and creative design resulted in his being seen by some as narcissistic, quick temper, arrogant, and dictatorial. But, his achievements are legendary and he's been compared with the great American inventor, Thomas Edison. At Macworld conferences, Jobs personally presented amazing new products and skillfully used his personal communication skills and charisma to inspire employees, customers, and stakeholders. Jobs' passionate leadership provided a clear vision for Apple's future and generated the trust of subordinates because they saw that he was not just driven by personal materialism or his own self-interests but also by wanting Apple to make the best products possible for consumers.[3]

In this chapter, we'll discuss relevant theories that suggest how appropriate leadership can influence the behaviors of salespeople and sales departments charged with

LEARNING OBJECTIVES

When you finish this chapter, you should be able to:

1. Understand the dynamics of leadership.
2. Contrast supervision, management, and leadership.
3. Identify the different sources of power for leaders.
4. Know the classic theories of leadership.
5. Apply the major contemporary theories of leadership to sales force management.
6. Communicate effectively with the sales force.
7. Overcome barriers to communication with the sales force.

the all-important revenue generating task. We'll also learn how and when different leadership approaches can be appropriate.

Foundations of Leadership

The forces shaping business and sales force management today are radically different from those of the past as there is now greater diversity in the labor force, intensifying global competition, and rapid advances in technology. Globalization has brought about fiercely competitive markets in which it's increasingly more difficult to remain profitable. Reengineering and downsizing have produced flatter, leaner organizations that require greater leadership at all organizational levels – not just in the executive suites.[4] Companies are placing a premium on recruiting managers with contemporary leadership potential and skills, because twenty-first century business and sales force management practices are necessarily going to be significantly different from those in the past.[5]

Research on leadership theory and practice is voluminous.[6] Some of the many ways to understand leadership include considering individual traits, behaviors, influence over people, interaction patterns, role relationships, occupation of an administrative position, and the perceptions of others regarding the legitimacy of leadership influence.[7] Generally, we can think of leadership as the process of motivating and enabling the task-related activities of team members,[8] and the ability to influence them toward the achievement of organizational goals.[9]

In the context of sales force management, leadership refers to the interpersonal process of communicating, inspiring, guiding, and influencing the behavior of subordinate salespeople toward the attainment of organizational objectives, goals, and values.[10] Our definition also includes self- and joint-leadership by salespeople, who may influence their peers on formal and informal sales teams.[11]

There are six important elements in our formal definition of sales force leadership. First, leadership is *interpersonal* because it affects others (followers or subordinates), who should be willing to accept directions from the leader (sales manager or supervisor). Second, leadership relies on *influence*, which stems from various forms of power that we'll discuss in the chapter. This implies an unequal distribution of power in favor of the sales manager. Third, sales force leadership is the ability not only to set goals, but also to *guide*, clarify, and chart the paths for salespeople toward goal achievement. Fourth, leaders *inspire* their subordinates (and sometimes their peers) to attain organizational goals. Fifth, leaders espouse ethical and moral *values* they expect their followers to subscribe to. Finally, as we'll discuss, leadership relies on *communication* to achieve organizational objectives, goals, and values.

Supervision, Management, and Leadership

Let's first distinguish between supervision, management, and leadership, which are widely considered to be overlapping functions. *Supervision* is closely monitoring the daily work activities of sales subordinates. All sales managers perform some supervisory duties, although direct supervision becomes less evident at higher levels in the sales force management hierarchy. *Management*, in general, deals with administrative activities that include planning, organizing, staffing, directing, and controlling the operations of a firm toward the attainment of its goals and objectives. These efforts tend to be *primarily* focused on the non-people, policy, and decision-making functions of a firm.[12]

Although leadership and management are related, management is primarily a *learned* process of guiding subordinates in the performance of formally prescribed duties. In contrast, *leadership* is an *emotional* process of exercising psychological, social, and inspirational influence on the people employed by the firm. In short, it's the ability to get people to do willingly what they would not readily do on their own.[13]

Most viable organizations recognize that their people are the key to business success and that leadership and management go hand-in-hand. A sales manager can be an effective planner and administrator, but not possess leadership skills. Conversely, an effective leader can inspire and engender enthusiasm, but not have the requisite managerial skills. Any organization is unlikely to succeed unless it can effectively both lead *and* manage its work force.[14] It's not surprising, therefore, that today's firms are seeking sales managers who exhibit flexible leadership capabilities and skills, because the twenty-first century business and sales force management environment is vastly different from the past.[15] A sales organization is a reflection of its leader. Shortcomings in sales force performance can usually be traced to inadequacy in sales force management, while superior performance is generally the result of outstanding leadership by sales managers.

Leadership and Power

Central to understanding how leaders wield influence over their subordinates is the concept of power. Power is the potential to influence the behavior of subordinates.[16] To influence subordinates, sales managers typically can draw upon five bases or sources of power shown in Figure 10.1: legitimate, reward, coercive, referent, and expert.[17] The first three stem from a leader's position and are forms of position power, while the latter two are forms of personal power.

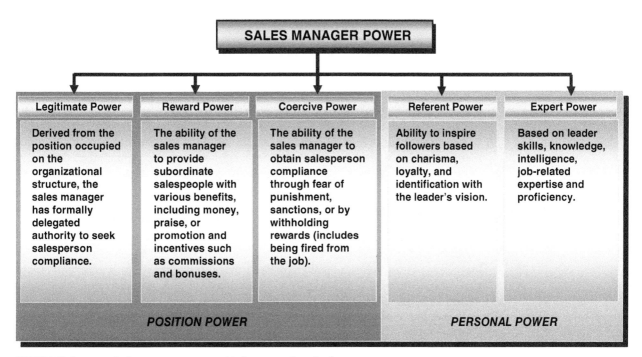

FIGURE 10.1 Sources of sales manager power and influence on the sales force.

Position Power Sources

Let's look at the forms of position power first. Most sales managers have access to three sources of power. *Legitimate power* is derived from the manager's position in the firm's hierarchical structure as well as the level of responsibility he or she is formally given. Often referred to as *authority*, legitimate power allows managers to govern sales department activities integral to achieving sales goals and objectives.

Reward power is the ability to provide salespeople with various benefits – salary, raises, commissions, bonuses, monetary incentives, promotions, interesting job assignments, preferred work schedules, sales territories, and clients – based on performance assessment. Reward power also includes important compensation issues, which we discuss in greater detail in Chapter 12.

Coercive power comes from the ability to withhold rewards or punish (even up to firing) and is primarily aimed at behavior modification through fear of sanctions. Most sales managers have access to all these position power sources and can use them in appropriate situations to influence the behavior of salespeople.

Personal Power Sources

Referent and expert power bases are derived from personal characteristics of the sales manager. *Referent power* is the ability to inspire salespeople to identify with and admire the sales manager because of his or her personal traits and charisma to such an extent that they're willing to change their behavior to resemble or be compatible with that of their leader. Superstar salespeople who perform at substantially higher levels than other salespeople also have referent power. Ben Feldman, whom many call the greatest salesperson who ever lived, epitomized referent power for his New York Life Insurance (www.newyorklife.com) colleagues as he inspired them to perform at higher levels.[18]

Finally, *expert power* is based on the sales manager's skills, knowledge, and special abilities that enable his or her work to exhibit the highest level of expertise. For example, sales managers who are highly educated and adept at technologically complex tasks, such as using sophisticated statistical sales forecasting or territory routing software, possess expert power.

Sales Force Management Implications

The major behaviors that sales managers can influence are the salesperson's commitment, compliance, and resistance.[19] When salespeople make a maximum effort and enthusiastically comply with the sales manager's directions, they manifest a sense of *commitment* to accomplishing sales objectives. With *compliance*, salespeople are not as enthusiastic but still may go along. *Resistance* is the most undesirable of the three behaviors, which occurs when salespeople reject the sales manager's plans by ignoring, pretend to comply with, or sabotage them. Table 10.1 presents the likelihood of eliciting each type of behavior by using the various sources of power. Sales managers who exercise expert and referent power are likely to achieve high commitment, while those just using legitimate and reward power are likely to only obtain compliance. Sales managers displaying coercive power usually meet with resistance from salespersons, who may also experience a sense of disconnection or alienation from the job, to the detriment of their performance.

| TABLE 10.1 |

Effects of Sales Manager Power on Salesperson Behaviors

Power source					Likelihood/Level of impact on			
		Commitment	Compliance	Resistance	Motivation/ Job effort	Job satisfaction	Job performance
Position power	1. Legitimate	High	High	Medium	Medium	Medium	Medium
	2. Reward	High	High	Medium	High	High	High
	3. Coercive	Low	Medium	High	Low	Low	Low
Personal	4. Referent	High	Medium	Medium	High	High	High
	5. Expert	High	Medium	Medium	High	High	High

The use of expert and referent power has been associated with increased sales force performance.[20] These two types of non-coercive power tend to increase sales force motivation as well. If salespeople are highly responsive to monetary rewards, a sales manager may also exercise reward power to augment performance.

Astute sales managers are likely to utilize all five sources of power at one time or another. The key is to know the appropriate source of power to use for each salesperson and in each situation.

Applying Classical Leadership Theories to Twenty-First Century Sales Force Management

Researchers' efforts to understand how leaders influence subordinates led to the development of three broad classical schools of thought about leadership: (a) the trait approach, (b) the behavioral approach, and (c) the contingency or situational approach. We'll look at those that are most germane to sales force management.

Trait Theory

The earliest leadership research – often referred to as the *Great Man* theory – concluded that great leaders are born, not made, and focused on identifying the personal traits that characterize them,[21] such as confidence, honesty, integrity, ambition, creativity, job-relevant knowledge, initiative, intelligence, extraversion, and drive. Later, researchers thought leadership traits were not completely inborn but could be developed through experience and learning. Moreover, it was soon observed that many good leaders did not seem to possess the desired or expected traits, and that even possession of these traits often failed to reliably predict leadership success.

Trait theory has been widely criticized because few studies have examined the same traits, and because it doesn't take into account the situational context of leadership. Stogdill completed a comprehensive review of over 100 trait theory studies, and found that only 5% of the traits appeared in four or more studies.[22] Moreover, there was a "chicken and egg" problem. For example, was George Washington a leader because he was self-confident, or was he self-confident because leadership responsibilities were thrust upon him at a young age? Other weaknesses of trait theory include studies seldom distinguished which traits are most or least important.[23]

Sales Force Management Implications No consistent list of leader characteristics has been uncovered. One researcher has, however, compiled a list of *behaviors* exhibited by proficient managers[24] that should be relevant considerations for effective sales managers:

- Clarify the mission, purposes, or goals of salespeople's tasks.
- Communicate assignments clearly to salespeople.
- Listen to salespeople's views and give them credit for their ideas.
- Make sure the resources needed for their assignments are provided.
- Clarify the evaluative performance standards for salespeople.
- Ensure that organizational rewards are worthwhile to the salespeople.
- Provide prompt feedback to salespeople on their performance.
- Show care and concern for individual salespeople without developing overt friendships that might convey favoritism.
- Merit and never violate the trust of the salespeople.
- Make the decisions that are yours to make, so that salespeople are not left in doubt.

While no single profile of traits can identify an effective sales force *leader*, many researchers believe that certain qualities are needed to be effective. For example, some hold that an effective sales force leader must work hard and be people-oriented. Others feel he or she must have the innate ability to take risks and be a decision maker. Table 10.2 presents a general perspective on the traits of a successful leader.

TABLE 10.2

Twelve Traits of Highly Effective Leaders

1. ***Courageous.*** Leaders set courageous examples for others to follow. As General George Patton once said, "Courage is fear holding on another minute."
2. ***A "big" thinker.*** Leaders see things in a larger perspective than others. They can help others to expand their thinking and imagination.
3. ***A change master.*** Leaders can create change, accept it, handle it, and move people in directions beneficial to everyone.
4. ***Ethical.*** Leaders are fair and just, loyal and conscientious in their work, and expect the same from others.
5. ***Persistent and realistic.*** Leaders set realistic goals and maintain commitment to them until they are accomplished.
6. ***Gifted with a sense of humor.*** A sense of humor can turn routine tasks into enjoyable experiences. Leaders are spontaneous and express their feelings.
7. ***A risk taker.*** Leaders take the initiative, are independent, and are willing to fail in order to succeed.
8. ***Positive and hope-filled.*** Leaders see good in a bad situation and have faith when others do not. They tend to be optimistic and elicit that from others.
9. ***Morally strong.*** Leaders value the power of truth yet are not judgmental in their morality.
10. ***A decision maker.*** Leaders know that not deciding is a decision, and that indecision wastes time, energy, money, and opportunity.
11. ***Able to accept and use power wisely.*** Leaders know that power can intimidate others, so they use it wisely to help others achieve their full potential.
12. ***Committed.*** The key to successful leaders is their commitment to their goals, their employees, and their company.

Leadership Behavioral Styles Theory

Because of the weaknesses associated with trait theory, many leadership studies have focused on identifying patterns of **leadership behavior**, or "**leadership styles**," shifting from who the leader *is* to what the leader *does*. Some leadership behaviors were found to be more effective than others.

Ohio State University and University of Michigan Studies Research conducted at Ohio State University identified two composite dimensions of leadership behavior styles: *consideration* (friendship, mutual trust, respect, support, and warmth) – sometimes called the "human relations" approach – and *initiating structure* (the extent to which leaders organize, clearly define, and clarify the tasks subordinates must perform) – sometimes called a "task orientation."[25] Although "high consideration, high initiating structure" tended to yield high employee satisfaction and performance, no single leader behavior surfaced as best for all situations. Moreover, few managers can be both task- and human relations-oriented.

Meanwhile, studies conducted at University of Michigan also sought to identify behavioral characteristics of effective leaders that were associated with building effective work teams and subordinate performance.[26] In these studies, the two dimensions of leadership styles identified were *employee-oriented* and *production or task oriented styles*, which are very similar to leader consideration and initiating structure facets, respectively. Employee-focused leaders set high performance goals and were supportive toward subordinates, whereas production-centered leaders displayed less concern with people's needs and were oriented toward maintaining schedules, reducing costs, making production efficient, and completing tasks; to them, people were a means to an end. The results revealed that job-centered leadership styles were associated with lower productivity and job satisfaction, while employee-oriented leadership styles led to higher work performance and job satisfaction.

Sales Force Management Implications Although a review found few studies that substantiated a significant relationship between the two dimensions of leader behavior and productivity,[27] the behavioral styles approach is appealing because of the widespread belief that people can learn and apply specific leader styles. Taken together, the Ohio State and University of Michigan studies suggest four leadership styles that may be effective for sales managers in varying situations; see Table 10.3.

As shown in Quadrant 1, a *high employee-oriented and low task-oriented leadership style* is appropriate if the sales force consists of highly motivated individuals who are dedicated to the task at hand, but require social support from superiors. This leadership style may be effective in influencing and managing experienced, high-performing salespeople, who tend to compete with one another.

A *high employee-oriented and high task-oriented leadership style* (Quadrant 2) is appropriate if the sales force requires social support from superiors, is not cohesive, and lacks a strong identity with the task at hand. This leadership is especially conducive when sales managers need to influence newly hired, inexperienced sales trainees.

When the sales force consists of highly motivated and experienced individuals who are socially mature and doing work they know and enjoy, a *low employee-oriented and low task-oriented leadership style* (Quadrant 3) is germane.

> **TABLE 10.3**

Leadership Behavioral Style Dimensions: Sales Force Management Implications

	Task Orientation	
	Low	**High**
High	**Quadrant 1:**	**Quadrant 2:**
	Leader focuses on achieving team harmony and individual need satisfaction. Less emphasis is placed on subordinate tasks.	Leadership strives to accomplish the job while maintaining a harmonious work team. Leader provides guidance on how tasks should be completed and is considerate of subordinate needs.
	Sales force management Implications: Appropriate to use when experienced, high-performing salespeople tend to be too competitive with one another.	**Sales Force Management Implications:** Appropriate in situations with newly hired, inexperienced sales trainees.
Low	**Quadrant 3:**	**Quadrant 4:**
	Largely passive, the leader does not provide structure and exhibits little consideration for subordinate needs allowing work and people to be self-managed.	Leader focuses on getting the job done by structuring tasks, but exhibits little consideration for subordinate needs.
	Sales Force Management Implications: Appropriate in situations with experienced, high-performing salespeople who know their tasks and enjoy the work.	**Sales Force Management Implications:** Appropriate in situations where experienced salespeople are required to do unpleasant, unfamiliar work.

Employee Orientation appears at left spanning the High/Low rows.

Sources: Based on Ohio State Leadership Studies. (1973) Dimensions of Leadership Style. In *Current Developments in the Study of Leadership* (ed. E.A. Fleishman and J.G. Hunt). Carbondale, IL: Southern Illinois University Press. Reprinted by permission of Southern Illinois University Press; Likert, R. (1979). From production- and employee centeredness to systems 1–4. *Journal of Management* 5:147–156.

As indicated in Quadrant 4, a *low employee-oriented and high task-oriented leadership style* is appropriate if the sales force consists of individuals who are socially mature and highly cohesive, but who do *not* understand or identify with the task at hand, such as learning new demanding technological skills that will augment their selling efforts.

Contingency Theories of Leadership

The inability to consistently explain the relationships between leadership and organizational effectiveness, and the assumption that high levels of leadership skill produce optimal results in *all* situations, are major drawbacks of the behavioral styles theory. These deficiencies gave rise to the third prominent line of thought: the contingency perspective.

Contingency theories generally suggest that an effective leadership style is largely predicated or contingent upon different situations.[28] While trait and behavioral leadership theories focus primarily on the leader, the contingency leadership approaches emphasize the interaction factors among the leader, followers, and situation-specific conditions. Interactions among the following factors have been identified as determinants of effective leadership: (1) the leader's personality and past experience;

(2) the expectations and behavior of superiors; (3) the characteristics, expectations, and behavior of subordinates; and (4) the behavior and expectations of peers. Implicit in this contingency perspective is the notion that leaders should be capable of adapting their leadership styles to match situational factors.

There are several contingency approaches, but we'll examine those specifically relevant to sales force management: Fiedler's contingency theory of leadership, the path-goal theory of leadership, theory H, leader-member exchange model, and substitutes for leadership.

Fiedler's Contingency Theory In developing the first comprehensive and perhaps most thoroughly researched contingency paradigm of leadership, Fred Fiedler incorporated leadership styles and the nature of the leadership situation.[29] Fiedler's research indicated that a leader's performance depends on two interrelated factors: (1) the degree to which the situation gives the leader control and influence and (2) the leader's basic motivation – whether toward accomplishing the task or toward having close, supportive relations with others. Leaders are either task- or relationship-motivated, somewhat equivalent to *initiating structure* and *consideration* from the Ohio State and University of Michigan studies discussed earlier. Specifically, Fiedler tried to discover which leaders most likely to develop high-producing teams: leaders who are very lenient or those who are highly demanding and discriminating in evaluating subordinates. His results indicate that the most effective type of leadership depends upon the following three situational variables:

1. **Leader–member relations:** Exerting the most important impact on the leader's power and effectiveness is his or her personal relationships with team members. Specifically, if subordinates respect, like, accept and trust the leader, leader–member relations are considered *good*; when leaders are disliked or not respected, leader–member relations are considered *poor*.
2. **Task structure:** The second most important factor in Fiedler's model is the degree to which the team's task is structured or clearly described with specific procedures to attain explicitly identifiable goals. The situation is considered *high* in structure when the tasks are well defined, *low* when tasks are ambiguous.
3. **Position power:** The third factor is the extent to which the leader can access coercive, legitimate, and reward powers to influence subordinates. A leader with no authority to evaluate, control, and reward is considered ineffective and possesses *weak* position power. Position power is *strong* when the leader can use the power bases to effectively induce subordinates to attain desirable goals.

Situations high on all three components are considered highly favorable (see Table 10.3) because (1) leaders can usually expect support from team members; (2) leaders can enforce their will with the legitimate power or formal authority of their positions; and (3) all members of the organization can more clearly define, delegate, control, and evaluate structured tasks.

Fiedler reported that a discriminating, task-oriented leader attitude is effective in *either* highly favorable or highly unfavorable situations. But when the situation is moderately favorable or moderately unfavorable, a more lenient and considerate leader attitude is best for higher team performance – as illustrated in Figure 10.2. When relationships with team members are moderately poor, position power is low, and a highly structured task is at hand, the leader should be more permissive and accepting in behavior and attitude.

Fiedler's contingency model of leadership effectiveness suggests that we can improve team performance by modifying either the leader's style or the team's task and situation. However, he believes that most organizations cannot afford expensive selection techniques to find talented leaders who fit specific job requirements.[30] Nor does training provide adequate answers to the problems of leadership.[31] The most reasonable approach is to tailor the job to fit the manager. Since the type of leadership called for depends on the favorableness of the situation, the organization can more easily alter the job than transfer managers or train them in different styles of interaction with team members. Such factors as the power associated with the leader's position, the task assigned to the team, or the composition of the team's membership can be changed.[32]

Sales Force Management Implications According to Fiedler's contingency theory, both relationship- and task-oriented sales managers can perform better under some situations than others. For example, a high-performing salesperson who is promoted to sales manager may fail because possessing a task-oriented leadership style may not match the demands of a specific situation. A sales manager's tasks are often complex and non-routine, such as motivating an older sales representative or building confidence in younger salespeople. Thus, to be an effective leader, the newly appointed sales manager will need to switch from a task-oriented to a personal, more relationship-centered style.

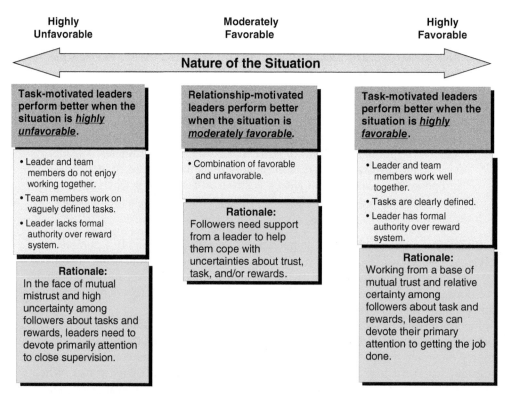

FIGURE 10.2 Fiedler's contingency theory of leadership.
Source: Kreitner, R. (2007). *Management*, 10th ed., 452. Boston: Houghton Mifflin.

The Path-Goal Theory of Leadership Path-goal theory extracts and extends the key elements of *leader consideration* and *initiating structure* around which behavioral styles theory is centered.[33] It also draws heavily on the *expectancy theory of motivation*,[34] which views motivation as a function of the degree to which increased effort will enable an individual to attain a valued outcome or reward.

The path-goal theory proposes that the leader can affect the level of satisfaction, motivation, and performance of team members by using appropriate leadership styles in several ways. The first is by making rewards contingent upon the accomplishment of organizational goals and objectives. Second, the leader can aid team members by clarifying their paths to those goals by removing obstacles to performance, and by ensuring their goals are compatible with the overall objectives of the organization. And third, the leader can increase the support and rewards valued by team members by determining which rewards are important and increasing these rewards consistent with their needs and wants.[35] Therefore, a leader's behavior is effective when team members view it as an immediate or future source of satisfaction.

According to the original formulation of path-goal theory, leadership styles were codified into four dimensions (see the following items 1–4).[36] However, in a more recent reformulation of path-goal theory, four additional behavioral facets were added by House (see items 5–8).[37] Collectively, these eight central behaviors which are "part and parcel" of the path-goal theory include:

1. **Participative leadership styles:** The leader consults with team members about work, task goals, and the paths to goals; leader shares information, and uses their suggestions before making a decision. Thus, team members are able to influence decisions about their jobs.
2. **Supportive leadership styles:** The leader displays personal concern, and is supportive, friendly, and sensitive to the needs of team members. This leadership style parallels *leader consideration,* the first dimension of the behavioral styles theory of leadership.
3. **Directive leadership styles:** The leader explains what the performance goal is, provides guidance and feedback, removes roadblocks, specifies rules, regulations, and procedures to be followed in accomplishing the task, schedules and coordinates work, and clarifies what is expected of team members. This leadership style is analogous to *initiating structure,* the second dimension of the behavioral styles theory of leadership.
4. **Achievement-oriented leadership styles:** The leader emphasizes the achievement of challenging tasks, the importance of excellent performance, and simultaneously shows confidence that team members will perform well.
5. **Path-goal clarifying leadership styles:** The leader defines the tasks (paths), and clearly identifies the results (goals) for which subordinates are held responsible. Further, the leader verifies that organizational goals are tied to rewards that are important to salespersons, and consistent with their needs and wants.
6. **Interaction facilitation leadership styles:** The leader proactively attempts to resolve and mediate conflicts, while simultaneously encouraging subordinates to coalesce, collaborate, and work as a team.
7. **Networking leadership styles:** The leader acts as a representative of the team and safeguards the interest of the team when interacting with influential managers in the upper echelons of the firm.
8. **Value-based leadership styles:** The leader formulates and articulates a vision, while passionately seeking support from and for subordinates.

While a leader can display *any* of these leadership styles concurrently, there are two classes of situations or contingency variables that moderate the leadership behavior–outcome relationship.[38] The first is identified as the environmental pressures and demands of the workplace such as the task structure (the extent to which tasks are defined and have explicitly developed work procedures), the formal authority system (the amount of legitimate power employed by leaders, the extent to which policies and rules are formalized to regulate the behaviors of subordinates), and the educational level of subordinates and their relationships in the work team.[39] The second variable, subordinate contingencies, includes personal characteristics of subordinates such as experience, perceived ability, skills, and needs.

Sales Force Management Implications We need to make three assumptions in order to effectively apply the path-goal theory to the sales force management setting. The first is that the sales force is made up of salespeople with independent as well as collective goals. The second is that the sales manager, by virtue of seniority, has access to economic, social, and psychological bases of power. Finally, we assume that individual salespeople and sales managers interact to coordinate accomplishment of sales tasks and activities.[40] Under varying conditions, sales managers should be able to use the appropriate leadership styles – shown in Figure 10.3 – to motivate greater sales force effort toward achieving organizational and personal goals, such as sales revenues, salesperson productivity, and job satisfaction.

For example, sales managers can employ a participative leadership style by eliciting suggestions and consulting with salespersons in decision-making, devising policies, and crafting sales strategies. This approach can be effective in increasing the

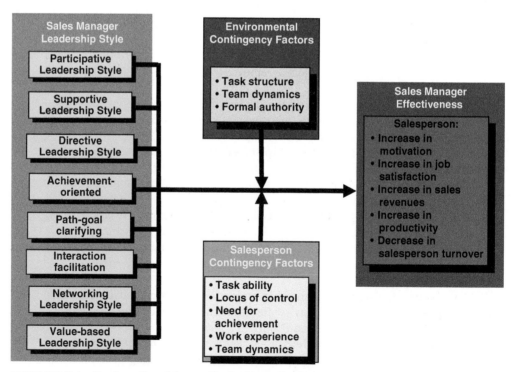

FIGURE 10.3 Extending the path-goal theory of leadership to sales force management.

salesperson's commitment, productivity, and performance. Sales managers can also employ participative leadership approaches for cultivating long-term customer relationships and even forging sales alliances with their competitors (discussed in Chapter 3). Together as partners, they can cooperate to create "win–win" outcomes. Oracle (www .oracle.com), Sun Microsystems (www.oracle.com/sun/), an enterprise software seller and a high-tech manufacturer of server hardware, workstations, and storage devices, took this strategy to a higher level by developing strategic partnerships with its competitors. Although the professional services division provides implementation expertise for its products, Oracle's salespeople partner with their software vendors and system integrators; then, as a team, they provide complete technology solutions for their customers by using participative leadership styles to make joint decisions. Rarely assuming the role of a "prime contractor," the firm opts to cooperate with its partners for mutual gain.[41] To augment your understanding of this "cutting edge" approach, visit websites, such as http://www.1000ventures.com/business_guide/mbs_mini_ spartnerships.html where you'll find articles, case studies, and slide shows on how participative leadership styles can be used for developing strategic partnerships.

Theory H Effective leaders match their style, from task-oriented to human relations-oriented, to the maturity and duties of the sales force. Experienced salespeople, used to operating largely independently, may resent a sales manager who exercises tight supervision and control over their activities. One way of visualizing possible leadership styles is to diagram them as the five areas of an automobile gearshift or the capital

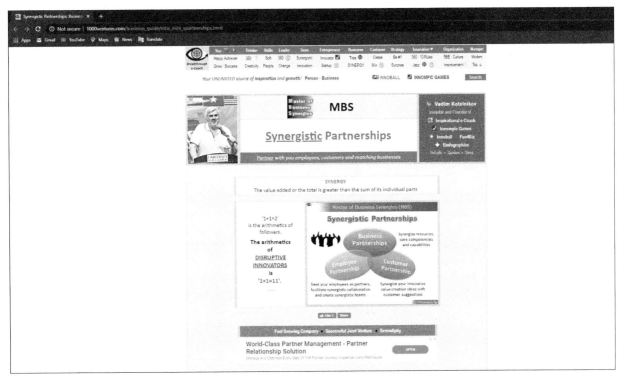

At www.1000ventures.com sales managers can discern how to use participative leadership styles for forging strategic partnerships.
Source: http://www.1000ventures.com/business_guide/mbs_mini_spartnerships.html.

1 **Autocratic**		3 **Democratic**
	5 **Consultative** **(neutral)**	
2 **Paternalistic**		4 **Laissez-faire**

FIGURE 10.4 Leadership styles based on Theory H.

letter "H," as shown in Figure 10.4.[42] A sales manager may need to shift among these styles as the composition and responsibilities of the sales force change. Xerox's Information Systems Group (www.xerox.com), which is responsible for copier and duplicator products, became one of the first companies to teach "situational leadership" to its middle-level and new first-level managers.[43]

Continuing the analogy of the gearshift, a sales manager exercises strong pulling power in first (autocratic) and second (paternalistic) gear, with the sales force largely dependent on the sales manager for rewards and punishments. In neutral (consultative), the sales manager exerts little push or pull and allows the salespeople to influence management decisions. In third (democratic) and fourth (laissez-faire) gear, the sales manager functions in a largely passive manner as salespeople operate quite independently. The real task of the successful sales manager is to select the style of leadership most appropriate for the individual salesperson, for the sales force as a whole, and for the particular sales situation.

No one leadership style fits all situations, and research indicates that about three-fourths of sales managers use at least two different styles to handle various members of the sales force. Effective leadership seems to call for flexibility and modification of style to match the changing sales situations. However, the sales manager must take care to be fairly consistent in handling each salesperson and team. Studies have indicated that the lowest morale usually comes about when a sales manager's style vacillates between an authoritarian approach at one time and a permissive approach at another. Capsule views of the five leadership styles are provided in Table 10.4.

Leader–Member Exchange Theory An interesting and intuitively appealing theory, leader–member exchange was an outgrowth of the incorrect assumption that leaders treat all their subordinates uniformly. Specifically, *not* all employees have similar relationships with their managers. Those whom a manager favors, consults, mentors, praises, trusts, and gives preferential treatment to belong to an "in-group" whom researchers call "cadres." In reciprocal exchange, each in-group subordinate makes greater efforts to increase performance, and exhibits greater respect and loyalty to the manager. Those assigned to an "out-group," however, are given less attention and privileges, and labeled "hired hands" by researchers. Thus, the group to which an individual is assigned will affect his or her short- and long-term opportunities within the firm.

Sales Force Management Implications Those salespersons a sales manager regards as being very high on (a) abilities, (b) motivation to assume additional responsibility,

> TABLE **10.4**

Extending Leadership Styles Based on Theory H to Sales Force Management

Leadership style characteristics				
Authoritarian	**Paternalistic**	**Consultative**	**Democratic**	**Laissez-faire**
• Tight control and rigid authority • Clearly defined tasks • Downward communication from sales manager	• "Kindly father knows best" • Authority is centralized with sales manager	• Two-way communication with sales force • Right to make final decision retained by sales manager	• Much authority delegated but sales manager retains the right to determine team consensus • Participatory decision making and division of work	• Leader responsibility abdicated and authority given to sales force • Primarily horizontal communication between sales force peers
Appropriate situation for leadership style				
Authoritarian	**Paternalistic**	**Consultative**	**Democratic**	**Laissez-faire**
• New or inexperienced salespeople • Disciplinary action needed • Emergencies • Complacent sales force	• Weak sales supervisors • Immature or inexperienced salespeople • Informal sales force leaders expressing discontent	• Well-trained, experienced sales force • Sales force works well as a team	• Small, well- informed sales force • Cooperative salespeople • Lots of time to make decisions	• Salespeople have expert knowledge • Nature of work guides salespeople
Inappropriate situation for leadership style				
Authoritarian	**Paternalistic**	**Consultative**	**Democratic**	**Laissez-faire**
• Mature, experienced salespeople • Teamwork and cooperation needed	• Mature, independent salespeople • Strong, competent sales force	• Inexperienced, poorly trained sales force • Sales force does not work well as a team	• Larger teams of Salespeople • Decisions must be made quickly • Salespeople are not sufficiently informed	• Salespeople are reluctant to make decisions • Nature of work is similar for all salespeople

and (c) trustworthiness are considered members of the in-group.[44] These salespersons have a high-quality relationship with their sales manager and receive considerable latitude, support, and attention; but, in return, they are expected to perform duties that go well beyond written job descriptions (e.g., service key customer accounts, collect overdue accounts, train inexperienced sales personnel). Salespeople whom the sales manager considers to be relatively low on the preceding three qualities belong to the out-group, thus they have a formal, lower quality, and less supporting relationship with their sales leader. Considered hired hands, the "out-group" salespersons perform tasks defined in their job description, nothing more. Of course, sales managers do not expect nearly as much from them as they do from salespersons in the "in-group." In addition, those salespersons a sales manager considers to be desirable task members and social partners receive more favorable performance reviews and interesting assignments than their counterparts who are regarded as less desirable.[45] While becoming a member of the "in-group" is desired by most salespeople, not all have the skills to be in that sales force category. Another interesting finding is that sales managers have less favorable reactions toward hired hands who perform ineffectively than cadres who perform ineffectively.[46]

Research has tried to determine whether certain factors differentiate cadres from hired hands, and findings to date reveal that cadres tend to have been with their managers longer and are more trusting and less suspicious of their managers than are hired hands.[47] Additionally, cadres, compared with hired hands, have been found to exhibit greater job satisfaction,[48] less role stress,[49] and higher performance.[50] Salespeople can attempt to cultivate a relationship with their sales manager that will lead to their becoming cadres.[51] Similarly, sales managers may seek to do the same with their superiors. Whether an individual has the ability or the aspiration to be a cadre, of course, is another issue. Some salespeople, as well as managers, may opt to be hired hands so as not to go beyond their "comfort zone" of industriousness. Although they may have the capacity to assume responsibilities that go well beyond their job description, they may simply be satisfied with their current job situation. The overall implications are that sales managers should focus on developing the selling skills and motivation of salespeople while displaying leadership behaviors perceived as trustworthy and objective. These sales manager behaviors are important for developing closer working relationships with salespeople who then will be more apt to perform in ways that will help them join the favorable "in-group."

Substitutes for Leadership Theory The substitutes for leadership theory were developed because existing theories didn't account for situations in which leadership is neutralized or replaced by characteristics of the subordinates, the task, and the organization.[52] First, salesperson characteristics, such as experience, need for independence, and professional orientation may serve to neutralize leadership behavior. For example, productive salespeople with a high level of professionalism may not need guidance on tasks. Second, challenging or intrinsically satisfying characteristics of the task itself may substitute for leadership. Finally, leadership may not be needed when company policies and practices are formal and inflexible. Preliminary research has provided support for these substitutes as partial replacements for leadership.[53]

Sales Force Management Implications The concept of substitutes for leadership is highly applicable to personal selling. In some situations, sales managers can be better leaders if they know when *not* to lead, choosing the management-by-exception approach instead. Further, the solitary nature of many sales jobs can mean that the salesperson and the sales manager will be physically separated and have little interaction. Thus, sales organizations often employ their own "leadership substitutes," mechanisms through which salespersons receive the needed guidance and support as they work alone. Here are some of the more popular substitutes:

- **Ability, experience, training, and knowledge:** Salespeople with the necessary training and preparation to perform the job in the field have less need to rely on the sales manager for job-related information or guidance.
- **Professional orientation:** Salespeople seek guidance and feedback from sales peers within the same sales team (or department) or from those outside the firm – noncompeting sales representatives or those in professional organizations such as Sales and Marketing Executives International and the American Marketing Association.

- **Task-provided feedback:** The job description, goals, and other parameters can indicate to the salesperson the level of his or her job performance. For example, percent of quota achieved to date, closing of a sale, loss of a sale, and customer complaints are accurate and immediate sources of performance-related information.
- **Organizational formalization and inflexibility:** The sales organization might choose to articulate explicit plans, goals, areas of responsibility, guidelines, and ground rules then employ them in a relatively rigid fashion. Such structure provides impersonal, yet formalized, direction.
- **Advisory staff:** Salespeople and sales managers are supported by an array of production, advertising, marketing research, pricing, and other departmental staff to aid in satisfying customers. They thus receive ad hoc, but ongoing, assistance as necessary.
- **Closely knit work group:** The sales organization fosters strong esprit de corps among the sales team that provides emotional support, encouragement, and friendship.
- **Compensation plans, quotas, and expense accounts:** These tools direct the salespeople toward the appropriate job behavior, providing guidance about what they should be doing on the job and how to execute their job tasks.
- **Customers and competitors:** Direct customer feedback can tell salespeople about the adequacy of their job performance, in the form of praise or purchase decisions. Indirect feedback can also come in the form of complaints or compliments to the salesperson's sales manager. Competitors' actions, such as raising or lowering market prices or offering favorable terms to a particular customer, can suggest what the salesperson should do in his or her territory to be successful.

Applying Contemporary Leadership Theories to Twenty-first Century Sales Force Management

So, now that you're familiar with the classical theories of leadership, you're probably wondering what it will take to be a successful leader in the twenty-first century. It's a fair question! The answer may well lie in the emerging schools of thought that include (a) transformational leadership, (b) Pygmalion leadership, (c) empowerment, (d) servant leadership, and (e) shared leadership.

Transformational (or Charismatic and Visionary) Leadership

The classic theories we've looked at so far all examine *transactional* leadership applications. In the context of sales management, transactional sales managers identify and clarify job tasks for salespeople and communicate to them how successful execution of those tasks will lead to receipt of desirable job rewards.[54] Today, however, interest is surging in *transformational* or *charismatic* leaders.[55] Let's discuss transactional leadership first, then turn to transformational leadership.

Transactional leaders recognize the immediate needs of their employees and communicate to them how those needs can be met through effective performance. In the context of sales management, these managers identify and clarify job tasks for their salespeople and communicate to them how successful execution of assigned tasks will lead to receipt of desirable job rewards.[56] As transactional leaders, they determine and define the goals and work that subordinates need to achieve, suggest how to execute their tasks, and provide feedback. The goals assigned salespeople usually have a short-term focus, can be based on effort and/or results, may or may not be quantifiable, and will depend on the sales subordinate's position and function within the sales organization.

Goals for the salesperson often include sales volume in dollars or units, new account acquisition, customer retention rate, percent of quota, willingness to assist new sales recruits, and knowledge of competition. The sales manager can reward successful performance with increased commissions, bonuses, salary increases, promotions to higher-level positions, recognition, trophies, transfers to larger territories, and praise. Conversely, the leader can react to poor performance with a wide array of negative contingent reinforcement methods, such as reduced compensation, intensified monitoring of activities, and reassignment.

Given the nature of the selling position, most sales managers use transactional leadership and seek to stimulate and direct their sales forces with contingent reinforcement (reward or punish salespeople based on their performance). In simple terms, transactional sales leadership consists of a contract between the manager and the subordinate. An example of this relationship is typified by the sign above a sales manager's desk that reads: "No orders, No money." Research has found that this leadership approach can have a favorable influence on salespeople's job attitudes and behavior[57] and on sales manager performance.[58]

While transactional leadership, which takes a short-term perspective to generate favorable results from the sales force, tends to be the most frequently used leadership approach in business today it has been criticized on several grounds. For example, time pressures on sales managers, poorly developed sales performance appraisal systems, unfair rewards systems for salespeople, absence of training for sales managers, and lack of control over company rewards by sales managers can all work against the effectiveness of a transactional leader.[59] Thus, an approach that has garnered growing attention of sales managers and senior management is *transformational leadership*, which adopts a long-term orientation by focusing on future needs.

Transformational sales leaders activate their subordinates' higher-order needs and encourage them to substitute company needs for their own. They raise salespersons' awareness of the value of their jobs, the consequences of their actions, and their importance to the organization. The result is more committed, more satisfied salespeople who are encouraged to surpass their own expectations and personal objectives for the good of the sales district and the company.[60] Transformational sales managers have the ability to gain extraordinary commitment from their salespeople through four key characteristics: *charismatic and visionary leadership, inspiration, intellectual stimulation, and individualized consideration.*[61]

Charismatic and Visionary Leadership Charisma is a "fire that ignites followers' energy and commitment, producing results above and beyond the call of duty."[62] Charismatic leaders are known to inspire and motivate people to willingly do more despite obstacles and personal sacrifice as well as transcend their own interests for the sake of the firm.[63] Charismatic sales managers create a strong emotional appeal among salespeople that exceeds ordinary esteem, affection, admiration and trust.[64]

They inspire through their confident attitudes, risk-taking tendencies, assertiveness, magnetic personalities, and frequently gutsy approaches. Salespeople often demonstrate total and unconditional belief in and identification with the vision of charismatic sales managers.

A *vision* is an attractive, credible notion of a future state that is not readily attainable. While vision is a key ingredient of charismatic leadership, visionary leadership includes articulating a realistic, credible, and attractive future that improves upon the present.[65] Thus, a visionary leader appeals to the hearts of subordinates and their desire to be part of something that will bring a bigger, brighter future.[66] Such leaders mobilize subordinate commitment toward the vision by communicating it, and institutionalizing change throughout the organization. Lee Iacocca, dynamic former President of Ford Motor Company (www.ford.com), then later CEO of Chrysler (www.chrysler.com), was a quintessential transformational leader who had both charisma and vision to transform companies and their managers into agents of change. Iacocca's personal charisma was so strong that he became the advertising pitchman on television for Chrysler and was largely responsible for turning the company from near bankruptcy to innovative success. Similarly, the legendary Herb Kelleher of Southwest Airlines (www.southwest.com) displayed the vision and foresight to create a uniquely successful airline committed to superior customer service delivered oftentimes in uninhibited and creative ways. Steve Jobs, co-founder and former CEO of Apple (www.apple.com), who epitomizes transformational leadership, inspired extraordinary loyalty to his vision of developing innovative and exciting products to improve the lives of people around the world. Some major characteristics of these exceptional leaders include: (1) a vision that is clearly articulated, (2) willingness to take risks to achieve the vision, (3) sensitivity to environmental constraints, (4) understanding follower needs, and (5) behaviors that are novel.[67]

Inspiration Inspirational leadership is the ability to articulate expectations to subordinates, communicate important purposes in simple ways, and use symbols to focus their efforts. Inspirational sales managers are emotionally arousing and reassuring to their salespeople, typically because they've "been there successfully before."[68]

Intellectual Stimulation A transformational sales leader stimulates salespeople intellectually by creating a readiness for change, and by encouraging them to use intuition to find new approaches for solving old and continuing problems or emerging ones. These leaders are capable of devising and introducing innovative prospecting and selling strategies, controlling sales force turnover, and maintaining the organization's stability by developing imaginative ways to recruit sales personnel. Salespersons under this kind of sales manager tend to readily offer their own ideas, become inspired in their problem solving, and think more critically and creatively.

Salespeople can benefit from maintaining a "learning log," which is a recording of each sales problem they confront, how they resolved it, and what they learned from it. The log allows them, and their peers, to review this material when they face similar problems in the future, rather than reinventing the wheel.[69] Sales managers at Amana Refrigeration (www.amana.com) went into the field to discover why their lead generation program did not produce a high rate of sales. They discovered that their more successful salespeople ignored most of the leads sent to them by distinguishing between customers who view the product as a commodity (and thus buy on price) and those who use it to differentiate their own products (the "real" prospects). Armed with this knowledge, Amana sales managers redirected sales force efforts toward identifying prospects and customers who were not price driven but were concerned mainly with the quality of the product.[70]

Individualized Consideration The fourth characteristic of transformational leadership is the manager's ability to treat each employee as an individual, supporting career development, and growth by providing mentoring, coaching, and counseling. Transformational sales managers show genuine concern for each salesperson rather than only for tasks, policies, administrative matters, or decision-making. Individualized attention paves the way for ongoing communication between the leader and the sales subordinate; evokes personal commitment and devotion; and allays fears, anxiety, and depression. Admittedly, frequent personal contact with field salespeople is often difficult because of their physical distance from the sales manager. Nonetheless, convincing salespeople to transcend their own self-interests for the benefit of the organization will be difficult without the sales leader's knowledge of, sensitivity to, and response to each salesperson's unique needs for growth and development. Bill Marriott, President of Marriott Corporation (www.marriott.com), practices individualized consideration by calling his firm's top producers every month to congratulate them. Imagine how motivating and empowering *that* phone call must be for the recipients!

In essence, then, transformational sales leaders are not content with the status quo and tend to develop salespeople who resemble and emulate them. They seek to "transform" the salespeople's perspective from a short-run, self-oriented one to a long-run, company (or work unit) orientation.

Transformational leadership has been found to be particularly effective in nonsales work contexts. Some preliminary evidence suggests that this leadership style has a favorable impact on salespersons[71] and sales managers,[72] but not necessarily a greater effect than that of transactional leadership. However, the two leadership styles can be used together to develop a favorable leadership perspective for both the company and the individual. Capsule views of transactional and transformational leadership are provided in Table 10.5.

TABLE 10.5

Extending Transactional versus Transformational Leadership to Sales Force Management

Transactional sales managers	Transformational sales managers
• Identify and communicate tasks to salespeople	• **Inspiration** – effectively communicate expectations; are emotionally arousing and reassuring to salespeople
• Recognize immediate needs of salespeople and suggest ways to meet more needs	• **Charisma** – have a vision, a sense of mission, and a strong emotional appeal for salespeople
• Suggest ways to execute tasks	• **Intellectual stimulation** – help salespeople become better at identifying and solving customer problems and needs
• Provide appropriate rewards and feedback	• **Individual consideration** – display individual consideration to salespeople through mentoring, coaching, and counseling

Sales managers can use different leadership approaches to effectively influence salespersons to go above and beyond the call of duty to help the organization be successful.

Pygmalion Leadership

Some effective sales managers communicate high but realistic expectations to their sales subordinates on the principle that positive thinking begets positive results. In other words, they try to shape subordinates' performance by communicating their high hopes for job success. The result is a self-fulfilling prophesy – sales managers get what they expect.

This leadership style is sometimes called the "Pygmalion" effect which comes from Greek mythology about the sculptor, Pygmalion, who fell in love with his own statue.[73] Pygmalion leadership is based on the central idea that "when a manager communicates high expectations to a subordinate, the subordinate is likely to raise the level of his or her own performance expectations."[74] (Sales Manager: "You have outstanding selling ability, and I'm confident you'll achieve your sales quota for this year." Salesperson: "Thanks, Boss, I really appreciate your support. You know what? I think I can achieve my quota, too, and maybe more.")

Salespeople can also develop high expectations for themselves without input from their managers and still perform exceedingly well (the "Galatea" effect). If, however, a sales manager articulates low expectations to a sales subordinate, low performance might well follow (the "Golem" effect) – negative thinking leads to negative results.

To use Pygmalion leadership effectively, sales organizations should encourage their sales managers to convey high performance expectations to their salespeople. At the same time, though, they also should try to increase the self-confidence of salespersons so that they will expect more of themselves and thus enhance their own productivity. Of course, sales managers should always avoid conveying low performance expectations to sales force members. Instead, they need to convince their salespeople that "they have untapped potential" and help them "believe that they can achieve more."[75]

306 Chapter 10 Sales Force Leadership

Leadership and Empowerment: Distributive Power Sharing Through Participative Management

In a departure from old-school thinking, the concept of empowerment focuses on distributing power to lower level employees. These employees often experience low levels of *self-efficacy,* or feelings of powerlessness and the belief that their work does not make any meaningful contribution to organizational performance. Another contributor to the spread of empowerment is that organizational hierarchies are becoming flatter and thus require stronger leadership and decision-making at lower levels.

Empowerment refers to the process of distributing power to subordinates, which makes them partners entrusted with legitimate authority and discretion in decision-making, and by providing rewards tied to company performance. Empowering employees means to recognize and release the potential power that people already have in their own reservoir of knowledge, experience, and internal motivation.[76] Because it allocates decision-making authority to better resolve problems, empowerment can help alleviate employee feelings of powerlessness and improve their self-efficacy.[77]

Participative management refers to the involvement of employees with management in shared decision-making that enables them to accomplish individual and organizational goals. Essentially, the philosophy behind empowerment is participative management, which gives subordinates a sense of ownership and responsibility by enabling them to play an integral role in decision-making, problem solving, goal setting, and instituting organizational changes. Participative management goes above and beyond simply eliciting ideas or opinions from subordinates. To feel self-worth and self-efficacy, employees must believe that their jobs have value. After being legitimately empowered, they are more likely to contribute to the accomplishment of organization goals. Participative management is associated with other organizational effectiveness criteria such as increases in subordinate job commitment, security, challenge, and motivation.[78] Figure 10.5 applies the idea of empowerment to sales management tasks along a continuum from high to low levels of shared power and authority.

Sales managers can take several steps to ensure the success of an empowerment program. First, they should ensure that their salespeople can attain job mastery by providing them with needed skills training.[79] Second, sales managers should give salespeople authority (legitimate power), responsibility, and control to make substantive decisions, including job performance procedures. In turn, salespeople should then be ready to be held accountable for results including organizational performance.[80] Third, sales managers should assign role models to mentor salespeople in their work.[81] Fourth, they can use reinforcement and persuasion to raise the confidence levels of salespeople, through praise, encouragement, and constructive feedback, plus offer emotional support to relieve job stress and anxiety.[82] Sixth, to make effective decisions, sales managers should provide their salespeople with access to financial and operational performance data.[83] Seventh, they should reward salespeople based on the extent to which they improve the firm's bottom line. For instance, a profit-sharing program might allocate a share of directly attributable profits to the sales department for rewarding the salespeople. Furthermore, subordinates ought be fairly rewarded for their work and even be allowed to choose how they get compensated.[84] Without results-based compensation and rewards, empowerment programs may not meet their intended objectives.

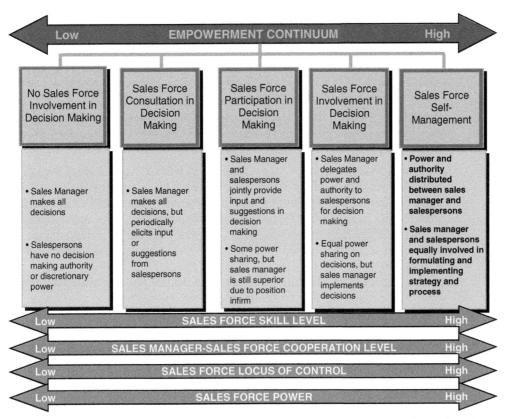

FIGURE 10.5 The Sales manager-salesperson empowerment continuum: Distributive power sharing through participative management.

Sales Force Management Implications Empowerment shifts decision-making to lower-level employees, and this may seem counterintuitive in the context of our earlier discussion of how sales managers can judiciously use power. But recall from Chapter 1 that the new definition of marketing entails "a set of processes for communicating and delivering value to customers and for managing customer relationships in ways that benefit the organization and its stakeholders."[85] Further, sales and marketing has moved from focusing on transactions to developing long-run mutually profitable customer relationships. Acting as boundary spanners between buyers and sellers, salespeople have found that their roles have shifted significantly to include customer relationship management (CRM), "the overall process of building and maintaining profitable customer relationships by delivering superior customer value and satisfaction."[86]

So what does empowerment mean for sales force management? First, because salespeople often work alone, they tend to have considerable freedom on the job. They can make decisions about which prospects or customers to call on (and in what order), the content of their sales presentations, their allocation of selling time versus nonselling time, and negotiating the selling price. Given this level of job latitude, sales managers want to empower their sales staff in a way that will allow adequate control over their activities while not inhibiting their sales productivity.[87] To bring out the creativity of their salespeople, many sales managers have empowered them by using "four levers of control"[88]:

- **Diagnostic control systems:** Sales managers establish and support clear performance goals for the sales force. The system allows them to monitor and correct their sales subordinates' progress toward such goals as sales, market share, and profitability.

- **Beliefs systems:** Sales managers communicate core values and a mission to the sales force. Thus, salespersons know what is acceptable behavior as their selling situations change.
- **Boundary systems:** Sales managers specify and enforce the rules of the game. Instead of having a blank check to execute their tasks, the sales team is allowed to operate within defined limits.
- **Interactive control systems:** Sales managers encourage learning within the sales department. Rather than simply believing that information alone is power, they believe that "we all need each other's input to be successful."

These four control levers allow for empowerment without "giving away the farm." Although many companies may employ some elements of each, successful sales managers make explicit use of all the levers when empowering their sales subordinates.

Second, to effectively implement an empowerment program, sales managers need to focus on: (1) enhancing salesperson skills, (2) developing salesperson character, (3) creating a culture of empowerment, and (4) providing empowerment opportunities. Ways of achieving these goals are shown in Figure 10.6.

Third, in light of their expanding CRM tasks that include building and maintaining long-term customer relationships, sales managers need to sufficiently empower their salespeople to effectively and efficiently perform their evolving roles. Empowerment may be difficult for traditional sales managers, who perceive it as a threat to their authority, but indications are clear that it offers high potential for success in today's

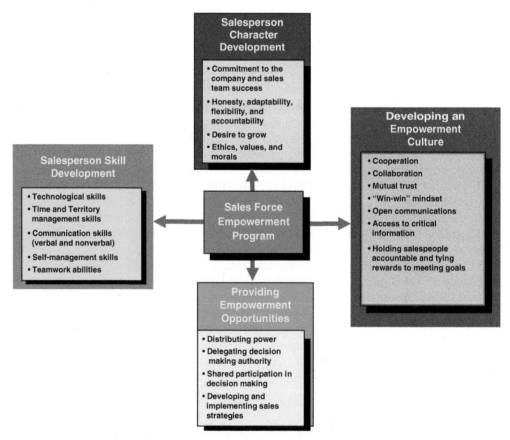

FIGURE 10.6 Implementing an empowerment program for the sales force.

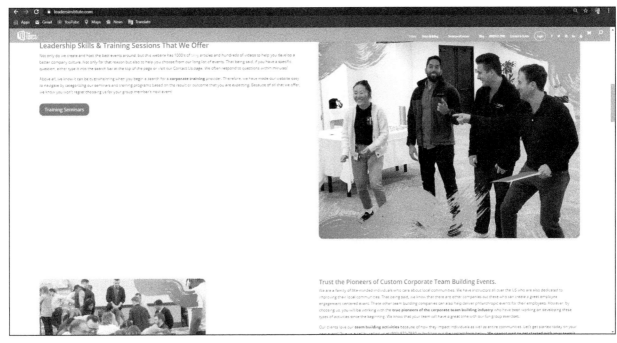

The Leaders Institute offers "cutting-edge" training programs on leadership and empowerment, which sales managers can enroll in to increase their managerial skills.
Source: https://www.leadersinstitute.com/.

business environment. To learn more about "cutting-edge" leadership and empowerment issues, sales managers can enroll in leadership and empowerment training programs offered by such organizations as the Leaders Institute (www.leadersinstitute.com).

Servant Leadership

Greenleaf, who is credited with coining the term "servant leadership" described it as leadership that strives in decision-making to consider and serve the needs of people first ahead of everything else.[89]

Organizations as well as individuals can exhibit servant leadership by focusing first on the well-being of the employees and other stakeholders in the company, including the communities in which they serve. Although Servant Leadership is often depicted as a "newer" theory, its philosophical foundation was laid over two thousand years ago in the life of Jesus Christ who said that the greatest in the kingdom to come would be the servant of all.[90]

Servant leadership is not about acting servile, obsequious, or submissive, but about proactively helping others (colleagues, customers, and communities) by identifying and trying to satisfy their needs in organizational decision-making. A servant leader in sales shares power with salespeople, considers their needs, and helps them develop to their full potential. Research has identified six key characteristics of servant–leader behavior, including empowering and developing people, humility, authenticity, interpersonal acceptance, providing direction, and stewardship. Servant leaders generally show and exercise the qualities of high moral values and empathetic communication with followers. They are concerned about the well-being and success of all company stakeholders, whether colleagues, customers, business partners, communities, or society at large. Servant leaders see themselves as stewards entrusted with the noble goal of developing and empowering followers to reach their full potential. This type of leadership includes aspects of charismatic and transformational leadership to encourage people to take pride in what they do and commit to working for the overall good of the organization. Studies have shown that servant leadership's "bottom-up" style of prioritizing the needs of subordinates causes them to become more engaged in their work because they feel that they have acceptance, social support, and backing from their leader-managers and colleagues. Research confirms that sales management style can be a crucial factor in the percent of sales force turnover as it demonstrates the organization's degree of concern and support for its salespeople.[91]

Servant leadership may also have a positive effect on the emotional health of employees because it relies heavily on one-to-one, empathetic communication with them to more fully understand their abilities, needs, desires, goals, and potential. Servant leadership is still going through the process of acceptance as a practical leadership theory in business because it's often viewed as an idealized way of thinking rather than a pragmatic, systematic process for effective management and leadership. Servant leadership may not be appropriate for every organization or situation, but it continues to attract more advocates among business leaders as it has been shown to be successful in improving the morale and performance of an organization, its people, and stakeholders. However, servant leadership will likely go through various modifications and adaptations before being widely adopted across business organizations.[92]

Shared Leadership

Shared leadership broadly distributes decision-making across the members of an organizational team, so it tends to be seen as horizontal, distributed, collective, dispersed, or collaborative group leadership instead of the traditional narrow "vertical" or "hierarchical" leadership that centers around one key individual or a small group of people. Shared leadership has been described as the distribution of leadership influence and decision-making across multiple team members instead of only the downward control of subordinates or followers by appointed or elected superior leaders. Exercising shared leadership becomes a dynamic and multifunctional group, collaborative, and social network process to which all team members are committed for their common good.[93]

Although relatively new in the business literature, the concept of shared leadership goes back at least several centuries to the early days of the Roman empire when its Senate exercised great power over the civil government in Rome and collectively approved or rejected the appointment of senators, top military officers, and the emperor. Using an overall team approach to decision-making, shared leadership consists of three basic dimensions which can be succinctly described as:

- **Shared purpose** that prevails when team members have similar understandings of their team's main objectives and take steps to ensure a focus on collective goals.
- **Social support** which is the extent to which team members actively provide emotional and psychological strength to one another. This may occur through overt acts of encouragement or expressed recognition of other team members' contributions and accomplishments.
- **Voice** or the degree to which a team's members have input into how the team carries out its purpose.[94]

With the increasing complexity and ambiguity of the strategic and tactical decisions that most organizations must make to successfully compete in rapidly changing market environments, no individual leader is likely to have the comprehensive skills and knowledge to effectively perform all the needed leadership functions. So, sharing leadership responsibilities across the organizational team members who bring different qualities and skill sets to deal with challenges and capitalize on opportunities seems to make sense because it can strengthen the organization's overall decision-making abilities. Studies show that the complexity of the work or tasks to be accomplished tends to act as a moderator on shared leadership-team effectiveness in that relationships and collaborative efforts are stronger when the work to be done is more complex. This can be explained by the greater interdependence, coordination, and information sharing necessary to accomplish work of higher complexity. Global expansion, restructuring, and merging of organizations across markets with different cultures are increasing the need for organizational flexibility and broader leadership knowledge and expertise. Shared leadership and more collaborative decision-making seem to offer higher potential to meet the challenging demands on modern business leadership.[95]

Other Emerging Issues in Twenty-First-Century Sales Force Leadership

Mentoring

One of the proven ways to develop leaders is through mentoring. A *mentor* is someone who systematically helps develop a subordinate's abilities through careful tutoring, personal guidance, and example. Mentors are typically strong, self-confident people who do not fear an aggressive young subordinate. They take risks in betting on perceived talent in subordinates and are an important source and stimulus for the development of leaders. Sales managers can be effective mentors by working closely with their salespeople. A form of mentoring that has recently gained popularity among sales managers is "curbstone coaching." In this practice, the sales manager remains with a salesperson during a sales call and provides a constructive critique immediately after the call. Many experts feel that tremendous improvements can be made if a sales manager can properly coach the salesperson about a sales call while the call is still fresh in his or her mind.[96] Sales managers must realize the importance of setting aside a few minutes after the sales call – either over a cup of coffee or on the way to the next appointment – to analyze what did or did not happen and what improvements can be made. If the sales manager can provide instant feedback that is truly helpful and acceptable to the salesperson, the payoff can be almost instantaneous. A few minutes of empathetic concern also can do a lot to boost a mentor's leadership ability.

Mentoring revisits the question posed at the beginning of the chapter: Can leaders be created? Mentors and senior sales managers can certainly create *better* leaders by helping young sales managers with various aspects of their careers.[97] For example, mentors can equip individuals with the skills, tools, and techniques to bring out their natural leadership talents. A solid background of information learned from mentors can give young sales managers the confidence they need to make critical decisions. Finally, a senior member of a company can do a great deal for an entry-level employee by instilling the values of curiosity, idealism, entrepreneurism, and commitment.[98] While implementing these strategies will not necessarily guarantee a leader, leadership talents can be revealed that may have been latent in an individual. For some additional insights on the development of leaders for the twenty-first century, see Sales Management in Action Box 10.1.

Box 10.1 | Sales Management in Action 10.1

Building Effective Sales Force Management Leaders for Today and Tomorrow

Intensifying global competition, multicultural customers, growing sales force diversity, and innovative sales and marketing channels have combined to make the search for effective sales management leaders increasing urgent. These potential "superstar" sales managers must exhibit exceptional leadership qualities and behaviors, including the following[99]:

- Treating salespeople more like partners or teammates than subordinates in achieving sales, profitability, and customer satisfaction goals.
- Empowering salespeople by providing them with profitability information about product and services and releasing decision-making authority that enables salespeople to negotiate and satisfy customers "on the spot" instead of having to obtain their sales manager's prior approval.
- Willingness to take risks and seize new opportunities for growth and improvement in all areas, instead of clinging to the status quo.
- Developing closer relationships with customers and more in-depth understanding of customers' businesses.

- Applying flexible motivational skills in working with a hybrid sales force across multiple sales channels, online and off-line.
- Persuading salespeople to embrace and share the organizational vision.
- Sharing successes with salespeople and sales support people by recognizing, rewarding, and celebrating the accomplishments, individually and collectively.
- Keeping up-to-date on the latest technologies impacting on buyer–seller relationships.
- Learning marketing skills in order to identify potential business opportunities and recommend strategies to senior management.
- Working closely with internal departments as a member of the total corporate team dedicated to satisfying customers profitably.
- Continually seeking ways to exceed customer expectations and bring added value to the ongoing buyer–seller relationship.
- Creating a flexible, learning, and adapting environment for all members of the sales team.
- Serving as a positive role model by exhibiting high standards of ethics and dedication to customer service and satisfaction.

Sales managers increase salesperson productivity by mentoring and providing guidance on sales data analysis.

Aleksandr Davydov/123RF

Diversity in Selling and Sales Force Management

Most organizations can benefit from increased diversity of gender, race, education, ethnicity, socioeconomic background, age, sexual orientation, political belief, religious affiliation, and other differences because their customers are diverse and becoming ever more so. Focusing on diversity in hiring and promotion can have an overall positive impact on the company's bottom line, especially when it comes to building your sales team's understanding of the changing requirements of customers. If your sales team is comprised of people with backgrounds that are essentially the same, they will likely approach market opportunities and challenges in very similar ways. A study by the *Harvard Business Review* found that a team with a member who shares the customer's ethnicity is over 150% more likely to understand that customer than is a team without such a member. The study also revealed that a lack of diversity in leadership presented a significant barrier to diverse perspectives being represented. In organizations without diverse leadership, women are 20% less likely than white men to win support for their ideas; people of color are 24% less likely; and LGBTs are 21% less likely. This lack of receptiveness for diverse perspectives can cost companies crucial market opportunities because it usually requires people from backgrounds similar to that of customers to fully understand and satisfy their needs and wants. What's more, prospects and customers like to see themselves represented in the make-up of the sales force and management at companies from which they are considering purchase of products and services. Recruiting, hiring, and retaining salespeople and sales managers with a variety of backgrounds, characteristics, and skill sets can have an overall favorable impact on the organization's success and employee morale. A major advantage of diversity is the ability to elicit a range of ideas and perspectives to solve company problems. Sales force diversity draws out more innovative ideas and creative approaches to market opportunities and challenges. Markets, both domestic and global, are becoming ever more diverse and changing rapidly along with the advancing communication technologies to reach them, so it's critical for companies to have selling teams that can keep up with and capitalize on oftentimes dramatic and sudden market developments.[100]

Guard Against Stereotyping

All organizations need to guard against stereotyping. Selling and sales management traditionally have been white male-dominated, but in the twenty-first century, women and minorities in growing numbers are rising to leadership roles as markets diversify. Studies show that in 2017, about 46% of marketing and sales managers were female. Average age for male and female managers was about the same with males being on average only four years older. Over 84% of the managers were white while Asian managers were the highest minority group at slightly over 6%. Clearly there is a need and opportunity for expanding the numbers of minorities in selling and sales management leadership but many companies complain that, although they are actively seeking to hire minorities, few seem interested in sales careers.[101]

Over the years, there have been innumerable studies conducted to determine whether there are significant differences between male and female salespeople and sales managers. These studies have generally shown that salespeople respond favorably to female sales leaders because women possess many qualities important to successful sales management.[102] For instance, women tend to be nurturing, interpersonally concerned, relationship oriented, socially sensitive, and expressive; to be highly involved with others; to value connection between themselves and others; to have a propensity for encouraging participation with subordinates; and to exhibit excellent communication skills.[103] Based on findings from these studies, some experts have concluded that women should use the same leadership approaches as male sales managers. Others contend that women should simply focus on doing their jobs by using their own innate qualities without trying to become male "management clones." Still other researchers argue that women sales managers should opt for an androgynous approach, using both male and female characteristics to advantage.[104] The bottom line seems to be that the interpretation of studies to date about gender differences in selling and management are varied and inconsistent. Therefore, the differences may not be attributable solely to gender. However, progress for women in sales focus management still lags. A recent study found that only 19% of women in sales are in leadership positions. Research by McKinsey & Company (www.mckinsey.com) reveals that the managerial roles held by women are more often in administrative support functions such as human resources while they are underrepresented in positions with profit and loss responsibility. However, the business climate is improving for women as they now make up about half of the U.S. workforce and almost 52% are in managerial or professional jobs. In sales, studies have found that saleswomen consistently achieve their assigned sales quotas at a slightly higher rate than do men. So what does all this mean for women sales managers? Advice from top female sales executives suggest that women should largely forget about the stereotypes because there are no proven inherent differences that make women less qualified for managerial jobs. Women and minorities are advised to focus on being superior manager-leaders by doing what all good sales manager should do, viz: support and motivate their salespeople, care deeply about customer satisfaction and loyalty, and ensure the achievement of sales and organizational goals.[105]

Communication

At its most basic level, leadership requires communication as a way of transferring ideas, facts, thoughts, and values from one person to another. Thus, communication is an essential component of leadership. Setting objectives and goals, organizing, staffing, forecasting, supervising, compensating, motivating, evaluating, and controlling the sales force – nearly all sales management functions – rely on communication. Open channels are especially critical when the sales organization must quickly adapt to a dynamic marketing environment. The typical manager spends more time communicating than doing anything else: 75% of an average day in face-to-face listening or speaking, 9% in writing, and 16% in reading.[106]

Communication is a two-way process that includes listening and reading body-language as well as speaking and writing. In fact, some of the best communicators follow this advice: "Always use your ears and mouth according to the number you have of each." Successful sales managers and salespeople are usually exceptionally good listeners. Many studies support the conclusion that good communication improves the productivity of an organization.[107]

Listening

One of the most overlooked qualities of a good communicator and thus of a good leader is *listening skill.* Listening provides managers with the bulk of the information they need to do their jobs. However, research shows that the average person is a poor listener, remembering only half of what is said during a 10-minute conversation and forgetting half of that within 48 hours.[108] Effective listening has become so necessary a component of business success that many companies train their employees in listening.[109]

There are four basic types of listening, and they differ not only in purpose but also in the amount of feedback or interaction that occurs:

1. **Content listening.** The receiver's goal is to understand and retain information and identify key points. The receiver asks questions and takes notes as the information flows primarily in one direction – from speaker to receiver.
2. **Critical listening.** The receiver's goal is to critically evaluate the message by looking at the logic of the argument, the strength of the evidence, and validity of the conclusions. There's a great deal of interaction in critical listening, as the receiver tries to uncover the speaker's point of view.
3. **Empathic listening.** The receiver's goal is to understand the speaker's feelings, needs, and wants in order to solve a problem. Less interaction occurs, as the receiver is attempting to gain insights into the speaker's psyche.
4. **Active listening.** This listening technique attempts to help people resolve their communication differences. Before replying to the speaker's comment, the receiver restates the ideas and feelings behind the speaker's comments to ensure mutual understanding. The goal here is to appreciate the other person's point of view, whether or not you agree.

Sales managers and salespeople can use these listening modes to build better relationships with one another and with customers. For example, sales managers can help alleviate any role ambiguities among their salespeople by honing their active listening skills. On the other hand, salespeople can learn a great deal about their customers by engaging in more empathic listening. Regardless of whether the sales management situation calls for content, critical, empathic, or active listening, sales managers can improve their listening ability by following the basic guidelines presented in Table 10.6.

Understanding Nonverbal Communication

Many communications experts feel that nonverbal communication has more impact than verbal communication, accounting for as much as 93% of the emotional meaning exchanged in most interactions.[110] *Nonverbal communication* takes place largely through body language: facial expressions, gestures, and body postures. Facial expressions (such as smiles, frowns, clenched teeth, or wrinkled brows) convey messages from approval to disapproval, from understanding to confusion. Gestures (such as nodding the head or shrugging the shoulders) can signal agreement, understanding, or indifference. Body postures assumed by superiors (bowing, slouching, or standing rigidly) can significantly affect subordinates' behavior. Even one's resting face while listening to others needs to be pleasant and not send a negative message. A timely smile, wink, or pat on the back by a sales manager can give salespeople positive feedback that is often more powerful than words.

Of the many forms of nonverbal communication, three of the most important to sales managers are communication by space, communication through dress, and communication with our bodies. For example, some customers may feel threatened if a salesperson is too close to them, violating their personal space during the sales presentation. Dress can affect perceptions that others have not only toward an individual and his or her message, but also toward the company the individual represents. To project a highly professional image, IBM (www.ibm.com) used to require its salespeople to wear conservative suits and white shirts, but it no longer required such conformity when many of its business customers began allowing their employees to dress more

TABLE 10.6

Ten Keys to Effective Listening

To listen effectively	The bad listener	The good listener
1. Find areas of interest.	Tunes out dry subjects.	Stays alert to opportunities. Asks, "What's in it for us both?"
2. Judge content, not delivery.	Tunes out if delivery is poor.	Judges content. Skips over delivery errors.
3. Hold your fire.	Tends to enter into arguments.	Doesn't make judgments until comprehension is complete. Interrupts only to clarify.
4. Listen for ideas.	Listens only for facts.	Listens for central themes.
5. Be flexible.	Takes intensive notes using only one system.	Takes fewer notes. Uses different listening approaches, depending on the speaker.
6. Work at listening and understanding.	Shows no energy output. Fakes attention.	Works hard. Exhibits positive body language.
7. Resist distractions.	Is distracted easily.	Fights or avoids distractions. Tolerates bad speaker habits. Knows how to concentrate.
8. Exercise your mind.	Resists difficult expository material. Seeks light, recreational material.	Uses heavier material as extra exercise for the mind.
9. Keep your mind open.	Reacts to emotional words.	Interprets the intended meaning of emotional words. Does not get hung up on them.
10. Capitalize on the fact that thought is faster than speech.	Tends to daydream with slow speakers.	Evaluates comments, mentally summarizes, weighs the evidence, before responding. Listens to changing tone of voice with different comments and observes body language.

Source: Adapted from Bovee, C.L. and Thill, J.V. (2008). *Business Communication Today*, 9th ed., 532. Upper Saddle River, NJ: Pearson Prentice-Hall.

Sales managers can use various techniques to communicate effectively with their salespeople.

informally. It's usually a good idea for salespeople to dress to fit the environment in which they're selling and the customers with whom they're interacting. Finally, the salesperson's ability to project confidence and professionalism by his or her posture and mannerisms and to be able to interpret the body language feedback of customers can significantly help the communication process. Learning to skillfully read and respond to the prospect's nonverbal communication will enable salespeople to make more flexible and effective sales presentations.

Sales managers can utilize the principles of nonverbal communication in two important ways. First, they can instruct the sales force on the proper handshake, eye contact, and attire to use during visits with prospects and customers. Second, sales managers can use their own confidence and the way they dress to boost their referent power among the sales force.

To find out how effective a communicator you are and to identify areas where you might improve your skills, take the communication "test" in Figure 10.7.

Breaking Down Communication Barriers

Perhaps the first step in enhancing communication is to identify the barriers that stand in the way. Let's look at organizational and individual barriers.

Use the scale, from 5 to 1, below to respond to the statements that follow. (In your answers, assume you're in face-to-face interaction with another individual. Be as objective as you can!)

Strongly Agree	Agree	Neither Agree nor Disagree	Disagree	Strongly Disagree
5	4	3	2	1

When I have face-to-face communication:

____ 1. I focus only on the other person.

____ 2. I try to maintain regular eye contact when the individual is talking.

____ 3. My nonverbal gestures communicate that I am listening carefully.

____ 4. I remain genuinely interested throughout the interaction.

____ 5. I ask for more details when I do not completely understand what the individual is saying.

____ 6. I paraphrase questions to make sure I understand before answering.

____ 7. I do not interrupt another who is speaking.

____ 8. I do not change the subject frequently when communicating.

____ 9. I never try to finish another speaker's sentences.

____ 10. I try hard to understand fully what the individual is saying verbally and nonverbally.

____ 11. I respond with useful statements rather than merely replying "yes" or "no."

____ 12. I offer relevant information in response to questions I'm asked.

____ 13. I show eagerness and enthusiasm in my responses.

____ 14. I answer questions at the appropriate time.

Assessing Your Communication Effectiveness

DIRECTIONS: It would be great if you scored a perfect 70, but very few people do. In fact, if your score *was* 70, it might be a good idea to let a friend objectively rate you on each question. Consider how you might improve on any questions where you rated less than 5.

FIGURE 10.7 Are you an effective communicator?
Source: Adapted from Ramsey, R.P. and Sohi, R.W. (1997). Listening to your customers: The impact of perceived salesperson listening behavior on relationship outcomes. *Journal of the Academy of Marketing Science* 25 (Spring): 127–137.

Organizational barriers. Communication problems are likely to occur between an employee and a supervisor because of the hierarchy of most organization structures. If the company objectives are not filtered down correctly to a salesperson, problems are sure to arise. Any barrier to communication from the sales manager may cause role perception problems for the salesperson and affect the salesperson's performance.

Individual barriers. Sales managers must be able to send clear and effective messages that the entire sales force can understand. Some individual barriers to communication that sales managers should readily recognize are conflicting assumptions, semantics, emotions, and communication skills.

Two individuals can hear the same message yet have *conflicting assumptions* about its meaning. For example, a client telephones a sales representative and asks her to ship an order "as soon as possible." The customer receives the order five days later and never orders from that salesperson again. To the client, "as soon as possible" meant "no later than tomorrow." To the salesperson, it meant a longer timeline so no special delivery request was sent to the shipping department!

Semantics, or the meaning of words, can cause communication failure. Most words have multiple meanings; some common words can have as many as 15–18. Communication barriers are sure to exist when two people attribute different meanings to the same words but don't know it.

All communication is influenced by *emotions.* When a person sends a message, feelings are attached to it; if the receiver of the message is unaware of or misinterprets those feelings, the intent of the message may be lost or misconstrued.

Finally, since *communication skills* vary greatly, some people are better communicators and thus often better leaders than others. Differences in communication skills are often due to education, training, or experience while others may be due to innate personality traits.

Overcoming communication barriers. Sales managers can overcome many barriers to communication if they acknowledge their existence and take the time necessary to work them out. Here are some useful strategies.

- *Regulate information flow.* Too much information can cause anyone to experience information overload. Establish a system that allows priority messages to receive immediate attention, and keep messages short; in fact, many communication experts recommend limiting messages to one page.
- *Provide and elicit feedback.* We've talked about the importance of *providing* feedback. Sales managers also need to *encourage* feedback from salespeople to ensure that they have understood the message. Respond promptly and respectfully to any nonroutine communications from the sales force to show your concern for their views and to encourage their early reporting of potential territorial problems or opportunities.
- *Use simple language.* Sales managers must use words *everyone* can understand. The larger the team you are addressing, the greater the chance of miscommunication. Avoid jargon or technical language and be sensitive to the diversity of your audience.
- *Practice effective listening.* Become familiar with the four types of listening and know when to apply them.
- *Keep emotions in check.* Emotions are in all communications, and they sometimes can distort the content of the message. A highly emotional sales manager can easily convey the wrong feeling in a message and create misunderstanding. Communicate when you are calm.
- *Give nonverbal cues.* Nonverbal cues help sales managers emphasize major points and express feelings. Make sure nonverbal codes reinforce your words so you don't send mixed messages.

- *Use the grapevine.* Don't be afraid to use the grapevine. It can help you send information rapidly without having to go through formal channels and it can be an excellent way to obtain feedback from the sales force. Make sure, however, that all information you convey is accurate and meaningful.

Chapter Summary

1. **Understand the dynamics of leadership.** In the drive for competitiveness, organizations are becoming flatter and leaner thereby requiring greater leadership skills at all organizational levels – not just in the executive suites because twenty-first century business and sales management practices are necessarily going to be significantly different from those in the past. Within the context of sales management, we can define leadership as the interpersonal process of communicating, inspiring, guiding, and influencing the behavior of subordinate salespeople toward the attainment of organizational objectives, goals, and values.

2. **Contrast supervision, management, and leadership.** Supervision, management, and leadership are related, but also quite different. Supervision entails performing tasks that deal with monitoring the daily work activities of subordinates. Management is primarily a *learned* process whereby subordinates are guided by formally prescribed duties toward the achievement of organizational goals. In contrast, leadership is more of an *emotional* process that involves the exercising of psychological, social, and inspirational influence on people.

3. **Identify the sources of power leaders possess.** Leaders may draw upon power from a variety of sources to enable them to accomplish their goals. These include *legitimate* power from formally delegated authority; *reward* power or the ability to provide subordinates with various benefits such as raises, praise, or promotion; *coercive* power which is the ability to punish or withhold rewards; *referent* power which is the leader's ability to inspire others, and *expert* power based on the leader's skills, knowledge, or special abilities.

4. **Apply the major classic theories of leadership to sales management.** Although there are a number of classical leadership theories, they can be broadly categorized into three approaches: (a) trait, (b) behavioral, and (c) contingency (situational). *Trait* theory contends that certain inherited traits such as honesty and drive determine successful leaders. *Behavioral* theory focuses on what the leader does and sees effective leadership as a result of two composite dimensions of leadership behavior or styles: consideration and initiating structure or task orientation. *Contingency* theory emphasizes the relationships among the sales manager, salespeople, and the sales situation. No one leadership style fits all situations and often sales managers must use more than one style to handle different members of the sales force. Moreover, effective leadership usually calls for flexibility to match changing sales situations. For example, effective leaders match their style with the maturity and duties of the sales force. One way of visualizing leadership styles is to diagram them as the parts of a four-speed automobile gearshift or the capital letter "H." The sales manager can *shift* leadership styles from *autocratic* to *laissez-faire* as the composition and responsibilities of the sales force change.

5. **Apply the major contemporary theories of leadership to sales management.** With dynamic changes in the global business environment, contemporary schools-of-leadership thought include (a) *transformational leadership*, (b) *Pygmalion leadership*, (c) *empowerment*, (d) *servant leadership*, and (e) *shared leadership*. Transactional leaders recognize the immediate needs of their employees and show them how their needs will be met by superior performance. Transactional leadership takes a short-term perspective to generate favorable results from the sales force. *Transformational* (or visionary and charismatic) leaders adopt a long-term orientation by focusing on future needs, and motivate salespeople to willingly do more despite obstacles or personal sacrifice. Sales managers encourage salespeople to surpass their own expectations and personal objectives for the good of the sales district and the company. Transformational sales managers gain extraordinary commitment from their salespeople through four key characteristics: *charismatic and visionary leadership, inspiration, intellectual stimulation, and individualized consideration.*

   Pygmalion leaders enhance the success of their salespeople by establishing high (but realistic) goals for their salespeople and communicating those aspirations to them with the expectation that sales performance will increase; that is, positive thinking begets positive results in that sales managers get what they expect – also known as the "Pygmalion effect".

   In flatter and leaner firms, there is a need for leaders at all levels. This has given rise to a forward thinking business philosophy known as *empowerment*, which can be defined as "recognizing and releasing into the organization the power that people already potentially have in their wealth of useful knowledge, experience, and internal motivation."

   Servant leadership first considers the needs and well-being of stakeholders (e.g., employees, customers, co-workers, and society) in all decision-making instead of the usual approach of focusing on profitability first.

   Shared leadership is in response to the increasing complexity and diversity of markets today which make it virtually impossible for any one person or even a small team to have the requisite knowledge and leadership skills to meet challenges and capitalize on dynamic market opportunities that may appear suddenly and disappear quickly. Shared leadership utilizes the ideas and abilities of members across the organization to make collaborative, informed decisions for the overall good of all.

6. **Communicate effectively with the sales force.** As an essential component of leadership, sales managers skillfully spend lots of time communicating in carrying out their sales management functions (setting objectives and goals, organizing, staffing, forecasting, supervising, compensating, motivating, evaluating, and controlling the sales force). *Communication* is a process whereby information is transferred and understood between two or more people. It's a two-way process involving listening as well as speaking, writing, and sending/reading body language for mutual understanding.

7. **Overcome barriers to communication.** Oftentimes, there are various communication barriers in a sales organization. Sales managers can overcome barriers to effective communication by providing feedback to subordinates, using straight-forward language, understanding nonverbal language, and by staying attuned to the organizational grapevine.

Key Terms

Leadership	**Contingency theory**	**Visionary leadership**	**Participative management**
Trait theory	**Path-goal theory**	**Empowerment**	**Mentoring**

Notes

1. Meindl, J.R., Ehrlich, S.B., and Dukerich, J.M. (1985). The romance of leadership. *Administrative Science Quarterly* 30 (March): 78–102; Pfeffer, J. (1977). The ambiguity of leadership. *Academy of Management Review* 2 (January): 104–112.

2. Martin, C.A. and Bush, A.J. (2006). Psychological climate, empowerment, leadership style, and customer-oriented selling: an analysis of the sales manager-salesperson dyad. *Journal of the Academy of Marketing Science*, 34 (Summer): 419–438; Hunter, M. (14 October 2014) 10 Reasons why leadership in sales is so important. https://thesaleshunter.com/10-reasons-why-leadership-in-sales-is-so-important/ (accessed 10 November 2019); Leimbach, M. Sales leadership: 2 key actions that increase sales performance. www.wilsonlearning.com/wlw/articles/s/lead-team-greatness (accessed 11 November 2019); Dubinsky, A.J., Yammarino, F.J., Jolson, M.A., and Spangler, W.D. (1995). Transformational leadership: an initial investigation in sales management. *Journal of Personal Selling and Sales Management* 15 (Spring): 17–31; Bass, B.M. and Avolio, B.J. (1994). *Improving organizational effectiveness through transformational leadership*. Thousand Oaks, California: SAGE; Bass, B.M. and Avolio, B.J. (1990). From transactional to transformational leadership: learning to share the vision. *Organizational Dynamics* 18 (Winter 1990): 19–31; Bass, B.M. (1985). Leadership: good, better, best. *Organizational Dynamics*, 13 (Winter): 26–40; Waldman, D.A., Bass, B.M., and Einstein, W.O. (1987). Leadership and outcomes of performance appraisal processes. *Journal of Occupational Psychology* 60 (September): 177–186; Edinger, S. (4 October 2012) Seven keys to sales leadership. www.forbes.com/sites/scottedinger/2012/10/04/seven-keys-to-sales-leadership/#434d32392cae (accessed 10 November 2019); Edinger, S. Sales (16 November 2018). Leadership is the key to executing strategy. www.forbes.com/sites/scottedinger/2018/11/16/salesleadership-is-the-key-to-executing-strategy/#2f9161d16957 (accessed 11 November 2019).

3. Sharma, A. and Grant, D. (2011). Narrative, drama, and charismatic leadership: the case of Apple's Steve Jobs. *Leadership* 7(1): 13–26; Henson, R. The leadership of Steve Jobs (11 November 2011). www.business.rutgers.edu/business-insights/leadership-steve-jobs (accessed 14 November 2019); Steve Jobs: The man who polished Apple. *The Sunday Times* (16 August):16.

4. Kouzes, J.M. and Posner, B.Z. (2003). *The Leadership Challenge*, 3rd ed. San Francisco, CA: Jossey-Bass Pfeiffer; Patel, S.(30 May 2019). Growing a company in a competitive or saturated market. https://sujanpatel.com/marketing/saturated-market/ (accessed 11 November 2019); White, J. (14 February 2019). Competitive advantage: definition, examples, and global impact. www.thestreet.com/personal-finance/education/what-is-competitive-advantage-14869235 (accessed 11 November 2019).

5. Bennis, W. and Townsend, R. (1995). *Reinventing Leadership*. William Morrow and Company, Inc.; Thacker, M. (8 August 2019). Six skills sales managers need to effectively lead a sales team. https://trainingindustry.com/articles/sales/6-skills-sales-managers-need-to-effectively-lead-a-sales-team/ (accessed 12 November 2019).

6. Yukl, G. (2006). *Leadership in Organizations*, 6th ed. Upper Saddle River, NJ: Pearson-Prentice-Hall; Bass, B.M. (1990). *Bass & Stogdill's Handbook of Leadership: Theory, Research, and Managerial Applications*, 3rd ed. New York: Free Press; House, R.J. and Baetz, M.L. (1979). Leadership: some empirical generalizations and new research generalizations. In: *Research in Organizational Behavior* (ed. L.L. Cummings, and B.M. Staw). Greenwich, CT: JAI Press; New study reveals top sales leadership challenges and priorities (12 June 2019). www.marketingdive.com/press-release/20190612-new-study-reveals-top-sales-leadership-challenges-and-priorities/ (accessed 13 November 2019).

7. Yukl, G. (2006). *Leadership in Organizations*, 6th ed. Upper Saddle River, NJ: Pearson Prentice-Hall.

8. Stoner, J.A.F., Freeman, R.E., and Gilbert, D.R., Jr. (1995). *Management*, 6th ed. Englewood Cliffs, NJ: Prentice-Hall; Hunter, M. (19 May 2017). What is sales leadership? https://thesaleshunter.com/what-is-sales-leadership/ (accessed 12 November 2019); Gschwandtner, G. (27 January 2015). What's the difference between sales leaders and sales managers? *Selling Power*. (18 February 2011). https://blog.sellingpower.com/gg/2015/01/whats-the-difference-between-sales-leaders-and-sales-managers.html (accessed 11 November 2019).

9. Robbins, S.P. and Coulter, M. (2006). *Management*, 6th ed. Upper Saddle River, NJ: Pearson Prentice-Hall; Colletti, J.A. and Fiss, M.S. (2006). The ultimately accountable job leading today's sales organization. *Harvard Business Review* (July–August): 125–131; Horne, K. (27 February 2019). What is leadership? We asked the greatest leaders in history. https://digital.com/blog/what-is-leadership/ (accessed 12 November 2019).

10. This definition is drawn from various sources, including: Dubrin, A.J. (1998). *Leadership: Research Findings, Practice and Skills*, 2nd ed. Boston, MA: Houghton-Mifflin; Yammarino, F.J., Dansereau, R., and Kennedy, C.J. (2001). A multiple-level multidimensional approach to leadership: viewing leadership

through an elephant's eye. *Organizational Dynamics* (Winter): 149–163: Hunter, M. (24 May 2016). What is sales leadership?: What is its impact with customers? www.salesforce.com/blog/category/sales-cloud.html (accessed 11 November 2019).

11. Ingram, T.N., LaForge, R.W., Avila, R.A., Schwepker, C.H., and Williams, M.R. (2006). *Sales Management: Analysis and Decision Making*, 4th ed. Mason, OH: Thomson South-Western; Ingram, T.N., LaForge, R.W., and Leigh, T.W. (2002). Selling in the new millennium: a joint agenda. *Industrial Marketing Management* 31(6): 559–567; Ingram, T.N., LaForge, R.W., Locander, W.B., et al. (2005). New directions in sales leadership research. *Journal of Personal Selling & Sales Management* (Spring): 137–154.

12. Colletti, J.A. and Fiss, M.S. (2006). The ultimately accountable job leading today's sales organization. *Harvard Business Review* (July–August): 125–131; Locander, W.B. and Luechauer, D.L. (2005). Are we there yet?" *Marketing Management* 14 (November–December): 50–52; Ledingham, D. Kovac, M., and Simon, H.L. (2006). The new science of sales force productivity. *Harvard Business Review*, (September): 124–133; Bursk, E.C. (2006). Low-pressure selling. *Harvard Business Review* (July–August): 150–162; Trailer, B. and Dickie, J. (2006). Understanding what your sales manager is up against. *Harvard Business Review* (July–August): 48–55.

13. Ingram, T. N., LaForge, R.W., Locander, W.B., Locander, W.B., MacKenzie, S.B., Podsakoff, P.M. (2005). New directions in sales leadership research. *Journal of Personal Selling & Sales Management* (Spring): 137–154; Edberg, H. (6 March 2019) 50 inspiring leadership quotes. www.positivityblog.com/quotes-on-leadership/ (accessed 11 November 2019).

14. Anderson, E. and Onyemah, V. (2006). How right should the customer be? *Harvard Business Review* (July–August): 59–67; Whitfield, J. (1985). Leadership, power, productivity and you! *Marketing Times* (September–October): 7–8; Rotenberg, Z. (9 May 2013). Sales management vs. sales leadership. http://www.insightssquared.com/blog/sales-leadership-vs-sales-management/ (accessed 13 November 2019).

15. Leadership power: the 7 types and how to use them. (3 October 2017 www.hrbartender.com/2017/leadership-and-management/leadership-power-types/ (accessed 11 November 2019); Manne, M. (3 March 2017). Four strategies every sales manager should be using in 2019. https://blog.hubspot.com/ sales/modern-sales-leader (accessed 12 November 2019); Re-invent sales for the 21st century. www2.deloitte.com/content/dam/Deloitte/uk/Documents/consultancy/deloitte-uk-reinvent-sales-pov-oct-2014.pdf (accessed 11 November 2019).

16. Newman, D. (3 October 2011). Power, influence, and leadership. https://fowmedia.com/power-influence-leadership/ (accessed 11 November 2019); Lunenburg, F.C. (2012). Power and leadership: an influence process. *International Journal of Management, Business, and Administration* 15(1): 1–9; Bass, B.M. (1990). *Bass & Stogdill's Handbook of Leadership: Theory, Research, and Managerial Applications*, 3rd ed. New York: Free Press; Yukl, G. (2006). *Leadership in Organizations*, 6th ed. Upper Saddle River, NJ: Pearson Prentice-Hall.

17. Hinkin T.R. and Scrieshiem, C.A. (1989). Development and application of new scales to measure the French and Raven (1959) Bases of Social Power. *Journal of Applied Psychology* (August): 561–567; Busch, P. (1980). The sales manager's bases of social power and influence upon the sales force. *Journal of Marketing* (Summer): 91–101; Busch P. and Wilson, D. (1976). An experimental analysis of a salesman's expert and referent bases of social power in the buyer-seller dyad. *Journal of Marketing Research* (February): 3–11. For other perspectives on sources of power, see: Rosenbloom, B. (2011). *Marketing Channels: A Management View*. Boston: Cengage; Coughlan, A.T., Anderson, E., Stern, L.W., and El-Ansary, A.I. (2006). *Marketing Channels*, 7th ed. Upper Saddle River, NJ: Pearson Prentice-Hall.

18. Thomson, A.H. (1980). *The Feldman Method: The Words and Working Philosophy of the World's Greatest Insurance Salesman*. Oakland, CA: Farnsworth Publishing Company; The selling legacy of Ben Feldman. (13 February 2016). prospectingprofessor.blogs.com/prospecting_professor/success_stories/index.html (accessed 4 September 2006).

19. Yukl G. and Tabor, T. (1983). The effective use of managerial power. *Personnel* (March–April): 37–44.

20. Kovach, M. (2016). The power dynamics that facilitate or inhibit organizational success. *Journal of Organizational Psychology* 16(2); 45–50; Ahearne, M., Mathieu, J., and Rapp, A. (2005). To empower or not to empower your sales force? An empirical examination of the influence of leadership and empowerment behavior on customer satisfaction and performance. *Journal of Applied Psychology* 90(5): 945–955; How to increase your expert power and become a better leader (11 June 2019). https://blog.toggl.com/increase-your-expert-power/ (accessed 11 November 2019).

21. Koch S.C. and Irle, K.W. (1920). Prophesying army promotion. *Journal of Applied Psychology* 4: 73–87; Stogdill, R.M. (1948). Personal factors associated with leadership: a survey of the literature. *Journal of Psychology* 25: 35–71; Stogdill, M.M. and Cooms A.W., eds. (1957). *Leader Behavior: Its Description and Measurement*, Research Monograph No. 88. Columbus, OH: Bureau of Business Research, Ohio State University; Cherry, K. (20 October 2019). The great man theory of leadership. www.verywellmind.com/the-great-man-theory-of-leadership-2795311 (accessed 12 November 2019).

22. Bass, B.M. (1990). *Bass & Stogdill's Handbook of Leadership: Theory, Research, and Managerial Applications*, 3rd ed. New York: Free Press; Cherry, K. (19 November 2019). Understanding the trait theory of leadership. www.verywellmind.com/what-is-the-trait-theory-of-leadership-2795322 (accessed 20 February 2020).

23. Gouldner, A.W. ed. (1950). *Studies in Leadership*, 23–24, 31–35. New York: Harper; McMahon, T.J. (2011). Leadership classics. *Strategic Direction*, 27(5); Avolio, B.J., Reichard, R.J., Hannah, S., Walumbwa, F.O., Chan, A. (2009). A meta-analytic review of leadership impact research: experimental and quasi experimental studies. *The Leadership Quarterly* 20: 764–784; Hoyt, C.L. and Murphy, S.E. (2016). Managing to clear the air: stereotype threat, women, and leadership. *The Leadership Quarterly (June)* 27(3): 387–399.

24. Adapted from Tagiuri, R. (1995). Managing. *Harvard Business Review* 73 (January–February): 10–11; Mango, E. (2018). Rethinking leadership theories. *Open Journal of Leadership (January)* 7(1): 57–88.

25. Stogdill, R.M. and Cooms, A.E., eds. (1957). *Leader Behavior: Its Description and Measurement, Research Monograph No. 88* (Columbus, OH: Bureau of Business Research, Ohio State University; O'Keefe, P. (29 December 2017). Leadership behaviors & skills that make leaders great. https://connect.edgetrainingsystems.com/blog/skills-and-behaviors-that-make-great-leaders-effective (accessed 12 November 2019).

26. Likert, R. (1979). From production-and employee centeredness to systems 1–4. *Journal of Management* 5: 147–156; Limsila, K. and Ogunlana, S.O. (2008). Performance and leadership outcome correlates of leadership styles and subordinate commitment. *Engineering Construction and Architectural Management* 15(2): 164–184.

27. Korman, A.K. (1966). Consideration, initiating structure, and organizational criteria—A Review. *Personnel Psychology* 19: 349–362; Roberts, K., Miles, R.E., and Blankenship, L.V. (2017). Organizational leadership satisfaction and productivity: A comparative analysis. *Academy of Management Journal* 11(4) (accessed 12 November 2019).

28. Kerr, S. et al. (1974). Towards a contingency theory of leadership based upon the consideration and initiating structure literature. *Organizational Behavior and Human Performance* 12: 62–82; Luenendonk, M. (27 January 2019). Leadership and the contingency theory (accessed 20 February 2020).

29. Fiedler, F.E. (1967). *A Theory of Leadership Effectiveness.* New York: McGraw-Hill; Robertson T. (25 January 2019). The advantages of Fiedler's contingency theory. https://bizfluent.com/info-10074476-advantages-fiedlers-contingency-theory.html (accessed 20 February 2020).

30. Fiedler, F.E. (1976). The leadership game: Matching the man to the situation. *Organizational Dynamics* (Winter): 6–16.

31. Fiedler, F.E. (1973). The trouble with leadership is that it doesn't train leaders. *Psychology Today*, (February): 23–30; Top leadership development challenges. www.sigmaassessmentsystems.com/leadership-development-challenges/ (accessed 10 November 2019); Oesch, T. (1 August 2018). Seven common leadership training challenges and their solutions. https://trainingindustry.com/articles/leadership/7-common-leadership-training-challenges-and-their-solutions/ (accessed 11 November 2019).

32. Behling, O. and Schriesheim, C. (1976). *Organizational Behavior: Theory, Research and Application.* Boston: Allyn and Bacon.

33. Evans, M.G. (1970). The effects of supervisory behavior on the path-goal relationship. *Organizational Behavior and Human Performance* 51 (May): 277–298; Path-goal leadership theory. www.nwlink.com/~donclark/leader/lead_path_goal.html (accessed 12 November 2019); House, R.J. (1971). A path goal theory of leader effectiveness. *Administrative Science Quarterly* 16 (September): 321–338; What is path-goal theory? https://pathgoal.com/path-goal-theory/ (accessed 12 November 2019); House, R.J. and Mitchell, T.R. (1974). A path-goal theory of leadership. *Journal of Contemporary Business* 3 (Autumn): 81–97.

34. House, R.J. (1971). A path goal theory of leader effectiveness. *Administrative Science Quarterly* 16 (September): 321–338; What is path-goal theory? https://pathgoal.com/path-goal-theory/ (accessed 12 November 2019).

35. House, R.J. (1971). A path goal theory of leader effectiveness. *Administrative Science Quarterly*, 16 (September): 321–338; House, R.J. and Mitchell, T.R. (1974). A path-goal theory of leadership. *Journal of Contemporary Business* 3 (Autumn): 81–97; Rosenbach, W.E., Taylor, R.L., and Youndt, M.A. (2018). *Contemporary issues in leadership*, 7th ed. New York: Routledge.

36. House, R.J. (1971). A path goal theory of leader effectiveness. *Administrative Science Quarterly* 16 (September): 321–338; House, R.J. and Mitchell, T.R. (1974). A path-goal theory of leadership. *Journal of Contemporary Business* 3 (Autumn): 81–97; House, R.J. and Dessler, G. (1974). The path-goal theory of leadership: some post hoc and a priori tests. In *Contingency Approaches to Leadership* (J. Hunt and L. Larson, eds.) Carbondale, IL: Southern Illinois University Press.

37. House, R.J. (1996). Path goal theory of leadership: lessons, legacy, and a reformulated theory. *Leadership Quarterly* 7 (Autumn): 323–352.

38. Cespedes, F.V., Gardner, A., Kerr, S., Kelley, R.D., Dixon, A.L. (2006). Old hand or new blood? *Harvard Business Review* (July–August): 28–40; Ingram, T.N., LaForge, R.W., Locander, W.B., MacKenzie, S.B., and Podsakoff, P.M. (2005). New directions in sales leadership research. *Journal of Personal Selling & Sales Management* (Spring): 137–154.

39. House, R.J. and Mitchell, T.R. (1974). A path-goal theory of leadership. *Journal of Contemporary Business* 3 (Autumn): 81–97.

40. Martin, C.A. and Bush, A.J. (2006). Psychological climate, empowerment, leadership style, and customer-oriented selling: an analysis of the sales manager-salesperson dyad. *Journal of the Academy of Marketing Science* 34(Summer): 419–438.

41. Lavinsky, D. (2 April 2013). Does your business have strategic partners? Why not? www.forbes.com/sites/davelavinsky/2013/04/02/does-your-business-have-strategic-partners-why-not/#3948f76f2731 (accessed 13 November 2019).

42. Stroh, T.F. (1974). *Effective Psychology for Sales Managers*, 59–70. West Nyack, NY: Parker Publishing); Landis, E.A., Hill, D., and Harvey, M.R. (2014). A synthesis of leadership of leadership theories and styles. *Journal of Management Policy and Practice* 15(2): 97–100; Khan, Z.A., Nawaz, A., and Khan, I. (2016). Leadership theories and styles: a literature review. *Journal of Resources Development and Management* 16: 1–7; Cherry K. (7 November 2019). The major leadership theories. www.verywellmind.com/leadership-theories-2795323 (accessed 12 November 2019).

43. Gumpert, R.A. and Hambleton, R.K. (1979). Situational leadership: how Xerox managers fine-tune managerial styles to employee maturity and task needs. *Management Review*

(December): 8–12; Cherry, K. (29 September 2019). The situational theory of leadership. www.verywellmind.com/what-is-the-situational-theory-of-leadership-2795321 (accessed 13 November 2019).

44. Castleberry, S.B. and Tanner, J.F. (1986). The manager–salesperson relationship: an exploratory examination of the vertical-dyad linkage model. *Journal of Personal Selling & Sales Management* 6 (November): 29–37; Babakus, E., Cravens, D.W., Grant, K., et al. (1996). Investigating the relationships among sales, management control, sales territory design, salesperson performance, and sales organization effectiveness. *International Journal of Research in Marketing* 13(4): 345–363.

45. DeCarlo T.E. and Leigh, T.W. (1996). Impact of salesperson attraction on sales managers' attributions and feedback. *Journal of Marketing* 60 (April): 47–66; Lipman, V.(16 January 2018). A common but overlooked management problem: playing favorites. www.forbes.com/sites/victorlipman/2018/01/16/a-common-but-overlooked-management-problem-playing-favorites/#33290e4435dd (accessed 12 November 2019).

46. Swift, C.O. and Campbell, C. (1995). The effect of vertical exchange relationships on the performance attributions and subsequent actions of sales managers. *Journal of Personal Selling & Sales Management* 15 (Fall): 45–56: Knight, R. (15 March 2017). How managers can avoid playing favorites. https://hbr.org/2017/03/how-managers-can-avoid-playing-favorites (accessed 12 November 2019).

47. Lagace, R.R. (1990). Leader–member exchange: antecedents and consequences of the cadre and hired hand. *Journal of Personal Selling and Sales Management* 10 (Winter): 11–19; Lunenburg, F.C. (2010). Leader–member exchange theory: another perspective on the leadership process. *International Journal of Management, Business, and Administration* 13(1): 1–5.

48. Flaherty, K.E. and Pappas, J.M. (2000). The role of trust in salesperson–sales manager relationships. *Journal of Personal Selling and Sales Management* 20(4)(Fall): 271–278; Tanner, J.F. and Castleberry, S.B. (1990). Vertical exchange quality and performance: studying the role of the sales manager. *Journal of Personal Selling and Sales Management* 10 (Spring): 17–27; Wolf, K.D. (23 February 2015). The right way to play favorites with your employees. www.inc.com/the-muse/the-right-way-to-play-favorites-with-employees.html (accessed 12 November 2019).

49. Van Breukelen, W., Schyns, B., and Le Blanc, P. (2006). Leader–member exchange theory and research: accomplishments and future challenges. *Leadership* 2(3): 295–316; Tanner, J.F., Dunn, M.G., and Chonko, L.B. (1993). Vertical exchange and salesperson stress. *Journal of Personal Selling and Sales Management* 13(Spring): 27–35; Shea, J. (10 August 2017). Are sales managers playing favorites? https://alignment-group.com/are-sales-managers-playing-favorites/ (accessed 12 November 2019).

50. Gerstner, C.R. and Day, D.V. (1997). Meta-analytic review of leader–member exchange theory: correlates and construct issues. *Journal of Applied Psychology* 82(6): 827–844; Manzoni, J.-F. and Barsoux, J.-L. (2007). *The Set-Up-To-Fail Syndrome*. Boston: Harvard Business School Press); Tanner, J.F. and Castleberry, S.B.

(1990). Vertical exchange quality and performance: studying the role of the sales manager. *Journal of Personal Selling and Sales Management* 10 (Spring): 17–27; Latoe, S. 12 Tips for dealing with a boss playing favorites. www.themuse.com/advice/12-different-strategies-for-dealing-with-a-boss-who-plays-favorites (accessed 12 November 2019).

51. Lopez, T. B. and McMillan-Capehart, A. (2002). How out-group salespeople fit in or fail to fit in: a proposed acculturation effects framework. *Journal of Personal Selling & Sales Management (Fall)* 22(4): 297–309; Backman, M. (3 July 2018). Your boss keeps playing favorites. Now what? www.fool.com/careers/2018/07/03/your-boss-keeps-playing-favorites-now-what.aspx (accessed 13 November 2019).

52. S. Kerr, S. and Jermier, J.M. (1978). Substitutes for leadership: their meaning and measurement. *Organizational Behavior and Human Performance* (December): 375–403; Avolic, B.J., Walumbwa, F.O., and Weber, T.J (2009). Leadership: current theories, research, and future directions. *Annual Review of Psychology* 60: 421–449.

53. Panagopoulos, N. and Oglivie, J. (2015). Can salespeople lead themselves? Thought self-leadership strategies and their influence on sales performance. *Industrial Marketing Management* 47 (May): 190–203; Mang, C.C. and Sims, H.P. Jr. (1987), Leading workers to lead themselves: The external leadership of self-managing work teams. *Administrative Science Quarterly* (March): 106–129.

54. Dubinsky, A.J., Yammarino, F.J., Jolson, M.A., and Spangler, W.D. (1995). Transformational leadership: An initial investigation in sales management. *Journal of Personal Selling and Sales Management* 15(2): 17–31; Bass, B.M. (1990). *Bass & Stogdill's Handbook of Leadership: Theory Research and Managerial Applications*. New York: The Free Press; Caille, B. (14 April 2018). 16 Advantages and disadvantages of transactional leadership. https://brandongaille.com/16-advantages-and-disadvantages-of-transactional-leadership/ (accessed 12 November 2019).

55. Skinner, S.J. and Kelley, W.W. (2006). Transforming sales organizations through appreciative inquiry. *Psychology & Marketing* 23(2): 77–93; Mehta, R. and Anderson, R. (1998). Global sales manager leadership styles: the influence of national culture, 362–367. In *Developments in Marketing Science: Proceedings of Academy of Marketing Science*; Abbott, T. Eight types of sales leadership styles. www.socoselling.com/8-types-of-sales-leadership-styles/ (accessed 12 November 2019).

56. Patil, A. and Shyam, N. (2018). How do specialized personal incentives enhance sales performance? The benefits of steady sales growth. *Journal of Marketing* 82(1): 57–73; Lopez, T.B., Hopkins, C.D., and Raymond, M.A. (2006). Reward preferences of salespeople: How do commissions rate? *Journal of Personal Selling & Sales Management* 26(4): 381–390; Griffin, M. *What are the best ways to reward salespeople? (8* August 2012). www.smartcompany.com.au/mentor/what-are-the-best-ways-to-reward-salespeople/ (accessed 12 November 2019).

57. Jones, E, Chonko, L., Rangarajan, D., and Roberts, J. (2007). The role of overload on job attitudes, turnover, intentions, and

salesperson performance. *Journal of Business Research* (July): 663–671; Dubinsky, A.J., Yammarino, F.J., Jolson, M.A., and Spangler, W.D. (1995). Transformational leadership: an initial investigation in sales management. *Journal of Personal Selling & Sales Management* (Spring): 17–31.

58. Jaramillo, F., Mulki, J.P., and Solomon, P. (2006). The role of ethical climate on salesperson's role stress, job attitudes, turnover intention, and job performance. *Journal of Personal Selling and Sales Management* 26(3)(Summer): 271–282; Russ, F.A., McNeilly, K.M., and Comer, J. (1996). Leadership, decision making and performance of sales managers. *Journal of Personal Selling & Sales Management* (Summer): 1–5; Higgins, K. (18 January 2018). Six simple metrics to accurately measure sales manager performance. https://trainingindustry.com/articles/measurement-and-analytics/6-simple-metrics-to-accurately-measure-sales-manager-performance/ (accessed 12 November 2019); What is transactional leadership: how structure leads to results. (8 May 2018). https://online.stu.edu/articles/education/what-is-transactional-leadership.aspx (accessed 12 November 2019).

59. Schwepker, C.H., Jr., and Good, D.J. (2010). Transformational leadership and its impact on sales force moral judgment. *Journal of Personal Selling & Sales Management* 30(4): 299–317; Bass, B.M. (1997). Personal selling and transactional/transformational leadership. *Journal of Personal Selling & Sales Management* 17(3): 19–28; Lee, C. (9 June 2014). How transformational leadership can boost sales. www.yesware.com/blog/transformational-leadership-can-boost-sales/ (accessed 11 November 2019).

60. Eisenbeiss, S.A., Van Knippenberg, D., and Boerner, S. (2008). Transformational leadership and team innovation: Integrating team climate principles. *Journal of Applied Psychology* 93(6) (November): 1438–1446; Russ, R.A., McNeilly, K.M., and Comer, J. (1996). Leadership, decision making and performance of sales managers. *Journal of Personal Selling & Sales Management* (Summer): 1–5; Behar, N. How to effectively set clear sales team expectations. www.salesreadinessgroup.com/blog/how-to-effectively-set-clear-sales-team-expectations (accessed 12 November 2019).

61. Gumusluoglu, L. and Ilsev, A. (2009). Transformational leadership, creativity, and organizational innovation. *Journal of Business Research* 62(4): 461–473; Bass, B.M. (1985). *Leadership and Performance Beyond Expectations*. New York: Free Press.

62. Babcock-Roberson, M.E. and Strickland, O.J. (2010). The relationship between charismatic leadership, work engagement, and organizational citizenship behaviors. *The Journal of Psychology* 144(3): 313, 326; Klein, J. and House, R.J. (1995). On fire: charismatic leadership and levels of analysis. *Leadership Quarterly* 6(2): 183–198.

63. Pauser, S., Wagner, U., and Ebster, C. (2018). An investigation of salespeople's nonverbal behaviors and their effect on charismatic appearance and favorable consumer responses. *Journal of Personal Selling and Sales Management* 38(3): 344–369; Williams, R., Jr., Raffo, D.M., and Clark, L.A. (2018). Charisma as an attribute of transformational leaders: what about

credibility? *Journal of Management Development* 37(6): 512–524; Friedman, W.A. (2006). Give me that old-time motivation. *Harvard Business Review* (July–August): 24.

64. Schwepker, C.H., Jr., and Good, D.J. (2010). Transformational leadership and its impact on sales force moral judgment. *Journal of Personal Selling & Sales Management* 30(4): 299–317; Dubinsky, A.J., Yammarino, F.J., Jolson, M.A., and Spangler, W.D. (1995). Transformational leadership: an initial investigation in sales management. *Journal of Personal Selling & Sales Management* (Spring): 17–31.

65. Robbins, S.P. and Coulter, M. (2006). *Management*, 6th ed. Upper Saddle River, NJ: Pearson Prentice-Hall; Parker, W.N. Visionary leadership. *SellingPower* (2 February 2010) www.sellingpower.com/2010/02/02/4679/visionary-leadership (accessed 12 November 2019).

66. Kinsey, A. (16 October 2018). What is visionary leadership? https://bizfluent.com/info-8721665-visionary-leadership.html (accessed 12 November 2019); Christensen, C.M., Marx, M., and Stevenson, H.W. (2006). The tools of cooperation and change. *Harvard Business Review* (October): 73–80.

67. Baldauf, A., Cravens, D.W., and Piercy, N.F. (2001). Examining business strategy, sales management, and salesperson antecedents of sales organization effectiveness. *Journal of Personal Selling & Sales Management* 21(2): 109–122; Conger, J.A. and Kanungo, R.N. (1998). *Charismatic Leadership in Organizations*, Thousand Oaks CA: Sage.

68. Dubinsky, A.J., Yammarino, F.J., Jolson, M.A., and Spangler, W.D. (1995). Transformational leadership: an initial investigation in sales management. *Journal of Personal Selling & Sales Management* (Spring): 17–31; Efti, S. How inside sales managers can be better at inspiring their sales teams. https://blog.close.com/inspire-your-team (accessed 11 November 2019).

69. Stavros, D. (1997). We kept reinventing the wheel. *What's Working in Sales Management* 5 (September): 5.

70. Marcil, B. (1997). We knocked on too many doors that would never open. *What's Working in Sales Management* 5(July):5; Why high-quality product content is critically important for sales (10 May 2016). www.manufacturing.net/e-commerce/article/13225250/why-highquality-product-content-is-critically-important-for-sales (accessed 12 November 2019).

71. Dubinsky, A.J., Yammarino, F.J., and Jolson, M.A. (1994). Closeness of supervision and salesperson work outcomes: an alternative perspective. *Journal of Business Research* 29 (March): 225–237; Yammarino, F.J., Dubinsky, A.J., Comer, L.B., and Jolson, M.A. (1997). Women and transformational and contingent reward leadership: a multiple-levels-of-analysis perspective. *Academy of Management Journal* 40(1): 205–222; Jaramillo, F., Grisaffe, D.B., Chonko, L.B., and Roberts, J.A. (2009). Examining the impact of servant leadership on salesperson' turnover intention. *Journal of Personal Selling & Sales Management* 29(4): 351-365.

72. Schwepker, C.H, Jr. and Good, D.J. (2010). Transformational leadership and its impact on sales force moral judgment. *Journal*

of Personal Selling & Sales Management 30(4): 299–317; Russ, F.A., McNeilly, K.M., and Comer, J. (1996). Leadership, decision making and performance of sales managers. *Journal of Personal Selling & Sales Management* (Summer): 1–5.

73. Whiteley, P., Sy, T., and Johnson, S.K. (2012). Leaders' conception of followers: implications for naturally occurring Pygmalion effects. *The Leadership Quarterly* 23(5): 822–834; Markin, R.J. and Lillis, C.M. (1975). Sales managers get what they expect. *Business Horizons* 18(June): 51–58.

74. Eden, D. (1992). Leadership and expectations: Pygmalion effects and other self-fulfilling prophecies in organizations. *Leadership Quarterly* 3(Winter): 271–305; Weaver, J., Moses, J.F., and Snyder, M. (2015). Self-fulfilling prophecies in ability settings. *The Journal of Social Psychology* 156(2): 179–189; Kierein, N.M. and Gold, M.A. (2000). Pygmalion in work organizations: a meta-analysis. *Journal of Organizational Behavior* 21(8): 913–928.

75. Business Psychology: Golem Effect vs. Pygmalion Effect (14 December 2017). https://www.brescia.edu/2017/12/golem-effect-vs-pygmalion-effect/ (accessed 20 February 2020). Eden, D. (1992). Leadership and expectations: Pygmalion effects and other self-fulfilling prophecies in organizations. *Leadership Quarterly* 3 (Winter): 294; Weaver, J., Moses, J.F., and Snyder, M. (2015). Self-fulfilling prophecies in ability settings. *The Journal of Social Psychology* 156(2): 179–189.

76. Uduji, J. I. (2013). Empowerment: an essential ingredient in modern sales force management. *Journal of Economics and Sustainable Development* 4(13): 62–72; Randolph, W.A. and Sashkin, M. (2002). Can organizational empowerment work in multinational settings? *Academy of Management Executive* (February):104; Seibert, S.E., Silver, S.R., and Randolph, W.A. (2004). Taking empowerment to the next level: a multiple level model of empowerment. *Academy of Management Journal* (June): 332–349; Mintzberg, H. (2004). Enough leadership. *Harvard Business Review*, (November): 22.

77. Yim, F.H.K., Swaminathan, S., and Anderson, R. (2015). Empowering salespeople: Does it work? In *Marketing Dynamism & Sustainability: Things Change, Things Stay the Same: Proceedings of the Academy of Marketing Science* (ed. L. Robinson, Jr.); Ford, R.C. and Fottler, M.D. (1995). Empowerment: a matter of degree. *Academy of Management Executive* 9(3): 21–31; Larsen, T., Rosenbloom, B., Anderson, R., and Mehta, R. (2000). Global sales manager leadership styles: the impact of national culture. *Journal of Global Marketing* 13(2): 31–48.

78. Sashkin, M. (1984). Participative management is an ethical imperative. *Organizational Dynamics* (Spring): 4–22; Jaramillo, F., Grisaffe, D.B., Chonko, L.B., and Roberts, J.A. (2015). Examining the impact of servant leadership on sales force performance. *Journal of Personal Selling & Sales Management* 35(2): 257–275.

79. Christensen, C.M., Marx, M., and Stevenson, H.H. (2006). The tools of cooperation and change. *Harvard Business Review* (October): 73–80; Attia, A.M., Honeycutt Jr., E.D., and Leach, M.P. (2005). A three-stage model for assessing and improving

sales force training and development. *Journal of Personal Selling & Sales Management* (Summer): 253–268; Leach, M.P., Liu, A.H., and Johnston, W.J. (2005). The role of self-regulation training in developing the motivation management capabilities of salespeople. *Journal of Personal Selling & Sales Management* (Summer): 269–281; Perry, M.L., Pearce C.L., and Sims, Jr. H.P. (1999). Empowered selling teams: how shared leadership can contribute to selling team outcomes. *Journal of Personal Selling & Sales Management* 19(3): 35–51.

80. Semler, R. (2000). How we went digital without a strategy. *Harvard Business Review* (September–October): 51–58; Briggs, E., Jaramillo F., Weeks, W.A. (2012). Perceived barriers to career advancement and organizational commitment in sales. *Journal of Business Research* 65(7): 937–943.

81. Brashear, T.G., Bellenger, D.N., Boles, J.S., and Barksdale Jr. H.C. (2006). An exploratory study of the relative effectiveness of different types of sales force mentors. *Journal of Personal Selling & Sales Management* (Winter): 7–18.

82. Ford, R.C. and Fottler, M.D. (1995). Empowerment: a matter of degree. *Academy of Management Executive* 9(3): 21–31; Boles, J.S., Johnston, M.W., and Hair, Jr., J.F. (1997). Role stress, work-family conflict and emotional exhaustion: inter-relationships and effects on some work-related consequences. *Journal of Personal Selling & Sales Management* 17(1): 17–28.

83. Bowen, D.E. and Lawler III, E.E. (1992). The Empowerment of Service Workers: What, Why, How, and When. *Sloan Management Review* (Spring): 31–39; Coy, R.W. and Belohav, J.A. (1995) An exploratory analysis of employee participation. *Group and Organizational Management* 20 (March): 4–17; Richards, K.A., Moncrief, W.C., and Marshall, G.W. (2010). Tracking and updating academic research in selling and sales management: a decade later. *Journal of Personal Selling & Sales Management* 30(3): 253–271.

84. Yang, S., Zhao, X., Shi, V., Liao, Y., and Zhu J. (2015). Joint determination of sales force compensation, production, and pricing decisions. *International Journal of Systems Science: Operations & Logistics* 2(3): 144–155; Podolske, A. (1998). Giving employees a voice in pay structures. *Business Ethics* (March–April): 12.

85. Dictionary of Marketing Terms: www.marketingpower.com; Vlachos, P.A., Theotokis, A., and Panagopoulos, N.G. (2010). Sales force reactions to corporate social responsibility: attributions, outcomes, and the mediating role of organizational trust. *Industrial Marketing Management* 39(7): 1207–1218.

86. Anderson, R.E. and Huang, R. (2006). Empowering salespeople: personal managerial and organizational perspectives. *Psychology and Marketing* 23 (February): 139–159; Kotler, P. and Armstrong, G. (2004). *Principles of Marketing*, 10th ed., 16. Upper Saddle River, NJ: Pearson Education International.

87. Ahearne, M., Mathieu, J., and Rapp, A. (2005). To empower or not to empower your sales force? An empirical examination of the influence of leadership and empowerment behavior on customer satisfaction and performance. *Journal of Applied Psychology* 90(5): 945–955: Martelli, L. (29 January 2016). Empowering

top salespeople to perform at their best – it's not all about the on-target earnings. www.salesforce.com/blog/2016/01/empow-ering-top-salespeople.html (accessed 13 November 2019).

88. Simons, R. (1995). Control in an age of empowerment. *Harvard Business Review* 73 (March–April): 80–88; Lee, A., Willis, S., and Tian, A.W. (2018). When empowering employees works, and when it doesn't. *Harvard Business Review* (March). https://hbr.org/2018/03/when-empowering-employees-works-and-when-it-doesnt (accessed 13 November 2019).

89. Sendjaya, S. and Sarros, J.C. (2002). Servant leadership: It's ori-gin, development, and application in organizations. *Journal of Leadership and Organization Studies*, 9(2) Fall: 57–64.

90. Dierendonck, D.V. (2011). Servant leadership: a review and syn-thesis. *Journal of Management* 37(4): 1228–1261.

91. Kashyap, V. and Rangnekar, S. (2016). Servant leadership, employer brand perception, trust in leaders and turnover inten-tions: a sequential mediation model. *Review of Managerial Science* 10(3): 437–461.

92. Parris, D.L. and Peachey, J.W. (2013). A systematic literature review of servant leadership theory in organizational contexts. *Journal of Business Ethics* 113(3): 377–393; Spector, P. (2014). Introduction: the problems and promise of contemporary leader-ship theories. *Journal of Organizational Behavior* 35(5): 597–746.

93. Carson, J.B., Tesluck, P.E., and Marrone, J.A. (2007). Shared leadership in team: an investigation of antecedent conditions and performance. *Academy of Management Journal* 50(5): 1217–1234.

94. Carson, J.B., Tesluk, P.D., and Marrone, J.A. (2007). Shared leadership in team: an investigation of antecedent conditions and performance. *Academy of Management Journal* 50(5): 1217–1234; Wang, D., Waldman, D.A., Zhang, Z. (2014). A meta-analysis of shared leadership and team effectiveness. *Journal of Applied Psychology* 99(2): 181–198; Pearce, C.L., Wassenaar, C.L., and Manz, C.C. (2014). Is shared leadership the key to responsible leadership? *Academy of Management Perspectives* 28(3): 275–288.

95. Kocolowski, M.D. (2010). Shared leadership: is it time for a change? *Emerging Leadership Journeys* 3(1): 22–32; Fitzsim-mons, D., Kames, K.T., and Denyer, D. (2011). Alternative approaches for studying shared and distributed leadership. *International Journal of Management Reviews* 13(3): 239–328; Pearce, C.L. (2004). The future of leadership: combining vertical and shared leadership to transform knowledge work. *Academy of Management Executive* 18 (a): 47–57; Boies, K., Lvina, E., and Martens, M.L. (2010). Shared leadership and team performance in a business strategy simulation. *Journal of Personnel Psychology* 9: 195–202; Goldsmith, M. (2010). Sharing leadership to maxi-mize talent. *Harvard Business Review*. https://hbr.org/2010/05/sharing-leadership-to-maximize (accessed 14 November 2019).

96. Quick, T.L. (1990). Curbstone coaching. *Sales & Marketing Management* (July): 100–101; Hackett, S. (11 December 2017). Coaching salespeople who don't want to be coached. https://brooksgroup.com/sales-training-blog/coaching-salespeople-who-don%E2%80%99t-want-be-coached (accessed 14 November 2019).

97. Jackson, Jr., D.W. (2006). Examining career development pro-grams for the sales force. *Journal of Business & Industrial Marketing* 21(5): 291–299; Phelps, T. (5 March 2019). A career in sales management. www.thebalancecareers.com/a-career-in-sales-management-2918242 (accessed 14 November 2019); Burke, C. (10 September 2015). Sales manager career paths. www.google.com/search?client=firefox-b-1-d&q=sales+management+career+path (accessed 14 November 2019).

98. Longenecker, C.O. and Neubert, M.J. (2005). The practices of effective managerial coaches. *Business Horizons* 48: 493–500; Brashear, T.G., Bellenger, D.N., Boles, J.S., and Barksdale Jr., H.C. (2006). An exploratory study of the relative effectiveness of different types of sales force mentors. *Journal of Personal Selling & Sales Management* (Winter): 7–18.

99. Updated and revised from Anderson, R.E. (1996). Personal selling and sales management in the new millennium. *Journal of Personal Selling & Sales Management* 4 (Fall): 17–32; Lassk, F.G., Ingram, T.N., Kraus, F., and Mascio, R.D. (2012). The future of sales training: challenges and related research ques-tions. *Journal of Personal Selling & Sales Management* 32(1): 141–154.

100. Kindane, M. Why increasing the diversity of your sales team improves your bottom line. www.nutshell.com/blog/increasing-sales-team-diversity/ (accessed 14 November 2019).

101. Marketing & Sales Managers. www.google.com/search?client=firefox-b-1-d&q=what+percent+of+sales+manages+are+min orities (accessed 14 November 2019).

102. Wood, J.A., Johnson, J., Boles, J.S., and Barksdale, H. (2014). Investigating sales approaches and gender in customer relation-ships. *Journal of Business & Industrial Marketing* 29(1): 11–23; Comer, L.B., Jolson, M.A., Dubinsky, A.J., and Yammarino, F.J. (1995). When the sales manager is a woman: an exploration in the relationship between salespeople's gender and their responses to leadership styles. *Journal of Personal Selling & Sales Manage-ment* (Fall): 17–32; Mandelbaum, A. Trends of women in sales. www.badgermapping.com/blog/women-in-sales/ (accessed 12 November 2019).

103. Mandelbaum, A. Trends of women in sales. www.badgermap-ping.com/blog/women-in-sales/ (accessed 13 November 2019); Burdett, E. (28 September 2015). The state of women in sales. www.peaksalesrecruiting.com/blog/the-state-of-women-in-sales/ (accessed 14 November 2019); Kirell, S. (25 October 2018). The power of women in sales: how to succeed in a male-dominated field. www.conductor.com/blog/2018/10/the-power-of-woman-in-sales/ (accessed 14 November 2019); Dubinsky, A.J., Comer, L.B., Jolson, M.A., and Yammarino, F.J. (1996). How should women sales managers lead their sales personnel? *Journal of Business & Industrial Marketing* 11(2): 47–59; Phelps, T. (26 November 2019). Learning from women in sales. www.thebal-ancecareers.com/ms-sales-professional-2918372 (accessed 20 February 2020).

104. Comer, L.B., Jolson, M.A., Dubinsky, A.J., and Yammarino, F.J. (1995). When the sales manager is a woman: an exploration in the relationship between salespeople's gender and their responses to leadership styles. *Journal of Personal Selling & Sales Management* (Fall): 17–32; Top 35 influential women in sales (30 October 2018). www.saleshacker.com/influential-women-in-sales/ (accessed 14 November 2019): Disney, D. (8 March 2019). The leading women in sales 2019. www.linkedin.com/pulse/leading-women-sales-2019-daniel-disney (accessed 14 November 2019).

105. Schreier-Fleming, M. Why aren't there more women in sales (and what to do about it). www.allbusiness.com/why-arent-there-more-women-in-sales-113047-1.html (accessed 14 November 2019); Dickstein, M. (15 May 2018). Women in sales leadership: how to help close the gender gap. www.spencerstuart.com/leadership-matters/2018/may/women-in-sales-leadership-how-to-help-close-the-gender-gap (accessed 14 November 2019); Mandelbaum, A. Trends of women in sales. www.google.com/search?client=firefox-b-1-d&q=women+in+sales+by+ava+mandelbaum (14 November 2019); Voria, R. Why we need more women in sales. www.forbes.com/sites/forbesbusinessdevelopmentcouncil/2018/01/17/why-we-need-more-women-in-sales/#17d9109d30ce (accessed 14 November 2019); Marshall, D. (8 March 2018). Six amazing women who are rocking it in sales. https://performio.co/insight/six-amazing-women-rocking-sales/ (accessed 14 November 2019).

106. Bovee, C.L. and Thill, J.V. (2008). *Business Communication Today*, 9th ed. Upper Saddle River, NJ: Pearson Prentice-Hall;

Why better communication skills lead to more sales success (6 June 2018). www.sandler.com/blog/why-better-communication-skills-lead-more-sales-success/ (accessed 14 November 2019); Wade, E. Boosting sales productivity with better communication: what you need to know. www.vonage.com/business/perspectives/boosting-sales-productivity-with-better-communication-what-you-need-know/ (accessed 14 November 2019).

107. Jones, E., Brown, S.P., Zoltners, A.A., and Weitz, B.A. (2005). The changing environment of selling and sales management. *Journal of Personal Selling & Sales Management* 25(2): 105–111; Albers, S., Raman, K., and Lee, N. (2015). Trends in optimization models of sales force management. *Journal of Personal Selling & Sales Management* 35(4): 275–291.

108. Pryor, S., Malshe, A., and Paradise, K. (2013). Salesperson listening in the extended sales relationship: an exploration of cognitive, affective, and temporal dimensions. *Journal of Personal Selling & Sales Management* 33(2): 185–196; The sales manager's guide to teaching active listening to salespeople (23 February 2016). https://salesdrive.info/guide-to-active-listening/ (accessed 14 November 2019).

109. Lassk, F.G., Ingram, T.N., Kraus, F., and Mascio, R.D. (2012). The future of sales training: challenges and related research questions. *Journal of Personal Selling & Sales Management* 32(1): 141–154.

110. Peterson, R.T. (2005). An examination of the relative effective of training in nonverbal communications: personal selling implications. *Journal of Marketing Education* 27(2): 143–150.

Chapter Review Questions

1. Is there a distinction between supervision, management, and leadership within the context of the sales department? Explain your perspective in detail. [LO 2]

2. Identify and explain the sources of power that leaders draw upon in exercising influence over their subordinates. [LO 3]

3. Define the concept of leadership. Describe what leaders do, then identify the traits of effective leaders? [LO 4]

4. Describe your understanding of the behavioral styles theory of leadership. What guidelines does it offer to sales managers? [LO 4]

5. Explain Fiedler's contingency model of leadership. What are the implications of this model for sales managers in influencing the behavior of salespeople? [LO 4]

6. Describe your understanding of the path-goal theory of leadership. What guidelines does it offer to sales

managers for influencing the behavior of salespeople? [LO 4]

7. Describe the leader–member exchange paradigm. Discuss its implications for sales managers seeking to influence the behavior of salespeople? [LO 4]

8. Identify and discuss the reasons why empowerment has become an important progressive management concept. What are the precepts of empowerment and the role of participative management? [LO 5]

9. Is the contemporary philosophy of empowerment similar to or different from the concept of traditional power being used by managers to influence subordinates? Explain your position in detail. [LO 5]

10. Describe servant leadership, then shared leadership. What are the similarities and differences between these two types of leadership and others like empowerment? What has caused the rise of these types of leadership

versus continuing to rely solely on traditional hierarchical leadership. [LO 5]

11. Which theory of leadership do you think is most sound? Discuss which theories you might apply during your career in sales management? [LO 5]

12. Define communication and suggest how sales managers might improve their own communication skills? [LO 6]

13. Think of some interactions you have had with people today. What kind of nonverbal communication took place? Were you conscious of your own nonverbal communication? [LO 7]

14. What are the common causes of communication barriers? How can a sales manager overcome these barriers? [LO 7]

Online Exercise

1. Use the Internet to find articles on contemporary leadership approaches being used by sales managers at two different organizations. How can you ascertain whether these leadership approaches are effective?

In-Basket Exercise

Recently hired as sales manager for a large industrial products firm, you have just received your first memo from the national sales manager. It addresses a very serious issue that's facing not only your company but your overall industry – "salesperson burnout." Your company's national sales manager believes that many of the salespeople in the company have plateaued and are no longer improving. He has requested your input regarding this issue at next week's regional sales meeting.

Discussion Questions

1. What are you going to recommend at the upcoming meeting?

2. Is there such a thing as a "plateaued" or "burned-out" salesperson?

3. What specific things can sales managers do as leaders to revitalize their salespeople?

Role-Play Exercise

Situation

You are the national sales manager for a large financial-services firm, and one of your regional sales managers has asked you for some advice. She is anticipating problems in one of her districts primarily because of the leadership style of one of her district sales managers. He is a highly successful sales veteran who believes in gaining compliance from his salespeople through fear and punishment. He makes it very clear to his salespeople that if they don't perform up to his standards, they *will not* receive bonuses and might even be fired. He firmly believes every salesperson can be replaced and salesperson turnover in his district is higher than in other district. Nevertheless, his sales district is one of the most profitable in the company. However, recently, she has heard rumors that some of the salespeople in his district have started deliberately ignoring his communications to them, and are making negative comments and spreading rumors about him to customers and other salespeople. None of the salespeople in his district have complained directly to her yet. But, nevertheless, she's worried that the salespeople in his district are becoming so turned off by his management style that some major sales force and customer problems may erupt soon and hurt the company's sales and reputation.

Role-Play Participants and Assignments

National Sales Manager – must give her regional sales manager advice on how to handle the situation.

Regional Sales Manager – feels the district sales manager's salespeople are nearing the point of open rebellion and that their behavior may harm the company's reputation with customers. Before discussing the situation further with the national sales manager, she needs to gather more facts and perspectives by first talking to the district sales manager then his salespeople.

District Sales Manager – not fully aware and maybe not even particularly concerned that his salespeople are becoming totally turned off by his management-leadership style.

School Suppliers, Inc. (SSI) is a national distributor of elementary and secondary school supplies. The company has fifty salespeople located in eight regional offices throughout the United States. The salespeople call on purchasing agents or principals at elementary and secondary schools in their assigned regions. Over the past decade, the Southeastern region has been one of the company's fastest-growing regions. Primarily because of the increasing population in Florida, SSI's Southeastern region has led the company in sales and is projected to be the strongest region for the next several years.

Howard Larsen, one of SSI's top sales reps over the past several years, was recently promoted to sales manager of the premier Southeastern region. Howard, age twenty-eight, was at first very pleased and excited to be managing one of the most promising regions within the company. After only four months as the sales manager of this region, however, he began to question his ability as a sales manager. Howard believes that he is having problems managing his salespeople.

Howard recently met with his close friend, John—who manages a large resort in the Orlando area—to discuss his problems with the sales force. He gave John a brief rundown of the situation: "Well, my problem concerns the way I'm leading my salespeople. Things seem to be going fine with five of my seven salespeople. Melissa and Jeff, who I just hired six months ago, are going great. They are both young and eager to learn. Both have been progressing well, with slight increases in sales volume over the last two months. They both have very little sales experience, so they do make a few mistakes now and then. However, both will take constructive criticism very well, as they continually want to improve their selling skills. Melissa and Jeff are both about my age. Therefore, they relate to me very well. I have no problems with my two new salespeople.

"Rhonda is perhaps one of my best salespeople. Everyone enjoys being around her. Rhonda can give the other reps a lift when they're down. Her own sales performance is exceptional. Rhonda regularly surpasses her quotas and actively seeks out new customers. Rhonda accepts my leadership as if I were the VP of marketing. I wish all my salespeople were like Rhonda.

"Robert is also a fun salesperson to manage. He's been out of college for only about two years. He's young and wants to do well in the company. Robert reminds me a lot of myself when I first started with SSI. He is very competitive and readily accepts my constructive feedback since he constantly wants to improve. I made a few sales calls with him last week, and he must have asked over twenty questions after each call about how best to handle selling activities.

He sort of looks on me as a big brother, and that makes him very easy to manage. To be honest with you, Robert is good for my ego.

"George is about my age, and if he has a problem, it's that he likes to goof off too much. George is good at bringing life and laughter into the job. He is well liked by everyone. However, he spends too much time bull-shooting with virtually everyone he encounters during the work day! Every so often I have to get after him to manage his time better. When I do, George picks up his pace and usually reaches his annual sales quota. George's lapses keep me on his case but I don't think he really minds being supervised. Actually, I think he realizes that a little bit of leadership now and then will help his sales performance."

"It sounds like things are going pretty well for you, Howard," John observed. "Five of your seven salespeople seem to be doing fine. Is it the other two salespeople who are causing you all that grief? I can't wait to hear about these two!

"Well, Fred is probably my biggest problem. He's a veteran salesperson who has been with the company for over thirty years. Fred started out by selling the liberal arts textbooks. In fact, he has been the top salesperson in the company several times in past years. However, since he's been working for me, his performance has fallen off sharply. His performance is not quite bad enough for me to recommend that he be fired. However, if it gets any worse, I'm going to have to do something.

"The biggest problem with Fred is that he doesn't listen to me. He is very hardheaded and seemingly feels insulted every time I tell him to do something. For example, the other day I told him that he wasn't spending enough time with some of his best customers. He angrily fired back that he was selling textbooks before I was born and that he has forgotten more about 'real world' selling than I've learned from textbooks.

"Recently, I've been going out of my way to work with Fred. I've asked him to go on recruiting trips with me, and I've tried to help make his job easier by offering to train him to do several sales related tasks on a laptop computer. In both instances, he rejected me by making up some feeble excuse. He refuses to listen to me, no matter how hard I try to win him over.

"Fred also shows me very little respect. He will sometimes address me as 'college boy' in sales meetings. Last week, he called me by that name in front of one of our largest accounts. I don't know how much more I can take from him.

"Warren is my other problem. Warren is about forty-eight years old and has been with the company for about ten years. He is a hard worker and normally reaches his sales quota. I think he resents me for having this managerial job at such a young age. It may sound paranoid, but I have the feeling that he wants my job and will do whatever he can to get it. Warren is very competitive and seems to be trying to undercut me and show people that he can do a better job managing the sales force than I can. Given his attitude, I have a difficult time being a leader to Warren because he's not a good follower.

"The way I look at it, I'm a fairly effective sales manager because five of my seven salespeople accept my leadership and are doing well. However, it really disturbs me that I can't do a better job with Fred and Warren. These two guys have the potential of being top salespeople. If they would change their attitudes and significantly improve their sales volume, I could have the best sales district in the company. I just don't know what to do to be a more effective leader to these guys!"

"I personally feel that you have nothing to worry about," said John. "You definitely have the ability to manage this sales force, or your company would never have promoted you. Howard, you need to build up your self-confidence so that these old guys don't bother you. Don't be afraid to boss them around. Remember, your company's future is with the younger and currently more successful people. I didn't become manager of a resort hotel by being afraid to boss people around."

Questions

1. Comment on Howard's leadership style. What kind of leader is he?

2. Do you agree with John's advice? Why or why not? Is John's leadership style different from Howard's? If so, how?

3. Should Howard take John's advice? Why or why not?

4. Should Howard change his leadership style in an attempt to be a more effective leader to Fred? To Warren? Why or why not?

5. Would a transactional or transformational leadership style help Howard? Please explain.

Case prepared by: Scott Widmier, Kennesaw State University

> **CASE 10.2** | ## Öhlins Chemicals: Resolving Communication Problems

Ulrik Johansson has been a junior salesperson for three years at Öhlins Chemicals, a Swedish-owned distributor of industrial chemicals and solvents, selling to markets in the European Union (EU) and the United States. Ulrik's sales position involved industrial sales (i.e. business-to-business) with no sales of consumer goods (i.e. one-to-many). All sales were professionally conducted in teams and developing long-term business relationships was important. In addition, Öhlins Chemicals had developed a very favorable reputation for its high quality industrial products and excellent customer service.

Öhlins Chemicals' reputation was very much dependent on effective management of relationships. Ulrik realized that selling industrial products requires excellent interpersonal skills because salespeople deal with a small number of customers, and upper management is often involved in making purchase decisions. Also, since the company had relatively few but important customers, the salespeople often need to be flexible in solving specific customer issues as well as personal needs – something that Ulrik learned and took advantage of early. Ulrik also realized that overly standardized procedures

in sales hampered his performance. He often looked for ways to improve sales on the basis of customer requirements, for example, through liberal use of the expense account for taking customers to lunches, dinners, and entertainment. While on several occasions he was asked by the accountants to explain big expenses, he was also rewarded for extraordinarily successful selling and contribution to the growth of the company.

The company recently decided to broaden its product mix and enter the textiles market, first in the United States and if successful move on to similar markets in Europe. The primary objective was selling to new customers and convincing past customers to purchase more. Twenty-four geographic sales areas were set up to sell the new line of textile products, and two salespeople were hired for each area. Ulrik Johansson, with his great experience from industrial sales, was one of them. The line of textile products included specialty woven, knitted, and braided fabrics for aerospace, marine, industrial, recreational, and medical applications. The textile products have characteristics similar to industrial chemicals, and a similar selling approach is often effective.

The company's strategic sales force management team suggested standardized routines to treat all customers in a similar way. Ulrik was not pleased with this approach, and argued that he and his team needed a less standardized approach and more flexibility for creative and individualized sales approaches. But the strategic sales management team responded that training is more difficult if standardized routines could not be utilized. Ulrik again requested that the strategic sales force management team allow the Öhlins textile sales force to use different sales approaches from the industrial chemicals sales force. He claimed that the most critical point in industrial sales is to leverage every relationship so it sustains and increases in sales volume, and this can only be achieved through committed, frequent, and long-term relationships. Finally, he argued flexibility and room for operational differences is a necessity.

About the same time, Öhlins hired a national sales manager for the textile division and its 48 salespeople. She reported directly to the executive vice president and was highly committed to the company's strategic objectives. Although this was Ulrik's formal supervisor, he also reported on a day-to-day basis to Joan Fleming, the district manager at his office. In contrast to the new national sales manager, his interaction with Joan was often very informal. Swedish work-culture includes "fika," which means gathering for a coffee and chat during workhours, and "after work" drinks out of the office. This was consistent with Ulrik's preferred type of interaction, both within the company and with customers. It also supported the flexibility to deviate from fixed routines, with room for improvisation and humor, and for bringing out the best in Ulrik's people skills.

Öhlin's senior management was eager to promote its new Wearever textiles product line. All the products in the line were made by suppliers but sold under their own brand names. Öhlins senior management was so eager to push the Wearever products to the market that they overlooked a number of serious problems, which were obvious to Ulrik with his insights at the operational level. The Wearever products sold well at first, but then distribution and warehousing problems caused delays in shipping orders. When customers did not receive orders on time they became very upset with Öhlins. At the same time, Öhlins was very inflexible in their pricing strategy while competitors were giving discounts for volume purchases, early payment, and other terms of sale. Ulrik's customers could not understand why Öhlins would not offer similar terms and as a result he began losing customers. Moreover, the CRM system Öhlins used to support sales force activities was outdated, and Ulrik frequently had to respond to customer inquiries or plan sales calls without having important account information. Ulrik sensed that Öhlins had become less flexible and more formal while pursuing new market segments too quickly.

Ulrik was a perceptive and committed salesperson. He visited with Öhlin's management on several occasions and shared his observations about emerging problems. He also talked with other salespeople and learned they were having similar experiences. After encouraging management to recognize and deal with the problems for almost a year without getting anywhere, Ulrik had had enough. He had been approached by another firm about a sales position and decided to leave Öhlins.

Questions

1. Explain the differences in industrial sales (i.e. business-to-business) vs consumer goods (i.e. one-to-many).

2. What are the different issues strategic sales managers see (i.e. standards and routines) and the issues operational sales person experience and how could these differences be solved?

3. How would you rate the leadership and communications skills of Öhlins management? Explain your rating.

4. What suggestions do you have for improving the leadership and communications activities of Öhlins sales managers?

5. What do you think Öhlins management could have done to keep Ulrik from leaving, even if all of his suggestions could not be implemented?

Case prepared by: Ossi Pesämaa, Luleå University of Technology, Sweden, and Peter Dahlin, Mälardalen University, Sweden

CHAPTER 11

Sales Force Motivation

In an era of rapid globalization, companies from all over the world are increasingly competing for survival or vying for a bigger piece of the pie. Some firms are waging virtual economic war versus competitors in the fight for customers,[1] and even urging their salespeople to use guerilla marketing tactics in selling.[2] It's clear that salespeople have one of the most critical, eclectic, and demanding jobs in business as they play a major role in determining whether or not their companies thrive in today's intensely competitive marketplace.

It's up to sales managers to make sure salespeople perform their jobs well.[3] This chapter provides a foundation for understanding sales force motivation. We'll not only review the major theories behind motivation, but we'll also show how to apply them to enhance sales force performance.

Foundations of Motivation

The concept of motivation has been the subject of intensive study.[4] Motivation has been defined as the set of processes both within and outside an individual that spurs the initiation, direction, intensity, and persistence of work related behaviors.[5] In the context of sales management, we define motivation as the set of dynamic interpersonal processes that cause the initiation, direction, intensity, and persistence of work-related behaviors of subordinate salespeople toward the attainment of organizational goals and objectives.

There are three important elements in our definition: First, *direction* means choosing the activities on which the individual will focus the effort (will the salesperson spend most of the time calling on prospects or on existing accounts?). Second, *intensity* refers to the amount of physical and mental effort expended on a given activity (how many sales calls will a salesperson make per day, and how much time will be allocated to other selling tasks?). Third, *persistence* refers to the duration for which an individual will exert the effort (will the salesperson make sales calls for eight hours straight?). Salespeople with a high degree of intensity and persistence will spend time and effort on those job duties that will bring them the greatest chance of achieving personal and organizational goals.

LEARNING OBJECTIVES

When you finish this chapter, you should be able to:

1. Understand the nature of motivation.
2. Apply contemporary theories of motivation to sales management.
3. Use reward and incentive programs to motivate salespeople.
4. See how sales contests and sales meetings can motivate salespeople and learn basic guidelines for coordinating them.
5. Apply organizational commitment, career stage, and empowerment to motivating salespeople.

Applying Contemporary Motivation Theories to Sales Force Management

We'll look at several theories of motivation that are especially relevant to sales force management, each offering intuitively appealing, but slightly different, explanations for why salespeople exert high levels of effort to reach certain goals.[6] The three categories of motivational frameworks are: (a) *content*, (b) *process*, and (c) *reinforcement oriented* theories. Depending on the situation and the composition of the sales force, sales managers will need to exercise their own individual judgments in deciding which motivation theory applies best.

Content Theories of Motivation

Content theories provide insights into employees' needs for rewards and recognition. They attempt to explain "why" human needs change. Understanding these theories can help sales managers design compensation plans and rewards that motivate by meeting the needs of salespeople.

Hierarchy of Needs Theory Maslow's well-known hierarchy of needs theory contends that people are motivated by a "hierarchy" of psychological growth needs.[7] In our sales context, it implies that salespeople come to their jobs already motivated and need only the opportunity to respond to the challenges of higher-order needs. Table 11.1 presents the priority of needs individuals seek to fulfill (beginning at the bottom) and that sales managers must consider. Remember that the stronger a given need, the greater its importance and strength. And second, the gratification of needs at one level in the hierarchy activates needs at the next-higher level.

Sales managers should use close personal contact to keep track of the level of needs most important to each salesperson, from the beginning trainee to the senior sales

---

TABLE 11.1

Hierarchy of Needs and Their Implications for Sales Force Management

Maslow's hierarchical levels	Salesperson's needs	Sales manager's task
Self-actualization needs	• Self-development • Creativity • Self-fulfillment	• Provide greater job control, freedom, self-development workshops • Provide greater job responsibilities, promotion opportunities
Esteem needs	• Recognition • Status	• Public recognition for achievement
Social needs	• Social interaction and friendship • Acceptance among peers and superiors	• Maintain close relationships with sales force • Sales meetings, newsletters, email, etc.
Safety needs	• Freedom from worry about security of jobs, incomes, medical expenses, etc.	• Provide a balanced package and fringe benefits
Physiological needs	• Food, shelter, overall health, basic human needs	• Be aware of general health and living conditions of sales force

representative. To avoid stagnating at any one level, salespeople must be given opportunities to activate and satisfy higher-level needs so they can be successfully motivated toward superior performances.

Existence, Relatedness, and Growth (ERG) Theory Only three need categories are posited by ERG theory, as follows: *existence* (Maslow's physiological and safety needs), *relatedness* (social and esteem needs), and *growth* (self-actualization needs).[8] Like the need hierarchy theory, ERG proposes that individuals will focus on higher-level needs as lower-level ones are satisfied; unlike need hierarchy theory, though, it suggests that people can move up and down the three-part hierarchy.

Sales managers can study each salesperson's location on the hierarchy and customize incentives to help fulfill individual unmet needs. This explicit positioning (preferably in writing) will help reveal which salespeople need guidance with personal problems, which could benefit from a pat on the back or a shoulder to lean on, which need more training, which can absorb greater responsibilities, and which might improve their productivity under a modified compensation or rewards plan.

Needs Theory Developed by David McClelland, needs theory says that employees develop certain needs over their lifetime based on life experiences.[9] Specifically:

1. *The need for power* reflects the need to control, influence, and have authority in their work and over others. Sales managers must recognize that many successful salespeople want greater control over their jobs and more influence on sales force decisions, so their input should be sought before important decisions are made.

2. *The need for achievement* is the strong urge to master and accomplish difficult tasks. Achievement-oriented people readily accept individual responsibility, seek challenging tasks, and are willing to take risks doing tasks they may serve as stepping-stones to future rewards. These individuals receive more satisfaction from accomplishing goals and more frustration from failure or unfinished tasks than the average person. Any achievement-related step on the "success path" may include rewards (positive incentives) or threats (negative incentives).[10]

   Sales managers should identify achievement-motivated salespeople and then give them personal responsibility for solving designated problems or achieving certain goals. Frequent, specific feedback is also essential so that these salespeople can know whether they are performing well or not. Managers may have to temper negative feedback because achievement-motivated people may quit if they feel they will be unsuccessful. Finally, competition among such salespeople can be intense and even damaging to the organization unless carefully monitored and controlled.

3. *The need for affiliation* is the desire to establish friendships, to have close working relationships with peers as well as customers, and to avoid conflict. Affiliative types like to work in groups and want to be accepted by others.[11] They are less self-centered, usually help bind the group together, and are less able to tolerate traveling jobs involving long periods of solitude.

In sum, although most salespeople have general needs for achievement, affiliation, and power, sales managers should learn the dominant needs of individual salespeople in order to devise specific strategies for motivating them.

Dual Factor Theory Also referred to as motivation-hygiene theory, the dual factor theory was formulated by Frederick Herzberg, who found two types of factors associated with the motivation of employees. One source is referred to as *motivators* because they are necessary to stimulate individuals to superior efforts. They relate to the nature or content of the job itself and include responsibility, achievement, recognition, and opportunities for growth and advancement. When present, they motivate salespeople; if absent, they demotivate them.[12]

Hygiene factors are extrinsic aspects of the job, such as company policies, pay level, fringe benefits, working conditions, and job security. They pertain to satisfying lower-level needs. When present, hygiene factors do not actually induce higher positive motivation in salespersons; their absence, however, leads to salesperson dissatisfaction and demotivation.[13]

In essence, then, only true motivators can stimulate greater sales force efforts according to this theory, while hygiene factors can be demotivating if absent and only neutral or unimpactful if present. Thus, being given increased responsibility can be particularly motivating to a salesperson. Whereas, working in a lucrative territory may satisfy the salesperson, but it will probably not motivate him or her, and working in a nonlucrative territory may reduce motivation.

Although this theory has received support in nonsales settings, its relevance in the selling arena remains questionable.[14] Nonetheless, one selling authority implicitly advocates its use stating: "Motivation is internal. . .. [sales managers] can't reach inside a rep's head and flip a switch. All. . . [they] can do is create an environment in which a rep's internal motivation takes over. In part that involves removing demotivators. It also involves good listening to find out what the rep's true motivators are."[15] This suggests that sales managers can improve salesperson productivity by maintaining hygiene factors (like a pleasant work environment) while providing motivators (like job enrichment). Some examples of job enrichment in the sales context include:

- Give salespeople a *complete natural unit of work responsibility and accountability* (specific customer category assignments in a designated area).
- Grant *greater authority and job freedom* to the salespeople in accomplishing assignments (let salespeople schedule their time in their own unique way as long as organizational goals are met).
- Introduce salespeople to *new and more difficult tasks and to challenges not previously handled* (opening new accounts, selling a new product on the Internet, or being assigned a large national account).
- Assign salespeople specific or specialized *tasks enabling them to become experts* (training new salespeople on "how to close a sale").
- Send *periodic emails and other communications directly to the salesperson* instead of forwarding everything via the sales supervisor. Of course, the supervisor must also know the information being sent to salespeople.[16])

Process Theories of Motivation

More dynamic than content theories, process theories emphasize the kind of goals and rewards that motivate people. Specifically, they try to explain the thought process of employees and identify the kind of activities and outcomes that fulfill their needs.

Sales managers can improve salesperson productivity by maintaining hygiene factors (pleasant work environment) such as an on-site day care facility for their sales force.

Equity Theory According to the equity theory of motivation, employees compare their relative work contributions and rewards with those of other individuals in similar situations. People experience inequity when they feel either under-rewarded or over-rewarded for their contribution relative to that of others. Although different individuals may respond in unique ways to inequity, most people who feel under-rewarded decrease their work efforts while people who feel overpaid tend to increase theirs. People may also distort their perceptions of their rewards and contributions relative to those of others. Finally, individuals may leave a perceived inequitable or unfair situation by quitting the job or changing the comparison group.[17]

According to equity theory, sales managers should learn how individual sales representatives feel about how their contributions and rewards compare with those of others. If some of the salespeople perceive inequity, the sales manager needs to find ways to either alter their perceptions, or if inequity really exists, remedy the situation.

Expectancy Theory First developed by Victor Vroom[18] and later modified by Campbell, Dunette, Lawler et al.,[19] the expectancy theory of motivation proposes that individuals contemplate the consequences of personal actions in choosing different alternatives to satisfy their needs. Because the motivation to perform is a rationally determined, carefully thought-out decision process makes this theory logically appealing. Expectancy theory was first applied to marketing in order to explain the performance level of salespersons.[20] According to expectancy theory, motivation (or effort) is a function of three elements: expectancy, instrumentality, and valence.

Expectancy is the salesperson's perception that exerting a given level of extra effort will lead to higher achievement. For example, the salesperson might believe that making 10% more sales calls per day will lead to a 75% or higher chance of achieving quota. Salespeople will likely increase their efforts when they think doing so will improve their performance outcomes. Not only is the degree of the expectancy estimate important, but so is its accuracy. If salespeople hold inaccurate expectancy beliefs, they are likely to expend effort on the wrong job activities.

Instrumentality is the salesperson's estimate of the probability that achieving a certain level of improved performance will lead to the attainment of certain rewards. For instance, the salesperson might believe there is a 50% chance that achieving quota will lead to a salary increase. If salespeople think that performing effectively will lead to rewards, they are likely to be more motivated. The accuracy of instrumentality beliefs is important. If salespeople hold inaccurate instrumentality perceptions, they're likely to focus on the activities for which they *think* they'll be rewarded, instead of those for which they *actually* will be.

Valence is the desirability of a potential outcome or reward that the salesperson may receive from improved performance. For example, a salesperson may have a strong desire for a promotion or a pay raise. To the extent that salespeople receive highly desirable rewards, their motivation is enhanced.

Symbolically, the motivation (or effort) expended by a salesperson is a function of the probability of an expectancy estimate multiplied by the probability of the instrumentality estimate multiplied by the valence for the reward:

$$\text{Motivation} = \left[E_i \times \left(\sum_{j=1}^{n} I_j \times V_{jk} \right) \right] \tag{11.1}$$

where

E_i = probability of an expectancy (How hard will I have to work to achieve this goal?)
I_j = probability of an instrumentality (What are my chances of receiving the reward)
V_{jk} = valence or desirability for the reward or outcome (How attractive is the reward?)

To motivate salespeople to greater efforts, then, sales managers should keep in mind that people tend to literally or subconsciously ask themselves: "What's in it for me – that is, what's my payoff, what's required of me (my costs or efforts expended), and what's my probability of success?" Unless sales managers can satisfactorily anticipate and provide answers for these questions, salespeople will not be motivated to expend greater effort.

Attribution Theory Extended from psychology, attribution theory identifies the reasons for a given outcome.[21] It contends that people are motivated to know why an event occurred and why they succeeded or failed at a certain task. For instance, a salesperson would likely be interested in determining why he or she lost a sale and might consider a list of attributions to explain the failure. An *internal* attribution is a reason *within* the salesperson that could have an impact on performance (such as ability, effort, skill, and experience); an *external* attribution is an explanation that lies *beyond* the realm of control by the salesperson (such as luck, territory or task difficulty, and unanticipated adverse circumstances). Whether an internal or an external rationale is given for the lost sale can influence the salesperson's subsequent behavior. A salesperson who thinks that he or she lost the sale because of poor effort or inadequate ability is likely to increase effort or seek training. However, the salesperson who perceives the sale was lost because of uncontrollable factors like bad luck or poor economic conditions will not likely change selling behavior (after all, the failure was not their fault). Management, then, must assist salespeople in making accurate attributions for success and failure; inappropriate attributions could lead them to make inappropriate responses.[22]

The outcome of the attribution process is that salespeople can choose either to *work harder* or to *work smarter*.[23] For example, calling on more accounts or putting in more hours is working harder. Changing the type or direction of effort is working smarter. Working longer hours and contacting more clients have long been among the primary objectives of sales managers for their salespeople. Yet attribution theory suggests they should concentrate on motivating salespeople to make better choices about the activities they perform – in other words, to work *smarter*. Sales managers can do this by helping sales reps direct their efforts better by searching for new customers, making tailored presentations for different types of customers, deciding which customers to visit more often, and devising creative selling strategies. By getting a better understanding of the causal attributions salespeople make, as well as the outcomes of those attributions, sales managers can add much to their understanding of the motivation of the sales force.

Goal-Setting Theory Goal-setting theory attempts to increase motivation by linking rewards directly to the individual's goals.[24] Sales managers should set specific goals for each of their salespeople on a regular basis. These goals should be moderately difficult to achieve, but they should be the type of goals that the salesperson will want to accomplish.[25] Unlike the traditional quota system, goal-setting theory integrates other motivational theories in an attempt to develop a reward system tailored to individual needs. Several management experts predict this approach to motivation will steadily gain in popularity.[26] Procedures for helping ensure the successful implementation of goal-setting are provided in Table 11.2.[27]

To learn more about cutting-edge motivation approaches, sales managers can enroll in training programs offered by specialized firms, such as the Sales Readiness Group (https://www.salesreadinessgroup.com/blog/how-to-motivate-salespeople), shown in Figure 11.1, to further develop their sales force motivation skills.

Reinforcement Theory of Motivation

The reinforcement perspective focuses on a unique approach to motivating people. It deals with the consequences of behavior, which managers can modify by using rewards and penalties, since individuals tend to repeat actions that result in rewards

---

TABLE 11.2

Goal-Setting Procedures for Motivating the Sales Force

- Involve the salesperson actively and openly in the goal-setting process
- Set realistic goals
- Meet and reset goals when conditions beyond the control of either party change, or when they prove to be unattainable because of unrealistic assumptions
- Fix goals that can be measured in tangible ways, such as time or dollar volume
- Incorporate the development of the measurement system into the goal-setting process
- Consider the measurement system in terms of real-time feedback
- Meet promptly with salespeople to determine the reasons for a goal shortfall
- Provide positive feedback on how to correct shortfalls
- Develop goals and a measurement system for the new corrective plan of action
- Provide timely public recognition for goal achievement

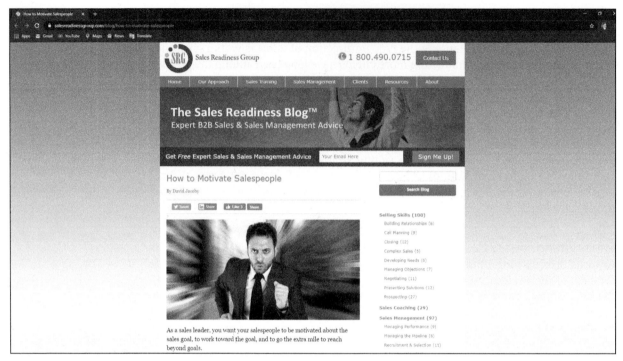

FIGURE 11.1 Sales force motivation training programs.

Sales managers can enroll in training programs offered by specialist firms, such as the Sales Readiness Group, and learn additional strategies for motivating their salespeople.
Source: https://www.salesreadinessgroup.com/blog/how-to-motivate-salespeople.

and avoid those that lead to punishment. Also known as organizational behavior modification (OBM),[28] which has been extended to the sales arena, this theory relies on the principles and techniques of learning to strengthen, maintain, or eliminate behaviors through an intentional and systematic application of rewards or punishments.[29] In essence, management engages in interventions that can influence employee behavior and thus motivation. Sales managers can take four approaches when utilizing OBM. Two of the approaches increase desired behavior through positive or negative reinforcement, and two are directed at decreasing undesirable behavior through punishment or extinction (eliminating the behavior).

Positive reinforcement provides a pleasant consequence for a desired behavior, like a bonus for opening new accounts. Negative reinforcement allows salespeople to avoid an undesirable outcome after displaying the desired behavior – for instance, those who achieve or surpass their annual quotas keep their jobs. Both kinds of reinforcement are intended to increase the likelihood that the desired behavior (opening new accounts, meeting quotas) will be repeated in the future.[30]

Punishment provides salespeople with an undesirable outcome when they display an undesired behavior (reducing the commission because the salesperson incorrectly estimated the cost of the sale). *Extinction* provides no positive reinforcement after an undesirable behavior (the sales manager starts a sales meeting on time rather than waiting for late arrivals). Both punishment and extinction are directed at eliminating, or at least reducing the frequency of an undesirable behavior. The ideal situation, of course, is to eliminate the unwanted behavior for good.

Sales managers must be aware of the frequency with which they reinforce sales-person efforts. *Continuous reinforcement* rewards the salesperson's positive behavior *every time* it's exhibited. *Partial reinforcement periodically* boosts the desired behavior such as by awarding a commission check only once a month rather than after every sale. Continuous reinforcement helps salespeople learn the desired behavior more quickly, but partial reinforcement often leads to more permanent learning.

For OBM to be successful, sales managers must know precisely what behaviors their salespersons should exhibit and avoid; then they should clearly articulate these behaviors and outcomes to them. Furthermore, sales managers need to determine what reinforcement schedules are necessary to bring about desired results.

Using Rewards and Incentive Programs for Sales Force Motivation

We now turn to one of the sales manager's most important tasks: initiating and direct-ing salespeople's intense and persistent work-related behaviors toward the attainment of organizational goals and objectives. Nucor Corp (www.nucor.com), a steel company that treats its workers like owners, demonstrates how a reward system can turn an underdog into an upstart nipping at the heels of giants in an industry almost deci-mated by intense global competition. Nucor has thrived by creating a performance culture based on a unique reward structure, which has been able to motivate its work force in all functional areas – including sales.[31] At Nucor, motivation focuses on the people on the front line of the business by talking to them, listening to them, and accepting the occasional failure. Built partially on symbolic gestures, each year every single employee's name goes on the cover of the annual report.[32] Most importantly, however, employees' income is tied directly to their performance,[33] Nucor exemplifies how employees will expend extraordinary effort if they are richly rewarded, treated with respect, and empowered.

So, you may now be thinking: "What administrative actions and strategies can I use to enhance sales force motivation?" Good question. The answer may well lie in the vast array of intrinsic and extrinsic rewards that can induce salespeople to exert higher levels of effort.

Extrinsic Rewards

Extrinsic rewards come from the organization, usually higher management, and are mostly financial in nature; examples include salary, commissions,[34] fringe benefits, perks, formal recognition, job promotions, employee stock ownership plans, profit sharing, gain sharing, stock options, and team-based compensation. Although they're a central part of extrinsic rewards, compensation plans and packages constitute the most important way in which employees are remunerated.[35] Thus, we discuss them separately in Chapter 12. Let's look at sales incentive programs first. [36]

Sales Incentive Programs As tools with tremendous potential motivating power, incentive spending is becoming a bigger part of many firms' budgets.[37] More than 70% of companies report that incentive programs are essential to the success of their over-all marketing plans.[38]

Among the more important motivators in financial incentive programs are cash, travel, and merchandise. When salespeople achieve or surpass a specified sales quota, they are often given a monetary bonus to reward them for their performance as well as to motivate them to continue this behavior. Travel rewards are used similarly. Some of the more popular destinations for travel incentives are Europe and the Mediterranean, Hawaii, the Caribbean, Bermuda, Mexico, and South America. U.S. companies spend many billions annually on incentive travel for top employees and customers.[39] Today's salespeople want choices in travel awards tailored to their particular interests and they often want to take their families with them. So, at a growing numbers of firms – including WebEx, a video-conferencing company, the range of travel rewards for salespeople who meet their annual sales quotas or other goals may include anything from a deep-sea fishing excursion to an African safari.[40] The most common items of merchandise used as a sales force incentive include plaques and trophies, consumer electronics, household goods, clothing, sporting goods, and travel accessories.

An effective sales incentive program can accomplish several important goals. Perhaps the main one is to increase total sales. Sales incentive programs can also help increase the number of new accounts brought into a company. Other benefits include helping launch new products, boosting morale, and reviving old products. For help in devising creative incentives, sales managers can turn to firms, such as **Incentive Logic (www.incentivelogic.com)**, that specialize in developing incentives to motivate the sales force.

Salespeople's self-selected sales incentives can be cost-effective ways to increase sales and sales force morale.[41] Among self-selected rewards, travel and merchandise

To devise creative sales incentives that augment the performance of salespeople, sales managers can consult with industry experts, such as Incentive Logic.
Source: https://incentivelogic.com/.

are among the most popular awards. There is also growing salesperson interest in less traditional incentives, for example, tuition assistance for themselves or their children and educational opportunities that could lead to career advancement.[42] The important implication for sales mangers is that salespeople are willing to extend themselves more when they are properly motivated by incentives they value most.

Promotion Opportunities An attractive career path with "promotion decision" stages at regular intervals (at least every three to five years) can keep many individuals motivated throughout most of their careers. Many people tend to become ego-involved with succeeding on the "fast track," and they continue to strive for the next promotion. To maximize motivational benefits from a career development plan, the sales manager must provide periodic feedback – at least yearly but more frequently in the early stages of career development. This feedback ought to come to salespeople through a comprehensive performance evaluation. Small sales units may find informal evaluations practical, but larger sales organizations need more formalized performance evaluation systems, supported by rating forms and written narratives maintained in the employee's personnel file.

In a simplified career path, sales trainees have an introductory or trial period of up to three years. By that time, the salesperson must either be promoted to the sales development stage or terminated from the company. Then, usually no later than their seventh anniversary with the sales force, the individual must be promoted to senior salesperson or let go. At this level, the individual may continue on a *career sales path* or switch to a *sales/marketing career path*. Although the decision to remain on the sales path is largely up to the individual salesperson, the opportunity to move into management depends upon performance evaluations, which we discuss in Chapter 14.

Intrinsic Rewards

Some rewards are psychological or behavioral in nature and seek to influence and satisfy internally experienced desires. These intrinsic rewards come from within the salesperson and include feelings of accomplishment, personal growth and development, enhanced self-esteem, and personal worth and recognition.[43] While monetary rewards are very important to most relatively new salespeople, the opportunity for advancement and promotion also are strong motivators for them.[44] Table 11.3, based on several studies, shows the variety of factors that motivate top sales performers.[45] Because research confirms that promotions and opportunities for growth are most attractive to salespeople in the early stages of their careers, we next discuss how sales managers can use such recognition to motivate the sales force.

Recognition For years, the majority of sales managers assumed that monetary rewards were most valued and therefore highest motivators for salespeople. Recently, however, sales managers across all industries are beginning to realize that while monetary rewards are initially motivating, non-financial incentives and intrinsic rewards, such as recognition, are critical in generating higher levels of performance over the longer run from the sales force.[46] In the words of a sales consultant: "I'll bet you'd be hard-pressed to find anyone in sales who doesn't crave the spotlight, the excitement, the personal validation that recognition brings. If they don't crave it, they probably shouldn't be in sales."[47]

There are many ways to give recognition to a salesperson. Several companies believe that creating a "fun" but competitive working environment in which everyone

> **TABLE 11.3**
>
> ## What Motivates Top Sales Performers?
>
> | Motivators | Description |
> |---|---|
> | **1. Need for status** | • Recognition is a key motivating factor for top salespeople as they seek greater respect, image, and reputation. |
> | **2. Need for control** | • While top salespeople like being with other people, they often also like to be in control and enjoy influencing others. |
> | **3. Need for respect** | • Top sales achievers like to be seen as experts who are able and willing to help and advise others. |
> | **4. Need for routine** | • It is a misconception that successful sellers thrive on freedom. Most like to follow a strict routine and are upset when it's interrupted. |
> | **5. Need for accomplishment** | • Money is only one of the many things that motivate top sales performers. In addition to a nice house, fancy cars, and expensive clothes, they continually pursue new challenges in their jobs to maintain enthusiasm. |
> | **6. Need for stimulation** | • Most outstanding salespeople have an abundance of physical energy and thrive on challenges. Therefore, they welcome new goals as ways of channeling their energy. |
> | **7. Need for honesty** | • Top sales achievers have a strong need to believe in the product they are selling. If they have doubts about the company or a new product line, they are likely to consider other employment. |
> | **8. Need for commitment from upper sales management** | • Salespersons need to be supported by their senior sales management in their quest for higher sales. This commitment is exhibited in the form of training, mentoring, and guidance provided by sales managers. |

is aware of others' accomplishments is an excellent form of motivation.[48] At Fel-Pro, a gasket manufacturer in Skokie, Illinois, any compliments the home office receives from customers are promptly relayed to the sales force. The corporate office believes it's important for salespeople to learn about customer compliments directly through their superiors.[49]

Many companies believe that giving salespeople symbolic rewards, such as plaques, rings, and memberships into elite sales clubs, can provide tangible public recognition that a higher paycheck or free trip may not. Money and other incentives are soon spent or consumed, but palpable recognition serves as a continual visible reminder to all of a salesperson's accomplishment. Xerox Corporation (www.xerox.com) has a President's Club for its top sales achievers. As one of Xerox's top salespeople explained, "The President's Club is what we all strive for because it's how our success is measured within Xerox."[50] While a free trip accompanies membership in the President's Club, the real motivator for most salespeople is being recognized as a member of that elite group. Many top-performing salespeople win monetary rewards year after year. What eventually becomes important is being recognized as a top salesperson. Bolstering the salesperson's ego becomes much more important than a monetary incentive can ever be.[51] Of course, no single form of recognition works for everyone. A good recognition program begins by finding each person's level of self-motivation or "start center,"[52] which may be activated by higher-order needs, such as appreciation and admiration that are unique to the individual. Some key factors a sales manager should consider in developing a recognition program for their salespeople are presented in Table 11.4.

TABLE **11.4**

Developing a Recognition Program

- The program should be based on objective *performance* only. No subjective judgments should be allowed.
- Everyone must have a realistic chance to win, and there should be awards for superior performance in several categories across the sales force.
- Awards should be presented in public, so that winners receive recognition in front of their peers.
- Award ceremonies must be conducted in good taste. A poorly done recognition program can leave employees uninspired to do their best.
- The awards program should be highly publicized to create awareness and involvement throughout the company.

Public recognition and awards for achieving excellence in sales productivity can be a powerful way of motivating salespeople.

Sales Force Motivation Strategies and Tools

If salespeople come to take a relatively stable plan for granted, compensation systems designed to attain organizational goals, can become ineffective. At that point, the sales manager needs other sales motivation strategies and tools that go above and beyond rewards. For example, sales training programs can motivate salespeople by creating feelings that the company is investing in them and sharing the latest information about new products, customers, and technology to employ in selling, which can increase the salesperson's self-confidence, enthusiasm, and career aspirations.[53] Two popular motivational strategies are holding sales contests and sales meetings.

Sales Contests

As a motivational device, the sales contest has the potential for undesirable as well as desirable results. Therefore, it is important that sales managers understand the goals that can be accomplished through sales contests, the essential decision areas in planning contests, and the potential pitfalls associated with them. Contest themes, rules, prizes, participation, duration, promotion, and post-contest assessment are important considerations in the planning and implementation of this motivational tool. However, all planning must begin with the specific purposes, goals, and objectives of the contest.

Sales Contests: Purposes, Goals, and Objectives Although astute sales contest planners will coordinate contests with current market conditions, contests can focus sales force attention on any particular goal area for short periods of time. For example, the purpose of a contest may be to motivate salespeople to increase the number of new customers, develop sales of a new product, counteract sales slumps due to seasonal variations, sell a more profitable product mix, cut costs, adjust quotas, reorder salespeople's priorities, and boost morale. In addition, sales contests might be designed to clear overstocked inventory, keep production lines running, encourage experienced sales personnel to recruit and train newcomers, develop creative prospecting methods, prepare call reports more efficiently, make more or better sales presentations, provide greater customer service, and enhance customer satisfaction. Sometimes, contests are designed subtly to get the sales force to reinstitute good work habits while focusing on some general goal like increasing sales volume. Some contests can be designed to achieve several complex goals. For example, the below *Sales Management in Action Box* 11.1 describes what may have been one of the first Internet-based sales contests. Potential objectives and rewards for sales contests are presented in Table 11.5.

Contests tend to produce the most effective results when only a small number of goals (one to three, ideally) are established. These goals should be consistent with the company's overall marketing strategy, understandable, achievable, and readily measurable.

Contest Themes Sales managers should ensure that contest themes are creative, novel, timely, implementable, promotable, visibly measurable, and self-image reinforcing. Variations of sports and games in season are frequently used as a contest theme, as are travel routes, mock battles, races, building construction, and clothing contests (in which the salesperson can wear to meetings whatever unique clothing or pin-on labels he or she wins). Sales contests must have an easily understood way to measure milestones of progress that can displayed for all salespeople to see how they're doing. Contest themes that

---

Box 11.1 | Sales Management in Action 11.1

Sales Force Contests Go Interactive

Along with motivating its sales force, MCI, a telecommunication company, wanted to give its service reps experience using the Internet. So, a sales contest called Cyber Safari was targeted to its 5,000 reps who had never used the Internet before. Salespeople won points for achieving each of 10 different objectives based on sales and revenues. Points could be redeemed for various prizes, ranging from trips to Monte Carlo, Hawaii, and Acapulco to home fitness centers, computers, and pianos. Salespeople used their laptops to find out their current rankings in the contest and to choose from the online catalog of prizes. This interactive sales contest helped MCI achieve its highest selling quarter in more than two years. What's more, the salespeople had competitive fun while learning new technology.[54]

TABLE 11.5

Sales Force Contest Objectives and Rewards

Motivators	Description
Increase dollar volume	• Prize to salespeople who increase sales (based on percentage of dollar increase over previous period). • Several prizes, with top producers awarded most expensive prize. Runners-up receive less expensive prizes. Points for each $1 of sales. Prizes won by salespeople in various career stages who earn the most points.
Stimulate more orders	• Prize for all salespeople who achieve their sales quota. • Points for each order, with fixed number of prizes for those with the most points. • Additional prize for meeting a secondary quota.
Increase demonstrations and complete call reports	• Prizes to those who make the most demonstrations and/or complete the most call reports. • Prizes to all who achieve their quota of calls and demonstrations.
Build higher unit sales	• Points for higher dollar or unit volume (based on past averages), with prizes for those who make the greatest percentage increases.
Add customers	• Points toward prizes for each new customer account, with bonus points for specific target account categories.
Secure prospects	• Points toward prize for each new prospect, with additional points for each prospect that becomes a customer within a specified period.
Build off-season business	• Dollar or unit-volume quota to earn prize during slow months. Two categories of prizes: first for salesperson, second for spouse or partner (e.g., a vacation trip).
Push slow item	• Points awarded for sales of slow-moving products in inventory, with prizes for biggest point getters.
Stimulate balanced selling	• Prizes to those who maintain best sales record for selling entire line during specified time.
Introduce new product	• Points toward prize for best sales record with new products. • Prize to salespeople who reach quota of customers who buy new product.
Increase use of displays	• Prize to salespeople for placing assigned quota of displays set-up.
Stimulate dealer tie-ins	• Prizes to salespeople who get most dealers to tie in with national advertising campaign.
Revive dead accounts	• Prizes to salespeople who reactivate most old accounts. • Prizes for greatest sales volume from formerly dead accounts.
Switch users to your brand	• Points toward prize for salespeople who switch customers from competitive product to ours.
Improve sales abilities	• Prizes to salespeople who score best on examinations after training period.
Reduce costs	• Prize to salespeople and managers who set best record of sales-to-costs ratio.
Build multiple sales	• Prizes to salespeople with best carload or multiple-sales of products.
Increase Internet usage among salespeople	• Prizes to salespeople with most new business generated from company webpages.

create great difficulties in implementation or include complex measurement processes should be avoided. Above all, salespeople should be able to identify psychologically with the contest theme, therefore it must not be so juvenile or silly that mature salespeople feel foolish when playing "the game." In fact, it's beneficial for salespeople to have substantial input into developing the goals and themes of the sales contest.

The theme can be seasonal, such as a summer contest or a special holiday contest, to persuade salespeople to put forth special efforts during vacation or holiday periods.

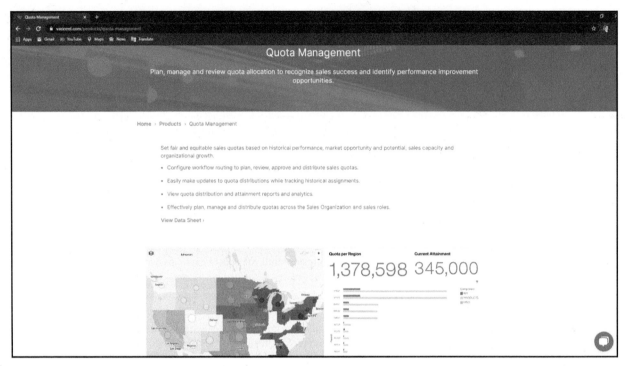

Sales managers can turn to industry experts, such as Varicent, to help develop quota management systems, as well as set equitable quotas based on historical performance, market opportunity, sales capacity, and growth expectations.
Source: https://www.varicent.com/products/quota-management.

Novelty themes can be related to the contest objective, to current events, to seasonal sports, or to other appealing common denominators. Regardless of the specific contest theme adopted, it must generate enthusiasm and stimulate the salespeople to react favorably. For example, one firm held a very successful "strip the brass" contest that had the effects of fulfilling the recognition needs of sales personnel. In this company, the president wore a very unusual digital watch, its marketing vice president was recognized by his elegant leather attaché case with raised edges, and the sales vice president had a wardrobe of designer shirts. During a two-week contest, replicas or reproductions of these three items were awarded to winners by the three executives (in person) in accordance with a formula that related productivity to the value of the prizes.

Contests can be designed for the entire sales force, for those with different levels of experience (such as junior or senior salesperson), or for horizontal business segments (such as those serving different customer categories, like government, institutional, or not-for-profit organizations). Grouping salespeople for contest purposes is consistent with the hierarchical segmentation approach to motivation, and it recognizes that different levels of salespeople tend to have different needs. Contests should be customized to each separate group of participants, with appropriate goals, themes, and awards reflecting their different career stages and reward preferences. For example, junior salespeople might be best motivated by the expectation of glamorous prizes, while senior salespeople might prefer a vacation trip with top officials of the company where they can share their views on company issues and later brag to their peers about their interactions with the "big bosses." In planning contests, sales managers should ensure as must as possible that everyone has an equal chance to win. Otherwise, the overall contest effect may sometimes be demotivational. Suppose, for example, that banks and savings and loan institutional buyers are the best prospects for products included in the contest scope, and that some salespeople have few of these institutions in their sales territories. Clearly these employees can become cynical about the whole sales contest.

Contest Rules Formulate contest rules to clarify goals and prevent abuses. Obsolete or deficient products as well as all unethical tactics must be deemed outside the ground rules of the contest. Rules should also be phrased so that they discourage salespeople from holding back orders before the contest, applying undue pressure on buyers during the contest, or suggesting that buyers can cancel their orders after the contest. It's important that the rules are used to orient the contest toward specific organization goals. For instance, restricting it to accounts not reported on call sheets for two months preceding the contest period might channel contest efforts more toward selling newly developed prospects. Finally, rules must clearly define the contest time period, the specific action (order, delivery, or payment) that will constitute a sale for contest purposes, and the exact basis for accumulating points for prizes.

Contest Rewards and Prizes Unless contest prizes include items that the majority of participants want, the contest will not be motivating. While many salespeople will say they prefer cash, more unusual and visible awards that winners can conspicuously enjoy, such as glamorous trips, luxurious boats, cars, sporting equipment, or home entertainment systems, serve as longer-lasting incentives for participants. Consideration of the salesperson's family also is important in selecting incentives. Awards ought to include something the whole family would enjoy, ensuring their involved support in cheering on their prospective winner.

Many corporations are turning to productive but fun travel as incentives – for example, providing inspirational training in exotic settings or conducting sales meetings abroad to reward salespeople who make the company's 100 Percent Club. Sales meetings have the advantage of being easily justified to top management, since they combine business and pleasure, family participation, highly visible recognition, and nontaxability while giving salespeople the chance to share spirited interaction with other high producers in the company.

oliveromg/Shutterstock.com

Using rewards, such as a fully paid vacation to exotic locales, sales managers can augment individual salesperson performance toward the attainment of organizational goals.

Salesperson Participation Sometimes, only senior salespersons have the opportunity to compete for the chance to go to national sales conventions or to be awarded membership in an elite group such as the President's Club or the Million Dollar Sales Club. Junior salespersons are more likely to have their own contests with public recognition awards such as a plague or business accessory (briefcase, cellphone, or luggage) presented by a top company official.

Most contests don't pit one salesperson against another but award prizes for achieving certain individual standards of performance. Experts disagree about whether it's better to have lesser prizes that nearly everyone can win, or expensive rewards that only a few can attain. Prizes must be at least attractive enough to motivate, because token prizes with little recognition value may kill the motivational effects of the contest. On the other hand, excessively expensive prizes may overemphasize competition and hurt sales force cohesiveness.

With firms increasingly emphasizing teamwork, sales contests also have the potential to increase the motivation of an entire sales team as well as individual salespeople. The same guidelines for goals and prizes hold for team-oriented contests. The major difference is that the contest winner is a team of individuals who all receive prizes.

Contest Duration Contests usually last between one and five months. Salespeople should have enough time to make at least one complete pass through their territories. Extra-effort pressures can be maintained for only a limited time before interest begins to lag. Contests that occur too regularly (at the same time each year) may come to seem routine and lose their incentive value, while contests that are unexpected often generate more enthusiasm.

Promoting the Contest The contest should be promoted with great fanfare to the sales force before it begins, in order to build enthusiasm. Personal letters and emails from management can announce and reinforce the imminent contest. It's important for sales managers to announce the exact nature and rules of the contest to all salespeople at the same time and in a dramatic fashion. Explanatory posters should be put up promptly after the contest is announced, and the company's website can be used to enable salespeople – no matter where their territories are located – to follow their relative progress in the contest. Some creativity in the presentation of the contest progress can add to the excitement and fun of the contest. For example, model race cars might show the daily or weekly progress of each salesperson "driver" by his or her relative position on a circular race track. All participants should get detailed, official feedback at frequent intervals unless the contest is not competitive, in which case each person's progress can be conveyed confidentially.

Assessing Contest Effectiveness A contest is like any other management tool: it requires the use of resources. Thus, management will want to assess whether the resources used in the contest were wisely invested. Determine whether the results of the contest exceeded its costs, whether contest objectives were achieved, how satisfied the sales force was with the contest, and what strengths and weaknesses were inherent in the contest. Obviously, there's no point in conducting a contest if the company is not better off afterward than it was before.

Potential Pitfalls of Contests While well-devised contests can accomplish multiple organizational and individual goals, the sales manager ought to recognize and avoid certain negative side effects. Contests can become so routine that they are expected, and sales reps consider awards as part of their yearly compensation. Another drawback is that contests can temporarily increase sales and thereby provide a means of disguising sales force shortcomings or sales management deficiencies. Like any over-used incentive, a sales contest eventually can begin to lose its motivational effects. Professional salespeople may sometimes look at a poorly designed or trivial sounding sales contest as beneath their dignity or self-image and decline to make extra efforts during it. It is always difficult to devise themes that are simultaneously fun and image enhancing for salespeople. Some sales managers feel that the money put into contests would provide a more continuous incentive if it were spread among high performers as pay increases instead. This approach can increase costs, however, and there is little to substantiate the idea that it would provide more benefits than sales contests.

While the major purpose of sales contests is to enhance motivation, sometimes they can end up *demotivating* the sales force. An improperly implemented sales contest can destroy morale among salespeople as well as negatively affect sales. For example, if sales contest rewards are earned by the same few salespeople year after year, some negative side effects are bound to occur. Everyone else starts to feel like a loser. And the winners, if the same few people all the time, usually do not need or benefit from the reward as much as some of the other salespeople would. Moreover, the contests can create jealousy in the sales force and make the consistent winners unpopular with their colleagues.

After sales contests end, some salespeople fall into a motivational valley, resulting in sales slumps. In such situations, sales managers need to provide positive encourage-ment to perk them up. The zeal to win contests can also lead to pressure-selling tactics, inventory overloading, outright cheating, and neglect of other customer relationships. Some general guidelines concerning what not to do with sales contests are presented in Table 11.6. Despite shortcomings, contests can provide a flexible and valuable mana-gerial tool if themes, rules, prizes, participation, duration, and publicity are tailored to organizational and salespersons' goals.

Sales Meetings

One of the most popular means of enhancing motivation is the sales meeting, be it national, regional, or local. Instead of utilizing the normal one-way communication from management to salespeople, sales meetings provide opportunities for two-way communication and interaction among all members of the marketing team – field and headquarters. The company comes alive at sales meetings, and names become

---

TABLE 11.6

Why Some Sales Contests are Losers

Setting unrealistic sales goals	• Salespeople may become frustrated trying to achieve overly optimistic sales goals.
Not adequately publicizing the sales contest	• All salespeople need to know about and understand the rules of the sales contest in order to fully participate.
Rewarding only one or a few winners of the sales contest	• When a sales contest rewards only a few top performers, the other salespeople may become discouraged and not increase their efforts during the contest. All sales-people need to have an opportunity to win various contest rewards.
Not including spouses or partners	• Salespeople need the support of their loved ones when making increased efforts to win a sales contest. Contest prizes should include vacation trips, merchandise, or other rewards that the entire family of the salespeople can enjoy.
Don't expect the sales contest to solve long-term problems in sales force performance	• Sales contests will not solve major sales force problems over the long-run. They are used primarily to offset sales slumps, get a temporary boost in sales, or introduce new products.

people as sales representatives, sales managers, marketing managers, and top company executives interact. Salespeople are able to see how their role as the field marketing arm of the company blends with headquarters' marketing activities.

Sales meetings are strategic "halftimes" in the selling game for communicating about new-product introductions, price changes, upcoming promotional campaigns, new policies, and overall company goals. They can help motivate salespeople to greater productivity by reminding them of the rest of the company's support efforts.[55] They can even motivate by surprising, entertaining, and motivating salespeople. For example, Northwestern Mutual Life salespeople wanted so much to take part in a family reunion-style sales meeting — which included country music star Wynona Judd — that each of them paid $1000 to attend. Sun Microsystems held a sales meeting that included a dance party and a day of river rafting in Colorado. Straus Discount Auto staged a wrestling match as part of its sales meeting. In the tag team match, a WWF champion and the CEO of the company took on several salesperson "Bounty Hunters." Creative sales meetings can boost morale and productivity for everyone involved.[56]

National, Regional, and Local Meetings Usually held once a year, *national meetings* may include the entire sales force or only a select group of top performers. Travel and lodging expenses for national meetings are considerable, and territorial opportunities or problems go unattended while salespeople are away. The benefits, however, may outweigh these costs. Sales representatives get the chance to exchange ideas with company management, experience a pleasant change of environment and a break in their normal routine, and often hear motivational talks by experts and/or celebrities so that they return to their territories with renewed enthusiasm. Especially when the sales force is relatively small and scattered, national conferences can be an important unifying device. *Regional conferences*, planned with a work-oriented agenda, can be less expensive for large corporations whose sales forces have more localized selling problems. *Local meetings* and seminars are the backbone of the communication system and usually give salespersons the greatest support. These regularly held meetings are important for bestowing timely recognition on salespeople, providing group interaction, and focusing sales training on solving territorial problems and creating selling opportunities.

Planning Detailed advanced planning is required for effective sales meetings. Regional or local meetings are generally held monthly or weekly in the regional or branch sales office, and success depends upon developing a strong agenda. Planning for national conferences, however, is much more demanding. Facilities must be reserved many months in advance, and goals, dates, programs, participants, and publicity must be arranged early on, often starting a year or more ahead of time. Usually, national sales conferences are held away from the immediate work environment, either at a resort area, if the purpose of the meeting is largely motivational, or at a hotel close to company headquarters, if training or information sharing are primary objectives. In planning sales meetings, there are several tasks:

- Establish meeting goals (from both the company's and the sales representatives' perspectives).
- Select a theme that integrates goals and communicates the overall purpose of the meeting.
- Develop a tentative agenda or program for the meeting and work up a preliminary budget.
- Finalize the program and budget, and send copies of the program to all attendees.
- Coordinate closely with all participants in the program to ensure they know their roles.

> **TABLE 11.7**
>
> ### Creating Memorable Sales Meetings
>
> - Before setting up and scheduling the meeting, sales managers should survey salespersons to learn what kind of information or training they would find most beneficial to them.
> - Choose meeting locations, entertainment, and activities that salespeople will enjoy and learn from.
> - Add a special element of surprise by not revealing ahead of time everything on the meeting's agenda, for example, a celebrity appearance or special gifts for attendees.
> - Give individual attention at the meeting by awarding salesperson accomplishments and recognizing special contributions.

- Provide handouts summarizing the main points of the meeting for salespeople to take home for further review.
- Evaluate the meeting in terms of goal achievement.

Some general guidelines to help create more memorable sales meetings are presented in Table 11.7.

Competitive Spirit The sales meeting provides management with an excellent opportunity to recognize sales accomplishments, to announce the names of sales leaders, and to award prizes to outstanding salespersons and sales managers. For instance, one company holds a three-day annual sales convention for district and division sales managers and their spouses. On the final evening, a formal dinner is held where manager-of-the-year trophies are given out in an "Academy Award" style, including requests for "the envelope please." Throughout the year, the company house organ builds up to the momentous occasion when the envelope will be opened by the president's spouse and the name of the manager of the year is announced. Another firm awards stock options to sales force members and uses the weekly sales meeting to announce the paper dollar gains of salespeople who own a substantial number of company shares.

Specialized Training Often, the national or regional sales meeting will offer management an excellent opportunity to train all salespeople simultaneously about how to introduce a new product or customer strategy. For example, one manufacturer of inexpensive costume jewelry held a training session at a national sales meeting to help company sales personnel handle a delicate problem. As the firm's merchandise was being sold off its racks at customer stores, retail clerks were filling in the company's racks with jewelry purchased from competitors. In frustration, company salespeople were removing the competitive products from its displays which upset the retail clerks. Discussions among the company's salespeople at the sales meeting were fruitful in developing a company-wide method of dealing with this troublesome matter. Some companies hold weekly sales meetings to analyze the activity or call reports of salespeople. Unidentified copies of call reports are distributed, discussed, and critiqued constructively by the sales manager to help all the salespeople do a better job in preparing their reports.[57]

Change of Pace The regional or national sales meeting is oftentimes viewed as a vacation with a purpose. Getting away helps salespeople unwind. Many firms hold their sales meetings at resort sites, where salespeople can enjoy golf, tennis, swimming, horseback riding, winter sports, and health club facilities in between business meetings. The announcement of a resort site, accompanied by a handsome brochure, will often cause prospective attendees to look forward to the meetings. Moreover, it tells them there will be enjoyable activities at the meeting in addition to business.

Videoconferences An efficient way to link several different locations together for one sales meeting is by having a videoconference. Rather than bringing the entire sales force of an organization together under one roof, videoconferencing links everyone via satellite and/or interactive video. One large company celebrated its one-hundredth anniversary by connecting over 2000 district sales managers in five cities for a video-conference. "We held a videoconference for the first time because we wanted every member of the sales force management family to be able to interact simultaneously and share the excitement coming out of the celebration," reported the manager of the company's sales meetings and conferences.[58]

A videoconference is an excellent way to inform and motivate the entire sales force of a company at one time with top management giving everyone the same message at the same time. Moreover, a teleconference to several locations enables top management not only to speak to each location simultaneously but also to tailor the content of each of the locations' meetings without having to hold separate regional meetings.[59] Given the success many companies are experiencing with videoconferences by using Zoom and WebEx, it's likely that they'll become a bigger part of sales meetings in the future.

Additional Perspectives in Twenty-First Century Sales Force Motivation

Let's now look at a few emerging perspectives that provide additional insights into sales force motivation.

Organizational and Job Commitment

Successful salespeople generally feel a close bond between themselves, their company, and their work. Organizational commitment is identifying with and internalizing the company's values and goals plus desiring to stay a viable member of the organization. Job commitment refers to the degree of involvement (high or low) that salespersons have for their job.

When salespersons feel committed to their organization and/or job, they feel ener-gized to be effective producers.[60] After all, their selling success will assist the firm in achieving its goals. Similarly, such success is likely to increase their positive attitudes toward — and subsequent commitment to — their job.[61] Such salespeople demon-strate strong dedication to their company and to the work itself. This sense of devotion can pack an emotional wallop. Research has found that both organizational commit-ment and job commitment can have a favorable impact on salesperson motivation.[62] Furthermore, the longer salespeople stay with the firm, the more knowledgeable they become about their customers; consequently, they're in a position to provide improved customer service and customer loyalty tends to rise.[63] Customer loyalty in turn increases salesperson job satisfaction and motivation.

Organizational Climate

Organizational climate consists of the perceptions salespeople have about their work situation and conditions. Whether favorable or unfavorable, these perceptions can affect salesperson attitudes about their job situation.

Organizational climate has four components: (1) job characteristics (role perceptions, opportunities, and problems in the job); (2) leadership characteristics (supervisory styles and salesperson/sales manager relationships); (3) organizational characteristics (company philosophy about managing salespersons); and (4) work group characteristics (formal and informal relationships among the salespeople).[64] Aspects of organizational climate that influence salesperson motivation include such factors as ethical climate, the considerateness of the sales supervisor, management's concern for sales subordinates, the level of company support and training, availability of adequate resources, the number of personal and career development opportunities, degree of trust in the sales manager, the degree of challenge in assigned goals, sales manager success in obtaining upper-management support for the sales force, and the opportunity for high earnings and promotions.[65]

Learning Orientation vs. Performance Orientation

Because sales managers typically have a short-term perspective, they tend to encourage their salespeople to adopt a performance orientation. That is, they predispose them toward working hard and generating sales. Indeed, a performance orientation works when salespeople are especially keen on receiving favorable assessments of their skills from management and peers. But, afraid that change will lead to failure, they may doggedly continue their traditional way of doing things, even if an alternate way would be better.

Compare this perspective to a learning orientation, which occurs when salespersons discover news ways of selling effectively. They're willing to take risks and try new approaches, even if doing so leads to mistakes; they value personal growth and development.[66]

More firms today are trying to enhance the learning orientation of their salespeople. Through careful and conscientious learning, salespeople *can* adopt improved methods for dealing with their customers, thus enhancing their selling skills and ultimately producing long-run gains for the firm.

Salespeople who use a learning orientation are zealous to acquire new knowledge, enhance their present skills, obtain new skills, and improve their overall performance for both the firm's customers, and themselves.[67] Research has found that a performance orientation has a different impact on salesperson motivation than a learning orientation does. Specifically, salespeople using a performance orientation have an increased propensity to "work harder" (increase their selling effort); salespersons utilizing a learning orientation also work hard but are more likely to "work smarter" too, and to gain knowledge about various selling situations, then adapt it to the sales situation at hand.[68] Working smarter is especially effective in enhancing salesperson productivity.[69]

Some salespeople set personal goals for themselves, in addition to the organizational and individual goals that have been set for them by or in concert with their sales manager. Personal goals can give the salesperson an "extra push," particularly because they have been tailored to the specific needs of the individual and the unique circumstances in their territories. In fact, salespersons who set specific goals for themselves and who believe that such goals are important to job success exert more effort than salespeople who don't.[70]

Salesperson's Career Cycle

Just like human lives and company products, salespeople, too, have a "life cycle" of different stages that evolve over time.[71] They pass through four distinct stages: the

> **TABLE 11.8**

Motivating Salespeople Throughout Their Career

Career stage	Salesperson characteristics	Sales force motivator
Preparation/ exploration	• Is in early phase of career • Is searching for comfortable position • Is likely to change occupation	• Use communication to build self-confidence and lower uncertainties
Development/ establishment	• Seeks stabilization in occupation • Sees career as very important • Strives for professional success and promotion	• Widen criteria for success • Introduce rewards for meeting challenges
Maturity/ maintenance	• Is concerned with retaining current position • Shows greater commitment to firm; less likely to switch jobs • Adapts to changes to keep performance at current level	• Reward creativity and self-reliance • Emphasize techniques for working smarter
Decline/ disengagement	• Exhibits declining performance • Psychologically disengages from work • Is preparing for retirement	• Reduce field selling hours and assign more staff functions like sales forecasting, training, or mentoring of junior salespeople

preparation or exploration stage, the development or establishment stage, the maturity or maintenance stage, and the decline or disengagement stage. Individuals go through these stages not only as a function of time, but also because of changes in their personal and professional lives or circumstances. At each stage, salespeople have different needs, skills, requirements, goals, and performance levels — and thus motivational concerns at each career stage can vary — as shown in Table 11.8.

In the *preparation/exploration stage* salespeople are concerned about finding an occupation in which they will succeed. They're likely to be new to the selling arena (or at least to the firm) and typically require extensive training. Their priority is to build up knowledge and skills and become conversant with the organization's policies and procedures.

When salespeople arrive at the *development/establishment stage*, they have become committed to the selling profession, seek stability in their professional and personal lives, and strongly desire professional success. This is the time when training must be converted into productive results. The *maturity/maintenance stage* requires holding on to what has already been achieved – position, status, image, and performance level. The salesperson may reach a "rated capacity" beyond which he or she is unwilling or even unable to go. In this stage salespeople prefer to sell smarter rather than harder and may well plateau at a desirable level.

In the *decline/disengagement stage* sales personnel may be preparing at least mentally for retirement or, if they haven't achieved much success, they may psychologically withdraw from the sales scene by making fewer calls per day or calling solely on existing accounts rather than on prospects. They may experience substantially reduced confidence in themselves and lose interest in their work.

How does motivation change from one career stage to the next? Research has found that preparation/exploration stage salespeople don't feel they're being rewarded for effective performance. In the development/establishment stage they place a heavy emphasis on receiving a promotion, while in the maturity/maintenance stage their level of motivation may be the same except for a decreased emphasis on receiving a promotion. Finally, decline/disengagement salespersons don't think they'll be adequately rewarded for achieving new accounts or their product quotas.[72] Another study found that salespeople in the exploration stage of their careers had greater material ambitions (desire for money and material things) than those in subsequent stages.[73]

Career Plateauing Despite the potential for substantial material and nonmaterial rewards, sales jobs are demanding, challenging, and even grueling. Career plateauing occurs when a salesperson no longer grows or develops in the position, or when the likelihood of the person's receiving additional responsibility is low. It occurs for three major reasons: (1) the salesperson's performance is deficient, (2) few opportunities for promotions or augmented responsibility are available in the firm, or (3) the individual has a preference or some constraint that prevents his or her taking on added responsibility. Plateauing is a vexing motivational problem for sales managers. Although the salesperson may still be a solid performer (but not necessarily), his or her performance is likely to have decreased at least somewhat. To elevate the salesperson's desire to move ahead and to increase the productivity level becomes a daunting challenge for management.

Salespeople at a plateau can manifest a number of adverse behaviors. They may reduce the number of calls they make per day or the amount of time they spend in the field. They may feel stressed out or burned out and unable to cope with either dilemma. Performance might decline across the board, or only on selected performance criteria. The salesperson may emphasize calling on existing accounts and considerably reduce the time spent prospecting. Absenteeism or sick days could noticeably rise. Boredom, frustration, moroseness, and even melancholy can envelope the individual. Unless drastic measures are taken, management may lose the services of a solid performer – and his or her behavior could even become contagious.

So what's a sales manager to do with a plateaued salesperson? Or better yet, what might be done to reduce the chances that sales force members will become plateaued? Although there are no sure-fire solutions to this problem, there are several substantive efforts sales managements can make[74]:

- Analyze and if necessary change the sales force selection process, to increase the chances of promoting salespeople with the skills or training potential necessary for increased job responsibilities.
- Review the job description of the advanced position, to determine whether the salesperson has the skills and abilities necessary to perform effectively in it.
- Consider reinvigorating underperforming senior salespeople in the last career stage by assigning them to staff or support activities such as sales forecasting, sales budgeting, sales training, or mentoring of junior salespeople.
- Provide different, more focused training for salespeople who have insufficient capacities for assuming additional responsibility but might be able to perform better in their current jobs.
- Consider changing the nature of the job – increase the number of sales activities the salespeople perform, use sales teams if feasible, and adopt relationship-selling principles to better serve customers.
- Explain to salespeople why their performance is deficient and work out strategies for addressing the sales problems.
- Maintain competitive compensation and promotional programs for salespeople at all career stages.
- Reduce stress and burnout by changing salespeople's assignments, providing techniques for managing these "twin evils," and facilitating development of *espirit de corps* within the sales organization so sales reps are encouraged to support and help each another.

- When promotional opportunities are minimal, encourage the poor performers to take early retirement or leave, provide extensive recognition in the form of titles, public praise, or pay raises to high performers who cannot yet be promoted, or coordinate personnel planning with strategic planning (match an employee's career needs with an appropriate position).
- Provide career information to salespersons – inform them of the consequences of their taking on or failing to take on additional responsibility.
- Create dual-career paths that can lead to improved matching of a salesperson's skills and desires with an appropriate position.

Empowerment and Participative Management

In the chapter on leadership, we talked about empowerment and participative management as ways to provide greater autonomy to employees. Now let's briefly revisit this cutting-edge business philosophy for its enormous potential to increase motivation.

Shifting, sharing, and delegating power to subordinates at lower organizational levels gives them greater authority to make decisions about how to perform tasks and instills a sense of ownership, and responsibility.[75] Empowered employees play an integral role in decision-making, problem-solving, goal-setting, and suggesting or instituting organizational changes. Consistent with Maslow's need theory, empowerment and participative management can heighten subordinates' self-efficacy – the feeling that they do meaningful work and have the ability to produce valuable outcomes-- leading to increased effort, greater motivation, and higher levels of performance.[76] Note, however, that empowerment programs may not produce motivation and desirable organizational goals if subordinates are *not* provided with information, knowledge (through training), enhanced power, and desirable rewards.[77]

Chapter Summary

1. **Understand the nature of motivation.** In an era of rapid globalization, companies from all over the world are competing for survival, larger market share, or highest profits. Firms are quickly learning that to thrive, not merely survive, they must increasingly rely on their salespeople to "do battle" with their competitor counterparts by skillfully interacting with prospects and customers on the front lines. Responsible for revenue generating and customer relationship activities, salespeople can help ensure that their firms succeed in this intensely competitive global economy. Recognizing the crucial role salespeople play in their firm's success, sales managers must devise and employ appropriate inducement strategies to increase salesperson **motivation** – the set of dynamic interpersonal processes that cause the initiation, direction, intensity, and persistence of work-related behaviors – to achieve organizational goals and objectives.

2. **Apply contemporary theories of motivation to sales management.** This chapter exposed you to the concept of motivation with an extended discussion of the relevant contemporary *content* theories of motivation (hierarchy of needs theory, ERG theory, needs theory, and dual factor theory), *process* theories of motivation (equity theory, expectancy theory, attribution theory, goal-setting theory), and *reinforcement* theory of motivation (organizational behavior modification theory), which can guide sales managers in stimulating

the sales force to exert extra effort needed to dramatically increase sales performance.

3. **Use reward and incentive programs to motivate salespeople.** While fulfilling financial needs is important to salespeople, research indicates that today's salespeople are increasingly motivated by extrinsic (financial) rewards as well as higher-order intrinsic (nonfinancial) rewards, such as need for respect, accomplishment, control, status, and honesty. Giving salespeople recognition via symbolic motivators, such as gifts (plaques or jewelry), simply verbal praise, or a pat on the back can instill a certain pride that a paycheck may not. Salespeople, in particular, can be motivated by the spotlight and personal validation that public recognition brings from success in their competitive work.

4. **Use sales contests and sales meetings to motivate salespeople.** Sales managers can choose from several motivational strategies and tools to implement their general approach to inducing higher performance from the sales force. Two of the most important motivational tools are sales contests and sales meetings. These tools, if implemented correctly, can significantly enhance the performance of individual salespeople and the entire sales force.

5. **Apply organizational commitment, career stage, and empowerment to motivating a sales force.** This chapter also discussed the emerging perspectives of organizational and job commitment, organizational climate, learning vs. performance orientation, salesperson's career cycle, and empowerment and participative management, which provided many insights for sales managers charged with motivating the sales forces of the twenty-first century.

Key Terms

Motivation
Hierarchy of needs theory
ERG theory
Needs theory
Dual factor theory
Equity theory
Expectancy theory
Expectancy (effort-performance linkage)

Instrumentality (performance-reward linkage)
Valence (the attractiveness of rewards)
Attribution theory
Goal-setting theory
Organizational behavior modification theory
Positive reinforcement

Negative reinforcement
Extrinsic rewards
Incentive program
Financial incentives
Intrinsic rewards
Nonfinancial incentives
Sales motivation strategies
Sales meetings

Organizational commitment
Job commitment
Organizational climate
Performance orientation
Learning orientation
Career plateauing
Empowerment
Participative management

Notes

1. Harasewych, A. (26 February 2015). Marketing warfare: Offensive strategy. http://andrij.co/blog/offensive-marketing-warfare/ (accessed 16 November 2019); Ries, A. and Trout, J. (1997). *Marketing Warfare*. New York: McGraw-Hill.; Competitive rivalry: The four strategies of marketing warfare (22 August 2013). https://ezyinsights.com/competitive-rivalry-the-four-strategies-of-marketing-warfare/(accessed 17 November 2019).

2. Wiener, A.Z. What is Guerrilla marketing? Seven examples to inspire your brand (30 July 2018) https://blog.hubspot.com/marketing/guerilla-marketing-examples (accessed 16 November 2019); Levinson, J.C. (1998). *Guerrilla marketing: Secrets for making big profits from your small business*, 3ed. Boston: Houghton Mifflin.

3. Colletti, J.A. and Fiss, M.S. (2006). The ultimately accountable job: Leading today's sales organization. *Harvard Business Review* (July–August): 125–131; Deeter-Schmelz, D.R., Goebel, D.J. and Kennedy K.N. (2008). What are the characteristics of an effective sales manager? An exploratory study comparing salesperson and

sales manager perspectives. *Journal of Personal Selling & Sales Management* 28 (1): 7–20; Cho, W. (3 October 2017). Why the sales manager's role is so important in contributing to organization success. www.linkedin.com/pulse/why-sales-managers-role-so-important-contributing-organization-cho (accessed 15 November 2019); Alton, L. (29 August 2017). The three most important things a sales manager does. www.inc.com/larry-alton/the-3-most-important-things-a-sales-manager-does.html (accessed 15 November 2019).

4. Friedman, W.A. (2006). Give me that old-time motivation. *Harvard Business Review* 84(7/8): 24; Mayer, D. and Greenberg, H. M. (2006). What makes a good salesman? *Harvard Business Review* (July–August): 164–171; Coutu, D. (2006). Leveraging the psychology of the salesperson: A conversation with psychologist and anthropologist G. Clotaire Rapaille. *Harvard Business Review* (July–August): 42–47; Thakor, M.V. and Joshi, A.W. (2005). Motivating salesperson customer orientation: Insights from the job characteristics model. *Journal of Business Research* 58 (5): 584–592; Here's what you should do to motivate your sales team. www.google.com/search?client=firefox-b-1-d&q=sales+force+motivation (accessed 19 November 2019); Alerecht, C. (1 September 2017). What motivates your sales force? https://info.zs.com/thecarrot/what-motivates-your-sales-force (accessed 19 November 2019).

5. Motivation and motivation theory. (10 February 2020). www.encyclopedia.com/management/encyclopedias-almanacs-transcripts-and-maps/motivation-and-motivation-theory (accessed 21 February 2020); Theories of motivation. https://businessjargons.com/theories-of-motivation.html (accessed 18 November 2019).

6. Chand, S. *Motivation theories: Top 8 theories of motivation – explained!* www.yourarticlelibrary.com/motivation/motivation-theories-top-8-theories-of-motivation-explained/35377 (accessed 17 November 2019); *Harvard Business Review on Motivating People* (2003). Cambridge, MA: Harvard Business School Press Books.

7. Maslow, A.H. (1954). *Motivation and Personality*. New York: Harper & Row; Lee, M.T. and Raschke, R.L. (2016). Understanding employee motivation and organizational performance: Arguments for a set-theoretic approach. *Journal of Innovation & Knowledge* 1 (3): 162–169.; ZoomInfo (5 November 2019). How to structure a sales team with Maslow's hierarchy of needs. https://blog.zoominfo.com/sales-team-structure/ (accessed 17 November 2019); Motivating salespeople–How managers can get it Wrong! (31 July 2014). http://salesstrategypitstop.theasggroup.com/2014/07/31/motivating-salespeople-how-managers-get-it-wrong/ (accessed 18 November 2019).

8. Alderfer, C.P. (1972). *Existence, Relatedness, and Growth*. New York: Free Press; Arnolds, C.A. and Boshoff, C. (2002). Compensation, esteem valence, and job performance: An empirical assessment of Alderfer's ERG theory. *The International Journal of Human Resource Management* 14 (4): 697–719; Robitaille, J. (11 February 2011). The value of ERG theory for managers. www.labmanager.com/leadership-and-staffing/2011/02/value-of-erg-theory-for-managers (accessed 17 November 2019).

9. McClelland, D.C. (1985). *Human Motivation*. Glenview, IL: Scott, Foresman; Tanner, R. (2017). Motivation: Applying Maslow's hierarchy of needs theory. https://managementisajourney.com/motivation-applying-maslows-hierarchy-of-needs-theory/ (accessed 18 November 2019).

10. Amyx, D. and Alford, B.L. (2005). The effects of salesperson need for achievement and sales manager leader reward behavior. *Journal of Personal Selling & Sales Management* 25(4)(Fall): 345–359; Five psychological theories of motivation to increase productivity (10 July 2019). https://contactzilla.com/blog/5-psychological-theories-motivation-increase-productivity/ (accessed 17 November 2019).

11. Gellerman, S.W. (1978). *Motivation and Productivity*. Stanford, CA: American Management Association, pp. 115–141.; Schacter, S. (1959). *The Psychology of Affiliation*. Stanford, CA: Stanford University Press.; Moriarty, T. (29 March 2014). Understanding the three types of needs: Achievement, affiliation, and power. www.plantservices.com/articles/2014/human-capital-types-of-needs/ (accessed 18 November 2019).

12. Ledingham, D.L., Kovac, M., and Simon, H.L. (2006). The new science of sales force productivity. *Harvard Business Review* 84(9): 124–133; Herzberg, F. B. (2003). One more time: How do you motivate employees. *Harvard Business Review* 81(1): 4–11; Herzberg, F.B., Mausner, B., and Snyderman, B. (1959). *The Motivation to Work*. New York: Wiley.; Mallin, M.L., Gammoh, B.S., Pullins, E.B.et al. (2017). A new perspective of salesperson motivation and salesforce outcomes: The mediating role of salesperson-brand identification. *Journal of Marketing Theory and Practice* 25 (4): 357–374.

13. Herzberg's motivation theory – Two factor theory https://expert-programmanagement.com/2018/04/herzbergs-two-factor-theory/ (accessed 18 November 2019); Herzberg's two-factor theory of motivation (15 May 2017). www.humanbusiness.eu/herzberg-two-factor-theory-of-motivation/ (accessed 19 November 2019).

14. McCarthy Byrne, T.M., Moon, M.A. and Mentzer, J.T. (2011). Motivating the industrial sales force in the sales forecasting process. *Industrial Marketing Management* 40 (1): 128–138; Berl, R.L., Williamson, N.C. and Powell, T. (1984). Industrial salesforce motivation: A critique and test of Maslow's hierarchy of need. *Journal of Personal Selling & Sales Management* 4 (May): 33–39.; Shipley, D.D. and Kiely, J.A. (1986). Industrial salesforce motivation and Herzberg's dual factor theory: A UK perspective. *Journal of Personal Selling & Sales Management* 6 (May): 9–16.; Marcos, J. and Franco-Santos, M. Motivating and rewarding the sales force. https://blog.som.cranfield.ac.uk/execdev/motivating-and-rewarding-the-sales-force (accessed 20 November 2019).

15. Miao, C.F., Evans, K.R. and Shaoming, Z. (2007). The role of salesperson motivation in sales control systems --Intrinsic and extrinsic motivation revisited. *Journal of Business Research* 60 (5): 417–425; Huggins, K.A., White, D.W. and Stahl, J. (2016). Antecedents to sales force job motivation and performance: The critical role of emotional intelligence and affect-based trust in retailing manager. *International Journal of Sales, Retailing, and Marketing* 5 (1): 27–37.; Moberg, C.R. and Leasher, M. (2011). Examining the difference in salesperson motivation among

different cultures. *American Journal of Business* 26 (2): 145–160.

16. Herzberg's two-factor theory of motivation (15 May 2017). www.humanbusiness.eu/herzberg-two-factor-theory-of-motivation/ (accessed 19 November 2019); Turner, P.K. and Krizek, R.L. (2006). A meaning-centered approach to customer satisfaction. *Management Communication Quarterly* 20 (2): 115–147; Dugguh, S.I. and Dennis, A. (2014). Job satisfaction theories: Traceability to employee performance in organizations. *Journal of Business and Management* 16 (5): 11–18.

17. Goodman, P.S. and Friedman, A. (1971). An examination of Adams' theory of inequity. *Administrative Science Quarterly* 16: 271–288; DeConinck, J.B. and Johnson, J.T. (2009). The effects of perceived supervisor support, perceived organizational support, and organizational justice on turnover among salespeople. *Journal of Personal Selling & Sales Management* 29 (4): 333–350.

18. Vroom, V. (1964). *Work and Motivation*. New York: Wiley.; Parijat, P. and Bagga, S. (2014). Victor Vroom's expectancy theory of motivation—An evaluation. *International Research Journal of Business and Management* 9 (September): 1–7.; Dininni, J. (30 September 2010). Management theory of Victor Vroom. www.business.com/articles/management-theory-of-victor-vroom/ (accessed 18 November 2019).

19. Campbell, J.P., Dunnette, M.D., Lawler III, E. E. and Weick, Jr., K.E. (1970). *Managerial Behavior, Performance, and Effectiveness*. New York: McGraw-Hill Book Company; Pousa, C. and Mathieu, A. (2010). Sales managers' motivation to coach salespeople: An exploration using expectancy theory. *International Journal of Evidence Based Coaching and Mentoring* 8 (1): 34–50.; Nasri, W. and Charfeddine, L. (2012). Motivating salespeople to contribute to marketing intelligence activities: An expectancy theory approach. *International Journal of Marketing Studies* 4 (1): 168–175.

20. Bagozzi, P.B. (1978). Salesforce performance and satisfaction as a function of individual difference, interpersonal and situational factors. *Journal of Marketing Research* 15(4): 517–531.; Shrestha, P. (1 November 2017). Expectancy theory of motivation. https://www.psychestudy.com/general/motivation-emotion/expectancy-theory-motivation (accessed 19 November 2019); Kohli, A. (1985). Some unexplored supervisory behaviors and their influence on salespeople's role clarity, specific self-esteem, job satisfaction, and motivation. *Journal of Marketing Research* 22 (November): 424–433; Teas, R.K. (1982). Performance-reward instrumentalities and the motivation of salespeople. *Journal of Retailing* 58 (Fall): 4–26; Teas, R.K. and McElroy, J.C. (1986). Causal attributions and expectancy estimates: A framework for understanding the dynamics of salesforce motivation. *Journal of Marketing* 50: 75–86.; Tyagi, P. (1985). Relative importance of key job dimensions and leadership behaviors in motivating salesperson work performance. *Journal of Marketing* 49 (Summer): 76–86; Ford, N.M., Churchill, G.A. and Walker, O.C., Jr. (1985). *Sales Force Performance*. Lexington, MA: D. C. Heath and Company.

21. Johnson, M.S. (2006). A bibliometric review of the contribution of attribution theory to sales management. *Journal of Personal Selling & Sales Management* 26 (Spring): 181–195; Dixon,

A. L., Forbes, L. P., and Schertzer, S.M.B. (2005). Early success: how attributions for sales success shape inexperienced salespersons' behavioral intentions. *Journal of Personal Selling & Sales Management* (Winter): 67–77; Sujan, H. (1986). Smarter versus Harder: An exploratory attributional analysis of salespeople's' motivations. *Journal of Marketing Research* (February): 41–49; Teas, R.K. and McElroy, J.C. (1986). Causal attributions and expectancy estimates: A framework for understanding the dynamics of salesforce motivation. *Journal of Marketing* 50: 75–86; Weiner, B. (2010). The development of an attribution-based theory of motivation: A history of ideas. *Journal of Educational Psychologist* 45 (1): 28–36.

22. Mallin, M.L. and Mayo, M. (2006). Why did I lose? A conservation of resources view of salesperson failure attributions. *Journal of Personal Selling & Sales Management* 26(4): 345–357; Fang, E., Evans, K.R. and Landry, T.D. (2005). Control systems' effect on attributional processes and sales outcomes: A cybernetic information-processing perspective. *Journal of the Academy of Marketing Science* 33 (4): 553–574; Dixon, A.L. and Schertzer, S.M.B. (2005). Bouncing back: How salesperson optimism and self-efficacy influence attributions and behaviors following failure. *Journal of Personal Selling & Sales Management* 25(4): 361–369; Farber, B. (19 February 2014). Seven reasons sales pros fail. www.inc.com/barry-farber/7-reasons-salespeople-fail.html (accessed 17 November 2019).

23. Harish, S. and Weitz, B.A. (1986). Sales training: The psychology of motivation. *Marketing Communications* 11(January):24–28; Furnham, A. and Fudge, C. (2008). The five factor model of personality and sales performance. *Journal of Individual Differences* 29: 11–16.

24. Fu, F.Q., Richards, K.A. and Jones, E. (2009). The motivation hub: Effects of goal setting and self-efficacy on effort and new product sales. *Journal of Personal Selling & Sales Management* 29 (3): 277–292; Fang, E., Evans, K.R. and Zou, S. (2005). The moderating effect of goal-setting characteristics on the sales control systems–job performance relationship. *Journal of Business Research* 58 (9): 1214–1222; Harris, E.G., Mowen, J.C. and Brown, T.J. (2005). Re-examining salesperson goal orientations: Personality influencers, customer orientation, and work satisfaction. *Journal of the Academy of Marketing Science* 33 (1): 19–35.

25. Cotteleer, M., Inderrieden, E. and Lee, F. (2006). Selling the sales force on automation. *Harvard Business Review* (July–August): 18–22; Ledingham, D., Kovac, M., and Simon, H.L. (2006). The new science of sales force productivity. *Harvard Business Review*, (September): 124–133; Examples of SMART goals for sales reps to dominate 2019 (6 February 2020). https://spotio.com/blog/examples-of-smart-goals-for-sales-reps-to-dominate-2019/ (accessed 21 February 2020).

26. Livingston, J. S. (2003). Pygmalion in management. *Harvard Business Review* 81(1)(January): 4–12; Eden, D. (1988). Pygmalion, goal setting and expectancy: Compatible ways to boost productivity. *Academy of Management Review* 13(4): 639–652; Yatham, G.P., Erez, M. and Locke, E.A. (1988). Resolving scientific disputes by the joint design of crucial experiments by the Erez-Yatham dispute regarding participation in goal-setting.

Journal of Applied Psychology 73(4): 753–772; Bernard, C. (7 April 2015). Sales management skills: are you a pygmalion or a golem? https://spotio.com/blog/examples-of-smart-goals-for-sales-reps-to-dominate-2019/ (accessed 20 November 2019).

27. Weaver, R.A. (1985). Set goals to tap self-motivation. *Business Marketing* (December): 55; Patel, S. (7 March 2018). How to set effective sales goals for your sales team. https://blog.mailshake.com/sales-goals/ (accessed 20 November 2019); Lunenburg, F.C. (2011). Goal-setting theory of motivation. *International Journal of Management, Business, and Administration* 15 (1): 1–6.

28. Skinner, B.F. (1953). *Science and Human Behavior.* New York: Macmillan; Stajkovic, A.D. and Luthans, F. (1997). A meta-analysis of the effects of organizational behavior modification on task performance, 1975–1995. *Academy of Management Journal* 40 (October): 1122–1149; Chonko, L.B. (1986). Organizational Commitment in the Sales Force. *Journal of Personal Selling & Sales Management* 6 (3): 19–28; Piercy, N.F., Cravens, D.W. and Lane, N. (2012). Sales manager behavior-based control and salesperson performance: The effects of manager control competencies and organizational citizenship behavior. *Journal of Marketing Theory and Practice* 20 (1): 7–22.

29. Scott, R.A., Swan, J.E., Wilson, M.E.et al. (1986). Organizational behavior modification: A general motivational tool for sales management. *Journal of Personal Selling & Sales Management* 6 (August): 61–70; Blanding, M. (26 March 2018). To motivate employees, give an unexpected bonus (or Penalty). https://hbswk.hbs.edu/item/to-motivate-employees-give-an-unexpected-bonus-or-penalty (accessed 20 November 2019).

30. Jelinek, R. and Ahearne, M.A. (2006). The enemy within: Examining salesperson deviance and its determinants. *Journal of Personal Selling & Sales Management* 26(4)(Fall): 327–344; Schwepker, C.H., Jr. and Good, D.J. (2004). Understanding sales quotas: An exploratory investigation of consequences of failure. *Journal of Business & Industrial Marketing* 19 (1): 39–48; Ledingham, D., Kovac, M. and Simon, H.L. (2006). The new science of sales force productivity. *Harvard Business Review* (September): 124–133; Zallocco, R., Pullines, E.B. and Mallin, M.L. (2009). A re-examination of B2B sales performance. *Journal of Business & Industrial Marketing* 24 (8): 598–610.

31. Byrnes, N. (2006). The art of motivation. *Business Week* (1 May) pp. 56–62; Dhawan, S. (14 March 2019). The Big List of Sales Incentive Ideas (Besides Money). www.copper.com/blog/sales-incentives (accessed 20 November 2019).

32. Chung, D.J. (2015). How to really motivate salespeople. *Harvard Business Review* https://hbr.org/2015/04/how-to-really-motivate-salespeople (accessed 20 November 2019); Mettler, R. (21 February 2017). Pros and cons of different types of sales compensation plans. www.salesforcesearch.com/blog/pros-and-cons-of-different-types-of-sales-compensation-plans/ (accessed 20 November 2019).

33. Kotler, P., Rackham, N., Krishnaswamy, S. (2006). Ending the war between sales & marketing. *Harvard Business Review* 84(7-8) (July–August): 68–78, 187; Zoltners, A.A., Sinha, P. and Lorimer, S.E. (2006). Match your sales force structure to your business

life cycle. *Harvard Business Review* (July–August): 81–89; Steenburgh, T. and Ahearne, M. (2012). Motivating salespeople: What really works. *Harvard Business Review* 90(7–8):70–75.

34. Lopez, T.B., Hopkins, C.D. and Raymond, M.A. (2006). Reward preferences of salespeople: how do commissions rate? *Journal of Personal Selling & Sales Management* 26(4)(Fall): 381–390; Kowalewski, S.J. and Phillips, S.L. (2012). Preferences for performance based employee rewards: Evidence from small business environments. *International Journal of Management and Marketing Research* 5 (2): 65–76.

35. Trailer, B. and Dickie, J. (2006). Understanding what your sales manager is up against. *Harvard Business Review* 84(7/8): 48–55; Brown, S.P., Evans, K.R., Mantrala, M.K. et al. (2005). Adapting motivation, control, and compensation research to a new environment. *Journal of Personal Selling & Sales Management* 25 (Spring): 156–167; Bursk, E.C. (2006). Low-pressure selling. *Harvard Business Review* 84(7/8): 150–162; Cespedes, F.V., Gardner, A., Kerr, S., Kelley, R.D.et al. (2006). Old hand or new blood?" *Harvard Business Review* 84(7/8): 28–40; Madhani, P.M. (2014). Compensation, ethical sales behavior, and customer lifetime value. *Compensation & Benefits Review* 46 (4): 204–218.

36. Christensen, C.M., Marx, M. and Stevenson, H.H. (2006). The tools of cooperation and change. *Harvard Business Review* 84(10): 73–80; Kuvaas, B., Buch, R., Gagne, M. et al. (2016). Do you get what you pay for? Sales incentives and implications for motivation and changes in turnover intention and work effort. *Motivation and Emotion* 40 (5): 667–680.

37. Murphy, W.H. (2004). In pursuit of short-term goals: Anticipating the unintended consequences of using special incentives to motivate the sales force. *Journal of Business Research* 57: 1265–1275; McCormack, M. (14 May 2015). How much should we budget for a sales incentive program? www.executivegrouptravel.com/blog/budgeting-for-an-incentive-program (accessed 20 November 2019).

38. Wenthe, M. Achieve sales and marketing alignment with incentives and recognition. www.itagroup.com/insights/achieve-sales-and-marketing-alignment-incentives-and-recognition (accessed 20 November 2019); Hatami, H., Huber, I., Murthy, V., Plotkin, C.M. (October 2018). Sales incentives that boost growth. https://managementisajourney.com/motivation-applying-maslows-hierarchy-of-needs-theory/ (accessed 20 November 2019).

39. White, M.C. (2007). Bon voyage as a bonus. *The New York Times* (13 March): c9; Harris, K. (25 October 2018). Sales incentive trips: A great way to reward your biggest performers. https://memoryblue.com/2018/10/sales-incentive-trips/ (accessed 19 November 2019).

40. Collins, T. (6 September 2019). Eighteen new sales incentives to improve performance. www.viktorwithak.com/18-new-sales-incentives-to-improve-performance/ (accessed 18 November 2019).

41. Bommaraju, R. and Hohenberg, S. (2018). Self-selected sales incentives: evidence of their effectiveness, persistence, durability, and underlying mechanisms. *Journal of Marketing* 82 (5): 106–124.

42. Zoltners, A.A., Sinha, P.K. and Lorimer, S.E. (3 August 2017). Are sales incentives becoming obsolete? *Harvard Business Review* (accessed 20 November 2019); Kearns, S. (1 February 2018). Sales incentives that motivate modern sales pros. https://business.linkedin.com/sales-solutions/blog/sales-leaders/2018/02/sales-incentives-that-motivate-modern-sales-pros (accessed 21 November 2019); Lane, J. (21 October 2019). Top 10 non-financial sales rewards to motivate reps. www.xactlycorp.com/blog/top-10-non-financial-rewards-to-motivate-employees/ (accessed 21 November 2019).

43. Colletti, J. A. and Fiss, M.S. (2006). The ultimately accountable job leading today's sales organization. *Harvard Business Review* (July–August): 125–131; Anderson, E. and Onyemah, V. (2006). How right should the customer be? *Harvard Business Review* 84(7/8): 59–67; Wietrak, E. (6 March 2017). External incentives and internal motivation – A perfect pairing to boost work performance https://scienceforwork.com/blog/incentives-motivation-performance/ (accessed 20 November 2019).

44. Brante, M. (2014). *Sales incentives and sales performance: The moderating effect of cultural dimensions*. Doctoral Dissertation, Coles College of Business, Kennesaw State University; Zoltners, A.A., Sinha, P. and Lorimer, S.E. (2012). Breaking the sales force incentive addiction: A balanced approach to sales force effectiveness. *Journal of Personal Selling & Sales Management* 32 (2): 171–186; Matta, R. (17 July 2017). Startups Lure salespeople with equity as an incentive. https://mattermark.com/startups-lure-salespeople-with-equity-as-an-incentive/ (accessed 21 November 2019).

45. Adamson, A. (26 June 2019). Want to stop rampant sales team turnover? Career ladders are the first step. https://blog.hubspot.com/sales/career-growth-opportunities-for-top-sales-performers-other-than-management (accessed 21 November 2019); Sales representative advancement opportunities (27 August 2018) https://study.com/articles/sales_representative_advancement_opportunities.html (accessed 21 November 2019).

46. Schultz, R.J. and Schwepker, C.H, Jr. (2012). Boomers vs. millennials: Critical conflict regarding sales culture, salesforce recognition, and supervisor expectations. *International Journal of Business Humanities and Technology* 2 (1): 32–41; Hunter, K. (24 July 2018). How employee recognition and incentives increase sales. https://blog.corecentive.com/how-employee-recognition-and-incentives-increase-sales (accessed 22 November 2019); Evans, P. and Wolf, B. (2006). Collaboration rules. *Harvard Business Review* 84(7/8): 96–104.

47. Alonzo, V. (1996). Recognition? Who needs it? *Sales & Marketing Management* (July): 45–46; Kuestrer, S., Homburg, C. and Hildesheim, A. (2017). The Catbird seat of the sales force: How sales force integration leads to new product success. *International Journal of Research in Marketing* 34 (2): 462–479.

48. Rutherford, B., Boles, J., Hamwi, G.A., and Madupalli, R. (2009). The role of the seven dimensions of job satisfaction in salesperson's attitudes and behaviors. *Journal of Business Research* 62 (11): 1146–1151; Patjug, K. (1 March 2019). Fifteen cool job perks that keep employees happy. https://www.businessnewsdaily.com/5134-cool-job-benefits.html (accessed 22 November 2019);

Happy sales team: Happy business (24 November 2015) www.sandler.com/blog/happy-sales-team-happy-business/ (accessed 17 November 2019).

49. Kipfelsberger, P., Bruch, H. and Herhausen, D. (2015). Energizing companies through customer compliments. *Marketing Review St. Gallen* 32 (1): 50–59; DiMisa, J. and Rinaldi, E. (22 December 2010). Paying sales reps for customer satisfaction www.shrm.org/resourcesandtools/hrtopics/compensation/pages/customersatisfaction.aspx (accessed 21 November 2019); McGovern, M. 21 Unique ways to motivate your sales team www.resourcefulselling.com/motivate-sales-team/ (accessed 22 November 2019).

50. Brennan, L. (1990). Sales secrets of the incentive starts. *Sales & Marketing Management* (April): 92–100; Patel, S. (7 June 2019). Seven sales team motivation strategies that cost you nothing. https://blog.mailshake.com/sales-team-motivation/ (accessed 12 November 2019).

51. Lin, Y. (2017). Praise sales personnel for talent or effort?: Person versus process-focused feedback, goal orientation, and performance. *Journal of Business & Industrial Marketing* 32 (8): 1073–1086; Metler, R. (14 February 2017). Four tips to show your sales team some love www.salesforcesearch.com/blog/4-tips-show-sales-team-love/ (accessed 22 November 2019).

52. Amyx, D. and Alford, B.L. (2005). The effects of salesperson need for achievement and sales manager leader reward behavior. *Journal of Personal Selling & Sales Management* 25 (4): 345–359; Panagopoulos, N.G. and Ogilvie, J. (2015). Can salespeople lead themselves? Thought self-leadership strategies and their influence on sales performance. *Industrial Marketing Management* 47 (May): 190–203.

53. Moncrief, W.C., Marshall, G.W. and Rudd, J. M. (2015). Social media and related technology: Drivers of change in managing the contemporary sales force. *Business Horizons* 58 (1): 45–55; Leach, M.P., Liu, A.H. and Johnston, W.J. (2005). The role of self-regulation training in developing the motivation management capabilities of salespeople. *Journal of Personal Selling & Sales Management* (Summer): 269–281; Rangarajan, D., Jones, E. and Chin, W. (2005). Impact of sales force automation on technology-related stress, effort, and technology usage among salespeople. *Industrial Marketing Management* 34 (4): 345–354.

54. Cohen, A. (1996). Sales contests go interactive. *Sales & Marketing Management* (July): 45–46; Lim, N., Ahearne, M.J. and Ham, S.H. (2009). Design sales contests: Does the prize structure matter? *Journal of Marketing Research* 46 (3): 356–371.

55. Golden, M. (21 November 2018). Conducting the perfect sales & marketing meeting: How to effectively reach alignment. https://business.linkedin.com/marketing-solutions/blog/sales-and-marketing/2018/effective-sales-and-marketing-meeting (accessed 22 November 2019); Anderson, R. and Rosenbloom, B. (1986). Conducting successful sales meetings. In: *The Handbook of Executive Communication* (ed. J.L. DiGaetani), 611–632. Homewood, IL: Dow Jones-Irwin.

56. Rantala, T. and Hanti, S. (2016). Identifying new innovations in diverse B-to-B sales meetings. *Proceedings of the International Society for Professional Innovation Management Innovation*

Conference (19–22 June): 1–13; Kaydo, C. (1998). Unforgettable meetings. *Sales & Marketing Management* (February): 71–76.

57. Tews, M.J., Nichel, J. W. and Bartlett, A. (2012). The fundamental role of workplace fun in applicant attraction. *Journal of Leadership & Organizational Studies* 19 (1): 105–114; Hitchcock, K. (1997). Should work be fun? *Sales Manager's Bulletin: Special Report* 1407 Section II (30 August 30): 3.

58. Matsuo, M. (2009). The influence of sales management control on innovativeness of sales departments. *Journal of Personal Selling & Sales Management* 29 (4): 321–331; Morgan, I. and Rao, J. (2003). Making routine customer experiences fun. *MIT Sloan Management Review* 45 (1): 93–95; Phelps, T. (20 November 2019). Top reasons why sales people are fun to be around. www.thebalancecareers.com/top-reasons-why-sales-people-are-fun-to-be-around-2918515 (accessed 22 November 2019).

59. Patel, S. (13 February 2018). Sales meeting ideas to keep your team motivated and focused https://blog.mailshake.com/sales-meeting-ideas/ (accessed 22 November 2019); Higgins, K. (14 June 2014). Six secrets to a successful sales meeting. www.entrepreneur.com/article/230689 (accessed 22 November 2019).

60. Aikhateri, A.S. and Abuelhassan, A.E. (2018). The impact of perceived supervisor support on employees turnover intention: The mediating role of job satisfaction and affective organizational commitment. *International Business Management* 12 (7): 477–492; Avlonitis, G.J. and Panagopoulos, N.G. (2006). Role stress, attitudes, and job outcomes in business-to-business selling: Does the type of selling situation matter? *Journal of Personal Selling & Sales Management* (Winter): 67–77.

61. Boles, J., Madupalli, R. and Rutherford, B. (2007). The relationship of facets of salesperson job satisfaction with affective organizational commitment. *Journal of Business & Industrial Marketing* 22 (5): 311–321; Jaramillo, F., Mulki, J.P. and Marshall, G.W. (2005). A meta-analysis of the relationship between organizational commitment and salesperson job performance: 25 Years of Research. *Journal of Business Research* 58(6): 705–714; Mulki, J.P., Jaramillo, F. and Locander, W.B. (2006) Effects of ethical climate and supervisory trust on salesperson's job attitudes and intentions to quit. *Journal of Personal Selling & Sales Management* (Winter): 19–26; Rozell, E.J., Pettijohn, C.E, and Parker, R.S. (2004) Customer-oriented selling: Exploring the roles of emotional intelligence and organizational commitment. *Psychology and Marketing* 21 (6): 405–424.

62. Rose, R.C., Kumar, N. and Pak, O.G. (2009). The effect of organizational learning on organizational commitment, job satisfaction, and work performance. *Journal of Applied Business Research* 25 (6): 55–65; Dubinsky, A.J. and Skinner, S.J. (1984). Impact of job characteristics on retail salespeople's reactions to their jobs. *Journal of Retailing* 60 (Summer): 35–63; Ingram, T.N., Lee, K.S. and Lucas, G.H. (1991). Commitment and Involvement: Assessing a sales force typology. *Journal of the Academy of Marketing Science* 19 (Summer): 187–197; Sager, J.K. and Johnston, M.W. (1989). Antecedents and outcomes of organizational commitment: A study of salespeople. *Journal of Personal Selling & Sales Management* 9 (Spring): 30–41.

63. Homburg, C., Muller, M. and Klarmann, M. (2011). When does salespeople's customer orientation lead to customer loyalty? The differential effects of relational and functional customer orientation. *Journal of the Academy of Marketing Science* 39 (6): 795–812; Reichheld, F.F. (1993). Loyalty-based management. *Harvard Business Review* 71 (March–April): 64–73.

64. Schetzsle, S. (2014). Salesperson-sales manager social interaction and communication quality: The impact on salesperson cooperation. *The Journal of Applied Business Research* 30 (2): 607–613; DeConinck, J.B. and Johnson, J.T. (2009). The effects of perceived supervisor support, perceived organization support, and organizational justice on turnover among salespeople. *Journal of Personal Selling & Sales Management* 29 (4). 333–350; Ingram, T.N., LaForge, R.W., Locander, W.B., MacKenzie, S.B. (2005). New directions in sales leadership research. *Journal of Personal Selling & Sales Management* (Spring): 137–154; Weeks, W.A., Loe, T.W., Chonko, L.B.et al. (2004). The effect of perceived ethical climate on the search for sales force excellence. *Journal of Personal Selling & Sales Management* (Summer): 199–214; Mulki, J.P., Jaramillo, F. and. Locander, W.B. (2006). Effects of ethical climate and supervisory trust on salesperson's job attitudes and intentions to quit. *Journal of Personal Selling & Sales Management* 26(1) (Winter): 19–26.

65. Schwepker, C.H. and Good, D.J. (2012). Sales quotas: Unintended consequences on trust in organization, customer-oriented selling, and sales performance. *Journal of Marketing Theory and Practice* 20 (4): 437–452; Román, S. and Ruiz, S. (2005). Relationship outcomes of perceived ethical sales behavior: The customer's perspective. *Journal of Business Research* 58 (4): 439–445; Babakus, E., Cravens, D.W., Johnston, M.et al. (1996). Examining the role of organizational variables in the salesperson job satisfaction model. *Journal of Personal Selling & Sales Management* 16 (Summer): 33–46; Tyagi, P.K. (1982). Perceived organizational climate and the process of salesperson motivation. *Journal of Marketing Research* 19 (May): 240–254; Tyagi, P.K. (1985). Relative importance of key job dimensions and leadership behaviors in motivating salesperson work performance. *Journal of Marketing* 49 (Summer): 76–86.

66. Gong, Y., Huang, J.C. and Farh, J.L. (2009). Employee learning orientation, transformational leadership, and employee creativity: The mediating role of employee creative self-efficacy. *Academy of Management Journal* 52 (4): 765–778; Limbu, Y.B., Jayachandran, C. and Babin, B.J. (2014). Does information and communication technology improve job satisfaction? The moderating role of sales technology orientations. *Industrial Marketing Management* 43 (7): 1236–1245; Silver, L.S., Dwyer, S. and Alford, B. (2006). Learning and performance goal orientation of salespeople revisited: The role of performance-approach and performance-avoidance orientations. *Journal of Personal Selling & Sales Management* (Winter): 27–38; Harris, E.G., Mowen, J.C. and Brown, T.J. (2005). Re-examining salesperson goal orientations: personality influencers, customer orientation, and work satisfaction. *Journal of the Academy of Marketing Science* 33 (1): 19–35.

67. Chonko, L.B., Dubinsky, A.J., Jones, E. and Roberts, J.A. (2003). Organizational and individual learning in the sales force: An

agenda for sales research. *Journal of Business Research* (56): 935–946; Misra, S., Pinker, E.J. and Shumsky, R.A. (2004). Sales force design with experience-based learning. *IIE Transactions* 36 (10): 941–952.

68. Chan, T.Y., Li, J. and Pierce, L. (2014). Learning from peers: Knowledge transfer and sales force productivity growth. *Marketing Science* 33 (4): 463–620; Artis, A.B. and Harris, E.G. (2007). Self-directed learning and sales force performance: An integrated framework. *Journal of Personal Selling & Sales Management* 27 (1): 9–24; Sujan, H., Weitz, B.A. and Kumar, N. (1994). Learning orientation, working smart, and effective selling. *Journal of Marketing* 58 (January): 39–52.

69. Guenzi, P., Baldauf, K.A. and Panagopoulos, N.G. (2014). The influence of formal and informal sales controls on customer-directed selling behaviors and sales unit effectiveness. *Industrial Marketing Management* 43 (5): 786–800; Sujan, H., Weitz, B.A. and Sujan, M. (1988). Increasing sales productivity by getting salespeople to work smarter. *Journal of Personal Selling & Sales Management* 8 (August): 9–19.

70. Fang, E., Evans, K.R. and Zou, S. (2005). The moderating effect of goal-setting characteristics on the sales control systems--Job performance relationship. *Journal of Business Research* 58 (9): 1214–1222.

71. Madhani, P.M. (2013). Realigning fixed and variable pay in sales organizations: A career life cycle perspective. *Compensation & Benefits Review* 42 (6): 488–498; Menguc, B. and Bhuian, S.N. (2004). Mehta, R., Anderson, R.E. and Dubinsky, A.J. (2000). The perceived importance of sales managers' rewards: A career stage perspective. *Journal of Business & Industrial Marketing* 1: 507–524; Menguc, B. and Bhuian, S.N. (2004). Career stage effects on job characteristic-job satisfaction relationships among guest worker salespersons. *Journal of Personal Selling & Sales Management* 24 (3): 215–227.

72. Miao, C.F., Lund, D.J. and Evans, K.R. (2009). Reexamining the influence of career stages on salesperson motivation: A cognitive and affective perspective. *Journal of Personal Selling &Sales Management* 29 (3): 243–255; Cron, W.L, Dubinsky, A.J. and Michaels, R.E. (1988). The influence of career stages on components of salesperson motivation. *Journal of Marketing* 52 (January): 78–92.

73. Hafer, J.C. (1986). An empirical investigation of the salesperson's career stage perspective. *Journal of Personal Selling & Sales Management* 6 (November): 1–7; Cron, W.L. (1984) Industrial salesperson development: A career stages perspective. *Journal of Marketing* 48 (4): 41–52.

74. Feldman, D.C. and Weitz, B.A. (1988). Career plateaus in the salesforce: Understanding and removing blockages to employee growth. *Journal of Personal Selling & Sales Management* 8 (November): 23–32; McConnachle, C. (21 February 2017). Seven causes for plateauing in sales. www.salesforcesearch.com/blog/httpwww-salesforcesearch-combid1532347-causes-for-plateauing-in-sales/ (accessed 23 November 2019).

75. Yim, F.H.K., Swaminathan, S. and Anderson, R. (2015). Empowering salespeople: Does it work? In Robinson, L (ed.) *Marketing Dynamism & Sustainability: Things Change, Things Stay the Same . . .Developments in Marketing Science: Proceedings of the Academy of Marketing Science*; Anderson, R.E. and Huang, R. (2006). Empowering salespeople: Personal managerial and organizational perspectives. *Psychology and Marketing* 23(February): 139–159; Conger, J.A. and Kanungo, R.N. (1988). The empowerment process: Integrating theory and practice. *Academy of Management Review* 13: 471–482.

76. Ahearne, M., Mathieu, J. and Rapp, A. (2005). To empower or not to empower your sales force? An empirical examination of the influence of leadership and empowerment behavior on customer satisfaction and performance. *Journal of Applied Psychology* 90 (5): 945–955; Shea, J. (5 June 2017). Good sales managers develop empowered salespeople. https://alignment-group.com/good-sales-managers-develop-empowered-salespeople/ (accessed 22 November 2019; Ford, R.C. and Fottler, M.D. (1995). Empowerment: A matter of degree. *Academy of Management Executive* (3): 21–31; Sashkin, M. (1984). Participative management is an ethical imperative. *Organizational Dynamics* (Spring): 4–22; Wagner, J.A. III (1994). Participation's effect on performance and satisfaction: A reconsideration of research evidence. *Academy of Management Review* 19 (2): 312–330.

77. Matthews, L. (2015). *Why empowering salespeople is a double edge sword. Doctoral Dissertation in Business Administration*, Coles College of Business, Kennesaw State University; Ahearne, M., Mathieu, J. and Rapp, A. (2005). To empower or not to empower your sales force? An empirical examination of the influence of leadership and empowerment behavior on customer satisfaction and performance. *Journal of Applied Psychology* 90 (5): 945–955; Anderson, R.E. and Huang, R. (2006). Empowering salespeople: Personal managerial and organizational perspectives. *Psychology and Marketing* 23 (February): 139–159; Skinner, S.J. and Kelley, S.W. (2006). Transforming sales organizations through appreciative inquiry. *Psychology & Marketing* 23 (2): 77–93; Bowen, D.E. and Lawler, E.E. III (1992). The empowerment of service workers: What, why, how, and when. *Sloan Management Review* (Spring): 31–39.

Chapter Review Questions

1. Define the concept of sales force motivation. Explain the important elements in the definition of sales force motivation. [LO 1]

2. Explain the meaning of *content* theories of motivation. Identify and discuss the key features of the different content theories of motivation. [LO 2]

3. Describe *process* theories of motivation. Identify and discuss the key features of the different process theories of motivation. [LO 2]

4. What are *reinforcement* theories of motivation? Identify and discuss the key features of the organizational behavior modification theory. [LO 2]

5. As a sales manager, which of the contemporary theories of motivation would you use to motivate your sales force? Why? [LO 2]

6. Discuss some extrinsic and intrinsic rewards that can be used in motivating the sales force? [LO 3]

7. Many sales managers face the problem of motivating top-performing salespeople who no longer respond to the incentive of more money. In such instances, how might you use salesperson recognition to motivate these salespeople? How would you develop a recognition program? [LO 3]

8. Discuss the reasons for using sales contests. What makes a good sales contest? [LO 4]

9. What advantages do videoconferences have over the traditional sales meeting? When might a videoconference be more appropriate than a large sales meeting at a specific location? [LO 4]

10. Explain the difference between learning vs. performance orientation and the relevance to motivating the sales force. [LO 5]

11. Identify and explain the four stages of a salesperson's career life cycle. Why might salespeople in each stage need different approaches for motivation? [LO 5]

Online Exercise

Using an Internet search engine find three firms that specialize in motivational training. What type of motivational training do they seem to be advocating? Is the focus on B2B selling, B2C selling, or both? Do they imply that one motivational approach will fit the entire sales force? What are the length and cost of each program? Where it is the training held? Who does the training, that is, what are their qualifications? What innovative topics will the sales force motivation training cover?

Role-Play Exercise

Situation

Several months ago, Fairlie Products, Inc. hired one of its most energetic, highly motivated, achievement-oriented college recruits in years. Lakisha had an overall 3.5 grade-point average while dual majoring in marketing and finance, was an officer in the business fraternity, and supported herself through school with a part-time sales job, so she looked like she couldn't miss as a new salesperson. However, Lakisha's manager Pedro just finished her first quarterly performance review, and things don't look good.

Role-Play Participants and Assignments

Lakisha – finished last in the region in sales volume and in generating new customer leads, but she really wants to succeed and hopes for time to prove herself.

Pedro – is confident that Lakisha has the brains, communication skills, and product knowledge to succeed, and is surprised by her poor performance. What should Pedro do in this situation? How can he choose the right motivational tools for Lakisha?

In-Basket Exercise

Today, you received your written annual evaluation from Caroline Jensen, the national sales manager for Specialty Metal Products Company. Last year, you received a large increase in salary plus a bonus because your district came in No. 1 in sales. This year, however, you're disappointed by your below average performance evaluation, small raise and lack of a bonus, primarily it seems because your district's sales performance was next to last. In reviewing your performance, Ms. Jensen noted that your district's poor performance seemed to be at least partially attributable to the sharp decline in sales by one of your senior salespeople, Roger Casey. Although her note didn't specifically say it, Ms. Jensen's comments clearly imply that she feels it's the responsibility of sales managers to keep their salespeople highly motivated so that they don't go through long sales slumps.

In a handwritten note attached to your performance evaluation, Ms. Jensen has suggested that you put Roger on notice that he will be moved out of field sales and shifted to a telemarketing job contacting small customers if his performance doesn't substantially improve in the next few months. If Roger's sales don't improve and he refuses the telemarketing job, then Ms. Jensen recommends terminating him because "we can't afford to carry deadwood on the payroll."

Signing a copy of your performance evaluation to return to Ms. Jensen, you also attach a note explaining: "Roger and his wife went through an unpleasant divorce at the beginning of last year. After that, he seemed melancholy, distracted, and without the old fire that drove his success for many years. Based on his 22-year successful sales experience prior to last year, I still think Roger has considerable potential. I knew that he was struggling last year, but I didn't want to add to his pressures at that time. Moreover,

I felt that he would be able to work things out and return to his old form. Of course, that didn't happen, but would you grant me six months to try to turn Roger's performance around?"

As part of your note to Ms. Jensen, provide a detailed outline of what you plan to do to motivate Roger.

Ethical Dilemma

You are the national sales manager for a large consumer goods company with a liberal travel and expense program for its salespeople. Many of your sales reps have large territories requiring a great deal of air travel. Your company always reimburses all travel expenses, but suggests that reps "search for the best possible airfares whenever traveling." Because of rising fares, your boss has asked you to do whatever you can to hold down air travel expenses. From a preliminary investigation of your reps' travel patterns, you discovered that the majority fly with only *one* airline. When you confronted them about this issue, most gave the same explanation: "All airlines charge about the same fares, so I stick with one airline so I can take advantage of the frequent-flyer programs!" Some of your

reps travel so frequently that they can accumulate five to ten *free* tickets a year!

Questions

1. Are the reps behaving ethically by flying with only one airline? Why or why not?

2. Should any or all of the sales force's free airline tickets be given back to the company to be used for future business travel?

3. What can be done to hold down air travel costs in this situation?

| CASE 11.1 | Schindler Pharmaceuticals: Motivating the Sales Force |

Amanda Miller, vice president of marketing at Schindler Pharmaceuticals, is beginning to question her company's various methods of motivating the sales force. Over the last year or so she has noticed a gradual decline in sales force morale. Sales among the top salespeople have been relatively flat, and from various conversations she has heard around the office, Miller believes her salespeople have become somewhat complacent and could use a good dose of motivation. The motivational techniques currently used at the company include a generous commission system, a promotion plan, sales contests, and sales meetings. In an attempt to determine if the motivational tools at Schindler are inadequate, Miller took a close look at them.

Management at Schindler believes the firm's compensation package can do a great deal to motivate salespeople to work harder. All salespeople are paid a fixed salary of $48,000 a year plus commissions on sales volume. The commission system is set up so the higher the sales volume, the higher the commission. Commissions for the sales force range from 6 to as high as 18%.

Miller believes this is a generous compensation plan and the "the sky's the limit" when it comes to salespeople's earnings at Schindler. According to Miller, who believes that "salespeople are highly motivated by money," there are very few problems with the compensation package at Schindler.

Another means of motivating the salespeople is Schindler's "promotion-from-within" program. Schindler is very proud of the fact that the majority of company executives started their careers in entry-level positions within the firm. Furthermore, all the marketing management personnel started in sales. The promotion-from-within program for the salespeople is set up so that the promotion is tied almost exclusively to sales performance. Salespeople that were top performers over the last several years are promoted.

Miller believes the promotion-from-within program is an excellent way to motivate the sales force. "Each person knows exactly where he or she stands and what it will take to move up the corporate ladder. If a salesperson wants to become part of the management group at Schindler, all it takes is a little hard work!" Miller's first job was as a sales rep for Schindler sixteen years ago, and he worked his way up to VP.

Schindler constantly uses sales contests as a motivator for its sales force. Despite the fact that Schindler's sales force is well compensated, management feels individuals can be motivated to reach their peak sales performance with sales contests. The company conducts a sales contest every year and is very careful to make the contest a fair one. The contest is set up to reward individual performance rather than just the top performers. Themes of the contest are changed yearly, as are prizes. While the prizes are usually trips to exotic locations, expensive gifts such as new cars and Rolex watches are given on occasion.

Once again, Miller has a difficult time finding fault with the yearly sales contests. "We have thoroughly done our homework concerning how to run sales contests, and I feel we are doing an excellent job of motivating our salespeople with these contests," says Miller. "When I was a salesperson, I couldn't wait for the chance to reach my next year's sales goal. By reaching this goal, I was assured of a free vacation to Jamaica or Tahiti or even a gold watch. These things motivated me to sell my heart out!"

Schindler's Atlanta, Georgia, headquarters has annually held a national sales meeting and five regional sales meetings. The national sales meeting is held at exclusive resort areas, usually in early June. The last six years' meetings were held at Knots Berry Farm, near Los Angeles, California; Colonial Manor, Williamsburg, Virginia; Kennedy Flight Center, Florida; French Quarter, New Orleans, Louisiana; Harrah's Club, Lake Tahoe, Nevada; and Disney World, Orlando, Florida. The meetings start on a Tuesday, last three days, and are considered an excellent means for announcing new-product lines. All of Schindler's top management and the board of directors attend, with the daytime devoted to business discussions and the nighttime set aside for recreation for management, employees, and their families. The national meetings are attended by approximately 100–150 people. Each year, the total attendance has increased by 10%. The national meetings have become extremely expensive and time-consuming to prepare. On the other hand, the regional meetings have proved to be more productive and far less expensive, primarily because of the lower transportation and lodging costs.

The effectiveness of both the national and regional meetings is being evaluated. When the regional meetings are held, Schindler sends eight top executives. The format is geared to seminars and workshops. Although the regional meetings appear to be better for technical instruction, they are not thought to be as valuable in strengthening total company morale. Miller has reviewed the major cost factors associated with the meetings and has listed several alternatives. They are as follows:

- Change the format of the national meeting to include technical instruction, thus eliminating the need for the regional meetings.
- Exclude the nighttime recreational activities.
- Hold meetings at less expensive locations.
- Send fewer top management personnel.
- Discourage relatives from attending the national meetings.

While the meetings are expensive, Miller believes they are great at building morale and improving communication between the salespeople and management. "It is important for all employees of a company to get together once a year in order to lift spirits and increase camaraderie," says Miller.

After evaluating the motivational tools that Schindler employs, Miller was having difficulty finding any problems. However, many of the other Schindler executives felt these motivators were a bit excessive given the recent lackluster sales performance from the sales force. The other executives are pressuring Miller to control some of the costs associated with the motivators, since it is very difficult for them to see how such motivators as sales contests and sales meetings contribute to the overall success of the company, especially during years of very marginal sales increases. As a response, Miller decided to use the new analytics feature in the CRM software program to analyze the financial incentive programs in terms of effectiveness and ROI. She hoped to provide an analysis that would interpret and communicate the relationship between the financial incentive programs and sales. In addition, she had recently read about nonfinancial motivators for salesforce management, such as recognition/appreciation programs and peer communities. Both of the initiatives could be implemented through a social media platform that sends push notifications about individual accomplishments to the group, and it provides a platform for the sales group to build a community of peer support. Prior to developing the analytics report and implementing the social media strategy, she had the following concerns and questions:

1. Will the CRM system already have data that is useful for her analytics report or will she need to collect new data?

2. Will nonfinancial motivators supplement the financial incentives and help drive sales to higher levels?

3. How can she actually measure the return generated by nonfinancial rewards?

Questions

1. Do you agree with Miller's evaluation of Schindler's motivational tools? Why or why not?

2. Would any of the theories of motivation presented in the chapter help Schindler to motivate its salespeople? If so, which ones?

3. If you were helping Miller with her analytics report, what type of data would you recommend that she look for in the CRM system?

4. Would a social media platform that provides for individual recognition and builds a sense of community help Miller? Why or why not?

5. What are the advantages and disadvantages of Schindler's promotion-from-within program?

6. Do you think Miller should implement one or more of her alternatives for changing the national and regional sales meetings? Explain.

Case prepared by: J. Michael Weber, University of Maine

| CASE 11.2 | Sales Actions Software, Inc. |

Sales Actions Software, Inc. sells time and territory management solutions targeted at small to medium size companies that cannot afford well-known brands of sales force automation (SFA) or enterprise software, such as Adobe Systems and Salesforce.com. Mary Collins, Sales Manager for Sales Actions Software, Inc., has been asked by the president to review and evaluate the motivational approaches used with the sales force. She believes the approaches used – social media messaging, sales contests, sales meetings, podcasts, newsletters, individual recognition, and targeted group sales training – make Sales Actions Software a desirable place to work. The president expressed some concern about how expensive a couple of the approaches were, however, such as sales meetings (because of the travel expense and loss of sales time) and podcasts (because of the production costs). In the past few years Sales Actions Software has experienced annual increases in sales in excess of 12%, but the gross margins on the various products range from 5 to 18%. The wide variations in gross margins and the perceived high cost of selected motivational approaches led the president to ask Mary to review her budget and suggest ways to consolidate and reduce expenses.

Mary first separated the motivational approaches into financial and nonfinancial. She believed the financial motivators were "the cost of doing business" and included commissions, bonuses, and sales contests. In contrast, sales meetings, podcasts, recognition, and targeted group sales training were nonfinancial motivators. Because she believed the financial motivators represented "the cost of doing business" and were directly tied to sales, less emphasis was placed on reviewing them.

Sales Actions Software holds one annual national sales meeting and five regional sales meetings. The national meeting is always held at an exclusive resort, usually in early June. The last five years were held at Colonial Manor, Williamsburg, Virginia; the French Quarter in New Orleans; Harrah's Club, Lake Tahoe, Nevada; Disney World, Orlando, Florida; and the hotel Westin, Maui, Hawaii. The meetings start on Tuesday, last three days, and are considered an excellent way to announce new products and significant product line extensions. All of Sales Actions Software's top management and board of directors attend, with the daytime devoted to business discussions and the nighttime set aside for recreation, except for one evening banquet. The national meetings are attended by approximately 120 people, and the number in attendance has been increasing by about 10% a year in the last five years. The meetings are expensive and require a lot of effort to plan. In contrast, the regional meetings are somewhat more productive and much less expensive, primarily because of the lower transportation and lodging costs and the fewer distractions.

The effectiveness of both the national and regional meetings needs to be evaluated. Ms. Collins has reviewed the two types of meetings and is considering several alternatives:

- Change the format of the national meeting to include technical instruction, thus eliminating the need for regional meetings.
- Eliminate nighttime recreational activities.
- Hold meetings at less expensive locations, particularly national meetings.
- Send fewer top management personnel.
- Discourage relatives from attending national sales meetings.
- Make the national meeting a reward for superior sales performance thus limiting the number of attendees.

The recognition approaches also needed to be reviewed. One program, referred to as "Pacesetters," recognizes the top-five pacesetters in each region. On a monthly basis the pacesetters, who are crowned the "Fabulous Five," are given recognition at monthly banquets, in the newsletter, and on the website. At the end of the year, a national "Fabulous Five," is identified and awarded a trip to company headquarters to meet with and be recognized by senior management. Other smaller programs include plaques, rings, and certificates for outstanding performance or identifying major new prospects.

Two types of training are used – individual training using podcasts and group training at monthly and regional sales meetings. Collins was influential in adding podcasts as a training method and also heavily involved in developing recent group training content and approaches. She is therefore finding it difficult to objectively evaluate these areas. The podcasts have been popular and frequently used based on the number of salespeople that have downloaded them. But the production costs are relatively high. There is no formal mechanism for evaluating their effectiveness. The group training topics included job descriptions, job analysis, sales techniques, and planning, and were directed more toward new recruits than experienced sales people. She sent out a lengthy questionnaire to evaluate these but the response rate was low. The reviews she received as well as informal feedback suggested the salespeople perceived the group training to be incomplete, inconsistent, and generally not very effective.

As Collins reviewed the various motivational approaches, she realized it was difficult to measure the effectiveness of any of the nonfinancial factors. Several senior managers argued it was foolish to continue spending on "frills," but Collins believed that in the software industry reputation and image are very important, not only in making sales, but also in attracting quality salespeople. In fact, Collins felt to some extent that an increase in the budget might be needed instead of a reduction, and that the more important issue might be how the budget is being spent instead of the size.

Questions

1. With respect to the motivational approaches (e.g., Maslow and Herzberg), what role does each of the nonfinancial factors play in motivating the sales force at Sales Actions Software? Are they motivators or demotivators, and why?

2. What kind of system could be developed to evaluate the intangible, nonfinancial motivational factors, and how might it be implemented at Sales Actions Software?

3. Should the nonfinancial motivators used by Sales Actions Software be changed, and if so how?

4. Do you agree with Collins' decision to not focus on the financial motivators, and if so why?

Case prepared by: Dan Goebel, Northern Arizona University, and Paul Christ, West Chester University

CHAPTER 12

Sales Force Compensation

"Show me the money!" This famous line by Tom Cruise in the iconic film *Jerry Maguire* shows that people often define success and power by the amount of money they earn. But, if you don't have the talent to become a highly paid entertainer, professional athlete, or entrepreneur, you can still gain a lot of control over your future earnings by starting an exciting, well-paid career in sales. Salespeople and sales managers are the direct revenue producers of their organizations, and in most organizations, those who bring in the money usually make the most. That's one major reason why sales force management is one of the higher paying jobs in America,[1] commanding six-figure compensation.[2]

LEARNING OBJECTIVES

When you finish this chapter, you should be able to:

1. Explain the reasons for regularly reviewing sales force compensation plans.
2. Describe the basic steps in developing compensation plans.
3. Compare the advantages and disadvantages of different methods of sales force compensation.
4. Be aware of developing trends in sales force compensation.
5. Understand the efficient and effective use of expense accounts and fringe benefits in compensation planning.

Although every employee directly or indirectly affects organizational performance, the firm's revenue-generating success largely rests on the performance of its salespeople. Thus, sales managers, who are ultimately accountable for the success of their sales organizations,[3] need to design compensations programs that clearly reward salespeople for superior performance.

How do you do this? To succinctly answer that question, let's turn to Jack Welch – the charismatic former CEO of General Electric (www.ge.com) for 30 years who responded: "By rewarding stars [the top 20 percent performers] in an outsized way that is soul-satisfying and financially satisfying." Top salespeople need to be openly recognized and fully compensated for excellent performance, which can also help their retention.[4] While the middle 70% of salespeople must be given more training and coaching to augment their performance, an effective reward program and compensation structure is perhaps the most powerful mechanism to spur average performers to achieve their full potential. Moreover, according to Welch, the bottom 10% who exhibit neither good results nor good behaviors should be "shown the door."[5] Welch believed that by moving out the bottom performers, firms can recruit new talent.[6] While his advice may sound harsh, it's hard to argue with his long-term success at General Electric.

Recall that in Chapters 10 and 11, we discussed how sales managers can use different leadership approaches and an array of intrinsic rewards and sales incentive strategies to motivate salespeople to higher performance levels. Many managers will tell you that the compensation plan is the most direct and powerful way to ensure productive sales force behavior. So, in this chapter, we turn our attention to how sales managers can design effective compensation structures[7] and extrinsic (financial) reward programs to stimulate higher levels of effort (motivation), thus contributing to superior salesperson performance, productivity,[8] and profitability.[9]

Sales Force Compensation Plans

Compensation is defined as all monetary payments as well as other benefits used to remunerate employees for their performance. Constituting a central part of extrinsic rewards, compensation plans and overall financial packages are the most important, least ambiguous way to remunerate salespeople.[10] Compensation is widely believed to be the single greatest motivator of salespeople,[11] although studies have revealed that managers frequently fail to determine what else motivates employees and to overestimate the importance of extrinsic rewards.[12] Sales compensation plans can be viewed as the "steering wheel" that enables management to directly drive salesperson performance in line with the company's goals.[13]

While there are a variety of ways employees can be rewarded – as shown in Table 12.1 – in general, firms use three main methods to financially compensate salespeople:

1. Straight salary – The salesperson receives a fixed amount of money at regular intervals, usually weekly or monthly.
2. Straight commission – The salesperson receives an amount that varies with results, usually sales or profits.
3. *Combination* – The salesperson receives a mix of salary and commission.

TABLE 12.1

Types of Sales Compensation Plans

Compensation plan	Nature of reward	Description
Hourly wage	Nonincentive based	Fixed pay per hour worked
Straight salary	Nonincentive based	Fixed salary paid in intervals as per contract
Straight commission	Incentive based	Pay based on sales results
Performance bonus	Incentive based	Discretionary pay based on individual or team performance
Merit pay	Incentive based	Pay based on exemplary performance
Profit sharing	Incentive based	Pay based on profits attained
Pay-for-knowledge	Incentive based	Pay based on skill augmentation and education degree earned
Stock options	Incentive based	Financial reward of company stock either given free or purchased at a discount
Flexible pay compensation	Incentive based	Pay based on a personal choice of compensation plan and benefits selected
Combination	Incentive based	Pay that includes a fixed salary, plus variable commission based on sales levels
Health insurance	Benefits based	Nonfinancial benefits in compliance with employment laws
Dental insurance	Benefits based	Nonfinancial benefits in compliance with employment laws
Pension plans	Benefits based	Nonfinancial benefits in compliance with employment laws
Social security	Benefits based	Nonfinancial benefits in compliance with employment laws
Others (education, travel allowances, etc.)	Benefits based	Additional payments disbursed as "perks"

Different salespeople respond uniquely to monetary rewards. Patrick Hughes, former vice president of sales and marketing for Blue Cross Blue Shield of Massachusetts (www.bluecrossma.com), analyzed salespersons' pay plans outside his industry for assistance in revising his company's plan because as he put it, "Salespeople, despite their market specialization, have one thing in common: they want to make lots of money."[14] Salespeople often see financial compensation as a way of "keeping score" among their peers, so they are understandably highly motivated by their "scorecard" (paycheck). To retain top sales performers, companies must maintain an attractive compensation package. Recruiting qualified salespeople has become so intense that some high-tech firms offer them signing bonuses.[15]

In examining the effect of various compensations plans on company profits, a seminal study identified five basic types of salespeople:

- ***Creatures of habit*** – They try to maintain their standard of living by earning a predetermined desired amount of money.
- ***Goal-oriented individuals*** – They prefer recognition as achievers by peers and superiors with money serving mainly as a by-product of achievement. They tend to be strongly sales quota oriented.
- ***Satisfiers*** – They perform just well enough to keep their jobs.
- ***Trade-offers*** – They allocate their time according to a personally determined ratio of work and leisure that is not influenced by opportunities for increased earnings.
- ***Money-oriented individuals*** – They seek to maximize their earnings. These people may sacrifice family relationships, personal pleasures, and even health to increase their income.[16]

Although this classic study of salesperson types was conducted years ago, the classifications still seem to hold generally true in today's sales environment. The sales manager must identify these basic types of salespeople and design a compensation package that will optimize total sales force efforts.

Sales managers can increase overall sales force productivity by designing compensation systems that recognize outstanding performance and reward salespeople accordingly.

Variable Pay Compensation Systems

Although the critical importance of rewards in motivating employees has been well established,[17] reward preferences, reward levels, reward satisfaction, and the perceived adequacy of such rewards by managers and subordinates may significantly differ.[18] Compensation and perks tend to increase at higher hierarchical levels of a corporation, thereby creating status and power differences, and reward inequality.[19] Studies also suggest that the importance employees assign to rewards differs according to their changing needs, career stage, and organizational level.[20] Furthermore, over the past few decades, the profile of the typical employee has changed dramatically with large numbers of minorities and women now at all organizational levels.[21] The U.S. work force today includes large numbers of dual-career households whose employers provide similar, overlapping reward or benefit programs in which only one spouse can participate. Moreover, many older employees have needs for rewards and benefits that may not be consistent with their chronological age, assumed family situation, or organizational level. Given these conditions, to be truly effective in improving productivity, management needs to design and implement reward systems, compensation structures, and benefit packages from which employees can make their own choices. In other words, managers must keep in mind that one size or option doesn't fit all in benefit programs or most anything else. Many firms have already adopted flexible, cafeteria-type compensation plans, which have become increasingly popular alternatives to standardized reward or benefit systems.[22] To learn more about designing and implementing innovative variable compensation plans that can be effective in augmenting sales force performance, visit websites, such as www.vault.com and www.kornferry.com.

Sales managers can employ companies like Korn Ferry to help design attractive variable compensation reward systems for the diverse needs of the modern sales force.

Source: https://www.kornferry.com/solutions/rewards-and-benefits/employee-rewards/variable-pay.

An innovative software provider delivering measurable improvements for customers, Varicent is also an industry-leading incentive compensation and sales performance management solutions provider that can provide guidance to sales managers.
Source: https://www.varicent.com/products.

Developing the Sales Force Compensation Plan

As shown in Figure 12.1, the seven distinct stages in the process of developing a compensation plan include: (1) prepare job descriptions, (2) establish specific objectives, (3) determine general levels of compensation, (4) develop the compensation mix, (5) pretest the plan, (6) administer the plan, and (7) evaluate the plan. If any of these steps are skipped or poorly executed, the compensation plan will not be as effective as it could be in motivating the sales force.

Preparing Job Descriptions

Sales managers need detailed, meaningful job descriptions before they can develop a compensation plan. They should systematically compare job descriptions – including responsibilities and performance criteria – to other sales positions in terms of their importance to the organization and whether they are current. Most job descriptions become dated over time as the technologies, goals, and strategies of the company

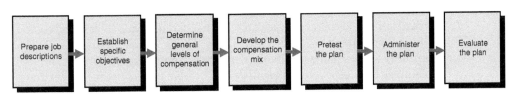

FIGURE 12.1 Stages in developing a sales force compensation plan.

change. Human Resource Department personnel are not able to keep job descriptions up-to-date without the regular input of the sales manager. Jobs of approximately equal value are usually assigned to the same grade level. For example, in the federal government, all jobs under civil service have been described, evaluated, and categorized vertically into grades ranging from GS-1 (the lowest) to GS-18 (the highest). On a horizontal basis, at any one civil service grade – say, GS-14 – there are different jobs, such as contract administrator or accounting supervisor. The U.S. Bureau of Labor Statistics (www.bls.gov) conducts national surveys every March to adjust the GS pay levels relative to private industry. Many companies also classify their positions, including sales jobs, by levels of responsibility.

Sales jobs typically vary on both vertical and horizontal levels. Vertical salesperson job positions may be sales trainee, sales representative, and senior sales representative. Horizontal jobs may be regular salespeople, missionary salespeople, or salespeople for specific customer groups like governments, nonprofit institutions, internet customers, or international companies. Each position, on both the vertical and horizontal scales, needs a separate job description for assignment of a minimum starting salary and a maximum salary, often determined by surveys of what other organizations within the industry are paying.

Establishing Specific Objectives

Compensation plans are designed to achieve certain organizational objectives, for example, larger market share, higher profit margins, introducing new products or services, winning new accounts, or reducing selling costs. Surprisingly, a large number of American companies use sales compensation plans that are inconsistent with their marketing goals. Many companies have a difficult time trying to keep their compensation plans in line with organizational objectives.[23]

These research findings about ineffective compensation plans are rather puzzling, since the procedure for establishing compensation plans that are consistent with organizational goals is relatively straightforward. Ready availability of sales data means that it is easier to measure the productivity of salespeople than that of most other types of employees. Moreover, firms can measure achievement of other organizational objectives, even when few sales are being made. For example, the number of sales presentations and demonstrations made to customers may be an important objective for making potential buyers aware of company offerings. Another quantifiable objective might be to increase the conversion ratio (orders as a percentage of sales presentations).

Any compensation plan may have several objectives, depending upon the needs of the specific company, sales manager, or salesperson. From the *company's or sales manager's* vantage point, the plan should stress:

1. *Control* – Sales managers prefer a plan that allows maximum control over how salespeople allocate their time.
2. *Economy* – Sales managers want a plan that offers a desirable balance between sales costs and sales results.
3. *Motivation* – Sales managers seek a plan that can motivate their salespeople to optimal performance.
4. *Simplicity* – Sales managers like a plan that is simple to administer, easily explainable to salespeople, and sufficiently flexible to ensure timely adjustments to changing market conditions and organizational goals.

From the standpoint of *sales representatives*, the compensation plan should offer:

1. ***Income regularity*** – Salespeople want to be protected from sharp declines in income so that their regular monthly expenses for home mortgage, food, and utilities can be paid without hardship.
2. ***Reward for superior performance*** – Salespeople like compensation in direct relationship to the amount of effort they expend and the results they obtain. Superior performance should reap superior rewards.
3. ***Fairness*** – Salespeople want their earnings to be equitable in terms of their experience and ability, the pay of coworkers, competitors' sales reps, and the cost of living.[24]

It's not easy for a single compensation plan to achieve all these objectives, especially since some objectives, such as economic conditions and income regularity, can often conflict.

Because their marketing situations and objectives are so diverse and variable, organizations across industries use a wide variety of compensation plans, from simple to complex. Regardless of the sophistication of the plan, it is important for sales force morale that sales reps be able to calculate their own expected earnings over a given pay period to facilitate their personal financial planning.

Determining General Levels of Compensation

Companies and industries with low average levels of compensation tend to suffer high turnover rates. Therefore, the level of compensation should be sufficiently competitive within the industry to attract and retain competent salespeople.

Several factors determine the basic level of pay for a sales force. The most significant ones are (1) the skills, experience, and education required to do the work successfully; (2) the income for comparable level jobs within the company; and (3) the level of income for comparable jobs in the industry (that is, the competitive environment). The relative importance of each of these factors will vary from one situation to another.

One approach to establishing general pay levels for sales positions is to assign numerical values to each job requirement. For instance, previous experience in sales might be rated high for a particular sales job (say, 8 on a scale of 1 to 10), and a college major in marketing may receive a value of 6. For another selling job, sales experience may be worth only 4. Sum the point values for all requirements to compare the importance of different sales jobs within and outside the organization. From this analysis, managers can obtain a rank order of jobs and assign a range of basic income to each level, as shown in the simple example in Table 12.2.

Usually, there is some overlap in salaries among the different job rankings, to allow for growth within each position based on the individual's experience, skills, and performance. For example, in civil service positions there is a range of salaries depending upon the individual's growth stage or seniority in that grade level. Unlike most jobs with designated pay ranges, however, salespeople at most companies earn commissions on all that they sell, so top-performing salesperson can often earn more than some senior executives.[25]

Living Costs Beyond the general level of compensation, any plan should be sufficiently flexible to adjust to area living costs. *Sales & Marketing Management* publishes an annual "Survey of Selling Costs," which identifies living costs by selected metropolitan statistical area. Sales managers can use this information to help establish the level of compensation for particular areas.

> ## TABLE 12.2
>
> ### Sales Position Analysis
>
> | Job requirements | Experience | Education | Test scores | | Total possible score |
> |---|---|---|---|---|---|
> | Total numerical values | 10 | 6 | 10 | | 26 |
> | | | *Minimum scores required* | | | |
> | Sales position | Experience | Education | Position scores | Totals | Pay level |
> | Sales trainee | 4 | 3 | 3 | 10 | Competitive within the industry to attract and retain new salespeople |
> | Sales representative | 6 | 4 | 6 | 16 | Higher than salary for sales trainee |
> | Senior sales representative | 8 | 4 | 8 | 20 | Higher than salary for sales representative |

Earnings Ceilings Should there be a ceiling on what an outstanding sales representative can earn? More specifically, should salespeople be able to earn more than their bosses? Although there are arguments on both sides of the issue, the answer depends on circumstances and management philosophies. Where ceilings are placed on earnings, management must set reasonable sales quotas and allow a range of salesperson earnings at least equal to other companies' salespeople in the industry. Otherwise, high performing salespeople are likely to leave for better earning opportunities elsewhere. In many progressive companies, no limits are placed on a salesperson's earnings as long as selling costs are kept within acceptable limits. For example, legendary magazine executive James B. Horton was a strong advocate of no ceilings on the salaries of sales representatives. When Horton was publisher of *Psychology Today*, an ad salesperson made the most money in the company and the sales manager had the second highest earnings. Horton received less money than either, which was fine with him because he knew that as the people in sales earned higher commissions, sales of the magazine grew so the cost per page in producing the magazine came down, and profits went up.[26]

Developing the Compensation Mix

Most contemporary sales organizations have found that a compensation mix of salary, commission, and/or bonus is more effective in achieving objectives and goals than salary or commission alone. Essential in this mix is the ratio between the regular salary and incentive pay. For most companies, salary is usually 70 to 80 percent of salesperson earnings with the rest coming from commissions.

Costs for Alternative Compensation Mixes Sales managers need to consider the costs of alternative compensation mixes before drawing up a compensation plan. Generally, straight-commission plans are most efficient at lower sales levels, but not at higher levels. Recognizing this, start-up companies often shift from commission only external sales agents to company salespeople earning salary plus commissions once sales volume has reached the critical level, and customer service becomes more important.

Table 12.3 illustrates, by means of a hypothetical small start-up firm, the impact on costs of alternative compensation mixes for three salespeople. At the lower sales volumes, the straight-commission plan is the most cost efficient. At the highest sales volume, however, straight salary is preferable. Salary plus commission for this small

Comparison of Costs for Alternative Sales Force Compensation Mixes

Salespeople	Compensation method		
Antonelli	Straight commission (10%) of $ sales		
Bartholomew	Straight salary ($2500/month)		
Cumar	Salary ($1200/month) plus commission (5% of $ sales)		
Monthly sales volumes	Name	Compensation costs	Cost-to-sales ratio (%)
$10,000	Antonelli	$1000	10.0
	Bartholomew	$2500	25.0
	Cumar	$1700	17.0
$15,000	Antonelli	$1500	10.0
	Bartholomew	$2500	16.7
	Cumar	$1950	13.0
$20,000	Antonelli	$2000	10.0
	Bartholomew	$2500	12.5
	Cumar	$2200	11.0
$25,000	Antonelli	$2500	10.0
	Bartholomew	$2500	10.0
	Cumar	$2450	9.8
$30,000	Antonelli	$3000	10.0
	Bartholomew	$2500	8.3
	Cumar	$2700	9.0

firm tends to be the most efficient just below the highest levels. Each compensation plan ought to be evaluated for effectiveness and efficiency versus alternatives at different sales levels.

In considering the breakdown of salary and incentives, sales managers must decide what degree of control is needed over the sales force activities, what amount of incentive is required to reach objectives and goals, and what the total costs are for the different compensation mixes. After answering these questions, sales managers must decide what proportion of each salesperson's total income should be earned through incentives and whether the incentive pay schedule should be fixed, regressive, or progressive.

Proportion for Salary Salaries should enable salespeople to meet everyday living expenses while encouraging them to perform tasks that are not directly measurable by sales, such as servicing customer accounts. But they should not be so high as to make the salesperson complacent or content with salary alone.

Proportion for Incentives Commission and bonus are the incentive parts of the compensation plan, and they typically require the salesperson to achieve some predetermined sales quota. Incentives are about 20% of earnings for salespeople at consumer products companies, and about 25% for reps at industrial products companies. However, for salespeople in business services, incentive pay may be 50–70% of their total earnings.[27]

Fixed, Progressive, or Regressive Incentives Fixed commission or bonus rates are the easiest to compute, but they do not offer salespeople much incentive for seeking higher, increasingly difficult levels of sales. Progressive incentive rates, which step up the percentage of commission or bonus awarded as sales volume grows past designated levels, are best when profit margins climb significantly after the break-even point is reached. Conversely, regressive incentives decline as sales increase: for example, 6% for all sales less than 1000 units, 4% for all sales from 1000 to 1500 units, and 2% for all sales over 1500 units. Firms may use regressive commission rates if there is a high probability of windfall sales from a scarce or innovative new product, or to keep salespeople from trying to earn higher commissions by overloading customer inventories. In choosing among fixed, progressive, or regressive commission plans, sales managers need to estimate the potential effects of each plan on overall profits and customer relationships.

Splitting Commissions A special administrative problem for sales managers is how to split commissions when two or more people worked on closing a sale. For example, a key or national account sales rep may call on the customer's headquarters, while other salespeople call on the customer's branch offices. Because disagreements may develop afterward as to who is most responsible for the sale, management should decide in advance how to divide commissions.

Types of Incentives Companies may consider a host of fringe benefits to reward high-performing salespeople (see Table 12.4). Although some are reserved for top-level management, fringe benefits, such as a company car and stock options are frequently made available to the sales force. Others, such as club memberships, are often given to salespeople to entertain customers. While Congress has limited some tax deductions that companies can claim for "entertainment facilities" – such as yachts, resorts, and hunting lodges – business-related entertainment expenses are still legitimate tax deductions.

Stock Options To retain top-quality people, sales organizations may offer stock options in proportion to the salesperson's productivity. A *stock option* is simply an awarded opportunity (an option) to purchase stock in the company at some future date at a preset price – usually lower than the prevailing market value. If the shares rise in price, the individual may buy them at the lower, preset price, sell them at a profit, and pay tax on the profit. When the price of the firm's stock is climbing, salespeople and

---

TABLE **12.4**

Types of Fringe Benefits Offered to the Sales Force

Company car	Low-or no-interest loans
Supplemental life insurance	Deferred compensation
Tax return preparation	Supplemental retirement benefits
Supplemental medical insurance	First-class air travel
Personal tax and financial planning	Relocation allowance
Country club membership	Stock options

managers may be reluctant to leave without exercising the options available at some future date. If stock options are awarded according to productivity, the company's hold on top performers increases. Some companies allow salespeople to make contributions after each sales order, which the companies match, to a special equity fund. When salespeople leave early, their own contributions are returned to them but they forfeit the company's contributions. These types of incentives are called "golden handcuffs," since they tend to hold people to a company. Sales Management in Action Box 12.1 explains how stock options work.

Sales managers can offer fringe benefits such as membership at a country club, which top salespersons can use for entertaining their clients during sales negotiations.

Box 12.1 | Sales Management in Action 12.1

Stock Option Inducements in Sales Force Compensation Packages

Ruth Bronsen, a sales manager for an office equipment manufacturer, earns approximately $165,000 annually in salary and bonus. In an effort to secure her services, a competitor offers the same salary plus stock options. If Bronsen accepts the competitor's offer, she will receive an official statement granting her the right to buy 5000 shares of the company's stock for $10 per share at some future date (when the market price is expected to be higher), usually two or three years hence so that management can evaluate her performance before she obtains windfall profits on the stock option. Some companies have terminated underperforming managers prior to the required waiting time for exercising the stock option, so many managers now insist upon an employment contract that extends beyond the exercise date of the stock option.

Pretesting the Plan

Managers must pretest and evaluate any compensation plan before adopting it. To identify its probable impact on profits, they need to compute the sales and potential earnings the new plan would have offered each salesperson over the past several years. The firm can then pretest the proposed plan in one or more sales divisions. This pretest should run long enough to evaluate its effect on achievement of organizational objectives. If the limited trial is successful, then the plan can be implemented throughout the sales force. Finally, because people often resist change, it is critical that committees of key affected employees help develop, approve, and implement any proposed new plan.

Administering the Plan

A compensation plan should be fair, easy to understand, simple to calculate, and flexible. As market conditions and organizational objectives change, the plan may need to be altered.

Sales are not always a fair or adequate measure of a salesperson's contribution. In times of product and service shortages, for example, allocating supplies to customers may become the company's major short-run objective. In general, the increasing demands on salespeople to perform such nonselling activities have led management to reevaluate basic compensation plans. Since only about a third or less of a salesperson's workday is typically spent in face-to-face selling, it is important to have a compensation plan that reinforces effective and efficient planning and time management by salespeople.

Most sales managers feel they should not disclose peer pay to the sales force. Pay experts generally fear that salary disclosure can lead salespeople to demand justification for pay differentials and increase friction and jealousy among employees. Therefore, most firms limit information to expected scheduling of raises and, perhaps, the prescribed range of salaries within different job categories.

But it's also possible that *lack* of pay information may negatively affect employee performance and satisfaction. Pay secrecy prevents people from judging their progress in relative terms. Some research has supported the position that greater disclosure can positively influence performance, satisfaction with pay, and acceptance of company promotional policies. One warning, though: Salespeople seem to become less satisfied with their superiors (at least initially) after implementation of open-pay policies. Also, organizations not capable of objectively measuring performance are likely to have difficulty with an open-pay system.

Evaluating the Plan

Before a compensation plan is set in concrete, even for a relatively short period, the firm should thoroughly evaluate it for consistency with the sales managers' goals of attracting desirable people, keeping them, and motivating them to achieve organizational goals. Once it's established, management must then continually review and evaluate the compensation plan to determine its ongoing effectiveness. This review can be done on a quarterly, semiannual, or annual basis as deemed necessary.

Advantages and Disadvantages of Different Compensation Methods

In the next several pages, we review the advantages and disadvantages of various compensation methods under changing market conditions and different sales objectives.

Straight Salary

New sales recruits prefer a base salary or drawing account so that they can depend on some regular income amount to plan and meet basic living expenses. At this early stage of their sales careers, dependable regular income is very important because sales may be initially harder to achieve as they are first trying to establish relationships with prospects and customers. Even more experienced salespeople may prefer straight salary compensation if sales are infrequent or unpredictable and/or seasonal.

Straight salary is most appropriate in the following situations:

1. *Team selling situations* – Several people – for example, a coordinating salesperson, a technical engineer, a marketing service representative, and a member of marketing management – cooperate as a team in making a sale. This approach is common in selling complex products or systems such as enterprise software.
2. *Long negotiating periods* – A year or more may be needed to make the sale of a complicated system of products and services or big-ticket items, such as private airplanes.
3. *Mixed promotional situations* – Advertising sometimes plays a vital role in selling, and the relationship between a salesperson's efforts and advertising may be difficult to evaluate. This is also true of "inside–outside" sales forces.
4. *Learning periods* – During the first year, a salary is usually required to attract new recruits into selling and to compensate the trainee, at least until commissions are large enough to provide an adequate living standard.
5. *Missionary selling* – Missionary selling jobs are nonselling jobs aimed at developing goodwill among customers (such as physicians, pharmacies, hospitals, museums, or government agencies that serve as product deciders or recommenders for their own patients, clients, or customers) by providing them with information, advice, products, service, and assistance in prescribing, recommending, or merchandising (setting up educational displays or advertisements).
6. *Special conditions* – Introducing a new line of products, opening up new territories, calling on new customer accounts, or selling in unusual market conditions (e.g., rapidly rising prices) are all special situations that may create salespeople anxiety about their earnings unless they have the security of a guaranteed salary.

At Xerox Corporation (www.xerox.com), district managers are expected to keep in tune with any unusual conditions in the marketplace so they can make adjustments in the compensation plan for their sales force. For instance, salespeople (who are directly affected by an unusual market condition) should have the option of switching from a combination compensation plan to a 100% straight-salary plan. This plan flexibility avoids instability of income and promotes satisfaction with the compensation plan in general. To ensure timely responses to the needs of the sales force and to monitor any changes in the environment, Xerox Corporation also evaluates its compensation plans each quarter.

Since earnings under a straight-salary method are independent of any productivity measures such as sales, profits, sales calls, or presentations, this method gives salespeople the security of a precise income. From the managerial perspective, the chief advantage of the straight-salary plan is that salespeople activities can be directed toward company objectives. Straight-salary plans are widespread in the aerospace, petroleum, and chemical industries, where service and engineering skills are particularly important to customers. In these industries, salespeople are more likely to think of themselves as customer consultants or sales engineers and often do not even carry the title "sales representative." Under a straight-salary plan, high productivity can be rewarded by annual salary increases. Overall, the straight-salary method of compensation has these advantages and disadvantages:

Advantages

- Provides security to salespeople, since they know their basic living expenses will be covered.
- Helps develop a sense of loyalty to the company.
- Increases flexibility in territorial assignments because salespeople are less likely to become attached to certain sales territories and customers.
- Gives a higher degree of company control over salespeople's activities.
- Permits rapid adaptation of sales force efforts to changing market demands and company objectives.
- Is simple to administer.

Disadvantages

- Provides no financial incentive to put forth extra effort.
- May increase selling costs because salaries continue even when sales are not being made.
- Often leads to income inequities, since the least productive salespeople tend to be overpaid, and the most productive underpaid.
- Leads to adequate, but not superior, performance.

Straight Commission

Straight-commission plans provide strong incentives for salespeople rather than security, but they tend to result in higher productivity and earning levels for salespeople than do salary-based compensation plans in similar organizations. Straight-commission plans are common in industries such as real estate, insurance, door-to-door sales, and party-based sales – such as Mary Kay Cosmetics (www.marykay.com) or Tupperware (www.tupperware.com).

Commissions are paid only for measurable achievements (usually sales volume), so straight-commission plans offer rewards and risks much like those assumed by entrepreneurs. To better control selling costs and increase sales productivity, the CBS Station Group (www.cbs.com) eliminated its salary structure for salespeople and adopted an all-commission plan.[28]

When compensated by straight commissions, less productive salespeople eventually resign; whereas under a guaranteed salary system, the sales manager would usually have to fire them.

Application of commission plans requires the sales manager to decide:

1. The base, or unit, upon which the commissions will be paid (dollar sales, units sold, or gross profits).

2. The rate to be paid per unit (usually expressed as a percentage of sales or gross profit).

3. The point at which commissions start (after selling the first unit or after reaching a sales quota).

4. The time when the commissions are paid (when the order is obtained, shipped, or paid for).

If salespeople are not paid their commission until the order is shipped, they will likely pressure plant managers to ship promptly. This means customer service is being improved at the same time that salespeople are looking out for themselves.

Companies without large working capital often use commissions as a method of keeping selling costs directly related to sales. Some companies prefer to use part-time salespeople or independent manufacturers' agents on straight commission, to avoid the administrative costs associated with collecting federal social security taxes, unemployment taxes, and income taxes. Whenever the company is not very concerned about service or developing long-term customer relationships, commissions are an effective way to obtain high sales.

Profitability Though commissions ought to be related to profits, management is often reluctant to reveal profit margins to salespeople for fear that they may quit and take the information to competitors. Yet salespeople should be able to compute their expected income. One solution to this dilemma is to divide products into profit groups and assign a different commission rate to each group.

Drawing Accounts Commission plans may include a draw, which is a sum of money paid against future commissions. A *guaranteed draw* is one that does not have to be repaid by the salesperson if he or she earns insufficient commissions. Thus, it acts like a salary but is lower than a straight salary would be. Commissions may be paid under varying conditions and times. Salespeople may receive commissions on all orders written, accepted, shipped, or paid for during a given period.

A draw, or advance, against future commissions is one way of giving salespeople the security of a fixed income while providing an incentive for greater productivity. As indicated in Table 12.5, a salesperson may receive a weekly draw of $2500, with 10% commission on all sales. Note that this sales rep's balance was negative until week 8, when sales volume reached a high enough level for total commissions earned to exceed the total draw against commissions. Throughout these weeks, however, the sales rep had some income security due to the fixed $2500 draw. With a high positive balance, the salesperson might reasonably request an increase in the draw. Generally, management's objective is to set the draw high enough to offer the needed security but low enough to prevent salespeople from falling too far behind their offsetting commission earnings. Some sales managers put upper limits on permissible negative draw balances.

If a salesperson's balance is negative at the end of the quarter, it is usually carried over to the next quarter. If this situation continues, however, the company should consider reducing the dollar draw amount or switching the sales rep to straight commission. In cases where a salesperson leaves with a negative balance on the statement, legal precedent does not call for the terminated employee to repay the deficit. Some companies use a negative commission system to control a sales rep's efforts. For example, if a customer terminates a machine lease, the salesperson assigned to that particular account would lose the original commission paid when the machine was placed. This type of policy helps ensure that salespeople do not neglect present or long-term customers. Many experts believe that whenever a sales force has a large

TABLE **12.5**

Salesperson's Earnings Statement with a Weekly Draw and 10% Commission

Week	Sales volume	Earned commissions	Weekly draw	Balance
1	0	0	$2500	–$2500
2	$10,000	$1000	$2500	–$4000
3	$15,000	$1500	$2500	–$5000
4	$25,000	$2500	$2500	–$5000
5	$30,000	$3000	$2500	–$4500
6	$40,000	$4000	$2500	–$3000
7	$45,000	$4500	$2500	–$1000
8	$50,000	$5000	$2500	+$1500
9	$45,000	$4500	$2500	+$3500
10	$55,000	$5500	$2500	+$6500
11	$60,000	$6000	$2500	+$10,000
12	$63,000	$6300	$2500	+$13,800
13	$75,000	$7500	$2500	+$18,800
Totals	$453,000	$51,300	$32,500	+$18,800

amount of pay at risk and more than 20% variation in earnings from month to month, the sales manager should consider whether the benefits of the draw program outweigh its negative points.[29]

The following are some advantages and disadvantages of straight-commission plans.

Advantages

- Income is directly related to productivity.
- Commission is easy to calculate, so salespeople can keep track of their earnings.
- There is no ceiling on potential earnings.
- Money is not tied up in salaries, because commissions are paid only when revenues are generated.
- Costs are proportional to sales.
- Salespeople have maximum work freedom.
- Poorly performing salespeople eliminate themselves by quitting.
- Income is based strictly on accomplishments, not on subjective evaluations by sales managers.

Disadvantages

- Excessive emphasis may be placed on sales volume rather than profitable sales.
- Salespeople have little loyalty to the company.
- Because of extreme fluctuations in earnings, many salespeople may face uncertainty about meeting daily living expenses for their families.
- There may be high sales force turnover rates when business conditions are slow.
- Nonselling activities like customer service, missionary or educational selling, and setting up displays are often neglected.

- Salespeople may overload customers with inventory, thereby straining long-term customer relationships.
- Windfall earnings may come about under expanding business conditions, which may be disturbing to sales management.
- Flexibility to split territories or transfer salespeople is diminished because of limited means of control over the sales force.
- Sales managers may become lax about recruiting, selecting, and supervising, since they may consider marginal salespeople acceptable under this compensation plan.

Bonus Compensation Plans Bonus plans provide a lump sum of money or stock for some exceptional performance, such as making a quota, obtaining a new customer account, or selling a desired product mix. Firms may pay bonuses for individual performances or group achievements and give them in the current period, distribute them over several time periods, or defer them until after retirement, when the salesperson is earning less money and will pay less tax. Most companies pay salespeople their incentive earnings annually. It is usually best for bonuses to be paid as soon as possible so they positively reinforce the desired salesperson behavior. If paid annually or semi-annually, a bonus tends to lose its effectiveness in stimulating superior performance. Finally, sales managers should not routinely allocate equal bonuses to all members of a team who achieve a certain goal. Instead, they should recognize individual contributions to the goal achievement so that marginal contributors are not rewarded equally with high producers. Probably the major advantage of bonus plans is their flexibility, allowing managers to quickly adapt individual and group efforts toward changing organizational objectives.

Combination Compensation Plans

Combination compensation plans combine two or three of the basic compensation methods. They usually include commissions and bonuses to motivate reps to achieve volume or profit goals, and salary to help attain less quantifiable goals, such as customer service, expense control, and long-run sales development. Combination plans are the most widely used of all compensation methods and more than 70% of companies favor them.[30]

The critical factor in a combination compensation plan is the selection of a target salary-and-incentive mix. The decision is not an arbitrary one. The sales manager needs to offer a salary high enough to attract talent, and an incentive sufficient to motivate. That means being familiar with the competitive compensation environment and the amount of incentive that will motivate the sales force, given the nature of the sales job. The compensation leverage ratio varies among companies, but it is generally 70–80% salary and 20–30% incentive.

No compensation plan will fit all situations. Combination compensation plans, however, are the most flexible of all approaches. These are some combination compensation plans that fit a variety of conditions:

1. **Salary plus commissions** – This combination is best when management wants to get high sales without sacrificing customer service. It is good for new salespeople, since it provides more security than straight commission.
2. **Salary plus bonus** – This combination is preferred for achieving long-run objectives, such as selling large installations or product systems or achieving a desired customer mix.

3. ***Salary plus commission plus bonus*** – This plan is appropriate for seasonal sales, when there are frequent inventory imbalances and when management wants to focus on certain products or customers.
4. ***Commission plus bonus*** – This plan is usually applied to group efforts, in which some salespeople call on central company buyers or buying committees while others call on store managers.

Here are the main advantages and disadvantages of a combination compensation plan.

Advantages

- Provides the greatest flexibility and control over salespeople, in that all desirable activities can be rewarded
- Provides security plus incentive
- Allows frequent, immediate reinforcement of desired sales behavior

Disadvantages

- Can be complex and easily misunderstood
- Can be expensive to administer, particularly if not computerized
- May fail to achieve management objectives if not carefully conceived and implemented

Which compensation method pays salespeople the most money? A recent survey revealed that a salary and incentive combination yielded the highest total pay to top salespeople.[31]

Visit various websites, such as www.primeum.com and www.axtria.com, to review case studies, white papers, industry research, and available webinars that can augment your understanding of sales force reward systems and incentive compensation plans.

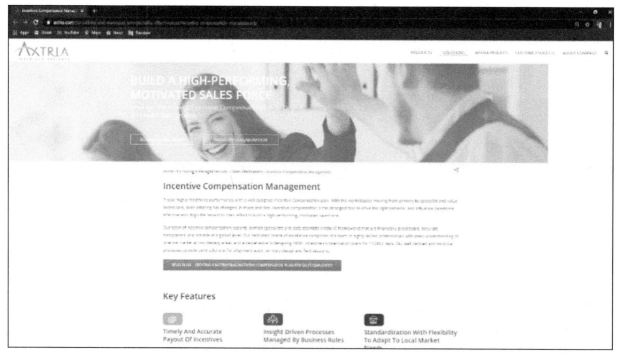

Sales managers can turn to specialist firms, such as Axtria, to help design combination compensation plans that can be effective in increasing sales force performance.

Source: https://www.axtria.com/consulting-and-managed-services/sales-effectiveness/incentive-compensation-management/.

Trends in Sales Compensation

Many recent changes in salesperson and sales manager compensation are expected to continue during the years ahead. These trends include the following:

- Tying the sales compensation plan to productivity plus retention
- Inclusion of customer satisfaction in the sales compensation plan
- More emphasis on international sales compensation

Compensation for Productivity and Retention

Companies are beginning to view sales compensation plans more broadly – as an investment in future sales productivity and retention of desired salespeople and sales managers. Thus, they are becoming more generous in compensating sales managers as well as salespeople.[32]

Due to years of cost cutting and downsizing, companies' sales forces have become rather lean. This puts added pressure on sales managers to retain good salespeople. So sales compensation plans must now not only attract new recruits but also retain the current salespeople. Increasingly, sales managers are offering high starting salaries and signing bonuses to attract new salespeople. At the same time, adjustments are being made to improve existing salespeople's compensation plans to keep morale high.[33]

Inclusion of Customer Satisfaction in the Compensation Plan

Another important trend in the business environment is the growing emphasis on customer satisfaction and relationship building. Managers are recognizing that high levels of customer satisfaction and retention are critical to profitability. Firms such as IBM (www.ibm.com), Xerox (www.xerox.com), Infiniti (www.infiniti.com), and Chrysler (www.chrysler.com) were among the early companies to include customer satisfaction-based incentives (CSBI) in their sales compensation plans.[34] Many companies today measure customer satisfaction as part of their sales compensation plan, and are likely to continue doing so in the future.[35]

Another related trend in sales compensation is customer sales teams and key account programs. Many companies are moving their salespeople into account-based teams. These companies believe they can better serve their customers by adopting a more customer-focused structure for their salespeople and compensation plan.[36] Key account salespeople or customer sales teams who call on the largest and most profitable customers are often the highest-paid salespeople in their companies. Their compensation plans are also tied to customer satisfaction. A national account manager for Monsanto (www.monsanto.com), with 15% of his compensation based on customer surveys. says, "You have to get your compensation tied to the relationships you have with your customers or upper management won't understand (how much you're worth)."[37]

International Sales Compensation

As U.S. firms continue to expand into international markets, they are being confronted with a range of circumstances that require them to adjust their sales compensation plans for indigenous salespeople.[38] For example, in the Far East, sales volume is the primary indicator of success, compensation is tied almost exclusively to this factor, and less weight should be placed on nonselling activities when developing a compensation plan. With wide cultural differences throughout the world, U.S. companies must carefully assess each country's culture before tailoring a sales compensation plan for that market.[39]

Commission for Sales Managers

While we've focused on methods of compensating salespeople, we should not overlook the obvious fact that sales managers are concerned about their own compensation, too. Logically, sales managers' compensation ought to be closely tied to the performance of the sales force, so many companies are awarding commissions or bonuses to sales managers for high performing sales forces.

Developing a sales manager's compensation plan can be challenging. First, the responsibilities of a sales manager are neither purely sales nor purely management. Good sales managers strike a balance between these two distinct goals: they continually strive for short-term sales, yet must also meet long-term corporate goals. Therefore, developing a sales manager's compensation plan solely on the basis of yearly sales performance may not be appropriate. Second, designing a sales manager's compensation plan is further complicated by the expectations of other functional areas of the organization. For example, financial executives may expect sales managers to control selling costs and be compensated accordingly, while marketing executives may want to reward a sales manager for emphasizing new products, market share growth, and the long-term image of the company. So companies should consider a blend of sales-oriented goals as well as organizational goals when developing a compensation plan for sales managers.[40]

Expense Accounts and Fringe Benefits

Expense accounts enable sales representatives to carry out necessary selling activities, while fringe benefits help provide them with personal security and job satisfaction. Although neither should be a means of augmenting income, salespeople often see them as important parts of the total compensation package, so we discuss them in this chapter. (We dealt with sales contests and other indirect monetary incentives used as motivational strategies in Chapter 10.)

Acknowledging the Importance of Selling Expenses

The costs associated with supporting salespeople in the field have been rapidly increasing and are expected to continue rising for the foreseeable future. The major sales expense categories – other than salary, commissions, and bonuses – are meals and entertainment, air travel, automobile rentals, and lodging. The increasing cost of lodging during the late 1980s single-handedly pushed the selling cost index to an all-time high. More recently, sales managers are beginning to voice concern over automobile expenses because the costs of new cars and ongoing maintenance have driven up the price of putting salespeople on the road.[41] To make matters worse, rising gasoline prices have increased the costs associated not only with automobiles but also air travel.

While selling costs have increased, they do represent expenses that are necessary and important for salespeople to carry out their jobs. In fact, sales managers have been known to consider travel and entertainment expenses as both "a tool and a curse."

Box 12.2 | Sales Management in Action 12.2

Corporations Toe the Party Line

The Tax Reform Act of 1986 reduced the amount of entertainment expenses that can be written off from 100% to 80%, and the days of "scandalous" entertaining appeared to be over. Nonetheless, many multinational firms continue to lavishly entertain their best customers and probably will continue to do so, even if the expenditure is not deductible at all. In fact, entertainment was "business as usual" at a recent Super Bowl, where 50-yard-line tickets selling for several thousand dollars each were provided to a few highly valued prospects and customers.

One of the most sought-after events on the corporate calendar is the Lawn Tennis Championships at the All England Lawn Tennis and Croquet Club – better known as Wimbledon. Seagram's is among the hundreds of multinational corporations that entertain guests at Wimbledon each year. Competition for space is tremendous, but IBM, British Petroleum, and Avis were among the fortunate few to fete prized clients with traditional tournament fare of champagne, cold salmon, and strawberries with cream. To help build company–customer relationships, Wexford International invited 60 of its customers and suppliers to a two-day golf tournament at a New Jersey country club. All this entertaining seems to be based on a business belief that companies and customers who play together, tend to stay together.

Firms must continue budgeting for these expenses, which are often critical to the company's sales growth and overall image. Many U.S. companies have found that providing entertainment to prospects and customers is akin to fertilizer used by the farmer because it increases the yield. Some firms take business entertainment expenditures further, as Sales Management in Action Box 12.2 demonstrates.

To accomplish sales objectives, every effective sales force must incur expenses. However, it is probably more realistic to see these not as expenses, but as investments that will yield future dividends. Because salespeople usually spend their own money for daily expenses, it is especially important to their morale that these outlays be quickly reimbursed. Most firms reimburse salespeople for items such as meals, lodging, auto expenses, business and personal phone calls home, drinks, and laundry costs while on the road.

Designing the Expense Plan

Any well-designed expense plan requires several building blocks. These are flexibility, equitability, legitimacy, simplicity, and affordability of administration.

Flexibility A plan that tries to relate selling expenses only to sales may discourage longer-run profitable sales activities, such as prospecting for new customers or providing special services. Thus, expense plans need to accommodate these other objectives.

Equitability An expense plan should be sufficiently flexible to ensure equal treatment of all salespeople regardless of their territory or sales assignment. Thus, the plan should take into account regional cost differences for food, lodging, and travel as well as expense variations for handling different types of customers or for doing different sales tasks. Each year *Sales & Marketing Management* calculates a selling cost index (SCI) for a typical five-day week for a salesperson working in each of 80 metropolitan markets. This index is used by many firms to determine appropriate reimbursement levels.

Legitimacy The plan should simply reimburse legitimate expenses, with neither profits nor losses for salespeople whether on the road or at the home office. Expense allowances should never be used in lieu of compensation. This would weaken the sales manager's control over the basic compensation plan, encourage expense padding, and violate federal income tax laws. Only expense accounts that reimburse salespeople for legitimate business expenses are nontaxable.

Simplicity Expense-account reimbursement policies must avoid legalistic language. Salespeople should easily understand which expenses are reimbursable so they have clear guidelines for making expenditures.

Affordability Too many organizations require excessive and redundant paperwork for reimbursement of expenses. An efficient expense control plan should minimize the clerical burdens for the reps and the sales office staff.

Controlling Expenses Through Reimbursement

Although salespeople on straight commission often pay their own expenses out of commissions, most companies reimburse their salespeople for legitimate selling expenses. Three basic reimbursement plans are widely used: unlimited, limited, and combination.

Unlimited Reimbursement Plans By far the most popular method of expense control, unlimited reimbursement allows salespeople to be reimbursed for all their necessary selling and travel expenses. No limit is put on total expenses, but sales reps must regularly submit itemized records of their expenditures. With the flexibility provided by unlimited payment plans, the expense variations in serving different customer types and territories or in performing diverse selling tasks are easily handled. This unlimited aspect may tempt some salespeople to be extravagant or to pad their expense accounts. While its flexibility allows sales managers some control in directing sales force activities, an unlimited payment plan tends to make forecasts of selling costs more difficult.

Limited Reimbursement Plans Under limited payment plans, expense reimbursement is restricted either to a flat dollar amount for a given time period (usually a day or week) or to an allowable cost per item (such as for a motel room, daily meals, or each mile of travel). To develop a limited payment plan, managers must study past company records to learn what the costs of meals, lodging, and travel have been over the years (using dollars adjusted for inflation). With this plan, sales managers can predict and budget expenses more accurately, reduce expense account padding, and establish unequivocal guidelines for spending by salespeople.

There are disadvantages, however. Salespeople may feel a limited plan indicates management's lack of trust. Such plans restrict those unusual (perhaps unallowable) expenses that might win or save a customer. And they make salespeople too conscious of reimbursement limits, to the possible detriment of sales and profits. They also tempt salespeople to switch reporting of expenditures from one-time period to another, to avoid going over expense ceilings. Finally, they require frequent revision of expense ceilings during inflationary periods and in different geographic locations; this may lead to confusion among salespeople about the current ceiling level.

Combination Reimbursement Plans Sales managers may consider a combination of the unlimited and limited expense reimbursement programs, in order to secure the advantages of both. One approach sets limits on certain items such as food and lodging

Although firms readily cover traveling expenses, sales managers should remember that keeping a close watch on expenses is an effective way of increasing profitability.

but not on transportation. Another variation of the combination plan relates expenses to sales. For example, the salesperson may be reimbursed for expenses up to 5% of net sales or be awarded a bonus for keeping expenses below 5% of net sales. Probably the greatest advantage of this approach is that it ensures that expenses do not get out of line in relation to sales. The major disadvantage is that it diverts some of the sales rep's attention from obtaining profitable sales to worrying about expense ratios.

Curbing Abuses of Expense Reimbursement Plans

Since few salespeople can afford frequent company travel on their personal funds, some means of immediate funding must be available to them. Unfortunately, travel advances have been a source of much waste and abuse. It is a temptation for salespeople to draw a larger advance than needed for a trip and to spend the full amount. Some companies have resorted to credit cards for salespeople, but these have proved so painful to use that travel expenses have been known to jump as much as 25% as the salespeople upgrade their out-of-town lifestyle.

Adjusting to Rising Selling Costs

As the costs of sales calls climb, many companies are being forced to rethink their selling strategies and tactics. One survey indicated that approximately 60% of companies take steps to make sure they're getting the best deals on all their travel arrangements.[42] More companies today are planning well in advance to get better air-fares and shopping airlines, hotels, car rental agencies, and websites to ensure they are getting the lowest possible prices. One of the most interesting responses to rising travel and entertainment expenses comes from a manufacturing company that developed a video as a substitute for face-to-face sales calls. Its sales force now does about two-thirds less traveling. According to the marketing manager of the firm, the use of the video saves the company substantial money each year in travel and lodging costs alone. The increasing use of the Internet is also helping to lower travel expenses for many companies. One of the key jobs of today's sales managers is to find creative ways to control rising personal selling costs.

Chapter Summary

1. **Meet the challenges of developing sales force compensation plans.** Developing a sales compensation plan is one of the most difficult tasks facing sales managers. In general, most salespeople are motivated by money, and for many salespeople the amount of money they make represents their "scorecard" of how well they are performing. The difficulty lies in developing a sales compensation plan that isn't too comfortable in that it fosters complacency, or one that is so aggressive in its goals that it actually demotivates the sales force. All salespeople are somewhat different, and to develop a plan to satisfy everyone is extremely challenging but a goal worth striving for.

2. **Follow the basic steps in developing a compensation plan.** When new compensation plans are developed or existing ones are revised, a systematic process should be followed. The seven distinct steps in the process of developing a compensation plan are to prepare job descriptions, establish specific objectives, determine general levels of compensation, develop the compensation mix, pretest the plan, administer the plan, and evaluate the plan.

3. **Compare the different methods of sales force compensation.** The three basic methods of sales compensation are straight salary, straight commission, and combination plans. Straight salary has the advantages of providing security, developing a sense of loyalty, providing more control over salespeople, and being simple to administer Its disadvantages are that it may cause a lack of incentive, increase selling costs, and lead to adequate but not superior performance. Straight commission has the advantages of relating income directly to sales, basing income strictly on accomplishments with no ceiling, and ensuring that costs are proportional to sales. The disadvantages of straight commission include an overemphasis on sales, neglect of nonselling activities, erratic earnings, and a loss of control by sales managers. Combination plans often provide the greatest flexibility and control while also providing security plus incentive. The disadvantages of a combination plan include the difficulty and expense in administering the plan.

4. **Evaluate the recent trends in sales force compensation.** The changing business environment has affected sales compensation planning for sales managers. Recent trends in sales compensation include tying sales compensation to retention as well as productivity, including customer satisfaction measures in the compensation plan, and growing emphasis on compensation for international salespeople.

5. **Control the use of expense accounts and fringe benefits in compensation planning.** Expense accounts enable salespeople to carry out necessary selling activities, while fringe benefits help provide them with personal security and job satisfaction. Although expense allowances and fringe benefits should not be used as a means of supplementing salespeople's income, they are often perceived by salespeople as important parts of their total compensation package. Any well-designed expense plan requires several building blocks. These basic criteria are flexibility, equitability, legitimacy, simplicity, and affordability of administration.

Key Terms

Compensation	Combination	Bonus	Draw
Straight salary	compensation plan	Progressive incentives	Expense account
Straight	Job description	Regressive incentives	
commission	Compensation mix	Fringe benefits	

Notes

1. Doyle, A. (20 November 2019). The highest paying management jobs. http://www.thebalancecareers.com/top-highest-paying-management-jobs-2061842 (accessed 22 February 2019).

2. https://money.usnews.com/careers/best-jobs/sales-manager/salary (accessed 21 September 2019).

3. Ripley, H. (1 August 2015). https://www.entrepreneur.com/article/247930 (accessed 22 February 2020); Colletti, J.A. and Fiss, M.S. (2006). The ultimately accountable job: Leading today's sales organization. *Harvard Business Review* 84(7–8): 125–131.

4. McFarlane, J. (5 August 2016). The top 25 reasons why salespeople are leaving your company. http://www.peaksalesrecruiting.com/blog/top-25-reasons-great-salespeople-leave/ (accessed 5 April 2016); Brashear, T.G., Manolis, C. and Brooks, C.M. (2005). The effects of control, trust, and justice on salesperson turnover. *Journal of Business Research* 58(3): 241–249; Aggarwal, P., Tanner, J. Jr. and Castleberry, S. (2004). Factors affecting propensity to leave: A study of salespeople. *Journal of Marketing Management* 14(1): 90–102.

5. Welch, J. and Welch, S. (2006). The case for 20-70-10. *Business Week* (2 October): 108; Welch, J. and Welch, S. (2006). Send the jerks packing. *Business Week* (13 November): 136.

6. Welch, J. and Welch, S. (2006). The case for 20-70-10. *Business Week* (2 October); 108. Brown, P.B. Should you fire 10% of your employees every year? Inc. (17 July 2017) (accessed 14 October 2019).

7. Kane, N. (13 May 2015). The importance of a good sales compensation plan. https://blog.janek.com/the-importance-of-a-good-sales-compensation-plan/ (accessed 26 September 2019).

8. Jordan, J. (8 June 2018). Sales productivity vs. Efficiency vs. Effectiveness. . . is there a difference? http://www.salesforce.com/blog/2018/06/sales-efficiency-metrics.html (accessed 26 February 2020); Durtan, D. (3 September 2019). 5 Strategies to drive sales productivity. https://seismic.com/company/blog/5-strategies-to-drive-sales-productivity/ (accessed 4 September 2019); Lucero, K. (9 May 2019). How to develop a sales compensation plan. http://www.xactlycorp.com/blog/how-to-create-sales-incentive-compensation-plan/ (accessed 3 October 2019); Ledingham, D., Kovac M. and Simon, H.L. (2006). The new science of sales force productivity. *Harvard Business Review* 84(9): 124–133; Brown, S.P., Evans, K.R., Mantrala, M.K. et al. (2005). Adapting motivation, control, and compensation research to a new environment. *Journal of Personal Selling & Sales Management (Spring)* 25(2): 156–167.

9. Chung, D.J. (2015). How to really motivate salespeople. *Harvard Business Review* 93(4): 54–61; Steenburgh, T. and Aherne, M. (2012). Motivating salespeople: What really works. *Harvard Business Review* 90(7–8): 71–75. Beasty, C. (1 January 2006). Dangling the carrot: Drive your sales force to profitability. http://www.destinationcrm.com/Articles/Editorial/Magazine-Features/Dangling-the-Carrot-Drive-Your-Sales-Force-to-Profitability-47693.aspx *CRM Magazine* (accessed 11 October 2019).

10. Johnstone, K. (16 Mary 2017). Responsibilities of a sales manager: The ultimate guide. http://www.peaksalesrecruiting.com/blog/responsibilities-sales-manager/ (accessed 13 October 2019; Trailer, B. and Dickie, J. (2006). Understanding what your sales manager is up against. *Harvard Business Review* 84(7/8): 48–56; Bursk, E.C. (2006). Low-pressure selling. *Harvard Business Review* 84(7/8): 150–162; Cespedes, F.V., Gardner, A., Kerr, S.. Kelley, R.D., and Dixon, A.L. (2006). Old hand or new blood? *Harvard Business Review* 84(7/8): 28–40.

11. Cabrera, C. (1 October 2014). 6 Reasons why sales commissions do work. https://www.google.com/search?client=firefox-b-1d&q=compensation+is+believed+to+be+the+best+motivator+for

+salespeople (accessed 10 October); Fatima, Z. (2017). Impact of compensation plans on salesforce motivation. *Review of Professional Management* 15(2): 70–76; Chamoro-Premuzic, T. (10 April 2013). Does money really affect motivation? A review of the research. https://hbr.org/2013/04/does-money-really-affect-motiv (accessed 13 October 2019); Gschwandtner, G. *Selling power* (1 February 2017). Seven non-cash incentives to motivate salespeople. https://blog.sellingpower.com/gg/2017/02/seven-non-cash-incentives-to-motivate-salespeople.html (accessed 12 October 2019).

12. The truth about motivating employees to be more productive. *National Business Institute Research* (accessed 11 October 2019); Mallin, M.L. and Mayo, M. (2006). Why did I lose? A conservation of resources view of salesperson failure attributions. *Journal of Personal Selling & Sales Management (Fall)* 26(4): 345–357; Dixon, A.L. and Schertzer, S.M.B. (2005). Bouncing back: How salesperson optimism and self-efficacy influence attributions and behaviors following failure. *Journal of Personal Selling & Sales Management (Fall)* 25(4): 361–369.

13. Charles, E.W. (27 September 2017). How to align sales rep behavior with company goals. http://www.xactlycorp.com/blog/align-sales-rep-behavior-company-goals/ (accessed 5 October 2019); Sales and marketing alignment. http://www.marketo .com/marketing-and-sales-alignment/ (accessed 6 October 2019); Chung, D.J., Huber, I., Murthy, V., Sunku, V., and Weber, M. (2019). Setting better sales goals with analytics. (9 July 2019). https://hbr.org/2019/07/setting-better-sales-goals-with-analytics (accessed 12 October 2019).

14. Montague, M. (28 February 2018). 9 tips for building a competitive sales compensation plan. http://www.google.com/search?client=firefoxbid%q=competitive+sales+compensation+plans (accessed 10 October 2019).

15. Corcodilos, N. What you need to know about signing bonuses. http://www.cmo.com/opinion/articles/2017/2/3/what-you-need-to-know-about-signing-bonuses.html#gs.73tkk5 (accessed 14 October 2019).

16. Paling, S. (21 October 2011). 4 signs a sales pro will be a good hire (Hint: Think Money). http://www.entrepreneur.com/article/220592 (accessed 3 October 2019).

17. Darmon, R.Y. (1974). Salesmen's response to financial incentives: An empirical study. *Journal of Marketing Research* 11(4): 418–426. Quain, S. (30 September 2015). 4 types of salespeople. https://smallbusiness.chron.com/4-types-salespeople-33679.html (accessed 3 October 2019); Metler, R. (21 February 2017). The five types of salespeople: Which one are you? http://www .salesforcesearch.com/blog/the-5-types-of-sales-people-which-one-are-you/ (accessed 4 October 2019); Lawler, E.E. (1987). The design of effective reward systems. In: *Handbook of Organizational Behavior* (ed. J.W. Lorsch), 255–271. Englewood Cliffs, NJ: Prentice Hall; Tyre, D. (11 June 2019). 4 Ways to design effective sales incentive programs. https://blog.hubspot.com/ sales/successful-sales-incentives (accessed 5 October 2019).

18. Wong, D. Seven non-cash incentives to motivate salespeople. *Selling Power* (1 February 2017) https://blog.sellingpower.com/ gg/2017/02/seven-non-cash-incentives-to-motivate-salespeople.html (accessed 6 October 2019); Dubinsky, A., Anderson, R.E. and Mehta, R. (2000). Importance of alternative rewards: Impact of managerial level. *Industrial Marketing Management* 29(5): 427–440.

19. Mahoney, T.A. (1990). Multiple pay contingencies: Strategic design of compensation. *Human Resource Management* 28(3): 337–347; Pfeffer, J. and Davis-Blake, A. (1987). Understanding organizational wage structures: A resource dependence approach. *Academy of Management Journal* 30(3): 437–455.

20. Dubinsky, A., Anderson, R.E. and Mehta, R. (2000). Importance of alternative rewards: Impact of managerial level. *Industrial Marketing Management* 29(5): 427–440; Wong, D. (2017). Seven non-cash incentives to motivate salespeople. *Selling Power* (1 February). https://blog.sellingpower.com/gg/2017/02/seven-non-cash-incentives-to-motivate-salespeople.html (accessed 6 October 2019); Lynn, S.A., Cao, L.T. and Horn, B.C. (1996). The influence of career stage on the work attitudes of male and female accounting professionals. *Journal of Organizational Behavior* 17(2): 135–150; Howtof, D. (19 July 2017). Seven ways sales incentives are changing. http://www.channelmarketerreport .com/2017/07/seven-ways-sales-incentives-are-changing/ (accessed 8 October 2019).

21. Gschwandtner, G. (21 February 2018). Why companies should want more women in sales (and How to get them). *SellingPower*. https://blog.sellingpower.com/gg/2018/02/why-companies-should-want-more-women-in-sales-and-how-to-get-them.html (accessed 22 February 2020); Tulshyan, R. (2015). Racially diverse companies outperform industry norms by 35%. *Forbes* (30 January 2015). http://www.forbes.com/sites/ruchikatulshyan/2015/ 01/30/racially-diverse-companies-outperform-industry-norms-by-30/#3748ded21132 (accessed 2 October 2019).

22. Cichelli, D. (25 January 2019). Seven trends in sales comp for 2019. http://www.worldatwork.org/workspan/articles/seven-trends-in-sales-comp-for-2019 (accessed 4 October 2019); Ryals, J. and Rogers, B. (2005). Sales compensation plans—One size does not fit all. *Journal of Targeting, Measurement & Analysis for Marketing* 13(4): 354–362.

23. Van Caster, S. (7 December 2018). 7 Common pitfalls that can derail incentive compensation programs. https://apttus.com/ blog/pitfalls-incentive-compensation/ (accessed 22 February 2020); James, G. (22 April 2019). How to align sales compensation with strategic goals. https://www.inc.com/geoffrey-james/ how-to-align-compensation-with-strategic-goals.html (accessed 3 October 2019).

24. Thacker, M. (22 August 2019). How to design a sales compensation plan that rewards performance and boosts revenue. http:// www.forbes.com/sites/forbescoachescouncil/2019/08/22/how-to-design-a-sales-compensation-plan-that-rewards-performance-and-boosts-revenue/#a7a0e45285cd (accessed 28 August 2019); Mahoney, T.A. (1990). Multiple pay contingencies: Strategic design of compensation. *Human Resource Management* 28(3): 337–347; Lopez, T.B., Hopkins, C.D. and Raymond, M.A. (2006). Reward preferences of salespeople: How do commissions rate?

Journal of Personal Selling & Sales Management (Fall) 26(4): 381–90; Erevelles, S., Dutta, I. and Galantine, C. (2004). Sales force compensation plans incorporating multidimensional sales effort and salesperson efficiency. *Journal of Personal Selling & Sales Management* (Spring) 24(2): 101–112.

25. Hamel, G. What percentage of profits should I pay my sales manager? https://smallbusiness.chron.com/percentage-profits-should-pay-sales-manager-37264.html (accessed 3 October 2019); Rose, D. What is the right sales manager commission percentage? https://cygnalgroup.com/sales-manager-commission-percentage/ (accessed 3 October 2019).

26. Love, B. (1985). Does your compensation plan inspire sales. *Folio* 14(3): 74–75; Nagori, M. (25 March 2019). Should sales managers make less than the sales professionals they manage? www.quora.com/Should-sales-managers-make-less-than-the-sales-professionals-they-manage (accessed 4 October 2019).

27. Chung, D.J., Kim, B. and Park, B.G. (2019). The comprehensive effects of sales force management: A dynamic structural analysis of selection, compensation, and training. *Harvard Business School* (working paper (30 June): 19–122); Lucero, K. (18 Febuary 2019). What is incentive compensation? https://www.xactlycorp.com/blog/what-is-incentive-compensation/ (accessed 5 October 2019).

28. Eckfeldt, B. (12 January 2018). Should you pay your sales people commission or salary? Here's how to decide. https://salesxceleration.com/straight-commission-sales-compensation-terrible-idea-8-reasons-why/ (accessed 6 October 2019).

29. Charles, E.W. (20 December 2018). What is draw against commission in sales? https://www.xactlycorp.com/blog/what-is-draw-against-commission/ (accessed 20 December 2018).

30. Hart, M. (6 January 2020). Everything you need to know about sales commission in 2019 (For Reps and Leaders). https://blog.hubspot.com/sales/sales-commission (accessed 22 February 2020).

31. Higuera, V. (6 March 2019). The average compensation percentage for sales reps. https://www.google.com/search?client=firefox-b-1-d&q=salesperson+compensation (accessed 10 December 2019).

32. Ciche, D. (25 January 2019). Seven trends in sales comp for 2019. www.worldatwork.org/workspan/articles/seven-trends-in-sales-comp-for-2019 (accessed 30 October 2019).

33. Evanschitzky, H. and Sharma, A. (2012). The role of the sales employee in securing customer satisfaction. *European Journal of Marketing* 46(3/4): 489–508; Pettijohn, C.E., Pettijohn, L.S. and Taylor, A.J. (2007). Does salesperson perception of the importance of sales skills improve sales performance, customer orientation, job satisfaction, and organizational commitment, and reduce turnover? *Journal of Personal Selling & Sales Management* 27(1): 75–88; Halliwell, S (12 June 2014). How to hire sales managers who are master motivators. https://www.peaksalesrecruiting.com/blog/5-secrets-for-hiring-sales-managers-who-are-master-motivators/ (accessed 16 December 2019).

34. Sager, I., McWilliam, G. and Hof, R. (1994). IBM leans on its sales force. *Business Week*, (7 February): 110.

35. Sharma, A. and Sarel, D. (2013). The impact of customer satisfaction based incentive systems on salespeople's customer service response: An empirical study. *Journal of Personal Selling & Sales Management* 15(3): 17–29;Chung, D.J. (2015). How to really motivate salespeople. *Harvard Business Review* 93(4): 54–61; Higuera, V. (6 March 2019). The average compensation percentage for sales reps. https://smallbusiness.chron.com/average-compensation-percentage-sales-reps-38188.html (accessed 3 October 2019); Meredith, H. (6 January 2020). Everything you need to know about sales commission in 2020. https://www.google.com/search?client=safari&rls=en&q=Meredith,+H.+Everything+you+did+to+know+about+sales+commission+in+2019&ie=UTF-8&oe=UTF-8 (accessed 21 February 2020).

36. James, G. (31 March 2014). 6 Ways selling will change by 2024. http://www.inc.com/geoffrey-james/6-ways-selling-will-change-by-2024.html (accessed 2 October 2019).

37. Wittenborn, C. (26 March 2018). Is your sales compensation plan aligned to your corporate objectives? https://salesbenchmarkindex.com/about-us/our-people/chad-wittenborn/ (accessed 6 October 2019); Sachse, E. (1 March 2016). In full alignment: Connecting sales compensation to company goals. https://www.worldatwork.org/docs/sales-compensation-focus/2016/03-14-2016/in-full-alignment-connecting-sales-compensation-to-company-goals.html (accessed 10 October 2019).

38. Madhani, P.M. (2015). Sales organization culture, compensation strategy, and firm valuation. *Compensation & Benefits Review* 47(4): 173–183.

39. Zoltners, A.A., Sinha, P.K. and Lorimer, S.E. (2015). There's no one system for paying your global sales force. *Harvard Business Review* (13 November). https://hbr.org/2015/11/theres-no-one-system-for-paying-your-global-sales-force (accessed 13 October 2019); Rouzies, D., Onyemah, V. and Iacobucci, D. (2017). A multi-cultural study of salespeople's behavior in individual pay-for-performance compensation systems: When managers are more equal and less fair than others. *Journal of Personal Selling & Sales Management* 37(3); 188–212; Segalla, M., Rouziès, D., Besson, M., and Weitz, B.A. (2006). A cross-national investigation of incentive sales compensation. *International Journal of Research in Marketing* 23: 419–33.

40. Meincke, J. (15 April 2019). How to set a sales manager compensation plan. https://blog.closeriq.com/2019/04/sales-manager-compensation-plan/ (accessed 15 April 2019); Rose, D. What is the right sales manager compensation percentage? https://cygnalgroup.com/sales-manager-commission-percentage/ (assessed 29 September 2019).

41. Rogers, W. The 16 do's of highly effective sales managers. www.salesforce.com/quotable/articles/effective-sales-managers/# (assessed 27 September 2019); James, G. (22 May 2014). 5 ways to reduce cost of sales. https://blog.getbase.com/5-ways-to-reduce-cost-of-sales (accessed 4 October 2019); Petrone, J. (2 February 2010). Reduce selling costs (without cutting your sales force). http://www.sellingpower.com/2010/02/02/3837/reduce-selling-costs-without-cutting-your-sales-force (accessed 14 October 2019).

42. Ibid.

Chapter Review Questions

1. Do you believe that most salespeople can be effectively "steered" by financial compensation? Explain. [LO 1]

2. What compensation mix do you think is best for creative selling of intangible goods, like estate planning advice? What mix would be best for a missionary salesperson (drug detail person) calling on physicians? A salesperson for large factory machines? A rep for office equipment? [LO 1]

3. What would be the ideal compensation package for the type of sales career you would consider? Would this "ideal" package change over the course of your career? [LO 1]

4. Identify and describe the various steps involved in devising a compensation plan. [LO 2]

5. What would you suggest to reduce selling costs? Do you think selling costs are like profitable investments and thus should not necessarily be reduced? Explain your answer. [LO 2]

6. Describe the advantages and disadvantages of different compensation methods. [LO 3]

7. What are the essential criteria for designing and implementing a sound bonus incentive program? [LO 3]

8. Discuss some of the recent trends in developing sales force compensation programs. [LO 4]

9. What method of reimbursing sales expenses would be best for a life insurance salesperson, a computer hardware sales rep, or an account executive who sells commercial time for a television station? [LO 5]

Online Exercise

Use the Internet to access Slideshare (https://www.slideshare.net/search/slideshow?searchfrom=header&q=sales+force+compensation/), Hubspot (https://blog.hubspot.com/sales/sales-compensation) and other similar knowledge exchange websites. Based on your research, develop a comprehensive sales force compensation checklist identifying financial rewards for remunerating the sales force.

Role-Play Exercise

Justifying the New Compensation Plan

Situation

You are the national sales manager for a large medical products company that sells a broad line of products to hospitals and pharmacies. After several years of fine-tuning your sales force compensation plan, you feel you've finally got it right to achieve corporate goals while maximizing sales force productivity. In brief, this plan, which was implemented six months ago, gives salespeople a weekly draw of $3000 plus 5% commission on sales, a 20% bonus for making quota, a 3% bonus for signing up each new account, and a special 5% commission on designated medical equipment that the company's product managers want emphasized. Your salespeople seem to like the new plan, and sales are steadily growing since its implementation. In fact, it looks as if each sales force region is going to reach its sales volume goals for the first time in years. The company doesn't provide executives below vice president with detailed profitability data so you are not able to calculate profits for different market factors (customer, product, territory, or salesperson), so your focus is on achieving the company's sales goals.

Today, you received a confidential memo from the vice president of finance for your company. In it, she informed you that a detailed financial analysis of revenues and expenses has revealed that the company is *losing* money in several areas and that cost reductions must be made throughout the company. An executive meeting has been scheduled for next week, and she has requested that you come prepared to discuss in depth the new sales force compensation plan.

Role-Play Participants and Assignments

National sales manager: You feel that you will be on the defensive at this meeting and will have to justify the sales force compensation plan to the senior executives.

Vice president of finance: She will come prepared with profitability data about sales territories, products, and customers. And, she will be asking tough, detailed questions about the new sales force compensation plan.

Other senior executives: They will probably ask many wide-ranging questions about sales force compensation, revenues, sales expenses, and profits.

In-Basket Exercise

After getting your first cup of coffee at work this morning before reading your emails, you notice a red envelope in your in-basket mail. You immediately recognize that distinctive red color as urgent correspondence from your company's national sales manager. Quickly opening the envelope and reading the letter inside, you're surprised to read that the company is getting a "rising tide of customer complaints" about poor customer service by your company's salespeople . . . .. and customer retention levels have "declined in each of the past three years." From the blunt wording of his letter, it's obvious that the national sales manager is under pressure to do something quickly to satisfy senior management. The last sentence of his letter puts it directly: "I want 'well-thought-out ideals with

supporting pro and con arguments' for changes in our sales force compensation plan by the end of the week from each sales manager." The company's current sales force compensation plan provides a relatively low salary and no team bonus but generous individual sales commissions. Since becoming a district sales manager, you have felt that some of the highest-earning salespeople might be neglecting customer service to maximize their commissions. "Wow," you think to yourself, "this is going to be a six-cups-of-coffee day."

Outline a new sales force compensation plan to improve customer service and retention without hurting sales force motivation.

Ethical Dilemma

You were recently hired as a sales manager for a successful financial services firm, and you're beginning to question the company's compensation plan. Salespeople are compensated on a salary-plus-commission basis. However, after a salesperson reaches a certain level of sales, commissions can run as high as 20%. This high commission rate, which can apply to over 100 different services, may be creating a situation that's not serving your customers well. After only a month on the job, you've received several calls from irate customers complaining that your company salespeople are too aggressive and have confused them into buying more financial service products than they need. You discuss this with one of your top salespeople, and he downplays the issue, stating: "With our

compensation system, selling only a few extra service products to each customer can mean the difference between earning $75,000 and $125,000 a year. And selling customers some extra financial services isn't really hurting them at all. In fact, everyone benefits!"

Questions

1. Is this salesperson acting unethically? Why or why not?

2. Should your company's compensation plan be changed? Why or why not?

3. How would you revise the compensation plan?

| CASE 12.1 | **AirComp, Inc.: How Compensation Influences Job Search** |

AirComp, Inc. is a U.S. manufacturer of industrial air compressors and other related products. The company worked with major retail chains such as Home Depot, Lowes, and Wal-Mart to develop a small, efficient air compressor for the industrial and commercial market. In turn, the large retailers marketed the compressors under their own brand names to painters, carpenters, bricklayers, and other people in small businesses. AirComp's own brand was introduced and developed by other merchandisers during the same time period. AirComp's image as experts in air compressor manufacturing was excellent among both the companies and the customers it served.

AirComp and many of the companies purchasing its air compressors recognized the growing trend in the do-it-yourself market. Many consumers were taking an

active interest in home-improvement projects and automotive repairs. This led to a tremendous market for do-it-yourself products. During this time, the marketing vice president and sales manager of AirComp, Inc., took an especially active interest in the demand for the company's smaller commercial line of air compressors. Close monitoring of the sales of small air compressors revealed that as consumers became more involved in do-it-yourself projects, many discovered the benefits of using small air compressors for home and automotive projects.

As a result of the tremendous growth of this market in recent years, AirComp, Inc., considered manufacturing a small, lightweight air compressor. After conducting several marketing research projects, AirComp developed a prototype of the product for further consumer testing and possible commercialization. The prototype had the following characteristics: It had a ¾-horsepower motor and a portable air compressor; did not require lubricating, and was virtually maintenance-free; it could do more than 50 tasks around the house and it weighed 12 pounds and came with a 14-foot cord and a kit of accessories. AirComp conducted additional research in the consumer market and found consumers liked its portability, its regulator dial, the ability to be attached to a wall in the garage or workshop, and its attractive design. AirComp then decided to enter the in-home consumer market with its new lightweight air compressor.

In developing the in-home air compressor market, AirComp faced the traditional problems of bringing a new product to market but it also needed to expand its sales force. Historically, the firm produced private-label air compressors for mass merchandisers. But it also sold to major accounts such as TruValue Hardware, Ace Hardware, and other large independent distributors. Unit sales were large, but there were a limited number of customers. The company had six full-time salespeople and a sales manager. To gain national distribution as quickly as possible, the firm contracted with a large number of manufacturers' representatives who collectively covered the United States. They called on smaller accounts and/or accounts that AirComp could not cover due to the small size of the internal sales force. The manufacturers' representatives were compensated through commissions and could have commissions computed on either a per-unit basis or a sliding-scale percentage of their invoice totals. Initially, both AirComp and the reps benefited. As the product became more accepted in distribution channels, the manufacturers' reps began to "cherry-pick" their accounts and ignored the smaller accounts in their territories. Recognizing this problem, AirComp decided to enlarge the size of its internal sales force and hired 16 new salespeople. Compensation was salary plus benefits and their role was to call on accounts the reps were bypassing. At the time of the decision to hire the "junior salespeople," the original six internal salespeople were promoted to national-account managers, handling only Lowes, Home Depot, Wal-Mart, Target, and similar chains.

Their compensation would be salary and benefits in addition to a year-end bonus on volume and profitability.

After a few years of having three different groups of salespeople (junior, national account, and manufacturers' reps), AirComp faced a serious problem with its junior salespeople. The junior salespeople pointed out that the manufacturers' reps continued to pick the large accounts in their territories, thus earning large commissions, while they had to make three times the sales calls for a minimal salary. In addition, junior salespeople felt the old guard had an unfair advantage with national accounts. Not only were they making considerably more, they also had much less responsibility in addition to their bonus opportunity. A summary of the annual compensation for each category of salesperson is shown in Table 1.

Despite the unusual makeup of AirComp's sales force, sales increased rapidly. The do-it-yourself market grew faster than AirComp management had anticipated. With the growth, however, came a great deal of competition. Although AirComp's sales force strategy had weaknesses, management felt they were doing an adequate job in the in-home consumer market. Salesperson turnover (loss of salespeople) for new sales reps remained high – 50% or more in some years – but there was never any problem hiring new salespeople. By 2020, AirComp's sales force had grown to 32 sales reps (six senior national-accounts reps and 26 new reps).

As competition in the in-home market slowed the growth rate at AirComp, Inc., management began thinking about separately targeting the small contractor segment of the market. As the consumer market expanded the small-contractor segment was virtually forgotten or was assumed to be part of the consumer market segment. Experts were projecting the home-improvement market would surpass $175 billion by the year 2022. Many of the products aimed at the home-improvement market were actually purchased by the thousands of small contractors throughout the United States.

While the tremendous growth during the past decade left many unsolved problems within AirComp's sales force, management wanted to get a jump on the competition in the relatively neglected small-contractor market.

TABLE 1

Compensation and Turnover for AirComp's Sales Force

Type of salesperson	Commission	Average yearly salary	Year-end bonus	Benefits	Turnover (%)
		Compensation			
Old reps (6)	None	$40,000–$50,000	$11,000–$20,000	$5000–$7000	0
Manufacturers' reps	$35,000–$40,000	None	None	None	0
New reps (26)	None	$28,000	None	$5,000–$7000	50+

Questions

1. Should AirComp enter the small-contractor segment with its product? Why or why not?

2. Give some suggestions on how the turnover problem among AirComp's new salespeople may be solved.

3. What are the major questions that must be answered before AirComp makes the decision to enter the small-contractor market? Should its sales force structure remain the same? Why or why not?

4. Assuming AirComp enters the small-contractor market and remains in the in-home consumer market, recommend a compensation program for the entire sales force. Be very specific in your recommendation. Include each of the seven steps of developing a compensation plan, as listed in the chapter, in your recommendation.

5. Would any of the recent compensation trends help AirComp with its problem? Why or why not? Be specific.

Case prepared by: Jim Boles, University of North Carolina, Greenville

---

| CASE 12.2 | **Juiced In Time Citrus Supply: Compensation and Sales Expenses** |

Juiced In Time Citrus Supply (JIT), located in Kissimmee, Florida, is a wholesaler of citrus farming supplies and equipment. Their main product lines include heavy-duty equipment such as pickers, forklifts, fruit washers, driers, and crating machines. Since being established 30 years ago, JIT has earned a reputation as one of the best citrus suppliers in the industry.

Ryder Ray assumed the position of sales manager for JIT less than 2 weeks ago. He was recruited from a large wholesaler of mining supplies in Morgantown, West Virginia. When Ryder's secretary presented him with the sales expense accounts for the past week, he almost fainted. He quickly asked her to double-check the figures, but she assured him they were correct. Ryder had been in sales for far too long to not recognize a padded expense account.

After checking the expense account records of all ten JIT salespeople for the past six months, Ryder realized that last week's expenses were not unusual. These numbers did not compare to industry norms, which quickly concerned Ryder. He walked out of the office and grabbed the first salesperson he came across. Chance Johnson happened to be in the wrong place at the wrong time.

When questioned about his expense account, Chance was noticeably a bit uncomfortable. After a few minutes, Chance insisted that he was tracking expenses in the manner he had been instructed. Chance then recommended that Ryder talk with the CEO. Chance reassured Ryder that the expense report is used to help make up for the low salaries provided to salespeople at JIT. Ryder thanked Chance for the information. Unfortunately, this conversation left Ryder more concerned than he was before his chat with Chance.

The next morning Ryder immediately talked to the CEO and found that Chance had indeed told the truth about the way padding the expense account was viewed at JIT. Ryder was very distressed. Not only was it illegal, but Ryder thought it reflected poor judgment by management because compensation and rewards should be tied to employee performance. After reflecting on it for several days, Ryder met with the CEO again. He told him he very much disapproved of the way the expense accounts were being handled and requested permission to change the reimbursement procedures so they would be more in line with industry norms. Ryder got the go-ahead from the CEO to take whatever measures he believed were best for the company.

That afternoon Ryder sat in his office trying to determine the best way to resolve the situation at hand. To help JIT better resolve this problem, Ryder researched the industry and found the information presented in Table 1. His research confirmed that instead of paying a competitive market rate of compensation, JIT paid much less than the industry average salary and commission and expected their employees to make up the difference by padding their expense accounts. Ryder understood the manner in which a company compensates employees sends a clear message about what management believes is important, which could cause JIT employees to believe the company is unethical in other business practices.

He wanted honest expense reporting, but wondered if it should be an open expense system or one with limits on the various types of expenditures salespeople were allowed to make. He also pondered how he would adjust the sales force's salaries to compensate for the tighter restrictions on expense accounts. Ryder knew that to attract and retain qualified employees, their pay should be linked to competitive market

TABLE 1

Sales Force Compensation and Selling Expenses

	JIT	Industry average
Compensation		
Salary	$38,000–$45,000	$44,000–$55,000
Commission	$10,000–$14000	$10,000–$20,000
Year-end bonus	None	$8000–$12,000
Selling expenses as a percent of sales:		
Meals and entertainment	8–12%	2–4%
Air travel	5–8%	4–5%
Lodging	7–10%	5–6%
Miscellaneous	4–6%	1–3%
Total Expenses as a percent of sales	24–36%	12–18%

rates for that industry and that employees tend to increase their performance when an organization implements a pay-for-performance method of payment.

Questions

1. Should any changes be made to the compensation at JIT? Why or why not?

2. How should Ryder approach the issue to ensure management does not frown on his actions and to avoid creating a morale problem among the sales team?

3. What type of expense budgeting should Ryder propose at JIT? Why?

4. Recommend an alternative compensation and selling expense plan for JIT. Justify your recommended plan.

Case prepared by: Nicole Dilg Beachum, University of Alabama at Birmingham

CHAPTER 13

Sales Organization Audit and Sales Analytics

We've covered organizing and developing the sales force in Part Two, then managing and directing in Part Three. Now, in Part Four, we'll examine two critical areas that fall within the realm of controlling and evaluating sales force performance. First, in this chapter, we'll concentrate on the overall sales organization audit and sales analytics for volume, costs, and profitability by key market segments to improve sales force effectiveness and efficiency. Our second topic – evaluating salesperson performance focuses our attention at the individual salesperson level which will be discussed in Chapter 14.

Some sales managers stress selling activities and sales volume while neglecting cost controls and profitability analysis. Although analyzing sales volume metrics is certainly helpful in evaluating and controlling sales effectiveness, it neglects the profitability of sales efforts – and high volume does not ensure high profits.[1] With the ever-increasing costs of selling, it's important that sales managers emphasize the profitability of sales efforts.[2] This requires conducting sales analytics on costs and profitability by important market segments (customers, product lines, and territories) and organizational units.[3] From such analyses, sales managers can redirect resources and expenditures to those areas where the return per dollar spent is highest. In this process, they should be able to assess the impact of formal and informal control mechanisms on the sales organization and salespersons, as well as on customers.[4] Thus, in this chapter we will show you how to analyze sales volume, costs, and profitability in order to assess sales force productivity.[5]

LEARNING OBJECTIVES

When you finish this chapter, you should be able to:

1. Understand the framework and process for carrying out a sales force organization audit.

2. Identify and describe the sources of information for conducting analytics on sales volume, costs, and profitability by market segments.

3. Explain the overall process and procedures for sales analytics on volume, costs, and profitability by territories, products, customers, and salespeople.

4. Describe the procedure for marketing costs and profitability analyses.

5. Provide the reasoning in sales analytics for using contribution costs versus full costs.

6. Illustrate the concept and explain ways to improve return on assets managed (ROAM).

Framework for Sales Force Organization Audit

Analysis of overall sales organization performance can be best approached through a sales force audit – a comprehensive, systematic, diagnostic, and prescriptive tool designed to assess the firm's sales force management process and to provide direction for needed changes and improved performance.[6] The approach sales managers use in conducting an audit depends on the purpose and perceived importance of the evaluation, the availability of needed information, management philosophy toward performance appraisals, evaluation skills of the raters, and the way the firm uses the results of the evaluation process in future planning. As shown in Figure 13.1, a sales force organization audit includes an evaluation of four areas:

1. *Sales force organization planning system* – Evaluates the sales department's goals and objectives, its overall sales force management program, and the program's deployment.
2. *Sales force organization environment* – Evaluates the external environmental factors (economic, sociocultural, competitive, technological, ethical, and political–legal) and the intra-organizational factors (company structure, sales-marketing department linkages, marketing mix).
3. *Sales manager qualities* – Assesses the adequacy of sales force management at all levels in terms of leadership, motivation, and communication skills as well as in empowering salespeople and seeking their participation in decision making.
4. *Sales force management functions* – Assesses the major sales force management functions of recruitment, training, compensation, supervision, forecasting, evaluation, quotas, sales, costs, and profitability analyses.

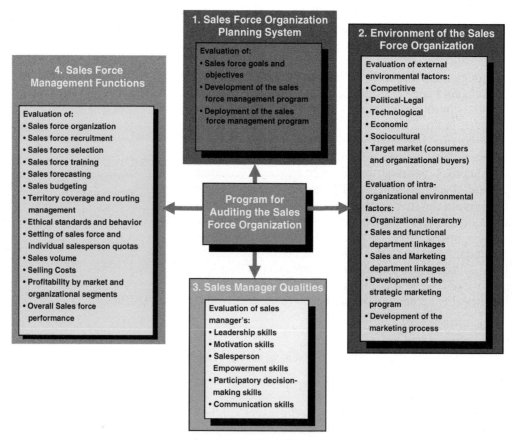

FIGURE 13.1 Conceptual model for a sales force organization audit.

When investigating each of these areas, the audit team will first acquire a wealth of information for identifying the sales organization's weaknesses and strengths, then offer recommendations about what the firm should do to address any deficiencies. Sales personnel, customers, the sales and marketing support teams, people in departments who interact with the sales organization (e.g., human resources, finance, and legal), internal company documents (marketing plan, sales plan, policy manuals, and surveys), industry publications, trade association data, and readily available published reports, newspapers, books, and periodicals can all provide valuable information. Auditors must be objective and unbiased, so oftentimes they will come from outside the sales organization or even outside the company.

Some managers may think that a detailed audit is an extravagance or questionable luxury, given the cost and time required. They prefer conducting audits only after some major problem has emerged. Waiting, however, until competition has become fierce, market share has eroded, key salespeople are leaving, or profitability has headed south may be too late to take corrective action that works. Therefore, it's advisable for sales managers to conduct a sales force audit regularly, preferably at least once a year. The cost of an audit is often offset by the potentially substantial returns from taking timely corrective action to solve sales force problems before they become large.

To learn more about conducting effective sales force organization audits, sales managers can engage professional firms, such as VanillaSoft (www.vanilla soft.com), which specialize in prescribing sales enhancement programs and practices.

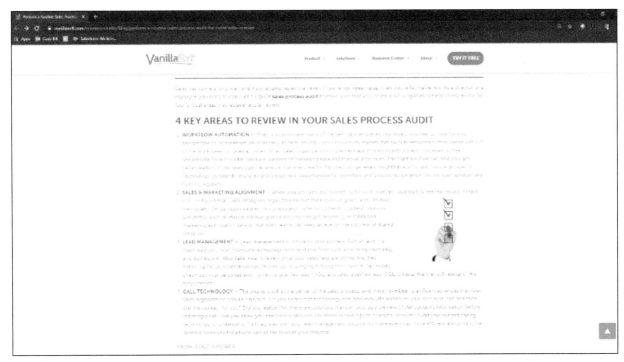

Sales managers can employ the services of firms, such as VanillaSoft, that specialize in conducting an unbiased, comprehensive, systematic, diagnostic, and prescriptive sales audit to assess the sales organization.

Source: https://www.vanillasoft.com/resource-center/blog/perform-a-routine-sales-process-audit-for-more-sales-success.

Sales Analytics

It usually takes considerable time and arduous efforts to complete a comprehensive assessment of the sales department's effectiveness and efficiency, but the payoff in improved sales productivity and overall company profits can be substantial. Let's now turn our discussion to conducting an analysis of sales volume, costs, and profitability because these are key factors by which we can quickly gauge the performance of the sales department. Total sales (or even profits) provide an incomplete picture of a firm's sales patterns. Sales managers need to analyze costs and profitability at the same time to reveal strengths and weaknesses of the company's different marketing units.

In analyzing the productivity of sales force efforts, sales managers should note the linkages among sales volume, selling costs, and profits by market segments.[7] To determine the profitability of different market segments, it's necessary first to analyze the sources of sales volume and then subtract the costs for producing those sales. Although the analytical task seems straightforward, it can present challenges, especially in assigning marketing costs (such as advertising, administration, or warehouse and office rent) that are indirect or common to more than one market segment across territories, products, and customers.

Since selling costs are really a subcategory of marketing costs, and because a combination of selling and marketing costs are required to produce sales, we'll use the more general term *marketing costs analysis* in our discussions. Moreover, the marketing and sales departments are inextricably connected with marketing activities creating expenses that support sales activities which generate direct revenue for the company. And, because both marketing and sales managers are more interested in profitability than in costs, we'll use *marketing profitability analysis* to describe the overall process of sales volume, costs, and profitability analysis.

Marketing profitability analysis requires an in-depth examination of the elements making up an organization's profit-and-loss or income statements. For managerial decision making, the traditional accounting statement expense categories need to be broken out into cost centers according to the purposes or functions for which the expenses (costs) were incurred. For example, a sales organization may pay employees for performing various functions such as direct selling, order processing, or sales administration. Salesperson earnings can be further allocated or traced back to territories, products, and customers from which they were generated. This type of analysis can be invaluable to sales managers for deciding whether to change some selling activities or alter the allocation of current efforts.[8] Let's discuss sales volume analysis first.

Sales Volume Analytics

Collecting, classifying, comparing, and evaluating an organization's sales figures is a process referred to as sales volume analysis. All organizations collect and classify sales data as the framework upon which to construct their accounting records and statements. To sales managers, sales figures are the most immediately visible and readily available means to judge how well the organization is performing. They regularly use sales analyses to compare current performance to past sales, competitors' sales, or forecasted sales. From these evaluations, management decides the direction and scale of future sales efforts. In some companies, sales figures are not always readily available due to a long sales cycle, as described in the Sales Management in Action Box 13.1.

Box 13.1 | Sales Management in Action 13.1

Sales Timing Can Be Everything

Analytics software sales at Cutting-Edge Technologies were unpredictable – up dramatically one quarter and sharply down the next. Company management wasn't able to accurately predict how much money was coming in and when, so operational planning became extremely challenging. Sales negotiations with government agencies are known for bureaucratic delays. In government sales, Cutting-Edge sales reps had to make sales presentations to large committees comprised of employees across several agency departments and work with various purchase decision influencers before closing its typical software sale of $80,000 to $120,000.

To try bringing more timely predictability to sales revenues, Cutting-Edge hired a new sales manager with strong analytical skills in selling metrics. She identified six distinct steps in the company selling process, ranging from identifying the key influencers within the prospect organizations

to developing the best strategies for successfully closing the deal after the sales presentation and demonstration. Utilizing Salesforce.com, an off-the-shelf CRM product, she began collecting and tracking key data at each stage in the selling process. She learned that salespeople needed at least 15 leads in the pipeline at any given time to generate a single sale. She began daily monitoring each salesperson's progress in the overall selling with the various prospect and customers to identify potential problems such as too few leads in the pipeline or insufficient contact with the key influencers at the different government agencies. When weaknesses were identified, the salespeople were counseled about how to get things back on track. By analyzing daily progress in each sales stage and ensuring prompt action to correct any problems, this resourceful sales manager was able to reduce quarterly revenue variations to less than 15%, and sales revenue planning for the company dramatically improved.

Key Considerations in Sales Volume Analytics Because sales volume analytics try to identify deviations between actual and expected sales performance of some marketing unit, then recommend action based on those deviances, sales managers first need answers to the following questions:[9]

- *How will we define a sale?* We can think of a sale in three ways: it can occur (a) when an order is taken, (b) when it is shipped to the customer, or (c) when the customer pays. Most companies consider a sale to take place at the time of shipment (and also use this date for recording and paying salesperson commissions), but some keep records for all three definitions to analyze what volume and type of orders make it through each of the stages. Whatever the definition, the firm must apply it consistently if sales comparisons across time periods are to be meaningful.
- *How will we measure sales?* Will we measure sales in dollars, physical units, and/ or as a percentage of total sales (e.g., product A sales as a percentage of total sales).
- *At what organizational level will we conduct the sales analytics?* Will we analyze sales for the overall sales organization, or will we also analyze them by region, district, or territory?
- *How will we break down the sales analyses?* Common categories include sales by territory, product (or product line), customer group (or individual customer), customer size, customer type (consumer, industrial, government, institutional, nonprofit) method of sale (phone, catalog, in-person, e-commerce), order size, distribution method, and salesperson.
- *What will we use as our basis (or bases) of comparison?* Popular bases include sales in prior periods, the fiscal period's sales forecast or sales quota, competitors' sales (or market share), and average sales for the period.

- ***What information sources will we use?*** Customer invoices, cash register receipts, salesperson call reports, salesperson expense reports, individual customer or prospect records, financial records, credit memos, and warranty cards can all provide information for conducting the sales analytics.

The most illuminating kind of sales analytics disaggregates the sales information into multiple marketing units or cross classifications. A territory-by-customer analysis will be more revealing than merely a territory or customer analysis alone. Similarly, a three-way sales analytics process (territory-by-customer-by-product) will uncover more information than a two-way (territory-by-customer) analysis. Additional gradations of sales information can be especially valuable in identifying weaknesses and strengths in the marketing units. Too much disaggregation of the data, though, may result in information overload – where management is simply inundated with sales information with which to make decisions. Thus, sales managers need to make a trade-off between the specificity of the sales information they desire and the time and resources they have to expend on the sales analytics.

Sources of Sales Information Depending upon the depth of sales analyses and the breakdown desired, the sources of sales information may vary widely. In a simple sales analytics process, only aggregate sales figures are needed for the desired market segment. But for comparisons with quotas, market potential, historical sales, or industrial averages, the sales manager will want much more information collected and classified. The sales invoice is the most important single source of sales information, but most

mangostar/123RF

A sales manager can ascertain how effective and efficient the sales force has been by examining sales, costs, and profitability data by different market segments or organization units which, in turn, can be used to design and implement more suitable sales strategies for accomplishing organizational objectives.

companies utilize other sources as well, depending on the types of analysis desired. Major sources of sales information are shown in Table 13.1.

Collecting Sales Data Firms usually report their sales figures in both dollars and units because inflation can distort dollar comparisons across different time periods. Sales data are frequently subcategorized by territories, product types, customer classes, order sizes, method of sales, time period, organizational unit, or salespersons to provide more meaningful information to management. Each subcategory can be further broken out for more in-depth analysis. For example, sales by territory can be broken out by product types, customer classes, and so on, as shown in Figure 13.2.

TABLE 13.1

Sources and Types of Sales Information

Sources and Types	Description of Data
Sales invoice	Customer name and address; products or services bought, sales in units and dollars; name of salesperson; customer's industry and/or trade channel; terms of sales, including discounts and allowances; method of payment; mode of shipment and freight costs.
Salesperson's call reports	Prospects and customers called upon; names of persons contacted; products presented or discussed; prospect or customer product needs and usage; orders obtained.
Salesperson's expense accounts	Itemized daily expenses for travel, lodging, food, and entertainment of prospects and customers.
Individual prospect/ customer records	Prospect or customer name and address; customer's industry or trade channel; number of calls by company salesperson; sales in dollars and units; estimated annual usage of each product type sold by the company; annual purchases from the company.
Internal financial records	Sales by major market segments (territories, customers, products, or salespersons); direct selling expenses; administrative costs; costs and profits by market segments.
Warranty cards	Basic demographic data on customers; where purchased; price paid; reasons for purchase; service expected.
Store audits	Dollar or unit sales volume; market share in product category.
Consumer diaries	Dollar or unit purchases by package size, brands, prices, special deals, and type of outlets where purchased.
Test markets	Dollar or unit purchases; market share; repeat purchases; impact of different marketing activity expenditures on sales.

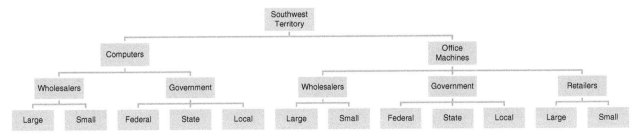

FIGURE 13.2 Subcategories of a sales territory.

Total Sales Volume In any sales analytics process, total sales volume figures are usually the first ones studied. Sales managers want to know the trend of sales over the past several years in terms of units and constant (un-inflated) dollars. Comparing relative changes in total industry sales with company sales gives the sales manager a benchmark for performance against competitors. Trends in company market share (company sales/industry sales) are excellent indicators of relative competitive performance. In Table 13.2, CENTREX Company's sales volume has risen faster than industry sales from 2014 through 2020, and sales (in constant dollars) have continued to increase. Even though these aggregate sales figures indicate that all is going well, an astute sales manager would resist the temptation to be complacent and go ahead with more in-depth sales analytics to see how sales force productivity might be improved.[10]

With the press of other duties, sales managers are often lulled into inattention to sales analyses when total sales figures appear favorable, because they forget the *iceberg principle*. Only about 10% of a floating iceberg is visible above the surface of the water. Yet it is the underlying 90% that can sink a mighty ship if the captain superficially evaluates the iceberg based only on its visible part. Favorable total figures can easily hide unprofitable market segments and unproductive sales activities. To uncover more of the iceberg, it is necessary to divide total sales figures into their successively smaller components. For example, we might start with an analysis of sales volume by territory, and then subdivide territorial sales to the individual salespeople who generated those sales. Next, we might look at each salesperson's sales by product lines. Finally, we can subdivide product-line sales into customer classes. Each sales manager will need to decide what type and how many breakdowns are needed to get at the desired underlying explanations for sales volume figures. Through this sequential process, sales managers can unravel the outer covering at each top-to-bottom hierarchical level to see exactly from where sales revenue and profits are being generated, as illustrated in Figure 13.3. Working with our data from Table 13.2, we can break out 2020 sales data by geographical territory, as shown in Table 13.3.

Sales Analytics by Territory Scanning the territorial classification in Table 13.3, we readily see that all the territories met or exceeded their quotas for the year, except for the Midwest region, which achieved 98% of quota and had the highest total sales. Although everything looks good overall, CENTREX Company's new sales manager,

TABLE **13.2**			
CENTREX Company Sales Versus Industry Sales (In Thousands of Dollars)[a]			
Year	**Industry Sales**	**Company Sales**	**Company Market Share (%)**
2014	$15,689	$2359	15.04
2015	$16,912	$2782	16.45
2016	$17,776	$3373	18.98
2017	$18,234	$3519	19.30
2018	$18,982	$3712	19.56
2019	$19,871	$3916	19.71
2020	$20,466	$4231	20.67

[a]Inflation-adjusted dollars.

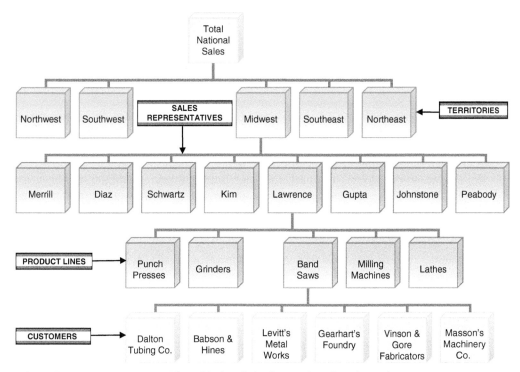

FIGURE 13.3 CENTREX Company: Hierarchical analysis of 2020 sales volume by market segments.

TABLE 13.3

CENTREX Company: 2020 Sales Analytics by Territory (In Thousands of Dollars)

Territory	Quota	Actual	Index Performance (Actual Sales/Quota)
Northeast	$845	$848	1.00
Southeast	$820	$840	1.02
Midwest	$890	$870	.98
Northwest	$815	$843	1.03
Southwest	$830	$830	1.00
Totals	$4200	$4231	1.01

Claudia Middleton, wants to investigate sales in each of the territories by breaking them out into subcategories. Before doing this, she reviews the procedure for assigning sales quotas to ensure that each quota was assigned fairly and based on one or more sound measurements of potential, such as *Sales & Marketing Management*'s annual "Survey of Buying Power Index." Middleton also considers any unusual conditions in the individual territories (such as more intense competition or a union strike) that might have adversely affected sales; or conversely, an anticipated shortage of the company's product that may have created windfall sales from customers stocking up ahead of time. If quota was barely achieved in a territory where industry demand was sharply up during the year, further investigation is called for. After considering each territorial circumstance for the period, the sales manager can start with the territory that suggests the most promise for productivity improvement. Since the Midwest territory was the only one to fall short of quota (.98), Middleton begins with that region's sales, broken out by sales representative, as shown in Table 13.4. Upon finding that the lowest-performing sales rep was Jared Lawrence, who reached only 82% of his quota, she decides to dig deeper into Lawrence's sales for the year.

Sales Analytics by Product Line Table 13.5 shows that Lawrence did a good job of reaching product quotas – except for band saws, for which he achieved only 20% of quota. In checking with the company's production manager, the sales manager learns there were no unusual quality control problems, shortages, or delivery problems on band saws. Furthermore, the marketing vice president said that there had been no recent change in the marketing mix for band saws in any territory and that total sales for band saws were running slightly ahead of last year. To probe a little deeper, Middleton decides to ask her sales administration assistant for a breakout of Lawrence's sales of band saws by customer.

Analysis of band saw sales by customer, shown in Table 13.6, reveals that one customer, Babson & Hines, accounted for Lawrence's poor performance on that product

TABLE 13.4

CENTREX Company: Midwest Territory 2020 Sales Analytics by Sales Representative (In Thousands of Dollars)

Sales Representative	Quota	Actual	Index Performance (Actual Sales/Quota)
Kim	$106	$110	1.04
Johnstone	$95	$93	.98
Merrill	$110	$112	1.02
Schwartz	$115	$117	1.02
Peabody	$110	$109	1.02
Lawrence	$130	$106	.82
Diaz	$116	$116	1.00
Gupta	$108	$107	.99
Totals	$890	$870	.98

TABLE 13.5

CENTREX Company: Sales Representative Lawrence's 2020 Sales Analytics by Product Line ($10,000s)

Product Line	Quota	Actual	Index Performance (Actual Sales/Quota)
Lathes	$53	$52	.98
Milling machines	$44	$49	1.11
Band saws	$60	$12	.20
Grinders	$37	$44	1.19
Punch presses	$46	$47	1.02
Totals	$240	$192	.82

TABLE 13.6

CENTREX Company: Sales Representative Lawrence's 2020 Sales Analytics by Customer

Product Line	Quota	Actual	Index Performance (Actual Sales/Quota)
Masson's Machinery Co.	1	1	1.00
Vinson & Gore Fabricators	2	2	1.00
Gearhart's Foundry	1	1	1.00
Levitt's Metal Works	1	1	1.00
Babson & Hines	24	0	0.00
Dalton Tubing Co.	1	1	1.00
Totals	30	6	.20

line. Babson & Hines was usually Lawrence's biggest customer by far and had been targeted for 80% of his entire sales quota for band saws. With a change of purchasing agent at Babson & Hines, however, the customer had switched to another supplier, leaving Lawrence out in the cold. Embarrassed about losing such a large account, which he had begun taking for granted, Lawrence said nothing to the new sales manager, hoping that he might regain some of the business later in the year or make it up by increasing sales on other product lines. Lawrence did not expect his deception to be picked up, because the previous sales manager seldom analyzed sales by market segments as long as overall sales were favorable. Claudia Middleton has a private conference with Lawrence following the next monthly sales meeting. She explains to him that in the future, she expects to be alerted immediately about sales problems so that she might provide assistance. Lawrence, relieved that he was not reprimanded for his mistake in judgment, leaves Middleton's office feeling respect for his manager's thorough analysis of sales force operations.

Lawrence's sales by customer illustrate the validity of the concentration principle (sometimes called the 80–20 rule), which asserts that the major portion (80%) of any organization's sales, costs, or profits often come from a small proportion (20%) of customers or products. If Lawrence had allocated his selling time with customers in proportion to sales, he might have retained the Babson & Hines account. Many progressive companies today use telesalespeople to make telephone and e-mail sales calls on small customer accounts, so that field salespeople can spend more time in face-to-face meetings with large accounts. Beyond revealing all kinds of valuable information about "who, what, where, when, and how" sales revenue is generated, sales volume analytics lay the foundation for the next stage in profitability analysis – the in-depth study of the costs of achieving sales.

Profitability Analytics

Although the sales volume analytics process is a useful control tool, it does not give the complete picture of the sales organization's effectiveness and efficiency because it neglects the attendant costs, profitability, and return on investment that were generated by the results. Thus, cost and profitability analyses are also needed.

Historically, sales managers have not been very cost or profit oriented. This is not to say that they don't recognize the need for profitable sales volume. They often make the mistake, though, of treating volume and cost control as two separate entities. Some sales leaders are so motivated to generate sales that they give little consideration to the costs of obtaining those sales. Others are shortsighted about cost-volume relationships. Furthermore, some sales managers incorrectly assume that the more their salespeople sell, the more money their firm is making. Sales managers, in pursuit of sales, are often reluctant to delete unprofitable products, drop unprofitable customers, or eliminate unprofitable territories. An ever-growing number of sales organizations are emphasizing a profit perspective in their evaluation process.[11]

Marketing costs analysis goes beyond sales volume analysis to investigate the costs incurred and the profits generated from sales volume. By subtracting the costs identified with the sales revenue from the various market segments or organizational units, we can determine the profit contributions of these segments and units.[12]

Sales managers should utilize all their resources to achieve that balance between sales volume and costs that will result in the highest long-run organizational profits. But it is often difficult to decide how to allocate these resources, because the precise impact of expenditures on different elements of the marketing mix – like advertising, sales promotion materials, sales calls, and post-purchase service – isn't readily measurable. Any effective marketing costs analysis requires cooperation among the sales manager, the headquarters marketing team, and the accounting department. One way to understand this need for integrated efforts is to consider input–output efficiency.

Input–Output Efficiency We need different mixes and levels of selling and supporting marketing efforts to achieve different sales objectives. The relationship between these inputs (marketing efforts) and the outputs (sales goals) is known as input–output efficiency.[13] To illustrate, suppose a regional sales division of Micro-Computer Solutions Corporation has the objective of selling 2000 new office computers during the year. The input is the mix and level of direct selling and supporting marketing efforts required to achieve the output, the sales objective. It is projected that to help introduce the new product to prospective customers, the sales force will have to make 3000 additional sales calls during the year, and 20 advertisements will be needed in selected trade magazines. In addition, the sales manager estimates that the inside office sales force will accept about 600 collect telephone calls inquiring about the new machines. A summary of these activities is presented in Table 13.7.

By dividing the dollar outputs by the dollar inputs ($1,000,000/$320,900), we derive an efficiency ratio of 3.116.

TABLE 13.7

MicroComputer Solutions Corporation: An Illustration of Input–Output Efficiency

Sales Efforts (inputs)	$	Sales Goals (Outputs)	$
3000 sales calls @ $100	$300,000	Sell 2000 new computers ($1,000 each) @ $500 gross margin	$1,000,000
600 telephone calls @ $1.50	$900		
20 trade magazine ads @ $1,000	$20,000		
Totals	$320,900		$1,000,000

Minimum Average Costs Many organizations fail to function most efficiently because they don't operate near the optimal point on their average cost curves, representing selling and supporting marketing costs. Instead of making 3000 sales calls based on a $10,000 market survey, it may be more efficient to mail out 6000 sales promotion brochures about the new product and make only 1500 sales calls on the best prospects identified by marketing research. By reallocating the mixture of direct selling and marketing support activities, the firm might achieve the same sales goal with greater efficiency ($1,000,000/$186,900 = 5.35), as shown in Table 13.8.

Cooperation Between Marketing and Accounting Departments Sales organizations often incur high average costs for selling tasks because they over-utilize direct selling activities and under-utilize their marketing support team. By cooperating with the marketing specialists in advertising, marketing research, or sales promotion, the sales force can often function much more efficiently. It behooves sales managers to attempt to operate at the optimal point on their average selling cost curve. As you can see in Figure 13.4, typically an optimal number of sales calls are required to operate at the lowest average selling cost per unit. At S1, reps are making an insufficient number of sales calls to produce desired sales, so per unit costs are high at C1. At S3, the sales manager is relying too heavily on costly sales calls, so per unit costs remain too high at C3. Only at S2 is the optimal number of sales calls being made to achieve the lowest per unit costs at C2. Beyond this optimal point, the sales manager ought to shift from sales calls to other marketing and promotional activities.

Historically, accounting systems have been concerned mainly with reporting aggregate financial data to stockholders and creditors in order to raise outside funds. Gradually, accounting statements were redesigned to provide analysis of production costs for internal management use. But only in recent years, with the widespread use of computers, have accountants seriously turned their attention to the analysis of marketing costs.

Due to their critical function as the revenue-producing arm of the company, marketing activities often constitute a company's largest total expenditures. To progressive accounting and marketing departments, analyzing marketing costs offers rewarding opportunities to cooperate in improving overall productivity. Three continuing

---

TABLE 13.8

MicroComputer Solutions Corporation: An Illustration of Minimum Average Costs

Sales Efforts (Inputs)	$	Sales Goals (Outputs)	$
1500 sales calls @ $100	$150,000	Sell 2000 new computers ($1,000 each) @ $500 gross Margin	$1,000,000
600 telephone calls @ $1.50	$900		
1 market survey @ $10,000	$10,000		
6,000 sales promotion brochures @ $1.00	$6,000		
20 trade magazine ads @ $1,000	$20,000		
Totals	$186,900		$1,000,000

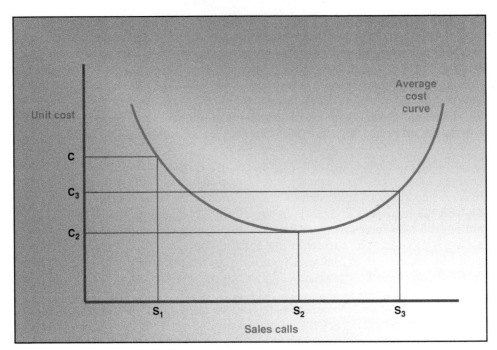

FIGURE 13.4 Average per unit sales cost curve for direct selling.

problems account for the long neglect of marketing costs analyses by accounting systems: (1) inadequate communication, (2) lack of marketing costs standards, and (3) inability to collect and analyze the huge volume of marketing data.

Inadequate communication between marketing and accounting managers arises partially from their different perspectives on the use of cost data. Accountants tend to see costs as an end, something to be reduced. Marketers, however, see such expenditures largely as a means to an end or investment to achieve higher sales. Sales managers are particularly sensitive to potentially adverse effects on sales if marketing expenditures are curtailed too much.

Accounting cost analysis is primarily designed to provide a historical financial record of overall company operations and to ensure that production costs stay within established standards. By contrast, marketing costs analysis is more concerned with future decisions; it seeks to learn the specific cost and profit contributions of different marketing efforts. While recognizing their different perspectives (costs versus investments) when analyzing marketing expenditures, accounting and marketing managers should try to cooperate with one another for the overall benefit of better understanding overall company efforts and productivity.

Lack of marketing costs standards has slowed the development of marketing costs analytics, and more companies might benefit from establishing a marketing controller position that would focus on developing better prediction and control mechanisms for marketing costs. However, based on experience and research, standard costs, including labor, material, and machinery resources needed to produce a certain output, can be predicted and standardized as norms in conducting production costs analyses. Unfortunately, the marketing outlays needed to produce a given level of sales are much less predictable, because results vary widely depending on the marketing mix selected for changing marketing scenarios. Marketing managers seldom can precisely determine the costs of inputs needed to achieve a desired sales level.

Moreover, many marketing expenditures, such as advertising and customer service, don't have an immediate, readily measurable impact on sales. They work over a period of time, making it difficult to identify sales results in one period with the marketing costs to achieve those sales.

In conventional accounting practice, most marketing expenses are charged off in the period incurred even though the results in sales usually come much later, while production costs are identified with per unit output which is held in inventory until sold. Even the terms *costs* and *expenses* highlight the accountant's difficulties with marketing operations. Accountants tend to speak of production costs and marketing expenses, suggestive of their different levels of specificity. Marketers often use the terms interchangeably but tend to think of marketing expenses as investments that will pay off in future sales. The challenge remains for accountants and marketers to find new approaches to managing marketing costs for improved profitability.

Inability to collect and analyze the huge volume of marketing data has long hindered the progress of marketing costs analysis. But with more sophisticated collection and computer analysis software, the mass of marketing data has become increasingly manageable. Today, even small firms often have access to the latest analytics software, which can handle the countless calculations necessary to compile and analyze marketing information in a timely fashion for decisions on sales force efforts and other marketing activities. Today's sales managers can receive full-color managerial charts and graphs, directly from computer printouts, summarizing the mountains of marketing sales volume, costs, and profit data in almost any form desired. Computer-generated graphics enable sales managers to more readily identify and respond to emerging opportunities and challenges in the marketplace.

Flying Colours Ltd/Photodisc/Getty Images

Managers from the sales, marketing, finance, and accounting departments need to work together to correctly calculate profitability by territory, market segments, product lines, and salesperson.

Benefits of Marketing Costs and Profitability Analytics Two terms – costs and expenses – have often been used interchangeably in describing marketing costs analyses. But costs tend to be specific and directly related to volume output, while expenses are more general or indirect expenditures; therefore, we tend to say *production costs* and *marketing expenses*. Marketing costs analysis recognizes that sales are achieved through marketing expenditures that contribute uniquely to profits. By identifying the productivity of different marketing expenditures, sales managers are able to improve the precision and productivity of their decisions in (1) allocating sales force efforts and sales department resources, (2) preparing sales department budgets, and (3) obtaining support for the sales force from other elements of the company's marketing mix.[14]

Numerous vendors offer sales analytics software, including Microsoft (www.microsoft.com), Salesforce (www.crm.com), Sisense (www.sisense.com), Tableau (www.tableau.com), Yellowfin (www.yellowfin.com), Board (www.board.com), Domo (www.domo.com), Qlik (www.qlik.com), Zoomdata (www.zoomdata.com), Birst (www.birst.com), Dundas (www.dundas.com), Looker (www.looker.com), Oracle (www.oracle.com), IBM (www.ibm.com), SAP (www.sap.com), and SAS (www.sas.com). Sales managers should check out the various websites that describe and compare the top sales analytics software to find the best fit for their specific needs.

In addition to diligently analyzing costs and profits by market segments using the latest analytics software programs, resourceful and insightful sales managers often can spot sales force inefficiencies needing correction by applying their common sense – with sometimes surprising benefits, as explained in the Sales Management in Action Box 13.2.

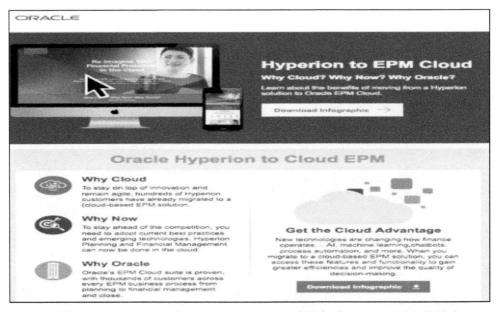

Sales managers can employ Enterprise Performance Management (EPM) software programs available from vendors, such as Oracle Hyperion, to systematically collect and organize data on sales revenues, marketing costs, and profitability to drive business, marketing, and sales analytics and, ultimately, improve sales force performance.

Source: https://go.oracle.com/LP=71702.

Box 13.2 | Sales Management in Action 13.2

Using common sense in sales analytics: Three examples

A sales manager for a medical device company observed that the commissions earned by salespeople varied dramatically with the "best" salespeople receiving up to ten times the dollar commissions of the apparently "worst" salespeople. Checking further, he found that the sales potential for the company's territories had not been updated in years. After updating the relative potential for the sales territories assigned different salespeople, he found that the salespeople with the highest commissions typically were assigned the highest potential sales territories. In essence, the company was rewarding the sales territory, not the salesperson's successful efforts.

An alert industrial products sales manager noticed that a territory that ranked fourth highest out of 250 territories in sales for the company had been vacant (no assigned salesperson) for many months. Further analysis revealed that the territory

had huge potential, so company sales might be readily and significantly increased by assigning salespeople to this territory.

After reviewing rising sales force travel expenses, a consumer products sales manager decided that it didn't make economic sense for the field salespeople to be calling on low-potential, remotely located customers. So, in the future, she decided that these accounts were to be covered by teleselling, direct mail, e-mail, and the company's Internet and extranet websites. By saving the travel time and costs expended in covering small accounts, salespeople were able to spend more face-to-face selling time with their larger accounts, and profits increased. What's more, the direct sales force retained over 80% of their total sales volume. Two personal benefits of reduced travel included more nights at home with their families for salespeople which substantially increased sales force morale.

Profitability Analysis Procedure In conducting a marketing costs (or profitability) analysis for a sales organization, sales managers can approach the analysis systematically by following these steps: (1) specify the purpose of the analysis, (2) identify functional cost centers, (3) convert natural expenses into functional costs, (4) allocate functional costs to segments, and (5) determine profit contribution of segments (Figure 13.5). Let's discuss each of these steps.

Specify the Purpose Sales managers must first decide the precise purpose of the analysis. That is, what do they want to determine the profitability of – sales territories, sales representatives, customers, product lines, or organizational units such as district or branch offices? Depending upon the answer to this question, the treatment of marketing costs will vary. Some costs may be direct for one segment but indirect for

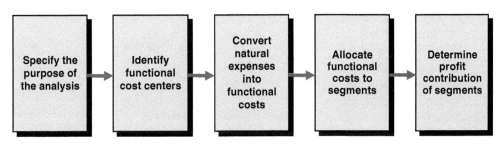

FIGURE 13.5 Marketing profitability analytics procedure.

another. For instance, a salesperson's salary is a direct cost to an assigned territory but indirect with regard to the different product lines or customer classes that he or she sells in that territory. Even compensation usually breaks down into fixed costs (salary) and variable costs (commission based on sales). By specifying the precise purpose of the analysis, sales managers are able to classify expenses as direct or indirect costs and as fixed or variable costs.[15]

Identify Functional Cost Centers Functional costs refer to reclassified natural expenses into the activities or functions for which they were incurred (e.g., "salary expense" reclassified into direct selling, transportation, or advertising function salaries).

As shown in Table 13.9, we can broadly categorize functional cost centers for sales organizations into: (1) order-getting costs, and (2) order-filling costs. Order-getting costs pertain to those activities that obtain sales orders, such as direct selling and advertising expenditures. Order-filling costs relate to those activities that follow the sale (such as order processing, packing, shipping, and delivery) and are necessary to fill a customer's purchase order. Each functional cost center should contain a group of directly related expenses instead of arbitrarily allocated ones.

Convert Natural Expenses into Functional Accounts In marketing costs analysis, natural accounting expenses (the traditional expense categories such as salaries, rent, depreciation, and insurance) used in accounting statements must be reassigned to categories based on the purpose of each expense. Because nearly all expense data are collected by the organization's accounting system, analysis ought to start with the traditional accounting statements. The most important of these is the profit-and-loss (or income) statement, which takes this basic form:

$$\textbf{Sales} - \textbf{Cost of goods sold} = \textbf{Gross margin} - \textbf{Expenses} = \textbf{Net Profit}$$

Traditional income statements are of limited value to sales managers because they fail to reveal the costs of performing different marketing activities. Working with the simplified income statement for the CENTREX Company Sales Department in Table 13.10, we have assigned the natural expense accounts to functional accounts in Table 13.11.

Salaries were spread to the functional areas where the recipients work. As Table 13.11 indicates, about $590,190 went to salespeople and the sales manager, $21,400 to a sales

---

TABLE 13.9

Functional Accounts for Marketing Profitability Analysis

Order-Getting Costs	Order-Filling Costs
Sales promotion and publicity	Product packing and shipping
Product and package design	Transportation and delivery
Advertising	Customer service
Sales discounts and allowances	Warehousing
Sales administration	Inventory control
Credit	Accounts receivable collection

TABLE 13.10

CENTREX Company: Sales Department Income Statement

Accounts	$ Expenses	$ Income/Profit
Sales		$11,466,683
Cost of goods sold		$6,923,491
Gross margin		$4,543,192
Sales expenses:		
Salaries	$831,110	
Commissions	$169,334	
Travel	$151,491	
Sales promotion	$20,115	
Advertising	$45,000	
Postage	$62,078	
Supplies	$160,623	
Rent	$188,606	$1,628,357
Net profit		$2,914,835

TABLE 13.11

CENTREX Company: Natural Expenses Assigned to Functional Areas

		Functional Accounts						
Natural Expenses		Direct Selling	Sales Promotion	Advertising	Sales Administration	Order Processing and Billing	Marketing Research	Packing and Shipping
Salaries	$831,110	$590,190	$21,400	$25,650	$64,250	$31,000	$27,340	$71,280
Commissions	$169,334	$169,334						
Travel	$151,491	$150,488					$1,003	
Sales promotion	$20,115		$20,115					
Advertising	$45,000			$45,000				
Postage	$62,078	$3000	$9,671	$212	$689	$794	$493	$47,219
Supplies	$160,623	$7716	$21,247	$2,023	$183	$928	$2,101	$126,425
Rent	$188,606	$79,186	$8,200	$5,300	$15,100	$23,400	$12,150	$45,270
	$1,628,357	$999,914	$80,633	$78,185	$80,222	$56,122	$43,087	$290,194

promotion specialist employed part-time in the sales office, $25,650 to an advertising specialist, $64,250 to two people in sales administration, $31,000 to a billing clerk, $27,340 to a marketing research staff specialist, and $71,280 to two people in the shipping department. Besides their regular salaries, all salespeople received a commission of 2% on sales. Since these commissions were directly related to sales, the entire $169,334 was charged off to the direct selling function. Travel expenses included $151,491 for food, lodging, and entertainment expenses incurred in direct selling efforts, and $1,003 spent by the marketing research specialist while coordinating a market study. As both natural and functional accounts, advertising in selected trade magazines required $45,000, and sales promotion materials cost $20,115. Postage expenses were incurred to some degree for every functional cost center but largely for the packing and shipping area. Expenditures for supplies, which were also spread over all the functional accounts, amounted to $160,623 – again mainly for packing and shipping. Finally, the sales department had to pay $188,606 in rent, and these costs are allocated to the functional areas in proportion to the floor space used by each activity.

Allocate Functional Costs to Segments To discover the profitability of separate organizational units or particular market segments, the sales manager must allocate the functional costs incurred by the unit or in serving the segment. Each marketing function or activity needs to be closely examined to find the factors that most affect the volume of work. In making the cost allocations, the sales manager might consider several bases, including selling time, number of sales calls, and actual space occupied.

Another frequently used but improper basis is to allocate functional costs according to sales volume. This approach tends to penalize sales productivity and efficiency. For example, if one sales territory accounted for 20% of total regional sales, it would be charged with 20% of the sales administration function costs of $80,222 in Table 13.10, regardless of the actual expenses and proportion of time spent by the sales manager and staff in working with that territory. In contrast, a particularly worrisome territory may have taken up 40% of total sales administration expenses and personnel time but be allocated only 5% of those functional costs to match its low sales volume. Using sales volume to allocate functional costs contravenes the very purpose of marketing costs analysis, since it ignores the actual costs incurred in different business segments while relying on a simple but irrelevant basis. Therefore, sales managers should allocate functional costs according to measurable variables that have a cause-and-effect relationship with the functional cost category. That is, the costs should change in proportion to the performance of the activity; so direct selling costs, for instance, should increase directly with the number of sales calls. Several bases for allocating functional costs to different identifiable segments are provided in Table 13.12.

Full Costs or Contribution Margin? Since marketing costs contain direct, indirect, fixed, and variable amounts, another major decision is whether to allocate full costs or only marginal costs (direct and variable) to the segments. Costs that are fixed and indirect are usually impossible to assign to segments except arbitrarily. Advocates of the full-cost (or net profit) approach argue that all costs can be allocated on some reasonable basis. Using the full-cost approach, we allocate total costs (whether variable, fixed, direct, or indirect), and determine the profitability of each segment by deducting cost of goods sold from net sales to arrive at gross margin. Then we deduct all other costs or operating expenses to derive net income for the segment.

On the other side of the controversy, proponents of the contribution margin (the sales price less direct costs and variable costs equals the amount the sale contributes to profits) approach claim that it's misleading to allocate costs that are not controllable and, therefore, not considered in marketing decisions. They believe only costs that are controllable (direct and variable) and traceable to a particular segment should be subtracted from the revenue produced by that segment. The reasoning is that these variable and direct costs would disappear if the segment were eliminated, while all other costs (fixed and indirect) would continue and have to be absorbed by other segments.

TABLE 13.12

Functional Cost Centers and Bases of Allocation

Functional Costs	Bases of Allocation		
	To Sales Territories	To Products	To Customers
Direct selling costs			
Salaries, incentive pay, travel, and other expenses of salespeople	Direct	Selling time devoted to each product	Number of sales calls multiplied by average time per call
Indirect selling costs			
Sales administration, sales training, marketing, research, field supervision	Equal charge to each salesperson	Selling time devoted to each product	Selling time devoted to each customer
Sales promotion costs			
Consumer or trade Promotions, e.g., trade discounts, coupons, contests, and point-of-purchase displays	Direct	Direct	Direct
Advertising expenditures			
Advertising department salaries and expenses, media costs	Direct or by circulation of media	Direct or by media space given each product	Charged equally to each account
Marketing research			
Cost of gathering information	Time spent researching each territory	Time spent researching each product	Time spent researching each customer
Transportation			
Cost of delivering goods to customers	Classification rate × weights of products	Classification rate × weights of products	Bills of lading
Order processing and billing	Number of customer orders	Number of customer orders	Number of customer orders
Packing and shipping	Number of shipping units, weights, or size of units	Number of shipping units, weights, or size of units	Number of shipping units, weights, or size of units

Yuri_Arcurs/Getty Images

A better understanding of sale force organization effectiveness and efficiency can be attained by critically examining sales, costs, and profitability data across product lines, customer types, geographic territories, and other market segments.

TABLE 13.13

Marketing Profitability Analytics: Full-Cost Approach Versus The Contribution Margin Approach

Full-Cost Approach	Contribution Margin Approach
Sales	**Sales**
Less: Cost of goods sold	**Less**: Variable manufacturing costs
Equal: Gross margin	**Less**: Other variable costs directly traceable to the market segment
	Equal: Contribution margin
Less: Operating expenses (including the segment's allocated share of company administrative and general expenses)	**Less**: Fixed costs directly traceable to products; Fixed costs directly traceable to the market segment
Equal: Segment net income	**Equal**: Segment net income

Moreover, any segment that produces revenues in excess of its direct and variable costs is making a contribution to profits by helping cover the organization's fixed expenses or common costs. In Table 13.13, we can see the essential differences between the full-cost and the contribution margin approaches to marketing costs analysis. Under the contribution margin concept, costs are categorized as either variable or fixed without regard to whether they pertain to manufacturing, marketing, or administrative activities. Then all the variable costs are deducted from dollar sales to determine the segment's contribution margin.

Advantages of the Contribution Margin Approach The trend in marketing profitability analysis favors the contribution margin approach, for two primary reasons. First, arbitrarily allocating fixed and indirect costs to segments merely confuses profitability analysis, since these costs continue even if the apparently unprofitable segments are eliminated. Second, the contribution margin approach considers the interrelationships among marketing activities and the synergism of their efforts. One marketing activity, such as advertising, both benefits from and supports other activities such as personal selling or sales promotion. Similarly, one product in a multiproduct line helps promote the image and sell the entire line.

We'll use the income statement for the CENTREX Company, depicted in Table 13.10, to compare the two approaches to allocating functional costs. As you can see in Table 13.14, the full-cost method shows product A suffering a net loss of $1,488 and product B earning a net profit of $682,154. From this analysis, management might decide to de-emphasize or even drop product A. However, the full-cost approach allocated $1,027,718 of administrative expenses on the basis of product A's percentage of total sales ($5,287,141 product A sales ÷ $11,466,683 total sales = .46 × $2,234,169 total administrative expenses = $1,027,718 product A administrative expenses). Thus, the arbitrary allocation of fixed costs was responsible for product A's net loss. Switching to the contribution margin approach (see Table 13.15) reveals that product A contributes $1,026,230 to covering total fixed administrative expenses of $2,234,169. If product A were eliminated, current total net profit of $680,666 would turn into a net loss of $345,564 because product B's contribution margin would be insufficient to absorb the additional burden of administrative costs. Progressive companies keep track of the profit contribution of sales regions and products on a monthly basis so timely marketing mix adjustments can be made.

TABLE 13.14

CENTREX Company Income Statement Analytics by Product Lines: The Full-Cost Approach

	Totals	Product A	Product B
Sales	$11,466,683	$5,287,141	$6,179,542
Cost of goods sold	$6,923,491	$3,562,734	$3,360,757
Gross margin	$4,543,192	$1,724,407	$2,818,785
Expenses:			
Sales expenses	$1,628,357	$698,177	$930,180
Administrative expenses	$2,234,169	$1,027,718	$1,206,451
Total expenses	$3,862,526	$1,725,895	$2,136,631
Net profit (loss)	$680,666	$(1,488)	$682,154

TABLE 13.15

CENTREX Company Income Statement Analytics by Product Lines: The Contribution Margin Approach

	Totals	Product A	Product B
Sales	$11,466,683	$5,287,141	$6,179,542
Variable costs:			
Cost of goods sold	$6,923,491	$3,562,734	$3,360,757
Sales expenses	$1,628,357	$698,177	$930,180
Total variable costs	$8,551,848	$4,260,911	$4,290,937
Contribution margin	$2,914,835	$1,026,230	$1,888,605
Fixed costs:			
Administrative expenses	$2,234,169		
Net profit	$680,666		

Determine Profit Contribution of Segments Although some sales managers still avoid cutting costs because they fear sales will simultaneously decline, more savvy sales managers want to identify unprofitable customer accounts, products, or territories that can be served less frequently or dropped. Unprofitable segments are endemic problems in virtually all sales organizations. In some companies, up to 50% of business elements lose money. Illustrating the concentration principle, commonly called the 80–20 rule, studies have found that often a relatively small percent of products, customers, orders, sales territories, and salespeople accounts for most profits. Studying profit contributions by segments invariably rewards the sales manager far beyond the time and effort spent in the analyses.

We can examine profit contributions by segments in two basic ways: (1) by individual segments or (2) by cross-classification of segments. When we study them individually, we examine segment categories sequentially; thus, the analysis may proceed from determining the profitability by one segment category, such as product class, and then move to territory or customer type, and so on until we have investigated all segments.

TABLE 13.16

Marketing Profitability Analytics of Individual Market Segments

Market Segments	Product X	Product Y	Territory 1	Territory 2	Customer A	Customer B	Customer C	Customer D
Sales	$805	$2995	$1610	$2150	$710	$900	$800	$1350
Variable costs	–$520	–$2340	–$1210	–$1650	–$540	–$670	–550	–$1100
Direct fixed costs	–$198	–$460	–$308	–$350	–$138	–$170	–145	–$205
Market segment profit contribution	**$87**	**$155**	**$92**	**$150**	**$32**	**$60**	**$105**	**$45**

TABLE 13.17

Marketing Profitability Analytics of Segments via Cross-Classification

	Territory 1		Territory 2	
Product X	Customer A	Customer B	Customer C	Customer D
Sales	$190	$120	$185	$310
Variable costs	–$115	–$73	–$128	–$204
Direct fixed costs	–$41	–$32	–$39	–$86
Market segment profit contribution	**$34**	**$15**	**$18**	**$20**

	Territory 1		Territory 2	
Product Y	Customer A	Customer B	Customer C	Customer D
Sales	$520	$780	$615	$1040
Variable costs	–$425	–$597	–$422	–$896
Direct fixed costs	–$97	–$138	–$106	–$119
Market segment profit contribution	**–$2**	**$45**	**$87**	**$25**

In a cross-classification analysis, we relate one segment to or define it more specifically by other segments. For instance, the sales manager may want to know the profitability of product X, sold to customer B, in territory 2.

In Table 13.16, we analyze the profitability of segments separately. All segments (products, territories, and customers) appear profitable when examined one at a time. But when we conduct cross-classification analysis of the three segments in Table 13.17, we learn that product Y is losing money with customer A in territory 1, and product Y is yielding only a low-profit contribution with customer D in territory 2. An alert sales manager would probably want to probe further by requesting a cross-classification that includes a breakdown by salesperson as well. Without seeing the interrelationships of segment profitability as provided in a cross-classification analysis, a sales manager might erroneously assume that all the individual segments are profitable.

Underlying Problems

Merely determining that certain cross-classified segments are unprofitable is not sufficient. The sales manager must next discover *why*. Have the salespeople been adequately motivated? Are they making efficient and effective use of their time? Is the competitive situation in these segments unique? Are product quality, customer service, and warranties satisfactory? Are prices competitive? How compatible and effective is the marketing mix supporting the field sales representatives? These plus many other questions should be asked and answered.

As important as marketing profitability analysis is, it may merely uncover symptoms. It's up to the sales manager to discover the specific underlying problems before attempting to improve profitability by making needed decisions, such as dropping segments, changing incentive plans, retraining or firing salespeople, or altering the marketing mix. Sales managers should not hesitate to obtain the help of marketing research specialists to identify problems and recommend solutions for improved segment profitability.

Return on Assets Managed (ROAM)

Profitability analysis is invaluable for comparing sales productivity by segment with the cost of activities performed to achieve those sales. Yet a critical financial management tool missing from profitability calculations is the total value of company assets (e.g., working capital in the form of accounts receivable and inventory) required to support the sales force functions. The ROAM by each segment of the business measures how productively the assets have been employed. We avoid using the term return on investment (ROI) here, since it usually refers more narrowly to capital investment (non-current assets) and owner's investment (net worth or equity capital). As shown in Table 13.18, ROAM is the profit margin on sales (net profit/sales) multiplied by the inventory turnover (sales/total assets used). When applied to a market segment, ROAM is the percentage return on the total assets used to generate the net profit, or contribution margin.

Using the data in Table 13.15, we can compute ROAM for product A (see Table 13.18). Assume product A required an investment in accounts receivable of $2,493,889 plus an inventory of $8,763,498 (for total current assets used of $11,257,387) in order to achieve its sales of $5,287,141 and its contribution margin of $1,026,230. By substituting these figures in the formula (see Table 13.18), we derive a ROAM of 9.12%.

Despite the obvious usefulness of ROAM calculations, one early study found that only about 10% of industrial firms were regularly using this tool, although nearly one-third were analyzing profitability by customer, salesperson, and territory.[16] One criticism aimed at the ROAM approach is that it tends to neglect the opportunity costs for capital invested in the assets.[17] Nevertheless, the most successful sales managers of

---

TABLE 13.18

Calculating Return on Assets Managed (ROAM)

$$\text{ROAM} = \frac{\text{Net profit}}{\text{Sales}} \times \frac{\text{Sales}}{\text{Total assets used}}$$

When applied to segment analysis on the basis of the contribution margin, the formula becomes:

$$\text{ROAM} = \frac{\text{Segment contribution margin}}{\text{Segment sales}} \times \frac{\text{Segment sales}}{\text{Additional assets used by the segment}}$$

$$\text{ROAM} = \frac{\$1,026,230}{\$5,287,141} \times \frac{\$5,287,141}{\$11,257,387} = 0.09116$$

today and tomorrow may gain a winning edge on other sales managers (in the eyes of superiors) by conducting marketing profitability analyses by market segments and making full use of ROAM.

Improving ROAM To increase the ROAM for specific segments, the sales manager has three options: (1) raise the profit margin on sales, (2) increase total sales while maintaining profit margins, and (3) decrease the relative dollar value of assets necessary to achieve sales. Raising the profit margins on sales requires the sales manager to conduct profitability analyses by segments to identify those that are yielding inadequate contribution margins. Then, he or she must decide to de-emphasize or eliminate efforts in these segments.

Increasing total sales while maintaining profit margins on sales requires the sales manager to seek more effective and efficient marketing mixes, so that the sales organization operates near its minimal average costs per unit of sales (as discussed earlier in this chapter). Market testing, under reasonably controlled conditions, may be necessary to find this optimal mix of headquarters and field marketing efforts. Therefore, it is vital for sales managers to include on their sales department staff a marketing research specialist who works closely with the headquarters marketing research department as well as with the field marketing representatives.

Decreasing the assets needed to obtain sales requires sales managers to cooperate with inventory managers to find that optimal trade-off between inventory levels and out-of-stocks. Both sales managers and accounting managers need to monitor the level of accounts receivables to ensure they remain within predetermined standards.

Increasing Sales Force Productivity and Profits

Revolutionary and evolutionary changes in analytics software and telecommunications technologies are helping sales managers in their unrelenting efforts to lower selling costs and increase sales force productivity,[18] and the possibilities for the future seem virtually unlimited.[19] With increasingly sophisticated software tools, the sales department and other functional areas (marketing, accounting, finance, operations) throughout a company can work synergistically to identify unprofitable market segments and take timely corrective actions that will significantly increase profits.[20] To motivate him to regularly conduct in-depth sales volume, marketing costs, and profitability analyses, one sales manager keeps a plaque on his wall with Benjamin Franklin's famous adage: "A penny saved is a penny earned."

Chapter Summary

1. **Understand the framework and process for carrying out a sales force organization audit.** This chapter discussed the importance of conducting sales, costs, and profitability analytics to assess the effectiveness of the sales force organization. Examining the performance of the overall sales organization can be accomplished through an in-depth sales force audit – a comprehensive, systematic, diagnostic, and prescriptive tool designed to assess the adequacy of a firm's sales force management process and to provide direction for improved performance and the prescription for needed

changes.[21] A sales force organization audit constitutes an assessment of four key issues: (1) sales force organization planning system, (2) sales force organization environment, (3) sales manager qualities, and (4) sales force management functions.

2. **Identify and describe the sources of information for conducting analytics on sales volume, costs, and profitability by market segments.** Although the *sales invoice* is the most important source of sales information, there are many other sources, too. Among the most important sources of sales information are salesperson call reports, expense accounts, prospect and customer records, internal financial records, warranty cards, cash register receipts, store audits, consumer diaries, and test markets results.

3. **Explain the overall process and procedures for sales analytics on volume, costs, and profitability by territories, products, customers, and salespeople.** Sales volume, costs, and profitability analyses involve the collection, classification, comparison, and evaluation of sales, costs, and profit figures by such subcategories as product types, customer classes, territories, and salespeople. Marketing costs analysis goes beyond sales volume analysis to determine the costs involved in generating sales. To determine the profit contributions of various market segments, marketing costs involved in generating the sales revenue must be subtracted. Using the concept of input–output efficiency, sales managers should consider several mixes and levels of selling and supporting marketing efforts to achieve different sales objectives. Especially important to improving overall company productivity is increased cooperation and understanding between the marketing and the accounting departments. Indeed, one of the sales manager's most important jobs is to use profitability analyses to increase the productivity and efficiency of sales force efforts by allocating resources to market segments providing the highest return per dollar spent.[22]

4. **Describe the procedure for marketing costs and profitability analytics.** Sales analytics, whether by territory, sales rep, product line, or customer, involves five major steps: (1) specify the purpose of the analysis, (2) identify functional cost centers, (3) convert natural expenses into functional costs, (4) allocate functional costs to segments, and (5) determine the profit contribution of segments.

5. **Provide the reasoning for sales analytics using contribution costs versus full costs.** Since marketing costs contain direct, indirect, fixed, and variable amounts, a critical decision is whether to allocate full costs or only marginal costs (direct and variable) to the market segments being analyzed. Advocates of the full-cost approach argue that all costs should be and can be allocated on some reasonable basis. Proponents of the contribution margin approach claim that it is misleading to allocate costs that are not controllable – and thus not appropriately considered in marketing decisions. They believe that only costs that are controllable (direct and variable) and traceable to a particular market segment should be subtracted from the revenue produced by that segment. The trend in marketing profitability analysis favors the contribution margin approach.

6. **Illustrate the concept of and ways to improve ROAM.** The ROAM by each market segment of the business measures how productively the assets, such as accounts receivable and inventory, have been employed. When applied

to a market segment, ROAM is the percentage return on the total assets used to generate the net profit, or contribution margin. Sales managers have three basic ways to increase ROAM: (1) raise the profit margin on sales, (2) increase total sales while maintaining profit margins, or (3) decrease the relative dollar value of assets necessary to achieve sales. This can be accomplished by salespeople selling more of the inventory and collecting more of the accounts receivable (i.e., unpaid customer invoices).

Key Terms

Sales force audit	**Costs versus**	**Direct costs**	**Contribution margin**
Sales volume analytics	**expenses**	**Indirect costs**	**Concentration principle**
Input–output efficiency	**Fixed costs**	**Functional costs**	
Standard costs	**Variable costs**	**Natural expenses**	

Notes

1. Francis, S. (21 May 2018). Is your goal volume or profit? *Strategic Pricing Solutions*. http://info.stratpricing.com/blog/volume-or-profit-goal-pricing-strategy (accessed 8 October 2019); Shavitz, J. (29 December 2017). To increase profitability focus on both the bottom and top lines. http://www.entrepreneur.com/article/305680 (accessed 17 October 2019).

2. Kelly, B., Melcher, R.C. and Wiley, S.F. (2013). With the right strategy, companies can increase profit margins on sales. *Industry Week* (23 July). http://www.industryweek.com/corporate-finance-amp-tax/right-strategy-companies-can-increase-profit-margins-sales (accessed 12 October 2019); Leung, S. (20 November 2015). Efficient vs. sufficient: How to improve key profitability ratios. http://www.salesforce.com/blog/2015/11/improve-key-profitability-ratios.html (accessed 19 October 2019; Colletti, J.A. and Fiss, M.S. (2006). The ultimately accountable job: Leading today's sales organization. *Harvard Business Review* 84(7–8): 125–131.

3. Zeisig, K. (20 February 2018). 12 must-have metrics to fuel your sales analytics. http://www.klipfolio.com/blog/sales-analytics-12-metrics (accessed 13 October 2019); Marr, B. 23 February 2016). The 9 best marketing and sales analytics every manager show know about. http://www.forbes.com/sites/bernardmarr/2016/02/23/the-9-best-marketing-and-sales-analytics-every-manager-should-know-about/#b16513e6b25d (accessed 15 October 2019); Sales analytics. http://www.techopedia.com/definition/30436/sales-analytics (accessed 14 October 2019); Best sales analytics software. https://www.g2.com/categories/sales-analytics (accessed 15 October 2019); 20 Best sales analytics software solutions of 2020. https://financesonline.com/top-20-sales-analytics-software/ (accessed 22 February 2020); 17 top sales analytics and sales intelligence reporting software. http://www.predictiveanalyticstoday .com/sales-analytics-sales-intelligence-reporting/ (accessed 16 October 2019; Garcia, M. (26 September 2017). How to calculate segment margins. https://bizfluent.com/how-6622493-calculate-segment-margins.html (accessed 15 October 2019).

4. Malek, S.L., Sarin, S. and Jaworski, B.J. (2018). Sales management control system: Review, synthesis, and direction for future exploration. *Journal of Personal Selling & Sales Management* 38(1): 30–35; Anderson, E. and Onyemah, V. (2006). How right should the customer be? *Harvard Business Review* 84(7/8): 59–67; Fang, E., Evans, K.R. and Landry, T.D. (2005). Control systems' effect on attributional processes and sales outcomes: A cybernetic information-processing perspective. *Journal of the Academy of Marketing Science* 33(4): 553–574; Cravens, D.W., Lassk, F.G., Low, G.S., Marshall, G.W., and Moncrief, W.C. (2004) Formal and informal management control combinations in sales organizations: The impact on salesperson consequences. *Journal of Business Research* 57(3): 241–248; Schwepker, C.H., Jr. and Good, D.J. (2004). Marketing control and sales force customer orientation. *Journal of Personal Selling & Sales Management* (Summer) 24(3): 167–179.

5. How to assess & audit your overall sales capability -- Rating your sales strength (14 July 2019). https://zorian.com/how-to-audit-your-overall-sales-capability-auditing-rating-your-sales-strength/ (accessed 15 October 2019); Sullivan, D. Sales audit procedures. https://smallbusiness.chron.com/sales-audit-procedures-75310.html (accessed 17 October 2019); Metler, R. (21 February 2017). How to measure your sales productivity. http://www.salesforcesearch.com/blog/httpwww-salesforcesearch-combid183097how-to-measure-your-sales-productivity/ (accessed 13 October 2019); Ledingham, D., Kovac, M. and Simon, H.L. (2006). The new science of sales force productivity. Harvard *Business Review* 84(9): 124–133.

6. Butters, H. (11 May 2017). How to audit your sales process; An actionable guide for business growth. http://www.saleshacker.com/sales-process-audit-practical-guide/ (accessed 11 May 2017); Dubinsky, A.J. and Hansen, R.W. (1981). The sales force management audit. *California Management Review* (Winter) 24(2): 86–95.

7. Kokemuller, N. Relationship of costs & sales volume to profits. http://www.google.com/search?client=firefox-b-1-d&q=linkage+between+sales+volume%2C+costs%2C+and+profitability (accessed 15 October 2019); Peavler, R. Introduction to conducting a cost-volume-profit analysis. http://www.thebalancesmb.com/how-to-do-cost-volume-profit-analysis-an-introduction-393475 (accessed 6 October 2019).

8. See, for example, Lambert, D.M. (Quarter 4, 2008) Which customers are most profitable? http://www.supplychainquarterly.com/topics/Finance/scq200804profitability/ (accessed 3 October 2019); Mewhiney, S. 8 Steps to successful profitability analysis. www.centage.com/8-steps-for-successful-profitability-analysis/ (accessed 1 October 2019); Bulent Menguc, B. and Barker, T. (2005). Re-examining field sales unit performance: Insights from the resource-based view and dynamic capabilities perspective. *European Journal of Marketing* 39(7–8): 885–909; Howell, R.A. and Soucy, S.R. (1990). Customer profitability—As critical as product profitability. *Management Accounting* 72(4): 43–47; Selnes, F. (1992). Analyzing marketing profitability: Sales are a dangerous cost driver. *European Journal of Marketing* 26(2): 15–26.

9. Five sales management trends for 2018. *Big Swift Kick* (26 January 2018). https://bigswiftkick.com/five-sales-management-trends-for-2018/ (accessed 11 October 2019); When is a sale a sale: Everything you need to know. www.upcounsel.com/when-is-a-sale-a-sale (accessed 4 October 2019).

10. How to analyze sales data to increase profits? (6 August 2018). http://www.quill.com/blog/tutorials/how-to-analyze-sales-data-to-increase-profits.html (accessed 2 October 2019).

11. Kumar, V., Sunder, S. and Leone, R.P. (2015). Who's your most valuable salesperson? *Harvard Business Review* 96(4): 62–68; Cravens, D.W. and Piercy, N.F. (2005). Sales management control research—Synthesis and an agenda for future research. *Journal of Personal Selling & Sales Management* (Winter) 25(1): 7–26.

12. For more insights on sales costs analyses, see Zeisig, K. (20 February 2018). 12 Must-have metrics to fuel your sales analytics. www.klipfolio.com/blog/sales-analytics-12-metrics (accessed 18 October 2019); Wright, T.C. What is profit segmentation? https://yourbusiness.azcentral.com/profit-segmentation-21059.html (accessed 3 October 2019); Nicholas, S. (3 October 2019). How are fixed and variable costs different? www.google.com/search?client=firefox-b-1d&q=allocating+sales+costs+to+fixed+and+variable+expenses (accessed 15 October 2019).

13. Rosenbloom, B. (2012). *Marketing Channels: A Management View* 8th ed. Boston, MA: Cengage.

14. Lewis, T. and Miller, J. (15 November 2018). How marketing can support the sales process. http://www.pr2020.com/blog/how-marketing-can-support-the-sales-process (accessed 7 October 2019); Patel, S. (30 June 2019). How sales and marketing can work together to maximize growth. https://sujanpatel.com/marketing/sales-marketing-can-work-together/ (accessed 14 October 2019).

15. For further insights, see Berry, T. Understanding fixed and variable costs and burn rate. https://articles.bplans.com/understanding-costs-fixed-vs-variable-burn-rate/ (accessed 5 October 2019).

16. Gallo, A. (2016). A refresher on return on assets and return on equity. *Harvard Business Review* (April). https://hbr.org/2016/04/a-refresher-on-return-on-assets-and-return-on-equity (accessed 5 October 2019); Boutwell, L. (22 December 2016). Using the ROAM method for sales training and coaching (Podcast 22 December 2016). www.brainshark.com/ideas-blog/2016/December/using-roam-method-for-sales-training-and-coaching (accessed 18 October 2019); Thomas, J.W. Basic sales analysis: Twelve ideas for anyone assigned the task of analyzing a firm's sales data. http://analytics-magazine.org/basic-sales-analysis/ (accessed 15 October 2019).

17. Higgins, K. (18 January 2018). 6 Simple metrics to accurately measure sales manager performance. https://trainingindustry.com/articles/measurement-and-analytics/6-simple-metrics-to-accurately-measure-sales-manager-performance/ (accessed 20 October 2019); Cron, W. L. and Levy, M. (1987). Sales management performance evaluation: A residual income perspective. *Journal of Personal Selling & Sales Management* (August) 7(2): 57–66; Twin, A. (1 September 2019). Return on assets managed defined (ROAM). www.investopedia.com/terms/r/return-on-assets-managed-roam.asp (accessed 13 October 2019); Higgins, K. (18 January 2018). 6 Simple metrics to accurately measure sales manager performance. https://trainingindustry.com/articles/measurement-and-analytics/6-simple-metrics-to-accurately-measure-sales-manager-performance/ (accessed 7 October 2019).

18. Burtan, D. (3 September 2019). 5 Strategies to drive sales productivity. *https://seismic.com/company/blog/5-strategies-to-drive-sales-productivity/* (accessed 9 October 2019); Jain, D. (20 November 2019). 10 strategies to improve sales productivity. https://aeroleads.com/blog/strategies-improve-sales-productivity/ (accessed 22 February 2020); Frost A. (4 September 2019). The ultimate guide to sales metrics: What to track, how to track it, & why. https://blog.hubspot.com/sales/sales-metrics (accessed 19 October 2019); Honeycutt, E.D. (2005). Technology improves sales performance—Doesn't It? An introduction to the special issue on selling and sales technology. *Industrial Marketing Management* 34(4): 301–304; Anderson, R.E. (1996). Personal selling and sales management in the new millennium. *Journal of Personal Selling & Sales Management* (Summer) 16(4): 17–32.

19. Sales productivity statistics you need to see ASAP (22 August 2019). http://www.brainshark.com/ideas-blog/2019/august/sales-productivity-statistics (accessed 11 October 2019); Frost A. The 5 most important sales performance metrics every rep and manager should track. https://blog.hubspot.com/sales/sales-performance-metrics (accessed 13 October 2019). Hunter, O.K. and Perreault, W.D. Jr. (2006). Sales technology orientation, information effectiveness, and sales performance. *Journal of Personal Selling & Sales Management* (Spring) 26(2): 95–113; Johnson, D.W. and Bharadwaj, S. (2005). Digitization of selling activity and sales force performance: An empirical investigation. *Journal of the Academy of Marketing Research* 33(1): 3–18; Dong-Gil, K. and Dennis, A.R. (2004). Sales force automation and performance: Do experience and expertise matter? *Journal of Personal Selling & Sales Management* (Fall) 24(4): 311–22; Jordan, J. (8 June 2018). Sales productivity vs. efficiency vs. effectiveness . . . is there a

difference? http://www.salesforce.com/blog/2018/06/sales-efficiency-metrics.html (accessed 17 October 2019).

20. Schiff, J.L. (19 November 2014). 7 Ways you can help your sales team be more effective. http://www.cio.com/article/2849367/7-ways-you-can-help-your-sales-team-be-more-effective.html (accessed 3 October 2019); Patel, N. 5 Essential ways marketing must change to support inside sales. https://neilpatel.com/blog/marketing-support-inside-sales/ (accessed 5 October 2019); What is sales support? http://www.tenfold.com/what-is/a-sales-support/ (accessed 3 October 2019); Behar, N. How to use technology in sales to improve performance. http://www.salesreadinessgroup.com/blog/how-to-use-technology-in-sales-to-improve-performance (accessed 4 October 2019).

21. Butters, H. (11 May 2017). How to audit your sales process: An actionable guide for business growth. http://www.saleshacker.com/sales-process-audit-practical-guide/ (accessed 8 October 2019); Altschuler, M. (1 March 2018). Sales operations demystified: What it is, why it matters, and how to do it right. www.saleshacker.com/what-is-sales-operations/ (accessed 4 October 2019; Dubinsky, A.J. and Hansen, R.W. (1981). The sales force management audit. *California Management Review* (Winter) 24(2): 86–95.

22. Kelly, B., Melcher, R.C. and Wiley, S.F. With the right strategy, companies can increase profit margins on sales. *Industry Week* (23 July 2013). http://www.industryweek.com/corporate-finance-amp-tax/right-strategy-companies-can-increase-profit-margins-sales (accessed 9 October 2019); Colletti, J.A. and Fiss, M.S. (2006). The ultimately accountable job: Leading today's sales organization. *Harvard Business Review* (July–August): 125–131.

Chapter Review Questions

1. Define a sales audit, and explain the four areas that constitute a sales force organization audit. [LO 1]

2. Identify and describe some sources and types of sales information that can be used for conducting a sales volume, marketing costs, and profitability analysis. What is the need to conduct these analyses? [LO 2]

3. How might the sales manager obtain greater cooperation with the accounting manager or marketing controller? Do you think sales managers have a communication problem in dealing with accounting managers? Explain. [LO 4]

4. Why has accounting generally focused on production costs instead of marketing costs analysis? [LO 4]

5. Do you think that we will ever develop standardized costs for marketing activities? Why or why not? [LO 4]

6. Discuss the benefits of conducting a sales volume, marketing costs, and profitability analysis. [LO 4]

7. Which side of the controversy between full-cost and contribution margin approaches to allocating marketing costs do you support? Why? [LO 5]

8. Why aren't more sales managers concerned about their ROAM? What would you suggest to increase their use of ROAM? [LO 6]

Online Exercise

1. Use the Internet to access SlideTeam (https://www.slideteam.net/search/go?ts=custom&w=sales%20analytics), Klipfolio (https://www.klipfolio.com/blog/sales-analytics-12-metrics) and other similar knowledge exchange websites. Based on your research, develop a comprehensive sales analytics checklist.

Role-Play Exercise

Preparing for the Seminar

Situation

Your national sales manager thinks that you, a district sales manager with a recent MBA and a dual major in Marketing and Finance, would be the best of his sales managers to help lead a seminar on sales volume, marketing costs, and profitability analysis. Staff people have been doing these analyses in the past, but the CEO has decided that he wants all sales managers to become familiar with the process and procedures and eventually to take over from the staff people. Your national sales manager left a voice mail message on your cell phone this Tuesday afternoon asking you to prepare an opening seminar presentation for this coming Monday on: (1) the overall purpose of sales volume, marketing costs, and profitability analyses, and (2) the sources of sales information.

Role-Play Participants and Assignments

District Sales Manager: Although you did earn a dual major in marketing and finance for your MBA, you're not very comfortable with accounting concepts and procedures. So, you're apprehensive about not being able to answer all the questions the other sales managers might come up with at the seminar. Some of them, in fact, might enjoy seeing you look foolish. To help prepare, you've asked two sales manager friends of yours from other companies to come over to your house Saturday afternoon to hear your presentation and ask challenging questions.

Two sales manager friends: Although they have been sales managers for several years, they have done only basic sales volume analyses – not marketing costs or profitability analyses. Nevertheless, they agree to come over to listen and to ask questions.

In-Basket Exercise

You are the national sales manager for a large and successful consumer products company. Today, your in-basket contains a memo from the company's chief operating officer. In the memo she indicates that, although sales have been increasing steadily, she would like you to cut your selling costs by approximately 15% to prepare for a projected sharp downturn in the economy. In addition, she feels that it would be beneficial to the organization if you could be "precise" in identifying those particular costs you plan to cut back to achieve the 15% reduction. She also states that the sales quotas for your sales force are not being lowered. In her words: "We must learn to achieve our annual goals by more creative and efficient use of our limited resources." She would like to meet with you on Friday to discuss these issues.

1. How are you going to respond to this memo?
2. Can you successfully argue against the COO's demands? If so, how?

Ethical Dilemma

You are the sales manager of the Northwest region for a medium-sized software manufacturer, and you're knee-deep in the process of analyzing quarterly sales volume, marketing costs, and profitability by different market segments. One thing surprises you: personal selling expenses seem about 10% higher this quarter than for the same quarter last year, even though inflation is up only about 2%. These increased selling costs are hurting profits compared to last year. Your company has a policy of reimbursing salespeople for all their legitimate selling costs – hotel, meals, travel, and customer entertainment expenses – although salespeople were expected not to spend extravagantly. Last year's sales were off company-wide because of a downturn in demand for your software products, which are a bit dated in comparison to those offered by competitors. You've heard that some salespeople are angry that their earnings are down, and it's rumored they feel the company is letting them down by not developing new software products for them to sell. To make up for their lower earnings, some salespeople are taking their families and friends out to dinner and entertainment and claiming on their expense accounts that they entertained customers. Although you consider such behavior unethical and unprofessional, you understand the frustration of the salespeople and their anger toward the company. You've decided this behavior needs to be dealt with forthrightly, but you don't want to make the salespeople even angrier. You've called a general meeting for all your salespeople this Friday morning, and you're now trying to work out exactly what you're going to say and anticipate their reaction.

Questions

1. How will you start off your comments to the salespeople who may be quite defensive about their behavior with regard to selling costs?
2. Since the salespeople seem to resent the company's failure to develop new software products for them to sell and apparently have made this an excuse for inflating their sales expenses. How will you handle this sensitive area?
3. What will you tell the salespeople about your future policy on reimbursing sales expenses?
4. In closing this meeting, will you promise or offer the salespeople anything to make them feel better?

Boudreaux's Rice Cake Company: The Value of Financial Reports and Big Data

Boudreaux's Rice Cake Company was started in 2014 by John Paul Boudreaux in Houma, Louisiana. John Paul had previously worked for Saint Pierre's Seafood Restaurant for six years as an assistant to the chef and was promoted to head chef after three years. As the head chef for St. Pierre, John Paul received many awards for his rice-based delights, and particularly rice cakes, and had several newspaper articles written about him. In fact, he became a local celebrity in the restaurant business in the Houma area, and many of his friends and family members believed he should start a business to market his rice-based products and rice cakes. After considering it for a couple of years, John Paul quit his job and put all his savings into Boudreaux's Rice Cake Company.

At first, John Paul concentrated his efforts on establishing his business on a regional basis. He prepared all the rice cakes himself, while his brothers James and Dwight called on grocery stores and supermarkets in Louisiana and the surrounding Gulf Coast area. Sales of Boudreaux's rice and rice cakes were better than anyone expected. Many of the grocery store managers who purchased the rice cakes were quite taken by his products and suggested that John Paul sell them to national supermarket chains. Within two years after John Paul started the company, his rice and rice cakes were being sold in all of the 48 contiguous states.

Over the years, John Paul added several new cakes and related product lines to his menu of products. A line of boudin, dirty rice, refrigerated meals, cracklins, and spices soon carried the "Boudreaux's" trade name. By, 2020 John Paul had 64 employees, including 28 salespeople and three regional sales managers. Joey LaBorde had been one of the three regional sales managers for the past five years, and when John Paul decided he needed a national sales manager he picked Joey. The first month on the new job went smoothly as Joey traveled through the other two regions to introduce himself. But after returning back to the home office, he began to realize that being a national sales manager involved a lot of paperwork, and required him to spend much more time in the office as well as in scheduled and unscheduled meetings. He did not like the paperwork or the time in the office, but he knew being national sales manager required him to grasp the "big picture" and to prepare and understand numerous reports.

At the end of the first three months, Joey received several reports from Boudreaux's financial department summarizing quarterly sales and profits (see Table 1). Reviewing these reports Joey saw that two of the company's regions had earned healthy net profits for the quarter, but the Midwestern region had a net loss of $40,269. Sales in the Midwestern region were $2.1 million less than the eastern region and nearly $2.7 million less than the western region. Yet selling expenses clearly were too high in the Midwestern region. Ninety percent of sales force compensation was straight salary and Joey remembered the Midwestern region had a lot of senior salespeople who were highly paid. Unless the compensation system changed, there wasn't much Joey could do about selling expenses in the region. One way to solve the problem might be simply to close the Midwestern sales region. It certainly did not make sense to keep losing money there. Joey wondered what the impact on the company would be if the Midwestern region were shut down.

Another financial report dealt with sales and profits by product in each region (Table 2). The company grouped its products into two basic categories: rice cakes and other products. This report showed that the only unprofitable product was pasta sold in the Midwestern region. Again, Joey wondered what would happen to overall company profits if rice cakes were dropped in the Midwestern region.

TABLE 1

Income Statement by Sales Regions

	Eastern Region	Midwestern Region	Western Region
Sales	$8,697,328	$6,543,121	$9,214,864
Variable costs:			
Cost of goods sold	$5,128,540	$5,210,533	$6,420,432
Selling expenses	$1,233,457	$1,025,732	$1,072,117
Fixed costs:			
Administrative expenses	$433,163	$347,125	$416,274
Total costs	$6,795,160	$6,583,390	$7,908,823
Net profit	$1,902,168	($40,269)	$1,306,041

TABLE 2

Income Statement by Product

	Eastern Region	
	Rice Cakes	**Other Products**
Sales	$5,362,192	$3,335,136
Variable costs:		
Cost of goods sold	$3,347,134	$1,781,406
Selling expenses	$703,118	$530,339
Fixed costs:		
Administrative expenses	$245,791	$187,372
Total costs	$4,296,043	$2,499,117
Net profit	$1,066,149	$836,019
	Midwestern Region	
Sales	$3,612,446	$2,930,675
Variable costs:		
Cost of goods sold	$3,060,050	$2,150,483
Selling expenses	$678,694	347,038
Fixed costs:		
Administrative expenses	$189,987	$157,138
Total costs	$3,928,731	$2,654,659
Net profit	$316,285	$276,016
	Western Region	
Sales	$5,423,517	$3,791,347
Variable costs:		
Cost of goods sold	$4,003,862	$2,416,570
Selling expenses	$621,664	$450,453
Fixed costs:		
Administrative expenses	$250,123	$166,151
Total costs	$4,875,652	$3,033,174
Net profit	$547,865	$758,173

Looking at several other reports provided by Boudreaux's financial department, Joey was drawn to one report showing each region's investment in inventory and accounts receivable (see Table 3). He was not sure what to do with this report, but he was extremely surprised to see how high accounts receivable and inventory were. The Supply Chain and Procurement department has a robust database of tracking information, with data on shipping times, delivery times, shipping volumes, vendor, and costs for all of the orders placed at every division of the company. The Marketing Department has also recently begun to monitor social media traffic for customers mentioning Boudreaux's Rice Cake Company on Twitter, Facebook, and Instagram. They have been able to link these social media posts to positive or negative feelings about certain products. Joey has a mountain of data at his disposal to try and diagnose issues in the Midwestern region. He has also acquired a new visualization software to help him slice the data and draw more targeted conclusions. Overall, Joey recognized there were problems, but being new in this job he was not sure how to analyze the data or what to do.

TABLE 3

Accounts Receivable and Inventory by Product and Region

	Eastern Region	
	Rice Cakes	Other Products
Accounts receivable	$3120,449	$1,872,312
Inventory	$8,881,479	$5,122,376
	Midwestern Region	
Accounts receivable	$2,120,287	$1,540,601
Inventory	$7,297,128	$6,482,120
	Western Region	
Accounts receivable	$2,311,483	$2,481,040
Inventory	$8,421,677	$7,120,432

Questions

1. What else besides high selling expenses might be contributing to the Midwestern region's problems?

2. What corrective action might Joey take given the information provided in the reports?

3. Should Joey drop the Midwestern region or just rice cakes? How can he use big data and sales analytics to help make his decision? Justify your recommendation.

4. Can Joey use the vast amounts of data and tools at his disposal to offer more targeted solutions for the Midwestern region? How about for the other regions?

5. What other financial reports should Joey request from the financial department to better understand the situation? Explain.

Case prepared by: Britton Leggett, and Jacob Whitmore, University of South Alabama

---

CASE 13.2 | # Omega Restaurant Supply: Using CRM to Justify Change

Omega Restaurant Supply is located in Houston, TX and serves full service restaurants throughout south, central and east Texas, as well as much of southeastern Louisiana. Omega provides a variety of restaurant supplies, from small items such as napkins, to large items such as industrial equipment. Omega recently implemented an advanced customer relationship management (CRM) system that includes a number of sales force automation processes. A primary goal for implementing the system is identifying the most and least profitable customers, and using that information to increase sales and profitability. After analyzing the report, the firm's sales managers arrive at several conclusions:

- Customers in larger metropolitan areas like Houston, Texas are more profitable than customers in rural areas, such as Jasper, Texas.

- National chains like Olive Garden and Flemings are among the most profitable customers.

- Independents are less profitable than larger chain customers.

- Salespeople with less than three years of experience, or more than 15 years of experience, generate less profit than do salespeople in the middle group (3–15 years of experience).

Sales managers at Omega are considering making some changes in an effort to improve the company's performance. The following changes have been announced based on an increased emphasis on profitability:

- The sales force will be reassigned so the salespeople with less than three years of experience are assigned only to chain accounts.

- Omega will expand its operations into the areas of Dallas, Texas and New Orleans, Louisiana.

- Omega plans to respond to the majority of sales calls to independent restaurant owners through email, video conferencing software, and an artificial intelligence platform.

Questions

1. Will these changes make Omega less or more profitable? Explain.

2. Are all of these changes in Omega's long-term best interests? Explain.

3. What potential problems could result from making these changes?

4. Are there additional changes you would suggest to help Omega succeed?

Case prepared by: Kathrynn Pounders, The University of Texas at Austin

Sales Force Performance Evaluation

Now that you know how to assess the effectiveness of the overall sales force organization, this final chapter will introduce you to the process and methods used in evaluating the performance of individual salespersons – an equally important component of controlling and monitoring the sales program. The success of the sales organization and the company depends largely on the performance of individual salespeople, who are responsible for the all-important revenue generating and customer relationship activities.[1] Appraising the performance of salespeople generally results in sales managers becoming better equipped to take appropriate measures to improve the productivity and performance of the sales force and its individual members.[2]

Sales Force Performance Evaluation

Performance is perhaps the single most important factor of concern to sales managers because the central purpose of the sales organization is to increase sales, market share, and profits.[3] Salesperson performance evaluation can be defined as a systematic process for establishing whether the salesperson's job behavior contributes to the fulfillment of a firm's sales objectives and for providing feedback to the individual. Before we start our analysis of sales performance evaluation procedures and methods, we need to discuss the purpose, challenges, and methods of conducting salesperson evaluations.

Purpose of Salesperson Performance Evaluations

The central reason to evaluate salespeople is to determine their performance and compare it with the established goals. Evaluation implies a process of systematically uncovering deviations between goals and accomplishments. When weaknesses are identified, the sales managers can devise and implement corrective methods.

When strengths are identified, management can use this information as a valuable aid for developing successful strategy and tactics in future periods.[4]

Performance appraisal can help ensure that managers: (1) recognize high-performing salespeople with increased compensation, awards, and promotion – or deny these benefits to poor performers and, when necessary, dismiss them; (2) identify training needs of salespeople; (3) anticipate sales force personnel requirements; (4) devise criteria for recruiting and selecting new salespeople; (5) mentor salespeople about their careers; (6) motivate and influence salespeople through leadership; (7) revise sales performance standards, policies, and evaluation procedures as appropriate; and (8) most importantly, augment salespeople's future performance. Overall, a comprehensive performance evaluation system for salespeople can provide a solid framework for setting and achieving organization goals, improve sales force management communication with salespeople, and increase the productivity of the sales force.[5]

Challenges in Salesperson Performance Evaluations

Evaluating salespeople is a challenging task, complicated by the nature of the selling job. First, salespeople typically work alone in the field and may have little direct contact with their sales managers. Second, salespeople usually have much more information about their sales territories than do their managers. They may use this information to their advantage, and to the possible disadvantage of their sales managers. In fact, research has found that information asymmetry between salespeople and their sales managers often leads to dysfunctional job behaviors.[6]

Third, salespeople engage in a multitude of activities. Determining which tasks to evaluate – and their relative significance – is not straightforward. Fourth, sales managers often do a poor job of evaluating salespeople simply because they dislike that task. They tend to feel uncomfortable having to assess the performance of their subordinates, and salespeople dislike being evaluated (particularly if the evaluation is somewhat negative). Yet, interestingly, one study reveals that positive performance feedback can enhance role clarity, satisfaction with the sales manager, and salesperson performance; moreover, even negative feedback can increase role clarity for the salesperson.[7]

And fifth, several factors that are truly beyond the salesperson's control contribute to individual performance.[8] These include differences in territory potentials, physical disparities in territories, competitive intensity, variations in company support, time allocation between account development and account maintenance, and salesperson tenure in and acclimation to the territory. Sales managers may overlook these uncontrollable factors during evaluation either because they forget, there's no system for including them or they don't know how to do so ("This is the way we've always done it!"), or the needed information to evaluate salespeople is unavailable.

Timing of Salesperson Performance Evaluations

Several studies indicate that performance appraisals are usually conducted by the salesperson's immediate supervisor and occasionally by a higher-level sales manager. Appraisals normally occur once a year, but sometimes semiannually and even quarterly. Evaluations include both objective (quantitative) and subjective (qualitative) measures. These are assigned different weights, usually with greater emphasis on objective measures. Sales managers generally provide feedback to salespeople in both written and oral forms.[9]

A Contemporary Approach to Sales Force Performance Evaluation

Using a systematic process for sales force performance evaluation – as shown in Figure 14.1 – the sales management hierarchical team's first step is to determine objectives and goals for the sales organization. Next, they develop the sales plan with specific strategies and tactics for achieving the objectives and goals. They set performance

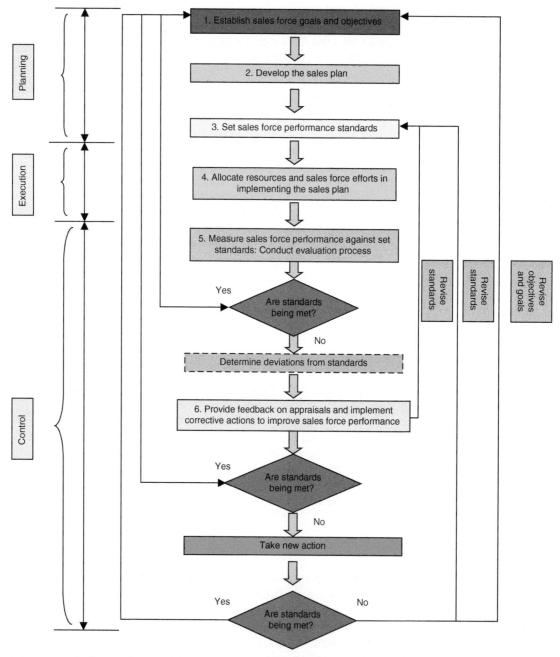

FIGURE 14.1 Sales force performance evaluation process.

Source: Adapted from Dalrymple, D. J. and Parsons, L. J. (1980). *Marketing Management* (2nd ed.). New York: Wiley, 622.

standards for all sales activities, and decide how best to allocate resources and sales force efforts. Next, it's time to put the plan into action. Finally, the team will monitor performance continuously, compare it to preset standards, and – if needed – make corrective decisions to bring any deviations back into line.

Establish Sales Force Goals and Objectives

After top management establishes the overall company's goals and objectives, the performance measurement and evaluation process for the sales organization can begin. The initial step is to formulate the longer-run aspirational goals that usually aren't easy to quantify. For instance, the sales organization may have a goal of being recognized by customers as the most service-oriented sales force in the industry. When long-run sales goals have been determined, the sales manager can focus on the shorter-run, more quantifiable targets, often called sales objectives. For example, annual objectives might include reaching 100% of sales quota, keeping sales expenses within assigned budgets, improving the ratio of selling to non-selling time by 20%, or increasing profitability on sales by 10%.

After sales force management has set sales goals and objectives, the next step is to ensure that salespeople understand, approve, and enthusiastically support them. Without open, two-way communication connecting these to the salespeople's personal goals, sales goals and objectives may become little more than "wish lists" without the organizational commitment needed for achievement.

Develop the Sales Plan

Goals and objectives indicate the "destination," a sales plan provides the detailed "road map" showing how to get there. As outlined in Table 14.1, the sales plan includes four major parts: (1) *situation analysis*, which identifies where the sales organization is now; (2) *opportunities and problems*, which indicate where it wants to go; (3) *action programs*, which outlines how best to get there, and (4) *performance evaluation systems*, which measure how much progress is being made toward the destination.

TABLE 14.1

The Sales Plan

I. **Situation analysis: "Where are we now?"**
   A. *Market situation and competitive environment*
      1. Size of the market (by major segments)
      2. Dynamics in the marketplace (e.g. shifts in customer purchasing behavior and competitive strategy changes)
      3. Market shares (by competitors, products, and customer classes)
      4. Strengths and weaknesses (of each competitor's sales organization and products relative to ours)
   B. *Product sales situation*
      1. Product types (by line items, sizes, models, etc.)
      2. Sales and distribution data (by geographic regions, territories, customer categories, or sales representatives)
      3. Markets served (by types of customer segments or end users)
      4. Customer profiles (by purchasing patterns and servicing needs)

<table>
<tr><td>

TABLE **14.1**

The Sales Plan (*Continued*)

II. **Opportunities and problems: "Where do we want to go?"**
   A. *Internal* (marketing and sales, R&D and technical, manufacturing/operations, financial, organization, personnel, etc.)
   B. *External* (market segments, competition, economic, political, legal, ethical, social, or international)
   C. *Planning assumptions and constraints*
      1. Internal company environment (estimate stability of objectives, goals, resources, management)
      2. External market environment (estimate short- and long-run marketing environment conditions)
   D. *Sales forecasts*
   E. *Contingency or dialectic planning* (based on different sets of assumptions from those in C, above)
III. **Action programs: "What's the best way to get there?"**
   A. *Strategies and tactics* (convert sales forecasts into resource, production, service, quotas, and budget needs)
IV. **Sales performance evaluation systems: "How much progress are we making toward our goals and objectives?"**
   A. *Set standards* of performance
   B. *Evaluate actual performance* versus planned standards
   C. *Take necessary corrective action* on variances from plan

</td></tr>
</table>

Set Sales Force Performance Standards

The next step is to set performance standards for the sales force. Performance standards are planned achievement levels that the sales organization expects to reach at progressive intervals throughout the year. They represent agreements between subordinates and superiors as to what level of performance is expected in some future period. One of the best ways to formalize this general agreement is in a detailed job description for the sales subordinate. An example of a job description for a sales representative at a major oil corporation is provided in Table 14.2.

In setting performance standards for the sales force, managers need to consider *efforts expended* as well as *results obtained*. Some variables bearing on performance are outside the sales representative's control, so results alone may not be objective measures. For instance, in many types of selling, there's a time lapse between efforts and results. This is especially true in business-to-business (B2B) sales, where tangible results may require several months of intense sales efforts before the prospective buyer makes a final decision. That's why sales managers must use qualitative, as well as quantitative, measures.

Key Sales Force Performance Factors

Although sales force managers are becoming more profit oriented in their focus,[10] the percentage of sales quota achieved has long been the ultimate performance criterion for salespeople. But because sales figures don't provide a complete assessment of a salesperson's job, most sales managers employ several variables to evaluate salesperson performance.

TABLE 14.2

Job Description for a Sales Force Representative

Position: **Sales force representative**
Immediate supervisor: District sales manager

Purpose of job: To manage a designated territory so that assigned objectives are achieved in the following categories: sales/profit, accounts receivable, rental income, and retail efficiency. These objectives can be largely accomplished by developing a strong network of dealers, salaried service station managers, consignees, agents, and distributors.

Regular assigned duties:

1. Plan and organize work in accordance with the TEAM system to achieve sales/profit plan in all categories.
   a. Analyze the accounts in the territory, using the *Quarterly Review and Replanning Guide*, to determine the opportunities and problems that can affect sales/profits, accounts receivable, rental income, and retail efficiency; determine what action plans would realize the opportunities and solve the problems.
   b. Prioritize opportunities and problems, determine which should be accomplished each quarter, and set objectives accordingly.
   c. Schedule and plans sales calls, set target dates to accomplish objectives.
2. Call on accounts on a planned basis.
   a. Solicit orders.
   b. Counsel dealers/managers and wholesalers on money management, hours, planned merchandising, appearance, and service; implement plans, programs, and methods that will contribute to the territory's objectives.
   c. Keep accounts receivable within established credit limits and collect all monies as required.
   d. Maintain dealer business in line with company objectives. Renew existing dealers' leases with consideration given to the interests of dealers and/or wholesalers as well as the firm.
   e. Conduct dealer meetings on subjects that can best be handled by group counseling and selling.
3. Recruit and interview lessee dealer/manager prospects following selection procedures; recommend acceptable candidates for management approval; arrange for training; negotiate and propose loans where applicable; install new dealers/managers using company guidelines. As required, recruit consignees.
4. Investigate customer complaints, resolve or, where necessary, refer to others for their handling.
5. Recommend appropriate maintenance of corporation-owned buildings and equipment.
6. Keep aware of competitive activity in territory and provide relevant information to dealers and the district sales manager.
7. Handle correspondence and reports pertinent to the territory and maintain adequate records.

All such standards should be: (1) relevant to job performance, (2) stable and consistent irrespective of the evaluator, and (3) capable of discriminating between outstanding, average, and poor performance. Variables in the larger marketing system such as product quality, price differences, and the level of promotional support should not distort the performance standards selected for measurement of sales force achievement.

Figure 14.2 shows three kinds of evaluation criteria for assessing salesperson performance: (1) outcome-based measures, (2) behavior-based measures, and (3) professional development measures. A larger inventory of these three categories of measures is identified in Table 14.3 parts 1–3. Let's look at each criterion.

Outcome-Based Measures Results generated by the salesperson fall into three categories: (a) sales results, (b) profitability indices, and (c) sales efforts (see Table 14.3, part 1) comprise outcome-based performance measures. Specific outcome-oriented criteria include sales volume, percent of quota, market share, gross margin, contribution margin, number of orders, average order size, number of new accounts, and number of lost accounts. Outcome-based performance criteria generally require

FIGURE 14.2 Sales force performance evaluation: outcome-based, behavior-based, and professional development measures.

relatively little monitoring of salespeople and minimal managerial direction or effort because they rely on straightforward objective measures of results.[11] In sales organizations that emphasize use of outcome-based criteria, salespeople tend to be especially bottom-line focused, extrinsically motivated, and self-oriented, but they also tend to be less accepting of supervisory direction.[12] The essence of outcome-based criteria is that they are quantitative and, therefore, objective. They afford easier comparison with a salesperson's prior performance, as well as with the performance of peers. However, the salesperson's activities or efforts, such as the number of sales calls made, tend to affect sales or expenses directly and also can be evaluated objectively.

The number of sales calls made is one among many measures of sales performance.

Behavior-Based Measures Each sales organization has to develop its own subjective behavior-based performance measures for evaluating the less-quantifiable sales-related activities. Examples of these qualitative criteria appear in Table 14.3, part 2. Sales managers tend to avoid using subjective criteria to evaluate salespeople because they reflect observations and opinions instead of objective measurements. Nevertheless, it's still important to consider subjective or qualitative measures in any evaluation because they can significantly affect a salesperson's performance and the

---

TABLE 14.3

Sales Force Performance Evaluation: Outcome-Based, Behavior-Based, and Professional Development Measures

1. Outcome-based measures

(a) Sales results

Sales orders

- Number of orders obtained
- Average order size (units or dollars)
- Batting average (orders ÷ sales calls)
- Number of orders canceled by customers

Sales volume

- Dollar sales volume
- Unit sales volume
- By customer type
- By product category
- Translated into market share
- Percent of sales quota achieved

Customer accounts

- Number of new accounts
- Number of lost accounts
- Percent of accounts sold
- Number of overdue accounts
- Dollar amount of accounts receivables
- Collections made of accounts receivable

(b) Profitability indices

Profit indicators

- Gross profit margin
- Net profit contribution
- Net profit margin by customer type
- Net profit margin by product category
- Return on investment
- Return on sales
- Return on sales costs
- Return on assets
- Return on assets managed

(c) Sales efforts

Sales calls

- Number made on current customers
- Number made on potential new accounts
- Average time spent per call
- Number of sales presentations
- Selling time versus non-selling time
- Call frequency ratio

Selling expenses

- Average per sales call
- As percent of sales volume
- As percent of sales quota
- By customer type
- By product category
- Direct selling expense ratios
- Indirect selling expense ratios

Customer service

- Number of service calls
- Displays set up
- Delivery cost per unit sold
- Months of inventory held by customer type
- Number of customer complaints
- Percent of goods returned

TABLE 14.3

Sales Force Performance Evaluation: Outcome-Based, Behavior-Based, and Professional Development Measures (*Continued*)

2. Behavior-based measures

Sales-related activities

- Territory management: sales call preparation, scheduling, routing, and time utilization
- Marketing intelligence: new-product ideas, competitive activities, new customer preferences
- Follow-up with customers
- Using promotional brochures and correspondence with current and potential accounts
- Customer relations
- Report preparation and timely submission

3. Professional development measures

Professional selling skills	*Professional knowledge*
- Product knowledge	- Willingness and ability to acquire new capacities
- Customer knowledge	- Sales force management potential
- Understanding of selling techniques	- Knowledge of the company and its policies
- Execution of selling techniques	- Knowledge competitors' products, marketing and sales strategies
- Quality of sales presentations	- Use of marketing and technical backup teams
- Communication skills	
- Cooperation with sales team	*Personal characteristics*
- Punctuality	- Enthusiasm
- Patience	- Motivation
- Initiative	- Judgment
- Resourcefulness	- Good citizenship
- Customer feedback (positive and negative)	- Ethical code of conduct
- Dependability	- Physical appearance
- Empathy	- Ambition
- Enthusiasm	- Stability
- Judgment	

company's reputation. It's vital for sales managers to develop an evaluation system that clearly identifies sales force goals and standards and encourages salespeople to perform in the desired manner.

Professional Development Measures Professional development criteria have a more indirect and longer-run impact on sales, so sales managers must evaluate them largely on a subjective basis. These criteria, identified in Table 14.3, part 3, fall into three areas: (1) professional selling skills, such as the salesperson's product and customer knowledge; (2) professional knowledge of company and competitors, such as awareness of organizational policies, and marketing and sales strategies; and (3) personal characteristics, such as enthusiasm, judgment, an ethical code of conduct, and personal appearance. Not all successful salespeople possess all or even most of these qualities. Research indicates that in many selling situations, some qualities are more important than others for success.[13] Sales managers place considerable emphasis on personal characteristics, and they are the most frequently used category of the three foregoing evaluation criteria.[14]

Combining Sales Performance Evaluation Criteria

Although some sales managers may emphasize outcome-based criteria and others behavior-based criteria when evaluating salesperson performance, it's preferable to adopt a hybrid approach that maximizes the strengths and reduces the limitations of each set of criteria.[15]

The appropriate combination of appraisal criteria depends on the specific selling framework and on the broad corporate, marketing, and selling objectives of the firm. In establishing goals for individual salespeople, sales managers should choose criteria that focus on the most important features of the sales job, provide a complete picture of the salesperson's performance, and are generally controllable by the salesperson. Obviously, these concerns need to be weighed against the availability of the information and the time and cost of obtaining and using it.

Sources of Information for Sales Performance Evaluations

Supervision and evaluation are interdependent and continuous processes. Field sales managers cannot work closely with subordinates without becoming aware of their strengths and weaknesses. Moreover, salespeople often discuss each other with members of management. Customers and prospects frequently praise or complain about different salespersons. A certain amount of informal, subjective appraisal of salespeople and their selling activities is both inevitable and desirable.

A major step toward improving the evaluation process occurs when the procedures become systematic, which may be difficult to achieve.[16] To assist in providing a systematic appraisal system, sales managers should collect evaluative information from a variety of sources.[17] The final rating of a salesperson's performance should be a composite of information received from many sources, with each source appropriately weighted. Company records, customers, prospects, other department managers within the company, and the salesperson's own input, can provide valuable performance information to the sales manager that is both outcome- and behavior-based.

The primary readily available source of quantitative information is company records. For example, how did the salesperson perform based on number of orders, sales volume, gross margin, selling costs, and profits? Such information about "how much" (available from company records) can be supplemented by data from other sources, including external ones. Field sales managers are best able to evaluate the quality of the salesperson's sales presentations, his or her work habits, rapport with customers and prospects, devotion to work, mental attitude, and integrity. Through regular interaction and/or joint sales calls on prospects and customers, the field sales manager can glean a wealth of qualitative information about the salesperson's performance. Also, time and activity studies of salesperson activities can indicate how much time is spent in various selling and nonselling activities and whether those time expenditures are worthwhile.

Activity reports turned in regularly by salespeople provide valuable information about effort such as prospecting methods, number and frequency of calls, number of presentations, or time spent entertaining clients. These reports are especially useful when combined with informal comments and solicited remarks from prospects or customers. Input from buyers at prospect and customer companies is fairly easy for the sales manager to obtain during order-verification phone calls or through questionnaires that seek information for improving the seller's offerings and services to customers.

Sales Dashboards

To quickly gain an overall perspective on the plethora of sales performance metrics, many firms have deployed sales dashboards that enable sales managers to assess the status of day-to-day sales and financial performance results as well as an up-to-date summary picture on the sales performance of each individual salesperson.[18] Moreover, many company dashboards also allow salesperson to immediately see their sales performance achievements vis-à-vis expectations on an assortment of performance indices – as identified in Table 14.3.

A sales dashboard is a diagnostic tool or graphically interface that displays valuable metrics or information about sales force performance. Somewhat like an automobile dashboard that enables the driver to obtain a fast overview of the car's key performance functions such as speed, gas tank level, or various warning lights, a sales dashboard quickly provides key information on critical sales performance metrics. The new mantra in the "science of winning" is to compete on analytics.[19] Thus, contemporary sales managers and their salespeople rely on analytics provided by sales dashboards of various types for monitoring day-to-day sales operations as well as longer-term activities. Information displayed on sales dashboards may differ widely depending on the industry, type of sales (B2B or B2C), size of the company, products or services, and objectives.[20] Sales dashboards should provide an effective, efficient way for sales managers to direct sales force efforts and for salespeople to see how they're performing. Like the automobile dashboard, the sales dashboard presents a fast overview of the ongoing progress of sales activities and whether changes are needed in strategies, tactics, or other efforts to achieve goals.

Microsoft (www.microsoft.com) and IBM (www.ibm.com) are software companies that specialize in the development of dashboards to track key business metrics for managerial decision-making across multiple sales channels, including digital.[21] For example, sales dashboards ought to include the critical sales metrics or key performance indicators (KPI) needed by sales managers to improve the interactions of salespeople with prospects and customers on sales calls and timely follow-up and servicing of accounts to increase customer satisfaction and loyalty. KPI is a numeric indicator of business performance for any activity important to a firm. Considered to be the "vital statistics" for a sales organization, Salesforce.com (www.crm.com) suggests that the perfect sales dashboard should display sales metrics, such as individual salesperson performance, pipeline performance, sales forecasts, the firm's competitors, product performance, leads by source, open calls, demos, visits, sales cycle, new business, upsell ratio, and win/loss rate.[22]

Numerous firms specialize in developing customized sales and business performance dashboards. While Salesforce (www.crm.com) is widely recognized to be the industry leader, many other firms, including Datapine (www.datapaine.com), Kipfolio Inc. (www.kipfolio.com), Sisense (www.sisence.com), InsightSquared (www.insightsquared.com), and Tableau (www.tableau.com), specialize in designing sales dashboards. Sales managers can use web-based software offered by these firms to easily design dashboards specifically customized for their sales force.

Sales managers also need to monitor and react to a number of big-picture metrics, including changes in markets and customer requirements, developments across

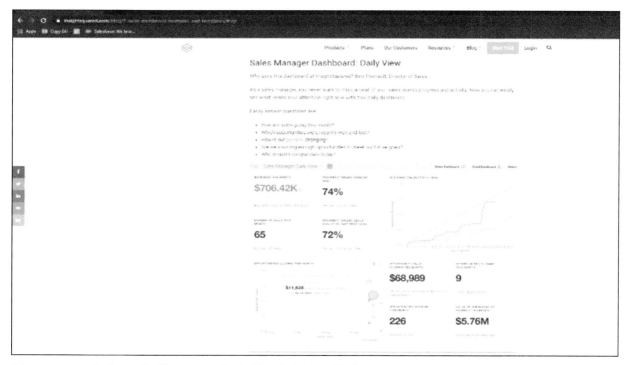

Sales managers and salespeople alike can use sales dashboards developed by firms, such as InsightSquared, that track and report key performance indicators and business metrics in one place to make informed data-driven decisions.
Source: https://www.insightsquared.com/blog/7-sales-dashboard-examples-and-templates/#rep.

multiple online and off-line distribution channels, progress toward achieving sales forecasts, profitability by different market segments (territories, customers, products, and salespeople), individual salesperson performance evaluations, and evolving opportunities and challenges in the macro-marketing/sales environment.

Management Information Needed From the Sales Dashboard

The exact metrics or information required from the sales dashboard will typically vary from company-to-company to fit unique needs. For example, companies such as SAP (www.sap.com) or Oracle (www.oracle.com) who sell enterprise software to major corporations need to closely monitor numerous ongoing interactions and activities with large customers over long periods of time to successfully negotiate large sales contracts, then closely oversee their implementation while ensuring customer satisfaction. So their sales operations require a vast amount of feedback information and actionable metrics. Each sales organization has to determine the KPIs to be monitored by the sales dashboard. Since sales strategies change over time, the dashboard must be flexible enough to readily adapt to any changes. In developing and maintaining a successful sales dashboard, it's critical to regularly analyze sales reports, sales goals, and the KPIs critical to timely, effective decision-making.

Dashboards can be strategic, analytical, operational, or informational. Strategic dashboards support managers at any organizational level by providing ready "big picture" overviews that help decision makers monitor the overall health of operations.

Sales dashboards of this type focus on high level measures of performance, and achieving forecasts. Dashboards for monitoring daily sales operations require ongoing updates of activities and events that are constantly changing and might require quick, decisive managerial response. Dashboards must provide analytics that enable sales managers to go deeply into the underlying breakouts of sales by market segments to make timely business data science driven decisions.[23] For large, enterprise-level sales teams, companies such as IBM (www.ibm.com) or Salesforce (www.crm.com) provide browser-based visualization of cloud-stored data, allowing users to access large, complex reports, and the ability to drill down into lower level data that would be largely inaccessible and therefore lost in overview metrics alone. Digital dashboards provide a data-oriented perspective allowing sales managers to determine more precisely how well each aspect of the sales organization is performing by capturing and reporting specific metrics from deep within the information gathered, instead of only a few "snapshots" of overall performance.[24] Dashboards also can be used to view historical records and performance over various time periods to compare with current performance.

Some key benefits of a digital sales dashboard ought to include the ability to:

- Improve overall sales force management decision-making based on the latest market intelligence
- Align sales organizational strategies and goals with those of the company
- View instant graphic presentation of important sales performance metrics
- Spot early-on the developing positive and negative sales trends in markets
- Display sales analytics that reveal performance efficiencies and inefficiencies
- Be able to quickly generate detailed reports for salespeople and management
- Gain instant access to a comprehensive overview of all sales operations
- Identify specific outliers in sales performance data, so that changes can be made on a timely basis

Indeed, in today's increasing complex and fiercely competitive world markets, no sales organization will be able to operate successfully for long without the benefits provided by an up-to-date sales dashboard using the latest technology to provide sales managers with needed information in readily understandable graphically displays for timely decision-making.

Allocate Resources and Sales Force Efforts

In the next step of the performance appraisal process (Figure 14.1), sales managers should allocate human, financial, and material resources for implementing the sales plan. This is necessary because sales managers control sales force efforts and activities by using quotas as well as standards for appraising the performance of individual salespeople (i.e. outcome-based, behavioral-based, and professional development criteria). Hence, to achieve desired sales goals and productivity objectives,[25] sales managers set sales quotas for their salespeople and for different sales units.

Types of Sales Quotas

Derived from sales forecasts, a sales quota is an objective to be achieved by a given time period assigned to a particular sales unit (such as the entire sales organization, or sales region, district, branch, territorial sales team, or individual salesperson).[26] It is a numerical motivational target representing a performance standard that is expected from the sales unit or salesperson. Sales quotas are effective control and evalua-tion devices, however, sales managers must assign them realistically and equitably according to valid differences in territorial potentials. Quotas are a supplement to direct supervision, like goal-setting[27] (see Chapter 11). Thus, they free up some of the sales manager's time for nonsupervisory duties.[28]

Sales quotas have several general purposes, including the following:

- To help motivate salespeople by providing an assigned sales achievement as an incentive
- To provide quantitative performance standards
- To control and direct salespeople's activities and efforts[29]
- To evaluate the performance of salespeople[30]
- To aid in controlling use of selling expenses

Different sales organizations may use quotas for a variety of reasons. In fact, the purpose for a quota dictates the kind of quota a firm utilizes. For example, if man-agement wants to increase profitability, it will most likely adopt a cost-reduction or profit-oriented quota. Or, to enhance market share, a sales volume-oriented quota may be assigned. Results of a study of 3,000 salespeople indicate how the intent of a quota may be blunted through salespeople's efforts (or lack thereof); specifically, up to 85% of salespeople have no documented plan for reaching their sales goals, thus suggesting that they think their quotas can be achieved with minimal planning and by relying on ad hoc sales tactics.[31]

Regardless of the kind of sales quota and its purpose, a quota plan (consisting of all quotas used in the sales department) ideally should possess the following features[32]:

- Realistically attainable
- Clear and precise in its definition
- Based on objective accuracy instead of subjectivity
- Easy to administer
- Allow for flexibility
- Seen as equitable by all the salespeople
- Include only quotas that represent critical salesperson tasks or responsibilities
- Enable regular feedback to salespeople about quota achievement progress

One sales force management expert offers additional requirements by suggesting that: (1) quotas should be attainable, but only with effort; (2) unreachable quotas are not motivating, but frustrating; (3) "creampuff" quotas do not induce extra effort; and (4) quotas should pertain to a salesperson's activities, not personality.[33]

What sales managers hope to accomplish will be a critical factor in determining the kind of quotas used. The rationale to use a specific type of sales quota is largely predicated by the quantitative and qualitative sales goals a salesperson is expected to achieve in a given time frame. Figure 14.3 shows four types of sales quotas: (1) sales volume, (2) financial, (3) activity, and (4) combination. Let's examine them more closely.

1. **Sales volume quotas.** A sales volume quota represents a sales goal (usually expressed in dollars or units). It is the most frequently used kind of quota because it is easy to understand and relates to a major sales department objective – generating sales. Sales volume quotas allow sales managers to aggregate different types of products, customers, or other market segments into a summary figure for comparison over time. The three different variants of sales volume quotas include: (a) dollar based sales quotas, (b) unit volume quotas, and (c) point quotas.

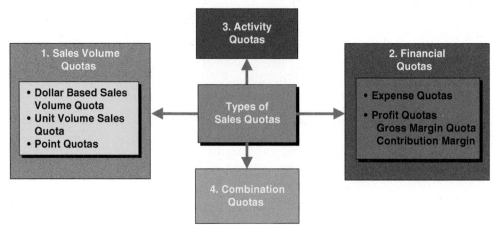

FIGURE 14.3 Types of sales quotas.

a. ***Dollar-based sales quotas.*** A dollar-based sales quota is typically used when a firm sells a large number of different products, prices are relatively stable, and prices reflect management's selling priorities (e.g. salespeople should emphasize one product line over another). Dollar-based quotas allow managers to compare sales to other dollar figures, such as selling expenses or commissions.

b. ***Unit volume quotas.*** A unit volume quota expresses the quantity of a product to be sold. A unit quota is especially advisable when sales reps are selling big-ticket items. Stating the quota in units can reduce the adverse impact that a dollar-based quota could have on salesperson morale and motivation. For instance, a quota of $1 million may look daunting to a salesperson even though each unit is $50,000. But, if the quota is set on a per unit basis, 20 units seems more reasonable. Companies selling a relatively small number of products with prices that are unstable also use unit-volume quotas.

c. ***Point quotas.*** To avoid having salespeople concentrate their selling efforts on a few easy-to-sell products or customers, sales managers often employ point quotas in lieu of or in addition to sales- and unit-volume quotas. Point quotas assign points that typically vary across products; this helps management encourage its salespeople to stress certain products over others. Some companies require salespeople to reach all point quotas before earning bonuses, thus ensuring a desired mix of product sales.

In setting sales volume quotas, the sales manager should start by comparing territorial potential with the salesperson's history of sales there. The salesperson and sales manager should always work together in developing a territory sales quota.

Sales volume quotas are generally established for a certain time period – and the shorter the time period, the more effective the quota. For this reason, many companies establish monthly or quarterly quotas unless sales are seasonal. For example, an annual quota guides college textbook sales reps because even though they work when school is in session (September to June), most of their orders do not come in until July and August, when many schools are closed for summer vacation.

2. **Financial quotas.** Rather than focusing on sales volume, financial quotas are established to control gross margin and net profit or expenses. Like sales volume quotas, these quotas can be applied to salespeople, regions, and product lines. Without financial quotas, many salespeople will gravitate toward easier sales whether they are the most profitable or not. Financial quotas help make salespeople aware of the cost and profit implications of their sales. By manipulating financial quotas, the sales manager can shift salespeople's efforts toward achieving specific company goals such as introducing new products, increasing market share in a given territory, developing new accounts, changing the customer mix, or attaining higher profit margins.

   Financial quotas have taken on increased importance as sales managers have begun to assume greater profit responsibility. Most successful companies realize that not all sales are profitable, so sales managers must be held accountable for the profit generated within their respective territories. There are two kinds of financial quotas: (a) expense and (b) profit.

   a. *Expense quotas.* Stated either as a percentage of sales or as a dollar amount, an expense quota is designed to make salespeople aware of the costs involved in their selling efforts. The idea behind its use is to force salespeople to be accountable for the expenses they incur. Only those expenses they can control (travel, entertainment, and lodging) belong in an expense quota. If salespeople start to pay too much heed to selling costs, however, they may overlook important selling activities like customer service.

   b. *Profit quotas.* Profit quotas focus on the profit generated through the sales department's selling efforts. A *gross margin quota* (sales – cost of goods sold = gross margin) makes sense when products have distinctly different production costs (and thus different gross margins). Management tends to set a higher quota for products having a larger gross margin than for those with lower margins. Some firms use a *contribution margin quota* (gross margin – direct selling expenses = contribution margin) when management wants salespeople to stress certain products and take responsibility for the expenses they can control (direct selling expenses). Other companies opt for a *net profit quota* (sales – cost of goods sold – direct selling expenses – indirect selling expenses = net profit). Managers selecting this kind of quota argue that ultimately the firm has to cover all expenses; therefore, they feel that sales personnel should be responsible for their role in reaching a designated level of profitability.

   Sales departments tend to prefer gross margin or contribution margin quotas over net profit quotas. Net profit quotas, after all, include expenses over which salespeople have little or no control over (like the sales manager's salary); the value of holding them responsible for such costs is questionable. Profit quotas are especially appropriate when salespeople engage in activities that can have a dramatic influence on company profit (like emphasizing one product line over another, or lavishly entertaining customers). Thus, sales managers can use these quotas to emphasize to high-volume salespersons that the company would rather have large profits than large sales volume. For example, Sam Barone sells the highest volume for Oracle Fasteners Company; however, he focuses on the easy-to-sell, low-margin products.

TABLE 14.4

Ratio of Sales Volume to Net Profit

	$ Sales price per unit	$ Profit margin per unit (%)	$ Volume per month		$ Profit margin per month	
			Sam Barone	Kaye Garcia	Sam Barone	Kaye Garcia
Product A	$20	$15.00 (75%)	$5,000	$30,000	$3,750	$22,500
Product B	$5	$3.00 (66%)	$5,000	$2,500	$3,000	$1,500
Product C	$2	$.50 (25%)	$40,000	$2,500	$10,000	$625
			$50,000	$35,000	$16,750	$24,625

Kaye Garcia, on the other hand, sells a somewhat lower volume, but she sells more expensive items carrying a greater profit margin. As shown in Table 14.4, although Barone sold $15,000 more than Garcia did, his total profit margin was almost $8,000 less than hers due to the type of product each of them emphasized.

This illustration is important to management because it points out the need to control the salesperson's selling emphasis. Salespeople receive an emotional boost every time they make a sale, so naturally they are going to try to make as many sales as possible. To do this they may emphasize the easy-to-sell items. By spending too much time on less-profitable products, the reps limit the company's opportunity to earn higher profits from its high-margin products. Granted, it may take a salesperson longer to sell higher-priced products, but the higher profits usually are well worth it to the company.

Salespeople also tend to spend more time calling on customers they feel more comfortable with. These customers, however, may not purchase in large quantities or may require many services. Thus, they can be far less profitable than other customers. Setting a quota on net profits encourages the sale of high-margin products over low-margin products.

While profit quotas are very desirable to some companies, they have some disadvantages. First, gross-margin or net-profit quotas are the hardest for salespeople to understand. Much of the cost information (particularly production costs) may not be readily available to them. Moreover, salespeople may not know they have achieved their quotas without frequent updates. Thus, because it is more difficult for them to know how well they're doing at any given time, they can get frustrated and lose motivation. Second, external factors, such as competition, economic conditions, or internal restrictions, (i.e. the inability to negotiate on price), affect the salesperson's net profit. Thus, profit quotas may be unfair because of the many uncontrollable factors.

Visit the website of a firm such as Optymyze.com (www.optymyze.com) to learn more about sales quotas, financial performance calculators, sales performance indicators, and sales skills assessments. At the website, you can also review free resources, such as sales articles, company testimonials, and case studies to augment your understanding of sales force performance appraisals.

To increase your knowledge of how sales quotas, financial performance calculators, and performance indicators are used in the sales force performance appraisals, visit the website of firms like Optymyze.com.

Source: https://optymyze.com/.

3. **Activity quotas.** To ensure that salespeople are conducting their tasks conscientiously, many companies require them to meet activity quotas, which are designed to control the many activities for which the salesperson is responsible. These quotas serve as guidelines for younger, inexperienced sales reps who may tend to overemphasize the wrong activities.

   The first step in setting an activity quota is to determine the salesperson's most important activities over a designated time period. These activities might include making sales calls on new prospects, setting up dealer displays, or providing special customer service. Before setting activity quotas, management should do research on how long it takes to perform these duties, how long it takes to travel throughout each territory, which activities should be given priority, and how much priority to give each activity. Finally, management must set a target level of performance, usually expressed as a frequency (see Table 14.5).

TABLE 14.5

Common Types of Activity Quotas

- Number of current customers or new prospects called on
- Number of product or service demonstrations made
- Number of displays set up
- Number of new accounts established
- Number of service calls made
- Number of dealer training sessions given

Activity quotas can be advantageous to both the salesperson and sales manager. If they plan their work carefully, salespeople should have no trouble meeting their daily activity obligations. Activity quotas also allow management to control the salesperson's selling efforts. Thus, they allow management to recognize sales reps for performing important nonselling activities and maintaining contact with infrequent customers who buy in large quantities. Finally, they quickly identify unmotivated, underperforming salespeople so that the manager can take corrective action.

One problem with activity quotas is that salespeople may not be motivated to perform these activities conscientiously or effectively; they may just go through the motions. So it's wise to use activity quotas in conjunction with sales volume quotas. Any slouching by the salesperson that is not revealed by the activity quota is sure to be indicated later by the sales volume quota. However, salespeople may become so preoccupied with the sales volume quota that they acquire bad habits – pressing for a quick sale, covering only large or existing accounts, and trying to bypass necessary stages in the selling process. For example, the salesperson may make the presentation before qualifying the prospect and waste time trying to sell to a person who lacks the ability to buy. Certain products may require several sales calls, yet because the salesperson is anxious to reach his or her sales volume quota, the buyer feels uncomfortably pushed and the negotiations are cut off early. For these reasons, activity quotas are generally best for salespeople who perform numerous nonselling functions.

4. **Combination quotas.** To control salesperson performance of both selling and nonselling activities, sales managers make use of combination quotas. They

In evaluating the overall performance of salespeople, sales managers should consider the accomplishment of various tasks assigned in activity quotas.

Graham Oliver/123 RF

generally use points as a common measuring tool to overcome the difficulty of evaluating the different units used by the other quotas. For example, dollars are used to measure sales volume, and the number of prospects called on is used to measure activities; by converting each unit to points, the sales manager can readily measure the salesperson's overall performance. Sales managers do this by computing the percentage attained for a specific quota and then multiplying this by a weight designed to show the relative importance of achieving that quota. This calculation is done for each individual quota, then all points are added together to provide a total score for the salesperson.

This method is shown in Table 14.6. Here, three sales reps are being evaluated on their attainment of three separate quotas: net profit, sales volume, and the number of new accounts established. Lanesha Freedman has the highest point total even though she had the lowest sales volume percentage of the three reps; she attained an extremely high percentage of her net-profit quota. Obviously, Freedman stressed the company's high-margin products. Julie Cangelosi did an excellent job establishing new accounts; however, the company did not assign as much importance to this quota as it did to the others. Chris Kwan came very close to attaining his full quota, but he did not do well in setting up new accounts.

This illustration points out some of the problems of combination quotas. First, they're difficult for salespeople to understand. Sales reps may get confused and put more emphasis on the less important activities. Second, salespeople have a hard time assessing their own performance and, thus, often do not know what needs to be improved. Therefore, it's important for the three salespeople evaluated in our Table 14.6 example to have computer access to up-to-the-minute feedback on their ongoing relative performances in obtaining new accounts, net profits, and sales volume versus

TABLE 14.6

Combination Quotas

Salesperson: Lanesha Freedman	Quota	Actual	% of quota	Weight	Quota × weight
Net profit	$50,000	$48,000	96	4	384
Sales volume	$100,000	$75,000	75	3	225
Number of new accounts	25	22	88	1	88
Total score = 697/8 = 87.125				8	697
Salesperson: Julie Cangelosi	**Quota**	**Actual**	**% of Quota**	**Weight**	**Quota × weight**
Net profit	$80,000	$52,000	65	4	260
Sales volume	$125,000	$105,000	84	3	252
Number of new accounts	25	25	100	1	100
Total score = 612/8 = 76.5				8	612
Salesperson: Chris Kwan	**Quota**	**Actual**	**% of quota**	**Weight**	**Quota × weight**
Net profit	$50,000	$38,000	76	4	304
Sales volume	$75,000	$73,000	97	3	291
Number of new accounts	15	9	60	1	60
Total score = 655/8 = 81.875				8	655

assigned quotas. There is always room for managerial creativity in setting sales goals and working with customers, as explained in Sales Management in Action Box 14.1.

Administration of Sales Quotas

For the quota system to effectively plan, control, and evaluate the sales effort, salespeople must be willing to cooperate with their sales managers. Some welcome the challenge of having their performance strictly monitored and measured, although many other salespeople dislike quotas. They become anxious and nervous when they are being evaluated so closely. Thus, management must "sell" the salespeople on the fairness and accuracy of assigned quotas and assure them that the quotas are a way for them to measure their own progress and reasonably attainable if the salespeople willingly accept them and expend an honest effort.

Set Realistic Quotas Salespeople must be motivated to sell effectively. If they feel their assigned quota is unrealistic, they will not be motivated to attain it. And if recognition, compensation, or job security is not dependent on quotas, then many salespeople may be less concerned about attaining any of them.

In setting quotas, different companies have different theories of attainability and motivation in mind. For example, some sales managers believe in setting an average quota, and then rewarding salespeople according to the percentage of quota achieved. This approach rewards salespeople for average work, but it also motivates many to continue working hard to achieve greater rewards for significantly exceeding quota. Xerox (www.xerox.com), on the other hand, sets quotas very high and rewards salespeople only for performance above and beyond their quotas. Xerox believes that rewards are for those who put forth an excellent performance, and that higher goals motivate most salespeople more. Easily achieved goals may cause some salespeople to slow down once they reach that lower bar.

To set accurate quotas, sales managers must closely relate them to territorial potentials while using sound, objective executive judgment. They must analyze the different markets and territories and make adjustments to ensure that quotas are fairly assigned based on market facts, so that salespeople willingly accept them.

Create Understandable Quotas Make the quota plan understandable, and carefully explained it to salespeople; otherwise, they may feel that management is trying to coerce them into giving more effort without comparable rewards. If salespeople fully understand their assigned quotas, they're more likely to view them as fair, accurate, and attainable.

TABLE 14.7			
Sales vs. Quota Performance Evaluation			
Salesperson: Delroy Hawkins			
Territory: Florida	**Actual**	**Quota**	**% of quota**
October 2020	$22,765	$25,000	91.1
October 2019	$21,050	$19,500	107.9
Year to Date: 2020	$267,567	$300,000	89.2
Projection: 2020	$321,081	$300,000	107.0

Include the Salesperson in Quota Setting Management can ease the sales reps' understanding of quotas by allowing them to participate in the quota-setting procedure. This not only enhances understanding, but also significantly reduces questions of inaccuracy, unfairness, and unattainability. The amount of input the salespeople should have depends on their experience, the amount of market information available, and the company's management philosophy.

Keep the Sales Force Updated Keeping salespeople updated on their performance relative to their assigned quotas reinforces the importance of the quotas, allows them to see their progress, and enables them to take timely corrective action to improve their performance. Sales managers should try to keep in close personal contact with their salespeople to encourage them and offer advice toward attaining quotas.

Maintain Control Continuously monitor and analyze individual salesperson performance, and then regularly provide up-to-the-minute information to each salesperson about progress toward his or her quota. Via e-mail, intranet website, or a sales dashboard (discussed earlier), the sales manager can provide salespeople with weekly or monthly charts, or a relative ranking of the entire sales force based on actual performance compared with quota. Some managers feel this disclosed ranking of all salespeople creates a competitive atmosphere that encourages poorly ranked salespeople to try harder so as not to be embarrassed. Others feel it can produce more harm than good, and they prefer to provide each sales rep with a chart monitoring just his or her progress toward quotas. One of these charts is shown in Table 14.7.

Measure Sales Force Performance Against Set Standards

Conducting the evaluation process enables measuring and comparing sales force performance against set standards. In smaller companies, the performance evaluation monitoring system (PEMS) may be largely informal, relying on the firsthand observations of supervisors. As an organization grows, managers are less able to closely monitor each employee's daily activities. So they turn to a more formalized PEMS.

Companies differ greatly in their approach to PEMS. Lockheed-Martin (www .lockheedmartin.com) requires managers in its Aerospace Division to write broad essays describing an individual's strengths and weaknesses. Most companies, however, try to quantify managerial observations and judgments by means of performance results, behavior, or personal characteristics. In their rush to develop quantifiable scores, organizations can lose sight of what they want the PEMS to do. Performance appraisal systems should help do three essential things for the sales manager and salespeople: (1) provide feedback to each salesperson on individual job performance, (2) help salespeople modify or change their behavior to include more effective work habits, and (3) provide information to sales managers to help in making decisions about promotion, transfer, and compensation of salespeople.

There are three successive stages in the effective implementation of a PEMS.

- *Performance planning* – Probably the most important phase of the PEMS; it allows the salesperson to ask the sales manager three key questions: "Where am I going?" "How will I get there?" "How will I be measured?"
- *Performance appraisal* – A continuous interpersonal process whereby sales managers give individual salespeople immediate feedback – recognition, praise, correction, or comment – on each specific task, project, or goal accomplished.
- *Performance review* – A periodic review of past performance appraisals summarizes where the salesperson is in his or her personal development. It should answer the question "How am I doing?" It should provide constructive feedback to help the salesperson improve performance, and lead into the next performance planning stage.

Even though the three PEMS stages lead into one another, sales managers should not assume they can deal with all three simultaneously in once-a-year, overall performance evaluations. *Performance planning* lays out goals and plans for achieving them, and explains how the individual will be evaluated. A well-constructed MBO (management by objectives) program (discussed later) can be invaluable in this stage. *Performance appraisals* are day-by-day, mini-evaluations on specific performances, while the *performance review* is a periodic summing up of these daily appraisals so that the salesperson can see where he or she stands.

Types of Performance Evaluation Techniques

Sales managers have a variety of evaluation techniques at their disposal. Each one, however, has limitations as well as strengths. When selecting evaluation approaches, consider the degree to which a particular method possesses the following characteristics[35]:

- *Job relatedness* – The evaluation method should accurately reflect the job behavior that leads to performance.
- *Reliability* – The method's measurement should be stable over time and consistent across raters.
- *Validity* – The method should accurately reflect what it is intended to measure.
- *Standardization* – The evaluation instrument and the way it is administered should be consistent throughout the sales organization.
- *Practicality* – The method should be easy to understand and use for both sales managers and salespeople, and neither too costly nor time consuming.
- *Comparability* – The method should allow for easy comparison across sales force members (those in the same and different jobs and in the same and different geographical areas).
- *Discriminability* – The method must be able to determine performance differences across salespersons.
- *Usefulness* – The method should be helpful for making decisions about promotion, compensation, and termination.

Sales managers should be required to periodically summarize each salesperson's performance in a permanent record, for the benefit of the salesperson in tracking personal progress and for the review of other sales and marketing managers. Ultimately, the nature of the sales job and the purpose of the evaluation process should determine which evaluation techniques sales managers use. Sales managers may use multiple evaluation methods simply because the sales job is complex (e.g., selling enterprise software), or they may opt for one approach if the job is relatively straight-forward (detail salesperson, for example).[36] The evaluation method they use should be related to the decisions that will flow from the evaluation, including potential promotion, higher compensation, or termination).[37] Four widely used evaluation technique are: (1) descriptive statements, (2) graphic rating scales, (3) management by objectives, and (4) behaviorally anchored rating scales.

1. *Descriptive statements.* Usually used in conjunction with some form of graphic rating scale, descriptive statements about a salesperson may be short responses to a series of specific criteria such as job knowledge, territorial management, customer relations, personal qualities, or sales results. Another approach, which various organizations including the military use, calls for an overall portrait of the individual's abilities, potential, and specific performance during this evaluation period. This essay-type appraisal backs up and should be consistent with quantitative ratings on different performance criteria. One overriding problem with descriptive statements is their subjectivity, both in the writing and the interpretation. Many sales managers fall into some predictable pattern of being too harsh, too lenient, or too neutral in their comments, so the appraisal is not well balanced. Moreover, many evaluators are simply not very capable writers, so their use of words may fail to accurately portray the salesperson. All sales managers need specific training in performance evaluation, particularly with making descriptive statements.

2. *Graphic rating scales.* There are several formats for the graphic rating scale, a kind of report-card-type rating. But in all cases, the sales manager must assign an individual a scale value for various traits, skills, or sales-related results. Two ways of doing this are the "semantic differential" and Likert-type scales. The semantic differential uses polar extremes to anchor several scale segments, usually five or seven, as shown in Figure 14.4. The manager rates the salesperson on some quality such as product knowledge from a numerical low of 1 (poor) to a high of 7 (excellent).[38]

   Likert-type scales provide descriptive anchors under each segment of the scale, as shown in Figure 14.5, so the sales manager can select which overall term best applies.

   Sales managers should try to avoid these report-card graphic ratings of generalized abilities, traits, or performances of individual sales reps. The word anchors are not very meaningful because of their subjective interpretation by the rater, the wide variation among salespeople, and their vague connection with actual performance.

3. **Management by objectives.** Sales managers are responsible for setting many sales performance standards for salespeople, but the salespeople must understand and accept these standards before developing their own plans for achievement. In management by objectives (MBO), the sales manager and the

Product Knowledge

Poor ___ ___ ___ ___ ___ X ___ Excellent
      1 2 3 4 5 6 7

FIGURE 14.4 Semantic differential graphic rating scale.

Product Knowledge

X
|_____ | _____ | _____ | _____ | _____ |
| **Unsatisfactory** | **Below average** | **Average** | **Above average** | **Outstanding** |

FIGURE 14.5 Likert-type graphic rating scale.

sales representative, jointly agree on the salesperson's specific goals or performance targets for the coming period. If they help set their own performance targets, salespeople are more likely to be committed to them and to devise realistic plans for their accomplishment.

In some companies, salespeople must prepare an annual "territorial marketing plan" outlining their strategy for obtaining new customers and increasing sales to current customers. This ensures that salespeople and sales managers agree on how goals are to be achieved – particularly when they participate in setting objectives and have give-and-take discussions about how to improve performances. Information derived from these territorial plans helps sales managers to more objectively evaluate the individual performances of salespeople. This process also encourages salespeople to do a better job of planning their work and reporting their activities.

At many companies, each salesperson has a written plan, reviewed quarterly with the sales manager. Periodic performance monitoring ensures sales reps are making acceptable progress toward goals and provides guidance for altering the planned strategies and tactics to get back on target. The final step is an annual performance appraisal, which leads to the setting of new objectives for the coming year. The MBO cycle is illustrated in Figure 14.6. The process is essentially the same whether applied to the entire sales force or to an individual salesperson. With each successive MBO cycle, sales managers and salespeople should find the process works more efficiently.

Sales managers should stress four principles in using MBO:

a. *Open communication* – Only a free exchange of views between sales manager and salesperson will result in realistic future commitments and agreement on specific actions needed to achieve goals and objectives.

b. *Mutual participation and agreement* – The salesperson must be an uninhibited, full participant in the MBO process with the sales manager, so that there is mutual understanding and agreement on objectives, plans, and performance evaluation.

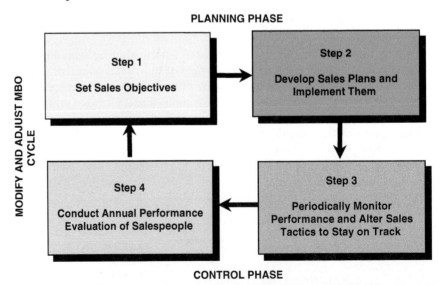

FIGURE 14.6 The MBO Cycle for sales force performance evaluation.

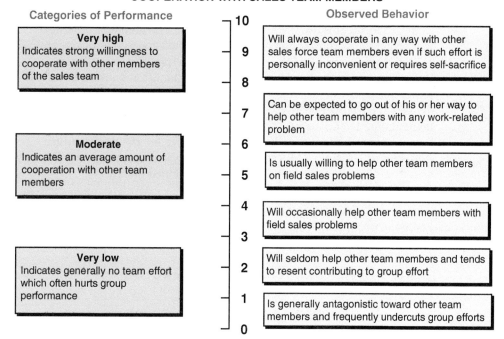

FIGURE 14.7 Behaviorally anchored rating scale.

c. **Coinciding goals** – Personal goals of the individual salesperson must be integrated with the overall goals of the organization so they are mutually reinforcing.

d. **Rewards for performance** – High-performing salespeople ought to be rewarded through public recognition as well as increased financial compensation. Public recognition enhances the value of the reward for high-achieving individuals and generally helps inspire other salespeople to do better.

4. **Behaviorally anchored rating scales.** Many rating systems attempt to overcome their inherent limitations by asking the sales manager to justify extremely high or low ratings. But this requirement tends to cause managers to avoid using scale extremes, resulting in a clustering of ratings. Another approach is to use a behaviorally anchored rating scale (BARS), shown in Figure 14.7. The BARS concentrates on measuring behaviors key to performance the individual salesperson can control. Consideration of specific behaviors also allows different sales managers to arrive at more consistent and objective evaluations, since the rating factors have similar interpretations.[39]

There are four basic steps to construct a sales-oriented BARS:

a. **Identify critical incidents**. Sales managers, salespeople, and customers describe specific critical incidents of effective and ineffective sales performance behavior and provide an actual example. These critical incidents are then condensed by the sales manager into a smaller number of performance categories. Some studies have obtained over a hundred critical incidents for a sales job before reducing them to about 10 sales performance dimensions.

b. **Refine critical incidents into performance dimensions**. The sales managers and salespeople who are developing the performance appraisal analyze the reduced set of critical incidents and then refine them into a still smaller set of performance dimensions – usually 5–12 – defined in general terms.

The critical incidents are then provided to another knowledgeable group of salespeople, who assign the incidents to appropriate performance dimensions. An incident is usually retained for the final BARS if 60% or more of the second sales group assign it to the same dimension as the first group.

c. ***Rate the effectiveness of the described behaviors.*** The second sales group rates the behavior described in the critical incidents as to how accurately it represents performance on the dimension, usually on a scale of 0–10. Incidents that have the lowest standard deviations (indicating greater agreement among raters) are kept for the final BARS.

d. ***Select a set of incidents as behavioral anchors for the performance dimension***. The final BARS consists of vertical scales, one for each dimension to be evaluated, anchored by the 6 or 8 retained incidents.

Although a true behavioral anchored rating scale takes time to develop, it is usually worth the extra effort because it allows for more precise, objective, and consistent ratings of salesperson by different sales managers.

Performance Evaluation Comparisons Between Salespeople

Many rating systems force sales managers to assign an overall score to each salesperson for comparison with other salespeople. Various formats have been used for such comparisons for salespeople, for example:

Compared to other salespeople I know doing the same job, this salesperson's performance is:

[ ]   Not quite as strong as most others
[ ]   About equal to most others
[ ]   Stronger than most others
[ ]   Far superior to most others

Comparison rating enables the sales manager to call all his or her salespeople "outstanding," even though some are more outstanding than others. A more direct comparison is rank ordering of all salespeople. Large sales organizations often gather several evaluations from different sales supervisors and managers for each salesperson. However, because each evaluator has his or her own tendency to be tougher or easier than other sales supervisors in rating salespeople, it is difficult to compare salespeople doing essentially the same job across sales districts. One way to minimize rater bias is to consider prior evaluations of each rater. In Table 14.8(a), first-year salesperson Ruth Saworski has been evaluated by five different sales superiors with an overall average rating of 80. As a matter of policy, the company has set 80 as the standard or average rating for salespeople. In Table 14.8(b), Ruth has been compared with four other first-year salespeople who are doing essentially the same work but have been rated by different sales supervisors. This comparison indicates that Ruth is about average in performance. But when we look at all others rated by the same sales supervisors and normalized to the company standard score in Table 14.8(c), Ruth is really a *below-average* performer. Her weighted normalized rating (which gives higher weight to raters who have considerably more prior ratings) is only 72.88, compared to the company's standard average rating of 80.

Comparisons like this provide for more overall objectivity of ratings by comparing performances based on normalized or standardized assessments. It prevents raters from unfairly inflating the ratings of their own people because their individual ratings establish a pattern to be used in normalization. In other words, each individual rating assigned by a sales manager is compared to his or her average rating.

TABLE 14.8

Evaluations of Salesperson Ruth Saworski

(A) Ratings of Ruth Saworski by different sales supervisors and managers

Rating	Rated by
80	John Becker, Assistant Sales Supervisor
85	Melinda Rao, Sales Supervisor
75	Kathy O'Shannon, Assistant Sales Manager
80	Andrew Rumanski, Sales Manager
80	Donovan James , Regional Sales Manager

80 = Composite Rating

(B) Comparison of first-year salespeople

Composite ratings	Ranking	Salesperson
88	1	Kathy Donnelly
82	2	Richard Staubach
80	3	Ruth Saworski
78	4	Charles Bruno
72	5	Janelle DePass

(C) Relative evaluation for salesperson Ruth Saworski

Rating	Rated by	Number of prior ratings	Weight assigned rating	Rater's average rating	Simple normalized rating
80	Becker	4	1	80	80
85	Rao	8	1	85	80
75	O'Shannon	7	1	80	75
80	Rumanski	18	2	90	70
80	James	15	2	87	73

Simple normalized rating: = Rating + (Company Standard Rating − Rater's Average Rating). To illustrate for Rumanski, $80 + (80 − 90) = 70$.

Weighting factor = Weight assigned rater × Number of prior ratings. For example, for James $2 \times 15 = 30$. Total weighting factors = 85 or $(4 + 8 + 7 + 36 + 30)$

Weighted normalized rating = (Weighting Factor × Simple Normalized Rating) − (Weighting Factors). Thus, Ruth Saworski's weighted normalized rating would be figured as follows:

Becker	(4×80)	$320/85 =$	3.76
Rao	(8×80)	$640/85 =$	7.53
O'Shannon	(7×75)	$525/85 =$	6.18
Rumanski	(36×70)	$2520/85 =$	29.65
James	(30×73)	$2190/85 =$	25.76
		$6195/85 =$	**72.88** Weighted normalized rating for Ruth Saworski

Sales Force Performance Evaluation Bias

Regardless of the evaluation criteria or methods, sales manager bias inevitably creeps into the evaluation process. To err is indeed human. But besides generating ill will and low morale, bias can lead to litigation against the firm (and the sales manager) if it strays to illegal personnel practices. Numerous studies have uncovered various management biases or errors that occur during salesperson performance appraisals.[40] Sales managers' social perceptions and judgments are likely to produce the different kinds of biases or limitations that are identified in Table 14.9:[41]

TABLE 14.9

Limitations of Sales Force Performance Evaluation Systems

Stereotyping – A sales manager develops a belief about some group as a whole (such as women) and then applies that belief to a salesperson in that group without considering the salesperson as an individual.

Contrast error – A sales manager allows the impression formed of one salesperson to affect the evaluation of another.

Similar-to-me error – The sales manager more favorably evaluates salespeople who are more similar to them on certain characteristics (attitudes, beliefs, interests, race, gender, and other demographic characteristics).

First-impression error – The sales manager permits the first judgment about a salesperson to strongly affect subsequent evaluations, regardless of change that has occurred within the salesperson.

Leniency or harshness error – The sales manager rates the salesperson at the extremes of the rating continuum (poor to outstanding) on all job criteria.

Escalation of commitment error – The sales manager evaluates salespeople personally hired (or recommended hiring) more highly than she evaluates others.

Fundamental attribution error – The sales manager attributes salesperson performance to certain factors within that individual (such as ability, effort, and skill) rather than to situational factors (such as environment, competition, and luck).

Self-serving bias – The sales manager attributes salespeople's successes to their guidance while attributing salespeople's failures to their efforts.

Central tendency – Some sales managers may be reluctant to take a stand, so they rate salespeople near the middle of the scale on all rating factors. Thus, little distinction is made among salespeople, providing minimal information for compensation or promotion decisions.

Psychological resistance to negative evaluations – A few sales managers suffer emotional distress when providing negative evaluations to salespeople, so they tend to avoid making negative evaluations.

Political concerns – To look good themselves and avoid creating problems on their watch, some sales managers will avoid giving any rating that is not acceptable to the individual salesperson.

Fear of reprisal – Due to fear of reprisal for discriminating among employees, some sales managers are especially careful to avoid giving negative ratings to anyone who might take legal action.

Varying evaluation standards – Some sales managers have very high standards and rate harshly; others may be relatively lenient.

Interpersonal bias – The sales manager's personal likes and dislikes may influence evaluations of salespeople. The chemistry between two people may be poor, and resultant friction can lead to evaluation bias. Conversely, salespeople may use personal influence techniques with the sales manager to bias their evaluations upward.

Questionable personality traits – Although many rating forms include personality traits (such as enthusiasm, resourcefulness, or intelligence) as indicators of selling performance, there is little research evidence to support this approach.

Organization use – Sales managers often give higher ratings to salespeople when the evaluation is for compensation or promotion purposes because they want to keep their people happy and see them do well in comparison to other organizational units. When appraisals are mainly for personal development of subordinates, however, sales managers tend to be more objective and willing to point out areas needing improvement.

Recency bias – Some sales managers are influenced too much by recent performance when evaluating individual performance, so behavior earlier in the rating period is neglected.

No outcome focus – Too many rating systems seem to have questionable validity and limited value for directing the growth and development of salespeople. They tend to rely on rating factors believed to be related to performance, but fail to indicate how the salesperson might improve performance.[42]

Inadequate sampling of job activities – Some sales managers may not know about or adequately observe behavior of all the activities in a given salesperson's assignment. Thus, the evaluation fails to include all-important aspects of the job, or job tasks may be included that are not part of the current job.

Providing Feedback and Improving Sales Force Performance

Sales managers must provide prompt, explicit, and meaningful feedback to their salespeople if they are to improve performance; otherwise the performance evaluation process is short-circuited and provides limited value for the salesperson or the company. Most sales managers readily give positive feedback to salespeople who are performing well, but many are reluctant to provide candid feedback to those who are performing poorly. Yet, the poorer performing salespeople are most in need of feedback about how to improve performance.

Providing Feedback on Sales Force Performance Appraisals

Earning praise from the boss can bring an emotional boost for successful salespeople. Such formal recognition enhances self-esteem, self-confidence, and motivation, and can spur many salespeople to even higher accomplishments. It also can provide direction and guidelines for future behavior because it indicates to the effective performers what they are doing well.

Even the poor and marginal salesperson should be promptly informed of his or her progress, standing, and need for improvement. Sales managers frequently hesitate to dismiss an ineffective producer. They hope (usually in error) that the poor performer will leave voluntarily, or they are reluctant to throw away the investment they made in recruiting and training the salesperson, or they fear legal reprisal if they dismiss the individual. Caution is commendable, but once it's clear that a salesperson is unlikely to improve, termination should be prompt so the manager's efforts can be redirected toward developing higher achieving salespeople. Jack Welch, former CEO of General Electric (www.ge.com), did not tolerate poor performance; annual evaluations at GE weeded out the bottom 10% of managers as explained in Sales Management in Action Box 14.2.

Box 14.2 | Sales Management in Action 14.2

Grading Managerial Performance

Jack Welch, the former charismatic CEO of General Electric (www.ge.com) for over 30 years, insisted that his managers grade their subordinate managers as A, B, or C performers. Moreover, he demanded that the bottom 10% of all managers each year be fired, so any manager graded "C" was at risk of losing his or her job. In this GE evaluation system, A-rated managers were those who demonstrated the critical four Es: *energy, energize, edge* (toughness), *execute*. The C-rated managers were considered a drain on the organization sapping the strength of others. In Welch's view, it was demotivating for other managers to see poorly performing managers kept on the payroll.

Although these tough evaluations appeared to work well for GE, other CEO's found them difficult to copy in their own companies. For example, when Jacques Nasser, former CEO of Ford Motor Company (www.ford.com), adopted Welch's practice of rating managers A, B, and C, then firing the lowest rated 10%, he triggered a Ford management rebellion that was a factor in his termination as CEO.[43]

Sales managers should provide prompt appraisal feedback so that salespeople can know how they're doing and take timely measures to adjust their performance.

Sales managers (like other supervisors) use one of the following approaches to provide feedback:[44]

- **Tell and sell** – The sales manager discusses both the positive and negative aspects of the salesperson's performance, makes a case for the validity of the evaluation, and seeks to get the salesperson to commit to performance improvement.
- **Tell and listen** – The sales manager describes the strengths and weaknesses in the salesperson's performance, listens to the salesperson's reaction to the results, and counsels in a nondirective way.
- **Problem solving** – The salesperson evaluates his or her own performance and reviews it with the sales manager in relation to previously agreed-upon goals. This approach seeks solutions to performance difficulties rather than simply focusing on them.

All three approaches have merit, depending on the situation. But, the problem-solving alternative is preferable in most selling situations for several reasons. First, it takes a proactive stance. Rather than waiting for problems to arise then react accordingly, salespeople (in concert with their manager) can try to identify situations that may need special attention in the future and then draw up a plan of action to prepare for them. Second, given the dynamism of the selling environment, being future oriented and seeking to uncover potential problems and opportunities before they develop will provide salespersons with enhanced ability to adapt. And third, given that sales personnel often work alone, they must be able to diagnose a situation and take appropriate action in the absence of a sales manager. The problem-solving approach provides salespeople with this experience.

Implementing Corrective Actions for Improving Sales Force Performance

After making a detailed evaluation, management needs to implement corrective actions based on that performance appraisal. In this context, "An evaluation program is of little benefit unless management carries through to the final stage: action. Isolating weakness and strengths is not an end in itself, because problems are not self-correcting and benefits are not self-generating. Yet, no action following diagnosis is an action – one that implies that the situation cannot be improved. Such situations rarely occur."[45]

At times management may feel uncomfortable admitting that the company, rather than the salesperson, is at fault. For example, the selling goals may have been set arbitrarily. When the salesperson's performance is below expectations through no fault of his or her own, then the company clearly is the culprit. In such instances, sales managers should revise the policies and/or plans or the various strategies used in their implementation, or they can adjust the objectives or standards either up or down to make them more realistic. When the salesperson is the ultimate reason for the lack of success, then taking corrective action requires redirecting the salesperson's efforts, enhancing his or her personal development, and sometimes modifying the organizational procedures or methods of operation to enhance individual performance.[46]

Before the sales manager presents an appraisal, the sales subordinate should be making a self-evaluation based on the same performance criteria, including suggesting ways to improve.[47] When the sales manager and the salesperson meet, they compare evaluations, discuss and reconcile discrepancies in evaluation perceptions, identify strengths and weaknesses in sales performance, uncover reasons for the performance-standard variances, and take corrective action (reinforce the salesperson's strengths and try to eliminate or reduce weaknesses). The appraisal interview should be an informal, two-way exchange that focuses on the causes rather than the results of the performance. The salesperson should be permitted to react to each segment of the appraisal, to suggest modifications of ratings, to explain any unique circumstances, and to recommend methods for the salesperson and sales management together to improve the individual's performance. In many ways, the appraisal interview is the beginning of an MBO plan where the salesperson and sales management work together in developing a set of goals, including performance targets for the next selling period. A final step is establishing the means for reaching these goals through self-development activities, formal retraining, or field-related actions by the salesperson's immediate sales supervisor.

A truly constructive performance evaluation can go a long way toward overcoming the angst associated with the process. Rather than viewing the evaluation as a report card, the sales manager and salesperson should consider it a progress report that provides feedback on how the salesperson is doing and outlines the path forward to attaining desired goals.

Applying Emerging Perspectives in Twenty-First Century Sales Force Performance Evaluation

We now focus on three emerging perspectives on sales force performance evaluation and the important insights they offer. Each perspective offers important insights for the salesperson being evaluated as well as for the evaluator.

360-Degree Performance Appraisals

Traditional sales force performance evaluation has been a top-down process, with sales managers evaluating salesperson performance. But salespeople interact with various constituents, not just their managers. So an innovative method called 360-degree performance appraisal –shown in Figure 14.8 –systematically elicits information on a salesperson's skills, abilities, and behaviors from all internal and external constituents with whom the salesperson has ongoing contact – the sales manager, sales team peers, subordinates, other departmental coworkers, purchasing managers, and accounts payable managers. It also includes a salesperson self-assessment,[48] thus providing performance feedback from many different perspectives.[49]

Salespersons can select their appraisers, but to gather data honestly, all ratings are confidential. The data-gathering is both multidirectional and multidimensional, though this means it can also be expensive and time consuming. Generally, 360-degree performance appraisals are able to capture information that other evaluation methods can't.[50] For example, because this method elicits input from customers, sales managers can understand their needs and in the process make adjustments to better serve them. Input from a salesperson's peers can help the manager reassign team members as needed to resolve conflict and improve cooperation and harmony. The statistically pooled results of this appraisal system are a rich source of information. Salespeople can use the feedback to make improvements in areas where they are deficient with the aim of augmenting performance and thus facilitating their growth and career development.[51] To facilitate 360-degree sales force performance appraisals, sales managers can turn to companies, such as Huron Consulting (www.huronconsultinggroup.com), Grapevine Evaluations, Inc. (www.grapevineevaluations.com), 360 Degree Cloud Technologies (www.360degreecloud.com), and Explorance, Inc. (www.explorance.com) that specialize in conducting these types of assessments. Alternatively, they can enroll in training seminars offered by companies such as Sales Training America, Inc. (www.salestrainingamerica.com) to learn how this innovative performance appraisal technique can boost company performance.

Although 360-degree performance evaluations have not supplanted traditional top-down assessments, they're gaining popularity. They fit well with flattening organizational structures, greater empowerment of employees, and working in teams, which are discussed next.

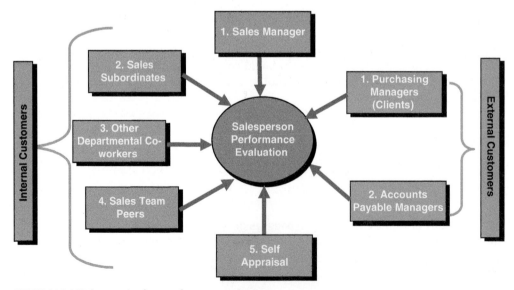

FIGURE 14.8 360-degree sales force performance evaluations.

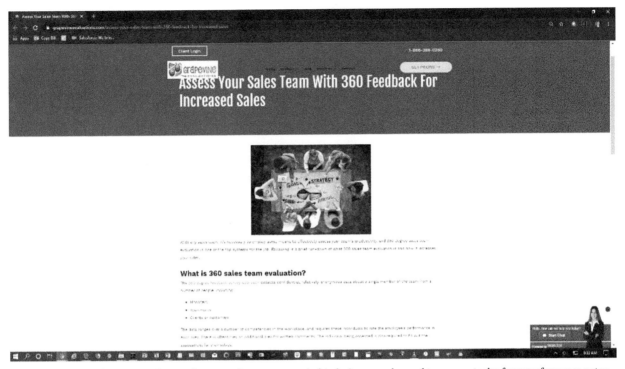

To learn more about how innovative 360-degree performance appraisal techniques can be used to augment sales force performance potential, sales managers can enroll in training seminars offered by firms, such as Grapevine Evaluations, Inc.
Source: https://www.grapevineevaluations.com/assess-your-sales-team-with-360-feedback-for-increased-sales.

Performance Appraisals of Team Selling

Appraising an individual salesperson's performance is a challenge; trying to evaluate members of a sales team, as a team and as individuals, can be even more complex. Problems include the use of systems that were established for individual evaluations, the difficulty of distinguishing between individual salesperson and group output, the need to customize performance measures to the type of team, and the problems of measuring inputs from cross-functional team members.[52]

Just like individual appraisal, team performance evaluation starts with selecting the relevant performance criteria and assessment methods. Both sales managers and team members should be part of the process. Some firms use a matrix that requires sales managers to identify the critical tasks of each team member, the relative importance of individual and group performance on each task, and the actual performance level on each task. Other companies ask each team member to rate all the other members on several critical performance dimensions, such as teamwork, leadership, productivity, and team relations. The sales manager then merges the ratings from all team members and arrives at a composite picture of team performance.

Performance Review Ranking System

Another recent trend is performance review ranking,[53] used by several firms that include Cisco Systems (www.cisco.com), Intel (www.intel.com), Hewlett-Packard (www.hp.com), and Microsoft (www.microsoft.com).[54] Sales managers evaluate each of their salespeople by *ranking* them on multiple performance dimensions using a scale, such as A = "excellent," B = "above average," C = "average," and so on.

Another approach is to place salespeople in performance categories such as the top 20%, the middle 70%, and the bottom 10%. In so doing, firms like General Electric (www.ge.com) have created meritocracies. How? In the words of former CEO Jack Welsh: "By rewarding stars [top performers] in an "outsized way that is soul-satisfying and financially satisfying; by developing the middle 70% with training and coaching; and the bottom 10% that have neither good results nor good behaviors are 'shown the door'."[55] The proponents of this system state that by moving out the bottom performers, managers can make room for new talent.[56] Although this method imposes a high degree of standardization, comparability, and discriminability, it has a poor standing on the remaining five features of performance appraisal techniques we discussed earlier. It is often based on subjective evaluations and can produce skewed results.[57]

In this chapter, we have discussed different concepts, approaches, and procedures for conducting sales force performance evaluations. Given the wide variety of market situations, company goals, and sales force compositions, there is no one best way to always perform this essential sales management function. Therefore, it is up to the sales manager to assess the overall sales environment and determine the approach that seems to work best for evaluating and improving the performance of his or her particular sales force.

Chapter Summary

1. **Carry out the sales force performance evaluation process using the outcome-based, behavior-based, and professional development measures.** Stages in the sales force performance appraisal process include: (1) establish sales force goals and objectives; (2) develop the sales plan; (3) set sales force performance standards; (4) allocate resources and sales force efforts; (5) measure sales force performance against set standards, that is, conduct the sales force performance evaluation process; and (6) providing feedback on sales force performance appraisals, and implement corrective actions plan to improve sales force performance. Three categories of evaluation criteria for assessing salesperson effectiveness are: (1) outcome-based measures, (2) behavior-based measures, and (3) professional development measures. Outcome-based measures can be separated into sales efforts, sales results and profitability indices. Sales efforts include such measures as number of sales calls made, selling expenses as a percentage of sales volume, and number of service calls. Sales results include measures, such as number of orders obtained, dollar sales volume, number of new accounts, and collections of accounts receivable. Profitability indices include net profit contribution, and performance as measured by financial/economic indicators, such as return on investment, return on sales, return on assets, and return on assets managed. Behavior-based outcomes include sales-related activities, such as customer relations, territory management, report preparation and timely submission, product knowledge, and personal characteristics. Successful sales organizations usually employ a mixture of quantitative and qualitative performance standards. Competence assessment, which tries to determine the characteristics needed to do a job rather than the specific tasks of the job, has been successfully used to select high-achieving salespeople. Professional development measures for assessing sales force performance include professional selling skills, professional knowledge, and personal characteristics.

2. **Develop different types of sales goals and objectives for preparing the sales plan.** After establishing long-run sales goals, the sales manager can focus on

the shorter-run, more quantifiable targets, called sales objectives, that should be aligned to the company's goals and objectives. For example, these goals may be to become the most service-oriented sales force in the industry or to increase profitability on sales by 10%. If these sales goals and objectives are not communicated to salespeople, they can become little more than "wish lists" without the organizational commitment needed for achievement. In essence, the sales plan provides the detailed "road map" showing how to achieve sales goals and objectives. It includes four major parts: (1) situation analysis, (2) opportunities and problems, (3) action programs, and (4) performance evaluation systems.

3. **Establish sales force performance standards.** Performance standards are planned achievement levels the sales organization expects to reach at progressive intervals throughout the year. Ideally, there should be agreements between subordinate salespersons and sales managers as to what level of performance is to be acceptable in some future period and they should be formalized based on the detailed job description for the sales subordinate. In setting performance standards for the sales force, managers need to consider *efforts expended* as well as *results obtained*. Business-to-business sales may require several months of intense sales efforts before the prospective buyer makes a final decision. Thus, where there's a time lag between effort and tangible results, sales managers must use qualitative, as well as quantitative, measures in setting sales performance standards.

4. **Allocate resources and efforts through sales quotas.** There are four types of sales quotas: (1) sales volume, (2) financial, (3) activity, and (4) combination. The rationale to use a specific type of sales quota is largely based on the quantitative and qualitative sales goals a salesperson is expected to achieve in a given time frame. Three variants of volumes quotas are: (1) dollar-based sales volume quotas, (2) unit volume quotas, and (3) point quotas. Two categories of financial quotas are expense quotas and profit quotas. Activity quotas are measured by factors such as the number of prospects called on, number of demonstrations made, number of displays set up, and number of new accounts established. While combination quotas are used when management wants to control the performance of both the selling and nonselling activities of the sales force. These quotas generally use points as a common measuring tool to overcome the difficulty of evaluating the different units across quotas.

5. **Describe sales dashboards and their important to sales force management decision-making.** Like automobile dashboards that provide an overview of car functions such as speed, gas tank level, or various warning lights, a sales dashboard provides key information at a glance on critical sales performance metrics. Dashboards can be strategic, analytical, operational, or informational. Strategic dashboards support managers by providing overviews that help decision makers monitor the general health of operations based on overall measures of performance like sales volume and progress toward achieving sales forecasts. Analytical sales dashboards enable sales managers to obtain detailed breakouts of sales by market segments; while dashboards for monitoring sales operations show updates of current activities and events that are changing daily and may require quick, decisive managerial response. Informational sales dashboards can be used to view historical records and performance from various time periods to compare with current performance. In today's dynamic, intensely competitive markets with fast moving complex technologies and customer preferences, sales dashboards are essential for successful sales management.

6. **List the major steps in the sales force performance evaluation monitoring system (PEMS).** An effective performance evaluation monitoring

system has three stages: performance planning, performance appraisal, and performance review. Specific steps in the performance measurement and evaluation process include: (1) establish sales goals and objectives, (2) develop the sales plan, (3) set performance standards, (4) allocate resources and sales force efforts in implementing the sales plan, and (5) evaluate sales force performance and implement corrective actions, if needed.

7. **Understand how to provide feedback and evaluation in order to improve sales force performance.** Four widely used evaluation technique are: (1) descriptive statements, (2) graphic rating scales, (3) management by objectives (MBO), and (4) behaviorally anchored rating scales (BARS). Descriptive statements about a salesperson may be short responses to a series of specific criteria, such as job knowledge, territorial management, customer relations, personal qualities, or sales results. Two commonly employed devices in graphic rating scales are "semantic differential" and Likert-type scales. The semantic differential uses bipolar adjective extremes to anchor several scale segments. Likert-type scales provide descriptive anchors under each segment of the scale. MBO involves mutual goal setting that is devised by the sales manager and the sales representative, who jointly agree on the salesperson's specific goals or performance targets for the coming period. BARS, which concentrates on measuring behaviors key to performance that the individual salesperson can control, includes four basic steps: (1) identify critical incidents, (2) refine critical incidents into performance dimensions, (3) rate the effectiveness of the described behaviors, and (4) select a set of incidents as behavioral anchors for the performance dimension. Traditional performance evaluation systems have limitations, including the halo effect, central tendency, varying evaluation standards, psychological resistance to negative evaluations, recent performance bias, no outcome focus, inadequate sampling of job activities, political concerns, fear of reprisal, interpersonal bias, questionable personality traits, and the influence of special organizational use. Prompt evaluation feedback is provided to salespeople, so they can take measures to enhance their performance by improving their selling skills and ultimately their sales performance through sales training programs. In evaluations of salespeople made by different sales managers, the relative degrees of leniency or harshness across sales managers can be adjusted for fairness by "standardization or normalization," i.e., putting the ratings of all salespeople on the same relative scale.

8. **Apply twenty-first century sales force performance appraisal methods.** Current developments in the area of sales force performance appraisals include: (1) 360-degree performance perspectives, (2) performance evaluations of team selling, and (3) performance review ranking systems. Just as in evaluating individual sales force members, team performance evaluation involves selecting the relevant performance criteria and employing appropriate appraisal methods. The 360-degree performance appraisal process systematically elicits information on a salesperson's skills, abilities, and behaviors from various individuals with whom the salesperson is in ongoing contact – all internal and external constituents, including the sales manager, sales team peers, sales subordinates, other departmental coworkers, purchasing managers, and accounts payable managers. Also included is a self-assessment, thus providing appraisal from many different perspectives. Performance review ranking entails sales managers evaluating each of their salespeople by *ranking* them using multiple performance dimensions and then placing them in different performance categories using a scale (e.g., A = excellent performance, B = above-average performance, C = average performance, D = satisfactory performance, and E = sub-par performance).

Key Terms

Salesperson performance evaluation

Performance standards

Outcome-based performance measures

Behavior-based performance measures

Sales dashboard

Sales quota

Sales unit

Financial quotas

Expense quotas

Activity quotas

Combination quotas

Performance evaluation monitoring system (PEMS)

Management by objectives (MBO)

Behaviorally anchored rating scales (BARS)

360-degree performance appraisals

Notes

1. Plaksij, Z. (16 September 2019). 10 reasons why salespeople need CRM. www.superoffice.com/blog/why-sales-people-need-crm/ (accessed 19 October 2019); Holland, J. (29 May 2015). 3 reasons salespeople hate CRM systems. https://blog.hubspot.com/sales/reasons-salespeople-despise-crm-systems (accessed 19 October 2019); Marincic, D. (21 February 2018). The most important part of crm implementation for salespeople. *Modern Sales Strategies* (21 February 2008). www.azamba.com/2018/02/21/the-most-important-part-of-crm-implementation-for-salespeople-is-to-get-involved-early/ (accessed 12 October 2019).

2. Davidoff, D. (24 September 2018). 5 strategies to reverse your sales productivity problem. https://blog.hubspot.com/sales/productivity-tips-for-salespeople-to-streamline-your-day-slideshare (accessed 11 October 2019); 13 Proven ways to increase the productivity of your sales team (10 February 2020). https://spotio.com/blog/improve-sales-productivity/ (accessed 23 February 2020).

3. Signorelli, B. (7 August 2019). 10 things I wish I knew before becoming a sales manager. https://blog.hubspot.com/sales/things-i-wish-i-knew-before-becoming-a-sales-manager (accessed 9 October 2019); Trailer, B. and Dickie, J. (2006). Understanding what your sales manager is up against. *Harvard Business Review* (July–August): 48–55.

4. Schroeder, S. (10 May 2017). Four ways to succeed at marketing in the age of information overload. https://spinsucks.com/entrepreneur/marketing-information-overload/ (accessed 10 October 2019); Overmyer, K. (4 January 2020). Why information overload shouldn't be a big marketing concern. http://www.skyword.com/contentstandard/marketing/why-information-overload-shouldnt-be-a-big-marketing-concern/ (accessed 23 February 2020); Hunter, G.L. (2013). Information overload: guidance for identifying when information becomes detrimental to sales force performance. *Journal of Personal Selling & Sales Management* 24(2):91–100.

5. Kesari, B. (2014). Salesperson performance evaluation: a systematic approach to refining the sales force. *International Journal of Multidisciplinary Management Studies* 4(6): 49–66; Stancu, L. (8 July 2019) 12 tips for evaluating sales reps performance. https://blog.insidesales.com/sales-performance/evaluating-sales-reps-performance/ (accessed 8 July 2019); How to effectively evaluate your salespeople and help them get better results.

(2 February 2016). https://salesdrive.info/effectively-evaluate-salespeople-get-better-results/(accessed 16 October 2019).

6. Ramaswami, S.N. Srinivasan, S.S., and Gorton, S.A. (1997). Information asymmetry between salesperson and supervisor: postulates from agency and social exchange theories. *Journal of Personal Selling & Sales Management (Summer)* 17(3): 29–50; Tabarrok, A. and Cowen, T. (6 April 2016). The end of information asymmetry (except when we want it). www.eugenewei.com/blog/2015/4/16/the-end-of-information-asymmetry (accessed 16 October 2019).

7. Dando, K. (27 April 2016). Role clarity: 7 Ways to set crystal clear expectations with your team. www.business2community.com/leadership/role-clarity-7-ways-set-crystal-clear-expectations-team-01528676 (accessed 20 October 2019); Boucherie, P. (2 August 2017). How to define sales roles to ensure more success. www.securitysales.com/columns/define-sales-roles-success/ (accessed 14 October 2019); Threlfall, D. (22 November 2016). How to turn your lowest performing sales team member into a top selling machine. https://resources.datanyze.com/blog/how-to-improve-lowest-performing-sales-rep (accessed 11 October 2019); Altschuler, M. (2018). Reality check: you're probably a bad salesperson if you possess any of these 11 qualities. *Sales Hacker* (9 January). http://www.saleshacker.com/bad-salesperson-qualities/ (accessed 17 October 2019); Meincke, J. (28 August 2018). 6 Tips for conducting sales performance reviews. *CloserIQ*. www.google.com/search?client=firefox-b-1 d&q=how+to+conduct+a+negative+evaluation+of+a+salesperson (accessed 4 October 2019).

8. St. Clair, D.P. (May 2018). Mixed methods study of factors influencing business to business (B2B) sales performance: the role of design attitude. Doctoral dissertation at Weatherhead School of Management, Case Western Reserve University.

9. Meincke, J. (28 August 2018). 6 tips for conducting sales performance reviews *CloserIQ* https://blog.closeriq.com/2018/08/sales-performance-reviews/ (accessed 11 October 2019).

10. Milano, S. (6 August 2018). How to analyze sales data to increase profits. www.quill.com/blog/tutorials/how-to-analyze-sales-data-to-increase-profits.html (accessed 17 October 2019); Barstow, S.R. Sales & profitability analysis. https://smallbusiness.chron.com/sales-profitability-analysis-76858.html (accessed 19 October 2019).

11. Madhani, P.M. (15 April 2015). Managing sales force performance: behavior versus outcome measures. *Compensation & Benefits Review* https://journals.sagepub.com/doi/abs/10.1177/0886368715581959?journalCode=cbrb (accessed 12 October 2019); Anderson, E. and Oliver, R.L. (1987). Perspectives on behavior-based versus outcome-based sales force control systems. *Journal of Marketing (October)* 51: 76–88.

12. Barker, A.T. (15 December 2014). Behavior-based and outcome-based sales force control systems: evidence from Canadian firms. https://link.springer.com/chapter/10.1007%2F978-3-319-13078-1_46 (accessed 21 October 2019); Rosen, K. (24 August 2019). Your salespeople hate being coached and why sales managers resist coaching them. http://keithrosen.com/2019/04/your-salespeople-hate-being-coached-and-sales-managers-resist-coaching-them/ (accessed 12 October 2019); Oliver, R.L. and Anderson, E. (1995). Behavior- and outcome-based sales control systems: evidence and consequences of pure-form and hybrid governance. *Journal of Personal Selling & Sales Management* (Fall)15(4):1–16.

13. Frost, A. (26 February 2019) The 5 most important sales performance metrics every rep and managers should track. https://blog.hubspot.com/sales/sales-performance-metrics (accessed 19 October 2019); Fernandes, P. (12 January 2018). 14 Important traits successful salespeople share. *Business News Daily* (13 October 2016). www.businessnewsdaily.com/4173-personality-traits-successful-sales-people.html (accessed 20 October 2019); Churchill, G.A., Ford, N.M., Hartley, S.W., and Walker, O.C. (1985). The determinants of salesperson performance. *Journal of Marketing Research* (May) 22(2): 103–118.

14. Bhattacharyya, B. (8 November 2019). 10 Essential characteristics of highly successful salespeople. *Sales Hacker* (25 June 2017). http://www.saleshacker.com/common-traits-successful-sales-people/ (accessed 10 October 10, 2019); Jackson, D.W., Schlachter, J.L., and Wolfe, W.G. (1995). Examining the bases utilized for evaluating salespeople's performance. *Journal of Personal Selling & Sales Management* (Fall) 15: 57–66.

15. Fatima, Z. (2015). Behavior based sales force control system for most effective sales organizations: a review based article. *Asian Journal of Marketing* 9(1): 1–11; Oliver, R.L. and Anderson, E. (1995). Behavior- and outcome-based sales control systems: evidence and consequences of pure-form and hybrid governance. *Journal of Personal Selling & Sales Management* (Fall) 15(4): 1–16.

16. Kesari, B. (2014). Salesperson performance evaluation: a systematic approach to refining the sales force. *International Journal of Multidisciplinary Management Studies (June)* 4(6); Morris, M.H., Davis, D.L., Allen, J.W., Avila, R.A., and Chapman, J. (1991). Assessing the relationships among performance measures, managerial practices, and satisfaction when evaluating the sales force: a replication and extension. *Journal of Personal Selling & Sales Management* (Summer) 11(3): 25–36.

17. Sources of appraisal information – sales management. http://www.wisdomjobs.com/e-university/sales-management-tutorial-309/sources-of-appraisal-information-10278.html (accessed 10 October 2019); Ahuja, B. (2017). Sales force evaluation and control, *Marketing* (10 April). www.slideshare.net/BHOOMIAHUJA1/sales-force-evaluation-and-control (accessed 11 October 2019); Hunter, G.L. (2004). Information overload: guidance for identifying when information becomes detrimental to sales force performance. *Journal of Personal Selling & Sales Management* 24(2): 91–100.

18. Velcu-Laitinen, O. and Yigitbasioglu, O.M. (2012). The use of dashboards in performance management: evidence from sales managers. *The International Journal of Digital Accounting Research* 12: 39–58.

19. Davenport, T.H. and Harris, J.G. (2009). *Competing on Analytics: The New Science of Winning*. Harvard Business School Press.

20. The perfect sales dashboard should have these 12 sales metrics. https://www.salesforce.com/products/sales-cloud/resources/sales-dashboard-tips/# (accessed 11 December 2019).

21. Flores, L. (2014). Digital dashboards: a tool for managing the effectiveness of digital marketing and integrated marketing communication, in *How to Measure Digital Marketing* (London: Palgrave Macmillan).

22. The perfect sales dashboard should have these 12 sales metrics. https://www.salesforce.com/products/sales-cloud/resources/sales-dashboard-tips/# (accessed 11 December 2019).

23. Davenport, T.H. and Harris, J.G. (2009). *Competing on Analytics: The New Science of Winning*. Harvard Business School Press.

24. Khatri, V. (2016). Managerial work in the realm of the digital universe: the role of the data triad. *Business Horizons* 59(6): 673–688.

25. Bauer, E. (2 November 2017). What are sales quotas (and why does your sales team need them)? http://www.google.com/search?client=firefox-b-1-d&q=sales+quotas (accessed 13 October 2019); Prater, M. (28 March 2019). The ultimate guide to setting sales quotas. https://blog.hubspot.com/sales/sales-quotas (accessed 12 October 2019).

26. Kulbyte, T. (28 January 2020). Sales quota: a step-by-step process for hitting your sales targets. Your guide on how to improve sales quota attainment (23 February 2020). www.superoffice.com/blog/sales-quota/ (accessed 19 October 2019); Rogers, W. (13 November 2013). 12 tips to improve sales performance. http://www.salesforce.com/blog/2014/11/12-tips-to-improve-sales-performance-gp.html (accessed 14 October 2019).

27. Zoltners, A.A., Sinha, P., and Lorimer S.E. (2019) 7 Ways sales teams can set better goals. *Harvard Business Review* (June). https://hbr.org/2019/06/7-ways-sales-teams-can-set-better-goals (accessed 19 October 2019); Harris, E.G., Mowen, J.C., and Brown, T.J. (2005). Re-examining salesperson goal orientations: personality influencers, customer orientation, and work satisfaction. *Journal of the Academy of Marketing Science* 33(1): 19–35; Silver, L.S., Dwyer, S., and Alford, B. (2006). Learning and performance goal orientation of salespeople revisited: the role of performance-approach and performance-avoidance orientations. *Journal of Personal Selling & Sales Management* 26(1): 27–38; Fang, E., Evans, K.R., and Zou, S. (2005). The moderating effect of goal-setting characteristics on the sales control systems-job performance relationship. *Journal of Business Research* 58(9): 1214–1222.

28. Green, A. (28 December 2018). The duties and responsibilities of a sales supervisor. *Career Trend* (28 December 2018). https://careertrend.com/list-6546197-duties-responsibilities-sales-supervisor.html; Childers, T.L., Dubinsky, A.J., and Skinner, S.J. (1990). Leadership substitutes as moderators of sales supervisory behavior. *Journal of Business Research* 21(4): 368–382.

29. Malek, S., Sarin, S., and Jaworski, B.J. (2018). Sales management control systems: review, synthesis, and directions for future exploration. *Journal of Personal Selling & Sales Management* 38(1): 30–35; Fang, E., Evans, K.R., and Landry, T.D. (2005). Control systems' effect on attributional processes and sales outcomes: a cybernetic information-processing perspective. *Journal of the Academy of Marketing Science* 33(4): 553–574.

30. Marsh, B. (30 November 2016). Why managing sales performance means measuring activities. *SalesForce*. www.salesforce.com/blog/2016/11/managing-sales-performance-activities.html (accessed 10 October 2019); Schwepker, C.H.Jr.,, and Good, D.J. (2004). Understanding sales quotas: an exploratory investigation of consequences of failure. *Journal of Business & Industrial Marketing* 19(1): 39–48.

31. MacDonald, S. (31 January 2020). 3 B2B sales strategies proven to win more customers. http://www.superoffice.com/blog/b2b-sales/ (accessed 23 February 2020); Clary, S.D. (8 February 2019). Three selling strategies to empower your salespeople. www.forbes.com/sites/forbesbusinessdevelopmentcouncil/2019/02/08/three-selling-strategies-to-empower-your-salespeople/#22c56ac85d0b (accessed 11 October 2019).

32. Bauer, E. (2 November 2017). What are sales quotas (and why does your sales team need them)? http://www.propellercrm.com/blog/sales-quotas (accessed 13 October 2019).

33. How to set goals and objectives for your business in 2019, *Business* (2 January 2019), http://www.business.gov.au/news/how-to-set-goals-and-objectives-for-your-business (accessed 14 October 2019); Prater, M. (28 March 2019). The ultimate guide to setting sales quotas. https://blog.hubspot.com/sales/sales-quotas (accessed 21 October 2019).

34. Kudo, E. (6 June 2019). Goal-setting collaboration: a how to guide for managers and employees. www.trustradius.com/buyer-blog/goal-setting-collaboration-guide (accessed 11 October 2019); Patel, S. (2 May 2018). How to set effective sales goals for your sales team. https://blog.mailshake.com/sales-goals/ (accessed 20 October 2019).

35. Kesari, B. (2014). Salesperson performance evaluation: a systematic approach to refining the sales force. *International Journal of Multidisciplinary Management Studies* 4(6): 49–66.

36. Sondhi, P. (21 April 2018). 5 Steps to an effective performance evaluation system. www.entrepreneur.com/article/312324 (accessed 14 October 2019); Crabtree, C. (27 March 2019). How to evaluate sales performance to improve your team's success. https://brooksgroup.com/sales-training-blog/how-evaluate-sales-performance-improve-your-team%E2%80%99s-success (accessed 20 October 2019). Muczyk, J.P. and Gable, M. (1987). Managing sales performance through a comprehensive performance appraisal system. *Journal of Personal Selling & Sales Management* 7(2): 41–52.

37. Schwartz, G. The best way to evaluate your sales reps: move past the numbers. www.surveymonkey.com/curiosity/best-way-evaluate-sales-reps-move-past-numbers/ (accessed 21 October 2019); Patton, W.E. and King, R.H. (1985). The use of human judgment models in evaluating sales force performance. *Journal of Personal Selling & Sales Management* 12(2): 1–14.

38. Altschuler, M. Reality check: you're probably a bad salesperson if you possess any of these 11 qualities. www.saleshacker.com/bad-salesperson-qualities/ (accessed 2 October 2019); Stancu, L. (8 July 2019). 12 tips for evaluating sales reps performance. https://blog.insidesales.com/sales-performance/evaluating-sales-reps-performance/ (accessed 22 October 2019); Atkinson, T. and Koprowski, R. (2006). Finding the weak links. *Harvard Business Review* (July–August): 22–23.

39. Klieger, D. M., Kell, H.J., Rikoon, S., Burkander, K.N., Bochenek, J.L., and Shore, J.R. (2018). Development of the Behaviorally Anchored Rating Scales for the Skills Demonstration and Progression Guide. *ETS Research Report Series* (December):18-24. https://onlinelibrary.wiley.com/doi/full/10.1002/ets2.12210 (accessed 21 October 2019;

40. Mayhew, R. How to eliminate bias and error in performance appraisals. https://smallbusiness.chron.com/eliminate-bias-error-performance-appraisals-11187.html (accessed 20 October 2019); Davis, K.F. (22 November 2017). Eliminate the bias in sales rep evaluations. https://toplineleadership.com/eliminate-bias-sales-rep-evaluations/ (accessed 23 October 2019). Marshall, G.W. and Mowen, J.C. (1993). An experimental investigation of the outcome bias in salesperson performance evaluations. *Journal of Personal Selling & Sales Management* 13(3): 31–48.

41. Poddar, S. (19 January 2015). Biases in performance management: how to overcome them? www.linkedin.com/pulse/biases-performance-management-how-can-overcome-sarajit-poddar-hrmp (accessed 10 October 2019); Gentry, J.W., Mowen, J.C., and Tasaki, L. (1991). Salesperson evaluation: a systematic structure for reducing judgmental biases. *Journal of Personal Selling & Sales Management* 11(2): 27–38; Ernst, R. (3 July 2019). Seven tips for identifying and managing behavior bias in performance evaluations (accessed 21 February 2020). www.forbes.com/sites/forbeshumanresourcescouncil/2019/07/03/seven-tips-for-identifying-and-managing-behavioral-bias-in-performance-evaluations/#339354337472 (accessed 23 October 2019).

42. See Lunenburg, F.C. (2012). Performance appraisal: methods and rating errors. *International Journal of Scholarly Academic Intellectual Diversity* 14(1): 1–9; Morris, M.H., LaForge, R.W., and Allen, J.A. (1994). Salesperson failure: definition, determinants, and outcomes. *Journal of Personal Selling & Sales Management* 14(1): 1–15; Marshall, G.W. and Mowen, J.C. (1993). An experimental investigation of the outcome bias in salesperson performance evaluations. *Journal of Personal Selling & Sales Management* 13(3): 31–47.

43. Slater, R. (2004). *Jack Welch on Leadership*, (New York: McGraw-Hill); Welch, J. and Welch, S. (2005). *Winning* (New York: Harper Collins). Gardner, O. (22 May 2017). Why Fields' departure echoes Nasser's past. http://www.autonews.com/article/20170522/BLOG06/170529983/why-fields-departure-echoes-nasser-s-past

(accessed 17 October 2019); Beard, B. (16 March 2016). 3 management mistakes I made firing underperforming sales reps. www.google.com/search?client=firefox-b-1-d&q=fire+underperforming+salespeople (accessed 20 October 2019); Nisen, M. (13 August 2013). Why GE had to kill its performance reviews after more than three decades. https://qz.com/428813/ge-performance-review-strategy-shift/ (accessed 19 October 2019).

44. Gallagher, B.J. (24 January 2019). The dos and don'ts of performance reviews, *AMA Articles*. http://www.amanet.org/articles/the-dos-and-donts-of-performance-reviews/ (accessed 11 October 2019); Lucero, K. (24 June 2019). Sales performance review best practices. http://www.xactlycorp.com/blog/sales-performance-review-best-practices/ (accessed 12 October 2019).

45. Mayhew, R. The importance of a follow-up evaluation. https://smallbusiness.chron.com/importance-followup-evaluation-75064.html (accessed 13 October 2019).

46. Kouloupoulos, T. (25 February 2018). Performance reviews are dead. Here's what you should do instead. www.inc.com/thomas-kouloupoulos/performance-reviews-are-dead-heres-what-you-should-do-instead.html (accessed 19 October 2019).

47. How to write and survive your self-assessment and performance review (19 September 2019). www.smartsheet.com/performance-review-self-assessment (accessed 13 October 2019).

48. Osing, R. (4 February 2015). Self-assessment: are you a sales standout? https://salespop.net/sales-professionals/self-assessment-are-you-a-sales-standout/ (accessed 18 October 2019).

49. Handrick, L. (20 December 2017). 360 Degree feedback: how it works & should you do https://fitsmallbusiness.com/360-degree-feedback-performance-review/ (accessed 21 October 2019); 8 intelligent questions for evaluating your sales reps performance. http://www.inc.com/barrett-riddleberger/8-intelligent-questions-for-evaluating-your-sales-reps-performance.html (accessed 22 October 2019).

50. Heathfield, S.M. (7 June 2018). Pros & cons of 360-degree feedback. http://www.thebalancecareers.com/360-degree-feedback-information-1917537 (accessed 12 October 2019); Toegel, G. and Conger, J. (2003). 360-Degree assessment: time for reinvention. *Academy of Management Learning and Education* 2(3):297–311.

51. Warren, L. (15 August 2018). Improv classes and no-phone time: 6 salespeople share tips for self-improvement. http://www.builtinnyc.com/2018/08/15/sales-tips-self-improvement (accessed 14 October 2019); Tracy, B. How to become a top salesperson by moving out of your comfort zone and building self-confidence.

http://www.briantracy.com/blog/sales-success/how-to-become-a-top-salesperson-by-moving-out-of-your-comfort-zone-and-learning-to-believe-in-yourself-self-confidence/ (accessed 22 October 2019).

52. Cherry, P. (7 March 2019). What good managers know about holding their sales team accountable. https://pbresults.com/Sales-Blog/good-managers-know-holding-sales-team-accountable/ (accessed 21 October 2019); Brennan, J. (27 March 2019). Evaluate your sales team's performance. http://www.advisorycloud.com/board-of-directors-articles/evaluate-your-sales-teams-performance (accessed 23 October 2019).

53. Zoltners, A.A., Sinha, P.K., and Lorimer, S.E. (2011). How to manage force sales rankings. *Harvard Business Review* (July). https://hbr.org/2011/07/forced-rankings-salespeople (accessed 20 October 2019); Hymowitz, C. (2001). Ranking systems gain popularity but have many staffers riled. *Wall Street Journal* (15 May 2001): B1; Gupta, G. (23 May 2018). Are you still using forced rankings? Please stop. http://www.forbes.com/sites/johnkotter/2018/05/23/are-you-still-using-force-rankings-please-stop/#153fccbc334d (accessed 22 October 2019).

54. Hassell, D. Rethinking your annual performance review process. http://www.15five.com/performance-review/ (accessed 15 October 2019); The 5 ways your performance review is failing Millennials (accessed 19 October 2019).

55. Welch, J. and Welch, S. (2006). The case for 20-70-10. *Business Week* (2 October 2006): 108; Welch, J. and Welch, S. (2006). Send the jerks packing. *Business Week* (13 November 2006):136; Grant, K. (14 November 2017). How to fire people like former general electric CEO Jack Welch. http://www.thestreet.com/story/14315785/1/how-to-fire-people-like-jack-welch.html (accessed 20 October 2019); Young, C. (17 February 2014). Why you need to practice "rank and yank" to remove C salespeople. http://www.therainmakergroupinc.com/blog/bid/157044/why-you-need-to-practice-rank-and-yank-to-remove-c-salespeopl (accessed 23 October 2019).

56. Welch, J. and Welch, S. (2006). The case for 20-70-10. *Business Week* (2 October2006): 108; Schwantes, M. (5 June 2017). Here's how good managers give bad employees feedback. http://www.inc.com/marcel-schwantes/heres-how-good-managers-give-bad-employees-feedback.html (accessed 14 October 2019).

57. Hymowitz, C. (2001). Ranking systems gain popularity but have many staffers riled. *Wall Street Journal* (15 May, 2001): B1; Walters, R. (14 April 2018). Guest blog: why Jack Welch's 10% rule is 100% ridiculous. https://creative.artisantalent.com/why-jack-welchs-10-rule-is-100-ridiculous (accessed 21 October 2019).

Chapter Review Questions

1. Identify outcome-based, behavior-based and professional development measures that could be used to evaluate sales force performance evaluations. In your opinion, which of these three categories of measures are most important for evaluating salespeople? Explain. [LO 1]

2. Discuss the multiple purposes behind employing sales quotas. [LO 4]

3. What are the features of an effective quota plan? [LO 4]

4. Identify and describe the four major types of sales quotas. Be sure to describe the different kinds of sales

volume quotas and financial quotas. In your opinion, which of these types of quotas can be effective for evaluating salespeople? Explain? [LO 4]

5. Name the three stages in a performance evaluation monitoring systems (PEMS), and describe the sales manager's role in each stage. In your work experience, what procedure or process has your superior used to evaluate you? [LO 5]

6. Identify and explain the characteristics different types of performance appraisal techniques should possess. [LO 5]

7. Explain the key features of the four widely used types of evaluation technique that include: (a) descriptive statements, (b) graphic rating scales, (c) behaviorally anchored rating scales, and (d) management by objectives. [LO 5]

8. Identify and describe the various limitations of sales force evaluation systems. Do you have any personal experience with these limitations as either a rater or a ratee? Describe your experience. [LO 6]

9. Explain the necessity of providing feedback on sales force performance appraisals. [LO 6]

10. Describe the key features, advantages, and disadvantages of 360-degree performance appraisals. Can a 360-degree performance appraisal help reduce appraisal bias? Why do you think this form of performance evaluation is being increasingly used? Explain. [LO 7]

11. Describe how a performance review ranking system can be used in evaluating sales force performance? [LO 7]

Online Exercise

Use the Internet to access SlideTeam (https://search .slideteam.net/powerpoint/Sales-Performance-Review), Hubspot (https://blog.hubspot.com/sales/ sales-performance-review-template) and other similar knowledge exchange websites. Based on your research, develop a comprehensive sales force performance appraisal checklist.

Role-Play Exercise

Appraising Salesperson Performance

Situation As a district sales manager, you conduct semiannual performance evaluations with each of your salespeople. You have been using the MBO approach to setting various annual quotas with each salesperson. Last year, all the salespeople agreed readily on the quotas that you jointly set. One of your salespeople, Raj Srinivasan, is not on track to reach several of his assigned quotas this year. Normally, in the semiannual performance of a salesperson, you jointly explore ways to take corrective action to get back on track toward achieving the assigned yearly quotas. After only a few minutes into his evaluation, Raj interrupts to complain that his sales quotas were set too high this year and that it is not possible for him to achieve them.

Role-Play Participants and Assignments District sales manager: You are somewhat irritated by Raj's complaint about his quotas being set too high because he agreed to them and jointly signed the letter establishing them for the year. Nevertheless, Raj has been an above-average salesperson for nearly five years at your company, so you're willing to patiently listen to his reasoning.

Raj: You are upset because you're fearful that you won't reach some of you assigned quotas for the year. At this six-month evaluation point, you're lagging significantly behind on some of the quotas. One of your complaints is that your territory was reduced at the beginning of the year when a new salesperson was hired. Several salespeople besides you were asked to give up a small part of their territories to create a new territory for the incoming salesperson. You feel that this reduction in territory has hurt your achievement of some quotas.

In-Basket Exercise

You were just hired as the national sales manager for a large retail organization, and your first task is to assess the company's salesperson evaluation system. You've asked several of the sales managers how they currently evaluate their salespeople. They all have indicated that their sales reps are ranked according to quarterly sales volume and that raises are based on these rankings. All the sales managers seem to believe this system provides a fair and objective annual appraisal of salespeople, even though you know it has many limitations.

However, you suspect their apparent satisfaction with the current system may really reflect their desire to avoid the extra work required to revise it.

Write a diplomatic but firm memorandum to all your subordinate sales managers expressing why you think the current sales force evaluation system needs to be revised and updated. In a concluding paragraph, ask them to provide feedback on how to improve the salesperson evaluation system within three weeks. Perhaps, you can offer an award for the best proposal.

Ethical Dilemma

One of your subordinate sales managers has just turned in a highly negative performance evaluation for the only female member of her sales force by assigning her to the *unsatisfactory* performance category. Her evaluation of the 24-year-old saleswoman, who was hired out of college two years ago, seems to be largely subjective and provides very little quantitative or objective written narrative support. The evaluation does not mention any failure to reach an assigned quota, complaints from customers, lack of product knowledge, or any other performance negative. Instead, the evaluation describes the saleswoman as self-centered, flirtatious around the salesmen, flippant with office staff, and detrimental to employee morale. In reviewing this saleswoman's

quantitative and qualitative performance for the year, you note that she has met all her quotas and received several letters from customers praising her for outstanding service. You suspect that the sales manager may resent this young woman for some reason and want her removed from her sales force. You realize you're facing a dilemma that needs to be resolved promptly. On one side, the young saleswoman may leave if she receives this highly negative evaluation. While, on the other side, your subordinate sales manager may take a job with a competitor if she thinks you're not supportive of her evaluation of the saleswoman. You don't want to lose either person because both are performing well. How will you handle this delicate situation?

| CASE 14.1 | **PARKSUNGCO Electronics: Employee 360-Degree Review** |

PARKSUNGCO is a very successful company, a leader in the highly competitive consumer and industrial electronics industry. Top management attributes much of this success to the drive for continuous improvement existing within the company. Senior executives encourage an aggressive, results-oriented approach among employees.

To enact the company's continuous improvement philosophy, the human resources department recently introduced 360-degree feedback as a component of the performance evaluation system. A 360-degree feedback approach involves assessing employees based on information provided by their supervisor, by the people they work with, and by customers.

In addition, employees are asked to evaluate their own performance.

Input for the 360-degree feedback process is obtained using questionnaires tailored to the position of the person being evaluated. One example is the 360-Degree Feedback Questionnaire for sales representatives, shown in Table 1. It asks about specific factors such as assessing territory market potential, influencing and selling, and managing the territory, as well as about more generally applicable topics such as communicating and managing self-development. Once completed, questionnaires are returned to the human resources department where individual factors are scored and totaled.

TABLE 1

360-Degree Feedback Questionnaire

Directions: Please complete this questionnaire about the person named below. The results of the questionnaire will be combined with others into a confidential report to him or her. Only ratings by the supervisor/manager will be identified. All other ratings are anonymous. When you have completed this questionnaire please return it to the Human Relations Department in the envelope provided.

Name of person being assessed:

Name of person giving feedback:

Your relationship to person being assessed: __Self __Manager/Supervisor __Peer __Client

Directions	**Rating Scale**
Please **circle** the number that reflects your view.	**1** = Below expectations **2** = Meets expectations **3** = Exceeds expectations **NA** = Not applicable or don't know

1. *Assessing territory market potential, setting objectives, and developing territory marketing plans*

a. Analyzing sales and market data	1	2	3	NA
b. Setting sales and product support objectives	1	2	3	NA
c. Developing territory marketing plans	1	2	3	NA

2. *Managing the territory*

a. Maintaining customer records	1	2	3	NA
b. Preparing call plans	1	2	3	NA
c. Developing work plans	1	2	3	NA
d. Budgeting and controlling expenses	1	2	3	NA
e. Handling administrative work	1	2	3	NA

3. *Influencing and selling*

a. Maintaining relationships with key influential contacts	1	2	3	NA
b. Establishing productive relationships with customers and their staff	1	2	3	NA
c. Identifying and confirming customer needs	1	2	3	NA
d. Making effective sales presentations	1	2	3	NA
e. Handling objections and closing	1	2	3	NA
f. Implementing corporate policies	1	2	3	NA
g. Developing new business opportunities	1	2	3	NA

4. *Communicating and maintaining effective working relationships*

a. Maintaining productive relationships with sales manager	1	2	3	NA

b. Developing productive relationships with appropriate corporate staff	1	2	3	NA
c. Contributing to the development of a strong team effort in the organization	1	2	3	NA
5. *Managing self-development/acquiring product knowledge*	1	2	3	NA
a. Gaining and maintaining product knowledge	1	2	3	NA
b. Participating in development programs	1	2	3	NA
c. Evaluating and improving job skills	1	2	3	NA
d. Managing his/her own career development	1	2	3	NA
e. Keeping up with the latest technology	1	2	3	NA

Questionnaire results are then provided to the ratee's supervisor or manager, who shares them with the individual in an appraisal interview, when objective performance measures (e.g. meeting sales targets) are also discussed. In the interview, the salesperson presents an appraisal of his or her own performance (see Table 2) for the previous year. This system is used to evaluate performance and set targets or quotas, and it is a significant factor in determining bonuses at the end of the year.

TABLE 2

PARKSUNGCO Electronics: Salesperson Self-Appraisal Form

Your Self-Appraisal Form

Directions

As part of a review of performance being conducted in your division, you are asked to complete a self-appraisal of your performance. The subject matter should include an opinion of what you feel are your major strengths and weaknesses and your accomplishments in reaching your goals for the past year. If you have not met your goals, then provide explanations for not meeting goals. You should also define areas concerning your job on which you and your sales manager agree as well as areas where you feel you do not quite see eye to eye. Also, comment on what you think can be done to help you do a better job at PARKSUNGCO.

It is important to understand that the performance review session is a method that enables you and your manager not only to discuss your performance but also to agree on mutually acceptable goals and seek ways to meet your needs as well as those of the company. The session should not be considered an inquisition or fault-finding process. When you meet with your sales manager, be sure to freely discuss all matters pertaining to your performance and your job.

After your performance review, your sales manager will submit your self-appraisal form and 360-Degree Performance Appraisal, plus a summary of your discussion, to the Human Relations Department, which maintains a confidential file on your job performance at PARKSUNGCO. Remember that this session is designed to help you progress in this company. Its success depends on cooperation between you and your sales manager.

Strengths

1. _____
2. _____
3. _____
4. _____
5. _____

Weaknesses

1. _____
2. _____
3. _____
4. _____
5. _____

Objectives
(Met and not met. If not met, please explain.)

_____
_____
_____
_____
_____
_____
_____
_____
_____
_____
_____
_____
_____
_____

Hana Lee was hired by PARKSUNGCO three years ago, right after she graduated from college. In her initial sales training, Hana was one of the top performers and was identified as a future outstanding salesperson at PARKSUNGCO. During her first two years at PARKSUNGCO, the bonuses were marginal, but she accepted the situation because she viewed this period as one for learning and self-improvement. Hana has just finished her third year with PARKSUNGCO, and this time she is upset with her year-end bonus. She believes the past year was her best year yet and that she deserves a much larger bonus. Hana's 360-Degree Feedback Questionnaire from her sales manager was outstanding. She received a rating of 3 (Exceeds Expectations) on all items except 3f, 4a, and 4b. For these items, she received a rating of 2 (Meets Expectations). Her total score for the 360-Degree Feedback Questionnaire was 66. Hana also feels she did exceptionally well on her Self-Appraisal Form. All the goals she set for the year were met, and any weaknesses that were listed have been overcome. Everything seemed to go well during Hana's management appraisal interview, and her sales manager said that he was impressed with Hana's progress and performance. After talking with several of her close friends on PARKSUNGCO's sales force, however, Hana found that some of her peers with scores of 55–60 on the 360-Degree Feedback Questionnaire received similar or even higher yearly bonuses.

Questions

1. What are the reasons for Hana's unsatisfactory year-end bonus?

2. Do you see any weaknesses with PARKSUNGCO's sales force evaluation system? What are they? Comment on both the 360-Degree Appraisal Form and the Self-Appraisal Form.

3. Are there areas that need to be evaluated that are not included in PARKSUNGCO's 360-Degree Appraisal Form? If so, what are they? Should weights be assigned to any of the factors listed in the 360-Degree Appraisal Form? Explain.

4. What should Hana do?

5. Develop an alternative evaluation system for PARKSUNGCO. Support your recommended system.

Case prepared by: Jose Casal, New Jersey Institute of Technology

---

CASE 14.2 — Midwest Risk Management: Performance Evaluation Systems

Douglas Powell, the southern district sales manager for Midwest Risk Management, has just returned from his company's annual sales and marketing meeting. At the meeting, the vice president of marketing announced the company's intentions to expand into the professional liability insurance market. Doug was instructed to take five salespeople from his sales staff of 25 and have them start developing the professional liability markets in his area, concentrating on lawyers and CPAs. In addition, he was given a first-year operating objective of obtaining a 10% penetration for the professional liability market in the southern district.

The selling tasks required in developing the market for professional liability insurance products are assumed to be quite different from those needed to sell the personal lines of insurance and risk management products. Doug was confident his district salespeople could do the job, but he was unsure about how to effectively assess their performance.

Background

The Midwest Risk Management Insurance Agency was started by Rick Henderson and Shane Williams. Both of them had experience working as insurance agents for national companies. The firm began as an independent agency selling personal lines of insurance, such as life, accident, and health coverage. After four years, the agency had almost $80 million of life, accident, and health coverage in force and employed ten agents who worked on commission and covered three states in the Midwest.

In 2018, the name of the company was changed to Midwest Risk Management to reflect its geographic growth and plans for product diversification. By this time, the company had approximately 70 agents working in four regional offices, with customers in five Midwestern states. The agency began to offer basic employee benefit plans, consisting of life, accident, and health insurance programs to small businesses with less than 50 employees. By 2020, Midwest had over $950 million of life, accident, and health insurance coverage in effect, with a sales force of 105 agents in five states.

Doug Powell has been the sales manager for the southern district three years. Under his supervision, the district has been either first or second in premium income generated. In addition, the level of turnover among the southern district's sales force was traditionally the lowest of the four regional offices in the company.

Midwest Risk agents sold life, accident, and health insurance policies underwritten by various national insurance carriers. Midwest's sales force compensation plan used three major components: (1) commissions based on premiums sold; (2) base salary; and (3) bonuses based on achieving quotas for a variety of sales activities that were drivers of selling insurance policies. Midwest Risk collected the premiums from the individual customers and kept an agreed-upon percentage of each premium payment to cover its sales expenses, administrative overhead, and profits. Part of that premium percentage went to pay the commissions of the agent who sold the policy. Agents were paid commissions based on a percentage of the premiums they generated. In addition, they received a base salary and quarterly bonuses for attainment of quotas. Quotas were developed by evaluating the market potential for writing new policies, or by adding to existing coverage. This potential was compared with the current estimated level of market penetration. Then, quotas were derived by mutual agreement between the salesperson and sales manager to increase market penetration. Paying bonuses for quotas such as these provided additional motivation beyond the commissions on premiums for salespeople to do the very hard work of opening new accounts and/or selling new products. Without such incentives salespeople tended to focus on their existing premium business and not invest their time in selling new customers and new products. The purpose of providing base salary was to give salespeople some level of security so that they could cover their living expenses, especially if sales commissions were low in a given month due to disruption in the market and a drop in Midwest's sales. This was not normally a problem for experienced Midwest salespeople who had a book of well-established customers and steady premium generation. However, there were times when an insurance market would become unstable, such as after a major natural disaster, and firms like Midwest occasionally saw significant dips in premium generation and providing security to salespeople during such times prevent unwarranted turnover. More importantly, a base salary was attractive to new salespeople who were just entering the field and enabled Midwest to recruit needed new talent to bolster their sales force, as a steady stream of their baby boomer generation salespeople were retiring and needed to be replaced. New salespeople were also attracted to and motivated by bonuses paid on conducting selling activities.

Doug attributed the productivity of the southern district to the talent of the sales force personnel and his ability to hire, develop and reward high performing salespeople. The current appraisal system consisted of Doug's comparison of each agent's premium income produced for the current year compared with the income generated from the previous year. Exceptions were noted and discussed with the individual agent. Doug then prepared an evaluation of each individual on the district sales force along with recommendations for how the salesperson could increase policies sold and generate higher levels of premium revenue, possible increases in commission rates for given products, or increases in base salary to reward

overall strong performance and encourage new business development. This report was forwarded to the vice president of marketing and was approved or revisions were suggested. The system had been developed by Doug when he became district manager and he felt it was an excellent blend of the strengths of three different salesperson compensation approaches that rewarded a wider range of sales performance and provided stability to allow new salespeople to build their business and more veteran salespeople to sell new products. Of course, no sales forces compensation system is perfect, but existing salespeople felt the system was fair and motivating and Doug was able to recruit and generally keep high potential new salespeople to the firm.

Lawyers, CPA's, engineers, or any individual who provides advice or services based on acquired expertise needs protection from lawsuits by clients. Professional liability insurance is designed for such needs. Frequently, one of the benefits provided by professional organizations is the vetting and endorsement of various insurance products for organization members at group rates. The individual members are typically contacted by the endorsed company through direct mail, followed by a sales call from the representative.

Doug knows that the company's decision to enter the professional liability insurance market will require that his salespeople perform a set of sales tasks quite different from those they are accustomed to performing. If Midwest Risk could become the endorsed supplier of professional liability coverage for bar associations or CPA organizations in each market of the southern district, the sales force would have access to a customer group of high potential. Gaining the endorsement of local, regional, and national professional organizations would do much to ensure Midwest's successful penetration of the professional liability insurance market.

The salespeople involved in the professional liability market spend a large portion of their time contacting officers of the target professional organizations, making presentations, and performing various missionary selling tasks in an attempt to win the organizations' endorsements. Consequently, any evaluation of the performance of the professional liability salespeople should take into account the amount of effort devoted to "non-selling" tasks.

In an attempt to handle this challenge, Doug wrote down the selling tasks required to sell life, accident, and health insurance (see Table 1). Beside the list of activities, he noted the percent of total effort his district salespeople typically devoted to each job. Doug listed the selling tasks he envisioned as necessary in developing and servicing a market for professional liability insurance. In the last column of the table, he placed question marks alongside the entries, since he was uncertain about the percent of effort needed for each task.

To ensure the "Percent of Effort" values are accurate, Doug asked the vice president of marketing if Midwest's sales force automation software could be used to set up quotas and track selling activities and outcomes. Doug thought the place to start was to ascertain what the industry standards were relative to sales activities in the professional liability insurance market. How much time did salespeople spend prospecting, calling on regional and national professional organizations, calling on local professional firms to sell liability insurance and other related tasks? He wondered if such data even existed and/or was readily available. He also thought that the firm should have a marketing plan that included personal selling but also direct mail and a digital and perhaps social media marketing tactics to build awareness for his agency to sell the product. He considered reaching out to the major professional liability insurance firms that Midwest represented and partner with them on developing a digital and social media marketing campaign to penetrate this market. For example, what were the popular social media industry sites where local professionals exchanged information? Was the issue of search engine optimization relevant to Midwest in marketing this product? Was it a useful marketing tactic for Midwest Risk Management to start a blog on one or more of these sites? How many sites should Midwest blog on? Should all of Midwest's professional liability

insurance salespeople set up a blog or should he centralize that function and contract with a professional writer. He was highly doubtful that all of his salespeople were good writers. He also began to have second thoughts on whether it made sense to create a series of activity-based quotas and considered that it would be much simpler to pay the salespeople a straight salary to develop the business for the first year or two. He could take that time to learn the business and what the key drivers of success were from a sales force management perspective and then develop a comprehensive sales force compensation package. Finally, he considered whether he should push back on top management's assumption that the new professional liability market warranted a specialized sales force. Why was selling this type of insurance so different from the other insurance lines carried by Midwest that it warranted a specialized sales force? Maybe the new product was more complex, but the sales forces was currently selling some very complex insurance products. The existing sales force likely had relationships with most of the professionals in their local areas. Nevertheless, it is often difficult to motivate commission salespeople to sell new products. Perhaps he could use blend of missionary salespeople and/or a marketing manager, especially one skilled in digital and social media marketing, to make it much easier for the existing sales force to sell professional liability insurance.

TABLE 1

Description of Required Selling Tasks

Life, accident, and health Insurance	Percent of effort	Professional liability insurance	Percent of effort
1. Prospecting for new accounts	0.20	1. Prospecting for new accounts (identifying new professional groups)	?
2. Contacting prospects	0.10	2. Obtaining endorsements for client affiliated professional groups	?
3. Qualifying prospects	0.05	3. Contacting prospects (group contacts through mass mailings)	?
4. Presenting the sales message	0.20	4. Qualifying prospects	?
5. Meeting customer objections	0.10	5. Presenting the sales message	?
6. Closing the sale	0.05	6. Meeting customer objections	?
7. Servicing the account	0.30	7. Closing the sale	?
		8. Servicing the account	?
		9. Maintaining client and professional group relationships	?

Looking at the two lists of activities, Doug began to realize that the selling tasks themselves were not so different but that the amount of time devoted to each task by the two types of salespeople was likely what would change. Keeping that fact in mind, Doug began to try to think of the best way to develop a marketing and sales force management plan for Midwest to penetrate the professional liability insurance market.

Questions

1. Could the vice president of marketing be premature in expanding into the professional liability market? Develop a marketing and sales force management plan for Doug to follow as he enters this new market. Should a specialized sales force be created to sell professional liability insurance or should Midwest use the existing sales force structure?

2. Evaluate Doug's current appraisal and compensation system for the specialized agents selling to the professional liability market. What are the current strengths and weaknesses of this system? What are other viable options?

3. Given the operating objectives for the professional liability market, which selling activities should be emphasized for the professional liability sales force? How much effort should be devoted to each sales task?

4. If a specialized sales force is the optimal structure for selling professional liability insurance, how would you develop standards of performance, quotas for the professional liability sales force? If the existing sales force is optimal structure, how would you motivate them to sell this new product?

5. Assuming a specialized sales force is created, how would you compare the productivity of the professional liability sales force with the performance of the life, accident, and health insurance sales force?

Case prepared by: Jim Strong, California State University, Stanislaus, and Paul Christ, West Chester University

GLOSSARY

360-Degree Performance Appraisals A performance evaluation system that provides a salesperson with comparative pooled and anonymous feedback from the sales manager, peers on the sales team, subordinates, and clients; often includes a self-assessment.

Acceptability A situation where a set of ideas or recommendations is allowed or tolerated.

Activity Quotas Those designed to control the many activities the salesperson is responsible for.

Adaptive Selling Modifying each sales presentation and demonstration to accommodate each individual prospect.

Analytical CRM Focuses on aggregating customer information electronically allowing target markets and opportunities for cross-selling to be identified better.

Approach The first face-to-face contact with the prospect.

ARIMA (Autoregressive Integrated Moving Average) A sophisticated forecasting approach based on the moving average concept.

Artificial Intelligence (AI) Refers to cognitive-like functions such as problem solving and learning that are performed by computer systems.

Attribution Theory Based on the assumption that people are motivated based on their perception of why an event occurred.

Augmented Reality (AR) A type of technology that superimposes a computer-generated image (can be text, picture, or sound) on a user's view of the real.

Behaviorally Anchored Rating Scales (BARS) Concentrates on measuring behaviors key to performance that the individual salesperson can control.

Behavior-Based Performance Measures Performance criteria that can be subjectively measured (e.g., product knowledge).

Blended Learning A system in which students learn via electronic and online media as well as face-to-face teaching.

Blockchain Systems A digital ledger that records transactions on many computers so that any involved record cannot be altered after being put in the ledger.

Bonus Payments made at the discretion of management for specific achievements.

Boundary Spanner Individuals whose role involves linking the organization's internal networks with external information.

Breakdown Approach A way of developing forecasts based on general economic conditions, typically projected gross national product (GNP) in constant dollars along with projections of consumer and wholesale price indexes, interest rates, unemployment levels, and federal government expenditures.

Budget Variances Differences between actual results and sales budget expectations.

Budgeting An operational planning process expressed in financial terms.

Build-Up Approach A way of developing forecasts based on primary research, new data collected for the specific purpose at hand.

Buying Power Index (BPI) A weighted combination of population, income, and retail sales, expressed as a percentage of the national potential, to identify a given market's ability to buy.

Canned (or Programmed) Selling Any highly structured or patterned selling approach.

Career Plateauing When a salesperson no longer grows or develops in the position or the likelihood of the person receiving additional responsibility is low.

Causal/Association Methods Methods that attempt to identify the factors affecting sales and determine the nature of the relationship between them.

Centralized Training Programs Training that is delivered in a central location, instead of away from the home office.

Charisma A mystical, inspirational quality that few people possess; the charismatic leader wins the emotional loyalty and enthusiasm of followers.

Click-Stream Analysis Involves drawing conclusions based on the path a customer takes while navigating information on the company web site.

Close The stage in the selling process where the salesperson tries to obtain the prospect's agreement to purchase the product.

Coaching A process in which a single individual provides guidance on how to improve performance, such as better selling approaches.

Codes of Ethics A set of rules that expresses the values of a firm by specifying, in writing, specific behaviors that are consistent or inconsistent with those values.

Coercive Power The ability of the leader to obtain compliance through fear of punishment, sanctions, or by withholding rewards including being fired from the job.

Combination Compensation Plan Plan that combines two or three of the basic compensation methods (e.g., salary plus commission). This is the most widely used compensation method.

Combination Quotas Those used when management wants to control the performance of both the selling and non-selling activities of the sales force.

Communication A two-way process whereby information is transferred and understood between two or more people.

Compensation Mix The relationship between salary, commission, and other incentives.

Compensation All monetary payments as well as benefits used to remunerate employees for their performance.

Concentration Principle Assertion that a relatively small percentage (20 percent) of products, customers, orders, sales territories, and salespeople account for a large percentage (80 percent) of profits.

Conferencing Holding a group meeting, often using electronic technology.

Consideration Sometimes called the "human relations" approach, this dimension of behavioral styles theory seeks to engender friendship, mutual trust, respect, and support of subordinates.

Contingency Planning A planning approach that considers possible future developments and identifies alternatives other than the initial one.

Contingency Theory A collection of leadership theories that suggests an effective leadership style is largely predicated (contingent) on the interaction among the leader, followers, and situation-specific conditions.

Contingency Events that are conceivable, but less likely than those based directly on the forecast.

Continuing Sales Training Program Training program that is ongoing instead of a single meeting.

Contractualism A philosophy that morality and ethics is based on contract or agreement.

Contribution Margin The sales price less direct costs and variable costs equals the amount the sale contributes to profits (contribution margin).

Cooling Off Rules Guidelines on how to defuse post-sale conflict. For major transactions (like real estate), the FTC and many states provide a 3-day period in which transactions can be canceled.

Core-Based Statistical Area A U.S. geographic area consisting of one or more counties (or equivalents) anchored by an urban center of at least 10,000 people plus adjacent counties that are socioeconomically tied to the urban center by commuting.

Correlation Analysis A statistical approach analyzing the way variables are related to one another or move together in some way.

Correlation Coefficient A measure of how much two variables are related to one another.

Costs versus Expenses Two terms that are often used interchangeably in describing marketing costs analysis. But costs tend to be specific and directly related to volume output, while expenses are more general or indirect expenditures (e.g., we tend to say production costs and marketing expenses).

Counting Methods Forecasting approaches that tabulate responses to questions on surveys or count the numbers of buyers or purchases.

CRM Intelligence Results when CRM software converts information into data that can be used in solving a sales manager's problem.

CRM A systematic integration of information, technology and human resources all oriented toward (a) providing maximum value to customers and (b) maximizing the value obtained from customers.

Customer Centric The customer becomes the heart of the business process.

Customer Commitment Represents the bonding, or affective attachment, between a customer and a sales firm.

Customer Lifetime Value The monetary amount representing the worth of a customer to a firm over the foreseeable life of a relationship.

Customer Portfolios Sets of customers who have something in common.

Customer Relationship Management A company-wide effort to satisfy customers across all "touch" points and provide personalized treatment of the most valued customers in order to increase customer retention and profitability.

Customer Retention Refers to the percentage of customers who will repeatedly purchase products from the selling firm.

Customer Share Represents the proportion of resources a customer spends with one among a set of competing suppliers.

Customer Value The net positive worth of a customer based on past, present, and future transactions.

Customer-Oriented Salesperson Motivated primarily by matching customers up with products that best address their needs.

D&B – Dun's Market Identifiers® (DMI) A directory produced by D&B, Inc. that contains basic company data, executive names and titles, corporate linkages, DUNS® (Data Universal Numbering System) Numbers, organization status, and other marketing information.

Data Mining Exploratory statistical analysis of the data in the data warehouse aimed at revealing relationships that allow customers to be targeted more accurately.

Database Marketing A computerized process for analyzing customer databases in a way that allows more effective selling by tailoring product and promotional offerings to a specific customer's sales patterns.

Decentralized Training Training delivered away from the home office.

Deliverability Refers to the proportion of email sent that is successfully delivered to the intended recipient.

Deontological A normative ethical theory that actions should be based on ideological or rule-based decision-making systems.

Diagnosis Identification of problems by examining symptoms.

Dialectic Planning Planning approach in which issues are discussed and various viewpoints are compared.

Differentiated Marketing Dealing with different groups of customers by offering a unique product for each group.

Direct Costs Those costs that can be entirely identified with or traced to a particular function or market segment, such as a territory, customer, or product. In a territorial analysis, for example, each territory would be assigned the cost of salaries for those salespeople working exclusively in that territory.

Draw A sum of money paid against future commissions. A "guaranteed draw" is one that does not have to be repaid in the event of insufficient commissions.

Dual Factor Theory Based on the assumption that the job itself contains sources of satisfaction and dissatisfaction as well as motivators.

Econometric Models Models developed to trace economic conditions in the United States by industry, with the objective of capturing, in the form of equations, complex interrelationships among the factors affecting either the total economy or the industry's or company's sales.

Effective Listening Becoming familiar with the four types of listening (content listening, critical listening, empathic listening, and active listening) and knowing when to apply them.

Effectiveness The extent to which a salesperson is successful in achieving their goals.

Efficiency The extent to which a salesperson is able to accomplish their assigned tasks with the least waste of time and effort.

E-Learning Learning utilizing electronic technologies to access training outside of a traditional classroom.

Employment Testing An objective way to measure traits or characteristics of applicants for sales positions and to increase the chances of selecting good salespeople.

Empowerment The process of distributing power to subordinates, which makes them partners entrusted with legitimate authority and discretion in decision-making and by providing rewards tied to company performance.

Equity Theory Based on the assumption that people compare their relative work contributions and rewards with those of other individuals in similar situations.

ERG Theory It espouses that individuals' needs can be subsumed under a three-category hierarchy of existence (physiological and safety needs), relatedness (social and esteem needs), and growth (self-actualization needs).

Ethical Dilemma A situation with alternate courses of action, each having different moral implications.

Ethical Maturity Development of salesperson leading to moral treatment of others prioritized ahead of short-term personal gains.

Ethical Stress Perceptions of ambiguity and/or conflict involving an ethical dilemma.

Ethical Work Climate A specific aspect of the organizational climate; it's the way employees view their work environment on moral dimensions.

Expectancy (Effort-Performance Linkage) The perceived probability by the salesperson that exerting a given level of effort will lead to higher achievement.

Expectancy Theory Based on the assumption that people are motivated to work toward a goal when they expect their efforts will pay off.

Expense Account Financial accounts that enable sales representatives to carry out necessary selling activities.

Expense Quotas Those designed to make the salesperson aware of the costs involved in their selling efforts.

Expert Power Subordinate compliance that is based upon the leader's skills, knowledge, intelligence, job-related information and expertise.

Exponential Smoothing A type of moving average that represents the weighted sum of all past numbers in a time series, placing the heaviest weight on the most recent data.

Extended Socialization Long-term training, job rotation, and involvement in corporate social activities.

Extrinsic Rewards Those rewards controlled by managers and customers (e.g., pay, bonuses, and promotions).

Financial Incentives Monetary reward for job performance; includes salary, commission, bonuses, stock options, or fringe benefits such as a company car, medical, dental and life insurance, or educational aid.

Financial Quotas Those established to control expenses, gross margin, or net profit for the various sales units.

Fixed Costs Those costs that do not change with sales volume, for example, salaries of the sales administration staff, office rent, and fire insurance.

Flexible Compensation Systems Also known as variable pay systems; pay based on a personal choice of compensation plan and benefits selected.

Follow-Up Customer service provided not just after the sale is closed, but throughout the selling process.

Fringe Benefits Indirect financial awards that help to provide salespeople with personal security and job satisfaction.

Functional Costs Reclassified natural expenses into the activities or functions for which they were incurred, for example, "salary expense" reclassified into direct selling, transportation, or advertising function salaries.

Geographic Control Unit A sales territory set up based on geographic boundaries.

Goal-Setting Theory It attempts to increase motivation by linking rewards directly to individuals' goals.

Governance The mechanism that helps ensure that the exchange is fair to all parties involved.

Green River Ordinances A U.S. city law prohibiting door-to-door solicitation.

Group Training Methods Training for several salespeople at the same time.

Hierarchy of Needs Theory A need theory; based on the assumption that people are motivated by a hierarchy of psychological growth needs.

Ideals Guidelines individuals apply to ethical and moral decisions – like the golden rule.

Incentive Program When salespeople achieve or surpass a specified sales quota, they are often given a monetary bonus to reward them for their performance as well as to motivate them to continue this behavior.

In-Depth Personal Interview A comprehensive, probing discussion of an individual's qualifications to be hired.

Indirect Costs Sometimes called common costs, which are incurred for more than one function or segment and thus must be allocated on some reasonable basis. For example, the sales manager's salary or office utilities would have to be spread among sales functions, sales territories, and other segments.

Individual Training Methods Training for a single salesperson.

Initial Sales Training Program Training that familiarizes new salespeople with the overall company and its basic policies and procedures.

Initial Screening A process designed to eliminate undesirable recruits as soon as possible.

Initial Socialization Exposure of new recruits to the firm that begins with the recruiting and selection process and ends with the initial orientation of the salesperson to the firm's procedures and policies.

Initiating Structure Sometimes called "task orientation," this dimension of behavioral styles theory reflects the extent to which leaders organize, clearly define, and clarify the tasks subordinates need to perform in attaining firm goals.

Input–Output Efficiency The relationship between marketing efforts (inputs) and sales (output) is a measure of a sales organization's efficiency.

Input–Output Models Complex systems showing the amount of input required from each industry for a specified output of another industry.

Instrumentality (Performance–Reward Linkage) The salesperson's estimate of the probability that achieving a certain level of improved performance will lead to the attainment of certain rewards.

Integrated Marketing Communication (IMC) The coordination of promotional elements (advertising, personal selling, sales promotion, public relations, direct marketing, and publicity) with other marketing mix elements (product, pricing, and distribution).

Intranet A restricted communications network within an organization.

Intrinsic Rewards Nontangible rewards that salespeople experience internally (e.g., personal growth and self-esteem).

Invalid Objections Irrelevant, untruthful delaying actions or hidden reasons for not buying.

Job Analysis The process of identifying the duties, requirements, responsibilities, and conditions of the job.

Job Commitment The degree of involvement (high or low) the salespersons have in their job.

Job Description A written description of the responsibilities and performance criteria for a particular position.

Job Qualifications The duties and responsibilities sales people must have to perform satisfactorily on the sales job.

Jury of Executive Opinion Sales forecast method based on key managers' best estimates of sales in a given planning horizon.

Leadership Behavior The leader's manner and approach in providing direction, implementing plans, and motivating people.

Leader–Member Exchange Theory A contingency leadership theory in which subordinates that a leader favors are given preferential treatment and assigned to an "in-group," whereas less desirable subalterns are placed in "out-groups."

Leadership Styles Different patterns of leader behavior, or "styles" employed to secure the subordinate compliance towards the attainment of organizational goals.

Leadership The interpersonal process of communicating, inspiring, guiding, and influencing the behavior of subordinate salespeople towards the attainment of organizational objectives, goals, and values.

Learning Objectives Goals to be achieved in and educational or training situation.

Learning Orientation When salespersons discover new ways of selling effectively.

Legitimate Power Derived from the position occupied in the organizational structure, the leader has formally delegated authority to seek subordinate compliance.

Machine Learning The ability for computers to perform functions that they are not specifically programmed to do.

Macroenvironment Largely uncontrollable factors, such as technology, competition, economy, laws, culture, and ethics, that are continuously changing and to which sales managers must adapt in overseeing the sales force.

Management by Objectives (MBO) Involves mutual goal setting devised by the sales manager and the salesperson, who jointly agree on the salesperson's specific goals or performance targets for the coming period.

Management The administrative activities that include planning, organizing, staffing, directing, and controlling the operations of a firm towards the attainment of its goals and objectives.

Managerial Training Training for managers in an organization.

Market Orientation Companies focus on making what could be sold, not selling what is made. A market-oriented firm focuses all activities on providing value for customers.

Market Potential A quantitative estimate, in either physical or monetary units, of the total sales for a product within a market.

Marketing Automation Routine marketing functions can be performed by digital and mechanical systems instead of human beings.

Marketing An organizational function and a set of processes for creating, communicating, and delivering value to customers and for managing customer relationships in ways that benefit the organization and its stakeholders.

Mass Marketing A way of dealing with customers by offering the same product to the entire market.

Mentor Someone who systematically helps develop a subordinate's abilities through careful tutoring, personal guidance, and example.

Mentoring An individual advises someone on how to change or improve their performance.

Metropolitan Statistical Area (MSA) A geographic region that consists of a city and surrounding communities for which the government reports statistical information.

M-Learning Learning across multiple situations using personal mobile devices such as an iPhone.

Moral Equity Inherent fairness of justice of a situation that considers all involved parties.

Moral Judgment A person's evaluation of the situation from an ethical perspective about what is or is not moral behavior.

Moral Philosophy The systematic approach in which individuals recognize and resolve decisions that include moral content.

Motivation The set of dynamic interpersonal processes that cause the initiation, direction, intensity, and persistence of work related behaviors of subordinate salespeople toward the attainment of organizational goals and objectives.

Moving Average Forecasts developed mathematically based on sales in recent time periods.

Multiple Regression A tool for forecasting a dependent variable like sales using several independent variables simultaneously.

NAICS (North American Industrial Classification System) A system for categorizing firms, formally adopted beginning with the 2002 Economic Census and the publication of the 2002 U.S. NAICS Manual.

Naïve Forecast The simplest judgment method, which assumes, naively, that the next period's sales will be the same as they were in the previous period.

Natural Expenses The traditional expense categories, such as salaries, rent, depreciation, and so on, used in accounting statements.

Needs Theory It posits that employees develop various needs–such as for power, affiliation, and achievement–over their lifetime based on life experiences.

Negative Reinforcement Avoiding an undesirable outcome after displaying the desired behavior (e.g., allowing those salespeople who achieve or surpass their annual quotas to keep their jobs).

Niche Marketing Offering a specialized product to an individual customer segment with specialized needs.

Nonquantitative Forecasting Techniques Subjective forecasts based on knowledgeable people's opinions instead of being analytically derived.

Nonverbal Communication Communication that takes place largely through body language, facial expressions, gestures, or body postures.

North American Product Classification System (NAPCS) A system for categorizing consumer products and service industries.

Objection Anything that the prospect or customer says or does that impedes the sales negotiations.

Objectives Targets to aim for in developing solutions to problems.

One-to-One Marketing Involves matching individual products with individual customers.

Online Conferencing Group discussions executed online with electronic devices.

Online Learning Learning online with electronic devices.

Operational CRM Focused on using information to improve internal efficiencies.

Opportunistic Behavior One fact of all relationships is that sometimes, one firm may take advantage of another firm.

Organizational Behavior Modification Theory It involves the use of various learning techniques to strengthen, maintain, or eliminate behaviors by using rewards or punishments.

Organizational Climate The way employees perceive the organizational culture.

Organizational Commitment Salespeople's identifying with and internalizing the company's values and goals and desiring to stay a viable member of the organization.

Organizational Culture The shared values, norms, and artifacts that provide the blueprint for behavior within a firm.

Organizational Ethics The study of how business people in an organization behave when facing a situation with moral consequences.

Outcome-Based Performance Measures Performance criteria that can be objectively measured (number of sales calls made each month).

Participative Management The involvement of employees with management in shared decision-making that enables them to accomplish individual and organizational goals.

Peer Behavior Employees' perception of the behavior in which colleagues go about their day-to-day job (particularly relevant for ethical environment).

Performance Evaluation Monitoring System (PEMS) System designed to provide feedback to salespeople on performance, to help salespeople modify or change their behavior and to provide sales managers information on which to make decisions on promotion, transfer, and compensation of salespeople.

Performance Objectives Goals for achieving a specified level of performance.

Performance Orientation When salespeople are especially keen on receiving favorable assessments of their skills from management and peers.

Performance Standards Planned achievement levels that the sales organization expects to reach at progressive intervals throughout the year; an agreement between subordinate and superior as to what level of performance is acceptable in some future period.

Policies and Rules Principles that govern selling and marketing conduct within the firm, sometimes summarized in a code of ethics.

Positive Reinforcement Providing salespeople with a pleasant consequence for having engaged in the desired behavior (e.g., providing a bonus for opening new accounts).

Power The potential capacity to influence the behavior of subordinates.

Pre-Approach The approach-planning stage of the selling process.

Pretraining Briefing Explaining what is expected when training occurs.

Price Discrimination Selling something at different prices to different groups that is disadvantageous to one or more groups.

Product Portfolio The set of products that a customer is responsible for selling.

Production Orientation Companies focus on processes allowing large-scale, efficient, and economic production.

Prognosis The likely outcome of a situation.

Progressive Incentives Increase the percentage of commission or bonus awarded as sales volume rises. Best when profit margins climb significantly after the break-even point is reached.

Prospecting First step in the SP, wherein salespeople find leads and qualify them on four criteria–need, authority, money, and eligibility to buy.

Purchase Intentions The likelihood customers will actually purchase a given product.

Push Technology Involves using data stored about a particular customer or customer group which helps send the particular customer information and promotional material at a time when the data suggests the customer will be interested in a purchase.

Quotas Sales goals for different sales territories and individual salespeople.

Recognition A non-financial reward used for motivation.

Recruiting Process A systematic procedure for recruiting salespeople.

Recruiting Finding potential job applicants, telling them about the company, and getting them to apply.

Referent Power The ability to influence subordinate compliance based on inspiration, charisma, loyalty, and personal identification with the leader.

Refresher Training Training following previous training to remind salespeople how to perform various tasks.

Regression Analysis A statistical approach to predicting a dependent variable such as sales, using one or more independent variables such as advertising expenditures.

Regressive Incentives Decrease the percentage of commission or bonus awarded as sales volume increases. Usually used where there is a high probability of "windfall" sales and a propensity to overload customer inventories.

Relational Exchange Recognition, by both buyer and seller, that each transaction is merely one in a series of purchase agreements between a buyer and a seller.

Relational-Based Governance Involves arrangements for sharing information and tasks between the buying and selling firm, but falls short of spelling out specific obligations for each party.

Relativism A doctrine that knowledge and morality exist in relation to a situation or context and is not absolute.

Retraining Training delivered a second or third time.

Return on Time Invested (ROTI) A financial assessment that helps salespeople spend their time more profitably with prospects and customers.

Reward Power The ability to provide subordinates with various benefits, including money, praise, or promotion.

Role Playing Practicing a role to improve and learning from an individual's behavior, such as a selling approach.

Routing Patterns The sequence and routing of calls specified by the sales manager.

RSS An information source that automatically provide updates.

Sales and Operational Planning Process (S&OP) An organized process that uses sales inputs to forecast business for upcoming periods of varying length.

Sales Budget A financial sales plan outlining how to allocate resources and selling efforts to achieve the sales forecast.

Sales Contests Relatively short-run competitive events designed to motivate and reward salespeople for achieving objective goals.

Sales Dashboard A diagnostic tool or graphically interface that displays valuable metrics or information about sales force performance.

Sales Emphasis An approach to selling that focuses on achieving sales goals.

Sales Ethics Subcompliance Culture The extent to which salespeople comply with the culture of the sales force in an organization.

Sales Ethics Subculture The ethical culture pertaining of the sales force to comply with its organizational code of ethics.

Sales Force Audit A comprehensive, systematic, diagnostic, and prescriptive tool designed to assess the adequacy of a firm's sales force management process and to provide direction for improved performance and prescription for needed changes.

Sales Force Automation (SFA) An integrated system of computer software and hardware that performs certain routine sales functions that formerly were performed with independent and often manual systems.

Sales Force Composite Sales forecast method based on sales force estimates of sales in the planning horizon.

Sales Management Ethics The specific component of organizational ethics that deals with ethical administration of the sales function and the actions of the sales force.

Sales Force Management The function of planning, direction, and control of the personal selling activities of a business unit, including recruiting, selecting, training, equipping, assigning, routing, supervising, paying, and motivating as these tasks apply to the sales force.

Sales Forecast A prediction of the future revenues for a specific product.

Sales Meetings Sales meetings provide opportunities for two-way communication and interaction among all members of the marketing team–field and headquarters.

Sales Motivation Strategies Techniques used to implement motivational theories or approaches (e.g., sales contests, sales meetings, promotion opportunities, and incentive programs).

Sales Potential The portion of market potential that one among a set of competing firms can reasonably expect to obtain.

Sales Quota A specific, quantitative goal, usually established in terms of sales volume; important in planning, control, and evaluation of sales activities.

Sales Subculture A component of the organizational culture that influences the ethical behavior of the sales force .

Sales Territory A geographic area that contains present and potential customers and is assigned to a particular salesperson.

Sales Training Development Process The process of designed to improve the training of salespeople in an organization.

Sales Training Training salespeople on how to improve their selling skills.

Sales Unit An individual salesperson, sales territory, branch office, region, dealer or distributor, or district.

Sales Volume Analytics The collection, classification, comparison, and evaluation of an organization's sales figures.

Salesperson Performance Evaluation A systematic process for establishing whether the salesperson's job behavior contributes to the fulfillment of a firm's sales objectives, and providing feedback to the individual.

Salesperson Workload Analysis An estimate of the time and effort required to cover each geographic control unit.

Scatter Diagram Graph that plots one variable against another to see whether there is a relationship.

Selection Process Choosing candidates that best meet the qualifications and have the greatest aptitude for the job.

Self-Efficacy Feelings of power and the subordinate belief in the ability to make a meaningful contribution in influencing organizational performance.

Semistructured Interview A combination of structured and unstructured interviewing approaches.

Situational Ethics Ethical actions that can be seen as acceptable in one situation but unacceptable in another.

Socialization The process of teaching new salespeople the acceptable and expected way to behave in the organization.

Stakeholders Company employees, suppliers, financial community, media, stockholders, special interest groups, governments, and the general public–all of whom have a stake, interest, and frequently opinions about the activities of the sales force.

Standard Costs Predetermined costs, based on experience and research studies, for achieving certain levels of volume. In production there are usually standard costs for direct labor, materials, and factory overhead. Marketing costs are much more difficult to standardize since they tend to be generated from non-repetitive activities.

Standard Industrial Classification (SIC) A uniform numbering system for categorizing nearly all industries according to their particular product or operation.

Straight Commission Payment for a given level of sales results; based on the principle that earnings should vary with performance.

Historically based on dollar or unit sales volume, but can be tied to measures of profitability.

Straight Salary A fixed sum of money paid at regular intervals. Most appropriate for team selling, long negotiating periods, mixed promotional mixes, sales trainees, missionary selling, and in special situations such as introducing new products or developing new customer accounts.

Strategic Partnerships The goals, strategies, and resources of buyers and sellers become so interconnected and intertwined that they develop an integrated, symbiotic relationship although still retaining their independent identities.

Strategy An action plan designed to achieve overall objectives.

Structured Interview An interview approach designed to ensure the same questions are always asked in the same order.

Supervision Tasks that deal with monitoring the daily work activities of sales subordinates.

Surveys of Buying Intentions Surveys that ask customers about their intentions to buy various products over a specified period.

Tactics Actions designed to achieve a specific objective.

Technology-Based Training Training delivered by technology instead of by an individual.

Teleology A philosophy that defines morality based on the consequences of the behavior.

Test Marketing A popular counting forecasting method for consumer packaged goods products.

Time and Territory Management Planning how salespeople can most effectively use their time to sell in the assigned territory.

Time Traps Situations that arise and take up more time than anticipated.

Time-Series Technique Use of historical data to predict future sales.

Touchpoint Refers to points in time when the customer and the company come together, either personally or virtually.

Trading Area A geographic area defined based on where a company does business with their customers.

Training Delivery Decisions Decisions about what is the best approach to deliver training to improve training objective

Training Needs Assessment Determining what training is needed to improve performance.

Trait Theory Leadership theory that focuses on identifying the qualities or personal traits of effective leaders.

Transactional Leadership Transactional leaders identify and clarify for subordinates their job tasks and communicate to them how successful execution of those tasks will lead to job rewards.

Transactional Selling A sales firm that acts consistently with the view that each and every interaction with a customer is a unique and independent event.

Transformational Leadership Transformational leaders adopt a long-term perspective. Transformational leaders gain extraordinary commitment from their followers through four key characteristics–charisma and vision, inspiration, intellectual stimulation, and individual consideration.

Trend Analysis A quantitative forecast whereby the dependent variable is sales, and the independent variable is time.

Trial Close Any well-placed attempt to close the sale; can be used early and often throughout the selling process.

Trust and Responsibility Defines how far people are trusted to behave in a responsible way and are held personally responsible for their actions.

Uniform Commercial Code A set of guidelines that governs commercial transactions in the United States.

Unstructured Interview An interview in which there is not a predetermined set or sequence of questions.

Valence (the Attractiveness of Rewards) The desirability of a potential outcome or reward that the salesperson may receive from improved performance.

Valid Objections Sincere concerns that the prospect needs addressed before he or she will be willing to buy.

Value An individual's selective perception of the worth of some activity, object, or idea.

Variable Costs Those costs that vary with sales volume, for example, travel outlays for salespeople calling on customers or commissions based on sales volume.

Vision An attractive, credible notion of a future state that is not readily attainable.

Visionary Leadership The ability to create and articulate a realistic, credible, and attractive vision of the future that improves upon the present situation.

Vulnerable When a party is at a disadvantage relative to another in sales negotiations due to ignorance, naiveté, and powerlessness or other factors.

Webinar A group meeting that is delivered online.

Wheel of Selling Depiction of the seven stages of the SP as a continuous cycle of stages carried out by professionals in the field of sales.

Wiki A website that has knowledge for individuals to access and use to understand concepts or guidelines.

INDEX